D0882654

The NEW ENCYCLOPEDIA *of* SOUTHERN CULTURE

VOLUME 10 : LAW AND POLITICS

Volumes to appear in
The New Encyclopedia of Southern Culture
are:

Agriculture and Industry   *Law and Politics*

Art and Architecture   *Literature*

Education   *Media*

Environment   *Music*

Ethnicity   *Myth, Manners, and Memory*

Folk Art   *Race*

Folklife   *Recreation*

Foodways   *Religion*

Gender   *Science and Medicine*

Geography   *Social Class*

History   *Urbanization*

Language   *Violence*

The NEW

ENCYCLOPEDIA *of* SOUTHERN CULTURE

CHARLES REAGAN WILSON General Editor

JAMES G. THOMAS JR. Managing Editor

ANN J. ABADIE Associate Editor

VOLUME 10

Law & Politics

JAMES W. ELY JR.   Law Section Editor

BRADLEY G. BOND   Politics Section Editor

Sponsored by

THE CENTER FOR THE STUDY OF SOUTHERN CULTURE

at the University of Mississippi

THE UNIVERSITY OF NORTH CAROLINA PRESS

Chapel Hill

This book was published with the
assistance of the Anniversary Endowment Fund
of the University of North Carolina Press.

© 2008 The University of North Carolina Press
Designed by Richard Hendel
Set in Minion types by Tseng Information Systems, Inc.
Manufactured in the United States of America
The paper in this book meets the guidelines for permanence and
durability of the Committee on Production Guidelines for Book
Longevity of the Council on Library Resources.
The University of North Carolina Press has been a member of the
Green Press Initiative since 2003.
Library of Congress Cataloging-in-Publication Data
Law and politics / James W. Ely, Law section editor ;
Bradley G. Bond, Politics section editor.
p. cm. — (The new encyclopedia of Southern culture ; v. 10)
"Sponsored by The Center for the Study of Southern Culture
at the University of Mississippi."
Includes bibliographical references and index.
ISBN 978-0-8078-3205-9 (alk. paper) —
ISBN 978-0-8078-5884-4 (pbk. : alk. paper)
1. Law—Southern States—History—Encyclopedias. 2. Justice,
Administration of—Southern States—History—Encyclopedias.
3. Southern States—Politics and government—Encyclopedias.
4. Political Culture—Southern States—Encyclopedias. I. Ely,
James W. II. Bond, Bradley G. III. University of Mississippi.
Center for the Study of Southern Culture. IV. Series.
F209 .N47 2006 vol. 10
[KF352]   975.003 s—dc22
2007049484
The Encyclopedia of Southern Culture, sponsored by the Center for
the Study of Southern Culture at the University of Mississippi, was
published by the University of North Carolina Press in 1989.
cloth   12 11 10 09 08   5 4 3 2 1
paper   12 11 10 09 08   5 4 3 2 1

Tell about the South. What's it like there.

What do they do there. Why do they live there.

Why do they live at all.

WILLIAM FAULKNER

Absalom, Absalom!

CONTENTS

In 1989 years of planning and hard work came to fruition when the University of North Carolina Press joined the Center for the Study of Southern Culture at the University of Mississippi to publish the *Encyclopedia of Southern Culture*. While all those involved in writing, reviewing, editing, and producing the volume believed it would be received as a vital contribution to our understanding of the American South, no one could have anticipated fully the widespread acclaim it would receive from reviewers and other commentators. But the *Encyclopedia* was indeed celebrated, not only by scholars but also by popular audiences with a deep, abiding interest in the region. At a time when some people talked of the "vanishing South," the book helped remind a national audience that the region was alive and well, and it has continued to shape national perceptions of the South through the work of its many users—journalists, scholars, teachers, students, and general readers.

As the introduction to the *Encyclopedia* noted, its conceptualization and organization reflected a cultural approach to the South. It highlighted such issues as the core zones and margins of southern culture, the boundaries where "the South" overlapped with other cultures, the role of history in contemporary culture, and the centrality of regional consciousness, symbolism, and mythology. By 1989 scholars had moved beyond the idea of cultures as real, tangible entities, viewing them instead as abstractions. The *Encyclopedia's* editors and contributors thus included a full range of social indicators, trait groupings, literary concepts, and historical evidence typically used in regional studies, carefully working to address the distinctive and characteristic traits that made the American South a particular place. The introduction to the *Encyclopedia* concluded that the fundamental uniqueness of southern culture was reflected in the volume's composite portrait of the South. We asked contributors to consider aspects that were unique to the region but also those that suggested its internal diversity. The volume was not a reference book of southern history, which explained something of the design of entries. There were fewer essays on colonial and antebellum history than on the postbellum and modern periods, befitting our conception of the volume as one trying not only to chart the cultural landscape of the South but also to illuminate the contemporary era.

When C. Vann Woodward reviewed the *Encyclopedia* in the *New York Review of Books*, he concluded his review by noting "the continued liveliness of interest in the South and its seeming inexhaustibility as a field of study." Research on the South, he wrote, furnishes "proof of the value of the *Encyclopedia* as a scholarly undertaking as well as suggesting future needs for revision or supplement to keep up with ongoing scholarship." The two decades since the publication of the *Encyclopedia of Southern Culture* have certainly suggested that Woodward was correct. The American South has undergone significant changes that make for a different context for the study of the region. The South has undergone social, economic, political, intellectual, and literary transformations, creating the need for a new edition of the *Encyclopedia* that will remain relevant to a changing region. Globalization has become a major issue, seen in the South through the appearance of Japanese automobile factories, Hispanic workers who have immigrated from Latin America or Cuba, and a new prominence for Asian and Middle Eastern religions that were hardly present in the 1980s South. The African American return migration to the South, which started in the 1970s, dramatically increased in the 1990s, as countless books simultaneously appeared asserting powerfully the claims of African Americans as formative influences on southern culture. Politically, southerners from both parties have played crucial leadership roles in national politics, and the Republican Party has dominated a near-solid South in national elections. Meanwhile, new forms of music, like hip-hop, have emerged with distinct southern expressions, and the term "dirty South" has taken on new musical meanings not thought of in 1989. New genres of writing by creative southerners, such as gay and lesbian literature and "white trash" writing, extend the southern literary tradition.

Meanwhile, as Woodward foresaw, scholars have continued their engagement with the history and culture of the South since the publication of the *Encyclopedia*, raising new scholarly issues and opening new areas of study. Historians have moved beyond their earlier preoccupation with social history to write new cultural history as well. They have used the categories of race, social class, and gender to illuminate the diversity of the South, rather than a unified "mind of the South." Previously underexplored areas within the field of southern historical studies, such as the colonial era, are now seen as formative periods of the region's character, with the South's positioning within a larger Atlantic world a productive new area of study. Cultural memory has become a major topic in the exploration of how the social construction of "the South" benefited some social groups and exploited others. Scholars in many disciplines have made the southern identity a major topic, and they have used a variety of methodologies to suggest what that identity has meant to different social groups. Literary critics have adapted cultural theories to the South and have raised the issue of postsouthern literature to a major category of concern as well as exploring the links between the literature of the American South and that of the Caribbean. Anthropologists have used different theoretical formulations from literary critics, providing models for their fieldwork in southern communities. In the past 30 years anthropologists have set increasing numbers of their ethnographic studies in the South, with many of them now exploring topics specifically linked to southern cultural issues. Scholars now place the Native American story, from prehistory to the contemporary era, as a central part of southern history. Comparative and interdisciplinary approaches to the South have encouraged scholars to look at such issues as the borders and boundaries of the South, specific places and spaces with distinct identities within the American South, and the global and transnational Souths, linking the American South with many formerly colonial societies around the world.

The first edition of the *Encyclopedia of Southern Culture* anticipated many of these approaches and indeed stimulated the growth of Southern Studies as a distinct interdisciplinary field. The Center for the Study of Southern Culture has worked for more than a quarter century to encourage research and teaching about the American South. Its academic programs have produced graduates who have gone on to write interdisciplinary studies of the South, while others have staffed the cultural institutions of the region and in turn encouraged those institutions to document and present the South's culture to broad public audiences. The center's conferences and publications have continued its long tradition of promoting understanding of the history, literature, and music of the South, with new initiatives focused on southern foodways, the future of the South, and the global Souths, expressing the center's mission to bring the best current scholarship to broad public audiences. Its documentary studies projects build oral and visual archives, and the New Directions in Southern Studies book series, published by the University of North Carolina Press, offers an important venue for innovative scholarship.

Since the *Encyclopedia of Southern Culture* appeared, the field of Southern Studies has dramatically developed, with an extensive network now of academic and research institutions whose projects focus specifically on the interdisciplinary study of the South. The Center for the Study of the American South at the University of North Carolina at Chapel Hill, led by Director Harry Watson and Associate Director and *Encyclopedia* coeditor William Ferris, publishes the lively journal *Southern Cultures* and is now at the organizational center of many other Southern Studies projects. The Institute for Southern Studies at the University of South Carolina, the Southern Intellectual History Circle, the Society for the Study of Southern Literature, the Southern Studies Forum of the European American Studies Association, Emory University's SouthernSpaces.org, and the South Atlantic Humanities Center (at the Virginia Foundation for the Humanities, the University of Virginia, and Virginia Polytechnic Institute and State University) express the recent expansion of interest in regional study.

Observers of the American South have had much to absorb, given the rapid pace of recent change. The institutional framework for studying the South is broader and deeper than ever, yet the relationship between the older verities of regional study and new realities remains unclear. Given the extent of changes in the American South and in Southern Studies since the publication of the *Encyclopedia of Southern Culture*, the need for a new edition of that work is clear. Therefore, the Center for the Study of Southern Culture has once again joined the University of North Carolina Press to produce *The New Encyclopedia of Southern Culture*. As readers of the original edition will quickly see, *The New Encyclopedia* follows many of the scholarly principles and editorial conventions established in the original, but with one key difference; rather than being published in a single hardback volume, *The New Encyclopedia* is presented in a series of shorter individual volumes that build on the 24 original subject categories used in the *Encyclopedia* and adapt them to new scholarly developments. Some earlier *Encyclopedia* categories have been reconceptualized in light of new academic interests. For example, the subject section originally titled "Women's Life" is reconceived as a new volume, *Gender*, and the original "Black Life" section is more broadly interpreted as a volume on race. These changes reflect new analytical concerns that place the study of women and blacks in broader cultural systems, reflecting the emergence of, among other topics, the study of male culture and of whiteness. Both volumes draw as well from the rich recent scholarship on women's life and black life. In addition, topics with some thematic coherence are combined in a volume, such as *Law and Politics* and *Agriculture and Industry*. One new topic, *Foodways*, is the basis of a separate volume, reflecting its new prominence in the interdisciplinary study of southern culture.

Numerous individual topical volumes together make up *The New Encyclopedia of Southern Culture* and extend the reach of the reference work to wider audiences. This approach should enhance the use of the *Encyclopedia* in academic courses and is intended to be convenient for readers with more focused interests within the larger context of southern culture. Readers will have handy access to one-volume, authoritative, and comprehensive scholarly treatments of the major areas of southern culture.

We have been fortunate that, in nearly all cases, subject consultants who offered crucial direction in shaping the topical sections for the original edition have agreed to join us in this new endeavor as volume editors. When new volume editors have been added, we have again looked for respected figures who can provide not only their own expertise but also strong networks of scholars to help develop relevant lists of topics and to serve as contributors in their areas. The reputations of all our volume editors as leading scholars in their areas encouraged the contributions of other scholars and added to *The New Encyclopedia*'s authority as a reference work.

The New Encyclopedia of Southern Culture builds on the strengths of articles in the original edition in several ways. For many existing articles, original authors agreed to update their contributions with new interpretations and theoretical perspectives, current statistics, new bibliographies, or simple factual developments that needed to be included. If the original contributor was unable to update an article, the editorial staff added new material or sent it to another scholar for assessment. In some cases, the general editor and volume editors selected a new contributor if an article seemed particularly dated and new work indicated the need for a fresh perspective. And importantly, where new developments have warranted treatment of topics not addressed in the original edition, volume editors have commissioned entirely new essays and articles that are published here for the first time.

The American South embodies a powerful historical and mythical presence, both a complex environmental and geographic landscape and a place of the imagination. Changes in the region's contemporary socioeconomic realities and new developments in scholarship have been incorporated in the conceptualization and approach of *The New Encyclopedia of Southern Culture*. Anthropologist Clifford Geertz has spoken of culture as context, and this encyclopedia looks at the American South as a complex place that has served as the context for cultural expression. This volume provides information and perspective on the diversity of cultures in a geographic and imaginative place with a long history and distinctive character.

The *Encyclopedia of Southern Culture* was produced through major grants from the Program for Research Tools and Reference Works of the National Endowment for the Humanities, the Ford Foundation, the Atlantic-Richfield Foundation, and the Mary Doyle Trust. We are grateful as well to the College of Liberal Arts at the University of Mississippi for support and to the individual donors to the Center for the Study of Southern Culture who have directly or indirectly supported work on *The New Encyclopedia of Southern Culture*. We thank the volume editors for their ideas in reimagining their subjects and the contributors of articles for their work in extending the usefulness of the book in new ways. We acknowledge the support and contributions of the faculty and staff at the Center for the Study of Southern Culture. Finally, we want especially to honor the work of William Ferris and Mary Hart on the *Encyclopedia of Southern Culture*. Bill, the founding director of the Center for the Study of Southern Culture, was coeditor, and his good work recruiting authors, editing text, selecting images, and publicizing the volume among a wide network of people was, of course, invaluable. Despite the many changes in the new encyclopedia, Bill's influence remains. Mary "Sue" Hart was also an invaluable member of the original encyclopedia team, bringing the careful and precise eye of the librarian, and an iconoclastic spirit, to our work.

Law and politics have provided a structure for the southern cultural identity, and they have offered prime expressions of cultural styles and ideologies associated with the American South. The region's laws sometimes diverged from those of the nation's, especially in de jure race relations in a white-supremacist South. The paternalistic, patriarchal, and socially hierarchical regional society authorized laws to reflect those outlooks. The region's religious culture found expression in the legal system, through antiliquor, antievolution, and antiabortion statutes. A court case, the Scopes Trial, is one of the region's most famous examples of its modern-traditional conflicts. A fictional lawyer, Atticus Finch, became a regional icon, a beloved and heroic figure in an era of social change.

Lawyers have often been politicians in the South, sharing in an oral culture that long prized storytelling and a down-home manner and making the combination of law and politics a natural one in this volume. Of course, politicians ranged from the intellectual Thomas Jefferson to the insurgent Huey Long, from the conservatism of Strom Thurmond to the liberalism of Bill Clinton— although the latter two certainly were not pure "types" of anything. The term "Solid South" expresses the degree of political unity that the region forged in national politics for a century after the Civil War, the term "courthouse clique" expresses the ruling power of local elites, and the term "Populism" acknowledges the persistent reformism that challenges conventional wisdom. The latter could be the progressive agrarian uprising of the 1890s or the reactionary counterrevolution of the decades after the 1960s. Cultural historians increasingly look beyond elections to find "politics" in the household economy, women's clubs, and black church life.

V. O. Key Jr., the political scientist whose landmark research in the 1940s documented the abiding patterns of southern politics, is still an often-quoted authority for understanding the historical distinctiveness of the region's political life. Key looked forward to a more rational politics than existed in his age, based in economic self-interest rather than the racial obsessions at the heart of so much southern political behavior in the era of Jim Crow segregation. More recently, the South's politics have truly been transformed in the last four decades. The Voting Rights Act empowered the once powerless African American population, who in turn helped reshape the Democratic Party in the South. One can chart a steady rise of the Republican Party in the South since the 1950s, but the 1990s were a watershed, with southern Republicans rising to national power as a result of Ronald Reagan's party winning both houses of Congress in the 1994 election. Three of the last four presidents have been born in the South (not counting George H. W. Bush, who is an adopted southerner), and the Republican Party has dominated recent presidential campaigns in Dixie. The region's continuing relevance to national politics is seen in debates that rage over whether the Democrats could win the presidency without the South. Meanwhile, Republican candidates in the last two decades have become competitive, for the first time since Reconstruction, in state and local contests, while Democrats, as seen in the 2006 elections, still succeed in congressional elections, gubernatorial races, and city and county governance.

The reference work categories established by James Ely and Numan Bartley for the law and politics sections of the original *Encyclopedia of Southern Culture* have held up well. In this new edition, new themes, including school prayer, culture wars, immigration policy and politics, and the image of the southern politician, have been addressed, and articles on political aspects of race, social class, and violence have been updated and added to the list of thematic entries. The politics articles in this volume include many historical entries that were not part of the politics section of the earlier *Encyclopedia*, providing needed context for readers of this volume. Both the law and politics subjects herein have new biographical and topical entries, providing broader historical coverage than in the previous volume and recognizing significant developments in the contemporary era. Certainly, there is fuller coverage than before given to African Americans, women, and Republicans in southern politics. And the extensive updating of the earlier thematic articles provides much of what is new in this volume.

The editors want to acknowledge the missing presence of Numan Bartley from this volume. His distinguished scholarship made him one of the great political historians of the South, and his insights in his overview essay on politics and his conceptualization of southern political culture remain germane to the contemporary South as well as to understanding its history. Bradley Bond has supplemented Bartley's overview with his own insights on southern politics.

Law

Scholarly interest in the legal history of the South has grown markedly. Pioneering essays and monographs on specialized subjects have appeared in recent years. Yet many topics have not been explored in a systematic way. The explosion of literature on southern legal history raises a fundamental question. What, if anything, is unique about the legal history of the South? Certainly legal norms and institutions in the South shared much with the nation at large. There were many ties between law in the South and national developments. Like jurisdictions elsewhere, southern states (except Louisiana, with its Spanish/French legal heritage) relied on English common law as the basis of their legal system. Southern state constitutions reflected the central values of American legal culture—resistance to arbitrary power, popular sovereignty, and protection of private property. In many areas of law, differences between regions seem to be matters of degree and timing, rather than basic divisions.

It is especially instructive in this regard to consider the Constitution of the Confederacy. In 1861 the southern states had an opportunity to fashion a new fundamental law. Instead, the Confederate framers produced a document that closely reflected the constitutional values of the nation as a whole. In most respects the Confederate Constitution was a copy of the United States Constitution. Despite some gestures toward the principle of state sovereignty and provisions protective of slavery, the Confederate Constitution asserted national authority over the states. However one assesses the motives of Confederate leaders, they did not envision a wholesale displacement of existing constitutional norms.

Yet, without overstating southern distinctiveness, it is difficult to escape the conclusion that the South's legal past was distinct in important respects. The challenge for historians is to capture the interplay between regionalism and national legal norms in shaping southern law.

Antebellum South. The peculiar legal needs of a developing plantation economy caused the jurisprudence of the Old South to diverge from national norms in some major ways. Historians have described antebellum southern society as patriarchal and particularistic, rooted in a class structure and in the traditional folkways of a scattered rural population. Unlike the modernizing commercial and industrial elites of the North, southern planters favored a nonbureaucratic legal system that left important public powers in the hands of private individuals. Preindustrial attitudes and behavior—clan loyalties, submission to community standards, an unwritten code of masculine honor—remained strong in the Cotton Kingdom long after they had been displaced elsewhere by the more impersonal mores of a market-centered legal order. Without the presence of slavery, however, these factors would have produced only minor legal differences between the South and the rest of the nation. Every state, after all, possessed some idiosyncratic laws and institutions that grew out of diverse settlement patterns, geographic conditions, and socioeconomic needs. Slavery alone unified the South and shaped a unique regional mentality that found expression in every aspect of antebellum southern culture, including the law.

The slave codes established a comprehensive system of social control that denied basic common law and republican values. Common-law doctrines protected a person's natural rights of life, liberty, and property; republican ideology encouraged enterprising individuals to share in the risks and profits of a developing capitalist economy. But market individualism and personal autonomy had no place in slave law. The master-slave relation, unlike the employer-employee relation, rested not upon voluntary agreement, but upon force. This raised the difficult task of reconciling two antithetical labor systems within a single body of law. Slave issues could not be completely divorced from the rest of American law, however, nor could masters always claim exclusive control over their slaves. Personal injuries, contracts, and crimes often involved nonslaveholding whites, and southern judges in such situations looked for guidance to the leading decisions of northern jurists. As the Civil War approached, capitalistic values made increasing inroads into the law of slavery and threatened to undermine even the status slaves had as "chattels personal."

In mortgage cases involving slaves, for example, some southern courts at first fashioned equitable remedies to preserve slave families and to give hard-pressed masters additional time to redeem their slaves. By the 1850s, however, judges had become more responsive to the legal claims of creditors and tended to treat slaves no different from other forms of property subject to forced sale. The treatment of slave victims and defendants in criminal cases followed a similar pattern. Although a few judges made common-law protections available to slaves through statutory construction, most agreed that slaves had no enforceable legal rights. The slave codes did prohibit the worst kinds of white abuse, such as maiming and killing, but penalties varied greatly, depending on whether the offender was a master, a lessee, an overseer, or a total stranger. Such a classification scheme strongly resembled that used to compensate any property owner for the loss or impairment of a valuable commodity.

Despite an emphasis on slave-based agriculture, antebellum southerners accepted much of the 19th-century legal culture designed to enhance commercial enterprise. Southern judges generally embraced modern contract law based on market values, as well as the doctrine of caveat emptor. Similarly, courts in the region embraced the concept of corporate charters as irrevocable contracts. Indeed, legislators enacted general incorporation measures to make the advantages of corporate enterprise widely available. Despite initial misgivings, southern lawmakers increasingly adopted limited liability for stockholders in order to encourage investments. In the same vein, southern lawmakers adopted strongly interventionist policies to encourage construction of railroads. State legislatures provided generous subsidies to railroad companies and even built some lines as a public enterprise. Southern judges, like their northern counterparts, upheld the delegation of eminent domain power to railroad companies.

For the enforcement of their laws and customs, southerners relied much more than other Americans upon informal agencies of social control. In every southern state, the judicial and police systems were rudimentary and weak, compared to the bureaucratic structures that existed in the North; and southerners sought extralegal solutions to many problems that would have been resolved elsewhere through litigation. The gentlemanly elite—large planters, merchants, and professionals—demanded reparation for personal insults on the dueling ground; slaveholders dispensed discretionary justice on their plantations, which resembled slave prisons in some ways, and convened special courts to settle neighborhood slave disputes; and slave patrols, made up in large part of nonslaveholders, served as a private police force to apprehend runaway slaves and prevent insurrections. As the antislavery movement intensified after 1830, local vigilance committees incited mobs to assault (and sometimes kill) abolitionist critics, while other vigilante groups meted out summary punishment to those who violated a community's moral standards, such as gamblers and prostitutes.

States' Rights. To defend their slave society against political interference from the more numerous free states of the Union, southern theorists developed a states' rights argument based upon a compact model of constitutionalism. In the Virginia and Kentucky resolutions of 1798 and 1799, Thomas Jefferson and James Madison contended that the states had delegated only limited powers to the national government and could interpose their authority to prevent the implementation of unwarranted federal policies within their borders. Antebellum law students, most of whom were self-taught, learned strict constructionist and states' rights principles from the appendix to St. George Tucker's edition of William Blackstone's *Commentaries on the Laws of England* (1803), the most widely read legal text in the nation prior to 1852. Southern law schools, such as the University of Virginia Law School, combined Tucker's Blackstone with later states' rights commentaries on the Constitution to train generations of elite practitioners and judges in the ways of "true republicanism." The proslavery argument culminated in the *Dred Scott* decision of 1857, in which Chief Justice Roger B. Taney held that Congress had an affirmative duty under the Fifth Amendment to protect slave property in all federal territories. When antislavery forces captured the presidency in the election of 1860, 11 southern states declared the constitutional compact broken and seceded from the Union to form a new government, the Confederate States of America.

The Confederacy had little time to establish its separatist claims. Four years of bloody fighting and military defeat left the South devastated, slavery abolished, and the national government in apparently firm control of the Reconstruction process. Legal differences between the South and other regions thereafter diminished perceptibly, as improved transportation and communication networks brought southerners into ever-closer contact with modern corporate America. The transition from patriarchy to mass society was slow and painful, however, and antebellum folkways continued to influence the developing law of labor relations, family relations, and civil rights.

The Impact of Indebtedness. The South's debtor position markedly influenced the evolution of law in the region. Although southern lawmakers sought to promote entrepreneurial activity, they were limited by a capital-scarce economy. The credit needs of an agricultural society and the capital intensive nature of slavery fastened indebtedness on many in the South. As a consequence, sympathy for the plight of debtors uniquely characterized southern law. Debt relief measures found a consistently receptive climate throughout much of southern history. In the post-Revolutionary era, for instance, the refusal of Virginia and Maryland planters to pay their debts to English creditors triggered a major constitutional controversy and aroused sectional tension. During the same period, southern legislatures passed numerous laws staying the collection of debts. Imprisonment of debtors was modified extensively, and attachment laws protected a wide range of personal property from execution. Even extralegal techniques were employed to frustrate the collection of debt. In 1785 a crowd in Camden, S.C., forcibly prevented the circuit judge from hearing any debt cases.

The boom and bust cycles of the 19th century fostered other policies to protect debtors in the South. Homestead provisions, protecting a family home from creditors, originated in Texas and spread quickly to other southern states.

Homestead laws have long been a subject of intense controversy. Nonetheless, in 1873 the Supreme Court of North Carolina upheld that state's homestead provision in sweeping language: "Exception laws are based upon policy and humanity; and they do not impair, but are paramount to debts. If under our circumstances our people are to be left without any exemptions, the policy of christian civilization is lost sight of, and we might almost as well return to the inhumanity of the Twelve Tables of the Roman law." As late as 1928 the Supreme Court of North Carolina adhered to this view in an opinion that quoted the poem "Home, Sweet Home." Indeed, perceived misuse of Florida's generous homestead provision was a source of controversy in the early 21st century.

Similarly, most scholars agree that the married women's property acts were designed primarily to protect a wife's assets from her husband's creditors. It is no coincidence that Mississippi initiated the movement to enact such laws in 1839 and that a number of other southern states rapidly followed suit.

The Civil War intensified the debtor status of the South. Recovering slowly from the conflict, an impoverished South continued to occupy a distinct place in the polity. Southerners were divided as to how to resolve their economic woes. Many sought to lure northern capital with tax exemptions and subsidies in order to encourage business growth. Yet other southern leaders looked askance at northern domination of the southern regional economy and resisted the imposition of national credit norms.

Sympathy with debtors, therefore, remained a major theme in southern legal history during the late 19th century. Two examples are instructive. A wave of debt repudiation swept across the South as debt-laden states and cities sought to scale down their bonded obligations and reduce interest payments. This repudiationist policy, which sharply divided southerners, imperiled future credit and produced a bumper crop of lawsuits. Louisiana repudiated the largest amount of public debt, but all southern states scaled down some part of their obligations. The debt repudiation litigation is too complex for treatment here. In short, some southern states found shelter under the Eleventh Amendment against suits by bondholders. One must bear in mind that much of the repudiated state debt was held by northern investors, and so the sectional implications were obvious.

Further evidence of southern support for debtors came in the fiery debates over a national bankruptcy law. Many southern lawmakers opposed enactment of national legislation and preferred to rely on state insolvency laws. The practice of allowing debtors to prefer certain creditors was deeply ingrained in southern society. Critics argued that a bankruptcy measure would oppress debtors and favor outside creditors. With little sense of irony, they maintained that bankruptcy would reduce debtors to slavery. By the 1890s many southerners still viewed debt in personal and localistic terms and were fearful of uniform methods of handling insolvency. The protection of local debtors, of course, conflicted with the interests of nonresident creditors.

The Law and Postwar Economic Adjustment. Since Emancipation made the law of master and slave irrelevant, southern planters sought new legal means to control a work force of "free" blacks. At first they insisted that the freedmen sign long-term written contracts that tied them to the land for a full year in return for share wages. Military commanders and officials of the Freedman's Bureau approved such arrangements, which promised to stabilize agricultural production and enable landless ex-slaves to become property owners in time. But the planters and their legal allies soon managed to circumvent the rights of tenants under existing law by constructing a novel system of sharecropping that was peculiar to the South. The cropper, unlike the tenant, had no possessory rights in the land he farmed but was merely a wage worker, subject in practice to whatever conditions his employer imposed. Farm credit legislation further contributed to a vicious debt cycle that impoverished many white yeoman farmers and brought croppers and tenants alike under the permanent control of a new business class of landlords and merchants.

The Redeemer legislatures of the post-Reconstruction 1870s enacted crop-lien laws that greatly increased the power of rural creditors. Landlord-tenant law had long recognized a landlord's right to seize the crop of a tenant who had not paid his rent; the new legislation extended the rental lien to cover all advances made by a landlord or merchant and exempted little or none of a debtor's personal property from attachment. If the sale of a particular crop did not repay all advances, a southern court would order that the remaining indebtedness operate as a preferred lien on future crops. The only way a poor farmer could escape from a mounting burden of debt would be to move away and find a new landlord, but lawmakers foreclosed this possibility by using the criminal law to enforce contractual duties. Antienticement statues made it a criminal offense for anyone to hire a laborer already under contract; other laws imposed criminal penalties upon those who failed to fulfill a contract after receiving money or other advances from an employer.

Black tenant farmers and sharecroppers suffered most from the neopaternalism of postwar labor relations. Just as the black codes of 1865–66 had attempted to compel freedmen to work, the contract-labor laws and analogous vagrancy statutes established a modern system of peonage in the South. A defaulting black farmworker might be arrested and returned to his workplace;

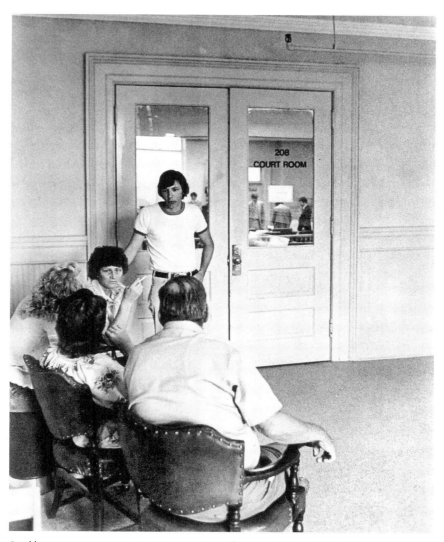

Outside a courtroom, Decatur, Ga. (Tennessee State Library and Archives, Nashville)

an unemployed stranger in town might be charged with vagrancy and put to work on a road gang or sent to a backwoods plantation until he earned enough money to pay his fine. Although the Thirteenth Amendment clearly prohibited such "involuntary servitude," peonage persisted in some southern areas for decades. By appealing to customary bonds of deference and personal loyalty, as well as comprehensive laws, southern landlords achieved a degree of control over their workforce unmatched by employers elsewhere in the nation. Local power structures did not begin to collapse until the emergence of New Deal

farm policies in the 1930s. As federal agencies set production quotas and regulated farm credit, southern agriculture lost its distinctive legal characteristics.
Mechanization after World War II displaced tenant farmers but hastened the
transformation of southern agriculture.

The industrial labor policies of the 20th-century South also warrant mention.
Southern states were reluctant to ban child labor. Southern legislatures were
slow to enact workers' compensation statutes—Mississippi, the last holdout in
the nation, did so only in 1948—while right-to-work laws proliferated. Strong
opposition to union activity resulted in persistently low rates of unionization.
In the absence of comparative studies of regional labor practices, however, the
distinctiveness of the southern experience remains unclear. The changes in class
relations introduced by the factory system may well have evoked similar responses from employers and lawmakers everywhere. By the 1930s, in any event,
the passage of the National Labor Relations Act, the Fair Labor Standards Act,
and other congressional measures effectively ended any lingering claims of regional autonomy, as the federal government began to regulate labor conditions
throughout the country. The southern labor market was increasingly integrated
into the national market. Regional wage differentials narrowed. By the start of
the 21st century the labor problems of the South were not unique, and legal
norms were adjusted accordingly.

Family and Religion. The late 19th century also witnessed the reconstruction
of domestic relations in the South. Although Mississippi inaugurated a nationwide movement toward married women's property acts in 1839, such laws gave
wives only limited control of their separate estates. They served in part to protect a woman's children and relatives by shielding family assets from the creditors of an improvident husband. Nonetheless, there was steady progress in
enlarging the property rights of married women. Southern lawmakers, moreover, steadily liberalized the grounds for divorce. Courts not only granted an
increasing number of divorces but also sometimes awarded alimony to wives.
Although anxious to preserve the institution of marriage, judges were often
sympathetic to wronged wives. In addition, southern courts increasingly broke
with common law and awarded custody of minor children to the mother. Thus,
southern states were part of a national trend to ameliorate the legal position of
unhappy wives.

The defeat of the Confederacy marked the end of a patriarchal slaveholding
society and left many southern widows in charge of one-parent households.
Courts responded to these realities by playing a more active supervisory role in

South and did much to eliminate regional differences in the conduct of criminal trials.

Civil Rights. In the field of race relations, southern resistance to change was particularly intense and unyielding. The U.S. Supreme Court undercut the nationalizing potential of the Thirteenth, Fourteenth, and Fifteenth Amendments by construing their provisions narrowly. In the *Civil Rights Cases* (1883), for example, the Court ruled that the Fourteenth Amendment prohibited only state violations of individual rights; acts of private discrimination remained subject to state, not federal, control.

Racist social policies were widely accepted in the United States during the late 19th century. But the South stood out with its insistence on a legalized color line to separate whites and blacks. The Supreme Court approved emerging segregation laws as reasonable exercises of a state's police power in *Plessy v. Ferguson* (1896). Reflecting the prevailing intellectual climate, Justice Henry Billings Brown noted: "In determining the question of reasonableness [a state legislature] is at liberty to act with reference to the established usages, customs, and traditions of the people, and with a view to the promotion of their comfort, and the preservation of the public peace and good order." Customary racial practices in the South thus gained new legitimacy at the hands of the nation's highest court. With the further imposition of poll taxes, literacy tests, and other electoral requirements in the 1890s, southern lawmakers completed a structure of racial subordination.

Vigilantes also flourished in the New South. The Ku Klux Klan, the most celebrated vigilante organization, arose during Reconstruction to preserve white supremacy by intimidating black voters and their Republican allies. In the 1920s and the 1950s a revived Klan resorted to further acts of violence and terrorism in defense of white hegemony. Such planned violence formed part of a larger pattern of regional lawlessness that included an alarming increase in lynchings between the 1880s and World War II. Most lynch victims in the South were black, and most lynchings went unpunished because of the obvious collusion that existed between law officers and local mobs. Antilynching organizations called repeatedly for strong federal legislation to remedy the problem. But southern senators filibustered all proposed antilynching bills to death, invoking states' rights and racist arguments that might have been lifted from the congressional slavery debates of the 1850s.

Civil libertarians, on the other hand, had never accepted the caste laws of the late 19th century. From the beginning, many black communities engaged in economic boycotts and other forms of protest against local segregationist

A jury section in a courtroom, Franklin, Ga. (Jack Delano, photographer,
Library of Congress [LC-USF-34-43941-D], Washington, D.C.)

measures. With the founding of the National Association for the Advancement
of Colored People (NAACP) in 1909, civil rights strategy began to be formulated
on an interstate basis. By the 1930s black NAACP attorneys launched a carefully
orchestrated legal campaign that culminated in *Brown v. Board of Education*
(1954). The *Brown* decision rejected *Plessy v. Ferguson* and held that segregated
schools violated the equal protection clause of the Fourteenth Amendment. Because of the long-standing and complex nature of the segregation issue, however, the Court granted state school boards a reasonable time in which to sub-
mit desegregation plans to federal district judges for their approval.

Southern authorities responded to *Brown* by vowing noncompliance. There
were calls for a return to antebellum policies of interposition and nullification;
police assaulted peaceful black demonstrators; and some state legislatures replaced their public schools with "private" institutions. Despite the rise of "massive resistance," however, southern whites remained deeply divided over civil
rights. The economic boom that accompanied World War II had accelerated
the urban and industrial development of the South and created a large middle
class of businessmen, professionals, and white-collar employees. These groups
feared economic instability more than integration and helped to mediate tense

racial confrontations, as in the Little Rock crisis of 1957. The Warren Court's reapportionment decisions strengthened urban voters by curbing the power of entrenched rural white minorities; both *Baker v. Carr* (1962) and *Reynolds v. Sims* (1964) struck down unrepresentative political structures in southern states. Yet the Second Reconstruction stalled until Congress passed a comprehensive Civil Rights Act in 1964 and the supplementary Voting Rights Act the following year. In 1982 the Voting Rights Act was amended to encourage creation of predominately black districts. Vigorous federal enforcement of these measures brought many changes to the social and political life of the South. For example, the number of black elected officials increased rapidly.

Still, the civil rights successes of the 1960s, as demonstrated by the rapid collapse of formal segregation, lost momentum in the 1970s. A decade later northern and southern cities and suburbs were growing more alike in a pattern of racially separate housing and schools. Although problems lingered, the South was no longer strikingly out of step with national policy on racial issues. The current debate over affirmative action in employment and higher education is national in scope and not regionally defined.

National Convergence. Southern legal culture today displays no striking deviations from national norms. The unique identity of aspects of southern law in the 19th century has largely come to an end. Even legal training has become standardized and homogenized through the accreditation requirements imposed upon law schools across the country. In such important legal fields as real property, torts, corporations, and commercial law, the South is becoming progressively less distinct from other sections of the country.

The continuing importance of religion and race to southern culture creates, though, particular contexts for the legal system in the South. Evangelical Protestants, for example, who dominate the region's religious picture, have objected to Supreme Court decisions banning prayer in schools since the 1960s, and they have continued to devise ways to test the decisions. Supreme Court cases in 1992 and 2000, both of which originated in southern states, declared student-led prayers at graduation and football games to be unconstitutional, but evangelicals have since then experimented with "spontaneous prayers" at football games, planned but without identifiable leaders, as a way to circumvent Court rulings.

In terms of race-based cases, the Supreme Court has exercised oversight on issues that grew out of the Voting Rights Act and its mandate for fair elections in southern states with a history of racial disfranchisement. Cases from North Carolina (1990) and Georgia (2000) found, however, the Court suggesting that legislatures not take race into account in drawing districts. High-profile trials of the murderers of civil rights heroes from the 1950s and 1960s have been significant in continuing to reinforce perceptions of race-based injustices in the South's historic criminal justice system while at the same time creating new images of a legal system redressing old wrongs. Finally, the South leads the nation in capital punishment executions and is part of a national pattern of what has been called a "school-to-prison pipeline" in which the number of blacks in prison has quadrupled since 1980.

MAXWELL BLOOMFIELD
Catholic University of America

JAMES W. ELY JR.
Vanderbilt University Law School

Edward L. Ayers, *Vengeance and Justice: Crime and Punishment in the 19th Century American South* (1984); Peter W. Bardaglio, *Reconstructing the Household: Families, Sex, and the Law in the Nineteenth-Century South* (1995); Maxwell Bloomfield, *American Lawyers in a Changing Society, 1776–1876* (1980); David J. Bodenhamer and James W. Ely Jr., eds., *Ambivalent Legacy: A Legal History of the South* (1984); W. Hamilton Bryson, ed., *Legal Education in Virginia, 1779–1979: A Biographical Approach* (1982); Harvey C. Couch, *A History of the Fifth Circuit, 1891–1981* (1984); Pete Daniel, *The Shadow of Slavery: Peonage in the South, 1901–1969* (1972); George Dargo, *Jefferson's Louisiana: Politics and the Clash of Legal Traditions* (1975); James W. Ely Jr., ed., *A History of the Tennessee Supreme Court* (2002); Fletcher M. Green, *Constitutional Development in the South Atlantic States, 1776–1860: A Study in the Evolution of Democracy* (1930); Larry J. Griffin and Don H. Doyle, eds., *The South as an American Problem* (1995); Ariela J. Gross, *Double Character: Slavery and Mastery in the Antebellum Southern Courtroom* (2000); Sally E. Hadden, *Slave Patrols: Law and Violence in Virginia and the Carolinas* (2001); Kermit L. Hall and James W. Ely Jr., eds., *An Uncertain Tradition: Constitutionalism and the History of the South* (1989); Paul DeForest Hicks, *Joseph Henry Lumpkin: Georgia's First Chief Justice* (2002); A. Leon Higginbotham, *In the Matter of Color: Race and the American Legal Process: The Colonial Period* (1978); Michael S. Hindus, *Prison and Plantation: Crime, Justice, and Authority in Massachusetts and South Carolina, 1767–1878* (1980); Timothy S. Huebner, *The Southern Judicial Tradition: State Judges and Sectional Distinctiveness, 1790–1890* (1999); Herbert A. Johnson, ed., *South Carolina Legal History* (1980); Richard Kluger, *Simple Justice: The History of* Brown v. Board of Education *and Black America's Struggle for Equality* (1976); Steven F. Lawson, *Black Ballots: Voting Rights in the South, 1944–1969* (1976); Thomas D. Morris, *Southern Slavery and the Law, 1619–1860* (1996); Gail W. O'Brien, *The Legal Fraternity and the Making of a New South*

Community, 1848–1882 (1986); William H. Pease and Jane H. Pease, *James Louis Petigru: Southern Conservative, Southern Dissenter* (1995); William M. Robinson Jr., *Justice in Grey: A History of the Judicial System of the Confederate States of America* (1941); A. G. Roeber, *Faithful Magistrates and Republican Lawyers: Creators of Virginia Legal Culture, 1680–1810* (1981); Judith Kelleher Schafer, *Becoming Free, Remaining Free: Manumission and Enslavement in New Orleans, 1846–1862* (2003); "Symposium on the Legal History of the South," *Vanderbilt Law Review* (January 1979); Mark V. Tushnet, *The American Law of Slavery, 1810–1860: Considerations of Humanity and Interest* (1981); Christopher Waldrep, *Roots of Disorder: Race and Criminal Justice in the American South, 1817–1880* (1998).

Civil Rights Movement

After the Civil War, many black leaders worked for equal status between blacks and whites. The most prominent spokesman for this aspiration in the early 20th century was W. E. B. Du Bois. The National Association for the Advancement of Colored People (NAACP) was founded in 1909, and a year later the National Urban League was organized. In *Buchanan v. Warley* (1917) the Supreme Court invalidated residential segregation laws as a deprivation of property rights without due process of law. During the 1930s the Court started to condemn the discriminatory administration of criminal justice in the South. Despite these early victories against racial discrimination, the nation made little progress in the field of civil rights until the end of World War II.

The emergence of New Deal social programs and the egalitarian rhetoric of World War II produced a change in American thought and helped to undermine the intellectual justification for racial segregation in the South. In turn, this development produced a gradual but significant shift in the role of the federal government. President Harry S. Truman identified his administration with the movement for equal rights. In 1948 Truman issued an executive order eliminating segregation in the armed forces. He also called for a Fair Employment Practices Commission and a ban on poll tax requirements for voting. Although Congress rejected Truman's legislative program, he established civil rights as a national issue. Moreover, the federal courts began to adopt a broader reading of the equal protection clause of the Fourteenth Amendment. During the late 1940s several Supreme Court decisions outlawed segregation in interstate transportation and higher education. This trend culminated with the historic 1954 decision in *Brown v. Board of Education*, which proscribed compulsory segregation in public schools as a violation of the equal protection clause.

Important new developments also took place at the state level and in the private sector. Several northern states passed laws against racial discrimination. In 1946 Jackie Robinson became the first black to play major league baseball. Four years later diplomat Ralph Bunche became the first black to win the Nobel Peace Prize.

The NAACP led the legal battle against segregation, working for civil rights legislation and instituting litigation to compel desegregation of public schools in the South. Despite the *Brown* ruling and pressure from the NAACP, only a limited amount of racial integration occurred in southern schools between 1954 and 1964. Most southern states rallied to the banner of "massive resistance" and sought to obstruct implementation of racial desegregation. President Dwight D. Eisenhower did not envision an active role for the federal government in promoting school desegregation. Nonetheless, he did send federal troops to Little Rock in 1957 when state authorities attempted to block implementation of a court-ordered desegregation plan.

Other organizations also struggled for equal rights. Foremost among these was the Southern Christian Leadership Conference, headed by Dr. Martin Luther King Jr. Late in 1955 blacks in Montgomery, Ala., under King's guidance, began nonviolent protest by instituting a successful boycott of the city's segregated bus system.

During the early 1960s the civil rights movement underwent several important changes. After a period of hesitation, President John F. Kennedy placed the executive branch of the federal government squarely behind desegregation efforts. In 1963 Kennedy endorsed a broad civil rights proposal to outlaw segregation in public accommodations. At the same time, many blacks grew impatient with the slow progress in achieving desegregation. Blacks increasingly resorted to direct forms of protest. There were sit-ins at segregated lunch counters and Freedom Rides that challenged segregation in transportation facilities. Defenders of segregation often employed violence against blacks or civil right workers in an attempt to halt their activities.

The civil rights movement may have reached its climax in August of 1963 when more than 200,000 persons took part in the March on Washington. King, who had emerged as the leading spokesman for the civil rights movement, delivered an impassioned plea for racial equality. President Lyndon B. Johnson responded to this initiative by calling upon Congress to enact sweeping civil rights legislation. The resulting Civil Rights Act of 1964 required equal access to public accommodations and outlawed discrimination in employment. The Voting Rights Act of 1965 suspended literacy tests in several states and strengthened federal protection of the right to vote. The Twenty-fourth Amendment, ratified in 1964, barred poll tax requirements for participation in federal elections. Subsequently the Supreme Court declared unconstitutional the poll tax in state elections. Thus, by the mid-1960s the civil rights movement had attained most of its original objectives, which concerned conditions in the South.

The late 1960s saw a marked shift in the goals of civil rights leaders. The large-scale migration of blacks to northern cities, which had begun by World War I, produced recurrent ethnic conflict in urban neighborhoods. Accordingly, the movement increasingly focused upon racial discrimination in the North. In particular, black leaders challenged residential segregation, poor schooling, high unemployment among members of racial minorities, and alleged police brutality. Given the heavy concentration of impoverished blacks in the inner-city areas, resolution of these problems proved extremely difficult. Indeed, civil rights gains hardly affected the living conditions of many northern blacks. A

A 1963 civil rights protest march with Martin Luther King Jr., in Washington, D.C.
(Warren K. Leffler, photographer, Library of Congress [LC-U9-10361-15], Washington, D.C.)

wave of urban riots across the North highlighted racial tensions and also served to alienate white opinion.

In addition, by promoting new remedies for discrimination, civil rights activists moved well beyond the national consensus in favor of equality. The busing of pupils from one neighborhood to another in an effort to integrate schools, although endorsed by the Supreme Court in 1971, threatened traditional neighborhood schools and was opposed by the vast majority of whites. Congress debated numerous proposals to restrict this practice. In *Milliken v. Bradley* (1974) the Supreme Court ruled against busing across school district lines to achieve integration between suburban areas and the inner city.

Initiated in the late 1960s, affirmative action policies in employment and university admissions were often perceived by whites as favoritism to members of minority groups and proved highly controversial. In 1978 the Supreme Court outlawed the use of quotas to increase the representation of racial minorities in university admissions but ruled that race was a factor that could be considered in the admissions process to further the goal of diversity. In a line of decisions in the 1980s the Court similarly sustained the legality of race-conscious remedies to remedy racial discrimination in the employment context. Thereafter, the Court seemed to shift course by tightening the evidentiary rule for proving employment discrimination, thereby making it more difficult for complainants to prevail in such cases. Moreover, in *City of Richmond v. J. A. Croson Co.* (1989), the justices held that a municipal plan awarding a set percentage of construction contracts to minority-owned businesses classified persons on a racial basis, in violation of the equal protection clause. With the Civil Rights Act of 1991, however, Congress rejected a number of Supreme Court decisions that curtailed employment discrimination lawsuits, expanded the definition of discrimination, and reaffirmed its commitment to affirmative action.

Criticism of affirmative action in higher education mounted in the 1990s. In *Grutter v. Bollinger* (2003) the Supreme Court upheld a state law school's use of race, along with other factors, to obtain a diverse student body. Yet in a companion case the justices limited reliance on affirmative action by striking down a policy of automatically preferring members of certain racial minorities. Such a mechanistic scheme seemingly operated much like a quota and was found to violate the equal protection clause.

The civil rights movement scored a symbolic victory in the late 1980s with the establishment of the Martin Luther King Jr. holiday. Fifteen years after Dr. King's death, President Ronald Reagan signed a bill into law making the third Monday of January a national holiday celebrating his birth and life. The first national celebration of the new holiday took place 20 January 1986. Nearly all states also have official King holidays.

Racial gerrymandering—the practice of drawing a state's legislative districts to create the maximum number of majority-black districts—emerged as a contested issue in the 1990s. In 1982 Congress prohibited states from adopting laws that diluted minority political strength. After the 1990 census, the Justice Department urged southern states to increase the number of minority-black districts, advising southern lawmakers that such action was required by the Voting Rights Act. The Supreme Court has inconclusively addressed racial gerrymandering in a series of confusing cases. In *Shaw v. Reno* (1993) the justices held that the Voting Rights Act does not require states to draw unusual and oddly shaped districts just to create majority-black districts. In *Miller v. Johnson* (1995), moreover, the Supreme Court explained that a state violated the equal protection clause if race was the predominant factor in establishing district lines. Yet the gerrymandering issue is complicated because the racial composition of legislative districts is closely intertwined with partisan voting patterns. The Court has sustained legislative districts created for political advantage rather than impermissible racial reasons. Thus, the mere fact that lines were drawn to create a black-majority district does not prove that lawmakers were motivated by race. The courts and the Justice Department continue to wrestle with this thorny question.

Efforts to desegregate primary and secondary schools slowed in the 1990s following Supreme Court decisions that made it easier for school systems to be released from federal court supervision. School districts dropped busing schemes in favor of voluntary desegregation programs and began to return to neighborhood schools. Neither Congress nor the executive branch has pursued policies to foster desegregated schools. The emergence of Latinos as the largest minority group in the United States has further complicated the desegregation process. As a result, schools in the South and across the nation are becoming more segregated. Although the *Brown* decision ended de jure school segregation, the prospects for achieving widespread racial integration remain elusive.

In the early 21st century the civil rights movement is less focused on the South and increasingly finds expression in the political arena. African American leaders are concerned with economic disparities in black neighborhoods and predominantly black schools. The issues of racial profiling, housing discrimination, and inadequate education are also high on the list of those concerned with civil rights. But the political climate renders uncertain the prospects for significant change.

JAMES W. ELY JR.
Vanderbilt University Law School

Raymond Arsenault, *Freedom Riders: 1961 and the Struggle for Racial Justice* (2006); Catherine A. Barnes, *Journey from Jim Crow: The Desegregation of Southern Transit* (1983); Taylor Branch, *Parting the Waters: America in the King Years, 1954–63* (1988); James W. Ely Jr., *The Crisis of Conservative Virginia: The Byrd Organization and the Politics of Massive Resistance* (1976); Michael J. Klarman, *From Jim Crow to Civil Rights: The Supreme Court and the Struggle for Racial Equality* (2004); Richard Kluger, *Simple Justice: The History of* Brown v. Board of Education *and Black America's Struggle for Equality*, rev. ed. (2004); Nick Kotz, *Judgment Days: Lyndon Baines Johnson, Martin Luther King Jr., and the Laws That Changed America* (2005); Anthony Lewis and the *New York Times, Portrait of a Decade: The Second American Revolution* (1964); Harvard Sitkoff, *A New Deal for Blacks: The Emergence of Civil Rights as a National Issue* (1978); J. Harvie Wilkinson III, *From Brown to Bakke: The Supreme Court and School Integration, 1954–1978* (1979).

Common Law

The reception of English common law by the American colonies along the southern Atlantic Seaboard was largely a consequence of the shared cultural heritage of the dominant English-speaking folk. The continued growth and development of the common law in the South, however, was principally determined by external influences: (1) availability of case reports and law treatises, (2) legal training of the bar, and (3) a common English language. These factors not only resulted in the preservation of the common-law inheritance of the settlers but promoted resistance to Benthamite codification efforts surfacing in New England. These influences also encouraged the transplanting of the English-based common law to the South's western frontier.

To the colonists, legal tradition was embodied in the common law, which was in essence a set of personal rights in the form of procedures that governed and restricted the exercise of sovereign power. The view of common law as tradition and custom, the inherent birthright of the English settlers, became preserved in the form of judicial decisions and statutes. This enshrinement of the common-law heritage would have perhaps succumbed to external political movements favoring codification, however, but for the conservative influences of the entrenched professional bar of the South and a body of legal literature that enunciated the common-law tradition.

Early colonial America had no regular school of law. Unless American lawyers were so fortunate as to study in England with its Inns of Court, professors of law at Oxford and Cambridge, and learned judges, they entered practice with little formal law education; that is, they only "read" law. For their instruction, post-Revolutionary lawyers depended upon such literary sources as William Blackstone's *Commentaries on the Laws of England*. One cannot overestimate the influence of Blackstone's *Commentaries* on the early bar of the American South. From this work, American lawyers acquired knowledge of natural law, common law, equity, and "the charter rights of Englishmen." Indeed, the *Commentaries* were probably more influential in the American South than in the British Isles. Blackstone's treatises remained the standard manual for the South's lawyers until the publication in 1826 to 1830 of Chancellor James Kent's *Commentaries on American Law*. These early sources of case law and commentary were at once highly traditional, grounded in precedents of actual experience, and capable of growth and adaptation. Thus, no perceived need existed for a comprehensive written code. Even though there were repeated attempts at codification in New England, all failed in the southern states (except, of course, in Louisiana, where a previous legal heritage prevailed before the entry of the common law).

Interior of law library, City Hall, Memphis, Tenn., date unknown (Ann Rayburn Paper Americana Collection, Archives and Special Collections, University of Mississippi Library, Oxford)

As Americans settled west of the original 13 states of the young Republic, not only did they carry with them the common law, but often they found that it preceded their arrival. The governor and the judges of the Northwest Territory, for example, adopted the Virginia Act of Ratification (1788), which put into force in the area the common law of England and all English statutes of general application. Similarly, when the Mississippi Territory was established in 1798, its law embraced most of the provisions of the Northwest Ordinance and Virginia Act of Ratification as regarded the common law.

Generally being bookish people, the early frontier lawyers and judges brought the common law with them rather than making their own law, especially in the Old Southwest. As Judge Thomas Rodney of the Mississippi Territory wrote: "Special Pleading is adhered to in our Courts with as much strictness, elegance and propriety as many of the States, so that even the young lawyers are obliged to read their books and be very attentive to their business or want bread."

In addition to the treatises and doctrinal writings of Blackstone, Kent, and Joseph Story, frontier lawyers had access to an abundance of both English and American case reports, evident in their frequent citation of English and early American case precedents. In that way, the English common law was transmitted westward across the American South.

ERNEST S. EASTERLY III
Baton Rouge, Louisiana

William Blackstone, *Commentaries on the Laws of England* (1765); Melvin E. Bradford, *A Better Guide than Reason: Studies in the American Revolution* (1979); Ernest S. Easterly III, *Geojurisprudence: Studies in Law, Liberty, and Landscapes* (1980); W. B. Hamilton, *South Atlantic Quarterly* (Spring 1968); Russell Kirk, *The Roots of American Order* (1974); A. Kocourek, *American Bar Association Journal* (October 1932); Roscoe Pound, *The Spirit of Common Law* (1921); David Ren and J. E. C. Brierley, *Major Legal Systems of the World Today: An Introduction to the Comparative Study of Law* (1978); A. G. Roeber, *Faithful Magistrates and Republican Lawyers: Creators of Virginia Legal Culture, 1680–1810* (1981); Louis E. Wolcher, *American Journal of Legal History* (July 1992).

Convict Lease System and Peonage

The convict lease system was the means by which southern states dealt with their post–Civil War prisoners. Under this regimen, convicts were leased to individuals or corporations, who thus acquired a captive labor force and at the same time agreed to supervise it. As a result, the industrial landscape of the New South was dotted with prison work camps and stockades, home to inmates who were overwhelmingly (roughly 90 percent) African American. At their worst, these facilities afforded examples of human misery that shocked contemporaries and gave southern corrections a bad reputation.

Apologists pointed out that the state governments were impoverished, that penitentiaries erected before the war were destroyed, and that state and local officials had no reliable mechanism of control over recently freed black populations. In fact, models for privately run prisons were already in place. As early as 1825, Kentucky had leased its inmates to a businessman who sought to turn the penitentiary at Frankfort into a factory. In 1846 Alabama legislators leased the "Walls" at Wetumpka to the first of a series of entrepreneurs. The lure of turning a debit into a credit through off-site labor appealed to postwar officials, Republicans, and former Confederates alike.

The convict lease system should be understood as a child of slavery. White southerners (and many northerners) believed that African Americans needed the tutelage of their former masters—that left to their own devices, freedmen would fall into idleness and crime. Judges imbued with these beliefs found themselves dealing with a range of behaviors (ranging from genuinely criminal acts to mere rudeness) that once would have been handled extralegally by plantation discipline. In the post-Reconstruction world such offenses were punished by hard labor for the state or county. Judges of the period exercised considerable discretion in sentencing, taking into account the labor needs of sheriffs or lessees. Sentences tended to be long. Of 1,200 convicts leased by Georgia in 1880, more than 500 were serving terms of 10 years or more. In Texas, with more than 2,300 incarcerated in 1882, only two men were sentenced for less than 10 years.

By the 1880s several states had given their convicts over to large corporations. This had the merit of administrative simplicity and was also financially attractive. Georgia in 1876 divided 1,100 prisoners among three companies, each of which agreed to pay the state $25,000 per year. Tennessee and Alabama made their arrangements with the Tennessee Coal and Iron Company (TCI). In 1890 more than 800 Alabama convicts worked in TCI mines, for which the state was paid more than $180,000—6 percent of its yearly income. It would be an oversimplification to argue that the South was following the "Prussian Road" of authoritarian development. On the other hand—in light of many alliances between entrepreneurs and ultraconservative Bourbon politicians—it is true that racial ideology and law converged for the benefit of New South industrialists. The latter gained both cheap labor and a ready-made strikebreaking force.

Yet the concentration of convicts made them more visible to journalists, reformers, and other critics of the system. An assertion made during the period was that convict leasing was worse than slavery—that, as Woman's Christian Temperance Union leader Julia Tutwiler said in 1890, it had all of slavery's evils without the personal contact and paternalism that she viewed as "ameliorating features." She was right to think that most lessees had few occasions to look upon their laborers as individuals and only the slightest economic motives to promote their welfare. The frequency of escapes was such that camp managers tended to fire lenient guards and to employ shackles and close confinement whenever possible. The results were poor sanitation and scandalously high mortality from disease and accidents. While 1 to 2 percent of northern prisoners died each year, death rates of 15 percent were not unknown in the South.

Critics of the system were a diverse group, including the African American leaders Booker T. Washington, W. E. B. Du Bois, and Mary Church Terrell, white women activists like Tutwiler and Georgia's Rebecca Felton, agrarian politicians and labor activists who opposed corporate power, and an intriguing number of well-placed, otherwise conventional whites who can be called "Bourbon reformers." The most celebrated of the latter was the Louisiana writer George Washington Cable, whose nonfiction work eloquently denounced racial discrimination and southern penal practices. These disparate elements did accomplish certain reforms in the 1880s and 1890s.

Administratively, these years saw the creation of stronger state regulatory boards, staffed by men who were acquainted with professional organizations such as the National Prison Association. Through these boards (and with persistent lobbying by women's organizations) the states mandated improved standards of housing, diet, and health care and began to provide educational facilities for inmates. During the same period, the states began to exclude female prisoners and minors from the camps, placing them in separate facilities. By the turn of the century, reformist and anticorporate influences were strong enough to put some states on the road to ending the lease system, initially by working convicts on state-owned farms. A leader in this development was Mississippi, which took steps to abolish the lease system in its 1890 constitution (interestingly, the same constitution that effectively disfranchised black voters) and had opened Parchman Farm by 1901.

For all these improvements the convict lease system was irretrievably flawed. This is evident in the career of R. H. Dawson, chief inspector of the Alabama Department of Corrections (1883–96). A true Bourbon reformer, Dawson saw himself as a mediator between the convicts and TCI, the state's chief lessee. Each prisoner was expected to produce 4,000 pounds of usable coal per day; Dawson worked to insure honest timekeeping and decent living conditions. To improve morale and fend off vice, he distributed writing materials and encouraged letter writing. Thus miners could stay in touch with their families and more easily report corporate rule-breaking. He gave each convict a card with two dates written on it: the date of the man's full-sentence release and the date of his "short-time" release for good behavior. For several years Dawson's methods seemed to work, and convicts had a fighting chance to survive prison—and to leave it with coal-mining skills, which many proceeded to put to use.

Yet in the 1890s TCI officials steadily undermined Dawson's achievements. Guards goaded prisoners into riots that wrecked their "short-time" status. Company bosses bribed or pressured inmates into overtime work in exchange for company scrip that fueled gambling and black market activities. Clearly, the lessees preferred to handle overburdened, dissolute men, and Dawson concluded that the kind of order he was promoting—prison run as a school of discipline—could not take hold within the convict lease system. Governor Thomas Goode Jones (1890–94) agreed, and under his administration the state prepared to shift its corrections to Mississippi-style prison farming. However, the Panic of 1893 touched off a crisis of state finance, and Jones's successors preserved the always-profitable mining lease.

The eventual decline of convict leasing came about as a result of several factors: middle-class concerns over child labor, illiteracy, and public health; election of progressive Democrats such as Georgia's governor Hoke Smith (a major actor in that state's 1908 abolition of the lease); and the "good roads" movement in Georgia, North Carolina, and other states, which shifted convict labor to the highways under state control. State sponsorship of private indentured labor ended with Alabama's 1928 laws terminating the convict lease. But public laws had little to do with the survival of a parallel regime—peonage—still very much alive in the 1930s.

Large numbers of African American farmers were sharecroppers who paid the landowner half their crops in addition to the value of supplies received. Declining prices of staple crops almost insured that they (and their white counterparts) fell deeper in debt each year, thus creating a class of hopeless debtors. When plantation owners compelled tenants to work out their debts, the result was peonage. Across the region, contract labor laws criminalized breach of contract, opening the way for shadowy collaborations between planters and local law enforcement. Under this system a justice of the peace would arrange for a defaulting debtor to be arrested and fined on charges that might or might not be entered on his books. The landowner would appear, pay the fine, and be granted custody. Now the peon had to work out the fine (and the rest of his indebtedness) or risk another arrest. Though such practices appear (correctly) to modern eyes as a crude restoration of master-slave relations, they also meshed perfectly with a long-lived stereotype of black folk and poor whites alike—that the working classes must be forced to work.

Peonage was widespread in the "cotton belt," in Florida's turpentine camps, and other settings of isolation and poverty. Nonetheless, in the early 1900s a number of federal officials, most of whom were Republicans, joined forces with black spokesmen and a sprinkling of Bourbon reformers to challenge these practices. Acting under an 1867 statute U.S. attorneys brought cases before District Judges Charles Swayne (Fla.), Thomas Goode Jones (Ala.), Emory Speer (Ga.), and Jacob Trieber (Ark.). Their greatest success came in Alabama, where Judge Jones and Booker T. Washington quietly supported a state case, *Alonzo Bailey v. Alabama* (1911), in which the U.S. Supreme Court overturned Alabama's contract labor law. Subsequently (*U.S. v. Reynolds*, 1914) the high court also struck down Alabama's practice of assigning prisoners to private citizens. Still, these victories did not end peonage. So long as debt reigned supreme, so long as planters and industrialists were patrons of local lawmen, the corrupt regime would flourish.

PAUL M. PRUITT JR.
Bounds Law Library
University of Alabama

Brent Jude Aucoin, "'A Rift in the Clouds': Southern Federal Judges and African-American Civil Rights, 1885–1915" (Ph.D. dissertation, University of Arkansas, 1999);

Mary Ellen Curtin, *Black Prisoners and Their World: Alabama, 1865–1900* (2000); Pete Daniel, *The Shadow of Slavery: Peonage in the South, 1901–1969* (1990); Matthew J. Mancini, *One Dies, Get Another: Convict Leasing in the American South, 1866–1928* (1996); Blake McKelvey, *American Prisons: A History of Good Intentions* (1977); David M. Oshinsky, *Worse than Slavery: Parchman Farm and the Ordeal of Jim Crow Justice* (1996); Paul M. Pruitt Jr., *Reviews in American History* (September 2001); Hilda Jane Zimmerman, "Penal Systems and Penal Reforms in the South since the Civil War" (Ph.D. dissertation, University of North Carolina, 1947).

Criminal Justice

The South has a long-standing reputation for violence and criminal disorder. It also has an image as a region where violent white men went unpunished and where, until recently, citizens frequently resorted to vigilantism to maintain order. Scholars have blamed the region's poverty, its racism, its pessimistic view of human nature, and even its debatable Celtic heritage for this crime and violence. Historians have suggested that an ineffective legal system intensified the combativeness of southern society.

Two themes from the Old South—frontier individualism and the plantation system—have served most frequently to explain the legal system's inability to deal with crime. No one has advanced these ideas with more assurance than W. J. Cash in his book *The Mind of the South* (1941). To Cash, an intense individualism, buttressed by a belief in white supremacy, blunted the development of law and government, while the growth of the plantation system kept the police power decentralized. An effective legal system was neither expected nor desired.

Historians have done little to rebut Cash's interpretation. Charles Sydnor, for example, declared that just as geographical distance isolated the westerner from legal restraints, so "the social order diminished the force of law in the South." For other scholars, the private discipline enforced by masters over their slaves found its counterpart in extralegal or illegal means of resolving disputes between whites.

Although an ineffective legal response to crime may be yet another burden of southern history, there are reasons to doubt traditional interpretations of its causes. Students of the westward movement are no longer so certain that the frontier experience was abnormally violent or excessively individualistic. Much of the frontier, including the South, was a peaceful place where settlers tried to maintain order and re-create community. The urban disorder of the 19th and 20th centuries, especially in the North, also makes it difficult to conclude that lawlessness was uniquely western or southern. Moreover, the idea that informal

Public execution, Carrollton, Mo., 1896. Well into the 20th century, such executions were considered an effective warning to other would-be criminals. (D. S. Cole, photographer, Library of Congress [LC-USZ62-79432], Washington, D.C.)

punishment of slaves diminished respect for legal process finds little support in recent scholarship. Several studies reveal a surprisingly high regard for due process in slave trials in the lower courts and upon appellate review. Thus, slavery may not have dulled the region's legal sensibilities, as many scholars have supposed.

Two other problems remain with older interpretations of southern criminal justice. Historians have rarely compared the southern experience with that of other regions, even though such comparisons are essential to the argument that an inefficient criminal process was peculiarly southern. A more fundamental weakness is that the literature on southern justice often has not examined the best evidence of the region's legal behavior, local court records.

Recent efforts to gauge the response of local courts to crime suggest the need to revise significantly—but not to abandon completely—standard themes advanced by historians, especially as they apply to the colonial and antebellum South. There is considerable evidence, for example, of the inability of local southern courts to complete prosecution in a large percentage of criminal cases. An examination of colonial courts in North Carolina found that only half of all bills of indictments brought before the General Court reached trial; almost one criminal action in three simply disappeared from the system. More dismal figures surfaced in a study of four counties in antebellum Georgia, where just one case in four reached a decision on the merits of the accusation. But in neither instance was the southern experience unique. Comparisons with local courts in colonial New York and antebellum Indiana revealed strikingly similar patterns of ineffective prosecution. Southern law enforcement, in other words, was not atypical in its inability to secure judgments in criminal cases; the problem was endemic to rural, prebureaucratic communities in both the North and the South.

Many of the patterns of prosecution in southern jurisdictions parallel those found elsewhere. Most criminal actions involved petty offenses, although prosecutions for felonies consumed much of the time courts devoted to criminal matters. Of the more serious crimes, theft and other property offenses appeared regularly on criminal dockets, with urbanizing areas devoting considerable prosecutorial energy to these cases. The available data suggest, moreover, that southern grand juries and prosecutors, like their northern counterparts, identified those without property as offenders in such cases.

Crimes against morality also occupied the attention of local authorities. Although the incidence of prosecution was less than in the colonies and states of Puritan New England, gaming, liquor-related offenses, and sexual immorality were frequent crimes before southern trial courts. These findings not only suggest a modification in traditional interpretations that emphasize southern laxity in crimes against morality but also in recent arguments that 19th- and 20th-century criminal process ignored such crimes in its attempt to protect the economic order. Perhaps crime as theft replaced crime as sin in the criminal codes of other states, but southern courts continued the effort to maintain a common morality.

Of course, violent crime and not theft or moral disorder gave the South its image as a lawless region. Tales of duels, murder, and assault were stock items in scores of travel accounts, newspapers stories, and grand jury presentments. Historians also have credited southerners with a readiness to settle private disputes with fists, dirks, or pistols. Examinations of felony indictments appear to confirm this conclusion. Crimes against persons were constant items on court dockets; some studies have discovered that almost 4 of every 10 indictments involved either petty or serious acts of personal violence. This circumstance, present in the earliest records, continues to exist. In the mid-1970s the southern states led the nation in these crimes. Forty-two percent of all murders in 1975 were committed in the South; and the region's fastest-growing urban area, Houston, had earned the name "Murder City" for its large number of capital crimes. In 2005 the murder rate in the southern Census region, per 100,000 people, was 6.6, compared with a northeastern rate of 4.4 and a national rate of 5.6.

While the South's rate of indictments for violent behavior surpasses the standards for other regions, it is inaccurate to claim that grand juries and circuit solicitors ignored violent crime or treated it casually. Instead, the figures suggest that prosecution of violent crime was a central concern of the legal system. In cases tried to a verdict, moreover, the violent offender stood little chance of acquittal, especially in jurisdictions with urbanizing areas. The degree of success enjoyed by courts in securing convictions in cases of violent crime underscores the social agreement that law and not private vengeance provided the most acceptable method of resolving personal conflicts. For most southerners, criminal justice remained a matter for the courts.

DAVID J. BODENHAMER
The Polis Center
Indiana University Purdue University Indianapolis

Edward L. Ayers, *Vengeance and Justice: Crime and Punishment in the 19th Century American South* (1984); David J. Bodenhamer, *Criminal Justice History* (1983); Bradley Chapin, *Criminal Justice in Colonial America, 1606–1660* (1983); Daniel Flanigan, *Journal of Southern History* (November 1974); Michael S. Hindus, *Prison and Plantation: Crime, Justice, and Authority in Massachusetts and South Carolina, 1767–1878* (1980); Richard E. Nisbett and Dov Cohen, *Culture of Honor: The Psychology of Violence in the South* (1996); Kathryn Preyer, *Law and History Review* (Spring 1983); Phillip J. Schwarz, in *Ambivalent Legacy: A Legal History of the South*, ed. David J. Bodenhamer and James W. Ely Jr. (1984); Donna J. Spindel and Stuart W. Thomas Jr., *Journal of Southern History* (May 1983); Christopher Waldrep, *Roots of Disorder: Race and Criminal Justice in the American South, 1817–1880* (1998); Christopher Waldrep and Donald G. Nieman, eds., *Local Matters: Race, Crime, and Justice in the Nineteenth-Century South* (2001); Alan D. Watson, *North Carolina Historical Review* (January 1991).

Criminal Law

Criminal law outlines standards of conduct for every member of the community and sets the punishment for violation of those rules. Its substance proscribes behavior that might variously be described as immoral, violent, disruptive of public order, or destructive of property rights and relationships. Its procedures seek to ensure that accused persons receive a fair hearing on the merits of charges against them. Yet, as sociologists, criminologists, and legal scholars have demonstrated in numerous studies, the law in operation at times bears little resemblance to its formal codes, maintaining a close, supportive relationship to the dominant class in society.

Historians have generally failed to study the South's criminal process. Nowhere is this neglect more pronounced than in the written and common law that defined criminal behavior. Available scholarship, however, tends to refute the traditional view of the South as a region with primitive, unenlightened penal codes. From the colonial period to the Civil War, southern legislators and jurists joined with reformers elsewhere to rid the law of the vast number of crimes and harsh punishments of 16th- and 17th-century England. Although the South moved to prescriptive or legislative law somewhat later than did New England, criminal law in the colonial South relied more heavily on English precedent. It was strongly affected by local interpretation and less reliant on biblical injunction than was true in the northern, especially Puritan, colonies.

The tenets of Revolutionary republicanism demanded a limitation on the power of the state, thus stimulating reform of the criminal law throughout the new nation, including the South. Heavily influenced by 18th-century rationalism, the writings of Montesquieu and Cesare Beccaria, and the codification efforts of Edward Livingston, southern legislators by the 1820s had drafted criminal codes that rivaled those of northern jurisdictions. In fact, some scholars have labeled Georgia's code of 1816 the first successful codification of criminal law in the new Republic. Reforms included a sharp reduction in the number of statutory crimes and in the punishments prescribed for their commission. Capital crimes for whites were limited to treason (rarely enforced), murder, arson, and rape of a minor; and imprisonment in a state penitentiary—originally created as a place for the reformation of the individual miscreant—became the norm for most other serious crimes. Criminal procedures conformed closely to the due process requirements of state and federal bills of rights, at least as interpreted by 19th-century judges and commentators. Recent studies of local trial courts, moreover, reveal that patterns of prosecution, conviction, and sentencing paralleled those found in nonsouthern jurisdictions with similar demographic and economic characteristics.

These reforms in the written criminal law did not, however, apply to slaves, and in practice their application to free blacks was uncertain and idiosyncratic. Separate laws for slaves, often called "black codes," prescribed different courts, fewer procedural safeguards for defendants, and harsher punishment upon conviction. In addition, enforcement of misdemeanors and even some felonies was often left to owners or overseers.

It would not be accurate to claim that trial and punishment of criminal slaves fell outside the legal system or that their treatment was totally at the whim of the master. Undoubtedly, justice at the local level varied widely, depending upon the locale, the ratio of blacks to whites, and the nature of the crime. But historians have probably overestimated the degree of discretionary justice attendant upon slave trials. Several studies reveal a surprisingly high regard for due process in the lower courts and upon appellate review. This result should not suggest that the white South was wedded to the concept of equal rights before the law for slaves, but rather that the application of due process in these cases satisfied the formal requirements of a legal culture without jeopardizing white control over blacks. Procedural safeguards for slaves and free blacks were, for example, at risk whenever black violence threatened the status quo.

In one area of criminal law, namely, statutory prohibitions of immorality, the South differed from the North. Laws against crimes such as adultery, fornication, intemperance, and gambling remained prominent in southern codes long after northern legislatures had shifted attention to property and economic crimes. Crime as theft may have replaced crime as sin elsewhere, but official regulation of immoral conduct continued to be a feature of the criminal law in southern states. It was no accident that prohibition and other moral crusades found ready reception in the South; the region's legal system had a long history of attempting to regulate morality.

Violence increased after the Civil War and abolition, causing changes in criminal law, including the leveling of misdemeanor charges against violators of racial separation. Extralegal actions, especially lynching and vigilante actions, were used for more serious violations of racial and moral order.

Except for the area of race, southern criminal laws in the 20th century resembled those in other regions of the country. Codes became more complex and defined more possible criminal actions as the South became more urban and industrial. But there remained some differences between South and North. Although details are sketchy, southern lawmakers and prosecutors appeared less willing to use criminal statutes to prosecute corporate offenders but did increase considerably the severity of punishment for individuals convicted of economic crimes, especially those involving racial violence. For example, some southern states by the 1930s had enacted laws that allowed the death sentence for convictions of armed robbery, a clear reversal of a two-centuries-long trend to limit the number of capital crimes.

Criminal law in the modern South is virtually indistinguishable from codes elsewhere. At least three reasons account for this: pressures from the federal judiciary and the U.S. Justice Department, especially in the area of civil rights; the growth of a professional bar in the southern states; and the incorporation of southern states into a national economy. In the interpretation and enforcement of these laws, however, regional differences remain because of the force of precedent in the Anglo-American legal tradition and because of the unique influence each community exercises in decisions to prosecute criminal violations and, through the jury, in decisions on individuals charged with crimes.

DAVID J. BODENHAMER
The Polis Center
Indiana University Purdue University Indianapolis

Edward L. Ayers, *Vengeance and Justice: Crime and Punishment in the 19th Century American South* (1984); Warren M. Billings, *Louisiana History* (Winter 1991); Bradley Chapin, *Criminal Justice in Colonial America, 1606–1660* (1983); Daniel Flanigan, *Journal of Southern History* (November 1974); Michael S. Hindus, *Prison and Plantation: Crime, Justice, and Authority in Massachusetts and South Carolina, 1767–1878* (1980); A. E. Nash, *Virginia Law Review* (February 1970); Kathryn Preyer, *Law and History Review* (Spring 1983); Mary M. Stolberg, *Journal of Policy History* 7, no. 4 (1995); Charles S. Sydnor, *Journal of Southern History* (February 1940); Christopher Waldrep, *Roots of Disorder: Race and Criminal Justice in the American South, 1817–1880* (1998).

Family Law

The rules of family law have varied significantly from one southern state to another since the 17th century. From the beginning of English colonization of the southern area of North America, the family law that prevailed there was English in the sense that marriage was monogamous and ordinarily indissoluble, and many, but not all, of the rules of succession followed contemporary English rules. Few disputes, however, turned on familial status, and, unlike England, in the South there was no system of courts of the established church to adjudicate them. Significant French and Spanish colonization in the southwestern region did not occur until the 18th century. In the Spanish settlements the law of Castille prevailed along with special rules promulgated for the Indies, and these principles replaced the custom of Paris on the formerly French territory of Louisiana in 1769. For a decade in the mid-18th century, a Spanish auxiliary bishop resided in Florida, and from the end of the 18th century, a Roman Catholic bishop was in New Orleans. But Episcopal jurisdiction was never exerted in a way that had any permanent effect on the further development of familial legal institutions.

MARRIAGE. In Virginia, until 1794, marriages were by law performed by an Anglican clergyman, but thereafter civil marriages by a magistrate were allowed.

Elsewhere in the English South, civil marriage and marriage by the rules of various nonconformist sects had been tolerated from the 17th century. Throughout the English South, the provisional governor's license to marry outside the established church could generally be substituted for the premarital ecclesiastical publication of banns and the marital ceremony. This sort of license was the predecessor of later marriage-licensing practices.

In the Spanish region, marriages were entered into in accordance with the formalities required by the Roman Catholic Church. In the absence of a priest, the Spanish military commandant acted as a notary with two witnesses and supervised written contracts to marry, contracts that were to be solemnized by a priest at the first opportunity. In the case of unions of non-Roman Catholics, this formality was frequently not followed by a later religious ceremony, because the participants tended to regard the civil formality as comparable to that generally available in English America.

As a consequence of the early lack of available religious officiants, in some areas during the 18th century informal (or common-law) marriage defined by agreement, cohabitation, and public notoriety was also recognized or went uncontested. In the 19th century this institution was particularly well rooted in the Lower South and Texas. Elsewhere in the South other legal doctrines accomplished many of the same results as the informal marriage, though without giving the marriage validity for all purposes. Today 10 of the 50 states and the District of Columbia recognize informal marriages (including the southern states of Alabama, South Carolina, and Texas); and where entered into by citizens of those states, the marriage can be dissolved only by divorce and not by agreement.

Some legal requirements, such as waiting periods before marriage, vary widely among the states. Other requirements, such as the minimum age for marrying without consent of a parent, guardian, or court, are fairly uniform nationwide. Only one southern state's minimum age for marriage without consent varies from age 18. In Mississippi, the minimum age is 15 for the woman and 17 for the man. The requirements for marriage *with* parental consent, however, vary widely, regionally and nationally. The minimum age for marriage with consent is 14 for both men and women in Alabama and Texas and for women in South Carolina; 16 for both sexes in Georgia, Virginia, and Tennessee, for men in South Carolina, and for women in Arkansas; and 17 for men in Arkansas. These are the lowest specified ages in the South, though not in the nation.

MARITAL PROPERTY. As under Spanish law, equal sharing of the gains of marriage (community property) between spouses continued to prevail in Louisiana and Texas and is still maintained there. In other former southern dominions of Spain, the English law of marital property quickly supplanted the Spanish law as those territories were incorporated into the United States. Whereas under Spanish law the personality of both spouses was distinctly recognized in law, under English law the married woman's legal capacity was largely merged into that of her husband. All of her movable property became her husband's on marriage, he had the power of management of her lands, and he owned the income derived from them. The married woman was given significant control over her lands and slaves first in the Arkansas Territory in 1835, in Mississippi in 1839, and later elsewhere (Alabama in 1848, North Carolina in 1849, and Tennessee in 1850). In Alabama a judicial means was provided as early as 1872 for a married woman to have her disabilities removed so that she might enter into business transactions. Similar legislation was enacted elsewhere. But unless complying with such requirements, married women in most of the South lacked general contractual power. (Spanish principles that recognized a married woman's capacity to enter into contracts generally survived only in Louisiana.) In order to protect her creditors who supplied a married woman with goods necessary for her subsistence and that of her children, the law generally recognized the wife as her husband's agent of necessity, so that he was liable on such contracts that she made. Married women did not acquire full contractual capacity throughout the South until the mid-20th century.

Though all the southern states protected certain necessary movable property, such as household furniture and tools of trade, from the claims of creditors, Texas extended this protection to the family home in 1839. The concept of homestead was rapidly adopted throughout the Lower South but not in Virginia or the Carolinas until the late 1860s. From the early 19th century, a number of states also gave the surviving spouse occupancy of the homestead during widowhood.

CHILDREN. In the social and economic conventions of the 17th century through the 19th century, the husband-father was the head of the family and was responsible for its support. All family members, including the wife, were identified by his surname. This name requirement no longer exists, although the practice is still widespread. Though the law traditionally has not imposed a duty on children to support needy parents, such a requirement for support has been provided generally.

DIVORCE. As in the states to the north, legislative divorce had been available in some southern states from the late 18th century (in Virginia and North Carolina as early as 1789 and 1794, respectively), and some legislative divorces were granted in almost every southern state. For a time Georgia, Mississippi, Alabama, and Louisiana required a prior judicial separation before a legislative divorce could be granted, and during the first half of the 19th century more than 300 legislative divorces were granted in Georgia alone. From the mid-19th century onward, legislative divorce disappeared in the South, as elsewhere in the United States.

Although judicial marital dissolution for a cause arising during marriage was introduced in Connecticut in 1667 and some other northern states followed this example, it was not available in the South until Tennessee so provided in 1798. Judicial authority to dissolve marital bonds soon followed in the Mississippi Territory, Louisiana, Georgia, and the Missouri Territory, but in the Upper South it was somewhat delayed (North Carolina in 1827, Texas in 1841, and Virginia in 1850). Divorce was finally provided in South Carolina in 1872. But only a few years after it was adopted in South Carolina, judicial divorce was abolished there, and it was not reinstituted until 1949. A single act of adultery of the wife and persistent adultery of the husband were generally recognized as grounds for divorce, and North Carolina and Virginia recognized no other grounds than marital infidelity until the early 20th century. Elsewhere cruel treatment, desertion, and incompatibility of disposition were recognized as additional grounds and, where recognized, these causes were relied on in most divorce cases.

When faced with the need to provide for the wife on divorce, the laws of most southern states restored her lands to her and ordered the ex-husband to pay her support (alimony) until her remarriage or death, rather than making a division of property (which usually meant the husband's property). Louisiana and Texas divided the community property on divorce, and in Louisiana, alimony might also be granted. Very limited ex-spousal support was not instituted in Texas until 1995. From 1872, alimony after divorce was not available in North Carolina but was restored to a limited extent in 1919. By the late 20th century all southern states allowed a division of property associated with the marriage.

Divorce occurred infrequently in the 19th century, but there was no question that the father had a continuing liability for the support of his minor children after a divorce. Though many statutes of southern states spoke in terms of "nullification" of a marriage by divorce, they specifically provided that the children of the marriage were nonetheless legitimate. There seem to have been few disputes as to parental fitness for custody of children, and on divorce of their parents, children of tender years were typically put in the custody of their mothers as a matter of course.

Existing patterns of family law remained largely intact in the South until after World War II. In the 1940s, divorce became more widely sought, but local standards were strictly maintained in some states, as in Virginia and North Carolina, or divorces were simply not made available, as in South Carolina. For some years Alabama courts tended to open their doors to outsiders by applying very lax standards of proving local residence, and some southerners also sought divorces in nonsouthern locations with lax residential standards. Divorce for marital incompatibility, breakdown of marriage (so-called no-fault or modified no-fault grounds for divorce), or living apart for a specified time (sometimes for one or one-and-a-half years) was available throughout the South, although Arkansas and Louisiana have instituted covenant marriage for which dissolution is somewhat more difficult. Arkansas, Louisiana, North Carolina, South Carolina, and Virginia were among the 12 states nationwide that did not have no-fault, or modified no-fault, grounds for divorce. By the late 20th century the custody of minor children was commonly awarded to fathers as well as to mothers. Mothers as well as fathers were also required to support minor children after divorce. Although reciprocal legislation was passed as interstate compacts to achieve enforcement of postdivorce support of ex-spouses and minor children, the system was too cumbersome to have much practical effect, and with greater population mobility, support orders became increasingly difficult to enforce.

During the 1970s and 1980s the states enacted uniform laws to govern jurisdiction for the modification of child-custody orders when parents and children moved from one state to another. At the same time, the federal government attempted to assist in the enforcement of child-support orders and to prevent abduction of minor children contrary to child-custody decrees. Although the laws do not seem to forestall such abuses, their resolutions have become easier to handle.

LEGITIMATION AND ADOPTION. Where English legal traditions were maintained, a child's rights of intestate inheritance rested on being the parents' legitimate offspring. Most southern states followed the model of the Virginia succession statute of 1785 in making children born out of wedlock legitimate as to their mothers, and legitimate as to both parents if they later married. Legitimacy as to the father who did not marry the mother required legitimation on the part of the father by administrative or legislative act.

In the legislative records of southern states from about 1810 there are increasing instances of changes of children's names. Many name changes were unrelated to legitimation, but some clearly had intestate succession as their object. But many legislative acts for legitimation began to be identified as such, and some legislative acts mixed the terminology of legitimation and adoption. Most southern states also provided for bastardy proceedings by which a father was required to support his illegitimate minor offspring; these proceedings, however, did not legitimate the children. As a further consequence of concern for illegitimate birth and orphanage of minor children, instances of legislative adoption in the South increased after 1820. First (for the entire nation in 1846) in Mississippi a judicial means of adoption was also provided, while Texas (1850) and Alabama (1851) provided for adoption by formal, administrative process. Both of these patterns were followed in other states and became the standard modes of adoption after the new state constitutions of the 1860s and 1870s made private legislative acts of adoption unavailable. Virginia, however, did not provide for judicial adoption until 1892.

SUCCESSION. By the end of the 18th century the rule of intestate succession in the English South in favor of the eldest male had been everywhere replaced by intestate inheritance in favor of all children equally, and parents were forbidden to create entails. Apart from the right of the surviving widow, however, a married man had the right to dispose of his property as he pleased and to disinherit children with or without cause, except in Louisiana and Texas. In 1856 forced inheritance of children was abandoned in Texas, but the right of descendants to inherit a portion of a parent's estate was maintained in Louisiana until 1981, when only those under 23 were protected from disinheritance. Only Louisiana also assured ancestors a share of a child's estate, though the ancestor could be disinherited for certain specified causes.

In most of the South, married women were not allowed to make an effective will as long as their husbands lived. But the law was otherwise in the former Spanish provinces and has so remained in Louisiana, Florida, and Texas. Married women did not obtain the power to make wills elsewhere in the South until the 19th century. Because in most of the South so much of a wife's property and its control passed to her husband at marriage, the married woman was provided (as under English law) with a dower interest in one-third of her husband's land if she survived him. During the late 19th century this principle was expanded in most of the South to a statutory right in both lands and movable property in favor of either spouse in the property of the other, despite any provisions made by will. In Louisiana and Texas, however, the surviving spouse was entitled to his or her half share of the community property, and in Texas, a share of the separate property of the deceased spouse.

In the 20th century no significant changes were made in the law of succession, except with respect to illegitimates who have attained the right of intestate inheritance in Louisiana and, in Texas, have been accorded the status of legitimates when paternity is proved during the father's lifetime.

SLAVE FAMILIES. In the era prior to the end of the Civil War a sizable part of the population—consisting of black slaves—was outside the legal scheme of familial relations, and that fact had a significant impact on social mores and legal institutions of the region for some time to come. In the subculture of slavery, which prevailed in all of the South until the fall of the Confederate government, the family was not a recognized legal entity. Marriage between free whites and blacks (free or slave) was generally prohibited (as it was in many other states at that time), and criminal sanctions were provided for breach of the rule. Legitimization of illegitimate children of color by a white parent was also generally forbidden. After the Civil War former slave unions were recognized as marriages, but legislation prohibiting and punishing interracial marriages persisted in most areas of the South well into the 20th century. With the repeal of anti-miscegenation laws, interracial marriages are now permitted.

JOSEPH W. MCKNIGHT
Southern Methodist University

Peter W. Bardaglio, *Reconstructing the Household: Families, Sex, and the Law in the Nineteenth-Century South* (1995); Jane T. Censer, *American Journal of Legal History* (January 1981); Carl N. Degler, *At Odds: Women and the Family in America from the Revolution to the Present* (1980); Neil R. Ferguson, *American Journal of Legal History* (April 1990); Joseph W. McKnight, *Southwestern Historical Quarterly* (January 1983); Donna Elizabeth Sedevie, *Journal of Mississippi History* (Fall 1995); *Texas Community Property Law: Conservative Attitudes, Relevant Change, Law and Contemporary Problems* (Spring 1993); Peter Wallenstein, *Magazine of Virginia History* (Winter 1995).

Labor Relations and Law

No other region in the United States has been so affected by labor shortages as the South, and problems stemming from this situation have been reflected in southern law. Early European colonists immediately discovered the need for workers, a need partially satisfied through Indian labor and slavery, European indentured servitude, and finally African slavery. Initial contacts between Europeans and Indians resulted in some work relations, but it did not solve the labor shortage problems for settlers. By the end of the 17th century, British traders in the Carolinas had resorted to an extensive Indian slave trade, particularly in the deerskin trade network, but wars and diseases terminated this experiment with forced Indian labor.

Indentured servitude was legally sanctioned by the British Crown and Parliament, and it enjoyed longer existence. Indentured servants were declared "persons" within the meaning of the law, but the right to their labor was distinctly the property of their masters. Servants did have the right to labor contracts, and these contracts usually secured passage to the New World for a period of labor to pay for this debt. Labor contracts could be modified once black servants arrived in the colonies. Conflicts soon arose between free whites, indentured whites, and black slaves; poor whites had only their labor to sell and having to compete with blacks in slavery eventually made it more difficult for them in the South. This led to the appearance of white guilds and unions, whose members adamantly refused to train either slaves or, often, free blacks.

In North America slavery was centered in the South. Some scholars believe that the southern plantation had labor needs that could not have been met in any other way. These economic needs spawned legislation designed to augment and preserve the labor system that evolved. Other historians posit that the evolution of labor law did not reflect the evolution of slavery but promoted it, aiming at industry and production. They contend that slavery could not have existed but for "positive legislation."

Laws, however, were not designed to guide the system but to regulate it. Corrections were not imposed until problems had already become evident. Much of the early labor legislation was directly borrowed from Barbados, where the English had vast legal experience in the control and marketing of slaves. South Carolina adopted the 1688 Barbados Slave Code in 1712; Georgia, which originally forbade slavery, followed, and Florida adopted the Georgia Code in 1822. Most of the laws were not aimed at particulars of slave existence but at the preservation of the labor institution itself.

By 1755 most of the southern colonies had adopted slave codes that included under their jurisdiction most Africans and persons of mixed blood, excluding most Indians. The lineage of a slave was also a factor because the child's status followed that of the mother. Any free black who remained in slave territory for 12 months or more might be enslaved, and a freedman could be reenslaved. Georgia and Florida required all free blacks to have a guardian appointed; there were criminal sanctions for any omissions.

Still, there were few actual labor laws in the colonial South. Not until after the colonial period did extensive labor legislation and litigation occur. The masters seemed to make up the rules as they went along, and only changes in the economy and political pressures eventually forced sophisticated labor legislation.

Labor legislation in the South after the American Revolution began to reflect more clearly certain applicable concepts of property. Slave ownership under southern state law was ownership of equipment capable of labor. Most of the laws governing slaves and the slave trade came to be based upon existing principles of property and, later, tort law. Most labor law was enforced on the plantation itself or in local municipal courts. Often punishments for slaves were quite harsh. Particularly stringent punishments, such as lashings or mutilations, were imposed for brawling and drinking. As the black population grew, southern states required identification papers and travel cards for slaves leaving their master's land for any reason.

Because the slave was property (as later defined in *Dred Scott v. Sandford*), the masters were taxed accordingly. Some states required an importation tax and also a yearly tax for keeping slaves. Trading in slaves was second only to the production of cotton as a mainstay of the southern economy; labor was big business. Importation costs were great for slave traders, so they preferred a domestic trade. Hence, the market was in some way stabilized by forbidding the importation of new slaves. This also kept the demand for labor high. Statutes were passed making it illegal to buy, use, possess, or sell any illegally imported slaves.

With the taxation of slaves and the reduction of the importation of slaves, a new business arose to meet the labor demand, slave renting. Most renting contracts were for 50 weeks with two weeks off near the Christmas holidays. The lessor held title to the slave, but the lessee assumed all responsibility for the slave. If the slave ran away, the lessee paid; if the slave committed a crime or tort, the lessee had the responsibility for making it right. The lessee was also responsible for food, clothing, and medical care of the slave, as well as paying the annual taxes for "owning" a slave. Southern courts heard a number of contract disputes concerning the rights of lessees and lessors in slave-rental relationships. The Georgia Supreme Court ruled, for example, in *Latimer v. Alexander* (1853), that the lessee of a slave was to be held responsible for reasonable medical costs, adding that any other ruling would undermine the labor system.

Clearly, any master could hire out a slave for any period of time, but a slave or former slave was not allowed to offer his own services for hire. If the temporary master allowed any harm to befall a slave, the lessor could demand compensation for loss of value. Sometimes the lessee found it easier and cheaper to purchase the slave rather than pay compensation. In later years slave insurance became available, and many rental masters required the lessee to purchase a policy before allowing the slave to leave.

The actual regulation of labor was left to the plantation owner, slave owner, or overseer. Any law enforcement thus became a private matter carried out upon private land. Almost every aspect of the slave's life was dependent upon the needs or the whims of the master. A few laws existed to control the time or type of his labor. Slaves were not allowed to work for themselves or on Sundays, and they were not to be kept in the fields more than 14 to 16 hours per day. Certainly by the advent of the Civil War, masters could determine the kind, degree, and time of labor to which slaves were subjected with minimal interference. Such was the state of southern labor law.

Immediately after the Civil War, most white southerners still thought of "labor" as black. Widespread rumors that labor would leave the South or that it would be unstable prompted efforts to restrain the newly freed blacks in their exercise of what are generally perceived as traditional individual contract rights of labor. Southern states devised a highly restrictive crop-lien system, which led to pervasive sharecropping that featured exorbitant rents and one-sided contracts. When blacks tried to leave the South for homesteading on the Great Plains, white southerners reacted by imprisoning the "exodusters" for debt or by using violence. Black codes were passed by southern legislatures, forcing many blacks to labor against their wishes. These took the form of restrictive work contracts, debt peonage, convict labor, and surety agreements.

Late 19th-century economic developments placed even greater stresses upon the labor-scarce southern society. The Industrial Revolution spread particularly to the southeastern states with their abundant water. The industrialization of the Piedmont occurred primarily with labor that was white and youthful. Most labor worked in cotton, textile, tobacco, or lumber mills.

Child labor was especially prominent in southern manufacturing, in part because poorer whites and blacks stayed on the farm, sending their children to work in the mills and plants. By 1889 Louisiana was the only southern state to limit child labor in manufacturing to certain ages (between 12 and 14, depending upon the industry), and by 1900 only Tennessee had any further age restrictions.

The end of the 19th century brought with it a young, progressive breed of politicians who wanted to use the law to reform society and fight the nation's social problems. In the South this fervor took the form of fighting for child-labor regulation. North Carolina was a leader in southern Progressivism, beginning with the election of Governor Charles Brantley Aycock in 1900. In 1903, during Aycock's term, the first child-labor law in North Carolina was passed after a campaign begun by southern ministers, such as Rev. Alexander J. McKelway, and by northern textile manufacturers. Many ministers reflected the public indignation at the maiming of young children by machinery.

North Carolina industrialists, however, fought child-labor laws with vigor. In the first major child-labor court test, *Fitzgerald v. Alma Furniture* (1902), the North Carolina Supreme Court ruled in favor of a nine-year-old boy who had suffered a smashed hand while working. The decision sent a message to the state legislature, which adopted child-labor legislation the next year. That legislation would be tested and upheld in North Carolina's courts in *Rollins v. R. J. Reynolds Tobacco Co.* (1906) and *Gaines Leathers v. Blackwell Durham Tobacco Co.* (1907). By 1909 all the southern states had adopted child-labor laws.

The federal government also passed child-labor legislation. In 1916 Congress approved, and President Woodrow Wilson signed into law, the Owen-Keating Act, which prohibited the passage into interstate commerce of any goods produced by child labor. This all-encompassing legislation was strongly opposed by southern industrialists, who supported a test case to the U.S. Supreme Court. In *Hammer v. Dagenhart* (1918) the Court held the Owen-Keating Act to be unconstitutional because it exceeded the commerce powers of Congress and preempted powers reserved to the states. The Charlotte, N.C., cotton mill involved in the case could continue to hire children and to have its products shipped interstate. The states were now left to regulate the age at which minors could work, and for the South it remained at 12 to 14 years.

Eventually the *Hammer* precedent was struck down. Under the New Deal, the Fair Labor Standards Act of 1938 incorporated virtually the same language as the Owen-Keating Act. This was tested in 1941 in *United States v. Darby*. Although *Darby* violated portions of the Fair Labor Standards Act that did not apply to child labor, the full act was held as constitutional. The fight for child-labor regulation at the national level was over, and southern employers, such as Darby of Georgia, had to adjust accordingly.

The shortage of labor and the attitude toward labor relations as a private rather than public matter created in the 20th-century South a climate hostile to unionization. Membership in unions was protected by the federal Erdman Act, enacted in 1898 in the aftermath of a national railroad strike. Section 10 of that act prohibited any employer from preventing an employee from becoming a member of a labor organization. The prohibition of "yellow dog" contracts was challenged by the Louisville and Nashville Railroad when it fired William Adair, a master mechanic, because he had joined a union. The U.S. Supreme Court decision in *Adair v. United States* (1908) validated "yellow dog" contracts. Conditions of employment were not deemed the proper sphere of national regulation, and the Erdman Act was overturned.

The Adair case and a particularly vicious longshoremen's strike in Galveston, Tex., in 1920 encouraged southern states to pass antistrike legislation, termed "right-to-work" laws. Texas implemented five right-to-work laws. The first, instituted by Governor W. Lee O'Daniel, made violence in the course of a labor dispute a penal offense. In 1943 Texas passed the Manford Act regulating unions. A 1947 law contained three sections that gave all workers the right to bargain individually without discrimination, but the legislature outlawed contract clauses providing for union security. The Parkhouse Act of 1951 placed contracts containing union-security clauses under the antitrust laws of Texas, and an act of 1955 made it illegal to strike or picket in order to force an employer to bargain with any except a majority union. By 1947 every southern state except Alabama and Louisiana had right-to-work laws, and in 1954 Alabama adopted one. Today only Louisiana is without right-to-work legislation in manufacturing.

Challenges to southern right-to-work legislation by labor have been fruitless. Exemplary was the Tennessee case of Joe Mascari, who questioned a union contract providing for a closed shop. In *Mascari et al. v. International Brotherhood of Teamsters et al.* (1948), the Tennessee Supreme Court upheld the Tennessee Open Shop Law and, furthermore, made the act retroactive to those contracts of a closed-shop nature signed prior to the act. Integrating the workforce, particularly in the textile and poultry industries, has been more fruitful in the post–World War II era.

JOHN R. WUNDER
University of Nebraska at Lincoln

David Brian Davis, *The Problem of Slavery in Western Culture* (1966); J. R. Dempsey, *The Operation of the Right-to-Work Laws* (1961); Herbert Gutman, *The Black Family in Slavery and Freedom, 1750–1925* (1976); Nell Irvin Painter, *Exodusters: Black Migration to Kansas after Reconstruction* (1976); James D. Schmidt, *Free to Work: Labor Law, Emancipation, and Reconstruction, 1815–1880* (1999); Almon W. Tauber, *Indian Slavery in Colonial Times within the Present Limits of the United States* (1970); William G. Whittaker, *Child Labor in America: History, Policy, and Legislative Issues* (2003); Peter H. Wood, *Black Majority: Negroes in Colonial South Carolina from 1670 through the Stono Rebellion* (1974); Harold D. Woodman, *New South–New Law: The Legal Foundations of Credit and Labor Relations in the Post-Bellum Agricultural South* (1995).

Law Schools

For most of the 19th century, studying in a law school was not the predominant method of preparing for admission to the bar in this country. Although law schools had existed in the South since the founding of the College of William and Mary Law School in 1779, most candidates for admission to the bar prepared by studying in a law office as required in many states by the rules of the local courts. If no such preparation was required, then self-study was the usual method, followed by an exam in open court. Study in a law school, however, conferred prestige and added to the credentials of the lawyers who attended. Not until the middle of the 20th century did law schools provide the only means of preparing for a career as a lawyer.

The introduction of lectures on law at the College of William and Mary in 1779 was the result of the efforts of Thomas Jefferson who, as governor of Virginia, suggested the establishment of a professorship of law and police. "Police" referred not to law enforcement but to government. George Wythe, a judge in the court of chancery in Virginia, was appointed the first law professor. His course of study was limited to one year and consisted of lectures with frequent moot courts. In 1824 the college began conferring degrees. The law school suspended operation during the Civil War and did not reopen until 1922. Many of the leaders of the post-Revolutionary bar of Virginia, including John Marshall, attended the lectures by George Wythe or his successor, St. George Tucker.

The second law school established in the South was at the University of Transylvania in Lexington, Ky. The law department was established in 1799 and continued until it was interrupted by the Civil War. It was the first to seek out and collect a law library, which was supported by fees from auctioneers in Lexington. The library held one of the largest antebellum law collections in the country. Many leaders of the American bar in the central area of the nation attended this school. Its course of study was typical of the period, consisting of lectures and moot court arguments.

Many of the law schools established in the antebellum South began as private endeavors of lawyers or judges and later were incorporated into a college or university. Joseph Henry Lumpkin apparently established such a "law school" in Athens, Ga., around 1843; the school was incorporated into the University of Georgia in 1859. Lawyers and judges found it profitable to teach students in their offices, but if these endeavors can be called "schools," it is difficult to establish their identities or determine the precise number that existed at any particular period. This continued to be true in states where unapproved law schools were permitted to operate.

If these proprietary schools are disregarded, approximately seven other law schools were established in the Southeast during the period prior to the Civil War. Generally, the courses consisted of a one-year program made up of lectures and moot court participation. Although such education may be considered primitive by today's standards, it was generally of higher quality than many of the lawyers received through training in law offices or self-study. The justification for the schools' existence was to provide a more thorough and systematic study of the law. This was not a barren period in the annals of legal education, for many of the founders of these law schools were intellectuals who experimented with various techniques of teaching. For example, students were encouraged to keep a "commonplace" book in which their notes were recorded.

Law schools continued to be founded at a slow rate in the South after the Civil War, but events in another part of the country were shaping legal education and laying the foundation for law schools to become the only means of preparation for the legal profession. In 1870 Christopher Columbus Langdell introduced at the Harvard University Law School the case method of teaching law. This system consisted of reading cases to extract "principles or doctrines" in a scientific manner to arrive at the fundamental legal doctrines. However, southern schools were reluctant to embrace this method of teaching and most held out for the lecture method into the 20th century.

Meanwhile, the American Bar Association (ABA) was responsible for founding the Section on Legal Education in 1890 and was instrumental in establishing the Association of American Law Schools in 1900. These organizations began to agitate for a three-year program of study and attendance of law school as the preferred method of professional preparation. The University of Tennessee Law School was the only southern charter member of the Association of American Law Schools, which indicates that school's early acceptance of the standards prescribed by these accrediting agencies. After 1910 such law schools as Texas, Kentucky, Georgia, Tulane, Vanderbilt, and Virginia became members, which conferred a greater prestige on them. In this period many of the better law schools began to hire academic law teachers rather than relying upon practicing attorneys as professors; this strengthened the method of teaching. During the decade of the 1920s, more southern law schools became members of the Association of American Law Schools and began to meet the standards prescribed by that association.

The Association of American Law Schools and the Section on Legal Education of the ABA soon began to have an impact on legal education in the South by periodic inspections of the facilities and the preparation of standards. These standards addressed such issues as the length of required study, methods of teaching, and physical facilities. These standards were suggested objectives for the schools to attain. The case method of teaching law as developed at the Harvard Law School in the late 19th century was strongly promoted as a replacement for the lecture method. The appointment of full-time law teachers was encouraged, and schools were especially encouraged to discontinue stressing local law. Attention began to focus on the physical facilities. The law library was an important adjunct to legal education, and it is not surprising that one of the earliest standards required that the collection include the reports of the highest court of the state and the U.S. Supreme Court, a selection of legal texts, and local and federal statutes. Until approximately 1950, law libraries were modest affairs, but after that date more emphasis was placed on expanding the collection to include English reports, all the American reports, and much more.

Another significant development in legal education after World War I was that law professors sought to further their knowledge by attending one of the more prestigious law schools of the East. In fact, by the last decades of the 20th century, an advanced degree had become a prerequisite for employment as a law professor. These changes were not brought about overnight but were incremental and can only be documented state by state as the bar examiners began to raise the requirements. As late as the end of World War II, a few southern law schools boasted of preparing individuals to practice law in the local courts. All of the ABA standards impacted legal education in the South. ABA approval was made a necessity as more states adopted a statute requiring graduation from an accredited law school as a prerequisite for admission to the practice of law. Most of the standards were objective rather than qualitative, based on the theory that better teaching methods would be the result of better libraries and facilities and the interaction of teachers. After World War II the number of law schools increased significantly as the demand for legal education mushroomed.

Acting under the doctrine of separate-but-equal education, three southern states founded all-black law schools—at North Carolina Central in 1939, at Southern University in Louisiana in 1947, and at Texas Southern University in 1947, where the law school was renamed the Thurgood Marshall School of Law when it moved to new quarters named for Justice Marshall in 1976. The faculties of the state university law schools were often used as the faculty at these black law schools. Desegregation has had little impact on these schools, which have kept their identities and, generally, their limited student body. The Supreme Court case of *Sweatt v. Painter* (1950), which mandated the desegregation of the University of Texas Law School, was a landmark in overturning legal support for racial segregation.

By the beginning of the 20th century, women had won the right to become members of the bar, but their numbers were small, usually limited to less than 5 percent of the student body. In the 1960s, this changed drastically as women came to constitute as much as 40 to 50 percent of the total student body.

ERWIN C. SURRENCY
University of Georgia

Abraham L. Davis, *Journal of Negro History* (Winter/Spring 1985); Robert F. Durden, *North Carolina Historical Review* (July 1990); Craig Klafter, *American Journal of Legal History* (July 1993); Michael D. L. Landon, *The University of Mississippi School of Law: A Sesquicentennial History* (2006); David John May, *The Pursuit of Excellence: A History of the University of Richmond Law School* (1970); Alfred Z. Reed, *Training for the Public Profession of the Law* (1921); John Richie, *The First Hundred Years: A Short History of the School of Law of the University of Virginia* (1978); E. Lee Shepard, *Virginia Cavalcade* (Spring 1988); Robert Stevens, *Law School: Legal Education in America from the 1850s to the 1980s* (1983).

Lawyer, Image of

Two types of lawyers have traditionally appeared in American fiction—conscientious, elite practitioners and predatory shysters. Although southern legal characters tend to conform to these basic stereotypes, they also embody distinctive regional values that set them apart from Yankee and western lawyers.

The typical antebellum practitioner, such as Philpot Wart in John Pendleton Kennedy's plantation novel *Swallow Barn* (1832), is a transplanted English gentleman. Warmhearted, courtly, and a bit eccentric, he can quote passages from the Greek and Latin classics as readily as citations from Coke and Blackstone. With ties of kinship and professional service to the planter class, he also shares the patriarchal ideology of slave owners. A staunch defender of slavery and states' rights, he recognizes the importance of unwritten law—local custom and community opinion—in regulating the behavior of white southerners.

Even extralegal violence, including dueling and vigilantism, may seem at times an appropriate means of settling personal disputes, and the lawyer is generally as willing to seek personal retribution in affairs of honor as the most thin-skinned of his clients. Judge York Leicester Driscoll in Mark Twain's *Pudd'nhead Wilson* (1894) thus reacts in characteristic fashion to the news that his nephew has taken an assailant to court: "You cur! You scum! You vermin! Do you mean to tell me that blood of my race has suffered a blow and crawled to a court of law about it?"

As a practitioner, the antebellum attorney takes a special interest in the plight of the legally disadvantaged, including women, paupers, and slaves. Ishmael Worth, the lawyer-hero of Emma Dorothy Eliza Nevitte (E.D.E.N.) Southworth's *Ishmael; or, In the Depths* (1863), wins fame by vindicating the legal rights of women before all-male juries; Edward Clayton, in Harriet Beecher Stowe's *Dred: A Tale of the Great Dismal Swamp* (1856), argues unsuccessfully for extending to slaves the legal protection granted as a matter of course to children and other dependents.

More paternalistic and emotionally involved in his client's affairs than his counterparts in other regions, the southern lawyer prizes equity above black-letter rules in all cases. Although he is quite familiar with abstract legal terminology and doctrine, he prefers to appeal directly to the feelings of jurors through spellbinding courtroom oratory in the manner of Patrick Henry. The image of the antebellum practitioner as a wise and chivalrous community leader has persisted in popular fiction, and it figured prominently in Hollywood's sentimental re-creation of the Old South in the movies of the 1930s and 1940s.

There was, however, a darker side to antebellum lawyering that found expression in fictional accounts of the frontier bar. Joseph G. Baldwin's humorous classic, *The Flush Times of Alabama and Mississippi* (1853), introduced a variety of lower-class, backwoods attorneys who used their minimal legal skills to exploit a gullible public. Typical of the breed was Simon Suggs Jr., who won his law license in a card game. Although the village pettifogger appeared in much northern fiction as well, he represented for southerners a peculiarly dangerous and subversive force. In a plantation society that cherished personal honor and customary practices, Suggs and his kind threatened to establish a new system of pecuniary values that had no place for patriarchal mores. As quintessential economic men, they repudiated all obligations except those dictated by self-interest. A clear line of descent links them to William Faulkner's unsavory Snopes clan in the 20th century.

The archetypal imagery of a divided profession—patricians versus rednecks—reappeared in Thomas Nelson Page's *Red Rock* (1898), Thomas Dixon's *The Clansman* (1905), and other Reconstruction novels. The legal villains in these works tend to be poor, white carpetbaggers and scalawags who are explicitly allied with Yankee businessmen in a conspiracy to "mongrelize" and industrialize southern society. Leading in a grassroots resistance movement against these alien forces is a younger generation of elite attorneys, who preserve the paternalistic outlook of their elders. Schooled in the racist tenets of social Darwinism, they equate southern "civilization" with white supremacy and invoke higher-law sanctions to justify disfranchisement and other assaults upon the legal rights of blacks. "We will take from an unprofitable servant the ballot he has abused," declares Charles Gaston, the hero of Dixon's *The Leopard's Spots* (1902). "It is the law of nature. It is the law of God." Dixon's ideas, dramatized in D. W. Griffith's powerful film *Birth of a Nation* (1915), reached mass audiences around the world.

Until the Warren Court precipitated a "Second Reconstruction" of the South by holding segregated schools unconstitutional in *Brown v. Board of Education* (1954), fictional lawyers continued to support the racist institutions they had helped create. The self-righteousness of Dixon and Page diminished percep-tibly, however, in works that dealt with race relations from World War I to mid-century. Here, the typical lawyer was a troubled liberal, who acknowledged the injustice of segregation and risked community censure by defending individual blacks who had been falsely accused of crimes. Yet he never attacked the system directly, because he believed that fundamental changes must await the erosion of custom and the growth of a more enlightened public opinion. Such ambiva-lence characterized the actions of Gavin Stevens in William Faulkner's *Intruder in the Dust* (1948), Atticus Finch in Harper Lee's *To Kill a Mockingbird* (1960), and Mary Winston—one of the few female attorneys in southern fiction—in Robert Rylee's *Deep Dark River* (1935).

As the civil rights movement intensified in the South during the early 1960s, the image of the tradition-conscious practitioner underwent a striking reevaluation. No reputable novelist of the Second Reconstruction had a kind word for diehard segregationists. In sharp contrast to the literary stereotypes of the late 19th century, legal characters who defended southern autonomy and customary racial practices were now perceived as villains, while NAACP attor-neys and other latter-day carpetbaggers received praise for forcing state and local officials to comply with national civil rights laws. The pattern is clearly dis-cernible in Jesse Hill Ford's *The Liberation of Lord Byron Jones* (1965), in which the mindless traditionalism of an aging small-town lawyer serves to radical-ize his young partner, Steve Mundine, who resolves: "Never again will I stand aside, defer to age and bigotry. We'll take it [the civil rights struggle] into the streets."

Female and black lawyers did not appear regularly in southern fiction until the 1960s. In scattered earlier works they were often treated with humorous condescension, and for black practitioners the transition from clown to hero was especially marked. Illustrative of popular attitudes in the 1920s were the Amos 'n' Andy–type sketches of black professionals in Birmingham, Ala., that Octavius Roy Cohen wrote for the *Saturday Evening Post*. From their comical antics it is a long step to the civil rights activism of David Champlin, the hero of Ann Fairbairn's *Five Smooth Stones* (1966). Champlin is as idealized a legal character as the virtuous Anglo-Saxons of Page and Dixon, whom he resembles in many ways. Like them, he uses his professional skills to liberate a worthy and long-suffering people.

With the nationalization of civil rights and the reemergence of two-party politics in the South, little remains of the shared values and siege mentality that once gave the region a sense of unique identity. Depictions of contemporary professional life reveal a notable absence of issues or practices that might be labeled traditionally southern. The television series *Hawkins* (1973–74), which starred James Stewart as a West Virginia attorney, contained no identifiably southern themes; and William Harrington's novel *Partners* (1980), which examines the careers of three women lawyers in Houston, Tex., might have been set as easily in any large city.

The popular television show *Matlock*, however, which ran from 1986 to 1995, evoked a contemporary South. Benjamin L. "Ben" Matlock was a folksy and colorful lawyer who played southern tunes on his banjoele and dressed in a signature light blue suit. Andy Griffith, who had created an enduring southern character in Sheriff Andy Taylor of Mayberry in the 1960s, was now Matlock, a down-home defense attorney with a pronounced southern accent and ways. The show was set in Atlanta and portrayed an older southerner navigating the modern world, albeit a bit cantankerously at times. The cartoon series *Futurama* parodies Matlock through a lawyer character who is a blue space chicken with a refined southern accent.

John Grisham's legal thrillers, and the films made of eight of them, represent popular portrayal of southern lawyers. The settings are sometimes in a traditional rural world, as in the five novels set in fictional Ford County, Mississippi. *A Time to Kill* (1989), Grisham's first novel, portrayed an African American father who kills the white man who raped his daughter, reversing a traditional southern narrative, with the community rallying around him. Grisham's settings are sometimes in newer landscapes of the South, with stories taking place in Memphis, New Orleans, and the Mississippi Gulf Coast. Attorneys are often young and inexperienced and frequently caught up in worlds of organized crime, corrupt corporations, great wealth, and unethical practices.

MAXWELL BLOOMFIELD
Catholic University of America

Maxwell Bloomfield, in *Law and American Literature: A Collection of Essays*, ed. Carl S. Smith, John P. McWilliams Jr., and Maxwell Bloomfield (1983); Joe Crespino, *Southern Cultures* (Summer 2000); James McBride Dabbs, *Civil Rights in Recent Southern Fiction* (1969); Mary Beth Pringle, *John Grisham: A Critical Companion* (1997); Floyd G. Watkins, *The Death of Art: Black and White in the Recent Southern Novel* (1970).

Massive Resistance

Coined originally by U.S. Senator Harry F. Byrd from Virginia on 25 February 1956, the words "massive resistance" denoted and embodied the white southerner's organized and all-out resistance to the effective implementation of the

U.S. Supreme Court's school desegregation decrees and to the subsequently intensifying civil rights movement in the South. Though the words themselves became the South's clarion call in the wake of the Supreme Court's May 1954 *Brown v. Board of Education* ruling and its following implementation order in May 1955, a genuine expression of southern white resistance to the federally initiated civil rights programs, which were destined to uproot the region's racial status quo, had already been detectable by the late 1940s.

In the presidential election year of 1948, when the Democratic National Convention, in spite of southern protest, adopted the strongest civil rights plank ever, a disgruntled group of some 6,000 southern delegates from 13 states gathered in Birmingham, Ala., and organized the States' Rights Democratic Party, or Dixiecrat Party. While the platform adopted by the Dixiecrats forcefully presented the case for states' rights, stressing the importance of such concepts as home rule and local self-government, the core of these southern Democrats' propositions revolved around their racial fears and anxieties. Interlocking the issues of states' rights ideology and white supremacy, the Dixiecrat revolt laid a solid foundation for the South's future massive resistance.

On 17 May 1954, when the Supreme Court unanimously outlawed legally imposed racial segregation in public schools in *Brown*, the worst nightmare visited many white southerners whose hostility toward the national Democratic Party, the federal government, and the probable increase of black civil rights activities had been intensifying. Resenting the ruling, some white southerners insisted that their cherished "segregated southern way of life" was God-ordained, and some, even though they were few in number, resorted to abominable forms of violence to defend the region's racial status quo. Still others resurrected and reintroduced a seemingly more sophisticated theory of states' rights constitutionalism to defy the Supreme Court decree and to combat the ever-intensifying civil rights movement in the South.

Immediately after the *Brown* decision, disaffected white southerners began to organize a number of private groups dedicated to the segregationist cause and anti-*Brown* enterprises. Among those, the Citizens' Council became the most vocal and widespread organization in the South. Organized in the summer of 1954 in the Mississippi Delta town of Indianola, Miss., the Citizens' Council symbolized and even personified the defender of the "segregated southern way of life," and it appropriately adopted the words "states' rights" and "racial integrity" on its organizational emblem. Despite the Citizens' Council's own claim that it was a nonpolitical, grassroots organization, its political influence soon stole over the state governments of the Deep South.

Though ordinary white southerners' involvement in the resistance move-

Protest rally at the Arkansas state capitol in response to the admission of the Little Rock Nine to Central High School, 1959 (John T. Bledsoe, photographer, Library of Congress [LC-U9-2919-25], Washington, D.C.)

ment was indispensable, what really made "massive resistance" massive and even respectable was the official and governmental sanction given by the southern states. Leading the crowd, on 1 February 1956 the Virginia state legislature adopted a so-called interposition resolution, whereby the state in essence asserted that the U.S. Constitution was a compact among the states and that each state could block actions of the Union unilaterally, adversely affecting the national interests and general well-being. More specifically, the resolution condemned the Supreme Court for usurping Virginia's inherent right to maintain racially separate public school facilities. The very next day, Alabama followed Virginia's example, and South Carolina adopted its own interposition resolution on 14 February.

While Virginia and the two Deep South states were on the verge of waging another Civil War, on 25 February 1956 Senator Byrd issued his fateful statement in Washington, D.C. Stressing the importance of unified southern support for interposition resolutions, Byrd called for "massive resistance" in the South to challenge the Supreme Court's school desegregation rulings. Inspired and heartened by Byrd, Mississippi and Georgia then adopted their resolutions. Mississippi would soon create a tax-supported agency to implement the resolves expressed in its interposition resolution—the Mississippi State Sovereignty Commission. Dubbed Mississippi's "segregation watchdog agency," the state sovereignty commission eventually became the most emphatic anti-*Brown* and anti–civil rights official agency throughout the South.

Along with the southern states' governments, their representatives in Congress added respectability to the resistance movement. On 12 March 1956, 19 U.S. senators and 82 representatives from the 11 former Confederate states approved and signed the "Southern Manifesto." In the manifesto, whose formal title was the "Declaration of Constitutional Principles," those 101 southern lawmakers pledged themselves to use all lawful means to bring about a reversal of *Brown*. By November, three other southern states—Louisiana, Florida, and Arkansas—had officially declared their opposition to the Supreme Court rulings.

In September 1957 the entire nation witnessed the first dramatic confrontation between a southern state and the federal government over school desegregation in Little Rock, Ark. The historic importance of the Little Rock crisis was that federal troops protected black civil rights in the South for the first time since Reconstruction. Moreover, the incident taught white southerners that the federal executive branch, though reluctantly, had now joined forces with the judicial branch in order to implement the *Brown* decisions in the South. Soon after the Little Rock incident, "massive resistance" attained its height, with "integration by federal might" and "race-mixing by bayonets" becoming the watchwords for the movement. By the end of 1957 the legislatures of 11 southern states had enacted some 200 segregationist and anti-*Brown* laws.

Legal battles and physical confrontations that pitted southerners against the federal government and civil rights organizations continued into the 1960s, and a series of traumatic and rapid-fire events on the civil rights front engulfed the region and, particularly, its Deep South states. Incidents such as the University of Mississippi desegregation crisis in September 1962, where Governor Ross R. Barnett's indecisiveness and irresponsibility eventually led to campus riots; Governor George C. Wallace's "standing in the schoolhouse door" during the University of Alabama desegregation ordeal in June 1963; and the brutal Neshoba County, Miss., murders perpetrated by members of the Ku Klux Klan in June 1964 during the Mississippi Freedom Summer Project, all gravely contributed to the demise of both the legality and the respectability of "massive resistance." Furthermore, the federal legislative branch finally threw its full support behind the other two branches to protect the constitutional rights of black southerners. In this respect, the passage of the Civil Rights Act of 1964 and the following Voting Rights Act of 1965 served the fatal blows to the South's already abating "massive resistance."

By the dawn of the 1970s, the vast majority of white southerners and their political leaders had realized that "massive resistance" was in fact massive fallacy. However, the eradication of the resistance movement's dark legacies and its negative impact on the region remains something with which the South, to this day, still struggles.

YASUHIRO KATAGIRI
Tokai University (Japan)

Numan Bartley, *The Rise of Massive Resistance: Race and Politics in the South during the 1950s*, 2nd ed. (1999); Jack Bass and Walter DeVries, *The Transformation of Southern Politics: Social Change and Political Consequence since 1945* (1995); Earl Black, *Southern Governors and Civil Rights: Racial Segregation as a Campaign Issue in the Second Reconstruction* (1976); Earl Black and Merle Black, *The Rise of the Southern Republicans* (2002); Dan Carter, *The Politics of Rage: George Wallace, the Origins of the New Conservatism, and the Transformation of American Politics* (1995), *From George Wallace to Newt Gingrich: Race in the Conservative Counterrevolution, 1963–1994* (1996); Hodding Carter III, *The South Strikes Back* (1959); David Chappell, *Inside Agitators: White Southerners in the Civil Rights Movement* (1994); Kari Frederickson, *The Dixiecrat Revolt and the End of the Solid South, 1932–1968* (2001); Yasuhiro Katagiri, *The Mississippi State Sovereignty Commission: Civil Rights and States' Rights* (2001); Michael J. Klarman, *From Jim Crow to Civil Rights: The Supreme Court and the Struggle for Racial Equality* (2004); Matthew Lassiter and Andrew Lewis, eds., *The Moderates' Dilemma: Massive Resistance to School Desegregation in Virginia* (1998); Alexander Leidholdt, *Standing before the Shouting Mob: Lenoir Chambers and Virginia's Massive Resistance to Public-School Integration* (1997); Jeff Roche, *Restructured Resistance: The Sibley Commission and the Politics of Desegregation in Georgia* (1998); Jeff Wood, *Black Struggle, Red Scare: Segregation and Anti-Communism in the South, 1948–1968* (2003).

Police Forces

Police forces in the South increasingly resemble their counterparts in other regions of the country. The civil rights movement of the 1960s and the influence of national standards of professionalism in law enforcement since the late 1960s combined to eliminate the distinctive features of southern law enforcement. With respect to role, organizational structure, personnel practices, operational procedures, and community relations, police forces in all regions of the United States share a high degree of similarity.

Prior to the civil rights movement, law enforcement agencies in the South were primary instruments in the maintenance of the racial caste system. Racial discrimination existed in both personnel practices and law enforcement policies. The civil rights movement swept away the more blatant forms of discrimination, and the increasing acceptance of professionalism in law enforcement supported the ideal of equality under the law. Racial problems persist today, but they are largely indistinguishable from similar problems faced by law enforcement agencies in other regions.

The primary responsibility for law enforcement in the United States is borne by the 3,300 county sheriffs' departments and over 13,500 municipal and township police agencies. Size rather than region accounts for the principal variations among these institutions. The Atlanta Police Department with 1,100 sworn officers, for example, has more in common with other big-city police departments across the country than with the small-town departments in neighboring parts of Georgia. By the same token, the two- or three-officer police department in Georgia is similar to the small-town police departments in other parts of the country.

Atlanta best exemplifies the impact of national influences on southern law enforcement. In the late 1970s the City of Atlanta hired Lee Brown as police commissioner. Not only was he black but he held a doctorate in criminology and had been the director of justice services (i.e., sheriff) in Multnomah County (Portland), Ore. The fact that he was from outside the South and had academic credentials was almost as significant as his race. By the early 1980s the Atlanta Police Department was one of the three in the entire country (Detroit and the District of Columbia were the other two) that had made substantial progress in the recruitment of black officers.

The county sheriff occupies a unique role in American law enforcement. The oldest law enforcement agency, with roots going back to the earliest English settlements, it has responsibility for all three branches of the criminal justice system. The sheriff polices rural areas, serves as an officer of the court, and maintains the jail. In addition, sheriffs in many states have important civil duties such as tax collection. An elected official, the sheriff has traditionally been one of the most important political figures in county politics. While the role of the sheriff has been greatly diminished in cities, where it is overshadowed by the municipal police, the office continues to be extremely important in rural areas.

The southern sheriff is a stock character in the entertainment and advertising media. The stereotype is still alive that portrays a fat, uneducated, and ill-trained person who is either a comic buffoon or a vicious racist. The inept Buford T. Justice in the *Smokey and the Bandit* movies and the corrupt Roscoe P. Coltrane of television's *The Dukes of Hazzard* are long-lived representations of the southern sheriff, although they are balanced by the folksy wisdom of a more positive image—Mayberry's Andy Taylor of *The Andy Griffith Show*.

In fact, southern sheriffs are no worse than their counterparts elsewhere in terms of physical condition, education, training, attitudes, or performance. Regardless of region, larger agencies tend to have higher standards than the very small rural agencies.

The number of sheriffs in the South who are black has grown since the 1970s to more than 5 percent of all southern sheriffs. Nat Glover, the sheriff of Duval County, Fla., since 1995, was the first African American to win that office in Florida since 1888. He runs a department of 2,500 with a yearly budget of $172 million. The South is home to nine of 24 female sheriffs in the nation. The nation's first female sheriff, Jacquelyn Barrett of Fulton County, Ga., was elected in 1992.

Municipal police departments fall into two general categories—big city and small town. Big-city departments are large and complex bureaucratic structures dominated by a military-style command. Civil service systems and collective bargaining agreements impose a high degree of rigidity on all personnel decisions. Southern police departments are somewhat less likely to have collective bargaining agreements between officers and their employers than are departments in other regions. This reflects the general weakness of organized labor in the South.

Big-city police departments have the most complex role of all law enforcement agencies. In addition to enforcing the criminal law, urban police spend most of their time as "peacekeepers." Officers are confronted with all of the social problems found in the urban context: crime, delinquency, family disputes, alcoholism, drug abuse, mental illness, and other problems arising from poverty and racial discrimination. In addition, the crowded urban environment generates conflicts over different standards of moral behavior.

The convergence of poverty and racial discrimination produces the most difficult problems for police. As the real and symbolic manifestations of the established legal order, police are inevitably in conflict with powerless groups.

This problem, generally labeled "police-community relations," is found in all urban communities. As a result of the civil rights movement and the drive to make law enforcement more professional, the police-community relations problem in southern cities is little different from that in other American cities.

Small-town police departments in the South, like their counterparts elsewhere, have a much less complex role. Even though the South as a region has a higher rate of criminal violence, particularly in terms of homicide, small towns have comparatively few serious crimes. Peacekeeping in small towns used to be primarily a matter of coping with minor acts of juvenile vandalism, although the spread of crack cocaine and crystal methamphetamine brought drug culture and related crimes into rural and small-town communities. Small-town police departments have an average of five or six officers. Professional standards, particularly in terms of personnel, are less stringent in small-town police departments than in big-city police agencies. Sheriffs in many fast-growing counties in the suburban South must deal with new kinds of residents in addition to longtime rural residents.

SAMUEL WALKER
University of Nebraska

John F. Heaphy, ed., *Police Practices: The General Administrative Survey* (1978); Michael G. Lindsay, *Arkansas Historical Quarterly* (Winter 2005); Elliott M. Rudwick, *Journal of Criminal Law, Criminology, and Police Science* (July–August 1960); Southern Regional Council, *Southern Justice: An Indictment* (1965); *USA Today* (16 December 1999); U.S. Department of Justice, *Sourcebook of Criminal Justice Statistics* (annual); U.S. Department of Justice, Federal Bureau of Investigation, *Crime in the United States* (annual); Samuel Walker, *The Police in America: An Introduction* (1982), *Popular Justice: A History of American Criminal Justice* (1980).

River Law

River law deals with rights of seamen, harbor workers, shippers, adjoining landowners, and various states where a river constitutes a boundary. Because of the tremendous volume of the waters of the Mississippi River and the relatively soft alluvial floodplain through which it courses, the southern states lying within the lower Mississippi River valley account for a large portion of this body of law. No distinctive "southern" law exists in this field, but the laws of southern states do differ from those elsewhere.

One of the most important property rights is that of the riparian owner—the person living adjacent to a waterway. The value of land bordering on a navigable stream far exceeds that of a parcel located away from the waters. It is access by commerce to the waters that gives the riparian land its value. As Justice Oliver Wendell Holmes noted, "A river is more than just an amenity, it is a treasure."

Most of the states of the Union follow the common law of England regarding land titles, but in determining the locus of state boundaries marked by navigable streams, the courts have looked to international law for guidance. International law and European custom suggest that when a navigable river constitutes the boundary between two independent states, the line defining this boundary is the middle of the main channel of the stream. However, the courts of the various states in early decisions reached differing conclusions as to what constituted the middle of the channel of a stream, some holding it to be a line equidistant from the banks at ordinary low water and others holding that it was a line marking the deepest water in the channel. The controversy was laid to rest in the case of *State of Iowa v. State of Illinois* (1892), wherein Justice Field, writing for the U.S. Supreme Court, concluded that the boundary should be "the middle of the main channel of the stream." This line has also been defined as the deepest channel, the principal channel, the track of navigation, and the thalweg.

As the bed of the river changes because of the gradual caving away of its banks and the concomitant building up of the opposite shore by the deposition of alluvion—a process called "accretion"—the boundary follows the migration of the river. However, during periods of great floods, the river sometimes leaves its old channel by cutting a new channel across the narrow neck of an elongated "point," followed in time by the adoption of the new channel by navigation.

Numerous disputes have arisen as to the apportionment of alluvion that has built up against a riverbank resulting in the creation of an elongated body of land called a "point," or "point bar." While all courts hold that this alluvion belongs to the owners of the banks to which it is attached, they are not at all in agreement as to how it is to be divided between coterminous owners of the banks. Generally, they all seek an equitable apportionment. The rule most often followed is that of allotting to each landowner as much of the new bank as would be in proportion to his ownership of the original bank. Thus, if A owned 500 feet and B owned 1,000 feet of old bankline and the new point bar measured 1,800 feet, A would be given 600 feet along the new bank and B would be allotted 1,200 feet, with the boundary connecting the old point of division with the new point of division by a straight line.

There is no uniformity among the states regarding the ownership of the beds of rivers, and each state determines its own laws. Thus, Mississippi holds that the riparian owner holds title out to the "thread" or "thalweg" of the stream, while in Louisiana, Arkansas, and Tennessee title is vested in the states. Again, there is no uniformity as to whether the "bed" stops at the low-water mark or high-water mark on the bank.

If an island forms on the bed of the stream by the deposition of alluvion, it becomes the property of the owner of the bed. However, if an island builds downstream to such an extent that it crosses the boundary of a downstream owner, the owner of the downstream bed gets title to as much of the island as is located on his portion of the riverbed.

All private rights in the bed and bank of a stream are subject to the superior right of navigation by the public. Therefore, the government can dredge or construct dikes in the interest of navigation. Structures that might cause an obstruction to navigation, such as piers and wharves, must first be authorized by public authorities.

M. EMMETT WARD
Vicksburg, Mississippi

School Prayer

In *The Provincials*, Eli Evans noted that Christian prayer was "a given" in southern public schools throughout most of the 20th century. Southern schoolteachers started off the day by saying a prayer, reading passages from the Bible, and delivering a brief message on godly character and morality before getting to the business of reading, writing, and arithmetic. When southern states expanded public education following the Civil War and up into the 20th century, religion became an integral part of the schoolhouse experience. Advocates of public education claimed that without the spiritual and moral foundation provided by religious activities the education of young southerners would be incomplete. Reba Wansley, a teacher in the South Carolina public schools, summed up the experiences of her educational colleagues: "For forty-one years, I have been teaching school. There has never been one single morning during these years that I have not read the Bible to my pupils and had prayer." These prayers, Wansley explained in 1962, had a positive impact on her students. Wansley's pupils informed her "that in our devotion every morning, they found the main thing that has helped them most through the years—whether on the battlefield, on their jobs, or in their home. If we, as teachers, don't give our pupils this instruction soon ours will be a godless nation, too."

A national survey conducted during the 1950s found that religion pervaded the South's public schools. Ninety-four percent of southern schools taught "spiritual values," compared with 75 percent of northeastern schools, 77 percent of midwestern schools, and 69 percent of western schools. Seventy-seven percent of public schools throughout Dixie conducted Bible reading. Northeastern schools had the second highest percentage of schools conducting Bible reading, with 68 percent. Ninety percent of southern districts surveyed held devotional services within their school systems. Only 9 percent of western school districts, 26 percent of midwestern districts, and 80 percent of northeastern districts held devotional exercises in the classroom. As indicated in these statistics, southern public schools did their part to ensure that the region earned its "Bible Belt" reputation.

Throughout the South, religious practices were normally left up to local school boards, the individual schools, or the classroom teachers themselves. State governments provided little guidance or interference on the teaching of religion in the classroom. With such practices in the hands of local communities comprised mainly of evangelical Christians, saying prayers and reading the Bible in a public school came naturally to most southerners. And most evangelical southerners had no doubt that prayer in the schools provided children with a firm foundation of morality and godliness. A native Tennessean fondly recalled morning devotionals, claiming that "hearing a prayer filled with sincerity made me a better citizen, a better employee, a better father, and a better neighbor." According to one Mississippian, religious exercises in the schools reminded young minds and souls that "reverence for God and His word was the number one priority."

U.S. Supreme Court rulings in 1962 and 1963 threatened the future of such cherished practices. In the 1962 case *Engel v. Vitale*, the Court ruled 6–1 that a prayer composed by the New York Board of Regents violated the establishment clause of the First Amendment. Though New York schools were not forced to use the prayer and the prayer was nondenominational, the majority opinion (written by Alabama native Hugo Black) declared that the state had overstepped constitutional boundaries when it began writing and recommending prayers for use in public schoolrooms. Just a year later, the Court found the practice of reading the Lord's Prayer and required Bible reading in public schools to be unconstitutional.

Following both decisions, southern members of Congress led the charge against the high court. Southern conservatives responded with an anger that had been previously reserved for the Court's ruling on school desegregation. South Carolina senator Strom Thurmond accused the Warren Court of continuing a perilous liberal trend that began with *Brown v. Board of Education*. After it rendered its decision in the *Engel* case, Thurmond took the opportunity to criticize the Court, saying it had "overstepped its bounds in loose and distorted interpretations of the Constitution on many occasions, but no court decision has shocked the conscience of the American people as has this one." Governor George Wallace of Alabama also spoke with a voice of defiance: "I don't care what they say in Washington, we're going to keep right on praying and reading the Bible in the public schools of Alabama." George Andrews, a fellow Alabaman and member of the U.S. House of Representatives, provided the most vehement retort: "They put the Negroes in the schools, and now they've driven God out."

Many white southerners interpreted the Court's antiprayer rulings as victories for the forces of atheism, communism, and immorality. Although the Court's ruling in *Engel* appeared to have limited effect on those states that did not compose official prayers or require schools to conduct religious activities, southerners left nothing to chance with the Court's rulings. Throughout the following decades, conservative white southerners repeatedly denounced the Court's prayer rulings in the halls of Congress and on the campaign trail. Some political leaders, such as Thurmond and Senator Jesse Helms of North Carolina, fought vigorously for a constitutional amendment that would protect prayer in the classroom but ultimately failed. In a 1966 vote on a school prayer amendment, 17 of the former Confederacy's 22 senators approved such an addition to the Constitution. Although the South made up only 22 percent of the Senate, 35 percent of those who backed the amendment were from southern states. In spite of determined southern support, the proposed amendment failed in 1966, as would others in later years. Southern states responded to failures at the federal level by passing "moment-of-silence" laws in the 1970s, though the Supreme Court later struck down those practices.

Failing to stand up for a school prayer amendment could be fatal to one's political fortunes in the South. Tennessee senator Al Gore lost his 1970 reelection bid to Republican Bill Brock largely because of Gore's opposition to a prayer amendment in 1966. That same year, Ralph Yarborough of Texas failed to hold his U.S. Senate seat thanks in part to his support for the Supreme Court's rulings on religion in the public schools. In the mid-1960s, North Carolina senator Sam Ervin became one of the most outspoken champions of strict church-state separation after initially opposing the Court's prayer rulings. Well into the 1980s the conservative Democrat routinely praised the Court for having a strict interpretation of the establishment clause. Unlike Gore and Yarborough, Ervin hung on to his Senate seat, but not before one constituent informed him that he shared "equal billing with the Devil" at revival services in North Carolina.

Although southerners clearly had hard feelings about the school prayer rulings, not all southerners rushed to condemn the Court. For nearly 20 years after the Court banned state-sponsored school prayer and Bible reading, the

Southern Baptist Convention issued numerous resolutions in support for these rulings, calling them triumphs for the separation of church and state. Leon Macon, the editor of the Alabama *Baptist*, broke ranks with most people in his state when he encouraged Baptists to "thank the Supreme Court for this decision [*Engel*] simply because such a required prayer is using the government to establish religion in our public schools." Some Southern Baptists especially feared that the entanglement of church and state would ultimately lead to the use of tax funds for Catholic parochial schools. Gore, a Southern Baptist, cited his church's historic support for church-state separation as the reason he opposed a prayer amendment. Maintaining a high wall between church and state was a major priority to the Southern Baptist Convention until the convention changed course and began to call for a school prayer amendment beginning in the early 1980s. Martin Luther King Jr. and major civil rights organizations such as the National Association for the Advancement of Colored People also backed the high court's decision, though in later years high-profile school prayer cases would unite blacks and whites in support of restoring religious practices to the public schools.

After the historic rulings of the 1960s, God could still be found in southern public schools. By no means were religious practices as widespread in the post-*Engel* period as they had been prior to the early 1960s. Supreme Court rulings in *Wallace v. Jaffree* (1985), *Jones v. Clear Creek Independent School District* (1992), and *Santa Fe Independent School District v. Doe* (2000) declared unconstitutional "moment-of-silence" laws, student-led prayers at graduation, and student-led prayers at football games, respectively. These cases infuriated conservative evangelicals. In light of these cases, many southerners agreed with David Barton, a conservative evangelical historian, who argued that rising problems with school violence, drug abuse, and teenage pregnancy could be traced to the declining presence of religion within public schools. Barton, along with Pat Robertson and Jerry Falwell, presented statistics showing what they believed to be a precipitous decline in the quality of American education and youth morals since 1962. The sense that public schools have become havens for godlessness and immorality has convinced many southerners of the need to send their children to private schools or, as seen in more recent years, to practice home-schooling.

Still, with most American schools in compliance with the Court's rulings, some southern teachers chose to follow the rebellious lead of George Wallace and continue praying with their students. In 1984 Jean Lancaster, a teacher from Greenville, Miss., told the *New York Times* that, every day prior to lunch, she would lead the class in a blessing. "If I forget to lead it, they remind me," she said. A 1980s study of religious activities in North Carolina public schools showed that prayer recitation and Bible reading continued on a regular basis in 39 of the state's 100 counties. The practice of student-led intercom prayers in many southern schools continued well into the 1990s. More recently, the terrorist attacks of 11 September 2001 sparked many religious conservatives, southern and nonsouthern, to call for the restoration of prayer in public schools. At the present, federal education guidelines, which are based on court precedent, state that teachers and school officials cannot lead religious activities. Religion may be discussed in classrooms and be taught as a subject, but it must be done in an academic and historical manner, not as a way to advance religion or to proselytize. Religious clubs, such as Bible groups and the Fellowship of Christian Athletes, are protected under the First Amendment and must be granted equal access to school facilities, according to the recent guidelines on religion in public schools. Though school prayer is no longer "a given," the Supreme Court's rulings have not completely barricaded religious practices from southern schools.

CHARLES WESTMORELAND
University of Mississippi

Joan DelFattore, *The Fourth R: Conflicts over Religion in American Public Schools* (2004); Bruce J. Dierenfield, *The Battle over School Prayer: How* Engel v. Vitale *Changed America* (2007); Richard Dierenfield, *Religion in American Public Schools* (1962); Charles Israel, *Before Scopes: Evangelicalism, Education, and Evolution in Tennessee, 1870–1925* (2004).

State Sovereignty Commissions

During the civil rights era of the 1950s and 1960s, a number of administrative commissions and legislative committees were created by southern states' governments to resist the civil rights crusades in the region. Though their names varied, these official agencies were bound together by common interests and purposes—defending the region's cherished "segregated southern way of life," devising both legal and extralegal means to circumvent the U.S. Supreme Court's desegregation rulings, propagandizing the vindication of states' rights ideology and racial separation, and suffocating any dissenters and deviators from the South's racial norms.

In the early 1950s, both reflective of the Dixiecrat revolt during the 1948 presidential election and in anticipation of the Supreme Court's impending school desegregation ruling, some Deep South states began to create legislative committees to protect their public schools from racial integration. The first such strategy-mapping segregationist committee was created by South Carolina in April 1951 when the state legislature established the South Carolina School Committee, also known as the Gressette Committee after its chair, State Senator L. Marion Gressette. Georgia then followed its neighboring state to organize the Georgia Commission on Education in December 1953.

Meanwhile, the Mississippi state legislature appointed a study committee officially called the Mississippi Legislative Recess Education Committee during the 1952 regular session. The committee's whole responsibility was to equalize the physical standards for black pupils with those for whites in the state's elementary and secondary educational systems in the hope that this equalization movement would influence the Supreme Court's upcoming school desegregation decision and, if possible, circumvent any federal court rulings unfavorable to the continuation of racial segregation in Mississippi's public schools. While reorganizing this study committee as the new State Education Finance Commission to have it supervise the construction of new public schools for black pupils and the consolidation of school districts in the state, the Mississippi legislature established the Legal Educational Advisory Committee in April 1954. In the name of preserving and promoting the best interests of both black and white Mississippians, the advisory committee, in substance, was vested with authority to draft segregationist laws to maintain racially separate schools in the state. The Legal Educational Advisory Committee would soon be converted into a tax-supported "permanent authority for maintenance of racial segregation" in Mississippi.

In the immediate aftermath of the Supreme Court's *Brown v. Board of Education* ruling in May 1954, Louisiana joined other Deep South states by creating the Louisiana Joint Legislative Committee on Segregation, better known as the Rainach Committee after an all-powerful state senator, Willie M. Rainach. A year later, the Supreme Court announced the implementation order of *Brown*, propelling southern states to organize "massive resistance" against what they termed "judicial tyranny" and the ever-intensifying civil rights movement in the region. An overwhelming mood of defiance to the federal government dominated southern states' legislative sessions in 1956. Virginia, Alabama, South Carolina, and Mississippi adopted the so-called interposition resolutions by the end of February, where these state legislatures expressed their strongest determination to defend the South against the "illegal encroachment" of the federal government.

In Mississippi, with defiance of the federal government at its height and inspired by the issuance of its own interposition resolution, the state lawmakers then turned to creating a tax-supported agency to implement the resolves expressed in the resolution. On 29 March 1956, with the blessing of Governor James P. Coleman, Mississippi created the Mississippi State Sovereignty Commission as part of the executive branch of its government "to do and perform any and all acts . . . to protect the sovereignty of the State of Mississippi . . . from encroachment thereon by the Federal Government." Though the State Sovereignty Commission in Mississippi was soon to be identified as the state's "segregation watchdog agency," neither the word "segregation" nor the word "integration" appeared in the carefully crafted bill that created the new agency. To be sure, however, federal "encroachment" was a periphrasis implying "forced racial integration," and "to protect the sovereignty" of Mississippi from that "encroachment" was a sophisticated, roundabout expression of the state's resolve "to preserve and protect racial segregation" in Mississippi.

Mississippi thus became the very first southern state to reinstate the word "sovereignty" of states' rights ideology in naming its anti-*Brown* and anti–civil rights state agency. With the aura of sophistication and respectability emanating from the word, the State Sovereignty Commission, for all practical purposes, was expected to maintain segregation at all costs and to wreck the National Association for the Advancement of Colored People and other civil rights organizations both in Mississippi and in her southern sister states. From its inception in 1956 to its practical demise in the late 1960s, the Mississippi State Sovereignty Commission, maintaining both public relations and investigative departments, was the most emphatic prosegregation and pro–states' rights governmental agency in the South. The Mississippi commission's heyday came about under the chairmanship of Governor Ross R. Barnett.

After the September 1957 Little Rock, Ark., school desegregation crisis, though it brought wretched consequences to southern segregationists, "massive resistance" reached its high point. Virginia created the Virginia Commission on Constitutional Government in 1958 as an official vehicle to carry on the state's "respectable" resistance to the civil rights movement. Then in June 1960, Louisiana established its own state sovereignty commission and the Louisiana Joint Legislative Committee on Un-American Activities. While the grand missions of the Louisiana State Sovereignty Commission were to paint the state's race relations in a rosy color and to alert the rest of the nation to the gradual encroachment on states' rights by the centralized federal government, the un-American activities committee, indicative of its name, took up the broadly defined "subversive hunt" in Louisiana. After all, the civil rights leaders, activists, and their sympathizers in the South could all be categorized as "subversives" in the sense that they willfully defied the region's white establishment and its long-cherished "segregated way of life."

In September 1962 the entire South witnessed the first dramatic and physical confrontation between a Deep South state and the federal government over the University of Mississippi desegregation crisis. Soon thereafter, at the behest of Governor George C. Wallace, Alabama belatedly organized its state sovereignty commission, as well as the Alabama Legislative Commission to Preserve the Peace, in 1963. As in the case of Louisiana, the Alabama State Sovereignty Commission devoted its time and energy mainly to public relations schemes, and the "Peace Commission" spied on civil rights activists.

Abominable racial incidents and irresponsible actions of die-hard segregationists ensued during the first half of the 1960s, and fatal blows were rendered to the white South's resistance movement with the passage of the Civil Rights Act of 1964 and the Voting Rights Act of 1965. Combined, these facts resulted in robbing both the legality and the respectability of the South's "massive resistance." Having virtually outlived its usefulness by 1968 to defend the state's racial status quo, the Mississippi State Sovereignty Commission, in its dying days, spent its resources on investigating anti–Vietnam War demonstrators, black nationalists, and campus radicals in the state, reflecting the transformation of the nation's political and social trends in the late 1960s. For the purpose of cracking down on these "new subversives," the state sovereignty commissions of Mississippi, Louisiana, and Alabama formed the Interstate Sovereignty Association in May 1968, but this cooperative scheme did not enjoy any longevity.

In June 1969, Louisiana's state sovereignty commission and its un-American activities committee were terminated. Having outlived the one in Louisiana, both the Mississippi State Sovereignty Commission and the Alabama State Sovereignty Commission faded away in 1973. By the time its death knell rang, Mississippi's "segregation watchdog agency" had ended up spending more than $1,542,000 to "protect the sovereignty" of the state.

YASUHIRO KATAGIRI
Tokai University (Japan)

Numan V. Bartley, *The Rise of Massive Resistance: Race and Politics in the South during the 1950s* (1969); Dan T. Carter, *The Politics of Rage: George Wallace, the Origins of the New Conservatism, and the Transformation of American Politics* (1995); Adam Fairclough, *Race and Democracy: The Civil Rights Struggle in Louisiana, 1915–1972* (1995); Erle Johnston, *Mississippi's Defiant Years, 1953–1973: An Interpretive Documentary with Personal Experiences* (1990); Yasuhiro Katagiri, *The Mississippi State Sovereignty Commission: Civil Rights and States' Rights* (2001); Steven F. Lawson, in *An Uncertain Tradition: Constitutionalism and the History of the South*, ed. Kermit L.

Hall and James W. Ely Jr. (1989); Neil R. McMillen, *The Citizens' Council: Organized Resistance to the Second Reconstruction, 1954–64* (1971); Jeff Roche, *Restructured Resistance: The Sibley Commission and the Politics of Desegregation in Georgia* (1995); William M. Stowe Jr., "Willie Rainach and the Defense of Segregation in Louisiana, 1954–1959" (Ph.D. diss., Southern Methodist University, 1989).

States' Rights Constitutionalism

States' rights constitutionalism holds that in the federal system the states retain certain rights and powers that cannot be taken from them, yet generations of southerners have tailored their constitutional views to fit changing social and economic realities.

Diversity characterized southern attitudes in 1787 toward relations between state and nation. Led by James Madison of Virginia, southern Federalists wanted a strong central government of enumerated powers that was also responsive to local self-interests. Ardent states' rights proponents, such as Patrick Henry of Virginia, denounced the new Constitution because it left unclear the balance between state and national powers. They also rebelled at Madison's successful effort in 1789 in preventing the insertion of the word "expressly" in the Tenth Amendment as a limit on national powers. Southern Federalists won important concessions for the peculiar institution of slavery in return for their support of the national constitution.

States' rights constitutionalism after 1787 evolved from a passive doctrine of resistance to national authority based on strict construction to an aggressive theory of state sovereignty. Southern proponents of the Constitution, like Madison and Thomas Jefferson, believed that the national government should remain sensitive to local self-interest and agrarian values. Thus, they resisted northern Federalist attempts to consolidate national power. Madison and Jefferson in 1798 most fully argued their position when they denounced the Alien and Sedition Acts. Their famous Virginia and Kentucky resolutions insisted on strict construction of the delegated powers of the national government and set forth the theory that a state might interpose itself between the citizenry and the national government in order to nullify a federal law. Few southerners supported the broad implications of the resolutions, and both Jefferson and Madison in the White House frequently adopted an expansive view of federal powers.

Economic depression and the large slave population in the Southeast during the 1820s radicalized states' rights constitutionalism. John C. Calhoun of South Carolina linked federal tariff policies to the region's economic woes. He pushed beyond the strict constructionism of Madison and Jefferson by asserting that the states could not only interpose their authority to nullify a federal law but also break from the Union altogether. During the nullification controversy of 1832, South Carolina's attempt to put Calhoun's theory into action faltered before Unionist sentiment in the Palmetto State, the leadership of Andrew Jackson, and the refusal of other southern states to lend support.

Under the pressure of the slavery expansion issue, states' rights constitutionalism emerged during the 1850s as a doctrine of power and not of right. Jefferson Davis of Mississippi replaced Calhoun as the South's most radical proponent of this view of states' rights. Confronted with a hostile antislavery movement in the North and declining power in Congress, Davis claimed that the federal judiciary was responsible for sustaining slaveholders' property rights in the new territories. Because the states were sovereign entities, Davis argued, the national government had a constitutional responsibility to protect slaveholders' rights aggressively. Ironically, northern antislavery forces resorted to the traditional Jeffersonian notion of states' rights as a passive restraint on the national government to justify their attempts to frustrate enforcement of the Fugitive Slave Act of 1850. The Supreme Court in *Dred Scott v. Sandford* in 1857 confirmed Davis's arguments, but it was a Pyrrhic victory; the social calculus of the peculiar institution and the election of Abraham Lincoln in 1860 culminated in the most extreme form of states' rights—secession. The ideals of local self-government and strict construction did retain vitality, however; the Confederate wartime effort, under Davis's leadership, suffered because authorities in the southern states refused to cooperate fully with the Confederate government in Richmond.

Confederate defeat marked the end of exaggerated claims for states' rights constitutionalism. Southern Democratic leaders in the post-Reconstruction era reaffirmed the traditional passive meaning of the doctrine in their successful efforts to deny free blacks the national protection of the Fourteenth and Fifteenth Amendments. The Supreme Court abetted this process in a series of decisions that culminated in the 1896 case of *Plessy v. Ferguson*. The justices sustained segregation by race in public places as long as the states provided equal facilities.

Events within and without the South during the 20th century undermined this coupling of states' rights and a dual system of race relations. The Supreme Court, beginning in the mid-1930s, broadened the interpretation of the commerce and other "elastic" clauses of the Constitution and accepted limited incorporation of the Bill of Rights into the Fourteenth Amendment. The justices enhanced the powers of the national government at the expense of the states.

Moreover, the moral legitimacy of states' rights ebbed as a result of southern resistance to ending de jure racial segregation. Following the Supreme Court's decision in *Brown v. Board of Education* in 1954, southern Democratic politicians orchestrated a strategy of massive resistance in order to prevent integration of public facilities. Governors Orval Faubus of Arkansas and George C. Wallace of Alabama resorted to Calhoun's exploded theories in futile attempts to block integration of public schools and universities. "States' rights" appeared in the South to be little more than a code word for racism.

The principle that the states retain certain distinct powers was given new emphasis by the Rehnquist Court. Led by Justice Lewis F. Powell, a small majority of the Court insisted that it should "restore" a balance of power between the states and the federal government. According to this sometimes-majority, the states were independent sovereigns that were "co-equal" with the federal government and the justices have a duty to weigh the competing interests of the states and the federal government, rather than merely upholding federal supremacy. As a result, the Court has invoked the long-neglected Tenth Amendment to block enforcement of federally created entitlements including the minimum wage, safe working conditions, welfare, social security, and medical and pension benefits. This view, however, does not apply uniquely to the South. The absorption of the region into the mainstream of American culture and the demise of the section's legally mandated dual system of race relations have made the South more like the rest of the nation. In the process, states' rights constitutionalism, shorn of its racist overtones, has experienced a modest rebirth.

KERMIT L. HALL
State University of New York at Albany

William Anderson, *The Nation and the States: Rivals or Partners?* (1955); Numan V. Bartley, *The Rise of Massive Resistance: Race and Politics in the South during the 1950s* (1969); Arthur Bestor Jr., *Journal of the Illinois State Historical Society* (Summer 1961); Daniel Elazar, *American Federalism: A View from the States* (1972); William W. Freehling, *Prelude to Civil War: The Nullification Controversy in South Carolina, 1816–1836* (1966); Alpheus T. Mason, ed., *The States Rights Debate: Antifederalism and the Constitution* (1972); Frank L. Owsley, *State Rights in the Confederacy* (1925); Mark Tushnet, *A Court Divided: The Rehnquist Court and the Future of Constitutional Law* (2005).

Supreme Court

Writing more than a half century ago, Charles S. Sydnor observed that the two traditional sources of authority in the South were the Bible and the Constitution. Relying on the Constitution, the region's leaders developed a cultural constitutionalism intended to protect regional values and institutions from external forces. At the heart of that cultural constitutionalism lay the political theory of states' rights, which preserved the powers of the states from any encroachment by the national government. The Supreme Court's interpretation of the Constitution remained compatible for a century and a half with the region's dominant values. But since the 1950s the Supreme Court has played a major role in reshaping the institutional structure of the region and forcing changes in the South's public values. As a result, Supreme Court decisions have become the focal point of many of the region's modern controversies.

By far the most significant area of judicial interpretation has been the Supreme Court's definition of the constitutional terms of race relations. During the course of a century, the Supreme Court sanctioned slavery, legitimized segregation, and ordered integration of public institutions. Through the antebellum period, a series of Supreme Court opinions sustained the institution of slavery. These cases culminated in 1857 with the *Dred Scott* case. In that case, the Court decisively confronted the conflicting values that circumscribed the slave owners' approach to the institution of slavery—the dilemma over whether slaves would be treated as property or as human beings. Dred Scott was a black slave who had been the property of an army surgeon. Scott had been taken by his owner into Illinois and into Wisconsin Territory, which was free territory under the Missouri Compromise. Scott eventually returned to Missouri with his owner. The surgeon died, and title to Scott passed to a New York resident named John F. A. Sandford. In 1846 Scott brought suit in the Missouri courts to obtain his freedom. He claimed that he had become a free person because he had been taken into free territory. The Missouri courts rejected Scott's plea, and his attorneys initiated a new suit in federal courts. After years of litigation, the Supreme Court held on 6 March 1857 that Scott could not sue for his freedom and that he was still a slave. Chief Justice Roger B. Taney argued that Scott could not sue because he was not a citizen. He was not a citizen because he was black and a slave. In effect, Scott had no rights under the Constitution.

The abolition of slavery in the aftermath of the Civil War placed race relations in a state of flux. By the early 1890s an increasingly rigid system of legal racial separation was in place throughout the region. The Supreme Court was unwilling to challenge the new system. In 1896, in the celebrated case of *Plessy v. Ferguson*, the Court gave constitutional legitimacy to the so-called separate-but-equal principle. The opinion feigned a commitment to the concept of equality but consigned black southerners to a status little removed from slavery.

During the next half century, carefully drawn constitutional challenges gradually chipped away at legal segregation. This legal strategy was slow and tortuous. The Supreme Court did not abandon generations of inaction and aggressively assert the basic political and civil rights of all citizens until 1954. In *Brown v. Board of Education* the Court attacked the separate-but-equal principle by concluding that in public education, separate facilities were "inherently unequal." In this manner, the segregated educational systems of the southern states violated the equal protection clause of the Fourteenth Amendment to the Constitution. Opponents of the *Brown* decision throughout the South placed blame, not on the Constitution, but on the Supreme Court's interpretation of the Constitution. In 1957 resistance to *Brown* was encouraged by 101 southern congressmen who signed the "Southern Manifesto," whereby they pledged "to use all lawful means to bring about a reversal of this decision which is contrary to the Constitution and to prevent the use of force in its implementation." Eventually, force was used and the Supreme Court's interpretation of the Constitution prevailed. The Court's attack on segregated educational institutions proved to be merely the first step in a long war against all forms of racial discrimination in the public life of the South.

The South's system of race relations was not the only element of the traditional southern value system to come under Supreme Court review. Agrarianism, however defined, has been an essential element of the distinctive regional culture that evolved over the last 200 years. A major source of continuing agrarian dominance in southern public life has been rural control over state legislative politics. By the 1950s, burgeoning urban areas in the region were severely underrepresented in state legislatures, while the rural areas and adjacent small towns enjoyed representation far in excess of what their declining populations would warrant.

In the 1962 case of *Baker v. Carr* the Supreme Court abandoned its longstanding decision not to intervene in legislative reapportionment matters. That case arose as a challenge to the 1901 Tennessee statute that had provided the method of periodically reapportioning the state legislature. Provisions of the law assured continued rural dominance of the legislature at the expense of the urban areas. The decision held that it was permissible to challenge the statute as a violation of the equal protection clause of the Fourteenth Amendment but provided little in the way of a remedy. Two years later the Supreme Court embarked on a course of simple majoritarianism in reapportionment matters. In *Reynolds v. Sims* the Court struck down a complex Alabama reapportionment plan and ordered the implementation of a reapportionment plan based on the principle of one man, one vote. The consequence of these decisions has been gradually to shift the locus of political power in the states from the rural areas to the cities. One other likely consequence may well be the gradual erosion of agrarianism as a dominant value in the culture of the region.

The third major element of the region's culture that has come under Supreme Court scrutiny has been religious fundamentalism. The flash points of the conflict between regional cultural values and the Supreme Court have been the school prayer issue and the teaching of evolution in the public schools. In each case, religious conservatives have been especially forceful in pressing their cause in favor of school prayer and against the teaching of evolution. In like manner, Supreme Court opinions have stood as the major bulwark against the widespread adoption of both these practices in the public school systems throughout the region. Rulings in these cases have raised opposition to the Supreme Court that was surpassed only by the desegregation cases. Unlike the desegregation and reapportionment cases, however, the school prayer cases have not altered the South's tradition of religious conservatism. If anything, the zealous defense of traditional religious values may strengthen their place in the pantheon of southern values.

Ronald Reagan appointed William Rehnquist chief justice of the Supreme Court in 1986, and the Rehnquist Court put new emphasis on the principle of states' rights, an idea long championed by southern politicians. Justice Lewis F. Powell led a small majority of the Court in promoting a balance between the powers of the states and the federal government. The justices used the Tenth Amendment, the constitutional source of sovereign state powers, to limit enforcement of federal entitlements in minimum wages, safe working conditions, and welfare.

The Supreme Court decisions that most evoke a southern context, though, have been in the Court's response to attempts to create black majority districts to encourage the election of African Americans. The Voting Rights Act requires such a result, but the Court has also been concerned with districts that are gerrymandered unfairly. After the 1990 Census, new black majority districts were created at many levels of government. The Court's *Shaw v. Reno* decision (1993) led to the elimination or redrawing of black majority congressional districts in six southern states. The court's 2003 decision in *George v. Ashcroft* approved a state legislature's plan to reduce minority strength in several districts.

The Supreme Court that reshaped the South's race relations in the mid-20th century continues to play a role in the region's legal evolution on racial issues.

ROBERT HAWS
University of Mississippi

Richard Cortner, *The Apportionment Cases* (1970); Don E. Fehrenhacher, *The Dred Scott Case: Its Significance in American Law and Politics* (1978); Michael J. Klarman, *From Jim Crow to Civil Rights: The Supreme Court and the Struggle for Racial Equality* (2004); Richard Kluger, *Simple Justice: The History of* Brown v. Board of Education *and Black America's Struggle for Equality*, rev. ed. (2004); Charles Lofgren, *The Plessy Case: A Legal-Historical Approach* (1987); Mark Tushnet, *A Court Divided: The Rehnquist Court and the Future of Constitutional Law* (2005).

Black, Hugo

(1886–1971) U.S. SENATOR AND
SUPREME COURT JUSTICE.
Through intelligence, grit, determination, and temporary alliance with the
Ku Klux Klan, Hugo Lafayette Black
rose from simple origins in the Alabama
hills to the U.S. Senate (1927–37) and
the Supreme Court (1937–71). During
34 years as an associate justice, Black,
whose only prior judicial experience
had been as judge of Birmingham's
police court, forged a reputation as
an eloquent defender of First Amendment freedoms. The seeming paradox
of a former Klansman evolving into
an ardent civil libertarian remains an
intriguing episode in Supreme Court
annals.

Son of a small-town merchant, Black
was born 27 February 1886 in Clay
County, Ala. He completed his formal
education in the two-year law school
of the University of Alabama at Tuscaloosa, in 1906. By the early 1920s he was
a highly successful damage-suit lawyer,
suspected by Birmingham's establishment of being a "Bolshevik" because of
his ties to organized labor. Black joined
the Klan in 1923 by swearing allegiance
to its principles, including white supremacy and anti-Catholicism. Thereby
he allied himself with a large, highly disciplined organization soon to dominate
state politics. The Alabama Klan of the
1920s reflected not only the prejudices,
ignorance, and inherent violence of numerous poor, white Protestants but also
their desire for a share in political and
economic power from which they had
long been virtually excluded. Undoubtedly, Black knew of the Klan's excesses

against individuals; evidently, his personal ambition persuaded him to believe that, over the long run, the Klan's
democratizing impact could prove
beneficial to these less-privileged and
underrepresented white Alabamians.
With the crucial aid of Klan-controlled
votes, Black achieved in 1926 the otherwise unattainable office of U.S. senator.
Although he had resigned from the
Klan for appearance's sake at the start of
his campaign, he remained politically
indebted to the Invisible Empire until
the early 1930s, by which time most
Alabamians had become temporarily
satiated with violence and appeals to
prejudice.

Senator Black proved an ardent New
Dealer, even alarming Franklin Roosevelt by advocating a 30-hour work week.
As a Senate investigator he dramatically
demonstrated his hostility to special
privilege and entrenched interests.
Black's progressive record, coupled with
the Senate's tradition of confirming its
members nominated to high office, led
Roosevelt to make him the first ap-
pointee in an ultimately successful endeavor to reshape the Court in favor of
federal activism in economic, political,
and social spheres. Despite the initial
skepticism of some of his judicial colleagues and a nationwide outburst over
his former Klan membership, Black
became a major intellectual force on the
high court, pressing his fundamental
concept that the guarantees of the Bill
of Rights are absolute and should bind
states as well as the nation. To the acute
dismay of many fellow southerners,
Justice Black sided with the Court majority to strike down legal segregation in

Hugo Black, U.S. Supreme Court justice, 1926
(Archives and manuscripts, Birmingham [Alabama] Public Library)

schools and public facilities; to advance the principle of one man, one vote; and to outlaw reading of official prayers in public schools. Through the unlikely instrument of the Klan, the Senate and the Supreme Court gained the services of a type of southerner rarely chosen for public office in the 20th century—a latter-day disciple of Jeffersonian and Jacksonian democracy.

VIRGINIA VAN DER VEER
HAMILTON
University of Alabama at Birmingham

Howard Ball, in *The Vision and the Dream of Hugo L. Black: An Examination of a Judicial Philosophy* (1975); Hugo Black Jr., *My Father: A Remembrance* (1975); Gerald T. Dunne, *Hugo Black and the Judicial Revolution* (1977); Virginia Van der Veer Hamilton, *Hugo Black: The Alabama Years* (1972), ed., *Hugo Black and the Bill of Rights: Proceedings of the First Hugo Black Symposium in American History on the Bill of Rights and American Democracy* (1978); Roger K. Newman, *Hugo Black: A Biography* (1994); Steve Suitts, *Hugo Black of Alabama: How His Roots and Early Career Shaped the Great Champion of the Constitution* (2005).

Black Codes

One legal response of southern white governments to the end of the Civil War and the passage of the Thirteenth Amendment was the adoption of laws purporting to bestow upon the newly freed men and women certain civil rights. Mississippi passed the first of these codes in 1865. They granted rights of blacks to hold personal property, intermarry, sue in state courts, swear out criminal warrants, and testify against whites under certain conditions.

The right to vote, however, was not given to blacks under these codes.

Black codes were in reality promulgated to control a newly fluid black labor force. For example, Section 1 of the Mississippi Black Code allowed blacks to sue and be sued and to acquire and dispose of personal property, but it limited their real property ownership to only incorporated towns or cities and severely hampered individual rural agricultural pursuits. Involuntary labor was authorized by statutes addressing vagrancy, peonage, work contracts, enticement, convict labor, and emigrant agency. Law and terror were successfully combined to enforce throughout the South what those who opposed black codes called a "new slavery."

Congressional Reconstruction required temporary abandonment of many of the black codes. After Reconstruction most states reconstituted the involuntary labor sections. These vestiges of the original black codes remained a part of southern social and economic life until the civil rights movement of the 1950s and 1960s.

JOHN R. WUNDER
University of Nebraska at Lincoln

Donald G. Nieman, ed., *Black Southerners and the Law, 1865–1900* (1994); Theodore B. Wilson, *The Black Codes of the South* (1965).

Brown v. Board of Education

On 17 May 1954 the U.S. Supreme Court ruled in *Brown v. Board of Education* that separate educational facilities for blacks and whites "are inherently unequal." With that decision the Court overturned the precedent of "separate but equal" set by the 1896 *Plessy v. Ferguson* case and prepared the way for the civil rights movement of the 1960s.

The National Association for the Advancement of Colored People (naacp) played a major role in the instigation of the case on behalf of Linda Brown, a black child denied admission to a Topeka, Kans., elementary school because of her race. *Brown* brought together five related cases from South Carolina, Delaware, Virginia, Kansas, and the District of Columbia, all of which challenged racial segregation as a violation of the equal protection clause of the Fourteenth Amendment. The arguments heard by the court centered on the intentions of the framers and ratifiers of that amendment.

In the brief, unanimous opinion delivered by Chief Justice Earl Warren, the Court ruled that the separate-but-equal doctrine, which held that racial segregation was permissible as long as equal facilities were provided for both races, was in violation of the equal protection clause. The justices wrote that the segregation of white and black children in public education "generates a feeling of inferiority" among the black children that could have an irreversible detrimental effect on the rest of their lives. In the spring of 1955 the Court heard arguments about how their *Brown* decision might be implemented. At the end of these arguments, the Court remanded the four cases back to the district courts with the order to take whatever steps were necessary to "admit to public schools on a racially non-discriminatory basis with all deliberate speed the parties in these cases."

The *Brown* decision and the Court's demand for swift integration did not bring about the immediate desegregation of public schools. The only school boards legally bound by the *Brown* decision were those named directly in the cases on which the Court ruled, and the only laws held unconstitutional were those specific laws cited by the plaintiffs. Ordinarily, rules of constitutional law decided by the Supreme Court are universally accepted and implemented where they apply. Technically, however, compliance is voluntary, and there was intense resistance to implementation of the controversial *Brown* decision. Some historians argue that the major significance of the decision was its triggering a white backlash against social change. The political branches of government were employed to speed integration. The threat by the Department of Health, Education, and Welfare (hew) under the Civil Rights Act of 1964 to withhold federal education funds from school districts that persisted in segregation policies was one such way of encouraging integration. Although some school districts began busing students from one neighborhood to another in an effort to achieve integration, many southern states sought to obstruct integration through "massive resistance," and in 1965 less than 10 percent of the South's black students were in integrated public schools.

The *Brown* doctrine, which said that segregated schools are illegal, was extended to apply to other public facilities through separate court cases involving, for instance, the segregation of beaches (in Maryland), golf courses (in Atlanta), and recreation facilities (in Memphis). Probably the most famous case ever decided by the Supreme Court, *Brown v. Board of Education* was the first step in major reform of not only public education but also race laws and policies in almost all aspects of American life.

KAREN M. MCDEARMAN
University of Mississippi

Robert Cushman, *Cases in Constitutional Law* (1975); "Forum: Reflections on the *Brown* Decision after Fifty Years," *Journal of Southern History* (May 2004); V. P. Franklin, *Journal of African American History* (Winter/Spring 2005); Michael J. Klarman, *From Jim Crow to Civil Rights: The Supreme Court and the Struggle for Racial Equality* (2004); Richard Kluger, *Simple Justice: The History of* Brown v. Board of Education *and Black America's Struggle for Equality*, rev. ed. (2004); J. Harvie Wilkinson III, *From Brown to Bakke: The Supreme Court and School Integration, 1954–1978* (1979).

Buchanan v. Warley

In the 1910s, tens of thousands of African Americans were migrating from rural areas to southern cities. Many of them took up residence in or near areas primarily occupied by whites. Whites, meanwhile, feared their property values would decline if African Americans moved into their neighborhoods, or worse, onto their streets. In some cities, whites used violence to keep African Americans out of their neighborhoods. However, white terrorism could not defeat the combined purchasing power of blacks in their pursuit of housing. Whites therefore turned to the government for assistance.

In 1910 Baltimore promulgated the first ordinance requiring African Americans and whites to live in separate areas. The Baltimore ordinance was imitated throughout the South. Between 1911 and 1913, Richmond, Norfolk, Ashland, Roanoke, and Portsmouth, Va., Winston-Salem, N.C., Greenville, S.C., and Atlanta, Ga., all passed residential segregation ordinances. When challenged in state courts, residential segregation ordinances met with some initial resistance, but on very narrow grounds. The laws, meanwhile, continued to spread. By 1916, Louisville, St. Louis, Oklahoma City, and New Orleans all had residential segregation laws.

Legal commentators, influenced by prevalent theories of "sociological jurisprudence," were nearly unanimous in their belief that such laws were constitutional. Nevertheless, the NAACP resolved to challenge these ordinances in court. The Louisville branch of the NAACP set up a test case. The Kentucky state courts upheld Louisville's segregation law, and the NAACP had little reason to be sanguine about its prospects before the U.S. Supreme Court. American racism was at its post–Civil War height, and the Court rarely strongly challenged prevailing social trends. In its Supreme Court brief, Kentucky emphasized the purported harms to society from race-mixing, playing to both race prejudice and sociological jurisprudence's fondness for pseudoscientific "social science."

Much to almost everyone's surprise, the Supreme Court unanimously held in *Buchanan v. Warley* (1917) that Louisville's segregation law was unconstitutional under the Fourteenth Amendment's due process clause because it violated property rights without a valid police power justification. Justice Oliver Wendell Holmes drafted a dissent, which he declined to deliver, apparently because he was unable to persuade any of his colleagues to concur.

Buchanan v. Warley did not have much of an impact on residential segregation, but it did benefit African Americans in several ways. First, *Buchanan* ensured that whites bore a far larger percentage of the cost of their discriminatory attitudes than they would have if de jure segregation had been approved by the Court. Second, *Buchanan* ensured that cities could not entirely exclude African American migrants. Third, *Buchanan* prevented residential segregation laws from being the leading edge of broader antiblack measures. Finally, the NAACP's victory in *Buchanan* ensured its survival and signaled an extremely positive turning point in the Supreme Court's jurisprudence on racial issues.

DAVID E. BERNSTEIN
*George Mason University
School of Law*

David E. Bernstein, *Vanderbilt Law Review* (May 1998); Alexander Bickel and Benno Schmidt, *The Judiciary and Responsible Government, 1910–1921* (1984); William A. Fischel, *Vanderbilt Law Review* (May 1998); Michael J. Klarman, *Vanderbilt Law Review* (May 1998).

Campbell, John A.

(1811–1889) U.S. SUPREME COURT JUSTICE.
John Archibald Campbell served as a justice of the U.S. Supreme Court from 1853 until 1861, when he resigned from the Court shortly after the start of the Civil War to return home to his native South and support the Confederacy.

Born into a prominent Georgia family, Campbell graduated from Franklin College (now the University of Georgia) at age 14 and briefly attended the West Point Military Academy before his admission to the Georgia bar when he was only 18. Campbell soon moved to Alabama, where he quickly became one of the state's leading attorneys. His Mobile office contained one of the South's finest libraries.

After arguing several cases before the U.S. Supreme Court and acquiring a national reputation as a voice of moderation amidst growing sectional tensions, Campbell was appointed an associate justice of the Court by President Franklin Pierce in 1853. During his years on the Court, Campbell frequently opposed the Court's growing solicitude for the legal rights of corporations, espousing in eloquent dissents his philosophy that the rights of private property were subordinate to the public interest. Campbell also was a staunch advocate of states' rights. Constitutional scholars generally agree that Campbell was an exceptionally able jurist and that he might have been remembered as one of the Court's more notable justices if he had remained on the Court for a longer time.

Campbell voted with the majority in the Court's notorious 1857 decision in *Dred Scott v. Sandford*, which held that a slave who had been taken to free territory remained a slave. Campbell continued to own slaves even after he became a Supreme Court justice, but he hoped that economic forces would make slavery obsolete, and he advocated various measures to ameliorate the harshness of slavery. Campbell, who believed that the federal government had no power to abolish slavery or limit its extension, voted in *Ableman v. Booth* (1859) to uphold the constitutionality of the federal Fugitive Slave Act of 1850.

Campbell publicly opposed the secession of southern states, including his home state of Alabama, following Abraham Lincoln's election to the presidency in 1860. After a futile attempt to begin peace negotiations between the Union and the Confederacy, Campbell resigned from the Court two weeks after the war began. The two other justices from Confederate states, James M. Wayne of Georgia and John Catron of Tennessee, remained on the Court. Nearly lynched by a pro-Confederate mob upon his return to Mobile, Campbell fled to New Orleans, where he established a law practice.

In 1862 Campbell reluctantly accepted a post as assistant secretary of war, with responsibility for enforcing the Confederate draft. In January 1865 Confederate president Jefferson Davis appointed Campbell to a three-man commission that met with Lincoln at Hampton Roads, Va., to attempt to negotiate peace. Shortly after the war's end in April 1865, Campbell was arrested on vague charges and spent four months in a military prison.

Bankrupt at the time of his release from prison, Campbell returned to New Orleans and reestablished a successful law practice, asserting for corporations many of the rights he had opposed during his years on the Court. Most notably, he served as counsel for New Orleans butchers who claimed that the state's regulation of their industry violated the new Fourteenth Amendment to the U.S. Constitution. Although the Court rejected this position in the *Slaughter House Cases* in 1873, it accepted many of Campbell's arguments during the late 19th and early 20th centuries, when the Court imposed significant restrictions of the power of the states to regulate business enterprises.

WILLIAM G. ROSS
Cumberland School of Law
Samford University

Henry Groves Connor, *John Archibald Campbell, Associate Justice of the United States Supreme Court, 1853–1861* (1920, 2004); Robert Saunders Jr., *John Archibald Campbell: Southern Moderate, 1811–1889* (1997).

Catron, John

(1781–1865) TENNESSEE SUPREME COURT CHIEF JUSTICE AND U.S. SUPREME COURT JUSTICE.

John Catron was Tennessee's first chief justice and the first Tennessean appointed to the U.S. Supreme Court. Born John Kettering in either Grayson County or Montgomery County, Va., to Johann Peter Kettering, a German immigrant, and Elizabeth Houch Kettering, Catron recalled late in life that he had been brought up on a farm, that he had been educated in the common schools of western Virginia and Kentucky and "in such academies as the western country afforded," and that he had been well versed in the Bible and

18th-century English novels, histories, and poetry.

He changed his surname to Catron and began reading law in Tennessee in 1812. Admitted to the bar in 1815, he served as a circuit solicitor general until 1817 and the next year moved to Nashville, where he married Matilda Childress in 1821. He was elected by the legislature to the Tennessee Supreme Court of Errors and Appeals in 1824 and named the court's first chief justice in 1831.

An intensely partisan Jacksonian throughout his judicial career, Catron engaged in public political debates and gave private political advice to the antebellum Democratic presidents with few qualms as a jurist about doing either. In a series of newspaper articles in 1829, for instance, he initiated President Andrew Jackson's war on the Second Bank of the United States, and on the eve of James Buchanan's inauguration in 1857, he urged the president-elect to prod Chief Justice Robert Grier into deciding how to vote in the *Dred Scott* case then pending before the Court and submitted remarks about the case for insertion into Buchanan's inaugural address.

With Catron's assistance, the Tennessee court established itself as an independent branch of the state government (it was not recognized as such by Tennessee's first constitution) and, although not libertarian in the modern sense, went further than the other antebellum southern courts to facilitate the private emancipation of slaves. A slave owner himself, Catron nonetheless declared for the court in *Loftin v. Espy* (1833) that

the slave's "rights of humanity" must be considered along with the slave owner's "rights of property."

In his last significant Tennessee opinion, *State v. Foreman* (1835), he abandoned several of his own earlier decisions enforcing treaties with the Cherokee Nation, resorted to a states' rights approach, and upheld extending the state's jurisdiction into the Cherokee Nation in defiance of the U.S. Supreme Court's ruling in *Worcester v. Georgia* (1832). His about-face in *Foreman* facilitated the Jackson administration's negotiation of a removal treaty with the Cherokees; the Treaty of New Echota (1835), which provided for the removal of the Cherokees to lands west of the Mississippi River, followed within three months of *Foreman*.

Failing to win election in December 1835 to a reorganized court under the state's newly ratified second constitution, Catron helped manage Martin Van Buren's presidential campaign in Tennessee in 1836.

As one of his last acts as president, Jackson on 3 March 1837 appointed Catron to the U.S. Supreme Court. As a Supreme Court justice, Catron is difficult to categorize. Although not a judicial activist, he consistently voted with the moderate nationalists on the Court to expand federal jurisdiction, and he voted in several decisions to uphold federal rather than state title to tidal lands within Alabama and Louisiana.

Nationalist in approach, but also illustrative of his unwillingness to interfere with the continuing legal viability of slavery, were his concurring votes in

Prigg v. Pennsylvania (1842), which sustained the constitutionality of the federal Fugitive Slave Act of 1793 and held that federal power to extradite fugitive slaves under the Constitution was exclusive, and in the unanimous decision in *Ableman v. Booth* (1859), which overturned the Wisconsin Supreme Court's effort to frustrate enforcement of the federal Fugitive Slave Act of 1850.

Catron also sided with the advocates of state sovereignty, however, and recognized that federal power had its limits. In *Dred Scott v. Sandford* (1857), which originated in Catron's circuit, he concurred with the Court's conclusion that Scott remained a slave because of the unconstitutionality of the Missouri Compromise of 1820, but not with Chief Justice Roger Taney's reasoning that the circuit court had been without jurisdiction in the case because African Americans were not citizens, within the original meaning of the Constitution, and therefore not entitled to litigate in the federal courts. He joined the Court's two unanimous states' rights decisions in *Ex parte Dorr* (1845), which denied a federal writ of habeas corpus for the leader of Dorr's Rebellion, and in *Kentucky v. Dennison* (1861), which refused to order the governor of a free state to comply with the Constitution's criminal extradition provision; and he dissented from the Court's decision in the *Prize Cases* (1862), which upheld President Lincoln's blockade of several southern ports at the outbreak of the Civil War without prior congressional approval.

A devoted Unionist during the Civil War, Catron left Nashville when Tennessee seceded from the Union. He returned to the city in 1862 under the protection of occupying federal troops and died there on 30 May 1865.

THEODORE BROWN JR.
University of Tennessee

Theodore Brown Jr., in *A History of the Tennessee Supreme Court*, ed. James W. Ely Jr. (2002); Tim Alan Garrison, *The Legal Ideology of Removal: The Southern Judiciary and the Sovereignty of Native American Nations* (2002); Timothy S. Huebner, *The Southern Judicial Tradition: State Judges and Sectional Distinctiveness, 1790–1890* (1999); A. E. Keir Nash, in *The Supreme Court Justices: A Biographical Dictionary*, ed. Melvin I. Urofsky (1994).

Daniel, Peter V.

(1784–1860) U.S. SUPREME COURT JUSTICE.

Peter V. Daniel, who served as a U.S. Supreme Court justice from 1842 to 1860, was born on 24 April 1784 in Stafford County, Va., to Travors and Frances Moncure Daniel. Privately tutored, he spent a year at the College of New Jersey (later Princeton) before returning to Virginia where he read law under Edmund Randolph. In 1808 he killed a rival in a duel. Throughout his life, Daniel frequently engaged in partisan political disputes, often publishing vitriolic letters in Richmond papers. He married Edmund Randolph's daughter, Lucy, in 1809.

Daniel served briefly in the Virginia House of Delegates and then for an extended period as a member of the Privy Council (1812–35), much of it as lieutenant governor. There he applied the principles of Jeffersonian agrarianism and strict constitutional construction articulated in the Virginia and Kentucky Resolutions of 1798. Willing to quibble over almost any perceived threat to the Constitution, even to the point of denying money to clothe militiamen, Daniel is more positively credited with using his position on the council to mitigate questionable sentences, harsh penalties, and forced confessions against slaves, including participants in Nat Turner's Rebellion of 1831.

Associated with the "Richmond Junto" and the Richmond/Albany Alliance, Daniel was a strong partisan of Andrew Jackson and Martin Van Buren, with whom he later split. He continued his partisan activities even after Jackson appointed him a U.S. district judge from Virginia. When Supreme Court Justice Philip Barbour died in 1841, Van Buren nominated Daniel and the outgoing Democratic Senate confirmed him. The incoming Whigs exacted some revenge by assigning Daniel to circuit duty in the remote areas of Arkansas and Mississippi.

Daniel's service on the U.S. Supreme Court was competent but hardly brilliant. He became known for reasoning from first principles, to which he strictly adhered, and for dissenting fairly frequently. He strongly opposed federal powers to incorporate banks, to fund internal improvements, to exercise admiralty jurisdiction within the rivers that flowed through U.S. boundaries, or to enact restrictions on slavery within U.S. territories. Daniel also opposed the idea that corporations were "persons" that could sue in federal courts, consis-

tently favored state over federal judicial jurisdiction, strongly supported the prerogatives of the jury, and favored the exercise of state powers over commerce and bankruptcy matters. He was often allied with Chief Justice Roger Taney, with whom he maintained an admiring friendship. Like Taney, Daniel did not think that the contract clause prohibited states from using their power of eminent domain to purchase bridges and other toll-generating structures on behalf of the common good, a position he outlined in *West River Bridge Co. v. Dix* (1849). Daniel was an early advocate of secession and voted with the majority in the *Dred Scott* decision of 1857.

His wife, Lucy, with whom he fathered a son and two daughters, died in 1847. A second marriage, to Elizabeth Harris of Pennsylvania in 1853, which ended in 1857 when she tragically died of burns, produced another son and daughter. After his second marriage, Daniel moved from Richmond to Washington, but he moved back after Elizabeth's death. Daniel died at his home on 31 May 1860 and was buried in Richmond's Hollywood Cemetery.

JOHN R. VILE
Middle Tennessee State University

Clare Cushman, ed., *The Supreme Court Justices: Illustrated Biographies, 1789–1995* (1995); John P. Frank, *Justice Daniel Dissenting: A Biography of Peter V. Daniel, 1784–1860* (1964); E. Lee Shepard, in *The Oxford Companion to the Supreme Court of the United States*, ed. Kermit L. Hall (1992).

Emigrant Agent Laws

In the first three and a half decades following the Civil War, labor recruiters known as "emigrant agents" played a key role in encouraging and financing African American migration within the United States. In particular, the agents recruited workers from Georgia, North Carolina, and South Carolina to the relatively high-wage, labor-starved "southwestern" states of Louisiana, Texas, Mississippi, and Arkansas. Emigrant agents lowered the information costs of migration by using their resources to advertise distant opportunities. Agents also often subsidized the economic costs of migration by either paying for or advancing the money for the migrants' train tickets.

Southern plantation owners rightly saw emigrant agents as a threat to their labor supply. They therefore lobbied state legislatures to pass laws placing prohibitive taxes on emigrant agents. The Georgia Supreme Court upheld an emigrant agent law, but the North Carolina and Alabama Supreme Courts each found their respective state laws unconstitutional for violating the tenets of laissez-faire jurisprudence.

Meanwhile, agents continued to ply their trade, moving tens of thousands of people, often in large groups. Group migrations were significant for several reasons. First, such migrations were sometimes a form of political protest, one of the few forms of protest in which disenfranchised African Americans could engage. African Americans would move to places where they were relatively well treated or had relatively good economic prospects. Second, in the era before the welfare state, emigrant agents helped groups of destitute African Americans flee areas devastated by flood, drought,

boll weevils, and other pests. Finally, and perhaps most important, mass migration, and even the threat of such migration, was crucial to improving the treatment of African Americans who did not migrate. In response to large-scale migrations, many farmers raised wages, improved living and working conditions, and, with the cooperation of local and state governments, granted greater educational opportunities and greater protection to African Americans in their property and person.

Robert A. ("Peg-Leg") Williams was the most successful emigrant agent of the late 19th century. However, Georgia's restrictive emigrant agent law prevented Williams from tapping that state's huge supply of African American labor. In 1889 he decided to ignore Georgia's law and was soon arrested. Williams appealed his arrest all the way to the U.S. Supreme Court, which rejected his appeal in 1900 in *Williams v. Fears*.

The result of the Supreme Court's ruling was widespread legal harassment of emigrant agents. By 1903, Alabama, Florida, North Carolina, and Virginia had enacted new emigrant agent laws, while the laws of Georgia and South Carolina remained in effect. Agent activity declined dramatically. The other southern states enacted emigrant agent laws when out-migration of African Americans rose dramatically during World War I.

Despite emigrant agent statutes, hundreds of thousands of African Americans managed to migrate both within and from the South after *Williams*. But the emigrant agent laws put a major obstacle in the path of emigrants, especially for rural African Americans who, without agents' help, had difficulty financing, or even receiving information about, emigration opportunities.

DAVID E. BERNSTEIN
George Mason University
School of Law

David E. Bernstein, *Only One Place of Redress: African Americans, Labor Regulations, and the Courts from Reconstruction to the New Deal* (2001), *Texas Law Review* (March 1998); William Cohen, *At Freedom's Edge: Black Mobility and the Southern White Quest for Racial Control, 1861–1915* (1991); William F. Holmes, *South Atlantic Quarterly* (Summer 1980).

Ervin, Sam, Jr.

(1896–1985) LAWYER AND U.S. SENATOR.

Samuel James Ervin Jr. graduated at age 26 from Harvard Law School in 1922. He subsequently practiced law with his father in Morganton, N.C., held various local and state offices, and from 1954 to 1974 served in the U.S. Senate.

Ervin's Senate career spanned a tumultuous era in the history of the South and the nation. Ervin viewed the South's dual system of race relations as a social reality that only the individual states could change. In the wake of the Supreme Court's 1954 decision in *Brown v. Board of Education*, he joined other southern members of Congress in signing the 1956 Southern Manifesto that denounced court-ordered integration. Ervin in 1960 filibustered the Eisenhower administration's civil rights proposals. He also opposed the civil rights acts of 1964, 1965, and 1968. Yet Ervin

was neither an apostle of massive resistance nor a racist. He rejected radical states' rights ideas of nullification and interposition. Moreover, on questions of civil liberties, where the racial issue did not threaten his political base in North Carolina, Ervin was liberal. He supported the 1966 Bail Reform Act and the 1968 Indian Bill of Rights.

Late in his Senate career Ervin emerged as a significant voice in constitutional matters. In 1971 he orchestrated the Senate attack on spying by army intelligence on civilians. More dramatically, as chair of the Select Committee on Presidential Campaign Activities, in 1973 he gave Americans a lesson in constitutional government during the Watergate hearings. His homespun stories, biblical quotations, and pointed questions captured the imagination of a national television audience. The commonsense wisdom of this country lawyer was more than a match for the Watergate conspirators.

Ervin believed that persons were only truly free when they accepted responsibility for their own lives. This notion paled before the historical realities of southern race relations, but it was an otherwise fundamentally correct insight into the nature of southern character. Sam Ervin the southerner, moreover, in his confrontation with Richard Nixon's White House, reaffirmed for all Americans the connection between this ideal and the value of limited constitutional government.

KERMIT L. HALL
State University of New York
at Albany

Sam Ervin, North Carolina country lawyer and U.S. senator. Photo taken in the 1970s.
(Southern Historical Collection, University of North Carolina, Chapel Hill)

Karl E. Campbell, *Journal of Church and State* (June 2003), *Senator Sam Ervin, Last of the Founding Fathers* (2007); Paul L. Clancy, *Just a Country Lawyer: A Biography of Senator Sam Ervin* (1974); Dick Dabney, *A Good Man: The Life of Sam J. Ervin* (1976).

Fifth Circuit Court of Appeals

Spanning the Lower South from Florida to Texas, the Fifth Circuit Court of Appeals was one of the regional federal circuit courts created in 1891. Following the 1954 decision of the U.S. Supreme Court in *Brown v. Board of Education*, the Fifth Circuit was called upon to supervise the dismantling of separate schools and the elimination of racial discrimination in the region. Dominated by several prominent liberal judges, notably Elbert P. Tuttle and John Minor Wisdom, the court repeatedly insisted upon compliance with desegregation despite widespread public hostility. Indeed, the Fifth Circuit has been described as "the nation's greatest civil rights tribunal." During the 1960s this court took the lead in fashioning new remedies for school segregation and devising streamlined procedures to expedite discrimination cases. One of the most celebrated matters handled by this court was the admission of James Meredith to the University of Mississippi.

Despite the generally liberal cast of school desegregation cases, the judges who constituted the circuit bench held widely differing opinions on many issues. The tribunal was racked by a bitter schism over the handling of contempt proceedings against Governor Ross Barnett of Mississippi and by the allegations of Judge Ben F. Cameron that the Fifth Circuit's three-judge panels were being stacked in favor of liberals. In addition to difficult racial cases, the Fifth Circuit was required to handle an extremely heavy volume of general litigation. In fact, the docket of the Fifth Circuit was dominated by cases involving economic issues, such as labor law and taxation. Proposals to divide the Fifth Circuit were blocked by desegregation proponents who feared that the resulting new circuits might prove to be more conservative. Instead, Congress repeatedly enlarged the size of the tribunal until it reached the unwieldy number of 26 judges. This was by far the largest circuit court in the federal system. Finally, despite lingering opposition from civil rights activists, Congress voted to split the Fifth Circuit, effective October of 1981. Alabama, Georgia, and Florida were placed in the newly created Eleventh Circuit Court of Appeals. Mississippi, Louisiana, and Texas remained within the revamped Fifth Circuit. In part as a result of new judicial appointments, the Fifth Circuit became more conservative on racial issues. For example, in *Hopwood v. Texas* (1996) the court struck down an affirmative action admissions program at the University of Texas Law School as a violation of the equal protection clause of the Fourteenth Amendment. This decision by the Fifth Circuit received widespread national attention but was superseded by a subsequent Supreme Court ruling in 2003 in another case.

JAMES W. ELY JR.
Vanderbilt University Law School

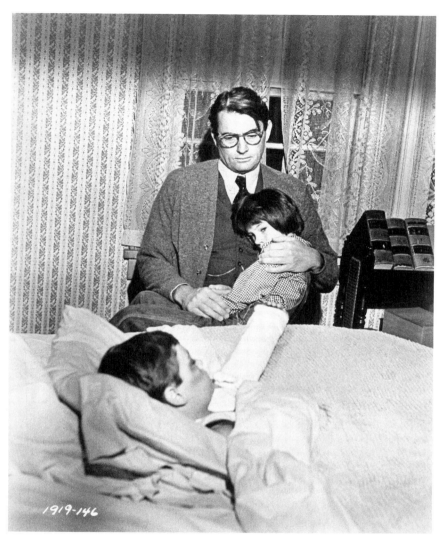

Gregory Peck as Atticus Finch in the film made from Harper Lee's Pulitzer Prize–winning novel *To Kill a Mockingbird* (1963) (Film Stills Archives, Museum of Modern Art, New York, New York)

Jack Bass, *Unlikely Heroes* (1981); J. Woodford Howard Jr., *Courts of Appeals in the Federal Judicial System: A Study of the Second, Fifth, and District of Columbia Circuits* (1981); Frank T. Read and Lucy S. McGough, *Let Them Be Judged: The Judicial Integration of the Deep South* (1978).

Finch, Atticus

A major character in Harper Lee's novel *To Kill a Mockingbird* (1960), Atticus Finch represents the conscience of the white South in the years before the advent of the Warren Court and the civil rights revolution. As a descendant of local slave owners, he well understands the deep-rooted racial prejudices that continue to exist in Maycomb, the small Alabama town in which he practices law during the Depression. Mild-mannered and scholarly, he is a stubborn idealist who believes in equality before the law for everyone, regardless of color or class. When Tom Robinson, a black man, is accused of raping the daughter of a poor white ne'er-do-well, Atticus is appointed by the court to defend him. Convinced of his client's innocence, he makes a determined effort to save his life, despite the growing opposition of the white community. His neighbors denounce him as a "nigger-lover," his children suffer insult and ridicule at school, and a mob threatens his life on the eve of the trial.

In the courtroom Atticus destroys the credibility of the prosecution's witnesses through skillful cross-examination. There is no proof that a rape occurred, he demonstrates, and strong circumstantial evidence suggests that the complainant, a lonely girl, was savagely beaten by her own father because she had made sexual advances to a black man. Reminding the white male jurors that "in our courts all men are created equal," Atticus pleads with them to abandon racial stereotyping and to decide the case on its merits.

After deliberating for several hours, the jury returns with a verdict of guilty, and Robinson is sentenced to death. The time has not yet come when southern juries will accept the word of a black man against that of any white man, Atticus explains to his children. Yet there are some indications that the grip of custom may be loosening. As a neighbor observes, only Atticus could have kept a jury out so long in a rape case. Through his gentlemanly appeals to shared southern values of honor and paternalism, he gradually persuades other white southerners to reexamine their inherited racial attitudes.

To Kill a Mockingbird received the Pulitzer Prize for fiction in 1961, and Gregory Peck won an Oscar for his portrayal of Atticus Finch in the movie version in 1962.

MAXWELL BLOOMFIELD
Catholic University of America

Joseph Crespino, *Southern Cultures* (Summer 2000); Eric J. Sundquist, in *The South as an American Problem*, ed. Larry J. Griffin and Dan H. Doyle (1995).

Foreman, Percy

(1902–1988) LAWYER.

As a defense lawyer, Percy Eugene Foreman combined his knowledge of law, his courtroom prowess, and his thirst for wealth to achieve legendary status in his native Texas and throughout the nation's legal community. His own celebrity status has attracted celebrated defendants and, in turn, been enhanced by his association with them.

Born in Polk County, Tex., in a backwoods area known as the Big Thicket, Foreman was the son of a former county jailer and sheriff. At eight years of age, he began earning money by shining shoes. He soon bought out his sole competitor in the town of Livingston and added a delivery business to his growing empire. By age 11 he was making as much money as most adults in the impoverished east Texas community. His next enterprise was loading cotton onto trains. While his bid of 25 cents per bale was low, he hired laborers at 8 cents per bale to do the actual loading. At 15 he quit school, and at age 16, having saved $6,500, moved to Houston. Subsequently he briefly attended Staunton Military Academy in Virginia before joining a Chautauqua company as an advance man. He delivered his first public oration as an 18-year-old with the company in Burnside, Ky.

Returning to his native state, Foreman enrolled at the University of Texas. He attended classes part of each year but continued to tour with the Chautauqua company as a circuit manager and lecturer. At age 25 Foreman completed law school, having served as president of the student body during his senior year.

In December 1927 Foreman formed a partnership with J. W. Lockett, with offices across from the Rice Hotel in Houston. The Rice remained a favorite Foreman hangout through much of his career. A few months after forming the partnership, he went to work for the district attorney in Houston. In 1929 he returned to private practice when his boss failed to win reelection. In 1933 Foreman became an assistant district attorney with a special interest in keeping gamblers from nearby Galveston out of Houston. In 1935 he again left the district attorney's office for private practice. His 1940 bid for election as district attorney failed.

Foreman's legendary status owes much to his record in capital punishment cases. By the late 1960s he had represented more than a thousand defendants in such cases, only one of whom had been executed; only 55 had even served time in prison. His most celebrated defendants include Jack Ruby, James Earl Ray, General Edwin Walker, and Candy Mossler.

Although part of his celebrity status stems from his successful record and the clients attracted by it, some of it derives from Foreman's being a member of that small fraternity of lawyers who have become wealthy doing criminal defense work. He received both his Houston home and a New York City co-op apartment as fees. His obvious early interest in making money did not abate over the years.

Foreman is the most famous of a special breed of southern attorney; Richard "Racehorse" Haynes and Warren Burnett are other examples. Although Foreman tried cases across the country, he had the physical stature—at 6′4″—and the down-home manner that made him the literal embodiment of that dominating courtroom presence, the Texas trial lawyer.

C. MARTIN WILSON III
Austin, Texas

Michael Dorman, *King of the Courtroom: Percy Foreman for the Defense* (1969).

Frank, Leo, Case

Described by Leonard Dinnerstein as "one of the most infamous outbursts of anti-Semitic feeling in the [history of] the United States," the Leo Frank case inspired formation of both the second Ku Klux Klan and the Anti-Defamation League of B'nai B'rith. The case began on Confederate Memorial Day in 1913 with the murder and mutilation of Mary

Portrait of Leo Frank, an innocent Jewish man lynched in Atlanta in 1915
(Library of Congress [LC-DIG-ppmsca-05650], Washington, D.C.)

Phagan, a 13-year-old employee of an Atlanta pencil factory. The mayor and an anxious populace, aroused by yellow journalism, demanded that the police find her killer quickly. They responded by arresting the victim's boss, Leo Frank. A Jew from New York, Frank rapidly became a focal point for the resentment toward factories and outsiders that rapid industrialization had ignited in southern traditionalists.

Frank's Atlanta trial took place in an atmosphere of public hysteria and amidst threats of mob violence. The prosecution, led by Solicitor Hugh Dorsey (who rode the publicity he gained from this case into the governorship), portrayed Frank as a lecherous employer who preyed on young factory girls. The state relied heavily on the testimony of Jim Conley, a black janitor with a criminal record, who claimed to have been asked by Frank to help him hide a body and to write two notes found next to Phagan's remains. Evidence available to police and prosecutors strongly suggested he, not Frank, was the killer. Nevertheless, the jury convicted the Jewish factory manager. Although he believed Frank was innocent, Judge Leonard Roane denied his motion for a new trial and sentenced him to death.

A good deal of new evidence soon surfaced, which raised further doubt about Frank's guilt. Efforts to secure a new trial failed, however, despite an appeal carried to the U.S. Supreme Court. The Court also spurned a petition seeking Frank's release on a writ of habeas corpus. He gained a temporary reprieve when Governor John Slaton sacrificed a promising political career by commuting his sentence to life in prison. Then, on 16 August 1915, a group of respectable citizens from Mary Phagan's hometown, Marietta, Ga., abducted Frank from the state prison farm at Milledgeville and hanged him.

Frank's death and the events preceding it aroused intense interest throughout the country. Governors, state legislators, and members of Congress joined more than 100,000 other Americans in efforts to save Frank's life. This outpouring of public sentiment and the nationwide press coverage of the case owed much to the efforts of Jewish leaders, who viewed this incident as a threatening manifestation of anti-Semitism, comparable to France's infamous Dreyfus affair.

Concerned Jewish groups persisted in trying to clear Frank's name, and evidence continued to surface. In 1982 a former office boy at Frank's factory, Alonzo Mann, came forward and said that he had seen another man carrying Mary Phagan's slain body. As of 1983, Governor Joe Frank Harris publicly supported a posthumous pardon of Leo Frank, but the Georgia Board of Pardons and Paroles refused to take such action. The Anti-Defamation League, the American Jewish Committee, and the Atlanta Jewish Federation submitted another petition focusing on the denial of justice to Frank, and the Board of Pardons and Paroles reversed itself and granted the pardon in March 1986, 71 years after the lynching of Leo Frank.

MICHAL R. BELKNAP
University of Georgia

Sit-in at Woolworth's store, Greensboro, N.C., February 1960
(Jack Moebes, photographer, Greensboro News and Record)

W. Fitzhugh Brundage, *Lynching in the New South: Georgia and Virginia, 1880–1930* (1993); Leonard Dinnerstein, *The Leo Frank Case* (reprint ed. 1999); Steve Oney, *And the Dead Shall Rise: The Murder of Mary Phagan and the Lynching of Leo Frank* (2003); Mary Phagan, *The Murder of Little Mary Phagan* (1987).

Greensboro Sit-ins

The sit-in demonstrations in Greensboro, N.C., marked an important turning point in the history of the civil rights movement. In February of 1960 four black college students sat down at a Woolworth's lunch counter and demanded service. Woolworth's, like other chain stores in the South, sold merchandise to all customers but denied black patrons the use of its lunch counters. The demonstrations rapidly grew in intensity. More black students participated and occupied the lunch-counter seats. White counterdemonstrators soon appeared. The incidents captured national headlines, and within a week sit-ins had spread to Winston-Salem, Durham, and other cities across the South. There was supportive picketing in the North against local branches of chain stores that denied service to blacks in the South.

At the end of February the students agreed to suspend their sit-ins while negotiations were in progress. When discussions failed to produce any resolution, direct action was resumed. Woolworth's then closed its lunch-counter operation. The students successfully mobilized the entire black community in support of their cause. Local blacks participated in an economic boycott and refused to patronize stores that would not serve them food. In the face of mounting business losses, Woolworth's quietly opened its food service in July to all persons.

It was ironic that Greensboro was the site for such a watershed in race relations. The home of five colleges, Greensboro had long enjoyed a reputation for moderation on the racial issue. City leaders had early announced that they would comply with the school desegregation requirements of *Brown*. Blacks, nonetheless, shared a sense of continuous frustration in achieving equal rights. Only minimal school integration had occurred by 1960, and other institutions remained racially separate.

This spontaneous action by Greensboro students provided a catalyst for a decade of direct, active protests. The Greensboro sit-ins altered the nature of the civil rights movement in two important respects. First, the sit-ins suggested new and more dynamic methods by which protests could be expressed. Shortly thereafter, the Freedom Rides began to challenge racial segregation in bus facilities. No longer were blacks content to await the often slow and elusive results of court decrees. Second, blacks were no longer willing to permit moderate whites to define civil rights objectives. Blacks were increasingly willing to jeopardize the goodwill of white moderates and liberals in order to follow their own agendas for social

reform, which would culminate in the black-power demands of the late 1960s.

JAMES W. ELY JR.
Vanderbilt University Law School

Taylor Branch, *Parting the Waters: America in the King Years, 1954–63* (1988); William H. Chafe, *Civilities and Civil Rights: Greensboro, North Carolina, and the Black Struggle for Freedom* (1980); Miles Wolff, *Lunch at the Five and Ten: The Greensboro Sit-Ins* (1970).

Herndon, Angelo, Case

The most famous civil liberties and civil rights case in Georgia during the 1930s centered on Angelo Herndon, a young black Communist. A native of Ohio, Herndon moved to the Deep South in the early Depression years in search of work and traded his fundamentalist Christianity for communism in 1930 while living in Birmingham, Ala. Assigned by the Communist Party to Atlanta, the 19-year-old Herndon organized a large interracial demonstration in June 1932, protesting the suspension of public relief. As a result, Atlanta police eventually arrested Herndon and charged him with attempting "to incite insurrection" against the state of Georgia, a capital offense. In his January 1933 trial, Herndon was represented by black attorneys Benjamin J. Davis Jr. and John Geer, who boldly challenged the exclusion of blacks from local juries, while the prosecuting attorneys responded with an emotional condemnation of communism. An all-white jury quickly found Herndon guilty and sentenced him to 18 to 20 years in prison.

The seeming injustice of Herndon's

conviction helped stimulate greater solidarity among Atlanta blacks and prompted a somewhat more assertive stance toward racial discrimination. Through vigorous publicity efforts the International Labor Defense, a communist-influenced legal defense organization, eventually turned the affair into a national cause célèbre. A team of prominent attorneys headed by Whitney North Seymour of New York City twice appealed the conviction to the U.S. Supreme Court, which in *Herndon v. Lowry* (1937) declared the Georgia insurrection law to be unconstitutional. After his release from prison, Herndon moved to New York City, where he remained active in radical causes and later helped to edit a literary magazine. Toward the end of World War II he left the Communist Party and eventually moved to Chicago, where he pursued a career in business.

Along with the more famous *Scottsboro* case in Alabama, the *Herndon* case symbolized the political use of the justice system to maintain racial subordination in the Deep South. Unlike *Scottsboro*, however, Herndon's prosecution under the insurrection law also raised a serious challenge to free speech and helped rally many civil libertarians to his cause. Although the Supreme Court eventually freed Herndon after nearly five years of proceedings, dramatic improvement in the status of blacks within the southern legal system had to await the advent of the civil rights movement in the mid-1950s.

CHARLES H. MARTIN
University of Texas at El Paso

Angelo Herndon, *Let Me Live* (1937); Charles H. Martin, *The Angelo Herndon Case and Southern Justice* (1976).

Iredell, James

(1751–1799) U.S. SUPREME COURT JUSTICE.

James Iredell was a lawyer, a political essayist, and a U.S. Supreme Court justice. Born in England of humble origins, Iredell came to America in 1768 to be the comptroller of customs at the port of Edenton, N.C. Soon after arriving there, he commenced the study of law under Samuel Johnston, who later became North Carolina's governor and one of its first two U.S. senators.

Iredell initially attained prominence as a leading essayist in support of American independence from Great Britain. As expressed by North Carolina's last royal governor, Iredell took "an open and eager part in rebellion." His treatise "Principles of an American Whig" predates, and bears unmistakable traces of consanguinity with, the American Declaration of Independence.

When North Carolina became an independent state in 1776, Iredell served it with distinction in several capacities. He was a member of a commission to prepare statutes for its government, draftsman of its initial court bill, one of its first three judges, its second attorney general, an original trustee of its university, and the initial reviser of its statutes.

As the former English subjects confronted the necessity of establishing a government for their infant nation, Iredell enhanced his claim to statesmanship. When the Philadelphia Convention proposed the federal Constitution, Iredell was the foremost advocate in his state for its adoption. He inaugurated the first public movement in North Carolina in favor of the document and wrote essays urging the birth of the new government. In particular, he responded to George Mason's 11 objections to the Constitution, closing with a resonant plea for establishment of the proposed government.

When North Carolina first considered ratification, Iredell was the floor leader for the Federalist forces. That convention refused to ratify, but Iredell continued to promote the Constitution by publishing and distributing the debates and by applying his considerable talents as a political essayist to the cause of the new government. When the Federalist cause finally prevailed, he was widely recognized as a principal architect of its victory.

George Washington sought "the first characters of the Union" for his initial judicial appointments. He found one in Iredell and named him to the original U.S. Supreme Court, where he served for almost a decade. During these years Iredell was close to Washington, John Adams, and their administrations and was their vigorous, highly partisan defender. He also served as a chronicler of important national events and personalities.

Iredell wrote opinions in only a few reported cases. Of these, only *Chisholm v. Georgia*, in which as the lone dissenter he supported the result that ultimately prevailed through adoption of the Eleventh Amendment, still receives juristic and scholarly attention. In *Alden v. Maine* (1999), a majority of the U.S. Supreme Court, frequently citing Iredell's dissent, viewed it as according with the original understanding of the Constitution, thus, as the dissenting opinion observed, rendering the Eleventh Amendment superfluous.

Like other justices of his era, Iredell spent most of his time traveling the federal circuits and doing the work of the circuit courts. The effects of a life Iredell described as one "of perpetual traveling, and almost a continuous absence from home" were harsh. The work, with the related travel and other hardships, took its toll on an already fragile physical constitution, and worn down by these rigors, Iredell died on 20 October 1799 at the age of 48. He is buried in the Johnston family cemetery in Edenton, N.C.

WILLIS P. WHICHARD
Campbell University

Lang Baradell and Donna Kelly, eds., *The Papers of James Iredell: Volume III, 1784–1789* (2003); Don Higginbotham, ed., *The Papers of James Iredell*, 2 vols. (1976); Griffith J. McRee, ed., *Life and Correspondence of James Iredell*, 2 vols. (1857–58); Willis P. Whichard, *Justice James Iredell* (2000).

Jaworski, Leon

(1905–1982) LAWYER.

Leon Jaworski, who became nationally recognized as the special prosecutor of the Watergate affair, was born in Waco, Tex., on 19 September 1905. He was the son of Rev. Joseph Jaworski, a Protestant minister of Polish birth, and Marie Jaworski, who was born in Vienna.

After deciding to devote his life to

a career as a trial lawyer, Jaworski attended law school at Baylor University, receiving his LL.B. in 1925; he then spent a year at the George Washington University School of Law and was granted the LL.M. in 1926. Returning to Waco to begin practice as a trial attorney, he was immediately successful, and he soon moved to Houston. His reputation spread rapidly, and in 1931, at age 26, he was asked to join one of the leading firms in that city, Fulbright, Crooker, and Freeman. He remained with this firm, becoming a senior partner in 1951. Fulbright and Jaworski became one of the largest and best-respected firms in Texas.

During World War II, Jaworski served in the Judge Advocate General's Corps, attaining the rank of colonel. He conducted the prosecution of Nazi prisoners of war in this country and then became the chief of the U.S. War Crimes Trial Section in the European Theater in the American zone of occupation, with headquarters at Wiesbaden. He personally prosecuted the first war crimes trials in Germany. In 1946 he returned to his law practice in Houston. His reputation continued to grow, and he became increasingly involved in civic and social affairs. He was elected president of the American College of Trial Lawyers in 1961, president of the State Bar of Texas the next year, and president of the American Bar Association in 1971. He received numerous awards, including 15 honorary degrees, and was an elder in the Presbyterian Church.

Jaworski's most significant accomplishment was the successful prosecution of the Watergate crimes. He served as director of the special prosecution team in 1973 and 1974; his expertise as a trial lawyer and his professional, dispassionate conduct exposed the burglary and obstruction of justice by President Nixon and his close associates. Jaworski died 9 December 1982 in Wimberly, Tex. His four books of memoirs are *After Fifteen Years* (1961), *The Right and the Power: The Prosecution of Watergate* (1976), *Confession and Avoidance: A Memoir* (1979, with M. Herskowitz), and *Crossroads* (1981, with D. Schneider).

W. HAMILTON BRYSON
University of Richmond

James Doyle, *Not above the Law: The Battles of Watergate Prosecutors Cox and Jaworski* (1977).

Johnson, Frank M., Jr.

(1918–1999) FEDERAL JUDGE.

Frank Minis Johnson Jr., was born on 30 October 1918 in rural Winston County, Ala. During the Civil War, Winston and other northwest Alabama hill counties with few slaves had little sympathy for the Confederate cause. After the war, Winston became a lone Republican stronghold in Democratic Alabama. Frank Johnson's father was active in GOP politics and was elected probate judge and a member of the Alabama legislature on the Republican ticket. Following law school at the University of Alabama and military service in Europe during World War II, Frank Johnson Jr. practiced law in Jasper, Ala., and, like his father, also became active in GOP politics. His services on behalf of Dwight Eisenhower's 1952 presidential campaign led to his appointment, in 1953, as U.S. attorney in Birmingham. In

Frank M. Johnson Jr., U.S. circuit judge. Photo taken in the 1980s.
(Frank M. Johnson Jr. Office, Montgomery, Alabama)

1955 Eisenhower appointed him to the U.S. District Court for the Middle District of Alabama in Montgomery, where he served until his appointment to a federal appeals court in 1979.

While a U.S. attorney, Johnson successfully prosecuted members of a prominent Sumter County plantation family on peonage and slavery charges, though such convictions had been rare since Reconstruction. As a district judge, he quickly gained a reputation as a vigorous defender of civil rights. During his first year on the federal bench, he helped to form a majority outlawing segregation on Montgomery's city buses. In the years that followed he issued numerous decisions on voting rights and became the first judge to order the names of qualified blacks added to county voting rolls. He also outlawed discrimination in Alabama's transportation facilities, libraries, agricultural extension service, and political parties; wrote the first statewide school desegregation decree; and placed numerous state agencies under permanent federal court order.

Judge Johnson's opinions on civil rights perplexed and angered his fellow white Alabamians, making him a convenient scapegoat for George C. Wallace and other race-baiting politicians. During his 1962 gubernatorial campaign, Wallace—Johnson's law school classmate and an associate of more than passing acquaintance—condemned "lying, scalawagging" federal judges, with Johnson his principal target. Court-baiting remained a familiar Wallace tactic for years after the 1962 election, and on at least one occasion, a Wallace aide urged Alabamians to ostracize federal judges, their wives, and children. Judge Johnson had become a pariah in his native state, however, even before the Wallace era in Alabama politics. Intermittently for 18 years, a dusk-to-dawn guard maintained a vigil at his home. His mother's home was bombed, crosses were burned on his lawn, and hate mail was directed to him. In 1975 his adopted son committed suicide. His son's emotional problems, some suggested, had their origins partly in the pressures to which his family had been subjected.

With increased black voter regis-

tration and the subsiding of race as the issue in Alabama politics, the attitudes of white Alabamians and the state's officialdom mellowed somewhat toward Judge Johnson. In the 1970s his landmark decisions mandating reform of Alabama's mental institutions and prisons prompted challenges from other quarters—critics who contended that Johnson and other activist judges were confusing their own social preferences with constitutional commands and encroaching unduly on legislative and administrative domains. Combined with his record on civil rights, however, such decisions served largely to enhance rather than damage his judicial reputation. His name was invariably mentioned when Supreme Court vacancies arose. In 1977 President Carter selected him to head the Federal Bureau of Investigation, but Johnson ultimately withdrew his name from nomination for medical reasons. In 1979 President Carter appointed Judge Johnson to the Court of Appeals for the Fifth Circuit. In 1981 the Fifth Circuit was split into two courts, and Judge Johnson became a member of the new Court of Appeals for the Eleventh Circuit, with jurisdiction over Alabama, Georgia, and Florida. He assumed senior status on the court in 1991 and continued serving until his death on 23 July 1999. Johnson had received the Presidential Medal of Freedom in 1995.

TINSLEY E. YARBROUGH
East Carolina University

Jack Bass, *Taming the Storm: The Life and Times of Judge Frank M. Johnson Jr. and the South's Fight over Civil Rights* (1992);

Robert F. Kennedy Jr., *Judge Frank M. Johnson Jr.: A Biography* (1978); Frank Sikora, *The Judge: The Life and Opinions of Alabama's Frank M. Johnson Jr.* (1992); Tinsley E. Yarbrough, *Judge Frank Johnson and Human Rights in Alabama* (1981).

Johnson, William

(1771–1834) U.S. SUPREME COURT JUSTICE.

Unlike most of his associates on the Supreme Court bench, William Johnson of Charleston was born to parents of relatively modest social position. His father, William Johnson (1741–1818), was a New York blacksmith who had moved to Charleston, S.C., in 1763 and married Sarah Nightingale of Charleston, whose father was the owner of a race track and several famous race horses. William, their second son, was born two days after Christmas in 1771, and shortly after the child's birth the elder William Johnson began his political career, which would include steady service in the South Carolina assembly, the Provincial Congress, and the state legislature until 1790. During the British occupation of Charleston the family suffered deportation while William's father was confined on a prison ship near St. Augustine, along with several other South Carolina patriot leaders.

The future Supreme Court justice was educated at Princeton and served his law clerkship with Charles Cotesworth Pinckney, a prominent Charleston attorney. Admitted to practice in 1793, Johnson became a successful trial lawyer and appellate counsel within three years of his admission. After six years legislative service in the South

Carolina House of Representatives, he was elected to the Court of Common Pleas, which entitled him to sit on the Constitutional Court of the state. In the spring of 1804 President Thomas Jefferson appointed him to serve as an associate justice of the U.S. Supreme Court.

Jefferson would have second thoughts about the political wisdom of this appointment. In some respects Justice Johnson's decisions on the bench reflected his earlier Jeffersonian-Republican political ideology. He strenuously dissented from the Marshall Court's majority opinion in *Fletcher v. Peck* (1810), which broadly expanded the scope of the federal Constitution's contract clause (Article I, sec. 10). A proponent of legislative primacy in government, Johnson objected to the Marshall Court's use of judicial review in many other cases. Yet he angered President Jefferson by declaring provisions of the 1807 Embargo Act unconstitutional because he felt they conferred excessively broad discretionary powers upon the executive branch of the federal government. Johnson also insisted that Congress's power over interstate and foreign commerce was exclusive, while Chief Justice Marshall and the Court majority left room for state legislative authority in these areas (*Gibbons v. Ogden*, 1824).

In 1822 ex-president Jefferson complained to Justice Johnson that he was not living up to expectations and urged him to begin to file separate opinions setting forth his personal views. Thereafter Johnson tended to write separate opinions more often, but he continued to concur silently with Court opinions he supported.

Perhaps the main reason for Johnson's alienation from Jefferson was the justice's variant view of the federal union. Although he was not a Federalist, Johnson viewed the national government as a creation of an agreement between the American people, the states, and the central government. He also supported generous construction of the Constitution's express powers, particularly as they affected foreign affairs and commercial matters. In this regard he represented a dissenting voice against southern views of states' rights and the compact theory of the federal union.

Justice Johnson's nationalism was put to the test when he invalidated the 1822 South Carolina statute that required the imprisonment of any free black seaman who left his ship in South Carolina (*Elkison v. Deliesseline*, 1823). While sitting as the U.S. circuit justice for South Carolina, Johnson held that the state statute was contrary to the foreign and interstate commerce powers conferred upon Congress by the Constitution. Secondly, the statute was contrary to the 1815 commercial treaty with Britain, and thus violated the supremacy clause of the Constitution. Thirdly, the statute was an attempt to circumvent the U.S. Supreme Court's ability to hear federal question appeals from the highest courts of the states. While South Carolina continued its persecution of black seamen by other means, Johnson's decision brought him into heated conflict with his Charleston neighbors. Thereafter he sharply limited the amount of time he spent in South Carolina. Shortly before his death in 1834, he moved his permanent residence to New York City, where he is buried.

HERBERT A. JOHNSON
*University of South Carolina
School of Law*

Herbert A. Johnson, *South Carolina Historical Magazine* 89 (1988); Donald G. Morgan, *Justice William Johnson, the First Dissenter: The Career and Constitutional Philosophy of a Jeffersonian Judge* (1954).

Lamar, Lucius Quintus Cincinnatus
(1825–1893) POLITICIAN AND U.S. SUPREME COURT JUSTICE.

L. Q. C. Lamar is best known for advocating sectional reconciliation in the post-Reconstruction Congress. He was elected to Congress from Mississippi in 1872. As one of the few southern Democrats in Congress, he developed and supported a program to harmonize the South with the rest of the Union. Lamar became nationally prominent when, in 1874, he took the occasion of the funeral of Charles Sumner, the radical abolitionist, to plead for rapprochement between North and South. Sumner had been a leading enemy of slavery, but he had also taken the position that the abolition of slavery had ended any reason for enmity between the regions. Lamar's eulogy for Sumner echoed these sentiments and called for the two regions to respect each other and reconcile. Lamar continued to champion a reintegration of the South with the rest of the nation through another term in the House, eight years in the Senate, and as secretary of the interior during Grover Cleveland's first term as president.

Lamar established his credentials for

Lucius Quintus Cincinnatus Lamar, Mississippi statesman and U.S. Supreme Court justice.
Photo taken between 1865 and 1880. (Library of Congress [LC-DIG-cwpbh-04887], Washington, D.C.)

championing the South with a distinguished antebellum career and wartime
service. He was born on 17 September
1825 in Georgia. He moved to Oxford,
Miss., in 1849, where he practiced law
and taught mathematics at the University of Mississippi. After a brief return

to Georgia, Lamar was elected to Congress as a Mississippi Democrat in 1857.
He drafted the Mississippi ordinance
of secession and rose to the rank of
lieutenant colonel in the Confederate
army. In 1862 President Jefferson Davis
dispatched Lamar as commissioner to

Russia, but Russian attitudes toward the Confederacy doomed his mission; Lamar never proceeded past Paris. He ended the war as judge advocate in a military court.

After the war and before reentering politics, Lamar held a full-time professorship at the University of Mississippi, where he headed the law department. He gradually returned to law practice and again became active in politics. In 1872, after Mississippi reentered the Union, but with Republicans still in political control, Lamar ran for Congress. Although Republicans prevailed in the other five congressional districts, Lamar won his race easily, becoming the first Democrat in Mississippi elected to Congress after the war. Lamar's leadership in advocating northern and southern reconciliation secured him a prominent position within the national Democratic Party. When, in 1884, the Democrats regained control of the presidency after a 24-year hiatus, Grover Cleveland chose Lamar for his cabinet as a symbol of the return of the South to national councils. In 1887 Cleveland nominated Lamar for the Supreme Court, as a further sign that the South had returned to power within the Union. Although Democrats were a minority in the Senate, the support of two Republicans and an Independent allowed Lamar's nomination to squeak past, 32 to 28. With this Senate confirmation in 1888, Lamar became the first southerner to be placed on the highest court since secession. Lamar's service on the Court was brief and was mainly important as symbolic of the reintegration of the South into the federal government. He suffered from poor health during his tenure and was only active on the Court for four years. Moreover, his legal qualifications were weak, and he felt inadequate in his new role. Despite his lack of influence on Supreme Court jurisprudence, the very presence of a southerner on the Court set a valuable precedent. Lamar died on 23 January 1893.

BEN BROWN
University of California, Berkeley

Wirt Armistead Cate, *Lucius Q. C. Lamar, Secession and Reunion* (1935); Edward Mayes, *Lucius Q. C. Lamar: His Life, Times and Speeches, 1825–1893* (1896); J. B. Murphy, *L. Q. C. Lamar: Pragmatic Patriot* (1973).

Little Rock Crisis

White southerners invoked the doctrines of states' rights and interposition to counter the NAACP's post–World War II campaign against de jure segregation. A few places in the Upper South immediately complied with the Supreme Court's decision in the 1954 case of *Brown v. Board of Education*, which overturned the doctrine of separate but equal, but throughout states of the old Confederacy, governments embraced a strategy of "massive resistance." The first major constitutional test of this strategy grew out of efforts to integrate the Little Rock, Ark., public schools.

The NAACP in 1956 brought one of its more than 50 post-*Brown* desegregation suits against the Little Rock Board of Education. Under federal court order, the board in September of 1957 proposed to admit a small number of blacks to formerly all-white Little Rock Central High School. Governor Orval Faubus invoked states' rights and

White mob marching from Arkansas state capitol to Central High to protest the admission of the Little Rock Nine to Central High School, 1959 (Library of Congress [LC-U9-2906-15], Washington, D.C.)

interposition as constitutional grounds to block the plan. Acting on the governor's orders, the Arkansas National Guard, accompanied by a jeering white mob, rebuffed black students. Faubus denounced as unconstitutional federal court orders directing compliance.

The Republican president, Dwight D. Eisenhower, responded to this attack on federal judicial authority by asserting the supremacy of the national government. He directed the attorney general to obtain an injunction against Faubus, who in turn withdrew the National Guard. The president on 25 September 1957 dispatched troops from the 101st Airborne Division to restore order and to force the admission of black students.

The tug-of-war between state and federal authorities continued until late 1959. The Supreme Court, in *Cooper v. Aaron* in September 1958, unanimously reasserted the supremacy of the federal government, denounced interposition, and reaffirmed the federal judicial power. Governor Faubus then implemented two statutes that authorized him to close the Little Rock schools. The Court in the 1959 case of *Faubus v. Aaron* unanimously declared these statutes in violation of the due process and equal protection clauses of the Fourteenth Amendment.

Little Rock Central High School reopened quietly in September 1959. Events of the preceding two years discredited die-hard segregationists' arguments that states' rights and interposition could thwart the massive social changes sweeping the South.

KERMIT L. HALL
State University of New York at Albany

Numan V. Bartley, *The Rise of Massive Resistance: Race and Politics in the South during the 1950s* (1969); Daisy Bates, *The Long Shadow of Little Rock: A Memoir* (1962); Benjamin Muse, *Ten Years of Prelude: The Story of Integration since the Supreme Court's 1954 Decision* (1964).

Marshall, John

(1755–1835) U.S. SUPREME COURT CHIEF JUSTICE.

Born in Fauquier County, Va., John Marshall was a prominent member of the Richmond legal profession before he accepted federal office, first as one of the ministers to France during the XYZ affair (1797–98), then as a member of the House of Representatives (1799–1800), and as secretary of state (1800–1801). Appointed chief justice in January 1801, he served for the remaining 34 years of his life during a period of unprecedented institutional change in the Court and unparalleled constitutional growth in American law. Marshall is best remembered for his articulation of the doctrine of judicial review (*Marbury v. Madison*, 1803), the use of the contract clause to defend private property against legislative seizures (*Fletcher v. Peck*, 1810; *Dartmouth College v. Woodward*, 1819), and his classic expositions and constructions of the interstate commerce power (*Gibbons v. Ogden*, 1824) and the necessary and proper clause (*McCulloch v. Maryland*, 1819). A former officer in the Virginia Continental Line, with combat service at the battles of Brandywine, Germantown, and Stony Point, Marshall supported ratification of the federal Constitution while a member of the Virginia Ratifying Convention and thereafter was a moderate Federalist deeply concerned for sustained economic growth of the United States.

Despite the rising tide of Jeffersonian Republicanism in Virginia and the split of the Federalist Party into factions following and opposing Alexander Hamilton, Marshall continued to be a political power in his native state. His outgoing personality and unaffected mannerisms won him friends and supporters. His "lawyers' dinners" were famous throughout the Old Dominion, and his gregarious approach to life persisted even after he received severe public criticism when he inadvertently shared dinner with Aaron Burr during the latter's trial for treason in Marshall's circuit court. Charming, chivalrous, and in later years flirtatious with women, the chief justice remained devoted to the ailing wife he had married in 1783 and who was the mother of their 10 children. Marshall treasured his associations with Virginians and loved the landscape of his native state, particularly the western mountains of his childhood. In the two years before his death, he was actively making plans to retire to the family homestead at Oak Hill.

Virginia made a strong impression upon Marshall and shaped him for national leadership. His father, Thomas Marshall, was surveyor for the Fairfax land interests in the Northern Neck and also served as sheriff for Fauquier County. It was Marshall's father who saw to it that his son had the appropriate educational background so that he would fit into the company of gentry families that dominated local and provincial government in the Old Dominion. Military service behind him, John was regularly elected to the House of Delegates, where he learned the give and take of legislative lawmaking, skills that would serve him well as leader of the small group of independent-minded justices that served with him on the U.S. Supreme Court. Service on Virginia's Council of State familiarized him with the political and economic planning that was essential to the shaping of constitutional and legal foundations for American prosperity. As Marshall's law practice grew, several landmark cases (*Ware v. Hylton*, 1796; *Hite v. Fairfax*, 1786; *Hunter v. Fairfax*, 1794) heightened his understanding of state authority during the Revolutionary War and the relationship between international law and the American federal system. In addition, his defense of the College of William and Mary against state seizure of its charter (1790) served as a precursor for his Supreme Court opinion in the *Dartmouth College* case.

Despite Marshall's federal judicial achievements, he nevertheless retained a preference for local government, based in part upon his experiences with the county court system that dispersed political authority in the commonwealth. At the same time, he appreciated the extensive legislative authority vested in the general assembly and the equally centralizing judicial authority in the general court, court of chancery, and court of appeals. As a consequence, Marshall was not a nationalist but rather an advocate of a federal government endowed with adequate authority to perform only those functions necessary for a national state. His economic preferences and views reflected a similar balance. Appreciative of the value of an agrarian lifestyle, Marshall foresaw the inevitability of economic diversification into commercial and industrial enterprise. Unlike many of his fellow Virginians, Marshall sought to provide a constitutional and legal structure that would encourage economic growth but at the same time to soften its impact upon the people. A contemplative and compassionate man, the chief justice brought to the national scene all that was exemplary in the Virginia of his day.

HERBERT A. JOHNSON
University of South Carolina School of Law

Charles F. Hobson, *The Great Chief Justice: John Marshall and the Rule of Law* (1996); R. Kent Newmyer, *John Marshall and the Heroic Age of the Supreme Court* (2001); David Robarge, *A Chief Justice's Progress: John Marshall from Revolutionary Virginia to the Supreme Court* (2000); Jean Edward Smith, *John Marshall: Definer of a Nation* (1996).

Morgan, Charles, Jr.

(b. 1930) CIVIL RIGHTS ATTORNEY.
Born in Cincinnati, Ohio, in 1930,
Charles Morgan was reared in Kentucky
and at age 15 moved with his parents to
Birmingham, Ala. He graduated from
the University of Alabama and received
his law degree from the same institution. Morgan first achieved national
prominence when he denounced the
September 1963 Birmingham church
bombing and blamed community attitudes for the tragedy. In the resulting
furor, Morgan left Birmingham. A year
later he became the regional director
for the American Civil Liberties Union
(ACLU) in Atlanta.

Throughout the 1960s Morgan was
involved in much of the litigation that
altered political and social life in the
region. He was instrumental in handling
lawsuits challenging racial segregation
in jury selection, state prisons, and the
choice of delegations to political conventions. Perhaps Morgan's most significant impact came as a result of *Reynolds
v. Sims* (1964), in which the Supreme
Court mandated equal population
districts for legislative bodies. Morgan
was one of the plaintiffs and successfully
argued the case before the Court. Subsequent litigation by Morgan forced a
reapportionment of the Alabama legislature.

Morgan also demonstrated a commitment to civil liberties. He defended
Captain Howard Levy at his court-
martial for refusing to teach derma-
tology to Green Beret aidmen. Morgan
also represented Julian Bond in the
early stages of his challenge to the 1967
action of the Georgia legislature denying Bond his seat because of his antiwar
political views. And Morgan appeared
on behalf of Muhammad Ali's claim to
be a conscientious objector in his prolonged fight against conviction for draft
evasion.

In 1972 Morgan moved to Washington and became head of the ACLU's
national office. He was one of the first to
call for the impeachment of President
Richard M. Nixon over the Watergate
scandal, and he persuaded the ACLU
board to adopt this position in September of 1973. Morgan resigned from
his ACLU post in 1976 when he was
criticized for publicly supporting fellow
southerner Jimmy Carter's presidential
bid. Always the maverick, Morgan then
organized his own law firm and began
defending corporations from assaults
on their rights. In the 1980s he successfully represented Sears, Roebuck, and
Co. against claims of sex discrimination
in employment practices in protracted
litigation. A skillful and dedicated advocate, Morgan once declared that "you
don't hire a lawyer to lose." He currently
practices law in Birmingham.

JAMES W. ELY JR.
Vanderbilt University Law School

Philip Kopper, *Washington Post Potomac*
(7 October 1973); Charles Morgan Jr.,
A Time to Speak (1964), *One Man, One
Voice* (1979).

Napoleonic Code

To prevent the complete adoption of
the Anglo-American common law
after the Louisiana Purchase (1803), the
largely French and Spanish residents of

Louisiana sought to preserve their Latin legal tradition by the reception and enactment of a civil code modeled after the projet of the Code Napoleon. On 31 March 1808 the territorial legislature of Orleans adopted a "code" drafted by Louis Moreau-Lislet and James Brown, titled the *Digest of Civil Laws Now in Force in the Territory of Orleans*. Printed in both English and French and patterned after the Napoleonic Code of France, this was indeed a digest, that is, a compilation of existing law, rather than a definitive and final statement of the law, a true code. Unlike the French code upon which it was based, the Digest of 1808 was not enacted in revolutionary times, nor was it intended to effect a national legal unification or extensive social transformation through legislation. It was not a break with the past, it did not abrogate the preceding law, and many of the radical ends that the authors of the French code championed were the very things Louisiana's inhabitants sought to avoid. This precursor of the modern civil code of Louisiana was mainly the result of a confrontation between competing cultures rather than a true codification effort.

The legislative act promulgating the Digest of 1808 stipulated that "whatever in the ancient civil laws of this territory . . . is contrary to the dispositions contained in the said digest, or irreconcilable with them, is hereby abrogated." In this clause, the earlier law was not necessarily abrogated. As the Superior Court of Louisiana observed in 1812, "what we call the Civil code, is but a di-gest of the civil law which regulated this country under the French and Spanish Monarchs." Moreover, unlike the products of legislative positivism associated with civilian codification movements at the time, the Louisiana "code" gave legal effect to custom. Spanish law, therefore, survived in Louisiana as an authoritative source of law as custom. The two major sources of Spanish law in Louisiana had been the *Recopilacion de Indias* and *Las Siete Partidas*. Indeed, because the Spanish had previously abrogated much of the former French law, the Digest of 1808 was largely a digest of Spanish law.

The Digest of 1808 did serve the purpose of preventing the erosion of the Roman civil law during the early high tide of the common law in Louisiana. It remained for Edward Livingston, sometimes called the "Bentham of American Jurisprudence," to awaken in Louisiana a zeal for true codification. Livingston, with Moreau-Lislet and Pierre Derbigny, drafted the Louisiana Civil Code of 1825, which repealed all civil laws and which was enacted by the state legislature. The authors asserted that "in the Napoleonic code we have a system approaching nearer than any to perfection." Although modified after the Civil War to reflect the abolition of slavery and reenacted as the Louisiana Civil Code of 1870, the version of the Napoleonic Code received by Louisiana in 1825 remains the fundamental basis of the state's system of private law. Thus, the Roman civil law has been preserved in Louisiana as a mixed jurisdiction in the midst of a basically American-style judiciary and in the face of general reception of the Anglo-American public law such as prevailed elsewhere throughout the South.

ERNEST S. EASTERLY III
Baton Rouge, Louisiana

R. Batiza, *Tulane Law Review* (April 1971); George Dargo, *Jefferson's Louisiana: Politics and the Clash of Legal Traditions* (1975); Ernest Easterly III, *Geojurisprudence: Studies in Law, Liberty and Landscapes* (1980); Shael Herman, *The Louisiana Civil Code: A European Legacy for the United States* (1993); Richard H. Kilbourne Jr., *A History of the Louisiana Civil Code* (1987); Robert A. Pascal, *Louisiana Law Review* (December 1965).

Parks, Rosa

(1913–2005) CIVIL RIGHTS ACTIVIST. The burden of 100 years of discrimination added to the weariness of a difficult day was just too much for the gentle black woman that early December day in 1955. Asked to give up her seat on a crowded Montgomery, Ala., bus to allow whites to sit down, Rosa Parks, once dubbed the civil rights movement's "most mannerly rebel," flatly refused.

Recalling that a year earlier a black teenager, Claudette Colbert, had been removed in handcuffs, kicking and screaming, for a similar offense, Parks felt sure the authorities would not repeat such a disgraceful performance. She was wrong. Summoned by the bus driver, the police arrested her and placed her in a cell with two other black women, one of whom would not speak to her. The other had attacked a man with an ax.

Born 4 February 1913 in Tuskegee, Ala., Parks was one of two children, and the only daughter, of Leona Curlee. Her mother was born on a tenant farm in Montgomery County. Raised in Montgomery, Parks attended Alabama State College and then worked as a clerk and an insurance saleswoman before becoming a tailor's assistant at the Montgomery Fair Department Store, where she was employed when the bus incident occurred. A former secretary of the Montgomery chapter of the NAACP, Parks also served as a "stewardess" (an assistant at communion services) at that city's African Methodist Episcopal Church.

"Rosa Parks was just the right person at the right time," civil rights activist E. D. Nixon later remarked. Nixon, an old friend of Parks and former president of the Alabama NAACP, paid her bail and asked if she would be willing to serve as a test case to challenge the legality of Montgomery's segregation ordinances. After receiving the support of her husband, Raymond, a barber at Maxwell Air Force Base, and her mother, she agreed and thereby stepped into history as the "mother of the civil rights revolution."

The real challenge to white supremacy came not from judicial action, however, but from the leadership of Martin Luther King Jr., the 26-year-old pastor of the Dexter Avenue Baptist Church, who launched the yearlong boycott of the bus system in Montgomery's black Protestant churches. The bus boycott, with its attendant violence on the part of the police and the white community and its hundreds of arrests, was the crucible from which King emerged as a nationally known leader.

After a 381-day boycott, the bus company capitulated and ended segregation on the city's public transportation network. On 13 November 1956 the U.S. Supreme Court ruled that bus segregation was unconstitutional.

Fired from her job as a result of her notoriety, Parks worked as volunteer for the Montgomery Improvement Association, which was formed to coordinate the bus boycott. In 1957 she moved to Detroit, where she became employed by Representative John Conyers of Michigan. Parks's husband, Raymond, whom she married in 1932, died in 1977. The couple had no children.

The catalyst that sparked the militant phase of the modern civil rights movement, Parks often expressed embarrassment at the adulation she received as the symbol of black resistance to injustice. Honored at the White House by President Jimmy Carter in February 1979, along with other notable elderly blacks including Jesse Owens and the Rev. Martin Luther King Sr., she was also awarded the Martin Luther King Jr. Nonviolent Peace Prize in Atlanta in January 1980. Detroit has named a street and a school after her.

During the last years of her life, Rosa Parks received a plethora of awards for her role in the American civil rights movement. In 1994 she received the Rosa Parks Peace Prize in Stockholm, Sweden, in 1996 President Bill Clinton awarded her the Presidential Medal of Freedom, and in 1998 she became the first recipient of the International Free-

dom Conductor Award given by the National Underground Railroad Freedom Center.

HELEN C. CAMP
New York City

Ebony (November 1980); *Los Angeles Times* (15 January 1980); *New York Times* (6 December 1955; 5 April 1978; 14 February, 24 February, 25 November 1979; 15 January 1980; 5 June 1982); *Southern Exposure* (Spring 1981).

Plessy v. Ferguson

In *Plessy v. Ferguson* (1896) the U.S. Supreme Court ruled in favor of the "separate but equal" principle in public transportation facilities for whites and blacks. In doing so it affirmed the role of states in controlling social discrimination, and, many argue, the decision actually promoted enforced segregation. The number of Jim Crow laws increased rapidly during the following years.

The case originated in Louisiana, which had a statute requiring separate-but-equal accommodations for whites and blacks on railroad cars. In 1892 Homer Adolph Plessy purchased a train ticket from New Orleans to Covington, La. Plessy, seven-eighths white and one-eighth black, sat in a "whites only" car and refused to move to a "colored" section. He was arrested for violating the "Jim Crow Car Act of 1890." The "Citizens Committee to Test the Constitutionality of the Separate Car Law," a group of 18 blacks, had instigated the incident, choosing Plessy as the example and making sure train officials knew his racial status. Their attorney was Albion Winegar Tourgee, a carpetbagger during

Reconstruction and author of the Reconstruction novel *A Fool's Errand*.

Four years later, the Supreme Court heard the case and voted seven to one (Justice David Brewer did not participate) against Plessy. In the majority opinion Justice Henry B. Brown wrote: "We consider the underlying fallacy of the plaintiff's argument to consist in the underlying assumption that the enforced separation of the two races stamps the colored race with a badge of inferiority. If this be so, it is not by reason of anything found in the act, but solely because the colored race chooses to put that construction on it." Furthermore, he wrote: "The argument also assumes that social prejudices may be overcome by legislation, and that equal rights cannot be secured to the negro except by an enforced comingling of the two races. We cannot accept this proposition. If the two races are to meet upon terms of social equality, it must be the result of natural affinities, a mutual appreciation of each other's merits and a voluntary consent of individuals."

Ironically, the only southerner then serving on the Court, Justice John Marshall Harlan, cast the sole vote against the final decision. In the minority opinion he asserted the equality of all men with regard to the civil rights "as guaranteed by the supreme law of the land." He stated, "Our Constitution is colorblind, and neither knows nor tolerates classes among citizens. In respect of civil rights, all citizens are equal before the law."

Not until the 1950s did Supreme Court decisions, most notably in *Brown v. Board of Education* (1954), begin to dissolve the Court's sanction of the concept of separate but equal. For more than a half century, the principle had dictated the social treatment of blacks, with "equal" facilities providing the legal rationale for segregation. Finally, though, what had been the minority opinion in *Plessy* became that of the majority, a belated response to Justice Harlan's statement that "the thin disguise of 'equal' accommodations for passengers in railroad coaches will not mislead any one, nor atone for the wrong this day done."

JESSICA FOY
Cooperstown Graduate Program
Cooperstown, New York

Henry J. Abraham, *Freedom and the Court: Civil Rights and Liberties in the United States* (1982); Catherine A. Barnes, *Journey from Jim Crow: The Desegregation of Southern Transit* (1983); J. Fickler Douglas, *Journal of Negro History* (Fall 1999); John C. Livingston, *Fair Game? Inequality and Affirmative Action* (1979); Frank T. Read and Lucy S. McGough, *Let Them Be Judged: The Judicial Integration of the Deep South* (1978); Barbara Y. Welke, *Law and History Review* (Fall 1995).

Powell, Lewis F.

(1907–1998) U.S. SUPREME COURT JUSTICE.

A private lawyer possessing no elective or judicial experience is seldom appointed to the U.S. Supreme Court. Lewis Powell, nominated to the Court in 1971 by Richard Nixon, was an exception.

A lifelong Virginian, Powell was born 19 September 1907 in Suffolk, Va. He received his law degree in 1931 from

Lewis F. Powell, U.S. Supreme Court justice. Photo taken in the 1980s. (Lewis Powell Office, Washington, D.C.)

Washington and Lee University. From 1937 to 1971 Powell was a member of a large, prestigious Richmond law firm. During this period he quietly established a reputation as one of the South's leading corporation lawyers, earned a handsome income, served as a director of 11 major companies, and was elected president of the American Bar Associa-

tion and the American College of Trial Lawyers. During the 1950s he served as chair of the Richmond School Board, steering a moderate course in the slow-paced desegregation of the public schools.

Powell's nomination met with less resistance from liberals than did several of Nixon's other choices for the Supreme

Court seats: unlike Harrold Carswell, Powell was judged to be highly competent; unlike Clement Haynsworth, Powell was seen as a racial moderate; and unlike William Rehnquist, Powell was not regarded as an uncompromising ideologue. In Powell, Nixon found the highly qualified southern jurist that he so desperately wanted to appoint to the Court.

As a justice, Lewis Powell did not assume a self-consciously "southern" stance. A regional orientation did not emerge in his opinions—even those touching Federalism or race. Favoring a "balancing approach" in constitutional adjudication similar to that of his avowed idols, Felix Frankfurter and John Marshall Harlan, Powell proved to be the swing vote in several close cases and the author of some of the Burger Court's most carefully wrought opinions. In 1972 he wrote a thoughtful majority opinion reaffirming the position that a wiretap is a search or seizure within the meaning of the Fourth Amendment. In his opinions on equal protection, Powell resisted the expansion of "suspect classifications."

Only in his opinions involving big business—perhaps because of his long service to large corporations—was Powell unable to maintain a stance of moderation. His aggressive support of big business is characteristic of the New South—a South no longer consumed by virulent racism but now willing to adopt strategies pioneered by northern corporation lawyers in the service of improved quarterly reports.

Powell's most famous opinion, *Regents v. Bakke* (1978), was characteristic of his balanced, trenchant, perceptive, and articulate legal analyses. In this landmark case that divided the Court and the country, Powell presented a lucid argument that invalidated racial quotas but upheld the concept of "affirmative action."

One scholar described Powell's work habits and temperament as being distinguished by "conscientiousness, thoroughness, craftsmanship, and sheer capacity for hard work." Powell was a particularly distinguished "lawyer's judge" among the Supreme Court justices.

JOHN W. JOHNSON
Clemson University

Leonard W. Levy, *Against the Law: The Nixon Court and Criminal Justice* (1974); Burt Neuborne, *The Justices of the United States Supreme Court* (1978); *Richmond Law Review* (1977).

Prather v. Prather

Prather v. Prather (1809), the first child-custody case in South Carolina that awarded control to a mother, captured the tension between change and continuity that characterized domestic relations law after the American Revolution. Most judges in the early Republic granted custody to women reluctantly because it cut against the grain of the traditional common-law commitment to paternal authority. There was no divorce in South Carolina before the Civil War, but the state's chancery court did grant legal separations. Jennet Prather petitioned the chancery court for a separation from her husband on the grounds of abuse, and she asked for custody of her infant daughter and two sons. According to her, William Prather had "used her extremely ill, and turned her out of doors"; he then began living with another woman "in open adultery."

There was little doubt that Jennet Prather's husband had treated her badly, and Chancellor Henry Desaussure showed few misgivings about awarding her a separation and alimony. He could not allow "such conduct, so inhuman in itself, so injurious to innocent and helpless women, and so mischievous to society, [to] pass unheeded and unchecked." But Desaussure obviously felt uneasy about challenging the common-law prerogatives of the father. In the chancellor's words, the father "is the natural guardian invested by God and the law of the country, with reasonable power over" his children. Only if "his paternal power has been monstrously and cruelly abused" would the court interfere "in the exercise of it." Desaussure, in the end, decided to award the father custody of the two sons, while giving the mother control of the daughter. Even this compromise left the chancellor uneasy, however, and he worried that the court was "treading new and dangerous grounds."

Desaussure's ambivalence reflected the extent to which the ideal of the male-dominated household still shaped southern family culture. As *Prather v. Prather* demonstrated, a growing conviction about the importance of proper child rearing and the role of motherhood led to increased custody rights for southern women. Even with the older children, the court insisted that Jennet Prather had a right to visit them "at all reasonable times." The expansion of custody rights after the American Revolution, however, left southern women with few gains in status outside the household because these new rights stemmed from a vision of mothers as innately suited for the task of nurturance within the home. The development of enlarged maternal prerogatives thus reinforced the restriction of white women in the South to the domestic arena, enclosed in a prison of male expectations.

PETER W. BARDAGLIO
Ithaca College

Peter W. Bardaglio, *Reconstructing the Household: Families, Sex, and the Law in the Nineteenth-Century South* (1995); Michael Grossberg, *Feminist Studies* (Summer 1983); Marylynn Salmon, in *Women, War, and Revolution*, ed. Carol R. Berkin and Clara R. Lovett (1980).

Roane, Spencer

(1762–1822) VIRGINIA JURIST.
Spencer Roane was born 4 April 1762, in Essex County in northern Virginia, the son of William Roane and Elizabeth Ball Roane, well-connected gentry. Roane studied law at the College of William and Mary under George Wythe, sharing Wythe's Revolutionary sympathies but not his subsequent Federalism. Instead, Roane allied himself with the Anti-Federalist Patrick Henry, marrying Henry's daughter Anne in 1786. Roane served as a legislator, but his interests were primarily legal. In 1789 he secured appointment to the General Court, which involved riding circuit as a trial judge and hearing criminal appeals. In 1794 he was elected to the state's highest tribunal, the Court of Appeals, a post he

would keep until his death on 4 September 1822.

Throughout his years on the bench, Roane proved a devotee of judicial review and the supremacy of constitutional law over legislative enactments. He affirmed the former in a 1793 case, *Kamper v. Hawkins*, overturning an act that sought to undermine the authority of Virginia's High Court of Equity. Supporting him in a separate opinion was St. George Tucker, who as a court of appeals judge would prove to be Roane's natural enemy. Like Wythe (whom he succeeded as professor at Williamsburg), Tucker's judicial temperament was cosmopolitan, assertive, and Federalist. Roane more closely resembled Edmund Pendleton, longtime presiding judge of the court of appeals, a consensus-builder whose jurisprudence was rooted in local institutions.

The years following Pendleton's 1803 death were difficult for the court of appeals. The legislature declined to fill vacancies, and by 1807 the court, reduced to three members, was controlled by Tucker. Roane's preference was for unanimous opinions achieved by conferences—the better to foster stability and prestige. Tucker, content with seriatim opinions, used conferences to fine-tune decisions. Tucker and Presiding Judge William Fleming ignored procedural reforms proposed by Roane in 1808 and 1809. On one occasion feeling especially provoked, Roane snatched a draft from Tucker's hands and threw it on the floor. Soon thereafter Tucker refused to hold conferences, whereupon Roane challenged him in open court. The feud ended with Tucker's resignation in 1811, following a legislative reorganization of the court.

Roane's confrontations mask the substance of his career. Historian Timothy Huebner calls him a transitional figure—devoted to protection of vested interests in the 18th-century manner, willing like southerners of the Revolutionary generation to limit slavery if it could be done without violating property rights, respectful of charters but unwilling to rate corporate freedom above public interest. In no sense did he equate judicial review with judicial lawmaking—unlike his counterparts of the mid-19th century. Always he was a Virginian, devoted to state sovereignty (as per the Virginia Resolutions of 1798) and prepared to defend his "country" with pugnacity.

These defenses were fully engaged by a series of cases appealed from the court of appeals to the U.S. Supreme Court involving the former holdings of a Loyalist, Lord Thomas Fairfax. Issues included title to lands seized and to properties bequeathed or sold, as well as the validity of quitrents that speculators (notably a group headed by Chief Justice John Marshall's brother) sought to collect. In *Fairfax's Devisee v. Hunter's Lessee* (1813), Justice Joseph Story brushed aside Virginia's dispositions and ruled for the Fairfax-Marshall side on the strength of protections in the Jay Treaty of 1794. But the court of appeals refused to enforce this judgment. In *Hunter v. Martin, Devisee of Fairfax* (1814), Roane attacked the constitutionality of Section 25 of the 1789 Judiciary Act, which authorized appeals from state to federal courts. Virginia could not be sovereign, he asserted, if her courts were subject to reversal by an outside tribunal.

The Marshall Court struck back in *Martin v. Hunter's Lessee* (1816) with Story's affirmation of the Supreme Court as ultimate arbiter—that is, that parallel lines of justice converged in Washington, D.C. In coming years Roane and Marshall would cross swords often via pseudonymous essays, Roane emerging as a leader of a "Richmond Junto" opposed to centralized government. He was no disunionist, though he contributed to the sectionalism that soon would startle Jefferson like a "fire bell in the night."

PAUL M. PRUITT JR.
Bounds Law Library
University of Alabama

Timothy S. Huebner, *The Southern Judicial Tradition: State Judges and Sectional Distinctiveness, 1790–1890* (1999); F. Thornton Miller, *Juries and Judges versus the Law: Virginia's Provincial Legal Perspective, 1783–1828* (1994); R. Kent Newmyer, *John Marshall and the Heroic Age of the Supreme Court* (2001).

Robinson, Spottswood W., III

(1916–1998) JURIST AND CIVIL RIGHTS LAWYER.
Spottswood Robinson was one of the most prominent black jurists in the United States. Born in 1916 in Richmond, Va., he graduated from Virginia Union University and then studied at Howard Law School, where he earned the highest scholastic average ever achieved at that institution. Robinson remained at Howard in a part-time faculty position for several years, divid-

ing his time between teaching and the private practice of law in Richmond. His legal career was interrupted by military service during World War II. Robinson subsequently left Howard and devoted his energies to real-estate law in Richmond and civil rights litigation for the NAACP. In the late 1940s he filed numerous lawsuits seeking equalization of facilities and teacher salaries between white and black schools in Virginia.

Throughout the 1950s Robinson served as southeast regional counsel for the NAACP, working with Thurgood Marshall. Noted for his clarity of expression and scrupulousness in handling details, Robinson played a major role in preparing and arguing *Brown v. Board of Education* (1954) before the Supreme Court. Following the decision in *Brown* he pushed actively for school desegregation across Virginia. From 1960 to 1963 Robinson was dean of Howard Law School. In 1961 President John F. Kennedy named him to the Civil Rights Commission. In October 1963 he was nominated by President Kennedy as the first black judge of the Federal District Court for the District of Columbia. Three years later President Lyndon Johnson appointed Robinson as the first black judge on the U.S. Court of Appeals for the District of Columbia.

Robinson wrote more than 300 opinions while serving the appellate court. He usually voted with the liberal wing of judges on that court, which has often been polarized along philosophical lines. In *Nixon v. Sirica* (1973) Robinson joined the majority opinion holding that the courts and not the president must determine the extent of executive privilege. Robinson also heard an early sexual harassment case and ruled that such conduct constituted sex discrimination proscribed by Title VII of the Civil Rights Act. He became chief judge of the D.C. Court of Appeals in 1981, only the second black to head one of the federal circuits. As chief judge, Robinson handled the administrative duties of the court and was instrumental in revamping its management structure. He took senior status in 1989 and died in 1998.

JAMES W. ELY JR.
Vanderbilt University Law School

Howard Law Journal, no. 1 (1977); Richard Kluger, *Simple Justice: The History of* Brown v. Board of Education *and Black America's Struggle for Equality* (1994); *Washington Post* (27 May 1981).

Ruffin, Thomas Carter

(1787–1870) JUDGE.
Born to a gentry family in Virginia and educated at the College of New Jersey (later Princeton), Thomas Carter Ruffin settled in North Carolina and found early success in politics and law. Although he served in the state legislature and as a presidential elector, disillusionment with politics during the 1820s caused him to focus on his legal practice. He acquired a reputation as an aggressive and effective lawyer, and in 1829 the North Carolina legislature elected him to the state supreme court. There he served until 1853 (from 1833 to 1852 as chief justice) and again briefly in 1859.

Ruffin's judicial opinions in some respects placed him within the mainstream of American legal development.

He relied on traditional common-law doctrines in criminal cases, expanded the power of eminent domain to promote the building of railroads, and contributed to the development of higher-law constitutionalism with his opinion in *Hoke v. Henderson* (1833), where he defined an appointed office as property with which the legislature could not interfere. Based on such achievements, eminent legal scholar Roscoe Pound included Ruffin on his list of the 10 greatest judges in American history.

Despite this record of moderation, Ruffin's slavery opinions made him one of the South's most extreme judicial defenders of the institution. His most infamous decision came in *State v. Mann* (1829), where he asserted that "the power of the master must be absolute to render the submission of the slave perfect." Ruffin held that a violent assault and battery upon a slave—the slave had been shot in the back while fleeing—did not constitute an indictable offense under common law. The ruling captured the attention of abolitionists, including Harriet Beecher Stowe, who modeled a fictional judge in one of her works after Ruffin. Although he later tempered the *Mann* decision by holding that a master could not kill his slave, Ruffin continued to be one of the southern judiciary's most outspoken proponents of racial control. He castigated his judicial colleagues in *State v. Caesar* (1848), a case involving a slave who killed a white man, for applying common-law principles so as to mitigate the charge from murder to manslaughter. Judges, he warned, should be "cautious against rash expositions, not suited to the actual state of things and not calculated to promote the security of persons, the stability of national institutions, and the common welfare." Such sentiments demonstrated Ruffin's stark unwillingness to sympathize with the plight of slaves when confronted with any potential threat to the dominance and security of whites.

Despite his attendance at the Peace Conference in Washington in 1861, Ruffin proved an ardent defender of the Confederacy and traditional southern values. The owner of two plantations and more than a hundred slaves, Ruffin served as president of the state agricultural society and in this capacity in 1855 delivered a proslavery address, in which he described a South composed of paternalistic masters and contented slaves. Though not nearly as famous as his firebrand cousin Edmund Ruffin of Virginia, Thomas Ruffin ranks among the most significant legal figures in the history of the South. He died in Hillsboro, N.C.

TIMOTHY S. HUEBNER
Rhodes College

Sally Hadden, in *Local Matters: Race, Crime, and Justice in the Nineteenth-Century South*, ed. Christopher Waldrep and Donald G. Nieman (2001); Timothy S. Huebner, *The Southern Judicial Tradition: State Judges and Sectional Distinctiveness, 1790–1890* (1999).

Scopes Trial

No other event of the 1920s captured the imagination of the public and the press as did the spectacle of the Scopes Trial. Held in the little Tennessee town of Dayton in a sweltering July 1925, the case of the *People of the State of Tennessee v. John Thomas Scopes* is probably the best-known trial in American history.

With passage of the Butler bill by the Tennessee legislature—a statute outlawing the teaching of evolution—several Dayton civic boosters accepted the offer of the American Civil Liberties Union to defend any teacher held in violation of the new law. Scopes, having just completed his first year as a science teacher at the local high school, agreed to act as the defendant. Ironically, Scopes probably did not, in fact, teach the theory of evolution.

The main actors in the drama came from outside Dayton. Clarence Darrow, the most famous lawyer of the day, defended Scopes with a staff including Dudley Field Malone and Arthur Garfield Hays. William Jennings Bryan, the three-time presidential hopeful and former secretary of state, led the prosecution team. H. L. Mencken, dubbing the developing spectacle the "Monkey Trial," led a horde of news personnel who descended on Dayton from around the nation and the world.

The trial opened on 10 July 1925 to the whirring of movie cameras and live radio coverage on Chicago station WGN. The courtroom crowd spilled over onto the lawn, and eventually Judge John T. Raulston moved the proceedings to the cooler temperatures outside.

The personalities and objectives of Darrow and Bryan did not, however, allow the trial to lessen its fever pitch. Bryan characterized the trial as a "duel to the death" between unbelievers and

John T. Scopes, the defendant in the famous Dayton, Tenn., "Monkey Trial," 1925
(Library of Congress [LC-B2-6377-12], Washington, D.C.)

Christians. The agnostic Darrow, on the other hand, fully intended to prove that the Butler law was unfair and unconstitutional. The initial subject of all this furor, Scopes himself, became a secondary figure. Judge Raulston did not allow scientific and technical testimony, and the trial degenerated into a personal battle between Darrow and Bryan, a conflict encouraged by an aggressive press corps.

A Darrow challenge to Bryan brought the Great Commoner to the witness stand near the end of the trial. Bryan proved to be conservative in his religious views but not a consistent fundamentalist. For example, he did not espouse a literal meaning for the Creation as taking place in a series of six 24-hour days. Actually, Bryan was consistent with his old populist leanings against monopoly, in this instance control of educational processes by educators and scientists. Moreover, his belief in a conservative social gospel scored natural selection as antithetical to reform. Darrow, one of the most clever courtroom orators in American history, was not as consistent in his reasoning. In the case of Leopold and Loeb, he defended the young men by arguing that they had been corrupted by naturalistic teachings; at Dayton, he defended just such instruction as proper.

The results of the trial proved inconclusive. Some liberals self-righteously believed the immediate posttrial death of Bryan to be fitting justice. The Rhea County jury found Scopes guilty and fined him $100. However, the Tennessee Supreme Court reversed the decision on a technicality, thereby removing the

possibility of a test case before the U.S. Supreme Court. Scopes left teaching and entered the oil business as a geologist. His sister was later dismissed from the Paducah, Ky., school system for teaching evolution.

Although only Arkansas and Mississippi followed Tennessee in passage of antievolution statutes, the Scopes Trial undoubtedly led to suppression of evolution instruction across the nation. Most science textbook publishers bowed to the apparent public will and deleted or de-emphasized sections on evolution. This trend lasted into the early 1960s. After publication of the Biological Sciences Curriculum study materials by the American Institute of Biological Scientists in the mid-1960s, a new round of antievolutionist activity began. Self-styled "creationists," who were usually fundamentalists, proposed equal-time statutes. Court decisions in 1982 and 1985 in Arkansas and Louisiana overturned state laws mandating that creation science, which is based on the Genesis account of creation, be given equal time in the classroom if evolution were taught. A study of high school biology instruction in Kentucky, Tennessee, and Indiana in the early 1980s indicated that most instructors placed a "moderate" stress on evolution, a conclusion suggesting that a balance or equilibrium has been reached on the subject of evolution instruction across the nation.

Since the Scopes Trial, a plethora of materials have both documented and interpreted this episode in Dayton. Perhaps the most famous of these, *Inherit the Wind*, a McCarthy-era adaptation of the Scopes Trial in play and movie forms, presented a version of the episode distorted by contemporary politics. Bryan College, located in Dayton, not far from the courthouse where the trail was held, stages its own dramatic account of the trial and has hosted discussions of creation science.

WILLIAM E. ELLIS
Eastern Kentucky University

Edward Larson, *Summer for the Gods: The Scopes Trial and America's Continuing Debate over Religion and Science* (1997); Lawrence W. Levine, *Defender of the Faith, William Jennings Bryan: The Last Decade, 1915–1925* (1965); Ronald L. Numbers, *Darwinism Comes to America* (1998); John T. Scopes with James Presley, *Center of the Storm: Memoirs of John T. Scopes* (1967); Ferenc Morton Szasz, *The Divided Mind of Protestant America, 1880–1930* (1982).

Scott, Dred, Case

Captain John Emerson of Missouri in 1833 purchased Dred Scott, an illiterate slave born in Virginia. Emerson took Scott to Illinois, to that portion of Wisconsin Territory embraced in the Missouri Compromise, and then back to Missouri. When Emerson died in 1843, putative ownership of Scott passed to John F. A. Sandford, Emerson's brother-in-law and executor. Three years later, Scott sued in the lower courts of Missouri claiming that his sojourn in free territory had made him a free man.

Scott's litigation consumed more than a decade. The Missouri Supreme Court in 1848 held that the laws of Illinois and Wisconsin Territory had no extraterritorial status in Missouri.

An 1887 portrait of Dred Scott (Library of Congress [LC-USZ62-5092], Washington, D.C.)

Scott in 1854 filed suit in the U.S. Circuit Court for Missouri against John Sandford, who had moved to New York. Judge Robert Wells rejected Scott's substantive claim, but he left open the question of the slave's citizenship. Scott appealed this issue to the U.S. Supreme Court.

The Court on 6 March 1857 issued its opinion in *Dred Scott v. Sandford*. A proslavery southern majority, led by Chief Justice Roger B. Taney, rejected Scott's claims. Taney struck down the Missouri Compromise, denied the power of Congress to abridge slaveholders' property rights, and held that a black person could not be a citizen of the United States within the meaning of the Constitution.

Taney's invocation of judicial authority complemented postnullification southern attitudes toward relations between nation and state. Southern leaders believed that their declining influence over the political branches of the national government dictated a greater reliance on the federal judiciary to protect slaveholders' interests. Yet the cost of obeisance to the Court in *Scott* was further division of the northern and southern wings of the Democratic Party and potential destruction of the Union.

Irony and tragedy plagued the South's efforts to harmonize states' rights, the rule of law, and a dual system of race relations. Although freed by a new owner following the Court's decision, Scott died of consumption on 17 September 1858. The postwar freedom of other blacks, to which Scott's case contributed, also proved ephemeral. After Reconstruction the South, with the blessing of the Supreme Court, reasserted the concept of states' rights to foster white supremacy, a concept that reigned until the civil rights changes of the 1960s.

KERMIT L. HALL
State University of New York at Albany

Don E. Fehrenbacher, *The Dred Scott Case: Its Significance in American Law and Politics* (1978); Paul Finkelman, ed., *Dred Scott v. Sandford: A Brief History with Documents* (1997).

Scottsboro Case

The Scottsboro case was the cause célèbre of American race relations in the 1930s. Touching on both the North's outrage at southern racism and the South's defensiveness about northern claims of moral superiority, this trial of nine black youths for rape in Scottsboro, Ala., reminded the nation of its failure to reconcile its image as the world's leader of democracy with the squalid reality of bigotry and repression daily faced by its black citizens.

On 25 March 1931 the deputy sheriff of Jackson County, Ala., reacting to reports of a fight among "hobos" on a Southern Railway freight train bound for Memphis, stopped the train at Paint Rock, Ala., and arrested nine black youths, jailing them at the county seat of Scottsboro. The deputy also removed several white hobos from the train, including two white women. Minutes later, the women accused the blacks of rape, and only courageous action by the Jackson County sheriff saved the blacks from a lynching. The first rape trial took place in Scottsboro just three weeks later, and despite the trumped-up nature of the charges, the jury convicted eight of the nine and sentenced them to death.

The severity of the youths' sentences galvanized public opinion throughout America. When an appellate court overturned the verdicts, the state of Alabama immediately launched a second prosecution of the "Scottsboro boys" in 1933. During the second trial, the International Labor Defense, an organization closely aligned with the Communist Party, defended the youths, and the case became front-page news. Five years of legal maneuvering followed in both the state and federal courts. In 1937 defense attorneys and the prosecution finally reached a compromise, which freed four of the defendants while sentencing the others to long prison terms. Not until 1950 did the last of the Scottsboro boys emerge from the Alabama prisons. For many southerners, the Scottsboro case marked a low point in 20th-century race relations because it starkly revealed white southerners' oppression of blacks.

CARROLL VAN WEST
Center for Historic Preservation
Middle Tennessee State University

Dan T. Carter, *Scottsboro: A Tragedy of the American South* (1969); James E. Goodman, *Stories of Scottsboro* (1994); Kwando Mbiassi Kinshasa, *The Man from Scottsboro: Clarence Norris and the Infamous 1931 Alabama Rape Trial, in His Own Words* (2002).

Slave Codes

The first statute reflecting slavery in the South was adopted by colonial Virginia in 1660. That law recognized a class of Africans as life servants, and it established as a punishment for white servants who ran away with black life servants the service time the black servant would have been required to render. This rather brief and simple act gave way within a generation to a complex code of laws concerning slavery in Virginia, which was a pioneer in this effort. In 1705 the Virginia legislature passed a two-chapter, 50-section slave code, one of the first such codifications in the South.

The Virginia Slave Code of 1705 clearly established two themes that would remain a part of slave codes in every southern colony and state. Slaves were defined by race, and this meant black persons; and slavery was associated primarily with a plantation economy. Provisions in the early Virginia Slave Code included sections on the torture and murder of slaves, the legal status of children whose fathers and mothers were slaves, penalties for failure to obey commands of a master, and restrictions on nonslave fraternization with slaves. The brutality of slavery is readily observed in Chapter 49, Section 37, which provided that "any slaves, against whom proclamation hath been thus issued, and once published at any church or chapel, stay out, and do not immediately return home, it shall be lawful for any person or persons whatsoever, to kill and destroy such slaves by such ways and means as he, she, or they shall think fit, without accusation or impeachment of any crime for the same." The section further allowed dismemberment of any slave caught and returned alive.

The first southern colonial slave codes and all subsequent codes encompassed three elements. First, they defined the slave status; second, they regulated the slave as a form of real property; and third, they delineated slaves' social behavior and provided legal forms for social control of slaves. This latter element reflected the southern white fixation on black slave insurrections. As the Civil War approached, slave codes added further restrictions on the personal freedoms of slaves, including the virtual abolition of manumission. By the 1850s slave codes in most southern states provided procedures for the expulsion of free blacks or their reenslavement with a master of their choice.

JOHN R. WUNDER
University of Nebraska at Lincoln

Eugene D. Genovese, *Roll, Jordan, Roll: The World the Slaves Made* (1972); William Goodell, *The American Slave Code in Theory and Practice: Its Distinctive Features Shown by Its Statutes, Judicial Decisions, and Illustrative Facts* (1969); Kenneth M. Stampp, *The Peculiar Institution: Slavery in the Ante-Bellum South* (1956).

Slave Patrols

The first slave patrols appeared in southern colonies during the early or mid-18th century: South Carolina passed its first patrol law in 1702, Virginia followed in 1726, North Carolina enacted laws for patrols in 1753, and Georgia instituted its patrols in 1757. These colonial assemblies drew upon their knowledge of slave control methods used in Caribbean slave societies when they established patrols. Other southern colonies and states would pass laws authorizing patrols until every state had them by the early 19th century. Patrollers (also called "paddyrollers," or "pattyrollers") used white-on-black violence to carry out their duties, and in many ways their actions mimicked the routine, nonpaternalistic side of master-slave relations.

Patrols were designed to supplement the sometimes ineffective mastery of white slave owners. To maintain control (theoretically) over slaves at all times, owners relied upon patrollers to police the roads and woods surrounding plantations. Like masters, patrols could and did use violence to enforce curfews and catch runaways. Working mostly at night, patrols had the legal authority to enter farms and slave quarters without warrants. They also worked in southern cities, which often established their own urban patrol groups. Urban patrols preceded, and in some cases supplanted, town police forces. As appointed local officials, patrols functioned like other civil officers—for relatively low compensation and little thanks. Fines for nonperformance kept some men on the job, and with enough money, one could hire a substitute to serve the typical three-month appointment to a patrol group. In the 18th century, patrols reflected a cross-section of southern white society, but by the 1830s in many southern states, patrollers were increasingly drawn from the lower social and economic tier of white communities. Slave owners and nonowners both served as patrols, although women and free blacks apparently did not.

In Virginia and South Carolina, and in many parts of the Deep South that copied South Carolina's patrol laws, patrollers were closely tied to local militia, often drawn directly from militia membership rolls. In North Carolina and Kentucky, however, the county courts had authority over the appointment and supervision of patrol groups. In North Carolina, parts of Virginia, and in most cities, patrollers were also paid for their efforts on an hourly or nightly basis.

Slave patrols were charged with breaking up unauthorized slave meetings at night, catching local runaway slaves, and stopping slave insurrections before they happened by taking preventative measures. As they moved through slave cabins, patrollers looked for missing persons but also for prohibited guns, papers, and means of communication.

Slaves found with stolen property or weapons would be punished summarily, and the goods confiscated (and frequently given to the observant patroller as a reward). Patrollers' activities brought them into conflict with slaves seeking fewer restrictions, and not surprisingly, slaves fought back against patrols. Folktales and oral-history narratives collected under the Works Progress Administration abound with stories of slave-patroller confrontations, and in rare cases, slaves committed acts of arson or murder to deter overly conscientious patrols from their duties. During rumored insurrections or wartime, patrols became more active, but in more common periods of peace, patrols might work only one night a week.

When slavery ended in the 1860s, slave patrols no longer had the legal authority to enter the homes and churches of African Americans, nor would former slaves permit them the same liberties. Nonetheless, behaviors common to prewar slave patrols (nightriding, white-on-black violence) continued under the guise of the Ku Klux Klan. Former bondsmen and slave owners alike commented on the striking similarity of the Klan's outrages to actions previously taken by slave patrols.

SALLY E. HADDEN
Florida State University

J. Michael Crane, *Journal of Mississippi History* (1999); W. Marvin Dulaney, *Black Police in America* (1996); Sally E. Hadden, *Slave Patrols: Law and Violence in Virginia and the Carolinas* (2001); E. Russ Williams, *Louisiana History* (Fall 1972).

Stone, George Washington
(1811–1894) JURIST.

George Washington Stone served on the Alabama Supreme Court from 1856 until 1865 and again from 1876 until his death in 1894, serving as chief justice from 1884. Reared in Tennessee, Stone read law in a lawyer's office in Fayetteville before moving to Alabama, where he was admitted to practice in 1834 and where he lived for the remainder of his life.

Stone's service on Alabama's high court spanned nearly four decades, encompassing historical periods that included the late antebellum period, the Civil War, post-Reconstruction, and the industrialization of the state in the final decades of the century. A prodigious worker, Stone authored over 2,400 opinions. Many were run-of-the-mill cases, but others offer a window into the changing times during which Stone sat as a state supreme court justice.

For example, as a judge in the antebellum period, Stone formulated a reasonableness standard as a limitation on the amount of force that the hirer of a slave could lawfully use to discipline him. In the post-Reconstruction era, Stone ruled on a case in which a buyer sought to enforce a contract to purchase land using by-then-worthless Confederate money, holding that a court of equity should not specifically enforce the contract. In the latter years of Stone's tenure, personal injury cases against railroads allowed him to help define doctrines such as proximate cause and contributory negligence that would be part of the tort law framework on into the 20th century.

Stone must also be held responsible for granting unfettered discretion to local jury commissioners, allowing them to exclude blacks from jury pools notwithstanding a U.S. Supreme Court ruling that their exclusion was unconstitutional. As a result of Stone's ruling, jury commissioners in Alabama were generally able to exclude blacks from jury venires until federal courts in the 20th-century civil rights era brought that practice to an end.

The most interesting of Stone's judicial opinions, though, were issued in a series of conscription cases during the Civil War. These involved the conscription laws adopted by the Congress of the Confederate States of America. In the first of these cases, Stone wrote a special concurring opinion holding that adoption of the conscription laws was within the powers of the Confederate Congress under the Confederate Constitution. In a subsequent case, Stone ruled that an individual who had procured a substitute and thus avoided service under the Confederacy's initial conscription law was not exempt under a second conscription act. In a later case Stone ruled that the right of the Confederate government to conscript an individual prevailed over the claim of the Alabama militia, in which he was already serving. The only circumstance presented by the conscription cases in which Stone believed the Confederate Congress exceeded its powers was an 1864 act repealing all previous exemptions; though the Alabama Supreme Court upheld the act, Stone filed a dissent.

One may find it surprising that an Alabama judge and his court would support the power of the central government (i.e., the Confederate Congress) just at the time that his state had adopted the ultimate measure of state autonomy by seceding. One obvious explanation is that the exigencies of wartime will often lead the most outspoken exponent of states' rights to concede power to the central government. But another may be that Stone was and always remained a Jacksonian Democrat, rather than a States' Rights Democrat in the John C. Calhoun tradition. Stone came to maturity in middle Tennessee at the time of the conflict over South Carolina's purported nullification of Jackson's tariff. When he came to Alabama in 1834, he found himself among Jacksonian loyalists who supported Old Hickory in the nullification struggle. Perhaps the nationalistic Jacksonian viewpoint acquired by the young lawyer in the early 1830s continued to influence the Alabama Supreme Court judge three decades later.

HOWARD P. WALTHALL SR.
Cumberland School of Law
Samford University

William H. Brantley, *Chief Justice Stone of Alabama* (1943); Thomas McAdory Owen, in *History of Alabama and Dictionary of Alabama Biography*, vol. 4 (1921); *Alabama Reports*, no. 100 (1895); Timothy S. Huebner, *The Southern Judicial Tradition: State Judges and Sectional Distinctiveness, 1790–1890* (1999).

Thomas, Clarence

(b. 1948) U.S. SUPREME COURT JUSTICE.

Clarence Thomas was the second African American appointed to the Supreme

Court of the United States. He replaced Thurgood Marshall, the first African American to sit on the Court and one of the most significant civil rights lawyers in U.S. history.

Thomas was born in 1948 in the dirt-poor town of Pin Point, Ga. Abandoned by his father and then given up by his mother, he was raised by his maternal grandparents in a segregated society. Through hard work, sacrifice, and sheer force of will—both his own and that of his grandfather—he graduated with honors from the College of the Holy Cross in Worcester, Mass., and then from Yale Law School. Seven years later, Thomas, who had become active in the black conservative movement after arriving in Washington, D.C., in 1979 to work for U.S. senator John C. Danforth (R-Mo.), was named assistant secretary for civil rights in the U.S. Department of Education by President Ronald Reagan. Ten months after that, he was appointed chair of the U.S. Equal Employment Opportunity Commission (EEOC)—the federal agency charged with enforcing the nation's equal employment opportunity laws.

During Thomas's tenure the EEOC shifted away from a group-based approach to civil rights enforcement to an individual-based approach. Thomas's rejection of group-based relief in civil rights cases—most notably, affirmative action—led civil rights groups to oppose his confirmation to the Supreme Court.

Thomas's Supreme Court confirmation process was arguably the most dramatic and divisive ever conducted. The NAACP, the nation's preeminent

civil rights organization, took the highly unusual step of opposing an African American nominee to the federal bench when it sought to block Thomas's confirmation on the ground that his record on civil rights was "reactionary." Others objected as well, most notably to Thomas's apparent willingness to invoke natural law in constitutional interpretation and to his seeming opposition to *Roe v. Wade*, the 1973 Supreme Court decision that legalized abortion. However, the issue that made all others pale in comparison was the allegation by law professor Anita Hill that Thomas had sexually harassed her during their tenure together at the Department of Education and at the EEOC.

After having been nominated by George H. W. Bush to replace retiring justice Thurgood Marshall, Thomas was confirmed to the Supreme Court on 15 October 1991, albeit by the narrowest margin in modern history (52–48). He fascinates the American people as few justices ever have. Although much of that interest can be traced to the controversy surrounding his confirmation process, his performance on the Court has received increasing attention over the years. Commentators initially tried to label Thomas as little more than Justice Antonin Scalia's loyal apprentice, but that label has been rejected by most observers who read Thomas's opinions.

Thomas has written many provocative opinions. In his civil rights opinions, he appeals to the principle of inherent equality at the heart of the Declaration of Independence. In civil liberties and Federalism cases, in contrast, he does what Robert Bork would have likely done had he been confirmed to the Supreme Court: he asks how the framers would have decided the question.

Thomas has been a member of the nation's highest court for over a decade. However, he is still a relatively young man and he has stated publicly that he intends to serve on the Court for "decades to come."

SCOTT GERBER
Ohio Northern University

Scott Douglas Gerber, *First Principles: The Jurisprudence of Clarence Thomas* (2002).

Tucker Family

Over several generations, the Tuckers of Virginia produced a number of eminent attorneys, jurists, politicians, legal educators, and authors, binding the family name inextricably to the legal and political culture of the Old Dominion and the South. Bermuda native St. George Tucker (1752–1827), progenitor of the main Tucker line, pursued a lengthy career as a state and federal judge, poet and political essayist, and law professor at the College of William and Mary. On the bench, Tucker's able decisions set important precedents during the formative years of Virginia jurisprudence. His opinion in *Kamper v. Hawkins* (1793) forcibly stated the doctrine of judicial review by holding the state constitution to be the supreme act of a sovereign people, with which all subsequent legislation had to conform.

Tucker wove a series of notes and annotations derived from his experience as a law teacher into appendices designed to identify areas of American practice that had diverged from English law in his five-volume edition of Blackstone's *Commentaries* (1803). He took occasion, too, to assert his objections to the institution of slavery and his hope for its gradual elimination. Though keyed largely to Virginia's law and practice, Tucker's edition of Blackstone rapidly emerged as an essential reference tool for student and practitioner alike throughout the South until superseded by later editions produced by other hands.

A distant Bermuda kinsman of St. George Tucker, George Tucker (1775–1861) acquired less fame as a lawyer than as an author and political economist. His best-known work, *The Valley of Shenandoah* (1824), provides a valuable view of Virginia's post-Revolutionary society and legal culture, while it takes the Tidewater gentry and the legal fraternity both to task for failures in leadership and professionalism. Most important, however, Tucker's book marks the first significant use of the plantation setting and the stereotyped southern slave in fiction. In his later works on political economy, some written while Tucker served as professor of moral philosophy at the University of Virginia, his earlier opposition to slavery becomes somewhat muted as his main focus turns toward a deep concern for public prosperity and a growing anxiety over the economic future of his section.

Henry St. George Tucker (1780–1848), son of St. George Tucker, made his greatest contribution as the state's highest judicial officer and as a legal writer. Thoroughly skilled in the application of complex principles of equity, he led the Virginia bench in pursuit of justice over legal technicality in opinions marked for their clarity of reasoning and legal scholarship. He exerted further influence over the legal culture of the South by training a remarkable generation of attorneys at his own private law school in Winchester and later at the University of Virginia. From his lecture notes he prepared in 1831 the two-volume *Commentaries on the Laws of Virginia*. This encyclopedic work became a handbook for practitioners as well as students.

The most prolific of the Tuckers, Nathaniel Beverley Tucker (1784–1851) parted from his father and brother to espouse extreme states' rights and proslavery positions in numerous contributions to Virginia newspapers and southern periodicals. After nearly two decades in Missouri as a modestly successful lawyer and jurist, Tucker assumed his father's old post as professor of law and government at the College of William and Mary. There, he imbued a receptive generation of aspiring attorneys with his own fiery brand of southern nationalism and secessionist rhetoric. His anxiety over northern domination of the South led to the prophetic *Partisan Leader* (1836), a novel that captured the spirit of states' rights proponents who foresaw the coming conflict. But Tucker also took the training of law students as competent advocates seriously. His broad approach to legal education blended the practical with the theoretical, particularly stressing the importance of procedure in the *Principles of Pleading* (1846).

After the Civil War, John Randolph Tucker (1823–97) assumed the family mantle of leadership in Virginia jurisprudence. Son of Henry St. George Tucker, this Winchester attorney served as Virginia's wartime attorney general and later became an influential Virginia congressman and dean of the law school at Washington and Lee University. A conservative southern Democrat and strict constructionist, Tucker simultaneously led his southern contemporaries in renewing their devotion to the federal Constitution and in understanding its usefulness to their section. He successfully defended Jefferson Davis against federal prosecution at the end of the Civil War but failed to win an appeal on behalf of a group of Chicago anarchists before the U.S. Supreme Court in the case of *Spies v. Illinois* (1887), which first contended that the Fourteenth Amendment incorporates the Bill of Rights. One of the first southerners elected to the presidency of the American Bar Association (1892–1893), Tucker wrote frequently on topics of concern to practitioners in the South. In the last years of his life, he stood firmly against the rising influence of Harvard and the developing case method of instruction in southern legal education.

E. LEE SHEPARD
Virginia Historical Society

Robert J. Brugger, *Beverley Tucker: Heart over Head in the Old South* (1978); W. Hamilton Bryson, ed., *Legal Education in Virginia, 1779–1979: A Biographical Approach* (1982); Mary H. B. Coleman, *St. George Tucker: Citizen of No Mean City* (1938); Charles T. Cullen, *St. George Tucker and Law in Virginia, 1772–1804* (1987);

John W. Davis, *John Randolph Tucker, the Man and His Work* (1949); Christopher Doyle, *Virginia Magazine of History and Biography* 106, no. 4 (1998); Robert C. McLean, *George Tucker: Moral Philosopher and Man of Letters* (1961); Tipson R. Snavely, *George Tucker as Political Economist* (1964); William R. Taylor, *Cavalier and Yankee: The Old South and American National Character* (1961).

Tuttle, Elbert P.

(1897–1996) FEDERAL JUDGE.
As chief judge of the Fifth Circuit Court of Appeals throughout the 1960s, Elbert Parr Tuttle provided leadership in the development of civil rights law comparable to that of Earl Warren on the Supreme Court. In a 1967 tribute to him, Chief Justice Warren praised Tuttle for combining "administrative talents with great personal courage and wisdom to assure justice of the highest quality without delays which might have thrown the Fifth Circuit into chaos." Tuttle and three other judges— John Minor Wisdom of New Orleans, Richard T. Rives of Montgomery, and John R. Brown of Houston—were disparagingly labeled "The Four" by an outraged fellow judge, who saw them as destroyers of the Old South he cherished.

Tuttle, Wisdom, Brown, and Rives shared a quiet passion that reacted to injustice and translated the Supreme Court's basic school desegregation decision into a broad mandate for racial justice and equality under law. They battled to make the law work during a period of social upheaval. They not only accepted the constitutional phi-

losophy that extended downward from the Warren Court but also reinforced it upward and outward, stretching and expanding the law to protect rights and liberties granted by the Constitution. They proved that change can come from below, provided there is an accepting climate in the structure above.

Born in California on 17 July 1897, Tuttle grew up in Hawaii, attending multiracial schools. He settled in Atlanta in 1923 after graduation from Cornell University Law School. In Atlanta he opened a law practice with his wife Sara's brother, William Sutherland, who had grown up in Jacksonville, Fla., and had clerked for Justice Louis Brandeis. As a lawyer, Tuttle won a landmark case before the Supreme Court establishing an indigent's right to counsel.

A World War II battlefield hero who became a brigadier general in the army reserve, Tuttle led a floor fight that seated the contested Georgia delegation that supported Dwight Eisenhower at the Republican National Convention in 1952. Following Eisenhower's election, Tuttle served as general counsel to the Treasury Department until 1954, when the president appointed him to the Fifth Circuit Court of Appeals. In his first 29 years on the federal bench, Tuttle wrote 1,225 opinions, reputed to be more than any federal judge in history, including 94 dissents.

Based on his belief in the theory of common-law development, Tuttle believed that "the law develops to meet changing needs . . . according to changes in our moral precepts." In civil rights cases that broke new legal ground, Tuttle explained: "I never had any doubt that what I was doing would be affirmed by the Supreme Court. It was the easiest field of the law I could write in. . . . The truth is, the black person in the litigation I sat in on was entitled to the result he got, under what the Constitution required."

In 1965 Harvard University awarded Judge Tuttle an honorary Doctor of Laws degree, stating, "The mind and heart of this dauntless judge enhance the great tradition of the federal judiciary."

After Congress split the Fifth Circuit in 1980, leaving it with Mississippi, Louisiana, and Texas and shifting Alabama, Florida, and Georgia into a new Eleventh Circuit, a subsequent act named the new Eleventh Circuit Court of Appeals building in Atlanta for Judge Tuttle. President Jimmy Carter already had awarded him a Presidential Medal of Freedom. Judge Tuttle died 23 June 1996.

JACK BASS
College of Charleston

Jack Bass, *Unlikely Heroes* (1981); Howell Raines, *My Soul Is Rested* (1977); Earl Warren, *Georgia Law Review* (Fall 1967).

Tutwiler, Julia

(1841–1916) EDUCATOR AND REFORMER.

Julia Strudwick Tutwiler was born 15 August 1841 in Tuscaloosa, Ala., third child of Henry and Julia Ashe Tutwiler. Raised near Havana in the Alabama Black Belt, she was influenced by the atmosphere of the Greene Springs School, run by her father from 1847 to 1884. Famous in its time, Greene Springs was primarily for boys but made no distinction between male and female students. Refusing to inflict corporal punishments, Tutwiler and his faculty urged their students to work for the betterment of humankind. A sincere if discreet critic of slavery, Henry Tutwiler owned slaves but allowed Julia to teach them to read.

Had she done nothing else, Julia Tutwiler's record as a language teacher and school administrator would have kept her memory alive. Her training, interspersed with early teaching at Greene Springs and elsewhere, was cosmopolitan—two years' study in Philadelphia, a semester at Vassar College, private instruction with the faculty of Washington and Lee University, three years' travel and study in Germany. Returning to Alabama, she taught from 1876 to 1881 at the Tuscaloosa Female College before being appointed principal of the Livingston Female Academy—after 1883, the Alabama Normal College. Named president in 1890, she served until her retirement in 1910, making ANC the state's outstanding teacher-training school. A progressive educator, Tutwiler was an earnest advocate of women's vocational education and collegiate coeducation. In 1893 her work as lobbyist and negotiator secured admission of women students at the University of Alabama.

From 1879, when she began to campaign for sanitary conditions in county jails, Tutwiler devoted much time to prison reform. In this work she was fortunate to have the support of fast-growing networks of women's organizations and clubs, from the local Tuscaloosa Benevolent Society to the national Woman's Christian Temperance Union (WCTU). Such groups did not openly challenge contemporary attitudes toward gender roles. Rather, they staked a claim to concerns (such as relief of the helpless, care of children, or support for the penitent) that were perceived as naturally falling within woman's domestic "sphere." As the WCTU's state "prison superintendent" after 1883, Tutwiler proved a relentless critic of Alabama's post–Civil War prison system. The practice of leasing the state's largely black convict population to industry was, she said, an abandonment of responsibility—worse than slavery.

Refusing to be sheltered, Tutwiler inspected mines and labor camps on a regular basis from the mid-1880s. Moving with assurance among legislators, wardens, and prison commission officials, she employed her many contacts, many of them former Greene Springs students, to lobby for improved facilities, for night schools and religious services for prisoners, separate facilities for women, and vocational schools for adolescent offenders. She and her allies secured enactment of several reforms between 1880 and 1900. On the other hand, her preferred tactic, moral suasion, was ill-suited to shake either the interests or opinions of New South elites. Like the Black Belt "Bourbons," the urban "Big Mules" desired cheap labor and mechanisms of racial control. Women reformers, labor leaders, and humane politicians of various stripes fought against these realities in vain. Operating until 1928, Alabama's convict

lease system would outlive Tutwiler by more than a decade.

Tutwiler's good works, writings, and public appearances (including efforts on behalf of temperance, women's suffrage, and international peace) made her the subject of hagiography well before her death on 24 March 1916. Contemporaries thought of her as "Miss Julia" the benevolent professor, or as the "Angel of the Camps." Certainly her career was transitional—bridging Old South and New, from Bourbon reaction to Progressive reform. Yet it may be more useful for modern students to see Tutwiler as the white female counterpart of Booker T. Washington. Both were administrators of schools; both believed in the transforming power of vocational education. Both were social reformers; but each was cautious, deferential when necessary. Each was rewarded by the Democratic power structure as semiofficial spokesperson of one or more marginalized groups.

PAUL M. PRUITT JR.
Bounds Law Library
University of Alabama

Anne Gary Pannell and Dorothea E. Wyatt, *Julia S. Tutwiler and Social Progress in Alabama* (2004); Paul M. Pruitt Jr., *Alabama Review* (July 1993), *Alabama Heritage* (Fall 1991), *Alabama Heritage* (Winter 1992); Mary Martha Thomas, *The New Woman in Alabama: Social Reforms and Suffrage, 1890–1920* (1992).

White, Edward Douglas

(1845–1921) U.S. SUPREME COURT JUSTICE.

The first sitting Supreme Court justice promoted to the chief justiceship,

Edward Douglas White was a jurist who carved a place for himself in legal history because of strong personality and longevity rather than legal brilliance.

The son and grandson of Irish Catholic judges, White was born in 1845 in Louisiana on his father's 1,600-acre sugarcane plantation. The young White was educated almost entirely in Jesuit institutions. After a brief, frustrating service as an aide-de-camp in the Confederate army, White apprenticed himself to a distinguished New Orleans lawyer and in 1868 was admitted to the Louisiana bar. White's affiliation with influential New Orleans law firms, coupled with the income from his Thibodaux plantation, provided him with the financial security to enter politics. His fortuitous association with the Redeemer governor Francis Nicholls ultimately won him the state legislature's selection to the U.S. Senate.

As a senator, White conformed to the dominant laissez-faire spirit of turn-of-the-century America except for a self-serving defense of the high protective tariff on imported sugar. In 1894 he was nominated for the Supreme Court by President (and fellow Democrat) Grover Cleveland. The choice of White to fill a Supreme Court vacancy in the midst of the Populist upheaval of the 1890s was intended by Cleveland as a device to bolster the southern wing of the Democratic Party.

On the Supreme Court, White used his hearty friendliness and access to the best parties in Washington to create a place for himself as one of the Court's social leaders. Although not characterized by a rigorous legal mind, White was a hard worker and possessed an absorbent memory that allowed him, upon occasion, to deliver his opinions without notes.

In 1910 President William Howard Taft nominated White for the chief justiceship. Apparently Taft wished to place someone in the Court's center seat sufficiently advanced in age (White was 64 at that time) to allow the position to become vacant again in a few years so that Taft himself could be appointed to head the Court. Although Taft eventually obtained his coveted judicial position, he had to wait until White's death, 11 years later, in 1921.

The traditional southern states' rights doctrines that White articulated as a senator from Louisiana were occasionally enunciated in his Supreme Court opinions. However, his judicial orientation was not self-consciously southern. White's status as a Confederate veteran did not keep him from developing a close personal friendship with Justice Oliver Wendell Holmes, a Boston Brahmin and Union veteran.

One biographer has referred to White's opinions as following a "jagged pattern," the product of "judicial whimsy." White's positions on such dominant legal concerns of the time as substantive due process and federal regulatory activity showed little consistency. In the *Insular Cases*, White introduced the novel but slippery doctrine that the Constitution followed the flag only for those overseas possessions properly "incorporated" by Congress. White's most famous contribution to public law was the creation of the "rule of reason" as a test for alleged restraints of trade: only those business combinations that were deemed "unreasonable," White argued, should be dismantled pursuant to the Sherman Antitrust Act. What White and his like-minded brethren meant by "unreasonable" was never articulated. This crude, pragmatic concept was White's principal doctrinal legacy.

JOHN W. JOHNSON
Clemson University

Robert B. Highsaw, *Edward Douglas White: Defender of the Conservative Faith* (1981); John Semonche, *Charting the Future: The Supreme Court Responds to a Changing Society, 1890–1920* (1978); James F. Watts Jr., in *The Justices of the United States Supreme Court*, ed. Leon Friedman and Fred I. Israel (1969).

Wisdom, John Minor

(1905–1999) FEDERAL JUDGE.
The "scholar" on the Fifth Circuit Court of Appeals during the turbulent battle over civil rights in the 1960s, Judge John Minor Wisdom "transformed the face of school desegregation law" in the absence of Supreme Court leadership. Born 17 May 1905 in New Orleans, Wisdom received a B.A. degree from Washington and Lee and an LL.B. from Tulane. As a young man, the New Orleans aristocrat became one of a handful of Republicans in Louisiana who openly argued that Huey Long's dictatorial control threatened democratic principles in the state. In 1952 Wisdom served as chairman of the 15-member Southern Conference for Eisenhower, which helped draft the former general to run for president. Wisdom played a significant role in the nominating convention, arguing successfully before the Credentials Committee for the seating of the contested Eisenhower delegation from Louisiana. President Eisenhower appointed Wisdom to the Fifth Circuit Court of Appeals in 1957.

In *U.S. v. Jefferson* (1967) Wisdom declared that school boards had "the affirmative duty under the Fourteenth Amendment to bring about an integrated, unitary school system in which there are no Negro schools and no white schools—just schools." The doctrine of affirmative duties developed by the Fifth Circuit shifted the burden from black plaintiffs to school boards and other public officials to end discrimination. It also helped lead to affirmative action programs to overcome the effects of past discrimination. "The Constitution is both color blind and color conscious," Wisdom wrote in *Jefferson*, "the Constitution is color conscious to prevent discrimination being perpetuated and to undo the effects of past discrimination. The criterion is the relevancy of color to a legitimate government purpose."

In his opinions in civil rights cases, Wisdom combined literary flair with a scholarly depth that left a major imprint on constitutional law. In *Jefferson*, he placed school desegregation in a larger historical and philosophical framework. "Brown's broad meaning, its important meaning," Wisdom asserted of the landmark 1954 Supreme Court decision, "is its revitalization of the national constitutional right the Thirteenth, Fourteenth, and Fifteenth Amendments created in favor of Negroes. This is the right of Negroes to national citizenship; their right as a class to share the privileges and immunities only white citizens had enjoyed as a class. Brown erased Dred Scott, used the Fourteenth Amendment to breathe life into the Thirteenth, and wrote the Declaration of Independence into the Constitution. Freedmen are free men."

Wisdom also wrote landmark opinions in cases that involved jury discrimination, voting rights, and affirmative action in employment, as well as in fields of law besides civil rights.

Congress in 1994 named the historic Fifth Circuit Court of Appeals building in New Orleans for Judge Wisdom. President Bill Clinton awarded him a Presidential Medal of Freedom. Judge Wisdom died 15 May 1999, two days before his 94th birthday.

JACK BASS
College of Charleston

Jack Bass, *Unlikely Heroes* (1981); J. Harvie Wilkinson III, *From Brown to Bakke: The Supreme Court and School Integration, 1954–1978* (1979).

Politics

During the 1970s southern political practices came to resemble more closely national norms. The election of a Deep South resident to the presidency in 1976 seemingly confirmed the region's newfound respectability. In earlier years, the South's political image had been a distinctive and largely negative one. Indeed, the region's long-established reputation as the home of demagogues, Dixiecrats, and disfranchisement contributed to making it a subject of endless interest, scorn, and puzzlement. V. O. Key's classic study *Southern Politics in State and Nation*, which appeared in 1949, began with the statement: "The South may not be the nation's number one political problem, as some northerners assert, but politics is the South's number one problem." After devoting almost 700 pages to a masterful examination of southern political practices, Key chose to title the final chapter of the book "Is There a Way Out?" Key closely associated southern political problems with three relatively distinctive southern political institutions: the one-party system, disfranchisement, and the pervasive ethos of Jim Crow segregation.

These institutions were crucial to southern electoral politics, particularly during the first half of the 20th century, but more recent scholarship has suggested that southern political problems were more deeply embedded in the region's social and economic fabric than the statement that "politics is the South's number one problem" would imply. Social and economic developments quite early in southern history were to have long-lasting significance for southern politics. Most important was the creation of an economy based on plantation agriculture and slave labor. Following the perfection of the cotton gin in the late 18th century, the rapid westward expansion of cotton and caste laid the foundation for southern unity. Slavery and plantation agriculture, although profitable for the planters who held the slaves, were not so materially beneficial for southern society as a whole. The purchase of slaves absorbed an enormous amount of southern capital, and the general self-sufficiency of southern agriculture debased the domestic market and hampered economic development. As a result, the antebellum South achieved little in the way of a "modern" economic infrastructure while at the same time it enjoyed a great deal of individual affluence.

Under these conditions, agrarian democracy flourished. Popular political participation shot upward during the 1830s, and voter turnout—in terms of the percentage of the eligible electorate that actually appeared at the polls—during the middle years of the 19th century was the highest it has ever been in south-ern history. Similarly, the South by the 1840s had developed a functioning two-party system. The relatively evenly balanced Whigs and Democrats competed vigorously for the favor of southern voters at all levels of government. It was the most thoroughly developed two-party system the South has ever had.

One of the explanations for such a vigorous assertion of democracy was that white southerners were in general agreement on substantive issues: land should be taken from Indians; agriculture should be promoted; slavery should be advanced; and the South should be defended from the meddling activities of antislavery advocates. A white male consensus on these points tended to pro-mote political democracy and two-party competition.

Herrenvolk Democracy and Paternalism. Southern democracy was herren-volk—that is, master race democracy, with political citizenship limited to white males—and, significantly, its origins were herrenvolk rather than popular. It is of symbolic interest that in August 1619 the first representative assembly to meet in English America convened in Jamestown, Va., where in the same month a Dutch warship sold the first 20 Africans known to have arrived in America, thus providing an early linkage between liberty and slavery. Developments in the South reinforced this paradoxical and symbiotic relationship. Rather early in American history, land hunger fueled growing hostility toward Indians. The need for labor on southern plantations was met by the importation of slaves. Thus, Edmund S. Morgan, in his important study of slavery and freedom in Virginia, concluded: "By lumping Indians, mulattoes, and Negroes in a single pariah class, Virginians had paved the way for a similar lumping of small and large planters in a single master class." Southern democracy not only limited political participation to a master race but rested directly on the exploitation of other races. Indeed, William J. Cooper has observed in *Liberty and Slavery* (1983) that "before 1860, free, white southerners could not conceive of holding on to their own liberty except by keeping black southerners enslaved."

Labor exploitation in the Old South, at least in the direct sense, normally meant whites exploiting blacks rather than each other. Such an arrangement undermined class conflict, encouraged what W. J. Cash termed a "Proto-Dorian" bond between whites, and fostered an autonomous independence that in some ways was conducive to citizenship and republican ideals, as the career of Thomas Jefferson would suggest. But despite generating high voter turnout among white males, herrenvolk democracy had severe inherent limitations. Not only did it rest squarely on racism and exploitation, it also limited the legitimate range of debate. Southern freedom and democracy, even before slavery came under attack from the outside, had tendencies toward "the savage ideal," which Cash described as "that ideal whereunder dissent and variety are completely suppressed."

The paternalistic social values that grew from master-slave relationships further influenced the ideological context of southern politics. Historians continue to disagree over the extent to which the South was capitalist and the extent to which it was a premodern, prebourgeois, traditional society, but whatever the ultimate resolution of the debate, southern social values were clearly different from those prevalent in the North. In the North, Jacksonian democracy marked the coming of age of a laissez-faire society and an ideology of free labor individualism that appealed to independent artisans, farmers, and businessmen; in the South, Jacksonian democracy did strengthen the herrenvolk civic concept of autonomous independence, but the region's forced labor system and the mutual dependence of masters and slaves also supported a patriarchal ideology. Southern thought tended to extol a paternal, organic, and hierarchical society, which contrasted with northern ideals of laissez-faire individualism, economic freedom, and legal equality. The southern paternal ethos projected, in the words of Eugene D. Genovese, "an aristocratic, antibourgeois spirit with values and mores emphasizing family and status, a strong code of honor, and aspirations to luxury, ease and accomplishment." Gunnar Myrdal, commenting on conservative southern political thought, pointed out in his epic, *An American Dilemma* (1944): "Slavery was only part of a greater social order which established an ideal division of labor and of responsibility in society between the sexes, the age groups, the social classes and the two races."

Herrenvolk democracy tempered by ideological paternalism produced for a brief period intense partisan competition. During the 1850s the two-party system collapsed under the strain of sectional strife. Following the Civil War and emancipation, the South again experimented with two-party politics. The Fourteenth and Fifteenth Amendments offered citizenship and suffrage to the newly freed blacks, and the black-oriented Radical Republicans in the South accomplished the remarkable feat of politically mobilizing the freedmen. Conservative whites reorganized under the Democratic banner. For varying periods of time, the southern states were battlegrounds for the contending Radical Republicans and conservative Democrats. Conservative whites organized the Ku Klux Klan and other terrorist groups, while the Republicans relied heavily upon federal forces for protection. The Democratic combination of terrorism and political rhetoric that appealed for herrenvolk unity proved successful, and Republicanism rapidly declined. The last of the Republican governments in the South collapsed in 1877, when southern Democrats and northern Republicans engineered a historic compromise whereby the southern conservatives accepted northeastern capitalist policies nationally in exchange for federal non-intervention in southern social affairs.

New South Politics. Effectively, the southern leadership tacitly acquiesced to the South remaining economically a colony of the North. The Civil War and Emancipation swept away the plantation prosperity that had marked the region's real economic problems. Bereft of capital, bound more closely to the North by postwar railroad construction, overwhelmed by the rapid growth of population and manufacturing above the Potomac, and hampered by northeastern-oriented tariff, banking, and other policies, the South provided cotton, lumber products, minerals, and other raw materials, and to a lesser extent, markets for the more advanced northern economy. A fundamental requirement imposed by the South's colonial dependency was cheap labor, and the maintenance of a cheap labor force was an underlying factor in the politics of the New South.

Presiding over these developments were the Bourbon Democrats. By controlling the Democratic Party machinery and by manipulating the race issue, the Bourbons were able to maintain themselves in office, and that fact ensured that state power would be exercised on behalf of the employing classes. But if the Bourbon system accomplished the rudimentary goals of those who were most likely to benefit from the South's colonial status, it was not particularly successful in providing political and social stability. The tensions and conflicts in southern society were severe. The Civil War, Emancipation, and Reconstruction left southern society deeply divided. The failure of plantation agriculture to restore prewar prosperity, the decline of the yeoman farmers, the breakdown of agricultural self-sufficiency, and the economic competition between black and white laborers produced further social stress and helped to explain the growth of lynching and other forms of social violence. The Populist movement of the 1890s grew out of this atmosphere and, indeed, brought to culmination a variety of long-simmering conflicts. So profound were the implications of the Populist radical critique of state and national policy that the conservative Bourbon Democrats responded with violence and with massive fraud in the casting and counting of ballots.

Unlike the antebellum era when the electorate was in general agreement on substantive policies, the New South was rent with social dissension. During the Reconstruction crisis, the conservative Democrats relied upon Ku Klux Klan terrorism to regain control of the southern states; during the post-Reconstruction era, they turned back independent insurgency by using their control of land, credit, and the law to influence the behavior of black voters;

and during the Populist crisis, they resorted to violence and fraud. Beyond that, they sought more institutionalized methods to ensure the social stability that ultimately rested on white supremacy and cheap labor. The result was the establishment of those institutions so ably described by V. O. Key: namely, disfranchisement, the one-party system, and Jim Crow segregation.

The disfranchisement of black people was such an obvious way to ensure political white supremacy and thereby to bolster the whole southern system of labor relationships that the surprising thing is conservative white southern political elites did not do it sooner. The explanation for the delay seems to relate to the ability of the Bourbons to manipulate the black vote and to earlier fears that disfranchisement might prompt federal intervention. The Democratic conservatives also demonstrated the willingness to support, often quite openly, the disfranchisement of whites. The president of the Alabama disfranchising convention of 1901 explained, "The true philosophy of the movement was to establish restricted suffrage, and to place the power of government in the hands of the intelligent and virtuous." Although such views were compatible with ideological paternalism, disfranchisement reversed the trend toward the expansion of democracy that had been evident in the antebellum South and the Reconstruction period. The high voter turnout of the antebellum era extended into the postbellum period. Voter turnout remained high after the enfranchisement of blacks, though it did begin to drop off following the end of Reconstruction. Despite this decline, voter participation remained respectable—above 50 percent of the eligible electorate in the former Confederate states—until the disfranchisement movement.

The conservative Democrats' disfranchisement of whites was not at all illogical. After all, inexpensive white labor was as important as black labor, and it was doubtlessly easier to maintain if the electorate were limited to "the intelligent and virtuous." But beyond this, the removal of the lower levels of the white working class from the electorate suggests the extent to which white sharecroppers and mill workers had already been relegated to what J. Wayne Flynt has termed "the Southern poor white caste." Prior to the Civil War, southern poor whites were a part of the overall population. In the New South, as Flynt says, "poor whites assumed many aspects of a caste system and were increasingly identifiable within the general population."

It is not entirely surprising that segregation, although having deep roots in southern history, assumed its particularly cruel Jim Crow form at approximately the same time as the disfranchisement movement. The motives for segregationist legislation were complex, but the Jim Crow system contributed substantially to social stability. It virtually guaranteed the continuing existence of cheap black labor, and it further divided the black caste from the poor white caste and encouraged each of them to direct hostility toward the other.

Segregation and disfranchisement not only served as formidable barriers to future Populist heresies but also strengthened the "Solid South." The one-party system discouraged the emergence of divisive issues at home while at the same time unifying southern political power nationally in defense of the region's peculiar social practices. During the first half of the 20th century, few southerners voted, and those who did voted overwhelmingly Democratic. When in 1924 Republican Calvin Coolidge received about 1,200 of South Carolina's approximately 50,000 presidential votes, Senator Coleman L. Blease exclaimed: "I do not know where he got them. I was astonished to know they were cast and shocked to know they were counted."

But if these reforms did place southern politics in the hands of "the intelligent and virtuous," there remains the question of just who "the intelligent and virtuous" were. Presumably they were not black southerners, who in the year 1910 made up more than one-third of the population of the former Confederate states. Thus, using 1910 figures, segregation placed 35 percent of the population and even more of the workforce in an inferior caste. Not all blacks were poor, of course, but discrimination ensured that most would be. The "intelligent and virtuous" also presumably did not include most of the poor whites. It is difficult to estimate the size of that group or even to define it in statistical terms, but huge numbers of whites labored at occupations not much different from positions held by blacks, and, defined in that manner, a fair estimate would be that the poor white class was probably no smaller than was the black caste around 1910. Thus, the black and white underclass made up approximately two-thirds of the southern population.

During the first four decades of the 20th century, the active southern electorate encompassed between one-fourth and one-third of the adult population, although the figures varied significantly from state to state. The "intelligent and virtuous" made up approximately one-third of the population, and southern election returns indicate that approximately one-fourth of the citizens voted. These figures seem to be compatible because not all people would have necessarily paid their poll taxes and made their way through all the other pitfalls that protected the polls from the voters even though they were otherwise sufficiently white to vote in the white primaries and sufficiently literate to deal with literacy and comprehension requirements. Thus, the bulk of southern voters were drawn from that third of southern society that was both whiter and more economically prosperous than the population as a whole; generally speaking, these "intelligent and virtuous" citizens included three more or less distinct so-

Banner with Huey Long's image hangs over the front steps of the Louisiana state capitol during the inauguration of Governor Richard Leche, Baton Rogue, 1936 (Louisiana State Library, Baton Rouge)

cial groups. One might be termed the plantation-oriented county-seat governing class; one could be called the uptown elites; and one was the white common folk.

The Governing Elite and the Common Folk. As the name implies, the "county-seat governing class" was the South's dominant political group. The Civil War and Reconstruction broke the national power of the planter class, but thereafter southern planters and their allies emerged victorious from the political wars of Reconstruction to become the most powerful social group in southern politics. Geographically concentrated in the region's lowland-plantation counties, the planter-merchant-banker-lawyer governing class set much of the tone for the politics of the region. They were the foremost defenders of the southern way of life, the most devoted proponents of Lost Cause mythology, and the most loyal adherents to paternal social values. They provided the basic hard-core support for Bourbon democracy, marshaled the conservative forces to turn back the Populist threat, and led the disfranchisement movement. V. O. Key was certainly correct when he stated, "The hard core of the political South—and the backbone of political unity—is made up of those counties and sections of the southern states in which Negroes constitute a substantial proportion of the population." At the crucial junctures in the politics of the New South, the plantation-and-county-seat governing class won the decisive engagements.

The greatest long-term potential threat to the power of the county-seat governing class was the uptown elite in the South's expanding cities. The term "uptown" denotes the leadership of the region's urban areas and suggests a Henry W. Grady / New South style of politics. Although lacking the authority and political prestige of the county-seat governing class, uptown elites were the South's most affluent people and, in some ways, the most strategically placed. They normally controlled the region's larger and more influential newspapers, banks, and other sources of influence. In addition to being the foremost proponents of the New South creed, they were leaders in the drive for segregation. They, of course, suffered from the South's being for so long so overwhelmingly rural—in 1910 only two people of every 10 in the former Confederate states resided in a town of more than 2,500. Furthermore, the widening economic disparity between the prospering cities and the poverty-ridden country contributed to an increasing rural hostility toward the cities, a fact that further limited uptown influence.

Normally uptown elites were the allies of the county-seat governing class. Not only did the two groups share class interest but southern urban prosperity was closely tied to the overall southern colonial economy. With a few exceptions, most notably Birmingham, southern cities served as the great distributing centers for the products that ultimately appeared on country-store shelves and as the centers for marketing and transporting southern cotton and raw materials to the North. Andre Gunder Frank has observed that Latin America "had a colonial class structure which inevitably gave its dominant bourgeoisie an economic self-interest in freely exporting raw materials and importing manufactured products." This applied equally to New South merchants and businessmen. The prosperity of the cities and towns was deeply enmeshed in existing economic arrangements. As a consequence, uptown elites remained only a long-term potential threat to county-seat power in the Solid South.

The largest of the three social groups was the common folk: the farmers, skilled workers, tradesmen, and all the others in southern society who found themselves situated between the black and white underclasses and the county-seat and urban elites. Lacking the ideological and political unity of the county-seat governing class and the strategic and material advantages of uptown, "The Man at the Center" lacked organization and consistent direction. The middle did, however, play a major role in New South politics. The middle was the social base for the southern demagogues. The Baltimore journalist H. L. Mencken lamented on numerous occasions the tragic descent of southern politics from the wise and aristocratic leadership of southern statesmen in the early years of the Republic to the unprincipled buffoonery of the 20th century and always assigned the cause for this catastrophe to the rise of southern poor whites. Mencken's contention that demagoguery was a poor white phenomenon was essentially nonsense. Southern poor whites did not vote, and the great era of the southern demagogues coincided precisely with the period when disfranchisement was most effective.

The common folk were the social base for demagoguery, and they were much courted at election time. Their attraction to the demagogues—who at least had redeeming value as spectator entertainment—suggests the extent to which they found the candidates of county-seat and uptown elites inadequate. The demagogues were overwhelmingly antiurban in their politics, if not necessarily their policies, a fact that indicates the extent to which the cities of the New South had become alienated from the countryside. To some degree, demagoguery was a politics of protest and insurgency, an antiestablishment thrust that, whatever its inadequacies, often gave ordinary whites more in the way of program and attention than they were apt to get otherwise. But most of all, demagoguery was a politics of frustration, resulting from the common folk's place in the social structure. The common white folk had the unenviable task of challenging those above while protecting themselves from those below, and any meaningful radical or semiradical assault on the power and pomp of those above would ultimately have involved those below, which incidentally was precisely what happened with Populism. The result was demagoguery—protest—and even on occasion moderate reform—without the disruption of the existing social order.

The Conservative Solid South. The South was a changing but—still in important ways—a premodern society with an underdeveloped colonial economy. The unfolding of the region's peculiar and vexing history led to the creation of a politically conservative Solid South that patterned southern political behavior for two-thirds of a century. So enmeshed were its economic, social, and political institutions that the Solid South's longevity is understandable. So undemocratic and exploitive were its arrangements that the criticisms directed against them seem unobjectionable.

Modernizing forces ultimately eroded the economic and social order that underlay the politics of the Solid South. The Great Depression of the 1930s and World War II fundamentally redirected southern development, although it required several decades for the region's people to absorb such a change, and certainly that was true of politics. Franklin D. Roosevelt and the New Deal responded to the Depression with a programmatic liberalism that won the support of huge numbers of southerners. The Roosevelt administration's *Report on Economic Conditions of the South* signaled a critical turning point in federal policy. Whereas national governmental policies had usually accepted and often buttressed the South's position as a colonial appendage of the northern economy, the report declared the economy of the South to be "the Nation's No. 1 economic problem—the Nation's problem, not merely the South's," thereby justifying the federal government's emerging role as an active sponsor of southern economic development. Although most agricultural historians are sharply critical of New Deal agricultural policies, which contributed so significantly to the depopulation of the southern countryside, the catastrophic condition of southern agriculture made any aid popular; and given the South's huge population of blacks and poor working-class whites, it is little wonder that New Deal liberalism won a very substantial following. Indeed, if public opinion polls are to be believed, the South was the most liberal area of the nation during the 1930s, and the solid Democratic South became even more solidly Democratic.

But despite the mass appeal of New Deal liberalism in the South, the region's politics was far more conservative than its people. New Deal liberalism was, of course, politically ineffective because a huge percentage of the South's black and white working people were both unorganized and voteless. Beginning in the mid-1930s, Solid South political elites increasingly turned away from the New Deal, allying instead with Republicans to form the conservative coalition in Congress. Thus, the area that opinion polls suggested was the nation's most liberal region produced the politicians who most successfully opposed the New Deal. Perhaps understandably, northern liberals chafed under such arrangements and persistently searched for ways to extend the liberal-labor-minority coalition into the South and thereby to transform southern politics.

The most formidable opponents of such a strategy were the Old Guard southern Democrats, who, with their prestige as the defenders of the Southland and their seniority in Congress, remained the most powerful element in southern politics. In Congress, they allied with Republicans in an informal but effective anti–New Deal coalition. The emergence of this coalition protected southern influence in Congress, but it also laid the foundation for an escalating sectional conflict within the Democratic Party. New Deal liberals sought to extend the New Deal coalition into the South. Southern conservative elites, while entrenched in Congress, fretted over liberal control of presidential politics and endeavored to restore their influence in national party affairs. This struggle between the northern liberal-labor-minority coalition and the once solid Democratic South was a crucial factor in American politics from the mid-1930s until the mid-1960s. The conflict escalated when President Truman asked Congress to enact civil rights legislation in 1948 and when later in the year the Democratic National Convention endorsed Truman's program.

Outraged southern conservatives responded with the formation of the Dixiecrats, and thereafter third-party movements in presidential politics were common. By depriving the national Democrats of southern electoral votes, southern conservatives hoped to force concessions from the party and to deadlock the electoral college, thereby creating an opportunity to negotiate another sectional compromise as their ideological ancestors had done to end Reconstruction in 1877.

Massive Resistance. The Supreme Court's *Brown v. Board of Education* desegregation decision in 1954 further inflamed the southern leadership. Old Guard conservatives launched a determined program of "massive resistance" to desegregation. If the southern states refused to obey the *Brown* decision, what could the Court eventually do but reverse the decision? To accomplish this task, southern conservatives adopted the hoary theory of "interposition" and sought to interpose state power between the federal courts and southern citizens. In practice that resulted in an astonishing variety of segregationist laws that spewed forth from the malapportioned southern state legislatures.

Like the third-party presidential movements, massive resistance began as an elite enterprise. The Old Guard conservative leadership, its ideological roots deeply anchored in Bourbon democracy, placed defense of the southern social system above such things as public education. They had been defending the southern way of life since the Compromise of 1877, and even in the 1950s the planter-merchant-banker-lawyer county-seat governing class that the southern conservatives represented remained a fundamental locus of political power.

During these years, the agenda for both the national liberals and the southern conservatives changed and, indeed, narrowed. Northern New Deal liberals had viewed southern problems within an economic context and had sought to expand political and industrial democracy. During the postwar era, northern liberals moved rather rapidly away from the perception of the South as "the Nation's No. 1 economic problem" to the position that the South was the nation's number one moral problem. Whereas New Deal liberals viewed southern social problems in class terms—as a conflict between haves and have-nots—postwar northern liberals tended to see the South in terms of a morality play featuring evil whites and virtuous blacks. A northern liberal agenda, then, which had once defined southern problems in relatively broad terms with profoundly meaningful implications for both southern whites and blacks, became narrowed to race as a moral issue. Similarly, while the southern conservatives defended a paternal order that encouraged such southern virtues as concern for family, kinship, community, church, roots, and place, they, like the liberals, reduced a broad range of values to the one issue of race, a massive resistance to desegregation.

Although originally promoted by conservative elites, the resistance to desegregation did ultimately become a popular reaction. As a result of federal court decisions and other factors, voter turnout steadily increased in the South, and by the late 1950s, the growing restiveness of black southerners and the gradual spread of desegregation made the race issue more salient to southern voters. The group that responded most positively to conservative appeals was the southern white common folk, the people who had often supported demagoguery in the past but who had shown strong proclivities toward New Deal reformism during the 1930s and 1940s. Thus, that social group upon which liberals had based so much hope for the future of liberalism ended up in the camp of the conservatives. The race issue—and the success of both the northern liberals and the southern conservatives in confining the political debate to that issue—completed the rout of the southern political liberals, who found themselves identified with the politically unpopular side of the controversy. Indeed, when the aging and declining southern Old Guard conservatives proved unable to turn

Leander Perez, Louisiana political leader and one of the original "Dixiecrats."
Photo taken in the 1950s. (Louisiana State Library, Baton Rouge)

back the desegregationist tide, working whites promoted their own spokesmen, the foremost of whom was George C. Wallace.

The Old Guard conservatives defined the issue as race, branded white liberals as traitors, and propounded a scorched-earth policy of closing the schools. The massive resistance strategy received its test when the schools actually started closing. In the fall of 1958 the governor of Arkansas closed the high schools in Little Rock and the governor of Virginia closed schools in a number of Virginia communities. The schools eventually reopened desegregated, but the process was repeated throughout much of the South. In the state of Georgia the crisis came in 1961 when a federal court ordered the admission of two black students to the University of Georgia. The state legislature had displayed the extent of its wisdom by enacting the usual bevy of massive resistance laws that included measures requiring that any desegregating institution be closed, that state funds be denied, that any instructor that taught mixed black and white students be arrested for felony, that any law enforcement official who failed to arrest a teacher for teaching in a desegregated classroom be himself arrested for felony, and so on. But in Georgia, as elsewhere, state authorities, when faced with the actual consequences of closing down the public schools and state universities, ultimately relented.

Leading the political opposition to closing the schools was the educated and affluent white middle class in the South's rapidly expanding cities and suburbs. Throughout the South it was the urban-suburban middle class, the heirs of the uptown elite, that organized the "save our school" movements in defense of public education. Avoiding the race issue, these campaigns merely insisted that public schools were essential to the continuing economic growth of the region. By endeavoring to avoid the race issue, the urban-suburban middle-class position was perceived as moderate, and in a massive resistance atmosphere its candidates for public office attracted the support of the rapidly expanding black electorate. Thus, the least materially affluent people in the South—the blacks— became the allies of the most affluent people in the South—the white business-professional-metropolitan elites.

Industrialization and Civil Rights. The middle-class uptown moderates provided much of the impetus for the drive to attract new industry. There was little novel in the notion that the South should endeavor to attract outside industry, although, as an important ideological force, its origins were relatively recent. The urban boosterism of the 1920s gained sustained momentum after the Great Depression had exposed the bankruptcy of southern agriculture and the economic thrust generated by World War II had propelled the South in the direction of further rapid economic growth. In 1936 Mississippi created its "Balance Agriculture with Industry" program, and thereafter all the other southern states created industrial development commissions. In the post–World War II period, southern state governments competed vigorously with a variety of programs and policies designed to offer services, tax concessions, and public subsidization to national and international corporations that chose to expand into the South. The old-style southern plantations gradually disappeared as agriculture became capital-intensive and mechanized, and the diversifying southern economy benefited from labor mobility more than from the coercive forms of labor control that had been such a central factor in the politics and ideology of the New South.

The economic growth ethos had wide appeal. It had been a favored liberal program in earlier years, although the liberals had sought industrialization with industrial democracy. It also appealed to Old Guard conservatives, who hoped to combine industrialization with segregation and paternal social values. While dominating the headlines with their frantic attempts to preserve the southern way of life, conservative governors and legislators also encouraged and funded industrial development programs, though generally taking less interest in them than did such moderate governors as Luther Hodges in North Carolina and Leroy Collins in Florida.

Indeed, the economic growth ethos provided one of the inspirations for the black protest movement. The black sit-in movement, which began in 1960, was in the beginning the work of young, educated, upwardly mobile blacks who wanted an opportunity to participate in the increasingly flourishing southern marketplace. The success of the black freedom movement in capturing the imagination of much of the nation ultimately forced the federal government to override the congressional Dixieland band and to enact the 1964 and 1965 Civil Rights Acts, which, when combined with other developments of this period, dismantled the social and political system that had for so long regulated wide areas of southern life. The 1964 act included an equality of economic opportunity provision that came to be interpreted in terms of affirmative action, and Lyndon B. Johnson's Great Society program did include what cynics came to call the "skirmish on poverty." These measures broadened enormously the opportunities for better-educated, more highly skilled, upwardly mobile black people. Lower-class blacks, while perhaps gaining psychological and even some social benefits from desegregation, remained about where they had always been.

As a result, despite the successes of the civil rights campaign, important elements of the black freedom movement turned steadily leftward. The Student Nonviolent Coordinating Committee, formed in 1960 to coordinate the student sit-ins, became a cadre of professional organizers. Rejecting the race-as-a-moral-issue argument, the SNCC workers developed a radical agenda that fueled their conflict, not only with the conservatives, but with both the southern moderates and the national liberals. Unable to find white allies, they carried their peculiar, semirevolutionary blend of socioeconomic realism and pan-African cultural romanticism into the great metropolitan ghettos of the nation in an effort to build black power bases from which to negotiate with the white power blocs.

Perhaps more significantly, Martin Luther King Jr. and the Southern Christian Leadership Conference, which in the beginning stood squarely within the national liberal mainstream in depicting the race issue as a moral question, also moved to the left. Breaking with the Johnson administration and with many southern moderates, King threw the resources of the SCLC into a poor-people's campaign that sought to restore a broadly based economic and social liberalism by uniting out-groups behind a demand for a massive Marshall Plan at home. King's assassination in the spring of 1968 was a mortal blow to whatever prospects the campaign may have had. These developments, combined with black rioting, mainly in northern ghettos, contributed to making the decade of the 1960s one of upheaval and conflict.

In the wake of these developments, southern Old Guard conservatives declined decisively. It was the county-seat Old Guard who suffered most directly from the demographic and economic transformation of the region, who benefited least from such political reforms as legislative reapportionment and black suffrage, and who most obviously lost prestige when unable to deliver on their massive resistance promises. The southern white common folk also lost in the political battles of the 1960s. Moving beyond the declining appeal of the Old Guard leadership, the white working class rallied under the banners of George Wallace and such lesser lights as Lester Maddox of Georgia. But the Wallace brand of popular resistance was essentially a negative program that was unable to sustain its appeal, as least without its most able practitioner to head it. The Wallace movement was in decline by the early 1970s, and any prospect that the Alabama governor might revive it terminated with the attempted assassination, and permanent crippling, of Wallace at a Maryland campaign rally in 1972. At any rate, white workers remained alienated from a national liberalism that for so long had placed them in the role of the heavies in the moral crusade for black rights, and they found little to applaud in President Johnson's black-oriented Great Society. Black southerners did of course benefit from the upheavals of the 1960s, but the failure of SNCC, the death of King, and the breakup of the civil rights movement left them with few viable options except—like the white working class—to support the southern moderate claim that economic growth would solve southern social problems.

As all this suggests, the basic result of the great political conflicts of the post–World War II years was to transfer the locus of southern political power from plantation-oriented county-seat elites to corporation-oriented metropolitan elites. The Republican Party, which was once anathema in the South, attracted increasing support from well-off suburbanites and from white southerners disenchanted with the national Democratic Party's liberal racial policies. The southern state elections of the early 1970s swept into office a wave of New South moderates and thereby signaled the triumph of a new political order. Reapportionment, the end of disfranchisement, desegregation, and the decline of the one-party system destroyed the institutional foundations of the old political system. If voter turnout was still low in the South, it was substantial when compared to the recent southern past, and it included a far greater range of citizens. The antebellum era and the modern age are the two periods in which southern citizens seem to have been most ideologically united and in which the South has had two-party politics and popular democracy.

The best known of the New South moderates was Jimmy Carter. Like other moderates, Carter welcomed black support and endeavored—especially symbolically—to recognize black aspirations. But most of all he championed continued economic expansion, rationalized governmental procedures, and looked to corporate elites for guidance. By the 1970s the economic growth ethos had come to dominate the formulation of southern state policy, and economic expansion had come to be seen as the panacea for southern public problems, in somewhat the same manner that slavery had once been seen as the key to antebellum development. Certainly, differences do exist in southern politics, but the range of debate has vastly narrowed.

In the 1970s, economic-development-as-political-ideology promised to obliterate the legacy of the three pillars of southern politics—disfranchisement, segregation, and one-party politics—and, like a rising tide, to lift all boats. In those transformative days, boosters proclaimed that race consciousness would become an obsolete consideration in political discourse and policy making because favorable treatment for developers and real estate brokers, public aid for industrial development, government antipathy toward labor, and perpetual low taxes promised to spark an economic boom. Economic progress promised to destroy the stimulus for the Proto-Dorian ideal. Unfortunately, because of the legacy of Jim Crow, the direct beneficiaries of such treatment were not generally of African American descent nor were they poor whites. But that seemed hardly to matter to political dons. In the prosperous, if not classless and raceless, New South, poverty, racism, and social injustice would disappear. Where once southern political life had been bolstered by three pillars, only one—"the economic growth ethos"—would sustain politics for future generations in the post–civil rights South. In the years since publication of the original *Encyclopedia of Southern Culture*, the appeal of economic development as panacea has remained strong, but the smoldering remains of race-conscious politics persist, too. While southerners, black and white, have found a way out of their peculiar politics, they have not made great progress toward creating a world in which race matters not. Neither has the nation.

Assessment of the course that the South has taken under the influence of the mantra of economic development produces mixed results. While government officials pointed to evidence of growth, such as automobile factories and other manufacturing concerns seduced to locate in the South by lavish public underwriting, the fact remains that outside of a handful of metropolitan areas, southerners are far removed from the mainstream of the national, much less the global, economy as anything other than consumers. Failure of the ethos of economic growth to lift all boats owes to the imbalanced focus on economic development in communities, rather than the development of individuals; it owes as well to the reluctance of business and governments—federal, state, and local—to invest in research. The prevailing vision of economic development so often promoted by politicians, a vision that starts—and often ends—with a handsome sign labeled "Industrial Park" in a weed-choked field, harkens back to the heyday of the "Balance Agriculture with Industry" program in the mid-20th century. To politicians who accommodate the desires of industrialists, economic development means the production of material goods, not the production of knowledge and novel applications of knowledge. Consequently, outside of the Research Triangle in North Carolina, the "New Economy" is to most southerners as foreign as the surface of the moon.

Ironically, although the South continues to lag behind other regions, the vocabulary that infused the economic growth ethos helped to draw the region into the national political discourse. So, too, did the nation's drift toward conservatism help the South suppress its image as the nation's number one political problem. When white and black Democrats entered into a peaceful coexistence, the Democratic Party ceased race-baiting and began kowtowing to industrialists and developers. In the post–civil rights epoch, southern politicians sounded each year increasingly more like politicians from the rest of the country than at any time in the 20th century. The nation as a whole taking a decided turn to the right—perhaps, considering the country's tormented history on the race question, a predictable development in the wake of civil rights reform—aided the perception that southern politics had become more like politics in the rest of the country. Southern politicians' traditional conservative pleas for less government, more local control of institutions, less gun control, and lower taxes echoed through national Republican circles, as former Democrats and "swing voters" in the South paved the way for Republican success in presidential elections.

The roots of the South's abandonment of the Democratic Party run as deep as southern politicians' uneasiness with the growth of the federal government during the New Deal and their rejection of World War II–era federal efforts to end discrimination in the workplace. The 1948 rupture of the Democratic Party and the lesser-known "Democrats for Eisenhower" movement in 1952 signaled a continuing disaffection with the national party in the South, and Barry Goldwater's 1964 campaign for president clearly pointed out to Republican Party presidential aspirants that the "solidly Democratic South" was a fading allusion. For his part, Republican president Richard M. Nixon recognized that the civil rights reforms had created a class of African American voters who would cast their ballots for the Democratic Party, the party of civil rights reform. After 1970, knowing that he could not draw a sizable black vote, Nixon embraced a "southern strategy" designed to attract white voters, even if a populist like George Wallace ran for president in 1974.

Moribund by the mid-1970s, the solidly Democratic South had plainly died by 1980. Ronald Reagan's xenophobic nationalism and his call for a smaller government resonated with white southerners. They flocked to his cause, broadening the base of the Republican Party from its once exclusive domain in the country club and taking it into the honky-tonk and the white, middle-class fundamentalist congregation. As candidate and president, Reagan promised a new day for plain white folk so long beaten down by affirmative action and high taxes, which covered the cost of busing children to school and other federal programs they believed benefited minorities. Reagan's Republican Party also found allies in evangelical groups, most significantly in Rev. Jerry Falwell's Virginia-based Moral Majority. Encouraged by white southerners who believed with equal fervor in the Bible as the inerrant word of God and in Ronald Reagan, the Republican Party took up the demagogic cry of "family values" and also gave wings to the antiabortion movement, which has now led many southern states to undermine the 1973 *Roe v. Wade* decision. The values of the Republican Party as defined by the Reagan revolution continued to find expression in the presidency of George H. W. Bush and his successors. At the national level, the Republican Party continues to garner widespread support, and the South is a linchpin in Republican presidential victories.

Even as the South embraced a new version of one-party politics on the national level, the Democratic Party continued to capture lesser offices, especially in contests that elected governors and members of the U.S. House of Representatives. A new breed of young Democrats, who had come of age in the 1960s and who felt at ease in a biracial world, led an effort to recast the party into a moderate one, while at the same time African American activists, as well as their intellectual heirs, entered seats of power. In the late 1980s, a triumvirate of moderate Democratic governors held office in Louisiana, Mississippi, and Arkansas. Although Buddy Roemer and Ray Mabus alienated their bases of support and lost reelection bids, William Jefferson Clinton made the moderate Democratic politics of the post–civil rights South a national phenomena when he was elected president.

Clinton campaigned on a platform that called for more jobs, better schools for all, higher taxes for the wealthy, universal health care, and welfare reform. An Ivy League–educated, redneck hipster, Clinton promised something to everyone and strove to occupy the middle of the political spectrum. In office, Clinton's health-care initiative failed to develop legs, but the mere conversation produced a backlash; and his "Don't Ask, Don't Tell" policy, intended to encourage toleration of gays and lesbians in the military, became fodder for conservatives. By 1994, Republicans, particularly in the South and the Midwest, were energized. Widespread endorsement of Georgia congressman Newt Gingrich's "Contract with America"—a call to conservatism that resonated with Reagan-era simplicity—helped produce the first Republican-controlled Congress since the 1950s. Responding to the political opposition that held a majority of seats in Congress, Clinton reached for middle ground and signed legislation to curtail the availability of public assistance programs to needy individuals. By embracing policies that Republicans advocated, the moderate wing of the Democratic Party made it difficult for the liberal wing to embrace enthusiastically its legislative success; alternatively, by virtue of the skin color of most of its members, the liberal wing, which tended to be home to African American politicians and which trumpeted the liberal promise of Clinton's first term, provided white voters an excuse to continue their self-exclusion from the Democratic Party. In the 1970s, the Democratic Party in the South was biracial, but by the 1990s, after the abandonment of the party by most whites, it had become almost as black in the popular imagination as the Republican Party was, in fact, white.

The days of overt race-baiting are ended, but like politicians in other parts of the country, southern ones use a coded language to communicate their fear and disdain for nonwhites and for legislation that appears to favor them. They talk about felons run rampant, unwed mothers, trickle-down economics, and the evils of a proactive government. The code is transparent. It serves chiefly to keep alive in mutated form the Proto-Dorian bond. More subtle ways for keeping race consciousness alive in southern politics exist, too. Gerrymandering of congressional and legislative districts complicates the racialized nature of southern politics. By unnecessarily creating black majority districts and white majority districts, legislators ensure that politicians do not have to talk or to legislate across the color line. Consequently, in white majority congressional and legislative districts, political discourse focuses on conservative issues: antiabortion legislation, low taxes, small government, individual responsibility, and economic development. Those districts, particularly suburban ones, provide the base of Republican Party support in national, state, and now even local elections. Among middle-class, white suburbanites, finding Democratic candidates to run for office has become difficult. Likewise, in black majority districts, Republican candidates for office are rare, and when they appear on ballots at all they do not threaten Democratic contenders. Only in districts that are more equitably divided among black and white residents are meaningful political dialogue and competitive elections for state and local offices across the color and class lines possible. One need only point to the campaigns and elections of African Americans Mike Espy and Douglas Wilder or the white Democrat Wayne Dowdy to prove the point.

Although the ethos of economic growth has seemingly cured many of the South's political ills, the legacy of Jim Crow, disfranchisement, and one-party politics remains. Yet, the South seems hardly peculiar any more. Indeed, the region is part of a broad belt of so-called red states that lean toward conservatism. In those states, concern is palpable that citizens have been left behind by the emerging global economy. Anxious citizens and politicians lash out at immigrants, homosexuals, big government, and a host of "-isms." For all its emphasis on economic growth as panacea for political discontent, the South has failed to conquer barriers to prosperity and education that continue to resemble the color line. In part that failure owes to a lack of commitment to equality. In part it owes to an antiquated vision of economic growth that privileges smokestacks and traditional manufacturing, the service industries, and suburban development. As long as southern politicians fail to connect their faith in economic growth to the development of individuals and the encouragement, indeed celebration, of creativity, the region will continue to suffer. Connecting that faith to individual development requires equitable allocation of resources regardless of race, class, sexual preference, or immigration status. It also requires a new vision of economic growth that emphasizes risk taking and investment in research and development. All things considered, one finds it difficult to imagine such a transformation, and it is equally difficult to imagine a transformation taking place in similarly situated regions elsewhere in the country. Likely, then, the South will continue, as it has over the last two decades, to embrace a political ideology and style of politics not particularly distinctive or southern.

NUMAN BARTLEY
University of Georgia

BRADLEY G. BOND
Northern Illinois University

Jonathan M. Atkins, *Parties, Politics, and the Sectional Conflict in Tennessee, 1832–1861* (1997); Tod A. Baker, Charles D. Hadley, Robert P. Steed, and Laurence W. Moreland, eds., *Political Parties in the Southern States: Party Activists in Partisan Coalition* (1990); Numan Bartley, *The Creation of Modern Georgia* (1983), *The New South, 1945–1980* (1995), *The Rise of Massive Resistance: Race and Politics in the South during the 1950s* (1969), with Hugh Davis Graham, *Southern Politics and the Second Reconstruction* (1975); Jack Bass and Walter DeVries, *The Transformation of Southern Politics: Social Change and Political Consequence since 1945* (1976); Dwight B. Billings, *Planters and the Making of a "New South": Class, Politics, and Development in North Carolina, 1865–1900* (1979); Earl Black and Merle Black, *Divided America: The Ferocious Power Struggle in American Politics* (2007), *Politics and Society in the South* (1987), *The Rise of the Southern Republicans* (2002), *The Vital South: How Presidents Are Elected* (1992); Bradley G. Bond, *Political Culture in the Nineteenth-Century South: Mississippi, 1830–1900* (1995); Dan T. Carter, *The Politics of Rage: George Wallace, the Origins of the New Conservatism, and the Transformation of American Politics* (1995); W. J. Cash, *The Mind of the South* (1941); James C. Cobb, *The Selling of the South: The Southern Crusade for Industrial Development, 1936–1980* (1982); William J. Cooper Jr., *Liberty and Slavery: Southern Politics to 1860* (1983); Joseph Crespino, *In Search of Another Country: Mississippi and the Conservative Counterrevolution* (2007); Stephen Edward Cresswell, *Multiparty Politics in Mississippi, 1897–1902* (1995); Anthony P. Dunbar, *Against the Grain: Southern Radicals and Prophets, 1929–1959* (1981); Thomas Byrne Edsall with Mary D. Edsall, *Chain Reaction: The Impact of Race, Rights, and Taxes on American Politics* (1991); John Egerton, *Speak Now against the Day: The Generation before the Civil Rights Movement in the South* (1994); Richard Florida, *The Flight of the Creative Class* (2005); J. Wayne Flynt, *Dixie's Forgotten People: The South's Poor Whites* (1979); George M. Fredrickson, *The Black Image in the White Mind: The Debate on Afro-American Character and Destiny, 1817–1914* (1971); William W. Freehling, *The Road to Decisions: Secessionists at Bay, 1776–1854* (1990); Eugene D. Genovese, *The Political Economy of Slavery: Studies in the Economy and Society of the Slave South* (1965), *Roll, Jordan, Roll: The World the Slaves Made* (1974), *The World the Slave-*

holders Made: Two Essays in Interpretation (1969); James M. Glaser, *The Hand of the Past in Contemporary Southern Politics* (2005), *Race, Campaign Politics, and the Realignment in the South* (1996); Douglas Hurt, ed., *The Rural South since World War II* (1998); Michael R. Hyman, *The Anti-Redeemers: Hill Country Political Dissenters in the Lower South from Redemption to Populism* (1990); V. O. Key Jr., *Southern Politics in State and Nation* (1949); Alexander P. Lamis, *The Two-Party South* (1984), ed., *Southern Politics in the 1990s* (1999); Steven F. Lawson, *Black Ballots: Voting Rights in the South, 1944–1969* (1976); David Lublin, *The Republican South: Democratization and Partisan Change* (2004); Donald R. Matthews and James W. Prothro, *Negroes and the New Southern Politics* (1966); Matthew C. Moen, *The Christian Right and Congress* (1989); Edmund S. Morgan, *American Slavery, American Freedom: The Ordeal of Colonial Virginia* (1975); Gunnar Myrdal, *An American Dilemma* (1944); Christopher J. Olsen, *Political Culture and Secession in Mississippi: Masculinity, Honor, and the Antipathy Tradition, 1830–1860* (2000); Nicol C. Rae, *Southern Democrats* (1994); Robert P. Steed, Tod A. Baker, and Laurence C. Moreland, eds., *Party Organization and Activism in the American South* (1998); Elizabeth R. Varon, *We Mean to Be Counted: White Women and Politics in Antebellum Virginia* (1998); Eric H. Walther, *The Fire-Eaters* (1992); Harry L. Watson, *Liberty and Power: The Politics of Jacksonian America* (1990); Samuel L. Webb, *Two-Party Politics in the One-Party South: Alabama's Hill Country, 1874–1920* (1997); Jonathan M. Wiener, *Social Origins of the New South: Alabama, 1860–1885* (1978); Bertram Wyatt-Brown, *Southern Honor: Ethics and Behavior in the Old South* (1982).

Cold War

The Cold War was the period of nuclear-armed competition between the United States and the Soviet Union, lasting from the end of World War II until the withdrawal of Soviet military forces from Eastern Europe in 1989 and the disappearance of the Soviet Union itself in 1991. Americans considered themselves the leaders of what they called the "free world," the noncommunist nations of Europe and the Americas. Much of the Cold War served as a contest between the Soviets and Americans for friendly relations and alliances with the new Third World nations of Asia and Africa, which emerged out of colonialism into independence following 1945.

U.S. policy makers believed that a key to waging the Cold War was American openness. In contrast to the secrecy and duplicity they associated with communists and the Soviet Union, they hoped that maximum exposure to Americans' essential decency and democratic practices would convince Third World peoples of the virtues of capitalism and Western-style democracy. In this regard, the South proved to be a stumbling block for the nation's Cold War purposes, particularly before 1965. Constituting a majority of the world's population, Third World peoples of color doubted that the treatment and status of African Americans south of the Mason-Dixon line made American society a model they wished to emulate. Racial discrimination abounded in the rest of the United States as well, but the South's legacy of rigid segregation and racial violence gave the region a particular prominence as Americans sought to convince others that their country was the leader of a truly free world.

Race reformers in the South used the logic of anticommunism to promote racial equality. Civil rights workers emphasized the close attention that Africans and Asians paid to the treatment of black southerners and the ease with which the Soviets used American racial discrimination and violence to undercut U.S. claims to being the leading apostle of freedom. This argument won out, for the most part, at the level of the federal government. The administrations of Harry Truman, John Kennedy, and Lyndon Johnson—and, to a lesser extent, Dwight Eisenhower—recognized this weakness and gradually moved the nation toward eliminating legal racial distinctions. Washington's Cold War priorities abroad eventually lent support to the work of the civil rights movement.

In their resistance to racial change, most white southerners in the first two decades after 1945 used the logic of anticommunism in a very different way. With support for civil rights outside the South growing, white supremacists in Dixie took up the slogan of anticommunism in part as a cover for preserving racial segregation. The few American communists enthusiastically supported racial equality, reactionaries noted, so it must be a subversive idea.

Indeed, racial equality was a subversive idea in most of the South before the mid-1960s, and white supremacists worked to associate it closely with communism. White southerners shared the genuine abhorrence of communism of most Americans, but their concern for preserving traditional racial hierarchies gave their anticommunism a particularly zealous and distorted cast.

The South benefited from the vast expansion of military spending that became standard during the Cold War. More than one-third of the federal funds for new military bases and defense industry contracts during World War II had gone to states of the former Confederacy, as warm weather and inexpensive land close to the coast made for attractive sites for training millions of new soldiers for service overseas. This was the starting point for the growth of the Sunbelt, which continued throughout the Cold War era and has done much to shape American society and politics ever since.

The South's distinctive racial mores during the first half of the Cold War engendered uncertainty about whether the region was more similar to or different from the rest of the country. Part of the uncertainty stemmed from the disproportionate influence that the region had in the nation's political life. The late 1940s and early 1950s marked the apex of southern influence in the U.S. Congress. Seniority rules and the one-party character of southern politics had elevated Dixie Democrats into the chairs of a majority of the most powerful committees in both the House and the Senate. Journalist William S. Whyte observed, "So marked and so constant is this high degree of Southern dominion . . . that the Senate might be described as the South's unending revenge upon the North for Gettysburg."

The South's influence reached into the executive branch as well. Almost all of the Cold War presidents displayed some kind of particular affection for the region. Truman, Johnson, and Jimmy Carter grew up in former slaveholding states. Eisenhower vacationed frequently in Georgia and spoke publicly of his respect for the Confederacy. Kennedy had the fewest personal ties to Dixie, but Richard Nixon ran his 1968 campaign on a "southern strategy" and remained solicitous of white southerners thereafter. Ronald Reagan campaigned for "states' rights" in Philadelphia, Miss., in 1980, and George H. W. Bush moved to Texas as a young man and considered it home thereafter. The South was a familiar and even intimate place to the men in charge of American foreign relations. From Truman to Johnson, American presidents viewed segregationist officials not as dire enemies in a struggle for control and direction of the American South, as did civil rights workers by the 1960s, but rather as a stubborn, backward-looking but respected part of the nation's leadership. These presidents also tended to share, to varying extents, the suspicion of segregationists that the civil rights movement was at least potentially subversive, if not actually communist-influenced.

The far-reaching changes that swept through southern society in the second half of the 20th century cannot be fully understood apart from the international context of the Cold War. The American civil rights movement fit in the larger story of decolonization—the international civil rights movement—and the Cold War struggle over world leadership and the meaning of "freedom." Despite their ties to the segregated white South, U.S. policy makers ultimately accepted the necessity and even rightness of desegregation as a Cold War imperative.

THOMAS BORSTELMANN
Cornell University

Thomas Borstelmann, *The Cold War and the Color Line: American Race Relations in the Global Arena* (2001); Pete Daniel, *Lost Revolutions: The South in the 1950s* (2000); John Egerton, *Speak Now against the Day: The Generation before the Civil Rights Movement in the South* (1994); Joseph A. Fry, *Dixie Looks Abroad: The South and U.S. Foreign Relations, 1789–1973* (2002); David R. Goldfield, *Promised Land: The South since 1945* (1987).

Congress

Southern concern for protecting distinctive regional interests has often focused on Congress, and the South has sent some of its greatest talent to that institution. South Carolina congressman and later senator John C. Calhoun, for example, developed a major American political theory for protection of minority rights in Congress. He maneuvered for decades in Washington, in a losing battle, to protect slave plantation interests. The growing antebellum North-South conflict erupted into outright violence on the floor of Congress in 1856, when South Carolina congressman Preston Brooks beat Massachusetts senator Charles Sumner with his cane as a stunned gallery watched.

Southerners in Congress have displayed a regional love of words through their oratory. John Randolph (1773–1833) of Roanoke, the eccentric Virginian of the early 19th century, was a brilliant extemporaneous speaker, quick-witted and frequently acrimonious. Like many later southern congressmen, he defended states' rights. The modern comic image of the southern congressman as "Senator Claghorn"—a verbose, obfuscating, loud speaker—was a satirical distortion of real-life individuals who powerfully used words.

Southerners in Congress also developed unusual skills at procedural maneuvering. Henry Clay (1777–1852) regarded himself as more western than southern, but this Kentucky congressman who served six terms as Speaker of the House of Representatives represented a slave state and displayed a seemingly regional talent for mastering the way Congress operates. He put together the Missouri Compromise (1820) and the Compromise Tariff (1833) that ended the nullification crisis, and his ideas became the basis of the Compromise of 1850. Southerners who later rose to prominence as congressional leaders because of unusual legislative skill included Speakers of the House John Nance "Cactus Jack" Garner, Sam Rayburn, and William Bankhead and Senate Majority Leader Lyndon Johnson. The filibuster became associated with southern congressional leaders in the mid-20th century, as James Eastland and John Stennis of Mississippi, Richard Russell of Georgia, Strom Thurmond of South Carolina, and others used it as a delaying tactic when Congress considered civil rights legislation.

The file of southern congressional notables would include those from a variety of political positions. Fire-eaters such as William Lowndes Yancey and Robert Barnwell Rhett were extremists in the defense of southern liberty, but Mississippi's Lucius Quintus Cincinnatus Lamar became a famed conciliator between the regions while serving in the House of Representatives (1873–77) and the Senate (1877–85) after the Civil War. Demagogues such as Cole Blease of South Carolina, Jeff Davis of Arkansas, Thomas "Tom-Tom" Heflin of Alabama, and Theodore Bilbo of Mississippi first achieved notoriety at the state level but then transferred their harsh racial rhetoric to the halls of Congress. Maury Maverick of Texas, though, was a great defender of civil liberties and equality; Lister Hill and John Sparkman of Alabama were famed as racial moderates; and Albert Gore of Tennessee and Ralph Yarborough of Texas were downright liberal on the issue. Southern congressional leaders such as Thomas T. Connally of Texas, J. William Fulbright of Arkansas, and John Tower of Texas have played an active role in foreign affairs, some as "hawks," others as "doves," but most committed to internationalism rather than isolation.

Southern political families such as the Bankheads of Alabama and the Byrds of Virginia have sometimes seemed to claim a genealogical interest in Congress. John Hollis Bankhead Sr. (1842–1920), for example, served in the House (1887–1907) and Senate (1907), while his sons John Hollis Bankhead Jr. (1872–1946) and William Brockman Bankhead (1874–1940) played key roles in the Senate and the House in the 1930s.

Southern Democrats dominated Congress in the 20th century. Their political longevity, their coalition with northern conservatives, and their ability to act in concert gave them a big advantage over other congressional factions. Southern one-party politics produced long careers in Congress for southern representatives and senators who, once secure as incumbents, rarely faced significant opposition. This factor, working in tandem with the legislature's seniority system, gave southerners the chairmanships of most major congressional committees. They strengthened that advantage in 1946 when many northern representatives and senators of equal seniority went down in defeat at the hands of Republicans. The southern Democrats parlayed their political windfall into a lasting advantage by renewing their cooperation with midwestern conservative Republicans in order to thwart subsequent legislative reform efforts until the Great Society of the 1960s. Congressional southerners acted as a unanimous power bloc, however, only in opposition to civil rights legislation. In the postwar era, opposing civil rights became the keystone of southern congressional unity, as it came to control southern politics generally.

When President Harry Truman made civil rights an important part of his 1948 reelection campaign, he directly threatened customary southern racial relations. Congressional southerners were able to defeat Truman's legislative moves because of their unity of purpose exercised through control of all major committees. Occasionally, civil rights legislation and initiatives did manage to pass through the House of Representatives, where the southerners could be easily outvoted. All these efforts were halted in the Senate, however, where southern senators, led by Richard B. Russell of Georgia, prevented civil rights bills from coming to a vote by waging filibusters and exploiting the chamber's tradition of unlimited debate. This legislative stalemate continued through Truman's term and into the Eisenhower administration until 1957, when the first civil rights bill since Reconstruction passed both houses. Nevertheless, that act and another approved in 1960 did little to change southern society, and both can be seen as tactical retreats by southern congressmen and senators, providing the illusion of progress while retaining the reality of white supremacy.

Meanwhile, other forces outside Congress were working to transform the South. The Supreme Court's 1954 *Brown v. Board of Education* desegregation decision and the 1957 use of presidential power to achieve integrated education in Little Rock, Ark., were beyond the reach of congressional southerners to stop or alter. In response to the Court, southern senators drafted, and southern House members signed, a 1956 "Declaration of Constitutional Principles," better known as the "Southern Manifesto." The document was little more than a condemnation of the *Brown* decision and a call for legal, peaceful resistance, using states' rights as a justification. Consequently, southerners in Congress were reaching the limits of their power by the early 1960s. With growing nationwide sentiment for a strong civil rights act, marshalled first by President John F. Kennedy and more effectively later by President Lyndon B. Johnson, reformers rammed through legislation in 1964 and 1965 that eventually transformed southern society and politics.

The civil rights acts and urbanization of southern society combined to transform the region's congressional politics. The subsequent decline of civil rights as a political issue encouraged a moderation of the South's political environment, which prompted the emergence of a wider spectrum of political concerns. The section's one-party political society began to weaken as the Republican Party gained footholds in a number of states. The advent of ultraconservative southern Republicanism and the attrition of the Old Guard through death and retirement encouraged younger southern Democrats to shift from opposing their party's leadership toward cooperation. These older southern Democrats softened their positions on race and other social issues to accommodate the rising numbers of black voters and a growing racial moderation by whites. Although neither a full-fledged two-party system nor a broad political spectrum emerged by the 1980s, the seeds for these vital parts of a political society were laid.

In Congress southern Democrats declined from their former position of dominance. As the southern Old Guard Democrats passed from positions of power, northerners took their places. The growing political diversity of the region further weakened the cohesiveness of the southerners in acting as a unit to support or oppose legislation. Finally, modifications in the seniority system diluted an important source of their legislative strength, since length of service no longer automatically assured access to positions of power. The distinctive southern identity in Congress had consequently declined by the 1980s.

In 1945 all 22 southern senators and 118 of 120 southern representatives in Congress were white, male Democrats. In the mid-1960s white southern Democrats headed about two-thirds of the committees in the House and Senate. With the Republican capture of both houses of Congress in the 1994 election, southern Republicans emerged as a powerful group of legislators. By the 1997 session, southerners held House leadership positions as Speaker of the House, majority leader, and majority whip. Southerners held similar Senate leadership positions, as majority leader and president pro tempore, and chaired such key committees as Appropriations, Rules, Ways and Means, and Foreign Relations. The Democratic capture of both Houses of Congress in the 2006 midterm elections brought a new nonsouthern leadership group into power. No southern senator chaired any committee, and only four southern House members chaired committees.

DAVID POTENZIANI
University of Memphis

Numan Bartley and Hugh Davis Graham, *Southern Politics and the Second Reconstruction* (1975); Jack Bass and Walter DeVries, *The Transformation of Southern Politics: Social Change and Political Consequence since 1945* (1976); Earl Black and Merle Black, *Politics and Society in the South* (1987); James MacGregor Burns, *The Deadlock of Democracy: Four Party Politics in America* (1963); Neil MacNeil, *Forge of Democracy: The House of Representatives* (1963); Matthew C. Moen, *The Christian Right and Congress* (1989); Robert L. Peabody and Nelson W. Polsby, eds., *New Perspectives on the House of Representatives* (1969); Nelson W. Polsby, *Congress and the Presidency*, 3rd ed. (1976); Frank E. Smith, *Congressman from Mississippi* (1964).

County Politics

Few if any popular perceptions of southern politics are more deeply ingrained than that of the courthouse "clique" or "ring." Film and fiction, scholarly tomes, and journalistic exposés have united in fostering an image of county governments dominated by self-serving officials closely aligned with business and agricultural wealth and exercising arbitrary, undemocratic control over local affairs. As with other generalizations about the South, this stereotype is more accurate for some eras than others, more applicable to some states and counties than to their neighbors. Nevertheless, a survey of the region's historical experience offers much support for this uncomplimentary appraisal of grassroots political conduct.

The beginnings of the courthouse cliques are readily discernible in the English origins of southern society. Acting for the crown, the king's counselors appointed militia officers, sheriffs, and justices of the peace in the counties of the mother country during the 1500s and 1600s. The justices of the peace constituted the linchpins of the system. Functioning collectively as members of county courts, they administered governmental affairs in the shires and handled routine judicial matters as well.

These practices exerted an enduring influence. Unlike their dissenting Puritan contemporaries to the north, who fashioned a distinctive amalgam of Calvinist theocracy and town-meeting democracy, the dominant groups in the colonial South willingly adopted the oligarchic governmental forms of Tudor-Stuart England—as modified to accommodate provincial needs and circumstances. Developments in Virginia set the pattern for the region. There the royal governors selected county officials, including justices of the peace. In the Old Dominion—as in England—the justices directed local affairs, establishing tax rates, regulating businesses, overseeing road maintenance, and performing a multitude of other functions. Drawn from the ranks of the plantation gentry and enjoying lifetime tenure on the county courts, the justices soon established

Political Rally, by John McCrady (1935) (Mr. and Mrs. Jack M. McLarty, Jackson, Mississippi)

a marked degree of independence from gubernatorial control. Most notably, they began to assert the right to fill vacancies in their ranks, and royal governors generally acquiesced in this claim by confirming the justices' nominees (as well as their choices for sheriffs and other county offices). Exercising peremptory control over local administration, members of the county courts also held considerable sway in elections to the House of Burgesses. Rule of, by, and for the planters thus became a fact of political life in Virginia and elsewhere in the region—in spite of sporadic protests by backwoods dissidents and other would-be reformers during the colonial and Revolutionary periods.

Indeed, the South's oligarchic county courts escaped significant change until the first decades of the 19th century. By that time, various abuses, including the appointment of excessive numbers of new justices and the consequent growth of court membership to unwieldy proportions (ranging upward to 90 men in some counties), demanded public attention. Professional lawyers led the assault by criticizing the planter-justices' lack of legal training, and charges of inefficiency, ineptitude, and corruption proliferated. More important, perhaps, democratic ideological currents of the Jacksonian era found obvious targets in the self-perpetuating county courts. This ferment produced dramatic results. Commencing in the new states of the Deep South cotton frontier and spreading throughout the region, legislative enactments and constitutional revisions transformed the tone and conduct of local politics. By the eve of the Civil War, voters in most of the southern states could elect their sheriffs, coroners, overseers of the poor, school commissioners, and constables. Life-tenured justices of the peace had given way to county judges chosen by state legislatures or the electorate for limited, specified terms. Although planters still occupied many positions in local government, they could no longer ignore the interests and wishes of ordinary voters.

These democratic trends broadened and deepened during the turmoil of the Reconstruction era, only to experience a stunning reversal during the white supremacist "Redemption" of the 1870s and 1880s. Appalled by the preeminence of scalawags, carpetbaggers, and blacks during the brief heyday of Radical Republicanism, the resurgent planter Democrats and their New South commercial-industrial allies moved inexorably to eliminate or neutralize potentially disruptive influences. Reflecting this antiegalitarian bias, popular election of local officials was replaced by legislative or gubernatorial appointment in Florida, Louisiana, and North Carolina, while violence and ballot box fraud hampered voter participation elsewhere, especially in closely contested Black Belt areas. Entrenched county officeholders provided the organizational cement for long-term Democratic hegemony, and successive generations of Republicans, Populists, and Independents railed against the abuses (real or imagined) of courthouse cliques and rings. Oligarchic control was, once again, the fashion at the grass roots.

One-party rule persisted almost unchallenged through the first half of the 20th century, but county-level politics in the "Solid South" was characterized by considerable diversity. Courthouse cliques generally exerted greater influence in lowland plantation districts than in comparatively egalitarian mountain or Piedmont areas. By the 1930s and 1940s, moreover, local officials in Louisiana, Tennessee, and Virginia tended to be closely aligned with dominant machine factions in their respective state Democratic parties, while county officeholders elsewhere in the region formed shifting, ephemeral alliances in state primary races. Courthouse politicos exerted particular influence in Georgia, where a county-unit system (similar to the federal electoral college) determined the outcome of statewide primary contests. Exemplifying yet other variations, county-seat political dominance in Alabama was typically enjoyed by probate judges; in Virginia, by circuit court judges; in Louisiana and Mississippi, by sheriffs with an abiding interest in the preservation of home rule over gambling and bootlegging in their jurisdictions.

Byzantine in its complexities, sometimes baroque in its manifestations, the courthouse regime constituted a bedrock reality of southern politics until the 1940s and 1950s. Even so, forces of change were omnipresent in the post–World War II years, eroding the authority and imperiling the permanence of the previously invincible cliques and rings. Urbanization, industrial growth, northern migration to the emerging Sunbelt, enhanced educational opportunities, and the advent of mass communications media were fashioning a more cosmopolitan social order, a South less attuned to one-party rule. In the aftermath of the New Deal, state and federal bureaucracies were on the rise, and they created alternative centers of power and influence. Most important of all, the civil rights revolution exerted a pervasive impact on the South. Encouraged by federal legislative enactments and judicial decrees, millions of blacks reentered the political process, while the Supreme Court's "one-man, one-vote" rulings bolstered the representation of urban residents at the expense of the old-style crossroads elite. Beset by external antagonists and internal stresses, the cliques and rings were in retreat throughout the region by the 1960s and 1970s.

Since then, African Americans have increasingly been elected as county officials, and women have also served as county sheriffs, supervisors, and administrators. Counties continue to represent state authority at the local level, providing law enforcement, construction and maintenance of bridges and roads, water and sewer services, disposal of solid waste, public libraries, recreational activities, assessment of ad valorem property taxes, and economic development. If no longer constituting political rings as in earlier southern history, county politicians retain considerable authority.

JAMES TICE MOORE
Virginia Commonwealth University

Monroe Billington, *The Political South in the Twentieth Century* (1975); V. O. Key Jr., *Southern Politics in State and Nation* (1949); Michael E. Stauffer, *The Formation of Counties in South Carolina* (1994); Charles S. Sydnor, *Gentleman Freeholders: Political Practices in Washington's Virginia* (1952), *The Development of Southern Sectionalism, 1819–1848* (1948); J. Devereux Weeks and Paul T. Hardy, eds., *Handbook for Georgia County Commissioners* (1998); C. Vann Woodward, *Origins of the New South, 1877–1913* (1951); Ralph A. Wooster, *The People in Power: Courthouse and Statehouse in the Lower South, 1850–1860* (1969), *Politicians, Planters, and Plain Folk: Courthouse and Statehouse in the Upper South, 1850–1860* (1975).

Culture Wars

In 1990 University of Virginia sociologist James Davison Hunter described the ideological "struggle to define America" as "culture wars." After presidential candidate Patrick Buchanan told the 1992 Republican National Convention that his campaign was a willing participant in "a religious and cultural war . . . for the soul of America," journalists had found a new term. Alluding to the fascist elements in Buchanan's use of the term, columnist Molly Ivins quipped that "it sounded better in the original German." Right language, wrong leader. Hunter had actually borrowed the term from Bismarck's 19th-century term *Kulturkampf*, applying it to the competing moral worldviews (or political philosophies) that have polarized contemporary America.

The culture wars, however, have several important links to politics in the South. First, the culture wars have roots in the same southern racial politics that greeted the civil rights movement. Many of these cultural combatants, like Moral Majority leader Jerry Falwell, first took to the public square inveighing against Martin Luther King Jr.'s social preaching and political involvements. Many religious leaders spoke for millions of conservative white southerners who opposed the activists of the civil rights movement and the politicians sympathetic to them.

Beginning in 1979, the fundamentalist takeover of the Southern Baptist Convention was sparked in part by Southern Baptist liberals' sympathy with the civil rights movement. Not coincidentally, 1979 also marked the beginning of the Moral Majority and the rise of the Religious Right. Falwell, Pat Robertson's Christian Coalition, and every Southern Baptist Convention president since 1979 have all been central figures in the culture wars. As it happens, all of them have southern accents. Hence, to an important degree, concern about race and the changes brought about by the civil rights movement was a catalyst that set in motion the Southern Baptist fundamentalist takeover movement, its involvement with the Religious Right, and its enlistment in the culture wars.

Second, the contemporary culture wars extended a conflict that began with the civil rights movement. After African Americans won the federal government over to a more inclusive image of the nation in the Civil Rights and Voting Rights Acts of the mid-1960s, the South led the rest of the nation in a white backlash against the gains of the civil rights movement. By the end of the Reagan administration, the movement had broadened its concerns, taken on a new name (the Religious Right), and converted the once Democratic Bible Belt into a new, solidly Republican South. Despite this transformation, however, the ideological warfare continues to center on the issue of racial and cultural diversity.

A Herblock cartoon from 1985 (Courtesy of the Herblock Foundation)

A third link is revealed by viewing the culture wars as evidence of a "southernization of America." Southern historian James C. Cobb finds that the "characteristic vices of the southern mind in 1940" had become the "defining features of the national mind" by the middle of the Clinton years. Journalist Peter Applebome put it most succinctly: "The most striking aspect of American life at the century's end—unimaginable three decades ago at the height of the civil rights era—is how much the country looks like the South." Discontents once peculiar to the conservative South had become nationalized.

After World War II, the South, whose insularity had previously protected it from serious incursions of pluralism, was challenged in ways strong enough to threaten its racial and religious status quo. The civil rights movement won its fight when the federal government became committed to its goals in the Civil Rights Act of 1964, the Voting Rights Act of 1965, and Lyndon Johnson's Great Society programs. It was a short-lived victory. When Johnson took office in 1963, a Harris poll found that only 31 percent of Americans believed that the federal government was pushing integration "too fast." A 1966 Gallup poll indicated that the percentage had risen to 72 percent. Thus, a national reversal began within three years of the high-water marks of the civil rights movement.

In addition to the Democrats' "capture" by the civil rights agenda and its commitment to the Great Society, middle-class white voters, especially in the South, were angered by the Watts riots of 1965, King's denunciation of the Vietnam War, and the civil disturbances after King's assassination. Making matters worse, other liberation movements (Indians, Women, Gays) and the anti–Vietnam War protests followed the civil rights example, and soon the losers in the civil rights wars now had more to disturb them than just racial diversity. Civil rights, Vietnam protests, the removal of public school prayer, *Roe v. Wade*, the secularizing tendencies of television, the growing violence in American life, and gay rights all created among conservative Americans a discontent with pluralism. Despite these cultural and religious transformations, racial change remained a central concern. Religious historian William R. Hutchison has argued that *Brown* bolstered the pluralist impulse more significantly than any other public policy change in the 20th century. In opposition stood a "counterpluralist" impulse that found its most powerful expression in the Religious Right. Predominantly white and Protestant—and southern, one might add— these counterpluralists, Hutchison observed, were not only troubled by the proliferation of minorities and new religions but fearful and angry about losing control of their "own country."

How did the racial concerns of the 1960s become broadened into the religious and cultural fears of the 21st century? Answer: George Wallace's "politics of rage"—another link between southern politics and the culture wars. Historian Dan Carter argued that, through the 1980s and 1990s, Wallace's issues "moved from the fringes of our society to center stage." Wallace did not create the conservative groundswell of the culture wars, but, Carter argues, he foresaw most of its themes. By his 1968 third-party run for the presidency, Wallace had broadened his criticism beyond the traditional racial politics of his "schoolhouse door" phase to a wider range of social battles that were later joined by the Moral Majority and the Christian Coalition. Yet beneath it all lingered the slightly domesticated racism that had earlier demanded "Segregation today, segregation tomorrow, segregation forever."

Since then, at least in the voices that have occupied the Oval Office, the Republican Party has largely become George Wallace without the southern accent. As the dean of southern historians, C. Vann Woodward, once put it, "southern white Democrats have been Republicanized and northern white Republicans have been southernized." Richard Nixon adopted a "southern strategy" designed to tap the region's discontent with the civil rights agenda. Ronald Reagan, who, like Wallace, had opposed the Civil Rights Act of 1964, launched his 1980 general election campaign for the presidency by announcing in Philadelphia, Miss., where three civil rights workers were murdered, his commitment to states' rights. Similar themes were a regular part of Republican strategies throughout the first Bush administration and in Newt Gingrich's tenure as Speaker of the House. In this era, Bill Clinton, a southerner so liberal as to flout traditional sexual ethics in both his public policy (Gays in the Military) and private life (the Lewinsky scandal), became the Antichrist to many in the Religious Right. And in the 2000 presidential campaign, George W. Bush helped secure southern votes and his party's nomination by viewing the use of the Confederate flag as a matter best left to the states.

Battles over the Confederate flag reveal the connections of southern politics and the culture wars in instructive ways. Many of its hot-button issues show up in the tangential arguments of flag defenders. When the city of Danville, Va., was roiled by the controversy, a flag defender charged, "It is precisely this type of thinking which has driven God and prayer from our classrooms." Still another reader compared Danville City Council member Joyce Glaise, who had criticized the flag's use, with the nation's most hated atheist, Madalyn Murray O'Hair: "We've already had one woman single-handedly try to bring down the morals of our nation by having prayer removed from our schools. Now you want to remove another vital part of our heritage." Reflecting nostalgia for the good old days, one writer commented, "I think most of the people who live here liked our town the way it used to be."

Similarly, Gov. Roy Barnes, reacting to threats of an NAACP boycott against the state of Georgia, led the Georgia General Assembly to change the state flag to a new design that made the Confederate emblem much less prominent. Southern heritage groups almost immediately declared war on Barnes, pledging to unseat him in his 2002 reelection campaign and distributing bumper stickers sporting the Rebel flag and the slogans, "Keep the Flag. Change the Governor" and "Boot Barnes." Democratic-turned-Republican legislator Sonny Perdue later launched a gubernatorial campaign promising to give the citizens of Georgia a referendum on the state flag. In one of the biggest upset victories in recent memory, Perdue defeated Barnes to become the first Republican governor of the state since Reconstruction. Most observers of Georgia politics agreed that tinkering with the state banner had cost Barnes his job and that Perdue had entered the governor's mansion wrapped in the Confederate flag.

One final link should also be noted. While it is often claimed that the issues of public school prayer or abortion triggered the Religious Right's late 20th-, early 21st-century political engagement, the actual impetus was in line with a more traditional southern political concern. Evangelical historian Randall Balmer reports on a 1990 conference attended by the luminaries of the Religious Right and sponsored by the Ethics and Public Policy Center, one of the movement's affiliate organizations. In public address to the conferees and private conversation with Balmer, Paul M. Weyrich, one of the central architects of the Religious Right, noted that their political action was triggered by the Carter administration's efforts to deny tax exemptions to Bob Jones University and other segregated Christian schools. Having spent 15 years attempting to galvanize evangelical voters on school prayer or abortion to no avail, Weyrich asserted—and other conferees confirmed—that it was the IRS threat against segregated Christian schools that enraged these conservatives and spurred them to action.

Thus, the Religious Right has watered the seeds planted by traditional southern politics while broadening its range of concerns and developing a more national appeal. Still, the center of its strength has been the South, and its central concern has blossomed from racial purity to the full bloom of religious and cultural diversity in America. As southerners have led the way in every American war, so they have been the most numerous and most enthusiastic recruits in the contemporary culture wars.

ANDREW M. MANIS
Macon State College

Peter Applebome, *Dixie Rising: How the South Is Shaping American Values, Politics, and Culture* (1996); Randall Balmer, *Thy Kingdom Come: How the Religious Right Distorts the Faith and Threatens America: An Evangelical's Lament* (2006); Earl Black and Merle Black, *Politics and Society in the South* (1987); Dan T. Carter, *The Politics of Rage: George Wallace, the Origins of the New Conservatism, and the Transformation of American Politics* (2000); Andrew M. Manis, *Southern Civil Religions in Conflict: Civil Rights and the Culture Wars* (2002); Oran Smith, *The Rise of Baptist Republicanism* (1997).

Demagogues

Political demagoguery is at least as old as the early Greek term (from *demos*, for "people," and *agog*, for "leader") for unscrupulous politicians who gain power by appealing to the electorate's emotions, passions, and prejudices. Throughout Western history, demagogues have symbolized the fear of privileged elites that expanding democracy inevitably degenerates into rabble-rousing. In America, no era or region has been free of demagogues, but the classic southern variety flourished with unusual vigor during the six decades between Reconstruction and World War II.

The term has been applied to successful southern politicians as diverse as Benjamin Tillman, Tom Watson, Jeff Davis, Coleman Blease, James K. Vardaman, Theodore Bilbo, Thomas Heflin, James and Marian Ferguson, W. Lee O'Daniel, Eugene Talmadge, and Huey Long. Their appeals to poor rural whites variously featured irresponsible campaign promises, flamboyant personal styles, violent rhetoric, appeals to racial and religious bigotry and anti-intellectualism, and attacks upon the predatory corporate interests. Mississippi's Bilbo denounced from the stump a typical pantheon of enemies of the common people: "farmer murderers, poor-folks haters, shooters of widows and orphans, international well-poisoners, charity hospital destroyers, spitters on our heroic veterans, rich enemies of our public schools, private bankers, European debt cancellors, unemployment makers, Pacifists, Communists, munitions manufacturers, and skunks who steal Gideon Bibles." As for the disfranchised and vulnerable blacks, Blease would "wipe the inferior race from the face of the earth." To Vardaman the black man was a "lazy, lying, lustful animal which no conceivable amount of training can transform into a tolerable citizen." Bilbo, who shot a black man on a Washington streetcar, called for solving the unemployment problem by shipping 12 million southern black citizens "back" to Africa. Not surprisingly, racial lynching flourished in such an atmosphere—Blease boasted that "whenever the constitution comes between me and the virtues of the white women of the South, I say to hell with the constitution."

W. Lee "Pappy" O'Daniel, Texas governor
and country-and-western musician, c. 1940
(Texas State Library, Austin)

These appeals understandably took root in an environment characterized by poverty, illiteracy, racism, Civil War and Populist defeat, agrarian decline, and a small-town and rural cultural barrenness that was only occasionally enlivened by revivals and political campaigns. Reinforcing this socioeconomic and cultural legacy were the South's one-party system and the direct (white) Democratic primary, which strengthened personality-centered stump politics at the expense of issue-focused debates, blurred policy continuities that linked incumbent regimes to policy outcomes, and invited the manipulation of faction-ridden legislatures by organized, well-funded lobbies against the collective interests of the "have-nots." As a result, victorious demagogues rarely implemented such promised and popularly mandated reforms as better schools, hospitals, roads, and pensions, and many of their regimes were riddled with corruption. Richard Hofstadter referred to this phenomenon as the "devolution of reform into reaction," whereby the highly educated Georgia Populist Tom Watson was transformed into the embittered baiter of blacks, Jews, and Catholics, and the modest attempts at reform under the Tillman regime in South Carolina degenerated into the empty promises of Blease, who as governor even opposed compulsory education and child-labor laws. As late as the mid-20th century, such common-folk champions as Governor Talmadge in Georgia and the Fergusons and O'Daniel in Texas would attack their state universities while corruption shaped their own administrations and swelled their pockets; as Talmadge explained, "Sure I stole, but I stole it for you." This in turn invited "good government" counterattacks by conservative elites who typically called for slashing both taxes and social services—which amounted, in the classic lament of Gerald W. Johnson, to a dismal choice between a "Live Demagogue or a Dead Gentleman."

The dominant stereotype of the southern demagogue masked considerable diversity and irony as well. These masters of the common tongue and taste generally enjoyed a superior education; champions of the downtrodden, they typically lived and retired in material comfort. Although most Deep South demagogues were race-baiters, their Rim South equivalents, such as Jeff Davis of Arkansas and W. Lee "Pappy" O'Daniel of Texas, generally were not. The most nationally spectacular embodiment of the triumphant demagogue, "Kingfish" Huey Long of Louisiana, staked his presidential bid against Roosevelt on the economic nostrum of "Share Our Wealth." But in Louisiana, Long not only refused to race-bait, he also refused to sell out, once elected, to the corporate interests he had attacked. After seizing near dictatorial control of Louisiana's government, Long taxed the extractive industries and delivered the roads, bridges, hospitals, schoolbooks, and utility regulation that his campaigns had promised.

Many political journalists of the 1930s viewed Long as a forerunner of American fascism and thereby demonstrated their misunderstanding both of the mainstream American political tradition and of its exaggerated southern variant. Contemporaries of Long watched Europe descend into a fascist nightmare, and with victory in World War II came an understandable surge of domestic social scientific interest in identifying the origin, structure, and location of America's equivalent fascist personality. University-based psychologists generated such test-battery inventories as the "f-scale" (for fascism) to identify the authoritarian personality, and sociologists employed the new tool of survey research to locate its distribution. But southerners proved to be no more inclined toward fascism than other Americans, primarily because America had no fascist tradition.

Southern demagoguery has always confused political analysts, because it tends to appeal simultaneously to the populist Left and to the bigoted Right. Neither tendency is alien to the American political tradition, but in the prostrate South from Reconstruction through the Great Depression, the bitterness of poverty and defeat was compounded by four warping political institutions—disfranchisement, the one-party system, malapportionment, and de jure Jim Crow—that whiplashed southern politics into a grotesque caricature of the American democratic ideal. Few contemporary observers understood that the pathological environment was temporary, and that its passing would reveal a deeper bedrock of regionally shared American political values.

World War II ushered in a belated surge of prosperity throughout the South, and with it slowly came the improved education and broadened political participation that would relegate the classic post-Reconstruction demagogues to history. Desegregation and the civil rights movement sparked a brief resurgence from the mid-1950s through the mid-1960s of the old demagogic strains, most notably in defiant governors Orval Faubus (Ark.), Ross Barnett (Miss.), George Wallace (Ala.), and Lester Maddox (Ga.). But the long and circular career of Alabama's Wallace testifies ironically not only to the depth of the South's racial tension but also to the strength of its populistic tradition and to the liberating effect of a genuinely democratic franchise, of two-party competition, of public education, and ultimately of the South's long submerged but abiding commitment to the norms and goals of American democracy.

HUGH DAVIS GRAHAM
University of Maryland, Baltimore County

William Anderson, *The Wild Man from Sugar Creek: The Political Career of Eugene Talmadge* (1975); Dan T. Carter, *The Politics of Rage: George Wallace, the Origins of the New Conservatism, and the Transformation of American Politics* (1995); Hugh Davis Graham, ed., *Huey Long* (1970); William F. Holmes, *The White Chief: James Kimble Vardaman* (1970); Gerald W. Johnson, *Virginia Quarterly Review* (January 1936); Stephen David Kantrowitz, *Ben Tillman and the Reconstruction of White Supremacy* (2000); Albert Kirwan, *Revolt of the Rednecks: Mississippi Politics, 1876–1925* (1951); Reinhard Luthin, *American Demagogues: Twentieth Century* (1954); Daniel M. Robison, *Journal of Southern History* (August 1937); Francis Butler Simkins, *Pitchfork Ben Tillman: South Carolinian* (1944); Robert L. Taylor Jr., *Tennessee Historical Quarterly* (Summer 1996); T. Harry Williams, *Huey Long* (1969), *Journal of Southern History* (February 1960); C. Vann Woodward, *Tom Watson: Agrarian Rebel* (1938).

Democratic Party

The Democratic Party in the American South began the 21st century fairly ominously. The first two presidential elections were Republican sweeps of the South, and they were followed by the publication of a politically fashionable book that argued that the national Democratic Party would be wise to "Whistle Past Dixie" and just forget the South. Even though three Democratic sons of the South, Lyndon Johnson, Jimmy Carter, and Bill Clinton, gave the Democrats their only presidential victories since the assassination of John F. Kennedy, the Democratic Party in the South was often perceived as fading almost to the sorry state of the Republican Party a century earlier. While that is certainly not the case, the glory days of Democratic dominance are gone.

The supremacy of the Democratic Party in the South between Reconstruction and World War II was mind-boggling. After the Civil War and Reconstruction, the Republican Party was viewed by the former Confederates as the party of the northern aggressors, and once those Confederate loyalists regained power after Reconstruction, Republicans were systematically ostracized from the political process. Between Reconstruction and the end of World War II, none of the 11 states of the old Confederacy had ever popularly elected a Republican U.S. senator. During this period, well over 90 percent of the delegation to the U.S. House of Representatives was Democratic, and with only a handful of exceptions, mostly in Tennessee, no Republican governor or presidential candidate had carried any of these states. Legislatures, city councils, mayors, judges, and sheriffs in every southern state, and especially in the states of the Deep South, were almost exclusively Democrats.

The most visible effect of a one-party South would bring its downfall. Southern Democratic Party officials of the early 20th century had been enormously successful in preventing progress toward racial equality. By World War II, with the eyes of the world watching the emergent world power of the United States, it became obvious that the South had an embarrassing system of racial apartheid. Partly because of that, the nation would no longer tolerate the racial policies that southern Democrats had promulgated. The national Democratic Party took its first firm stand in favor of black civil rights at the 1948 Democratic National Convention in a dramatic move that would break the loyalty of these white southerners to the party.

At the Democratic presidential nominating convention, a young senator from Minnesota, Hubert Humphrey, delivered a rousing address. Humphrey had spent a few years studying political science at Louisiana State University, where he learned about the populism of Louisiana's legendary governor Huey Long. There he also witnessed firsthand the ravages of racial discrimination in the Deep South. He returned to Minnesota with a passion to change things. At the 1948 convention, Humphrey electrified the crowd with a speech that convinced a bare majority of delegates to pass a strongly worded civil rights plank in the party platform. With the results of that vote in hand, hordes of southern delegates walked out and with a dramatic flourish effectively signaled the end of Democratic dominance in the South. Two of those delegates, South Carolina's Strom Thurmond and Mississippi's Fielding Lewis, headed an alternative presidential ticket that replaced the Democratic Party on the ballot and carried Louisiana, Mississippi, Alabama, and South Carolina. The successes of this States' Rights Party, or the "Dixiecrats" as they were commonly called, signaled the coming end to Democratic hegemony in the region.

Although Democrat Harry Truman was elected president without those four normally Democratic states, the defection made both parties cautious and somewhat accommodating to southern Democrats on the race issue in the decade that followed. Subsequently, the wholesale move away from the Democratic Party in the South was held in check. After the assassination of President John F. Kennedy, President Lyndon Johnson made passage of the Civil Rights Act and the Voting Rights Act a priority for the Democratic Party. In 1964, with now Vice President Hubert Humphrey as Johnson's running mate, the Democrats ran with a clear civil rights message that was anathema to the southern Democratic stand of only a few decades earlier. The Republicans nominated Arizona's Barry Goldwater who, for reasons that presumably had nothing to do with racial attitudes, did not support passage of the Civil Rights Act or the Voting Rights Act. The contrast of the two parties' stands had an enormous effect on two-party politics in the South. For the first time in their history, Mississippi, Alabama, Georgia, and South Carolina voted Republican. And in Mississippi, where the large African American population was effectively disfranchised, Mississippi white voters propelled Goldwater to an 87 percent popular-vote landslide in a state where a Republican presidential, senatorial, or gubernatorial candidate had never won a popular majority. While Democrats won the election handily, Democratic hegemony in the South had ended.

The breakthrough success may have shaken Democrats, but it presented the national Republicans with a dilemma. Republicans wanted to hold onto these new party converts but didn't want to be perceived as the party of racial intolerance. Enter Strom Thurmond and Richard Nixon. In 1964 the "Dixiecrat" standard-bearer switched to the Republican Party and began helping Republican presidential candidate Nixon in his 1968 bid for the presidency. They, with the notable help of Thurmond's political adviser Harry Dent, devised the now-legendary "southern strategy" to keep these new Goldwater Democrats in the Republican column. The bridge from anti–civil rights to the more palatable "tough on crime" was a natural one that appealed to these southern white segregationist voters. With segregationist candidate George Wallace (D-Ala.) on the presidential ballot as an independent in 1968, Nixon only won South Carolina from among the Goldwater southern states, but the seeds were planted for an effective strategy to convert these Goldwater Democrats to Republicans.

The Democrats clearly knew what had hit them. By the early 1970s, Republicans were beginning to have some successes in offices and places where Democrats had long dominated. Perhaps poetically, the first Republican elected to the U.S. Senate from the South filled the Texas seat vacated by Lyndon Johnson when he became vice president. Democrats worked hard to keep control, and in 1976, when Georgia governor Jimmy Carter was the Democratic nominee for president and swept every southern state except Virginia on his way to the White House, the newly integrated Democratic Party seemed to be back on top.

While the Civil Rights Act and the Voting Rights Act that passed under Democratic stewardship may have pushed away some white southern segregationists, they clearly opened the door for the newly enfranchised and substantial African American minority. And African Americans loyally voted for Democrats as they entered, and remained a part of, the southern political system. While Republicans may have been the party of Abraham Lincoln, it was the Democrats who had taken the next step and led the civil rights and voting rights revolution. As black presidential candidate Al Sharpton said in a speech to the 2004 Democratic National Convention, "It was those that earned our vote that got our vote. We got the Civil Rights Act under a Democrat. We got the Voting Rights Act under a Democrat. We got the right to organize under Democrats." Black voters became a significant and often critical part of any statewide Democratic majority in the South. Smaller political subdivisions, such as congressional districts, cities, counties, and judicial districts, often formed both a racial and partisan majority that elected countless African American Democratic officials throughout the South. In the early 1970s Democrats began electing a new breed of southern politicians that created an economic, biracial, populist coalition and won governorships and other statewide races. However, in the decades that followed, this Democratic biracial coalition would slowly become a less common exception rather than the rule.

In spite of African Americans' loyalty to the Democratic Party, Republicans began to win Senate and House seats and eventually state offices as well. By 1980, however, the partisan divide seemed to increase beyond racial issues. Republican Ronald Reagan, more than Thurmond, more than Goldwater, more than Nixon, found a way to appeal to a majority of southern whites that had lasting impact. With Reagan, Republicans crafted a message of social conservatism on issues like abortion, prayer in public schools, and eventually gay marriage that would trump the economic, populist appeal of the Democrats and would fade the racial issue into the background. In order to win, Democrats had to neutralize these social issues by trumpeting the same conservative positions as Republicans and hope the electorate would vote on the basis of the Democratic record on working-class economic relief. Therefore, in order to win statewide office,

Democrats in the South were often steadfastly at odds with their nonsouthern counterparts on social issues but consistent on domestic spending and tax policies.

By the end of the 20th century, Democratic success in the South depended on convincing a socially conservative majority that the party had more to offer than the national party's liberal stances on social issues. This was especially true concerning white voters. Black voters in the South were socially conservative as well, but the Democratic Party's consistency on economic and racial issues afforded it enough goodwill to keep these voters as very loyal Democrats. However, because of the national party's position on social issues, Democrats have had trouble winning elections in the South for federal offices. Southern sons Bill Clinton and Al Gore together were only able to win a few southern states. As the images of the parties have nationalized, especially white, rural, socially conservative voters and politicians have changed their voter registration and habits to the Republican Party, and more and more state and local legislators and state, county, and city officials are Republicans.

The once dominant Democratic Party in the South is down but far from out and a far cry from the predicament of the Republicans a century earlier. Democrats control many state legislatures, governorships, and other statewide offices. As of the 2006 midterm elections, Democrats hold a small majority in the House and an even narrower one in the Senate, but few of those gains were made in southern states.

WAYNE PARENT
Louisiana State University

Jack Bass and Walter DeVries, *Transformation of Southern Politics: Social Change and Political Consequence since 1945* (1976); Earl Black and Merle Black, *Politics and Society in the South* (1987); V. O. Key Jr., *Southern Politics in State and Nation* (1949); Thomas F. Schaller, *Whistling Past Dixie: How Democrats Can Win without the South* (2006).

Dixiecrats

In 1948 several southern Democrats rejected the liberal leadership of their national party and pursued an independent course. At issue was President Harry Truman's proposal on civil rights that advocated an antilynching law, a permanent fair employment practices commission, desegregation of the armed forces, and elimination of the poll tax. After a special committee of the Southern Governors' Conference unsuccessfully sought concessions on civil rights from the Democratic National Committee, many southerners, fearing the destruction of their regional traditions, considered a revolt against the national party. Under the guidance of Fielding Wright of Mississippi, Frank Dixon of Alabama, Strom Thurmond of South Carolina, and Leander Perez of Louisiana, disgruntled southerners launched a grassroots organization in the region.

When the South failed to prevent the nomination of Truman at the Democratic National Convention in Philadelphia and suffered reversals on civil rights, the rights of states to control tideland oil reserves, and the two-thirds rule, several delegates bolted. Six thousand southerners, mainly from Mississippi and Alabama, met later in Birmingham. Influenced by Charles Wallace Collins's *Whither Solid South?* (1947) and seeking to force the presidential election into the House of Representatives, these states' rights supporters "recommended" a separate ticket of Thurmond and Wright. Although race was clearly their key concern, the States' Rights Democrats included, in addition to white supremacists, antiunion industrialist oilmen and constitutional conservatives who abhorred civil rights and communism. Branded "Dixiecrats" by Bill Weisner of the *Charlotte News*, the dissident southerners advanced no positive programs, sought primarily to save the South from the clutches of political modernism, and reflected a historical consciousness that romanticized their regional past and social heritage.

Although States' Rights Democrats generally opposed the creation of a separate southern party, they seized control of the party machinery in Alabama, Mississippi, Louisiana, and South Carolina. Thurmond carried these four states, where he appeared on the ballot as the Democratic nominee and received 1.2 million votes, but Truman triumphed in the remainder of the South and won the election. Throughout the controversy, most prominent southern leaders stayed within the Democratic Party. After the election, the Dixiecrat movement evaporated. The South's vocal dissent in 1948, however, forecast the sectional unrest of the following decades, weakened the region's loyalty to the Democratic Party, and prepared the way for future political realignment.

EDWARD F. HAAS
Louisiana State Museum
Tulane University

Richard C. Etheridge, "Mississippi's Role in the Dixiecrat Movement" (Ph.D. dissertation, Mississippi State University, 1971); Kari Frederickson, *The Dixiecrat Revolt and the End of the Solid South, 1932–1968* (2001); Robert A. Garson, *The Democratic Party and the Politics of Sectionalism, 1941–1948* (1974); Gary C. Ness, "The States' Rights Democratic Movement of 1948" (Ph.D. dissertation, Duke University, 1972).

Emancipation

Emancipation troubles southern culture, raising issues that make many, regardless of race, uncomfortable. Emancipation is a story of liberation and loss, of identities gained and identities shattered, a history that places conflict and domination at the center of the region's past. Representing the promise of freedom and equality on one hand and the broken dream of plantation slavery on the other, Emancipation is above all else a shared history of conflict. Yet where does a revolution—one that pitted southerner against southerner—fit in the construction of a common southern identity or a shared southern culture? This dilemma so challenges the South that Emancipation has been quieted and domesticated in the myths of the region.

The dominant white southern parable of Emancipation transforms the moment of freedom from a political act to a personal one. Freedom, according to this story, left African Americans bereft, compelled to return home to their white folks. In *The Unvanquished*, William Faulkner recounted the tales of his youth, writing that those "who had followed the Yankees away . . . [had scattered] into the hills [to] live in caves and hollow trees like animals I suppose, not only with no one to depend on but with no one depending on them, caring whether they returned or not or lived or died or not." Noble white southerners, such as the Sartorises, took African Americans back in, both the faithful Ringo, who had never left, and the unfaithful Loosh, who had walked off declaring, "I going. I done been freed . . . ; I dont belong to John Sartoris now; I belongs to me and God." According to Faulkner and his peers, whether African Americans claimed freedom or not, the end result was the same: former slaves returned to the plantation household.

Our national narrative recognizes the political significance of emancipation, emphasizing that Abraham Lincoln waged a four-year bloody civil war to free the slaves. Yet this story elides the fact that it was not Lincoln, the U.S. military, or the federal government that freed the slaves. The push for emancipation began in the South.

Enslaved black southerners freed themselves during the Civil War, altering the course of the war and the nation. In what historian Steven Hahn writes was "the most sweeping revolution of the 19th century, [slaves] shifted the social and political course of the Atlantic world." Because of their actions, the U.S. Congress adopted the Thirteenth Amendment in 1865, abolishing slavery across the nation. Emancipation, therefore, is largely a southern story defining a region and a people.

At the outset of the Civil War, slaves identified President Abraham Lincoln and the Union army as their allies in the struggle for freedom. Yet the Lincoln administration was a reluctant partner. As Lincoln stated in 1862, "My paramount objective in this struggle is to save the Union and is *not* to either save or destroy slavery. If I could save the Union without freeing any slave I would do it, and if I could save it by freeing all the slaves I would do it; and if I could save it by freeing some and leaving others alone I would also do that. What I do about slavery, and the colored race, I do because I believe it helps to save the Union." Southern institutions, including slavery, would be respected in order to bring the South back into the nation.

As early as May 1861, African Americans declared themselves free by running away and entering Union army camps. Throughout the antebellum era, slaves kept informed about national politics. Using their positions as domestic servants, artisans, and draymen, black southerners circulated news gathered on and off the plantation. Each time the conflict over slavery entered the national debate, African Americans took notice and crafted an image of the North as a place of salvation. The Civil War brought the North into the South. The land of liberty suddenly lay within reach. As the Union army invaded Virginia, South Carolina, and the Mississippi River valley, slaves stood ready to run for freedom.

The first African Americans who ran for Union lines were similar to those who ran away before the war. They were young adults (predominately men) without children. Making policy as they waged war, Union generals responded to the freedpeople's exodus in a number of ways. General John C. Frémont simply freed every slave who came within his lines. Outraged, Lincoln removed him from his command. General Benjamin Butler decided to keep former slaves within his lines not as free people but as "the contraband of war." Slaves, he reasoned, were valuable property—instruments of war—that could be used to assist either the Confederacy or the Union. From Butler's perspective it was better to have slaves serve the Union than the enemy. As word spread that Butler permitted the black southerners to stay and work within his lines, hundreds of slaves began to make their way to Union lines across the South. In August 1861 the U.S. Congress responded by passing the First Confiscation Act, which declared that those black southerners employed directly by the Confederate military could be held as "contraband." All others should be returned to their masters. Refusing to mark such distinctions, slaves began to travel into Union lines in great numbers, with women and children joining the men. They liberated themselves. Slowly, Congress reacted, passing the Second Confiscation Act in July 1862, stating that all slaves held in rebel territory could be legally seized by the Union. Eventually over 400,000 slaves freed themselves by walking into

Union lines. Laying claim to their bodies and to the right of self-determination, they denied slaveholders' rights of mastery. Subsequently, on 1 January 1863, the Emancipation Proclamation freed slaves held in the Confederacy.

For every African American who left the plantation, hundreds remained behind. One did not have to run away to claim liberty. Freedom could be won at home. In what W. E. B. Du Bois named "the General Strike," many African Americans on the plantations refused to work efficiently for the slaveholders while others refused to work for masters at all. Instead, African Americans stayed at home and went to work for themselves.

African Americans claimed freedom as southerners. Liberty, for most, rested on family, land, and the crop because each promised a kind of self-sufficiency and independence from outsiders. Black and white southerners shared these values, and this fact brought them into direct conflict.

Many, but not all, white southerners refused to share public space or political power with black southerners. Viewing emancipation as a zero-sum game, planters felt that their freedom would be sacrificed if African Americans became fully free. Many whites would not acknowledge African American claims because the land, family, and the crop (not to mention the political and civil rights that went with them) were integral to white identity and power. To grant African Americans rights threatened an erasure of white manhood.

Emancipation exposed the fiction of white men's independence. Planter men found themselves "dependent" on free labor, "dependent" on their women for financial support, and, in the case of the wounded, literally "dependent" on others for mobility. More profoundly, as black southerners took up arms and asserted their claims, they challenged what the white man saw as *his* household—*his* land, *his* crops, and *his* workers. As plantation slavery dissolved, mastery, whiteness, and manhood all lost their mooring.

White southerners fought back, limiting black southerners' access to voting rights, civil rights, the public sphere, and freedom from fear. Each limitation took a toll on the public remembrance of Emancipation. Immediately following the war and up to the turn of the century, black southerners celebrated Emancipation Day with parades and speeches, retelling the story of how they won their freedom. As each southern state imposed segregation (and turned a blind eye to lynching), violence disrupted and finally stopped these celebrations across much of the South. States filled the silence created in the absence of Emancipation Day ceremonies with newly minted histories that defamed Reconstruction, credited the Yankees with Emancipation, and depicted black southerners as either bestial or childlike. Black southerners—Carter Woodson, Pauli Murray, Susie King Taylor, and Anna Julia Cooper, to name just a few—

responded with histories of their own. The history of Emancipation became a segregated history and, in many ways, it still is. The history of Emancipation tends to be written either as an African American freedom struggle (the study of "Emancipation" and "Reconstruction") or as the study of whites' loss, mourning, and nostalgia for an invented past (the study of "the Lost Cause").

Yet Emancipation is a shared history, one that reminds us of how brutal, contested, and revolutionary that sharing has been. If southern culture emphasizes stasis, tradition, and a common identity, then Emancipation represents its opposite—the struggle between white and black, slave and free, rights and privilege. Emancipation disturbs southern myth by exposing the fact that each of these histories is dependent on the others. Far from being opposed, southern culture and Emancipation are contingent upon one another. Southern culture, in large part, is the act of forgetting Emancipation and its implications. Manners, congeniality, and honor work to paper over conflict and to refuse to speak of southerners' unpleasantness to southerners. Emancipation, therefore, is an unspoken referent, a hidden heart, of southern culture.

NANCY BERCAW
University of Mississippi

David W. Blight, *Race and Reunion: The Civil War in American Memory* (2001); Elsa Barkley Brown, in *The Black Public Sphere: A Public Culture Book* (1995); W. E. B. Du Bois, *Black Reconstruction in America: An Essay toward a History of the Part Which Black Folk Played in the Attempt to Reconstruct Democracy in America, 1860–1880* (1935); Laura F. Edwards, *Gendered Strife and Confusion: The Political Culture of Reconstruction* (1997); Barbara Jeanne Fields, *Slavery and Freedom on the Middle Ground: Maryland during the Nineteenth Century* (1985); Eric Foner, *Nothing but Freedom: Emancipation and Its Legacy* (1983), *Reconstruction: America's Unfinished Revolution, 1863–1877* (1988); Joseph T. Glatthaar, *Forged in Battle: The Civil War Alliance of Black Soldiers and White Officers* (1990); Thavolia Glymph and John J. Kushma, eds., *Essays on the Postbellum Southern Economy* (1985); Steven Hahn, *A Nation under Our Feet: Black Political Struggles in the Rural South from Slavery to the Great Migration* (2003); Mitchell A. Kachun, *Festivals of Freedom: Memory and Meaning in African American Emancipation Celebrations, 1808–1915* (2003); Clarence Mohr, *On the Threshold of Freedom: Masters and Slaves in Civil War Georgia* (1986); James L. Roark, *Masters without Slaves: Southern Planters in the Civil War and Reconstruction* (1977); Armstead L. Robinson, *Bitter Fruits of Bondage: The Demise of Slavery and the Collapse of the Confederacy, 1861–1865* (2005); Leslie A. Schwalm, *A Hard Fight for We: Women's Transition from Slavery to Freedom in South Carolina* (1997).

Foreign Policy

The southern experience in world affairs reflects variations on a set of ideas common to much of the American experience. Southerners have identified with internationalism especially through multilateral organizations focused on European matters and Anglo-American cooperation. Southerners also have shown signs of isolationism: a "nonentangling" outlook usually aimed at Europe and Britain but sometimes at Latin America, Africa, or the Pacific. Finally, a strong strain of expansionism persisted through much of the South's antebellum as well as postbellum experience. This belief in the justice of southerners' increasing their influence over foreign places has often appeared in conjunction with territorial growth and colonialism but, in other instances, it has surfaced in a nonterritorial form—expansion for trade and investment as well as for religious reasons. A review of the major episodes of the South's history in world affairs reveals internationalism, isolationism, and expansionism at work in particularly southern ways, that is, until the late 20th and early 21st centuries, and places the South's experience in world affairs within the broader context of ideals and self-interest in American history.

Like most American viewpoints, southern ideas about the world began with the activism and assertiveness spawned by the Renaissance, Reformation, and Enlightenment. Through these movements Western people increasingly perceived the improvement of their condition on earth as a matter of religious mandate. Although this concept of progress is a well-established part of New England's history, the people of the southern colonies had much the same cultural background and reflected a similar optimism and fervor. Abundant natural resources, removal from the "decadent" Old World, a Puritan zeal even in the predominant Anglican churches, a liberal belief that "property" was a matter of "right" and the key to "individual freedom"—here were cornerstones of a powerful sense of what later would be called "Manifest Destiny" and progressive idealism in the developing culture of the colonial South. Southern colonials also responded to less idealistic forces. An unending frontier and brutal Indian fighting, plus more fighting and diplomatic intrigue against Spanish and French colonials, were all part of the unavoidable realities of living in a Western society and competing for empire in the new world. Because of these experiences, Anglos in the southern colonies developed a high tolerance for violence (though they rarely enjoyed, much less excelled at, soldiering) and became effective in pursuit of economic and political self-interest. By the end of the colonial era, two key ingredients of the South's future foreign policy outlook had begun to surface: a faith in its mission (idealism) and a pursuit of realpolitik (materialism and self-interest).

During the American Revolution and the early national period, most views articulated in the South reflected these two strains of expansionism in equal, balanced proportions. A powerful array of southern expansionists—George Washington, Thomas Jefferson, James Madison, James Monroe, and Henry Clay—helped guide the nation through the first and second wars with Britain and onto a course of continental and foreign expansionism seen in the acquisition of Louisiana, Florida, and Missouri and also in the development of the Monroe Doctrine. The vast majority of southerners thrived in the mainstream of Jeffersonian expansionism. Sensitive to what soon would jell as "the southern interests," that is, slavery and export economics, a subsidiary group of southern congressmen dissented, however, from the goal of a neighborly reciprocity with Latin America. This sectional self-interest would soon broaden and carry considerable weight.

Indeed, the transition from the Jeffersonian to the Jacksonian era brought major changes. Those southerners uninvolved with slavery continued to reflect the old balance of ideals and self-interest. Some slave owners did, too, but for the other Jacksonian planters, ideals quickly became subordinate to self-interest as abolitionists began to attack their "peculiar" labor institution. When the West realigned with the Northeast on the tariff issue, the already defensive planters became even more fearful. A new congressional alliance might ban slavery from the territories and weaken the South's role in national affairs. Thus, in the three decades before the Civil War many planters who feared social and economic ruin showed little enthusiasm for the mission of expansionism. With a steely, defensive tone, they advocated territorial growth for their own sectional self-interest. If President James K. Polk was chiefly a commercialist with national goals, he still made good use of the South's practical and materialistic political focus—as well as the missionary idealism among other elements of the South—as he maneuvered the nation through its final transcontinental thrust to the Pacific. Ironically, the planters' realpolitik was a far less effective force in the policy when it was channeled by its own sectional leaders. The southern dream of a Caribbean empire remained just that, a dream. And when secession and war finally came, the southern strategy of a supposedly hard-nosed realpolitik lacked the deft diplomacy to translate this approach into the foreign negotiations essential to a Confederate victory.

After the Civil War, embittered by defeat at the hands of what they understood to be an imperialistic Northeast, many white southerners who once had been expansionists took antiexpansionist stances regarding much of the northeastern-controlled U.S. foreign policy. Southern views of the late 19th century reflected misgivings about American expansion into Hawaii, Cuba,

Puerto Rico, and the Philippines. Still, by 1898 most southerners ultimately surrendered to the patriotism generated by the action against Spain, showing cautious interest in the anticipated opening of Caribbean and Pacific markets. Yet they still talked incessantly about the pain and dislocation a similar surge of Yankee imperialism had brought to their own region just half a century earlier and characterized that type of expansionism as contrary to key American principles of self-determination and autonomy. They also focused on contemporary problems spawned by the new foreign expansionism: the annexation of non-whites could cause further conflict in already strained race relations. Over half the southern senators voted with the anti-imperialist opposition to the Treaty of Paris. In short, more than party politics was involved. Isolationism—generated out of anti-imperialist principles and racism—grew to consensus in the postbellum period. Such a tormented reversal made certain southerners appear ambivalent, and many downright insular, as they reacted to America's rise to world power.

Yet a small, vocal, and powerful group within the emerging middle class showed signs of being anything but isolationists. To publicists such as Alabama politicians John Tyler Morgan and Joseph H. Wheeler, both acclaimed veterans of the Confederacy, the American mission of the late 19th century remained as justified as it had been in the days of Jefferson. But these two also represented some key differences. Morgan worried that a growing national expansionism would create a burgeoning U.S. government and military, which, unchecked, could turn on "southern autonomy" interests—the South's various components of sectional uniqueness—much as it had between 1860 and 1865. Wheeler, by contrast, after rekindling his old friendship with the greatest of all Yankee entrepreneurs, J. P. Morgan, showed little concern about northeasterners gaining control over the Philippines as well as Birmingham, Ala., and waxed eloquent about a northeastern-controlled national government and economy being not only good for foreign policy but a key to southern modernization. Still, on racial objections to world power they were together, blithely responding that the problem could be solved with segregation. With ideals and self-interest harmonized in classic Gilded Age liberalism, these "new southerners" would simply export the emerging institutions of their own region.

In the 20th century, Wheeler's, not Morgan's, views on national government and foreign expansionism gradually prevailed as the dominant view of the South. The ascendancy of Woodrow Wilson spurred southern expansionism to rapid and full recovery. Many white southerners, even some of the lower classes, perceived President Wilson's crusade for a moral and legal world order receptive to American influence as clear indication of "the return of the South" to international prominence. In fact, with the exception of a few isolated cases like Mississippi's James K. Vardaman, southerners identified with Wilson's notion of international order as something brought back to life from the presidency of another great southerner, Thomas Jefferson. That historical connection had serious flaws. Although born a southerner, Wilson derived his internationalism primarily from experiences with idealistic liberals of the Northeast, some with abolitionist roots and most with far less pragmatism than the sage of Monticello. Yet as Civil War memories dimmed and sectional reconciliation offered industry and profits as well as psychological security, southerners grasped at Wilsonian internationalism as "a southern idea" reunited with American patriotism. Southern Wilsonians actually were motivated as much by the practicalities of New South economics and politics as by a renewed enthusiasm for the American mission. Still, they followed Wilson straight through the crusade of World War I and then down his unpragmatic approach to the League of Nations.

The ironic and contradictory outlook—balanced, Jeffersonian expansionism advanced through the medium of relatively strong idealism—did not die with Wilson. During the 1920s and 1930s, the League of Nations Association and the Carnegie Endowment for International Peace, two organizational bridges between the Wilsonianism of World Wars I and II, recruited far more effectively in the South than in any areas beyond a few urban centers in the Northeast where they were based. Indeed, between the wars, southern voices dissenting from Wilson's internationalism were uniquely few. And when war reopened in Europe in 1939, a regional arm of the Carnegie Endowment, the Southern Council on International Relations, worked to convert this regional sentiment into political support for President Franklin D. Roosevelt's developing war policies. After the war, Southern Council members and other southerners urged acting on the second chance at realizing the dream of Wilsonian internationalism—the United Nations. Nevertheless, in the early 1950s, shortly after the creation of the UN, most southerners turned against the organization because it seemed ineffective in achieving the Wilsonian goal of blocking the growth of socialist and communist power. They also feared Joseph McCarthy's attacks on supporters of organized internationalism. Such a waning interest in internationalism did not place southern leaders at odds with others associated with the general goals of Wilsonianism; on the contrary, it brought them closer together. The Cold War caused most Americans once committed to internationalism to move to the right and to espouse American rescue of the world through collective security agreements, economic expansionism, and interventionism. Considering this trend, the South's interventionist sentiment in the Korean War and in the initial stages of the Vietnam War appeared synchronized to late 20th-century American expansionism.

Other than a few antiexpansionist mavericks like Florida's Claude Pepper, there have been only two major exceptions in this recent harmony between southern and national attitudes. In the 1950s and 1960s, Richard B. Russell of Georgia and many other southern leaders balked at sending economic aid to the nonwhites of Africa, Latin America, and the Mideast, whereas many expansionists and the few enduring internationalists from other sections generally supported these measures. Southerners feared that competing low-technology products might be developed in these lands with the assistance of American funds. More important, southerners exhibited a racial reaction to nonwhites that was triggered by the civil rights movement at home. In some ways this attitude resembled the isolationism reflected by southerners in the years following the Civil War; in other ways, momentarily setting aside modern racial sensitivities, it bore out Senator Morgan's concern about foreign policy creating a powerful U.S. government that then attacked "southern autonomy." On the other hand, just as stabilization of southern internal affairs gradually eased southern insecurities after the turn of the century and resulted in a new interest in expansionism, so did the slackening of the civil rights movement a century later contribute to increased southern political support for numerous foreign aid projects.

At roughly the same time, the late 1960s and early 1970s, another peculiarly southern attitude emerged. At this time certain high profile southerners in Washington—and the majority of their constituencies—followed Mississippi's James Eastland in opposing withdrawal of American troops from Vietnam long after most other Americans had accepted the limits of interventionism. At least as early as World War I, southerners had seemed excited about formal military activity abroad because of investments and jobs it provided within the generally poor southern population: economic opportunities in home-front war industries and military bases, plus "jobs" abroad through actual military service. These same considerations, coupled no doubt with the southerners' relatively high tolerance for violence and strong anticommunist sentiments, encouraged what was characterized as a prolonged southern militarism in the Vietnam episode. In time, this attitude, too, gave way to internal forces, taking down with it the presidency of Texan Lyndon Johnson.

As increased black voting power raised issues of human rights in southern politics and elevated Andrew Young and other advocates of economic aid to national prominence, the interventionist strain of southern expansionism lost out. Simultaneously, the economic development of the Sunbelt created more jobs and a slightly larger middle class of whites and blacks. These upwardly mobile businessmen and professionals lived off corporate profits and often looked to reports from the local chapter of the Council on Foreign Relations for appropriate responses to world problems. They advocated whatever moderation in American policy was necessary for American capitalism to reverse its energy shortages and trade imbalances and to establish more influential relations with developing nations.

Finally, out of this moderated expansionist consensus, in which ideals were increasingly harmonized with self-interest, there emerged Georgia's Jimmy Carter. President Carter's approach to foreign policy has been criticized for its lack of cohesiveness, its case-by-case "engineer's approach" to world problems in need of consistent U.S. policy, and a poorly planned intrusion in Iran. Yet Carter's advocacy of expanded American trade was complemented by an equal emphasis on human rights, reduction of nuclear arms, and other progressive internationalist goals. If this policy reflected little that was uniquely southern, more often than not it was attuned to the influence the United States might expect to have in a given area of the world, especially Africa, where Carter benefited from the advice of his close friend from Georgia, Andrew Young. Moreover, U.S. policy did indeed appear effective with the Camp David Talks aimed at peace in the Middle East. Still, frustrated near the end of his term, Carter gravitated toward a post–World War II bipolarity, a military buildup against the Soviet Union, as his chief foreign policy agenda. With the demise of the internal issue of race, the southerner in the White House did not look as much like the southern as the *American* cold warrior.

Ultimately, under two distinctly nonsouthern presidents, Ronald Reagan and George H. W. Bush, a strong extension of Carter's focus on the Soviet Union figured into the demise of its empire and the end of most strains of the Cold War. Yet this did not mean an end to complexity in foreign policy; quite the contrary. With another southerner in the White House, the former Arkansas governor William Jefferson Clinton, U.S. policy focused on encouragement of democracy abroad, with less emphasis on human rights and more on the "enlargement" of U.S. access to foreign markets. Despite his accent, Clinton seemed quite the American centrist who benefited from a strong economy at home while remaining relatively unsuccessful on foreign policy matters except those influenced by America's "hot" economy. When the former Texas governor George W. Bush succeeded Clinton, here was a third recent southerner in the White House who had little foreign policy experience. Tragically, Bush would gain that experience almost overnight as foreign-based terrorists launched devastating attacks on New York City and Washington, D.C.

Hence in the nation's first 150 years, southerners increasingly showed relatively unique southern ideas in foreign policy and delivered certain well-experienced foreign policy leaders to deciding junctures in American history. In the late 20th century and early 21st century, however, the demise of a uniquely "southern way of life" with regard to race and economics (if not football, music, and food) produced a southern foreign policy sentiment more harmonious with the rest of America's. From another perspective, in the minds of most educated Americans and certainly many historians, Woodrow Wilson provided the substantial ideological foundation of the predominant foreign policy sentiment of the 20th-century South. Actually, however, the viewpoint that helped most recent southerners reclaim at least some of their once-powerful role in world affairs was not so much Wilsonian internationalism but, rather, the more basic Jeffersonian approach, that of harnessing ideals to self-interest (minus the earlier agrarian/racial rhetoric) to pragmatically achieve national influence abroad. In the early 21st century, it was this less sectionally distinctive, but more confident, cultural prism that most southerners looked through as they focused on the world.

TENNANT S. MCWILLIAMS
University of Alabama at Birmingham

Henry Blumenthal, *Journal of Southern History* (May 1966); Alexander DeConde, *Journal of Southern History* (August 1958); Joseph A. Fry, *Dixie Looks Abroad: The South and U.S. Foreign Relations, 1789–1973* (2002); George L. Grassmuck, *Sectional Biases in Congress on Foreign Policy* (1951); Alfred O. Hero Jr., *The Southerner and World Affairs* (1965); Charles O. Lerche Jr., *The Uncertain South: Its Changing Patterns of Politics in Foreign Policy* (1964); Tennant S. McWilliams, *The New South Faces the World: Foreign Affairs and the Southern Sense of Self, 1877–1950* (1988); Robert E. Osgood, *Ideals and Self-Interest in American Foreign Relations* (1953); Paul Seabury, *The Waning of Southern "Internationalism"* (1957).

Government Administration

Government administration in the South has traditionally been considered less professional, less vigorous, less accountable, and more affected by personalized political influences than administration in other regions. To a considerable extent, this distinctiveness can be attributed to southern governments' having typically had a much smaller revenue base on which to finance public programs. The administrative establishment had fewer employees per capita, salaries were lower, merit systems were less feasible, and professionalism and administrative effectiveness were less developed. However, much of what has been distinctive about southern government administration is not a simple result of the traditionally low level of personal wealth in the South. The special character of partisan and interest-group politics also influences the quality and nature of administration. Consequently, southern government administration may continue to be somewhat distinctive even as the region catches up with the rest of the nation economically.

Perhaps the most important actor in southern government administration is the governor. There is something paradoxical about the way this office has been viewed by political and historical observers. V. O. Key Jr. classified most southern states as "loose factional systems," because they were characterized by an "issueless politics" and an inability to "carry out sustained programs of action." The absence of a viable, well-defined system of party competition created a situation in which political power was not effectively tied to partisan forces. Thus, southern governors have not normally been required to enforce party platforms or to follow party preferences in administrative appointments. Instead, they have often had considerable personal control over government jobs, roads, purchasing, and local public improvements. In short, southern governors have traditionally possessed notorious personal power, making them highly unpredictable and yet, in the absence of a cohesive party organization and effective party competition, weak in terms of policy effectiveness.

The institutional weakness of southern governors was historically reflected in (1) their lack of exclusive responsibility for budget development, (2) their relatively restricted appointment powers, and (3) their inability in many southern states to succeed themselves. In addition to the weakness of the gubernatorial office, the formal administrative procedures of southern state agencies have not traditionally been subject to the kind of "judicialization" accomplished long ago on the federal level and in most other states. Administrative hearing and rule-making procedures were subject to fewer procedural requirements, raising questions about the thoroughness and accountability of such activity. Government administration in southern states, as a result of all these factors, was often fragmented, personalized, and unprofessional when compared with that in nonsouthern states.

The interest-group situation in the South has been rather ambiguous. Some researchers have concluded that organized groups were effectively unopposed by countervailing interests, suggesting that interest groups have been more powerful in the South than elsewhere. Others, most notably Mancur Olson Jr., argue that the historically brief period of stable industrialization in the South has prevented the development of groups devoted to collective action. Labor unions, for example, remain less numerous and less powerful in the South than elsewhere. One can, therefore, construct and support arguments suggesting that the South is characterized by "strong" or "weak" interest groups, depending upon one's interpretations.

Actually, either view lends support to the idea that southern politics has not been characterized by persistent, institutionalized conflict among well-established interest organizations to the same degree as are the politics of non-southern states. Government administration was more particularized, less "open," because interest groups did not appeal to broad interests any better than do the fragmented, one-party political machines. A professional, cohesive, merit-oriented bureaucracy is, in part, a response to the kind of effective, broad-based patterns of political influence that traditionally have not characterized the South. Ironically, such influences should be less developed both in states with weak interest groups and in those with organized interests not effectively opposed by others.

Much of what has been distinctive about government administration in the South is rapidly disappearing. Southern governors are becoming more powerful. Since 1986 all southern states have established four-year terms for their governors, and all but one, Virginia, allow governors to serve more than one term. According to a recent study on state party organization, "regional differences in organizational strength have declined . . . as the Republicans in the South developed modern party organizations and the Southern Democrats were forced to follow." As industrialization in the South completes its "catching up" process, the interest-group climate should become like that in other states as well. Personality in southern politics and government is so well established a factor, though, it will likely endure for some time to come.

MARCUS ETHRIDGE
University of Wisconsin at Milwaukee

Council of State Governments, *The Book of the States* (2006); Virginia Gray, Herbert Jacob, and Kenneth Vines, eds., *Politics in the American States: A Comparative Analysis* (1983); V. O. Key Jr., *Southern Politics in State and Nation* (1949); Alexander P. Lamis, ed., *Southern Politics in the 1990s* (1998); Sarah Morehouse, *State Politics, Parties, and Policy* (1981); Laurence W. Moreland, Tod A. Baker, and Robert P. Steed, eds., *Contemporary Southern Political Attitudes and Behavior: Studies and Essays* (1982); Terrel L. Rhodes, *Republicans in the South: Voting for the State House, Voting for the White House* (2000); Ira Sharkansky, *The Maligned States: Policy Accomplishments, Problems, and Opportunities*, 2nd ed. (1978); Kevin B. Smith, ed., *State and Local Government, 2007* (2007).

Ideology, Political

American political ideology is celebrated in the catchwords of our everyday life—"freedom," "democracy," and "equality." The political culture of the United States includes both the noble ideas of the founding documents, the Declaration of Independence and the Constitution (particularly the first 10 amendments), and the reality of conflict among citizens based on race, ethnicity, class, and region. The development of a distinctive southern political ideology was part of this broader culture. At times in open conflict with theoretical national sentiments, it was based on regional conflict with the North and eventually overrode the subcultures and bands of dissenters within the region.

A distinctive southern political ideology was elusive in the colonial South. The foundations of a system of belief different from that of the nation were there in the beginnings of the plantation system and large-scale black slavery, but the lack of any generalized American nationalism meant no southern regionalism existed either. The years from the Declaration of Independence (1776) to the Missouri controversy (1819–20) were a transitional period in the history of southern political ideology. The South participated fully in the creation of the American system of government and in the political ideals of the new nation. Its greatest leaders—Washington, Jefferson, and Madison—were from southern states, with Jefferson remaining the central figure of American political democracy. But sectionalism lurked everywhere, and the requisite compromises of the 1789 Constitution, particularly those concerning slavery and centralization versus state powers, reflected the South's emerging political differences. Nevertheless, the transitional years left no record of blatant assertion of southern difference or serious calls for a southern polity.

The Missouri controversy was a landmark in the growth of a southern political ideology. The debate gathered up all the bundles of an emerging sectionalism—the division of power between North and South, slavery, the pattern of the growing national economy, and more significantly, the meaning of American democracy and its values, however compromised they were by intergroup conflict. The debate impelled southerners to define their political views in relationship to the North and to articulate their separate political culture. By the 1830s and 1840s, events such as the nullification crisis, the growth of antislavery movements, and the Mexican War overwhelmingly channeled sectional political differences into the single stream of the slavery question. In its defense of slavery, the South slid into a political orthodoxy and social conservatism that adjusted the political and social reform movements of the first half of the 19th century to a southern standard. The South's greatest politician of this period, John C. Calhoun, defended southern political differences. Calhoun created a political ideology that attacked democratic values and accepted class- and race-stratified authoritarianism—an ideology that was more distinctive and more at variance with that of the Founding Fathers than any other major American political philosophy of the time.

Recently scholars have shown the importance of paternalism to southern ideology. Defenders of slavery believed that southern society was a hierarchical one, marked by accepted obligations and responsibilities on the part of everyone from the slave to the planter. Eugene D. Genovese has even argued that the personal relationships inherent in paternalism worked against "solidarity among the oppressed by linking them as individuals to their oppressors." The concept of personal honor became closely tied to paternalism as a guiding concept of the antebellum elite.

During the crucial years of the 1850s and 1860s, the southern political ideal of orthodoxy and conservatism transformed itself into the radical concept of separate southern nationalism; only the massive defeat of the Confederacy killed the dream. The Old South's political ideals did not wither away in the bitterness of conflict and defeat. Instead, the modern political South was born, and the struggle of Reconstruction only confirmed its distinctive political ideology built around a tense amalgam of rugged, freewill individualism, states' rightism, white supremacy, social conservatism, paternalistic class divisions, and political loyalties to systems that protected these principles.

The values of a white, male-dominated democracy (herrenvolk democracy) and the master-race cultural views of southern planters persisted after the Civil War. The emerging capitalist entrepreneurs in the New South's commerce and industry seemed more captive to this political ideology than such figures elsewhere in the nation, and a distinctive form of conservative politics emerged. It favored a rural county elite ideology that was frankly class-centered in the paternalistic ways of the plantation and the cotton mill. As Numan Bartley wrote: "The transfer of political leadership from plantation-oriented county-seat elites to business-oriented metropolitan elites was a long, complex, and divisive process."

After Reconstruction, political change came slowly to the South. The ideology of orthodoxy and conservatism weathered the Populist challenge and the subsequent Progressive movement. Southern politicians overwhelmingly supported the Democratic Party and used their power to protect all things southern. But the interwar years of the 1920s and 1930s created visible cracks in the foundation of the southern system, and widespread economic changes after the 1940s and 1950s remade southern politics. The civil rights revolution, the impact of a postwar American culture of television, shopping malls, big cities, and major league sports, and the national acceptance of southern music suggested that the Americanization of Dixie had occurred. The result was that southern political ideology began to look suspiciously American. As elsewhere, groups divided or came together on the basis of race, income level, lifestyle, occupation, place of residence, education, and various transient issues. Southerners now gave ardent homage to all the value words of the American political tradition. By the 1980s, journeys to the southern political land revealed fewer exotic, strange, or even different phenomena than earlier. National polling data suggested the South in the 1980s remained the nation's most conservative region on great and small economic and social questions, but its controlling ideologies found ready allies all over the country. At least in terms of political ideology, it no longer appeared to be the "nation within a nation" that V. O. Key described late in the 1940s.

The 1990s were polarizing along liberal-conservative lines. The Republican Party's southern strategy since the 1970s worked to separate conservatives from the Democratic Party, using veiled racist appeals in some cases but increasingly making broader, ideological appeals on cultural and economic issues. Ronald Reagan's fiscal conservatism, anti–big government message, and attraction to the Religious Right made a new Republican Party base in the South. Newt Gingrich's Contract with America in 1994 conveyed a precise, ideological agenda that contributed to the sweeping Republican Party victory that year. President Bill Clinton was a southern Democratic moderate, but his policy proposals on national health care enabled Republicans to paint his administration as liberal—at least in his first term. Since the 1960s, southern Democrats have been painted as the party of liberalism by conservative Republicans because of national Democratic Party positions. Studies suggest southern Republicans are much more ideologically cohesive than southern Democrats, whose black constituents tend to be more assertive of the role of the national government and of social reform proposals than southern whites.

JAMES A. HODGES
College of Wooster

Joseph A. Aistrup, *The Southern Strategy Revisited: Republican Top-Down Advancement in the South* (1996); Numan Bartley, *The Creation of Modern Georgia* (1983), *Reviews in American History* (December 1982), with Hugh Davis Graham, *Southern Politics and the Second Reconstruction* (1975); John Bass and Walter DeVries, *The Transformation of Southern Politics: Social Change and Political Consequence since 1945* (1976); Dwight B. Billings, *Planters and the Making of a "New South": Class, Politics, and Development in North Carolina, 1865–1900* (1979); Charles Bullock III and Mark J. Rozell, eds., *The New Politics of the Old South: An Introduction to Southern Politics* (1998); W. J. Cash, *The Mind of the South* (1941); Eugene D. Genovese, *The Political Economy of Slavery: Studies in the Economy and Society of the Slave South* (1965); Dewey Grantham, *The Democratic South* (1963); V. O. Key Jr., *Southern Politics in State and Nation* (1949); Alexander P. Lamis, ed., *Southern Politics in the 1990s* (1999); John McCardell, *The Idea of a Southern Nation: Southern Nationalists and Southern Nationalism, 1830–1860* (1979); John Shelton Reed, *The Enduring South: Subcultural Persistence in Mass Society* (1972); Jonathan M. Weiner, *Social Origins of the New South: Alabama, 1860–1855* (1978); Bertram Wyatt-Brown, *Southern Honor: Ethics and Behavior in the Old South* (1982).

Immigration Policy and Politics

As the 21st century begins, the United States has become an immigrant destination once again. In 2005, according to U.S. Census statistics, the immigrant population of the nation—legal and illegal—stood at 35.2 million people, or about 12 percent of the total U.S. population of 300 million. In 1910 immigrants made up about 15 percent of the nation's population, but the current immigrant proportion represents a dramatic increase compared to immigration patterns over most of the 20th century.

Latino immigrants from Mexico and Central America comprise the largest group among the new immigrants. As a result of this new immigration, some 42.7 million Hispanics, including illegal immigrants, resided in the United States in 2005, and the number was growing by 3.6 percent a year. By comparison, overall U.S. population has been increasing at about 1 percent per year. Just two years earlier, in 2003, Hispanics first surpassed African Americans as the nation's largest minority. Large numbers of new immigrants, some 11 to 12 million at the end of 2005, are illegal, and 80 percent of them are Latinos from Mexico and Central America. During the 1990s about half a million illegal immigrants arrived annually, but that number spiked after 2000. Between 2000 and 2005 some 7.9 million immigrants—legal and illegal—entered the United States, making this the highest five-year period of immigration in American history.

The American South has attracted large numbers of Latino newcomers. Some 65 percent of the Latino population currently resides in just four states— California, Texas, Florida, and New York. Texas and Florida have long had high proportions of Hispanics—35.5 percent and 19.6 percent, respectively, in 2005. However, a rising percentage of Hispanics have settled in other southern states. From Georgia to North Carolina, and from Arkansas to Alabama, Hispanic

TABLE 1. *Hispanic Population Increase, 1990–2005, Twelve Southern States*

State	1990 Census	2005 Estimates	Increase	% Increase	% of Total Population
North Carolina	76,745	533,087	456,342	594.6	6.3
Arkansas	19,876	126,932	107,056	538.6	4.7
Georgia	108,933	625,028	516,095	473.8	7.1
Tennessee	32,742	172,704	139,962	427.5	3.0
South Carolina	30,500	135,041	104,541	342.8	3.3
Alabama	24,629	99,040	74,411	302.1	2.2
Kentucky	22,005	69,702	47,697	216.8	1.7
Virginia	160,403	438,789	278,386	173.5	6.0
Mississippi	15,998	43,275	27,277	170.5	1.5
Florida	1,574,148	3,414,414	1,840,266	117.0	19.6
Texas	4,339,874	7,903,079	3,563,205	82.1	35.5
Louisiana	93,067	123,066	29,999	32.2	2.8
Total	6,498,920	13,684,157	7,185,237	110.6	4.6

Sources: U.S. Census, 1990; U.S. Census estimates, 2005.

Note: States are ranked by percentage of Hispanic growth, 1990–2005.

population rocketed upward during the 1990s and the first decade of the new century. According to the 2005 U.S. Census estimates, the Latino population of southern states included, for example, 43,000 in Mississippi, 439,000 in Virginia, 533,000 in North Carolina, and 625,000 in Georgia (see Table 1). Southern metropolitan areas—Atlanta, Memphis, Nashville, Charlotte, Charleston, Birmingham, Raleigh-Durham, and the Virginia portion of the Washington, D.C., metro—all have large and rapidly growing Hispanic populations. Because of acknowledged census undercounts, the actual numbers are likely much higher. But whether census statistics or the higher estimates offered by local experts are accepted, one pattern is evident: major demographic and cultural transformations have been taking place all across the South.

Jobs and economic opportunity have provided the magnetic pull attracting Latino workers to the southern states. In small towns in northern Alabama, Hispanics labor in poultry processing, agricultural work, and hosiery, garment, textile, furniture, and plastic manufacturing. In Atlanta, Charlotte, Birmingham, and other metro areas, they work in landscaping, roofing, construction, restaurant, janitorial, and service jobs. In Dalton, Ga., the self-proclaimed "Carpet Capital of the World," more than 20,000 Hispanics make up the majority of the labor force in the area's 120 carpet factories. In small fishing villages along the North Carolina coast, hundreds of Mexican women with special H-2B visas have replaced African American women in the seasonal crab processing industry. Throughout the Southeast, farm labor has been transformed in recent decades as Hispanics have replaced blacks and now make up a huge percentage of the farm labor force. In Kentucky, Virginia, and North Carolina, tobacco growers primarily hire Latinos for tobacco farm work. All across the South, fruit and vegetable farms, plant nurseries, timber companies, poultry plants, carpet and textile factories, and construction firms rely heavily on Latino newcomers.

What accounts for the sudden surge of Latino migration to the United States and to the American South? Essentially, these recent demographic and cultural transformations are linked to major changes in American immigration policy and economic policy. First, American immigration policy has had a shaping impact on cross-border labor migration patterns. Throughout the 20th century, Mexican labor migrants moved back and forth across the border in response to employment opportunities in the United States. During the 1920s, for instance, when restrictive congressional legislation dramatically reduced European immigration, Mexican labor migrants found easy access to American jobs in agriculture, manufacturing, and service work, primarily in California and the southwestern states, but also in such cities as Chicago, Detroit, and Minneapolis. With the unemployment crisis of the Great Depression in the 1930s, local governments encouraged or forced the repatriation of some 400,000 Mexican workers to their homeland. During the domestic labor shortage of the World War II years, the federal Bracero Program regularized the temporary recruitment of as many as 4 million Mexican migrant farmworkers annually, mainly in the Southwest. The program officially ended in 1964, but Mexican farmworkers continued their migratory ways, utilizing the job networks established during the Bracero era.

In the mid-1960s the U.S. Congress overhauled American immigration policy. The 1965 Immigration and Nationality Act scrapped the national-origins quota system that had heavily favored the immigration of people from western Europe. The new law opened up immigration from Latin America and Asia. In the distribution of immigrant visas the 1965 law preferred highly educated and skilled newcomers, as well as the relatives of citizens and permanent residents. Conceived in the civil rights era as a policy reform, the 1965 act subsequently opened the door for an unanticipated but massive wave of new legal immigrants, especially from Latin America, the Caribbean, and the entire Pacific Rim.

The door opened for some, but not for others, especially those with little education and few job skills. Needless to say, illegal immigration from south of the border continued, eventually prompting passage in 1986 of the Immigration Reform and Control Act (IRCA). Controversial from the very beginning, the new law powerfully restructured Hispanic migration to the United States, eventually turning the American South into a new immigration destination. IRCA beefed up border controls and supposedly imposed tough new sanctions on employers who willfully hired undocumented immigrants. Under pressure from big agricultural interests and proimmigrant groups, Congress added an amnesty provision to IRCA, granting permanent residency—the famous green card—to about 3 million illegal immigrants, including 2.3 million Mexicans, who could document at least five years of work and residence in the United States.

Those amnestied under IRCA subsequently had full labor rights and the freedom to move within the United States in search of better opportunities. They also gained the right to bring family members from Mexico, potentially as many as 9.2 million additional Mexican migrants. In addition, IRCA policies eventually encouraged amnestied Mexicans and their families to seek citizenship—an outcome speeded up by Mexican legislation in the late 1990s permitting dual U.S.-Mexican citizenship. IRCA's amnesty provisions suggested the contradictions in U.S. immigration policy, seeking to curb illegal Mexican migration while simultaneously granting permanent residency to millions. In addition, the implementation and enforcement of IRCA's provisions were deeply flawed, and employer sanctions were never enforced.

The new Latino migration to the South coincided with IRCA's amnesty provisions. Free to move about the country, amnestied Mexicans in California and the Southwest found new labor markets in the Southeast. Subsequent chain migration, legal and illegal, brought relatives and friends from home communities to new southern destinations.

New border regulation had an impact, as well. The tighter border controls of IRCA and a subsequent program in 1994 called Operation Gatekeeper eventually diverted labor migrants away from traditional destinations such as Texas and California. As a result, Mexican immigration patterns became national rather than regional. The same forces encouraged undocumented workers to stay longer, or even permanently, to avoid the now more difficult border crossings. In short, IRCA had huge unanticipated consequences. In 1986 immigration reform was supposed to solve the illegal immigration problem, but 20 years later, the problem had gotten much bigger and the proposed solutions looked a lot like those implemented in 1986.

Economic policy has had an important impact, as well. Essentially, Hispanic migration is a reflection of global market forces at work—U.S. businesses want low-wage workers to boost profit margins. Facing weak economies at home, Mexican and Central American immigrants are attracted to U.S. jobs that pay wages substantially higher than they could earn at home. These same market forces explained the mass migration of European immigrants to the United States during an earlier period of globalization—the industrial era at the end of the 19th century.

Recent national economic policies have accentuated migration trends. New free-trade policies, such as the 1994 North American Free Trade Agreement (NAFTA), encouraged the migration of capital and labor. A restructuring of regional, national, and global economies undermined older forms of production in the South, such as in agriculture, steel, textiles, and apparel. At the same time, new economic investment poured into the region as American and foreign capital sought cheap labor, new markets, and government incentives. The region's new economy features many foreign-owned auto plants in Alabama, Tennessee, Kentucky, Mississippi, and South Carolina. It also features innumerable food processing plants for poultry, hogs, and seafood, industries that rely on Hispanic workers. In the decade 1995–2005, for instance, about half of all poultry processing in the United States came to be concentrated in four low-wage, antiunion southern states with rising Latino populations—Alabama, Arkansas, Georgia, and North Carolina. The largest hog butchering plant in the world, owned by the Smithfield Packing Company and employing more than 3,000 Hispanic workers, can be found in Tar Heel, N.C. In addition, rapid population growth in southern states and Sunbelt cities has created an immense service economy and a consequent demand for low-wage labor.

NAFTA envisioned an era of economic integration and free trade between the United States, Mexico, and Canada. Its promoters argued that capital investment in Mexico would invigorate its economy and keep Mexican workers at home. Once again there were unanticipated consequences. NAFTA stimulated American capital flows to the maquiladora region along the border, a form of outsourcing and cheap labor for American manufacturers. But the end of tariff protections undermined Mexican manufacturing in other parts of the country, leading to extensive Mexican deindustrialization. Similarly, cheap American food exports badly damaged Mexican agriculture. These consequences, along with the devaluation of the Mexican currency in relation to the dollar, led to high unemployment and even lower wages in Mexico. Not surprisingly, working in the United States seemed a better alternative to still larger numbers of Mexicans.

Globalization has meant the transfer of capital, goods, and jobs across national borders, but the other side of that equation is the movement across the southwestern border of low-wage workers in search of opportunity or economic survival. Capital mobility and labor mobility seem to be inextricably linked. Taken together, then, the globalization of markets and shifting immigration policy—both NAFTA *and* IRCA—stimulated and diversified the migratory flows of Latino labor, with the results we see now in the American South and across the nation.

The convergence of globalization and changing immigration policy has brought a transnational, low-wage, mostly Mexican and Central American labor force to the land of Dixie. This new human migration has produced substantial social, cultural, and demographic change in a region where change has always been slow and received with skepticism, if not hostility. Latino migration has added a new dimension to the black-white racial binary that has characterized southern history. Farms and factories and employers of all kinds now seek out Latino workers for their work ethic, especially their willingness to work long hours for low pay. Nationally and regionally, immigration has stoked concerns about the resulting social and economic costs, while igniting new forms of nativism as well. Issues of job competition, especially for African Americans, remain unresolved. Many southerners are troubled by the large numbers of illegal immigrants among the newcomers and by the sense that immigration is out of control.

The immigration policy disputes raging across the nation since the 1990s have their counterparts in the American South. Big agriculture, poultry and construction companies, and small businesses throughout the region have argued that immigrant labor is essential to do the work that Americans will not do. Southern politicians at every level have complained about lax border controls and ineffective enforcement of IRCA provisions on the hiring of illegal immigrants. At the national level, Congress has debated new immigration legislation, but without result to date. Some Congressmen have promoted amnesty for illegals, or a new guest-worker program; others want to send undocumented immigrants home, build a wall along the southwestern border, or impose other forms of border control. The nation seems evenly divided on these issues, with both Democrats and Republicans divided among themselves as well. President George W. Bush, for example, supported a new guest-worker program, but most Republican politicians disagreed with the proposal.

In the absence of federal action on immigration, cities and states have begun taking matters into their own hands. Some southern governors, such as Alabama's Bob Riley, have used state police to enforce federal immigration statutes.

Many local governments, such as Huntsville, Ala., and Athens, Ga., have enacted local ordinances cracking down on local employers of illegal immigrants. Conflicts over language use, drivers' licenses, homestead exemptions, college tuition, and access to social and medical services divide residents of small towns and big cities across the South. Whatever Congress may eventually legislate, most of the region's new immigrants are here to stay. Anti-immigration fever has infected the politicians and the media pundits. Meanwhile, the immigrant newcomers have been adapting to life in a new land, while also building ethnic communities based on common culture and tradition. The South seems to have embarked on what might become a long-term process of Latinization, duplicating what has already happened in other parts of the United States with other immigrant populations.

RAYMOND A. MOHL
University of Alabama at Birmingham

James C. Cobb and William Stueck, eds., *Globalization and the American South* (2005); Leon Fink, *The Maya of Morganton* (2003); Douglas S. Massey, Jorge Durand, and Nolan J. Malone, eds., *Beyond Smoke and Mirrors: Mexican Immigration in an Era of Economic Integration* (2002); Raymond A. Mohl, *Journal of American Ethnic History* (Summer 2003); Arthur D. Murphy, Colleen Blanchard, and Jennifer A. Hill, eds., *Latino Workers in the Contemporary South* (2001); James L. Peacock and Carrie R. Matthews, eds., *The American South in a Global World* (2005); Victor Zuniga and Ruben Hernandez-Leon, eds., *New Destinations: Mexican Immigration in the United States* (2005).

Jacksonian Democracy

The source of the political division of antebellum America into Jacksonian and Whig parties lay in the expansion of the market economy in the years between the War of 1812 and the Civil War. Acceptance of the values of the marketplace and resistance to those values each implied a conception of the meaning of freedom. For Jacksonians—dedicated to defending the ideal of economic and social self-sufficiency and fearful of being exploited by centers of power in the society—freedom was something the citizenry had by right, although evil, anti-democratic forces were attempting to take it away. People were free when they were dependent on no one else for their livelihood and welfare. Movements and institutions whose success would diminish the existing autonomy of the individual were thus authoritarian and inimical to the American experiment. For Whigs, freedom was not something Americans already had but something for which they perpetually strived. People became free by fulfilling their potential, by becoming all that they could be. The shackles of ignorance and poverty were their greatest enemies; the expansion of knowledge and opportunity were their principal security. Morality and justice required that citizens cooperate in order to build a better social order for all.

These differing definitions of freedom carried with them differing notions of the proper role of government. Whigs sought the enactment of programs intended to break the bonds that they felt held the mass of Americans in economic, social, or moral bondage: governmental aid for the construction of railroads, roads, and canals; protective tariffs; central regulation of the currency supply and the banking system; the establishment of public schools; the prohibition of the sale of liquor; and the creation of hospitals to cure the insane, institutions to train the deaf and blind, and penitentiaries to redeem criminals. Jacksonians generally regarded all such programs as the products of paternalistic elitism. They thought it intolerable that ordinary citizens should be taxed to benefit railroads, factories, and banks; that their private conduct should be regulated; that their children should be forcibly indoctrinated with alien, urban ideals.

The Jacksonians campaigned for the abolition of all property qualifications for voting and office-holding, hoping that a broadened electorate would use the government not to assist the growth of corporations but to restrict and ultimately to destroy them. But beyond such activities, which they considered defensive, Jacksonians sought limited government, states' rights, and strict construction of federal and state constitutions. They viewed their political party as a trade union of the electorate through which ordinary citizens, individually weak, could band together and use their numbers to counterbalance the power of the wealthy. Whigs, on the other hand, were often doubtful that poverty-stricken, ill-educated citizens were capable of appreciating what was actually in their own best interest. Whigs conceived of their party as a sort of religious denomination, an organization of believers seeking to convert and to save the society at large. Though practical political considerations quickly led Whig politicians to abandon their early defense of restrictions on voting and office-holding, they continued to insist upon examinations for admission to such professions as law and medicine—examinations that Jacksonians frequently opposed.

In the Lower South, the origins of Whiggery lay in the use of nullification-ist doctrines to insist upon the right of each state to expel the Indians within its boundaries. The ease with which these nullifiers embraced the broad-constructionist program of the national Whig Party in the late 1830s is an index of the degree to which ideology in the region was an extension of self-interest.

Those merchants and planters who had eagerly sought the opening of Indian lands for speculation and commercial exploitation also eagerly awaited roads, railroads, and the easy credit promised by a national banking system. Although the majority of planters supported the Whigs, planters were not the cutting edge of the party; the intellectual leaders of Whiggery were the urban merchants and factors, whom the planters envied and emulated. The strength of the Jacksonians, in contrast, was usually to be found concentrated in those areas of the region most isolated from large-scale market agriculture.

In the Jacksonian period the attitudes and programs at issue between the parties in the South were essentially the same as those at issue throughout the nation. The expansion of the market economy and its values was a national phenomenon, and the response to it was national, embodying fears and hopes as real in the South as in the North. However, states' views toward one institution—slavery—differed. Slavery was an integral assumption in the ideology of each party. Jacksonians conceived of it protecting communities of self-reliant small farmers from the marketplace; as they saw it, with slaves to supply plantation labor, the white, independent yeomanry could not be converted into a proletariat, subservient to planters and capitalists. Whigs thought slavery a mechanism of social mobility, another of the many happy institutions facilitating the efforts of the industrious to achieve economic success. Both regarded it as essentially American, a bulwark of the freedom and democracy that were the Republic's distinguishing characteristics. Therefore, when proposals to exclude slavery from the western territories gained popularity in the North, both Jacksonians and Whigs in the South concluded that the absence of slavery from the territories would lead to the establishment in them of a hierarchical, un-American society, on the northern model.

Just before the advent of the party period in the early 1830s, Lower South factions that would become Jacksonians and Whigs were united in desiring the expulsion of the Indians—the Jacksonians so that settlers could establish independent farms on the Indians' lands and the Whigs so that the territory could be brought into the expanding American economy. The end of the party period in the mid-1850s found Jacksonians and Whigs throughout most of the region equally united in desiring slavery in the West—the Jacksonians because it would permit the yeomanry to be secure from the exploitation of the rich and the Whigs because it would promote the settlers' material advancement. In the intervening decades, however, the issues dominant on the national scene—banking, tariffs, and aid to internal improvements—revealed the sharply differing conceptions of freedom held by the more upwardly mobile and by those less willing to take risks in both the South and the nation at large. The salience for a time of this set of issues permitted the definition of the two parties in the southern states.

With the collapse of the Whig Party in the 1850s the Democrats lost their social and ideological coherence. A group of ambitious younger Democratic politicians, who generally accepted the label "Young America," began to use aspects of Jacksonianism, especially its devotion to laissez-faire and strict-constructionist doctrines, in ways that defended rather than attacked commercial and industrial interests. Adopted in most instances as well by the leaders of the Republican Party during the 1850s, these ideas became the ideology of America's dominant culture after the Civil War, which has often been called, though misleadingly, "social Darwinism."

Reconstruction in the southern states led to virtually all whites in the region becoming Democrats and had the effect in the late 19th century of depriving the yeoman constituencies—to which southern Jacksonianism had most strongly appealed—of a political party dedicated to defending them from rival sectors of society. And the heretical "social Darwinist" formulation of the Jacksonian creed deprived them, in some measure, of their familiar ideology upon which to ground a protest against their evident marginalization, in the South as elsewhere. The elimination of the public domain, and with it the squatter who had lived upon it, as well as the end of the open range for the grazing of livestock with the passage of fencing laws, left the yeomanry's economic and social position increasingly precarious. Yet important elements of the Jacksonian tradition persisted, particularly in the most isolated, small-farming areas of the South. Its influence is to be seen in the Independent movement of the late 1870s, in the Farmers' Alliance of the 1880s, in the Populist movement of the early and mid-1890s, and, indeed, in the appeals of popular political leaders well into the 20th century.

J. MILLS THORNTON III
University of Michigan, Ann Arbor

J. L. Blau, *Social Theories of Jacksonian Democracy, 1825–1850* (2000); Richard E. Ellis, *The Union at Risk: Jacksonian Democracy, States' Rights, and Nullification Crisis* (1990); Lacy K. Ford Jr., "Social Origins of a New South Carolina: The Upcountry in the Nineteenth Century" (Ph.D. dissertation, University of South Carolina, 1983); Steven Hahn, *The Roots of Southern Populism: Yeoman Farmers and the Transformation of the Georgia Upcountry, 1850–1890* (1983); Lawrence F. Kohl, "The Politics of Individualism: Social Character and Political Parties in the Age of Jackson" (Ph.D. dissertation, University of Michigan, 1980); J. Mills Thornton III, *Politics and Power in a Slave Society: Alabama, 1800–1860* (1978); Harry L. Watson, *Jacksonian Politics* and Community Conflict: The Emergence of the Second American Party System in Cumberland County, North Carolina (1981); Rush Welter, The Mind of America, 1820–1860 (1975).

Jeffersonian Tradition

Thomas Jefferson is invariably linked in the American mind with such concepts as liberty, freedom, and democracy. Indeed, the Jeffersonian tradition, as a general pattern of recognizable beliefs and behavior, provides much of the basis for America's liberal tradition. Through Jefferson, Charles M. Wiltse writes in *The Jeffersonian Tradition in American Democracy* (1960), "the political liberalism of accumulated centuries passed into the American democratic tradition, where it helped to mold the American way of life." To basic liberal tenets Jefferson added his own strain of agrarian thought, which praised the superiority of a self-sufficient, agricultural lifestyle. The independent yeoman farmer became a symbol for American democracy, and the image has persisted, particularly in the South, into the 21st century.

Southerners have invoked Jefferson's precepts on numerous occasions since his death in 1826. For much of America's history the South has served as "a kind of sanctuary of the American democratic tradition," according to David M. Potter. Until comparatively recently the region was still a bastion of Jeffersonian ideals, at least for liberal critics of American society. There, Jefferson's agrarian descendants carried on resistance to the crass commercialism and capitalism of the Northeast and Midwest.

Following themes elaborated by Frederick Jackson Turner in the late 19th century, Americans easily linked the frontier with the development of democratic institutions and economic opportunity. Turner's "frontier thesis" exalted the role of the West, yet agrarian democracy and frontier democracy share obvious similarities, as William E. Dodd later noted in *Statesmen of the Old South* (1911). One of the first historians to realize the implications of agrarian democracy, Dodd asserted that the "real South" was precisely the South of Thomas Jefferson. Any conservative, hierarchical developments, as opposed to progress along democratic, equalitarian lines, were mere aberrations from true southernism. Dodd subjected his thesis to little critical evaluation, and later writers have disputed his findings. But his version was not entirely lacking in historical foundation. Jefferson and the Jeffersonian tradition originated in the South, and for much of American political history the region has supported men who shared such ideas.

Southerners have invoked, in addition to Jefferson's agrarian philosophy, a number of other principles that can be traced to the intellectual and political heritage of the third president. His name is often associated with arguments sustaining states' rights, and southerners cite his authorship of the Kentucky Resolution of 1799 as evidence of his opposition to the extension of federal power. Inhabitants of the region recall his arguments against Alexander Hamilton's plans for industrialization, national banks, and tariffs, and much of America's antiurban tradition can be traced to Jeffersonian origins as well. Ironically, for all his praise of yeoman farmers as God's "Chosen People," Jefferson eventually admitted the need for commerce and manufacturing, and his immediate successors in the White House acquiesced in the chartering of a Second Bank of the United States and the development of a tariff policy. Slavery also received considerable attention in Jefferson's writings, but his recommendations for abolition did not endear him in the South. Few southerners would admit that such ideas represented Jefferson's settled policy.

Jefferson's commitment to liberalism, grounded in the 18th-century Enlightenment, provided the intellectual foundation for his writings on agrarianism, states' rights, and restricted governmental power, as well as his opposition to slavery. The most widely known examples of his ideas on liberal political theory appear in the Declaration of Independence and in other sources, including his *Notes on the State of Virginia*. His liberalism contributed to the practical reforms that connected his administration with those of Andrew Jackson, Woodrow Wilson, and Franklin D. Roosevelt. Both Jeffersonian agrarianism and idealism surfaced in the programs advocated by the Populists in the 1890s and in the writings of the Nashville Agrarians in the 1930s.

Jefferson's influence in the South remains difficult to assess precisely. The region unquestionably cherished his agrarianism and his defense of states' rights, but his more liberal, equalitarian doctrines languished there in the years after independence. By the "era of good feelings" Jefferson was viewed as the defender of states' rights in his native Virginia, where his principles coincided with powerful economic and political interests. The nullification movement in South Carolina contributed to the transformation of his image in the South. The patriot who was eulogized in 1826 as the "Apostle of Liberty" became the "Father of States' Rights."

Jefferson's Kentucky Resolution enhanced his position among nullifiers, because his words in that document implied that nullification of an unconstitutional federal law was a legitimate procedure. Nullification, Merrill D. Peterson asserts in *The Jefferson Image in the American Mind* (1960), "was the pivot upon which many state rights Jeffersonians swung toward the policies of sectionalism, slavery, and secession." At the very least, the Jeffersonian tradition was linked to the South's cause, and the episode also demonstrated that Jefferson's ideas could be appropriated for purposes alien to the original intent.

The nullifiers were not the only faction in Jacksonian society to rely on the Jeffersonian tradition. Jacksonian democracy itself revived essential Jeffersonian themes that were modified and strengthened by new influences in the 1830s and 1840s. In the *Age of Jackson* (1945) Arthur M. Schlesinger Jr. defines Jacksonian democracy as a "more hard-headed and determined version of Jeffersonian democracy," adding that democrats had to accept that new era's industrialism, with its factories, mills, labor, banks, and capital—all distasteful to orthodox Jeffersonians. The latter's view of independent yeomen as the nation's unique class of producers had to be enlarged to accommodate urban wage earners.

In the meantime, defenders of slavery still invoked Jefferson, noting that the Virginian had owned extensive property in slaves throughout his life. At the same time, the Wilmot Proviso linked the Jeffersonian heritage with the growing opposition to the extension of slavery into the western territories. The proviso revived the language and intent of the old Northwest Ordinance of 1787, which banned slavery in the states of the Old Northwest. Jefferson made no contribution to that legislation, although he had proposed a similar ban on slavery in Congress's 1784 land ordinance. Congress had rejected that restriction, only to add its own to the Northwest Ordinance. Southerners viewed Jefferson's alleged authorship of the antislavery provision as one of his "fatal legacies," but most doubted that he ever favored outright abolition. Later, southerners advocated the concept of popular sovereignty in Jefferson's name, for it implied frontier individualism, self-government, and local control. Even Stephen A. Douglas described his brainchild, popular sovereignty, as "the Jeffersonian plan for government in the territories."

As the South's leaders gradually retreated from the democratic idealism of the Jeffersonian tradition, the Democratic Party lost a degree of its identity, and its spokesmen seemed opposed to the doctrines that many Americans typically defined as being Jeffersonian or liberal. In the 1850s the new Republican Party easily incorporated the Jeffersonian commitment to human rights, antislavery, and agrarian democracy, adopting the powerful rhetoric of "free men and free soil" that composed an idealistic image. And in the political upheaval that flowed logically from the compromises of 1850, the Republican platform corresponded to what most Americans imagined to be Jeffersonian and "in essentials," Merrill D. Peterson adds, "with what had in fact been Jeffersonian."

After the Civil War, Democratic leaders called for a return to Jeffersonian principles, but Jefferson's influence in the party remained limited until the

1880s and 1890s. Only in 1892, for example, did the party's platform openly re-affirm allegiance to the principles formulated by the third president. As for the New South of the postwar era, its dynamic leaders preached industry, business, and progress. By the 1880s such tendencies in the region stimulated the rise of a vocal group of Jeffersonian critics. The oratory of such men as Robert L. Dabney and Charles C. Jones conjured up the polemics of John Taylor of Caro-line and reflected more clearly the influence of Thomas Jefferson than Jefferson Davis. These critics saw the growing cities of the South much as Jefferson and John Taylor had earlier described urban centers—"sores on the body politic."

By the 1890s some southern Jeffersonians had drifted toward the Populist Party, and in that era of agrarian revolt they emphasized the radical side of the Jeffersonian tradition. Although men like George G. Vest of Missouri and John Sharp Williams of Mississippi remained within the Democratic Party, Tom Watson's disillusionment led him to the Populist Party, where he worked to re-vive the agrarian alliance of earlier years. The Populist-Democratic fusion and the ensuing defeat of William Jennings Bryan in 1896 destroyed Watson's hopes and those of most agrarians in the South.

When Populists invoked Jefferson's philosophy in the 1890s, they harked back to the lost world of independent cultivators, doing so at a time when the South yearned to advertise its new, modern outlook. At the same time, agri-culture had become more of a business and less of a way of life. Still, Populists evaded their critics by appealing to the body of native southern tradition and doctrine that dated back to the writings of the Revolutionary period. More-over, southerners recalled the ideas upon which their ancestors relied when they provided the leadership against Hamilton's Federalists and later against the Whigs. The Texas Populist "Cyclone" Davis campaigned with volumes of Jefferson's collected works tucked under his arm, and in response to questions responded, "We will now look through the volumes of Jefferson's works and see what Mr. Jefferson said on this matter." Professor Dodd is likely correct in his contention that Jefferson would have been a Populist in 1892.

With the Populist defeat the Jeffersonian tradition entered a period of qui-escence, although Woodrow Wilson invoked his name and praised his philoso-phy in the years before World War I. By the 1920s the Jeffersonian tradition was of limited value in America; clearly its agrarianism was of little worth in the Jazz Age, and liberal reform found few successful advocates. Yet in the next de-cade, Franklin D. Roosevelt's administration was keenly aware of its intellectual and political roots in the liberal tradition of Jefferson, and such measures as the Civilian Conservation Corps reflected the president's personal commitment to the land. Roosevelt, too, shared a Jeffersonian suspicion of the crowded atmosphere of large cities and feared their detrimental impact on people. As a result of the New Deal's response to the Great Depression, the Democratic Party of Thomas Jefferson became the Democratic Party of Franklin D. Roosevelt.

Jeffersonian ideals flourished in the 1930s, according to a newspaper columnist who declared, "Everyone has a kind word for him. Nearly everyone writes a book about him." Jeffersonian agrarianism enjoyed a special resurgence in some parts of the South, following publication of *I'll Take My Stand: The South and the Agrarian Tradition* (1930). The essays by the Twelve Southerners, or Nashville Agrarians, praised the agrarian way of life while damning the modern, industrial New South. The book stimulated a vigorous debate in southern intellectual circles, but this last agrarian revival ran its course before the end of the decade. Still, the movement testified to the tenacity and vitality of the Jeffersonian tradition. For southerners, Jefferson's writings served as a bulwark against unwanted change and as a defense for the southern way of life. If the Jeffersonian heritage could not exclude the forces of progress or defuse the power of an ever-expanding federal government, those concepts always offered a calm, self-sufficient alternative to the exigencies of modern life.

More recently, controversies over Thomas Jefferson's relationship with one of his slaves, Sally Hemings, brought attention to the centrality of race in American identity, going back to Jefferson's ambivalent views of slavery.

GEORGE M. LUBICK
Northern Arizona University

R. B. Bernstein, *Thomas Jefferson* (2003); Daniel J. Boorstin, *The Lost World of Thomas Jefferson* (1981); Jan Ellen Lewis and Peter S. Onuf, *Sally Hemings and Thomas Jefferson: History, Memory, and Civic Culture* (1999); Peter S. Onuf, ed., *Jeffersonian Legacies* (1993); Merrill D. Peterson, *The Jefferson Image in the American Mind* (1998), ed., *Thomas Jefferson: A Profile* (1968); David M. Potter, in *Myth and Southern History*, ed. Patrick Gerster and Nicholas Cords (1974); Twelve Southerners, *I'll Take My Stand: The South and the Agrarian Tradition* (1930); Clyde N. Wilson, *From Union to Empire: Essays in the Jeffersonian Tradition* (2003); Charles M. Wiltse, *The Jeffersonian Tradition in American Democracy* (1960); C. Vann Woodward, *Origins of the New South, 1877–1913* (1951).

Legislatures, State

Though governors and senators have been famous as individuals, the office of state legislator has best embodied the stereotype of the southern politician. The white male lawyer cum country bumpkin who rants against Yankee capitalists, spouts racial slurs, and is careless toward public policy embodies the stereotype.

Whatever the validity of that image in the past, it is far from accurate in the 21st century. Southern legislatures as institutions and legislators as members have been in the midst of changes for a good while. Although some of these changes reduce regional differences, others underscore the distinctiveness of the South. Much of the change has come as a result of legislatures' gaining the power to counterbalance that of southern governors.

In the last half of the 20th century similar developments in southern and nonsouthern legislatures reduced regional differences. State legislatures in the 1950s, for example, commonly met only in biennial sessions, with an especially large proportion of southern legislatures fitting this pattern (70 to 90 percent). By 2003, only four of 11 southern states met biennially. The shift to annual sessions has been an important step toward active and informed participation in shaping state public policy.

Southern state legislatures traditionally had more committees than did their northern counterparts, but the number of committees per legislature in both the North and the South has been reduced dramatically in the last three decades. In the process, the disparity between the two regions has lessened. Both changes—increase in frequency of sessions and reduction in the number of committees—were vigorously advanced in the 1960s and 1970s as essential reforms to increase the capacity of legislatures to act. Both trends have been as fully felt in the South as nationally.

Likewise, legislatures throughout the country became quite similar by the 1980s in the availability of staff support for members and committees. By then a quarter of the legislatures in each region provided professional assistance, and close to a majority of states provided only secretarial and other nonprofessional assistance. Today 10 of 11 southern states provide year-round staff support for legislators, usually as shared assistance for committee work, but sometimes serving individual legislators. Another indication of interregional similarities among state legislatures is seen in their attempt to control federal funding. Both state governors and legislatures want control over the disposal of these funds. About a quarter of the states, North and South, leave considerable discretion to their governors, but about 40 percent of the legislatures in each region take active steps both to monitor and to decide upon the allocation of such federal funds.

Regional differences, however, still persist. Southern legislatures, for example, on the average consider fewer bills per session but enact a larger number and a higher proportion of all bills introduced than do those outside the South. In 2003 southern legislators introduced 21,593 bills and passed 4,110 of them, which represented about twice as many bills as introduced in nonsouthern states and about twice as many passed as elsewhere in the nation. A higher proportion of southern states lack home rule for municipalities than in other regions, despite the fabled southern belief in localism, and thus a sizable number of bills must be processed to accommodate local requests.

Though the South has traditionally been the locale of strong, flamboyant governors, reforms in recent decades have greatly strengthened the capacity of legislatures to act independently of the governor. The South has adopted, to a greater extent than elsewhere, provisions for "sunset" review of programs and administrative agencies. Over half the southern legislatures may review and terminate the full range of administrative agencies, whereas legislatures elsewhere are much more limited in the scope of their review. Southern state legislatures depend upon regular committees to conduct agency reviews, but legislatures elsewhere tend to rely more upon specialized review bodies.

Perhaps the greatest changes that have taken place in southern legislatures involve membership. Members in the past were almost exclusively white, male, rural Democrats. The narrowness of representation came not only from strong political ties to the Democratic Party but also from the selection of legislators from multimember districts that were malapportioned to favor rural areas. Judicial decisions on reapportionment combined with Department of Justice rulings under the Voting Rights Act of 1965 required state legislatures throughout the country to shift to single-member districts drawn in accordance with the location of population. Thus, in keeping with national trends, southern legislatures have become more urban and suburban, and less rural, than previously. An integral part of these changes has been an increase in the election of blacks, Republicans, and women to the legislatures.

By 1982 the number of black state legislators in the South was triple that of 1971, while their numbers had increased by less than half in legislatures in the rest of the country. In 1971, of all black state legislators in the country, 24 percent sat in southern capitals; by 1982, that proportion had risen to almost 41 percent. The average southern state legislature in 1971 had two black members, by 1982 the number had grown to six, and by 1993 to 23. Legislatures that once fostered Jim Crow laws now have the nation's largest numbers of black representatives.

Until the 1990s, the most distinctive feature of southern legislatures remained the partisan dominance of the Democratic Party. A southern legislature in the 1950s without a single Republican was not uncommon. In 1951, seven of the 13 southern states had no Republican solons. In 1961 Democrats controlled on average 95 percent of the seats in both the upper and lower chambers of southern legislatures. The Democratic dominance in the South during the 1950s and the 1960s was even more pronounced when compared with state legislatures throughout the rest of the country, where Democrats averaged only 40 percent of the seats. In 1981, across the 13 states used in this analysis (the 11 states of the Confederacy, plus Oklahoma and Kentucky), the Democrats averaged 80 percent of the House seats and 84 percent of the Senate positions. Though southern states had frequently elected Republicans for both governor and U.S. senator and supported Republican presidential candidates through the 1980s, Republicanism had not trickled down into the essentially local-district elections of state legislatures.

The 1990s were a dramatic time for the Republican Party's advance in the South, and for the first time a partisan surge occurred at the state legislative level. In the 1990 elections, Republicans controlled 27.8 percent of southern legislative seats. After the 1996 elections, Republicans had 40 percent of those seats. The 2000 elections saw the Republicans reach 43 percent of legislative seats, and that figure rose to 46.7 percent in the 2002 midterm elections.

Notable differences exist among the southern state legislatures themselves. Variations within the South in partisanship, structure, and behavior persist. The strong South Carolina legislature stands in contrast to the gubernatorial-dominated Louisiana legislature. Still, southern state legislatures are a definable group in contrast with those in the rest of the nation. Having experienced dramatic changes and especially growing power since World War II, they remain distinctive institutions with their southern political outlook.

DAVID M. OLSEN

E. LEE BERNICK

University of North Carolina at Greensboro

Council of State Governments, *The Book of the States* (biennial eds., 2004, 2006); Virginia Gray, Herbert Jacob, and Kenneth Vines, eds., *Politics in the American States: A Comparative Analysis* (1983); Ronald J. Hrebenar and Clive S. Thomas, *Interest Group Politics in the Southern States* (1992); Malcolm E. Jewell, *Legislative Representation in the Contemporary South* (1967), *Representation in State Legislatures* (1982); V. O. Key Jr., *Southern Politics in State and Nation* (1949); Alexander P. Lamis, in *The American South in the Twentieth Century*, ed. Craig S. Pascoe, Karen Trahan Leathem, and Andy Ambrose (2005); Terrel L. Rhodes, *Republicans in the South: Voting for the State House, Voting for the White House* (2000); Alan Rosenthal, *Legislative Life* (1981); Ronald E. Weber and Paul Brace, *American State and Local Politics: Directions for the Twenty-first Century* (1999).

National Politics

Alexis de Tocqueville, the oft-quoted French visitor to the young American Republic in the 1830s, observed in *Democracy in America* (1835), "Two branches may be distinguished in the great Anglo-American family, which have hitherto grown without entirely comingling; the one in the South, the other in the North." Politically, that was not entirely true at the time, but it would soon become so. The South had been an integral part of national life in its first half century, providing talented leaders such as Jefferson, Madison, Jackson, and Marshall, and during the 1840s and early 1850s southern politics were intertwined with the nation's. Whigs and Democrats competed on similar levels in the South as elsewhere, and the region's electorate participated at the same high rate as other Americans of that time.

The South's political goals were, of course, somewhat different from those of the rest of the country because of its economy. Madison had stressed in *The Federalist* no. 10 how "the possession of different degrees and kinds of property" influences "the sentiments and views of the respective proprietors." This creates "a division of the society into different interests and parties," or factions. The slave economy, a rural and agricultural one, produced a faction of planter elites from the Black Belt areas—where the fertile topsoil was deep and dark—who fought from the constitutional period to Tocqueville's time for a certain agenda. In the Philadelphia convention of 1787 this influential class shaped several provisions of the new Constitution to their ends, among them the infamous Three-Fifths Compromise, a 20-year protection against halting the importation of slaves, and a $10 tax limit on those brought in, plus a prohibition on direct taxes on personal wealth or income. In ensuing decades they engaged repeatedly in the titanic tariff struggles against the northern manufacturing interests who sought to protect themselves from foreign goods while the planters sought free trade.

Madison had explained in his seminal essay that the federal, republican form of government could effectively rule over an enormous territory through an array of formal checks and balances to fragment elite power and through divided constituencies to do likewise for mass sovereignty. An advantage of this system would be the "security afforded . . . in the greater obstacles to the concert and accomplishment of the majority." By the time of Tocqueville's visit, such protections were becoming increasingly important to the slaveholding elite for a host of reasons.

At the time of the passage of the Constitution, the populations of North and South plus their economies and political balance were roughly equal, but that was changing as the nation began its second half century. The economic advantages of the northern manufacturing and commercial interests grew steadily, while the admission of new western states began to alter the political alignment. Whereas the North had grown to some 13.5 million by 1850, the South grew to only 9.5 million. These and other adverse trends led John C. Calhoun to bemoan to southerners in the 1830s on the Senate floor that "we are here but a handful in the midst of an overwhelming majority." The eminent historian Richard Hofstadter wrote in *The American Political Tradition* of that critical era: "The Southern leaders reacted with the most intense and exaggerated anxiety to every fluctuation in the balance of sectional power. How to maintain this balance became the central concern." It would remain so for the next 150 years.

Thus, the southern planter elite embarked on a futile struggle to maintain a semifeudal, agrarian, and racially stratified society. This eventually made residents of the region the only Americans (until Vietnam) ever to lose a war and the sole ones ever to be governed by a conquering military occupation force. After the war the struggle resumed as the elite Bourbons, or "Redeemers," as they came to be called, reestablished the state Democratic parties, engineered the removal of the Reconstruction governments in the Compromise of 1877, and moved in the 1880s and 1890s to isolate Republicans to the upland areas that had opposed secession, to squelch the radical populist uprising of small farmers, and to establish Jim Crow in the turn-of-the-century constitutions. Thus, the "solid South" was built on one-party politics, racism, formal and informal disfranchisement of the masses, malapportionment in favor of Black Belt areas, and—perhaps most important of all—regional autonomy from national politics and, in particular, undesirable policies on racial matters.

The foremost scholar of Dixie politics, the late political scientist V. O. Key Jr., said of this solid South system in his brilliant study in 1949: "The coin of southern politics has two sides; on one is seen the relations of the South as a whole with the rest of the nation; on the other, the political battle within each state. And the two aspects are, like the faces of a coin, closely connected." He traced how the relatively small white minority of the Black Belt counties ruled Dixie through the unchallenged hegemony of the Democratic Party. Democrats won, for example, 113 of 114 gubernatorial elections and 131 of 132 senatorial ones from 1919 to 1948. Also, with the single exception of 1928, when five rim states abandoned the wet, Catholic, urban New York Democrat Al Smith, Dixie gave all its electoral votes to the Democratic ticket in the 17 presidential elections from 1880 to 1944.

Such loyalty provided the region's elite enormous leverage in national politics, particularly in Congress, where the solid bloc of southern Democratic senators consistently controlled the Senate and the overwhelmingly Democratic southern congressional delegations likewise controlled the House. The seniority system adopted in 1910 for choosing chairpersons promoted the South's members into positions of great power, so that by the 1950s Dixie, with some one-fifth of the total population and number of states, commanded approximately 60 percent of the committee chairs. Because of their power and because of the practice of senatorial courtesy, southern senators greatly influenced the federal judiciary, especially at the lower levels. And until 1936, the requirement that Democratic presidential nominees acquire two-thirds of the delegate votes gave the South an effective veto over unacceptable candidates. The thoroughness with which regional autonomy was achieved through these and related devices is highlighted by the observation of W. J. Cash, a full century after Tocqueville, that the South "was not quite a nation within a nation, but the next thing to it."

The use of this power to resist nationalizing, industrializing, and egalitarian trends greatly retarded the economic, political, and social development of the region. In 1938 President Roosevelt assembled a major Conference on Economic Conditions in the South, stating that the "South presents right now the Nation's No. 1 economic problem." Key would write at midcentury, "The cold hard fact is that the South as a whole has developed no system or practice of political organization and leadership adequate to cope with its problems." Racially, the historic gulf between white and black southerners flared into violence often in the civil rights years, during the Little Rock school crisis in 1958, the University of Mississippi riots in 1962, at Selma in 1965, and in many other locales as well.

The oligarchic, one-dimensional, closed, and inflexible solid South system that served Black Belt elites so well was shattered in the 1950s and 1960s. These two decades were the watershed years between the politics begun so long ago by Calhoun and his generation and the politics of the current generation. Many developments in this era transformed the style and substance of southern politics, from the region's increased prosperity to the reemergence of a two-party system with John Tower's election to the Senate from Texas in 1961 on the Republican ticket, victories of the Goldwater forces in 1964, Republican gains in the off-year congressional elections of 1966, and Nixon's wins in 1968 and 1972. The black protest movement was led by a native son, Dr. Martin Luther King Jr., and the national Democratic Party's push for civil rights resulted in the Civil Rights Act of 1964 and the Voting Rights Act of 1965. In the seminal court case, *Brown v. Board of Education* (1954), the Supreme Court ruled that segregated schools were in violation of the Fourteenth Amendment's "equal protection clause," and another case, *Baker v. Carr* (1962), began the process of fair apportionment.

The American nation embarked on its third century with over 4 million southern blacks registered to vote. There were 2,000 black officials in the region; its schools were more desegregated than the rest of the country's; it boasted a rapidly growing population, an expanding economy, and a developing two-party system. In the states of Mississippi, Louisiana, and Georgia, blacks constituted approximately 25 percent of the electorate and were a force to be reckoned with throughout the South. In a real sense, the election of 1976 that brought a southerner to national power was, like that famous one a century earlier, one of redemption. Walker Percy summed up the change nicely in the late 1970s: "The South has entered the mainstream of American life for the first time in perhaps 150 years, that is, in a sense that has not been the case since the 1820s or '30s."

The South's role in contemporary national politics is much more akin to the pre-Calhoun, pre–Civil War era than to the century or more of political resistance and isolation that followed. National issues, from abortion to foreign affairs, educational reform, and budgetary matters, are as important in the South as elsewhere. Presidential elections are now vigorously contested throughout Dixie. In 1984, for example, South Carolina native Jesse Jackson made a credible race for the Democratic nomination, and the 13 March southern primaries in Alabama, Florida, and Georgia proved of crucial importance to him. Jackson's campaign and the primaries, dubbed "Super Tuesday" by the media, received extensive national attention.

Jackson's campaign symbolized the importance of religion to recent elections in the South. The Religious Right became a dynamic force in its support for Ronald Reagan, and organizations like Moral Majority, and later the Christian Coalition, mobilized evangelical Protestants to become more active in politics. In addition to the role of Baptist minister Jesse Jackson, Virginia Pentecostal preacher Pat Robertson also ran for president in 1988, using his cable television network to promote a greater evangelical participation in politics.

Southern political leaders who exercised great national influence in the 1980s included such Republicans as Senator Jesse Helms (N.C.), former Senate majority leader Howard Baker (Tenn.), and then-assistant minority leader in the House Trent Lott (Miss.). Democratic senators Sam Nunn (Ga.), Lloyd Bentsen (Tex.), and John Stennis (Miss.) wielded significant power on the other side of the aisle, and Jim Wright (Tex.) was Speaker of the House. Governor Lamar Alexander of Tennessee, a Republican, assumed the chair of the National Governors' Conference in 1985, while former mayor Ernest Morial of New Orleans, a Democrat, served as chair of the National Mayors' Conference in 1986.

Because of the changing political scene in the South, plus dramatic population growth—which saw every southern state outstrip the national average of 11.4 percent in the 1970s, thereby giving the region eight additional congressional seats and electoral votes—and an economic performance better than the nation as a whole, America was in the midst of a historic shift in power to the "Sunbelt," the South and West.

The 1990s saw southerners playing an even more prominent role in national politics. In 1992 the Democrats nominated two white southerners, Bill Clinton from Arkansas and Al Gore Jr. from Tennessee. They were moderates who had worked with the Democratic Leadership Council to nurture policy positions that would be less liberal than previous Democratic Party platforms. The ticket did better in the South than any Democratic presidential and vice presidential candidates since Jimmy Carter, capturing Arkansas, Georgia, Kentucky, Louisiana, and Tennessee. The ticket did not, however, win a majority of white voters. Clinton became unpopular in the South after assuming the presidency. In the pivotal 1994 midterm election, which brought Republican control of both houses of Congress, the Republicans in the South gained 19 seats in the House of Representatives and four in the Senate.

Clinton and Gore were reelected in 1996, with 49.2 percent of the popular vote nationwide. They won Arkansas, Tennessee, Louisiana, Kentucky, and Florida in the South, but lost Georgia, a state they had captured four years earlier. The Republicans maintained control of Congress after 1996, though. In the impeachment of Clinton, his chief prosecutors were a House leadership team dominated by white southern Republicans. Among his chief defenders were black southern Democrats, including veterans of the civil rights movement.

Southerners were, in general, notable congressional leaders in the 1990s. During the 1997 session, for example, Newt Gingrich (R-Ga.) was Speaker of the House, Richard Armey (R-Tex.) was House majority leader, and Tom DeLay (R-Tex.) was House majority whip. Southern members chaired the key House committees of Appropriations, Ways and Means, Commerce, National Security, and Intelligence. In the Senate, Vice President Al Gore Jr. (D-Tenn.) was president of the Senate, Strom Thurmond (R-S.C.) was president pro tempore, and Trent Lott (R-Miss.) was majority leader. Southerners chaired such leading Senate committees as Appropriations, Rules, Foreign Relations, Government Affairs, Armed Services, Intelligence, and Energy and Natural Resources.

The national parties nominated white southerners as their standard-bearers in the 2000 presidential election, George W. Bush from Texas and Al Gore Jr. of Tennessee. The South played a key role in Bush's victory. The eleven former

Confederate states all gave him their electoral votes, totaling over half of the electoral votes required to win. Bush won by significant margins in all southern states, except Florida, where the election was so close that it took seven weeks and a five–four Supreme Court decision to reward Florida's votes, and the election, to Bush.

The Republicans did well in the 2002 midterm elections, which were held in the aftermath of the 11 September 2001 terrorist attacks. The party regained narrow control of the U.S. Senate and added to its majority in the House of Representatives. Bush was reelected in 2004, over John Kerry, the Democratic Party nominee from New England. Bush swept the South, with notable support from grassroots evangelical white voters.

By the midterm 2006 elections, the Iraq War had become the dominating issue of national politics, with support for Bush dramatically declining throughout the nation. The Republicans lost control of Congress to the Democrats, but few southerners were among the new congressional leaders.

JIMMY LEA
University of Southern Mississippi

Numan Bartley and Hugh Davis Graham, *Southern Politics and the Second Reconstruction* (1975); Jack Bass and Walter DeVries, *The Transformation of Southern Politics: Social Change and Political Consequence since 1945* (1976); Earl Black and Merle Black, *The Vital South: How Presidents Are Elected* (1992); Charles Bullock III and Mark J. Rozell, eds., *The New Politics of the Old South: An Introduction to Southern Politics* (1998); W. J. Cash, *The Mind of the South* (1941); William C. Havard, ed., *The Changing Politics of the South* (1972); V. O. Key Jr., *Southern Politics in State and Nation* (1949); Alexander P. Lamis, ed., *Southern Politics in the 1990s* (1999), *The Two-Party South* (1984); Donald R. Matthews and James W. Prothro, *Negroes and the New Southern Politics* (1966); Nicol C. Rae, *Southern Democrats* (1994); Oran Smith, *The Rise of Baptist Republicanism* (1997); T. Harry Williams, *Romance and Realism in Southern Politics* (1961).

New Deal

Agriculture was the South's major economic activity in the 1930s; and New Deal farm programs—such as the Agricultural Adjustment Act (1933), the Resettlement Administration (1935), and the Bankhead-Jones Farm Tenancy Act (1937)—by cutting production, raising farm income, and pushing southerners from farm poverty to southern and nonsouthern cities, created the basis for the sweeping change soon to come to the largely rural South. Along with the agricultural revolution, the New Deal infusion of federal money disrupted the cycle of poverty, and the region's economy began to merge with that of the nation. New Deal labor legislation, such as the National Labor Relations Act (1933), the Social Security Act (1935), and the Fair Labor Standards Act (1938), helped to spur the first significant unionization of the country (one of every four workers by the end of the 1940s). The South, with its major industry, textiles, overwhelmingly nonunionized, was the most underunionized region of the country, with all the attendant cultural and economic impact of nonunionization. In the nation's poorest region, the Federal Emergency Relief Administration provided limited but badly needed amounts of money to fund welfare programs; and the Public Works Administration (1933), Civilian Conservation Corps (1933), and the Works Progress Administration (1935) offered public service work to the unemployed.

At first the personal popularity of Franklin D. Roosevelt and his Depression-fighting New Deal programs meant solid support among southern politicians and southern voters. But New Deal politics and programs threatened white supremacy and lessened the power of local oligarchies. The centralizing tendencies of the New Deal menaced the basic institutions of southern life. The subsequent slow defection of southern Democrats from the New Deal created a new conservative southern political culture.

The role of the New Deal in creating the modern political economy of southern society remains controversial. Statistical study indicates that the Dixie economic miracle dates from the 1940s. Ambiguity surrounds the New Deal years in the South. In many ways, the New Deal nationalized southern culture, and the South became by the 1940s not the nation's number one economic problem but its ever-growing, ever-Americanizing region. The persistence, however, of such cultural patterns as racial segregation, dire poverty, and rural and small-town control kept the South looking more old than new. The New Deal, with its host of centralizing agencies and its nationalized political ideology, changed the Old South but did not destroy it. Only the war years, the racial revolution of the 1950s and 1960s, emigration, and the postwar prosperity of industrialization and urbanization would do that.

JAMES A. HODGES
College of Wooster

Roger Biles, *The South and the New Deal* (1994); James C. Cobb and Michael V. Namorato, eds., *The New Deal and the South* (1984); Pete Daniel, *Agricultural History* (July 1981), *Breaking the Land: The Transformation of Cotton, Tobacco, and Rice Cultures since 1880* (1985); Gary Fink and Merl Reed, eds., *Essays in Southern Labor History: Selected Papers, Southern Labor History Conference, 1976* (1976); Frank Freidel, FDR and the South (1965); Elena C. Green, ed., *The New Deal and Beyond: Social Welfare in the South since 1930* (2003); Donald H. Grubbs, *Cry from the Cotton: The Southern Tenant Farmers' Union and the New Deal* (1971); Jack Irby Hayes Jr., *South Carolina and the New Deal* (2001); Michael Holmes, *The New Deal in Georgia: An Administrative History* (1975); Janet Irons, *Testing the New Deal: The General Textile Strike of 1934 in the American South* (2000); John B. Kirby, *Black Americans in the Roosevelt Era: Liberalism and Race* (1980); William E. Leuchtenberg, *The White House Looks South: Franklin D. Roosevelt, Harry S. Truman, Lyndon B. Johnson* (2005); Robert S. McElvaine, *The Great Depression, 1929–1941* (1984); Paul E. Mertz, *New Deal Policy and Southern Rural Poverty* (1978); John Dean Minton, *The New Deal in Tennessee, 1932–38* (1959); Harvard Sitkoff, *A New Deal for Blacks: The Emergence of Civil Rights as a National Issue*, vol. 1 (1978); George B. Tindall, *The Emergence of the New South, 1913–1945* (1967).

One-Party Politics

The disfranchisement of practically all blacks and many white have-nots in the period between 1890 and 1910 decimated the Republican and Populist Parties in the South and left the region with only a single important political party. In the era of classic one-party politics, roughly 1910–50, Democrats monopolized state offices and deterred serious opposition in general elections. The national political interests of white southerners were likewise managed exclusively by Democrats; the region regularly cast all of its electoral college votes for Democratic presidential candidates and sent virtually only Democrats to the House of Representatives and the Senate.

As a consequence of the decline in meaningful interparty competition, general elections in the region became empty rituals. Less than one-fifth of the eligible electorate voted in any four-year wave of gubernatorial general elections in the South from 1920 through 1951. Interest in electoral politics, meager as it was, shifted to the relatively new arena of Democratic nominating primaries, which were initially regarded as voluntary organizations open only to whites. In the Democratic primaries, turnout usually exceeded one-fifth of the eligible electorate but never included as many as three-tenths of the potential electorate in the 1920–51 era. One-party politics helped to "anesthetize" or "sterilize" between two-thirds and four-fifths of the region's white adults. As a consequence, politicians representing the interests of more affluent southerners usually triumphed over spokesmen for the region's have-nots.

In the 1950s the campaigns that counted in the South were conducted as a politics of faction rather than a politics of party, as a struggle among groups of rival Democrats as opposed to a battle between Democrats and Republicans.

Election posters along a Mississippi roadside, 1968 (William R. Ferris Collection, Southern Folklife Collection, Wilson Library, University of North Carolina at Chapel Hill)

It is useful to distinguish between "faction" (any subunit of a political party) and "factional system" (the pattern of competition among factions). Students of factional systems have typically followed V. O. Key's lead in identifying three varieties of intraparty competition, based on the number of factions seeking a particular office and the distribution of the first primary vote among the factions: unifactionalism, where one faction wins a commanding majority of the vote; bifactionalism, where the vote is divided more or less evenly between two factions; and multifactionalism, where the vote is split, not necessarily evenly, among three or more factions.

By far the most common electoral situation in the 1920–49 era was multifactionalism, which appeared in 70 percent of the first gubernatorial primary elections. This outcome was hardly surprising. Because ambitious politicians were plentiful while opportunities to win the governorship were rare, multifactionalism would have been the natural mode of intraparty competition once the Democratic Party's dominance in general elections had been established. The most plausible deterrent to multifactionalism is the candidacy of an incumbent governor, whose usual advantages in campaign fund-raising, name and face recognition, patronage, and the like should discourage some potential challengers from running. Southern governors, however, were denied by law from succeeding themselves in states with four-year terms; though succession in states with two-year terms was constitutional, most governors limited their aspirations to two two-year terms. Accordingly, most gubernatorial primaries in the South were efforts to fill open seats, which simply reinforced the attractiveness of the governorship to many candidates.

The other patterns of factional cleavage appeared less frequently. Unifactionalism was present in approximately one-fifth of the gubernatorial contests and was the most common form of factional competition in only a single state (Virginia). Bifactional cleavage was even less likely to occur (13 percent of the elections). Tennessee and Georgia provided most of the examples of conflict between two groups of rival Democrats.

When the form of intraparty competition is related to the type of faction that usually wins nomination, four central tendencies can be distinguished in intraparty politics in the southern states: bifactional primaries won by successful, durable factions (Tenn.), unifactional primaries won by successful, durable factions (Va.), multifactional primaries won by successful, durable factions (La., Miss., Ala., N.C., and Ga.), and, as the most chaotic and disorganized of all systems, multifactional primaries won by moderately successful, transient factions (Fla., Tex., S.C., and Ark.).

In national presidential politics, the solid South actually ended during the mid-20th-century period covered by Key in *Southern Politics*. Not since 1944 have all 11 former Confederate states voted for the Democratic presidential nominee. The most recent approximation of regional solidarity for the Democrats occurred in 1976, when 10 southern states were carried by Jimmy Carter, but it was short-lived and a poor imitation of the real thing. The disintegration of the solid South has deprived the national Democrats of crucial electoral college votes and has required them to be disproportionately successful outside the South in order to win the presidency.

Southern congressional delegations remained overwhelmingly Democratic for a longer period. From the late 1930s until the late 1950s, most nonsouthern Senate and House seats were held by Republicans, and only the Democrats' near monopoly on southern Senate and House seats enabled them to control both houses of Congress. The weakness of the Democratic Party outside the South permitted conservative southern Democrats to exert considerable influence on public policy and, in particular, to prevent passage of meaningful civil rights legislation. Once the white conservatives from the region lost the ability to control the agenda of race relations, the rationale for sending only Democrats to Congress from the South was weakened considerably.

In recent decades the Republican Party has dominated presidential elections in the South, with George W. Bush, for example, winning all 11 former Confederate states in the 2004 campaign. The campaigns are often competitive two-party contests, though, not approaching the one-party Democratic Party dominance of the early 20th century, which rested on a restricted electorate.

MERLE BLACK
University of North Carolina at Chapel Hill

EARL BLACK
University of South Carolina

Earl Black and Merle Black, *Politics and Society in the South* (1987), in *Contemporary Southern Political Attitudes and Behavior*, ed. Laurence W. Moreland, Tod A. Baker, and Robert P. Steed (1982); Charles Bullock III and Mark J. Rozell, eds., *The New Politics of the Old South: An Introduction to Southern Politics* (1998); Bradley C. Canon, *American Journal of Political Science* (November 1978); Malcolm E. Jewell and David M. Olson, *American State Political Parties and Elections* (1978); V. O. Key Jr., *Southern Politics in State and Nation* (1949); J. Morgan Kousser, *The Shaping of Southern Politics: Suffrage Restriction and the Establishment of the One-Party South, 1880–1910* (1974); Nicol C. Rae, *Southern Democrats* (1994).

Partisan Politics

The dominance of a one-party political system in the South after the Civil War and into the mid-20th century belies the existence of earlier two-party systems in the South. Party systems before the Civil War were influenced by the same concerns of personality, ideology, and organization as elsewhere in the country.

The first partisan conflict in the southern United States emerged in the 1790s and led to the appearance of the Federalist Party and the Democratic-Republican Party. The Federalists in the South were strongest in South Carolina and, to a lesser degree, Virginia and North Carolina. It was a party of merchants, planters, lawyers, editors, speculators, and those, in general, who profited from the national financial politics of Alexander Hamilton in the George Washington administration. The Federalists declined after 1800, though, as Thomas Jefferson's Democratic-Republicans gained control of the presidency and Congress in that year's elections. Jefferson's party was strong in the South and West from its beginnings and came to stand for local control of government, financial conservatism, and an ideology of individual freedom. The party gradually absorbed Federalist supporters and policies until the South—like the nation—had a virtual one-party system from 1816 to 1828.

After the election of Andrew Jackson as president in 1828, a new party system slowly appeared—the Democratic Party of Jackson and the Whig Party of Henry Clay and Daniel Webster. Recent studies suggest little philosophical or class difference between the groups, with the personality of Jackson and the organizational techniques of the Democrats at first giving them dominance in the South as elsewhere.

The Reconstruction era after the Civil War witnessed the first partisan conflict between blacks and whites in southern history. Blacks identified with the Republican Party—which had emerged as a northern, free-soil political group in the 1850s and was the party of Emancipation—while most southern whites moved into the Democratic Party. The latter called itself the conservative Democratic Party through most of the late 19th century to separate itself, to a degree, from the national Democrats and to attract pre–Civil War Whigs. From the end of Reconstruction in 1877 to the 1960s, partisan politics in the South was, in most areas, conducted within a one-party framework.

The annals of American regional partisan change have rarely, if ever, witnessed such a dramatic transformation as occurred in the South from the 1960s to the present. When the national Democratic Party effectively advocated equal rights for blacks in the early 1960s, the rationale for the South's unique one-party system collapsed, blacks entered the political process with strong federal support, and the present top-heavy two-party system took hold throughout the 11 states of the former Confederacy.

The overriding purpose of the one-party system was to preserve white supremacy, the argument being that if whites divided their votes blacks would hold the balance of power. This reasoning was destroyed in the mid-1960s when national Democratic leaders "betrayed" the white South and pushed passage of the Civil Rights Act of 1964 and the Voting Rights Act of 1965. The partisan impact of these events was reinforced by the highly publicized opposition to the Civil Rights Act of 1964 by Republican presidential nominee Barry Goldwater. In November 1964 President Lyndon B. Johnson won a landslide Democratic victory nationwide, but Goldwater swept the Deep South, carrying Mississippi, always an extreme case, with 87.1 percent of the vote.

The national Democratic Party's civil rights activism unleashed a torrent of Republican activity in the region. The fuel for this GOP spurt was white antagonism toward all things remotely connected with the national Democratic Party integrationists. Figure 1 pinpoints the Republican leap forward to the mid-1960s. There was, however, another feature to the GOP's rise that was separable, if not always separated, from the race issue. With the collapse of the one-party system, the economic and philosophical divisions found in party politics outside the South—dating from the class-oriented New Deal realignment—had an opportunity to descend into the region's emerging partisan structure. Thus, in the forefront of the nascent southern GOP movement were well-to-do businessmen and professionals seeking to help along this process in order to give the region's economic conservatives a permanent home. And the southern Republican Party made its most faithful converts among those attracted by the party's conservative position on economic-class issues.

Simultaneously, however, the race issue became enmeshed in the emerging class-based, two-party system that seemed to be taking hold in the post-1964 period. Twisted into the situation was the logical compatibility of conservative economic-class Republicanism with the racial protest. The GOP, as the party philosophically opposed to an activist federal government in economic matters, gained adherents also from those who objected to federal intervention to end racial segregation in the states.

Steady Republican growth ended in the early 1970s when the race issue abated sufficiently to result in a mild resurgence on the part of the region's transformed Democratic Party, which had gradually shed its segregationist leaders after blacks entered the electorate in large numbers. Figure 1 reflects this mid-1970s Democratic gain by showing a dip in Republican fortunes in those years. The resurgence was accomplished by clever white Democratic poli-

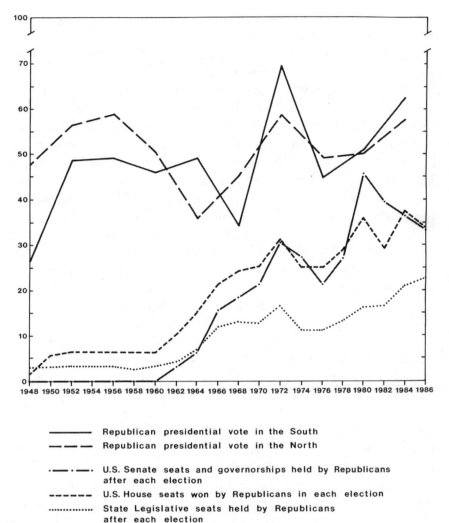

FIGURE 1. *The Uneven Growth of the Republican Party in the South, 1948–1986.*
Source: Alexander P. Lamis, The Two-Party South *(1988).*

ticians who recognized that the post–civil rights era offered them the potential to put together an effective black-white alliance. This biracial coalition was composed of those traditionally Democratic white voters who returned to their party in the 1970s as the race issue eased and of southern blacks, who carried strong Democratic allegiance in gratitude for what the national party did for them during the 1960s. It became a mere matter of arithmetic in some states—especially in the Deep South—for the Republicans to realize that this black-white Democratic alliance arrayed against them was a powerful one indeed.

The irony present in the situation—namely, that the traditional party of segregation in the South should become the home of, and dependent on, black voters—did not escape Republican notice. One Georgia Republican Party chairman ruefully bemoaned the existence of this diverse Democratic coalition that had demolished the once bright GOP potential in his state, complaining that there was "no tie-in" between the twin pillars of the Georgia Democracy— rural, small-town whites of south Georgia and blacks. "They're as far apart as night and day," he noted. And yet, "They're voting hand in hand, and . . . they're squeezing the lives out of us."

This disparate southern Democratic coalition contained serious tensions. Through the early 1980s the alliance held together—although the national victory of Ronald Reagan in 1980 gave the southern GOP a boost—primarily as the result of the canny maneuvers of white moderate leaders, who were its chief beneficiaries. These leaders walked a political tightrope that required Olympian balancing because racial distrust and class antagonisms constantly threatened to divide the coalition's contradictory elements.

In the 1990s the South entered a strikingly new phase of its 30-year experience with two-party politics. During the first two-thirds of the decade, the Republican Party made stunning advances, achieving majority status for the first time. After the 1996 election, the Republican Party held 23 of the 33 governorships and U.S. Senate seats in the 11 former Confederate states, an overwhelming 69.7 percent. In that same election, Republicans in the South won 56.8 percent of the region's U.S. House seats. At the state legislative level, the slowest area of politics to be affected by the Republican rise, the GOP reached 40 percent of the seats (see Table 2).

Bill Clinton, the savvy, nationally oriented veteran Democratic governor of Arkansas, won the presidency in 1992 and 1996, overcoming the national party's persistent weakness in the South and winning, in 1992, four southern states— Arkansas, Georgia, Louisiana, and Tennessee. Clinton campaigned in 1992 as a moderate, a "new Democrat," although as president he pursued such liberal policy proposals as national health care. The 1994 elections brought Republicans control of both houses of Congress, after an anti-Clinton, antigovernment, strongly ideological campaign by the Republicans. Georgia's Newt Gingrich became the symbol of this victory and the new Speaker of the House of Representatives. Clinton overcame Republican successes to win the presidency again in 1996, capturing Arkansas, Louisiana, and Tennessee in the South.

Another southerner, Albert Gore Jr., served as vice president under Clin-

TABLE 2. *Republican Percentage of All State Legislative Seats Nationally, 1966–1999*

Election Year	All States	Southern States	Nonsouthern States
1966	41	16	54
1968	43	17	62
1970	39	16	51
1972	40	19	50
1974	32	14	41
1976	32	13	42
1978	36	16	46
1980	40	18	50
1982	32	17	47
1984	42	22	51
1986	40	23	48
1988	40	25	47
1990	39	26	46
1992	41	29	47
1994	48	36	54
1996	47	38	51
1998	47	39	51
1999	47	42	49

Source: National Conference of State Legislatures.

ton and was the Democratic Party presidential nominee in 2000. The disputed election, which was settled by a five-to-four Supreme Court decision about the decisive Florida vote, brought Texas governor George W. Bush to the White House. Bush won the electoral votes of all 11 southern states. Republicans made gains in the midterm congressional races of 2002, and Bush was reelected in 2004, again winning all the South's electoral votes. Discontent with the Iraq War led to a Democratic Party resurgence in the 2006 midterm election, with the Democrats regaining control of both houses of Congress. Although the Republicans dominated much southern political activity in the 1990s, elections were even then often closely contested, with Democrats continuing to rely on the potential of a biracial coalition for success.

ALEXANDER P. LAMIS
Case Western Reserve University

Lance Banning, *The Jeffersonian Persuasion: Evolution of a Party Ideology* (1978); Numan Bartley, *The Rise of Massive Resistance: Race and Politics in the South during the 1950s* (1969); Jack Bass and Walter DeVries, *The Transformation of Southern Politics: Social Change and Political Consequence since 1945* (1976); Earl Black and Merle Black, *The Rise of the Southern Republicans* (2002); Charles Bullock III and Mark J. Rozell, eds., *The New Politics of the Old South: An Introduction to Southern Politics* (1998); William J. Cooper Jr., *Liberty and Slavery: Southern Politics to 1860* (1983); Alexander Heard, *A Two-Party South?* (1952); Richard Hofstadter, *The Idea of a Party System: The Rise of Legitimate Opposition in the United States, 1780–1840* (1969); V. O. Key Jr., *Southern Politics in State and Nation* (1949); Nick Kotz, *Judgment Days: Lyndon Baines Johnson, Martin Luther King Jr., and the Laws That Changed America* (2005); Alexander P. Lamis, in *The American South in the Twentieth Century*, ed. Craig S. Pascoe, Karen Trahan Leathem, and Andy Ambrose (2005), *Southern Politics in the 1990s* (1999), *The Two-Party South* (1984); Richard P. McCormick, *The Second American Party System: Party Formation in the Jacksonian Era* (1966); Nicol C. Rae, *Southern Democrats* (1994); C. Vann Woodward, *Origins of the New South, 1877–1913* (1951).

Politician, Image of

American popular culture has long conveyed stereotypes of the American South, and politics is no exception. Fred Allen's nationally broadcast radio program of the 1940s, for example, included a frequent appearance by Senator Beauregard Claghorn, "from the deep South, that is." He made puns and bellowed, "That's a joke, son!" This unreconstructed southerner claimed "the only train ah ride is the Chattanooga Choo-Choo"; when he passed Grant's tomb "ah shut both eyes." He never, of course, went to Yankee Stadium, and he never went to the New York Giants field, the Polo Grounds, "unless a southpaw's pitchin'." The *Richmond Times Dispatch* editorialized about this "bombastic bumbling, brou-ha-ha of the air waves" and the ways he undermined a realistic view of southern politics. Senator Claghorn, nonetheless, soon became a cartoon character—a rooster, of course—in the short features seen in American movie theaters.

Political scientist V. O. Key Jr. noted around the same time that "outlanders regard southern politics as a comic opera staged on a grand scale for the amusement of the nation." Key's view came in the aftermath of generations of colorful demagogic political leaders from the rural South who had so shaped perceptions that the national culture remained fascinated with them. The survival of such images continues, as seen in Sean Penn's portrayal of the Huey Long–like governor Willie Stark in the recent film version of *All the King's Men*, which had all the arm-waving, incoherently drawling mannerisms that American audiences associate with "classic" southern politicians.

Political leaders in the South, in fact, have represented a diversity of styles and images. One might begin with Virginia in the early national period when the refined intellectual Thomas Jefferson symbolized the planter-in-politics, albeit a down-to-earth one who eschewed many of the high-styled precedents of his Virginia predecessor as president, George Washington. Patrick Henry, that eloquent rhetorician, embodied a democratic insurgency that appealed to the masses in more emotional ways than Jefferson did, surely presaging a later southern demagoguery. Andrew Jackson was the next generation's democrat, a rough-hewn character who symbolized a southwestern energy that would transform the region's political outlook into one empowering the common folk, although leaving a hierarchical planter regime in a position of unusual authority in the southern version of the young republic.

The movement of settlers onto the southwestern frontier and the deepening North-South sectional conflict in the decades from 1810 to 1860 saw the rise of a new group of politicians who responded to yeomen's and poor whites' resentment of the upper-class planter elite. Political debate included social-class issues. Southern whites before the Civil War voted as frequently as those in other parts of the nation, responding to candidates who appealed to their class interests. Like charismatic evangelical preachers from the same era, these politicians appealed to the emotions of their mostly farmer, hill country, and piney woods constituents. Franklin Plummer, for example, stirred up his east Mississippi voters against the Delta planters of that state, while W. R. W. Cobb from Alabama rode popular support to election as governor, congressman, and senator. Plummer was the congressman who first suggested the idea of free land for homesteaders, a popular plan on the frontier. Cobb's outlook was clear from the campaign song he used, "Uncle Sam Is Rich Enough to Give Us All a Farm." The image of the southern politician responding to the plain folk thus traces this far back in southern history.

The antebellum South also saw the deepening image of the southern politician as an extravagant orator. W. J. Cash long ago argued that the southern white on the frontier became "one of the most complete romantics and one of the most complete hedonists ever recorded." Overlooking Cash's own over-the-top language, one grants the cultural authority that was invested in political talk that entertained. Cash went further, arguing that this romantic political rhetoric preempted the development of a realistic, interest-oriented politics, such as developed in the Northeast and Midwest. The politics of the Old South became "an arena wherein one great champion confronted another or a dozen, and sought to outdo them in rhetoric and splendid gesturing." Historian Kenneth Greenberg has more recently affirmed the importance of honor and symbolic behavior in antebellum southern culture, including its politics. South Carolina congressman Preston Brooks's beating of Massachusetts senator Charles Sumner on the floor of Congress in 1856 for a violation of the southern code of honor represented a particularly dramatic example of a political act that would live long in national and regional memory, although interpreted differently in each place. Promoters of southern secession in the 1850s, such as Alabama's William Yancey and South Carolina's Robert Barnwell Rhett, became known as "fire-eaters" for their inflammatory rhetoric that intentionally stirred passions against the North.

Southern whites saw their politicians as their defenders against an aggressive and wicked nation, through the Civil War and Reconstruction and even long after that time. Southern military leaders, the Lees and Jacksons and Stuarts, rather than politicians like Confederate president Jefferson Davis or Vice President Alexander Stephens, were the great heroes of the Lost Cause. Reconstruction gave southern whites persistent images of hated political types, whether northerners who ran for office (carpetbaggers), southern whites who cooperated with the Yankees (scalawags), or black politicians, whom whites portrayed as ignorant, venal, or manipulated by northerners. The freed slaves, though, invested considerable meaning in such African American political figures as Hiram Revels and John Lynch.

With Redemption, the ending of Reconstruction, southern politics was dominated by Bourbon politicians famous for representing planter interests or those of the emerging southern industrial system. They were high Victorians, genteel in their manners and high-flown in their rhetoric. They appealed to the memory of the antebellum plantation and the Lost Cause heroism to create a backward-looking politics that empowered themselves as the presumptive champions of traditional regional ways. They oversaw the restriction of the southern electorate, virtually excluding blacks from voting and, through the poll tax and other measures, many poorer whites as well.

The dominance of these Bourbon politicians never went unchallenged, with independent political parties and individual politicians raising issues that mainstream politics ignored. Reformers should be seen as a major southern political type. The neglect by the Redeemers of the economic interests of southern farmers led in the 1880s and 1890s to an agrarian revolt, which produced a new group of political leaders who helped solidify the image of the southern politician. The Redeemers made the Democratic Party *the* party of the South, but agrarian reformers were torn whether to remain inside it and campaign for their economic changes or start an independent movement. The Populists represented a fundamental critique of American capitalism's exploitation of workers, and their movement represented a quest for a truly democratic politics. Using appeals to social-class interests, the reformers put together a shaky white-black coalition, although the southern political establishment eventually used appeals to white supremacy and southern tradition (as represented by the Democratic Party) to defeat this insurgency.

After 1900 the New South political establishment continued its dominance but absorbed some of the grassroots issues that agrarian reformers had pressed. The Progressive reformers were typically more urban and middle class than the agrarian insurgents had been, and they improved schools, roads, and health care. The Progressive type of southern politician favored reforms to make society more stable and virtuous, although the neglect of black southerners was a notable aspect of the era.

The marginalization of the Republican Party, which had become associated with blacks during Reconstruction, created a one-party system in which factionalism became a dominant theme. Personality politics appeared in the Progressive era, especially with the adoption of the primary system for nominating candidates, which promoted more direct political appeals to the masses than earlier. Demagogues sprouted throughout the southern countryside, appearing often as reformers but just as often betraying the economic interests of their constituencies once in power, while at the same time building new political machines. The demagogues represented the maturation of a dominant image of the colorful rural politician as a southern type. Their campaigns entertained the southern electorate. Rallies included barbecues, country music and hymn singing, and boundless rhetoric. Mississippi's Theodore Bilbo, like other politicians in his era, perfected a flashy dress to gain attention: red suspenders (snapped for dramatic effect), a bright checked suit pattern, flaming red necktie, diamond stickpin, and a stylish, brimmed felt hat. Politicians such as James Vardaman (Miss.), Jeff Davis (Ark.), and Eugene Talmadge (Ga.) were masters of anecdotal rhetoric, with mimicry of blacks and city folks a favored technique, followed by a superficial but stirring consideration of political issues. Campaigning often descended into what Bilbo called a "family fight," characterized by argumentation that he referred to as "cuss-fighting."

The demagogues appealed to the social-class interests and cultural values of rural voters. Huey Long, who served as governor and U.S. senator from Louisiana in the late 1920s and early 1930s, was the most renowned example of the demagogue in the national culture, although he was not typical in all ways. Long did not, for example, appeal to the racial prejudices of white voters, and he was the most extreme of southern politicos in building a ruthless political machine. He increased state services by challenging the entrenched planter-business establishment, which, like most of the region's state establishments, had long ignored the problems of the working classes. During the Depression, Long became a national figure with his proposals for radical economic redistribution.

The demagogue image remained a dominant one through much of the 20th century, augmented by the powerful presence on the national scene of such congressional leaders as Richard Russell (Ga.), Sam Rayburn (Tex.), and Strom Thurmond (S.C.). They usually abstained from the harshest racial rhetoric, while at the same time defending Jim Crow and striking a statesmanlike pose. The 1950s and early 1960s saw race rise to preeminence as a political issue in the South and nation, and both the demagogues and congressional statesmen rallied to massive resistance. Governors Orval Faubus (Ark.), Ross Barnett (Miss.), and George Wallace (Ala.) reactivated a harsh racial rhetoric, while congressional leaders used their parliamentary and rhetorical skills to delay, compromise, or gut proposed legislation to change the southern way of life.

The end of Jim Crow and disfranchisement brought fundamental change to the southern political system with the rise of the Republican Party and the transformation of the Democratic Party into one that rested on a biracial coalition. The 1970s witnessed the emergence of new southern political types—African American politicians, moderate Democrats, and conservative Republicans. The Black Belts, where the African American population was concentrated, had, when blacks could not vote in the South, been dominated by white elites, but the political empowerment of blacks after the Voting Rights Act (1965) brought black politicians into state and local offices for the first time since Reconstruction. In 1972 Barbara Jordan (Tex.) and Andrew Young (Ga.) became the first modern African American congressional leaders from the South, and in 1989 L. Douglas Wilder (Va.) became the first African American to win the office of governor in a southern state.

White Democratic leaders quickly adapted to the new realities of a biracial electorate. Ernest S. Hollings of South Carolina was the first U.S. senator elected after the passage of the Voting Rights Act, and he illustrated an evolution of the southern politician in this era. He retained the folksy manner and down-home style long associated with demagogues and mainstream politicians alike, yet he consciously appealed to his new black constituency, supporting Senate efforts in 1969 to expand programs to fight poverty and malnutrition that still affected rural whites and blacks in his state. A group of moderate Democratic governors, elected in the 1970s and early 1980s, symbolized a Democratic Party renewal. Among this new breed were Reuben Askew (Fla.), Dale Bumpers (Ark.), Bill Clinton (Ark.), Jimmy Carter (Ga.), James B. Hunt Jr. (N.C.), and William

Winter (Miss.). They advocated efficiency in government operations and progressive policies on social issues. The elections of Carter and Clinton as presidents dramatically symbolized national acceptance of a New South political image. Of course, national media also portrayed Carter as a bumbling farmer and Clinton as a redneck Bubba at times, but, nonetheless, their national success moderated southern stereotyping.

The election of Texan George W. Bush in 2000 and his reelection four years later solidified the most recent image of the southern politician—the conservative Republican. Californian Ronald W. Reagan, elected president in 1980, had an enormous impact in the South, stimulating the development of an ideologically based party, appealing in both the region's growing suburbs and the rural areas that once were the center of the Democratic Party establishment. The landmark 1994 election, which brought Republicans to power in both houses of Congress, was especially important in making such southern Republicans as Newt Gingrich (Ga.), Tom DeLay (Tex.), and Trent Lott (Miss.) the recognized new leaders of southern politics. Balancing probusiness economic policies, a moralistic social agenda, and the techniques of modern political organization, these leaders dominated national politics for a decade until disillusionment with the Iraq War and Bush's other policies brought Democrats back to power in 2006.

Whether Republicans or Democrats, contemporary southern politicians more closely resemble their national party members than ever before. It is an age of blow-dried and media-sophisticated politicians.

CHARLES REAGAN WILSON
University of Mississippi

Jack Bass and Walter DeVries, *The Transformation of Southern Politics: Social Change and Political Consequence since 1945* (1976); Benjamin A. Botkin, ed., *A Treasury of Southern Folklore* (1949); W. J. Cash, *The Mind of the South* (1941); Dewey Grantham, *The South in Modern America: A Region at Odds* (2001); Alexander P. Lamis, ed., *Southern Politics in the 1990s* (1999); Stephen A. Smith, *Myth, Media, and the Southern Mind* (1985); T. Harry Williams, *Romance and Realism in Southern Politics* (1966).

Populist Party

Adherents of the People's Party, launched formally in 1892, were commonly known as Populists. The nucleus of the third party was the combined strength of the southern and northern branches of the Farmers' Alliance, which had grown from a local protective association of Texas cattlemen and farmers, formed in 1875 to combat cattle and horse thieves, into a formidable national body. Local, county, state, and national chapters developed coordinated programs designed to achieve economic reform and benefit the agricultural classes. Southern Alliance warehouses, exchanges, and stores engaged in numerous ventures in cooperative buying and selling. As its lecturers and newspapers denounced the impoverished condition of the agrarians, the Farmers' Alliance promoted social and educational activities for farmers and their families.

The South produced a number of national leaders, such as Leonidas L. Polk of North Carolina. Dr. Charles W. Macune, an itinerant reformer, edited the *National Economist* from the Farmers' Alliance headquarters in Washington, D.C. Macune championed the subtreasury plan, which would enable farmers to store perishable products in local warehouses and receive loans on their goods while waiting for better prices. Its principles were later adapted by the New Freedom and the New Deal administrations of Woodrow Wilson and Franklin D. Roosevelt. In the 1890s the subtreasury plan became the basic economic demand of the Southern Alliance. It was denounced as dangerous socialistic heresy by the ruling Democrats, a group of conservative politicians often called Redeemers, or Bourbons, after the conservative ruling house of France that was returned to power following the overthrow of Napoleon. The Alliance was both specific and general in its program that decried the results of the convict lease system, low farm prices, one-crop agriculture, the crop-lien system, and tenant farming. As the spokesman for the agrarians, the Alliance denounced high land taxes, exorbitant freight rates by largely unregulated railroads, and fertilizer producers who sold spurious brands at inflated prices. The Alliance launched a successful campaign against the jute manufacturers who held a monopoly on the bagging used to wrap cotton. Bankers who charged unreasonable interest rates were condemned as enemies of the indebted farmers.

In the South the Alliance worked to restore a diminishing sense of worth and dignity among farmers. The Alliance was one of the first national orders to admit women to membership. Although unable to aid the party as voters, women contributed to its social and educational programs. Later, some of the women became editors of Alliance and Populist newspapers. Ministers of the gospel, primarily evangelical Protestants, assumed leadership roles in the order from the first.

The first black Alliance, known as the Colored Farmers' Alliance, was organized in Houston County, Tex., in 1886, and later that year a state organization was formed. Black Alliances were set up in other states, and in March 1888 a national convention was held at Lovelady, Tex. Blacks had separate national, state, and local organizations, although white orders accepted them, and often Alliances held joint meetings and cooperated in their objectives. Scholars have debated the degree to which Populists advocated benefits for African Americans, but the evidence is strong that they did.

At first the Southern Alliance backed Bourbon Democrats who pledged themselves to enact the subtreasury plan and other reform measures. The Alliance strategy was to gain control of the Democratic Party and pursue its program from within the power structure. The leaders anticipated success because farmers represented a majority of the population and of the ruling party. Things went awry when the Bourbons reneged on campaign promises, and it seemed probable that the Southern Alliance would copy its counterparts in the Midwest, breaking away and forming a third party. Yet an immediate and similar southern defection proved difficult because the Democrats had controlled the states politically since the end of Reconstruction. Their strength was based on honesty in government, fiscal conservatism, and white supremacy. Any divisive issue threatened a return to the horrors (more imagined than real) of Reconstruction and Republican rule. Certainly the relationship of black and white Alliance men alone was cause for alarm. Most white southerners wanted to maintain white supremacy and looked to the Democratic Party as the sacrosanct instrument of its preservation.

As the Alliance program faltered, desperate white farmers turned finally to a third national party: the People's Party, also called the Populist Party. Their sense of despair led them to abandon the "party of the fathers," which they considered no longer sensitive to their needs. Populism had many facets and was not confined to farmers, but when viewed as the sum of its parts, it was a class movement. The southern experience was distinct and unique. Southern Populism drew its foot soldiers from the ranks of farmers, many of whom were bedrock Alliance men. That was so even though some Alliance leaders—Benjamin R. Tillman in South Carolina and James S. Hogg in Texas, for example—refused to leave the Bourbon Democrats and branded the Populists as dangerous radicals.

Realizing the need for additional support, southern agrarians broadened their party's appeal. The Populists were as concerned about political democracy as they were about any other reforms and adopted as party shibboleths "Free Ballot" and a "Fair Count." In 1892 the Populists ran a national ticket as well as candidates for local, state, and congressional offices and in 1896 made their climactic effort, again at every level. That year southern Populists were undergirded, as usual, by their farmer ranks. (Some planters were Populists, but most large landowners lived in Black Belt counties where they controlled the black vote by various means of economic and even physical coercion and had long since made political deals with the other power bases: urban industrialists, businessmen, lumbering interests, textile owners, and mine operators.) The agrarians reached out to and succeeded in securing support in small towns and cities from labor unions, immigrants, and nonunion workers in textile mills and mines. Blacks in counties where they could vote without intimidation gave the Populists powerful support. In North Carolina and Alabama, many Republicans fused with the Populists and, despite their obvious philosophical and political differences, made common cause in the effort to defeat the Democrats. Particularly conspicuous were individual Populist leaders in individual southern states and a solid phalanx of newspaper editors who, despite being outnumbered by Bourbon editors, formed the Reform Press and fought the Democratic journalists with powerful resolve.

The 1896 Populist national ticket was doomed to failure despite the appeal of its "Free Silver" platform (a plan to promote inflation and ease the debt burden by having the nation coin silver at an increased ratio to gold). The reasons for defeat were many but came primarily because the Democrats also adopted free silver and because William Jennings Bryan was nominated for president by both Populists and Democrats, thereby splitting the reform vote. In addition there were other factors that included race, a lack of campaign funds, traditional loyalties, and poor organization. At the state level, southern Populist candidates stood small chance of victory against massive fraud and intimidation. There were widespread examples of stolen ballots, stuffing of ballot boxes, voting by dead people and by voters long since moved away, threats, and physical intimidation. Illegal electioneering tactics (much of it defiantly and proudly admitted later) by Bourbon Democrats defeated the Populists in many local, state, and congressional races in 1896. Nothing like it had been seen since Reconstruction. After 1896 the Populists maintained their party apparatus but were never again a major player at the national level.

Populists openly sought black support in most southern states. If their appeals fell short of promoting social equality, such a program was not credible in the 1890s. Even so, many Populists declared that skin color bore no relation to political freedom and economic opportunity. If part of the Populists' courtship of African Americans was based on political expediency, their commitment to improved race relations was significantly greater than that of the Democrats or Republicans. The reality of the Populist threat in 1896 was seen in the southern reaction of white conservatives. Blacks were legally disfranchised, usually by new state constitutions and state laws that simply eliminated African Americans as voters on grounds other than race. The devices used included direct primary elections, poll taxes, literacy tests, and property requirements for voting that targeted both blacks and a large number of poor whites.

Yet, in the long run, Populist principles prevailed, and almost without exception Populist demands were adopted later by both major parties. Monetary reform, a mass of regulatory laws affecting American society and the nation's economy, was enacted. At their best, men like Reuben F. Kolb and Joseph C. Manning in Alabama, Thomas E. Watson in Georgia, Hardy Brian in Louisiana, and a host of political philosophers, editors, and other politicians viewed Populism correctly as a movement. It was an upheaval, a native radicalism whose power base was largely rural but also contained other reform elements that aimed to change national and state inequities. The Populists insisted that all citizens should share in the bounty of America, and the principles of the People's Party still resonate in the rhetoric of contemporary politicians. Populism is deeply embedded in America, and, conceding the movement's imperfections, what the Populists stood for remains timeless.

WILLIAM WARREN ROGERS
Florida State University

Robert F. Durden, *The Climax of Populism: The Election of 1896* (1965); Helen G. Edmonds, *The Negro and Fusion Politics in North Carolina, 1894–1901* (1951); Lawrence Goodwyn, *Democratic Promise: The Populist Moment in America* (1976); Sheldon Hackney, *Populism to Progressivism in Alabama* (1969); Steve Hahn, *The Roots of Southern Populism: Yeoman Farmers and the Transformation of the Georgia Upcountry, 1850–1890* (1982); Richard Hofstadter, *The Age of Reform: From Bryan to FDR* (1955); William F. Holmes, *Agricultural History* (Fall 1990); Robert C. McMath Jr., *American Populism: A Social History* (1992), *The Populist Vanguard: A History of the Southern Farmers' Alliance* (1975); William Warren Rogers, *The One Gallused Rebellion: Agrarianism in Alabama, 1865–1896* (1970).

Progressivism

A far-flung series of movements encompassing diverse aspects of early 20th-century public life rather than a single phenomenon, Progressivism profoundly affected the modern South. Occurring across the United States, this social movement arose in response to industrialism, urbanism, and a new sense of nationhood; it also embraced the post–Civil War economy of railroads and an internationalized market economy. Viewing industrialism positively, members of the middle classes of the newly emerging towns and cities dominated Progressive movements. Rejecting the localism of 19th-century rural America and accepting the realities of the industrialized world, these urban reformers sought to restructure politics and public institutions in areas such as education, moral habits, public health, and child welfare.

Although many Progressives were male, a notable number were female. New roles for women shaped the course of reform, as middle-class women immersed themselves in social uplift and in efforts to recast institutions related to children. White and African American women led efforts to modernize the curricula and facilities of public schools, to regulate the use of children in mills and factories, and to institute new measures of child welfare. Southern women's efforts as foot soldiers and leaders in social reform moved them toward a single political reform: obtaining the vote. Although by 1910 the primary objective of Progressive southern women had become suffrage, the opposition of antisuffrage groups (the "antis") frustrated these state-level campaigns, and suffragists sought a national constitutional amendment. The Nineteenth Amendment was submitted to the states on June 1919, and it achieved ratification after Tennessee, on 18 August 1920, became the 36th and final state to endorse the amendment.

A strong moral fervor drove the reformers' enthusiasm. Overwhelmingly Protestant, Progressives were informed by an evangelical zeal to perfect human society. They wanted to purify southern society by rooting out vice and prostitution, and their most determined efforts focused on eliminating the manufacture and distribution of alcohol. Prohibitionism occupied a prominent position in Progressive era social reform; attempts to destroy the liquor traffic represented the most successful social reform in the South. The Anti-Saloon League, an organization originating in Ohio in the 1890s, organized state chapters across the South and, by the early 1900s, succeeded in persuading legislatures to enact local option ordinances banning breweries, distilleries, and saloons. Southern prohibitionists participated in efforts to ratify the Eighteenth Amendment, which was adopted in 1919.

Progressives in the South resembled their counterparts elsewhere in the United States. But at least two considerations made southern Progressivism distinctive. The first reflected how matters of race and white supremacy dominated the reform agenda; the second was the ways in which southern poverty shaped the goals, objectives, and methods of reformers. Among their most important objectives was a desire to change the practice of politics, public policy, and governance. Hostile to mass democratic politics, which they saw as an obstacle to efficient government, they took various measures to regulate the ballot, refashion voting practices, introduce political primaries (which, though democratic, also replaced parties' traditional means of nominating candidates), institute anticorruption measures (which limited parties' access to funds), and inaugurate civil service reforms (which limited the patronage powers). But these reforms occurred within the construct of white supremacy: while introducing political reform, southern states also barred African Americans from voting through methods such as the poll tax and literacy test. In truth, most southern Progressives were white supremacists who believed that black voting mistakenly arose during Reconstruction; ridding the system of African American participation, they believed, would be the most effective way to "reform" politics. But without black political power, the public policy revolution that reformers sought and partially accomplished in education, social welfare, and public health inordinately benefited white southerners at the expense of African Americans.

The poverty of the South also shaped a distinctive agenda. Much of that poverty was rural poverty. In general, reformers favored the reorganization of southern farming through the introduction of modern business methods: the system of county agricultural extension agents, which became established as a national, federally run program in 1914, first started in the South. County agents pioneered new methods in farming; female home demonstration agents, working for the extension service, preached the new gospel of the modern household to southern women. At the same time, southern Progressives sought to expand, modernize, and consolidate the isolated, community-controlled one-room schools that dotted the southern landscape. Other reformers began efforts to refashion the health practices of black and white southerners, focusing on the multitude of parasites, nutritional deficiencies, and diseases that plagued the countryside.

In the end, Progressivism left a mixed legacy in the South. The Progressives' reforms promised change, progress, and expanded opportunities, especially for women, for new forms of public involvement. Seeking far-reaching changes, in many instances Progressives encountered resistance from a powerful tradition of community control and localism. Indeed, by the 1920s, competing traditions of modernization and traditionalism squared off in the South, and a sort of dialogue between these forces continued throughout the 20th century.

WILLIAM A. LINK
University of North Carolina at Greensboro

Hugh Bailey, *Liberalism in the New South: Southern Social Reformers and the Progressive Movement* (1969); Glenda Gilmore, *Gender and Jim Crow: Women and the Politics of White Supremacy in North Carolina, 1896–1920* (1996); Dewey W. Grantham, *Southern Progressivism: The Reconciliation of Progress and Tradition* (1984); Jack Temple Kirby, *Darkness at the Dawning: Race and Reform in the Progressive South* (1972); William A. Link, *The Paradox of Southern Progressivism, 1880–1930* (1992).

Protest Movements

When Tom Watson, the onetime Georgia Populist, was asked the difference between his campaign and the one run by William Jennings Bryan, he replied, "Bryan had no everlasting and overshadowing Negro Question to hamper and handicap his progress: I HAD." Historians may quarrel about what makes the South different from the rest of the nation—a Lost Cause, secession, poverty, an agrarian tradition, race. But most would agree, along with Tom Watson, that the issue of race relations has dominated, hindered, and shaped protest movements in southern society.

The South emerged from the Civil War as a region committed politically to the Democratic Party. The Democrats had supported both slavery and secession. Moreover, white southerners blamed the Republican Party for Reconstruction, which allowed black folks to participate in the political process, an activity that implied racial equality. That was a concept the vast majority of southern whites repudiated. In addition, Reconstruction occurred simultaneously with the first postwar panic (1870–76); Republicans were thus identified with depression and agricultural poverty. By 1877 the "Solid South" stood solidly for the memory of the Confederacy and the Democratic Party.

There were, however, cracks in the frame that held the Solid South together. Isolated areas with large black populations elected some Republicans to public offices. Within the Democratic Party, both agrarian and conservative—sometimes called "Bourbon" or "Redeemer"—constituencies existed. The latter, committed to the New South, warned agrarians that to break with the Democrats would simply bring those black Republicans back into power, destroying both the white man's party and any chance for economic prosperity. Instead, Redeemers argued, the cost of government should be held down, white immigration into the region encouraged, crops diversified, and government stabilized, through the auspices of the Democratic Party; eventually, they argued, such acts of austerity and change would bring new industries and prosperity to the New South.

Until 1885 or so, most farmers were willing to heed such pleas. The agrarians, however, always applied pressure to the uneasy alliance between the conservative haves and the farming have-nots. Consequently the Patrons of Husbandry, or "the Grange," as it was more popularly called, enlisted 220,000 white southern farmers into its cause. The organization advocated crop diversification, economic cooperatives, and social and educational activities but eschewed politics. Where possible, it sent representatives to Redeemer constitutional conventions. There Grangers took the lead in defeating poll-tax provisions, passing laws that defined railroads as public carriers, and supporting any measure that held down the cost of government. The Patrons of Husbandry opposed both Republicans and third parties. Certainly the issue of race and politics inhibited Granger political protest, yet the organization's limited dissent from the New South orthodoxy was always watched with suspicion by the more conservative Redeemers.

The organization did train potential political protesters. Indeed, some contemporary observers maintained that the Greenback crusade attracted so many Grangers that the Patrons of Husbandry died. The Greenbackers, who wanted to issue legal tender notes to counteract agricultural depressions, organized third parties in Arkansas, Alabama, Texas, Kentucky, West Virginia, and Mississippi—all states with large Granger constituencies. These protest movements ran candidates for local offices in 1876 and for statewide offices in 1878 and 1880, when James B. Weaver was a presidential candidate. The party, although optimistic, ran well only in Texas, Oklahoma, and Kentucky. Tom Watson explained its failure: "The Democrats . . . wrote Greenback platforms, and then said to receding Greenbackers, 'Don't leave your old party; get your reforms inside the party; we white people of the South cannot afford to divide.'" Thus the policy of the Democratic Party toward political dissenters in the Solid South was to co-opt, use racial issues to divide, and promise moderate reforms. To a large measure, that policy never changed, and never did it succeed as well as in its defeat of southern Populism.

Populism grew from a sizable number of agricultural societies that appeared as the Grange declined. Historians have designated the Farmers' Alliance, first organized in Lampasas, Tex., in 1875, as the oldest of these voluntary associations. After intermittent stops and starts, the organization began again in 1879 and claimed 50,000 members by 1885. That same period, however, produced organizations throughout the South, such as Reliefmen in Mississippi, Brothers of Freedom and Commonwealth Organizations in Louisiana, the Cross Timbers of Texas, the Arkansas Agricultural Wheel, and the Farmers' Union of Louisiana. In short, southern farmers awaited only a charismatic leader to unite them in an agrarian crusade.

Charles W. Macune of Texas was that man. In 1886 he took over the Texas Farmers' Alliance. Within two years, he joined that organization with the Farmers' Union of Louisiana and the Agricultural Wheel of Arkansas, and the National Farmers' Alliance and Industrial Union, called the Southern Farmers' Alliance, was born. By 1890 the Southern Alliance claimed 3 million members, recruiting not only in all the southern states but in Kansas and the Dakotas as well. In addition, 1.3 million black people joined an affiliate known as the Colored Alliance. These organizations advocated free silver, improved public services, governmental control or regulation of public transportation, no convict leasing, repeal of the national bank act, fairer taxation laws, national and state election reforms, and the subtreasury plan. By 1890 no southern politician could ignore Alliance demands.

Ironically, Macune's organization spun off a political party more radical than most of its members. The key was the subtreasury plan. Macune proposed that subtreasuries be located throughout rural areas and that these government warehouses loan farmers, at 1 percent interest in legal tender notes, up to 80 percent of the value of staple crops. This plan attacked both banks and furnishing merchants and created a flexible currency. Orthodox Democratic politicians could not endorse this scheme, even when radical members of the Alliance demanded that local and state officeholders embrace the subtreasury, warning that failure to do so would mean that farmers would choose an opposition candidate. The result was a third-party movement that spread throughout the South during the depression years of the 1890s. The Populist Party would divide and destroy the Alliance, but it became the major challenge on the left to Democratic hegemony in the Gilded Age.

Democratic politicians struck back in two ways. First, the party moved to the left. James S. Hogg of Texas, John B. Gordon of Georgia, James Z. George of Mississippi, Ben Tillman of South Carolina, and Zebulon Vance of North Carolina, for example, all argued that they supported Alliance platforms but opposed such radical measures as government ownership of railroads and the subtreasury. They in turn passed moderate reforms, such as commission regulation, and spoke for free silver. Their slight move to the left prevented a massive switch of dirt farmers from the Democratic to the Populist Party.

The second maneuver was even more effective politically, longer lasting, and absolutely devastating to Populist hopes. The Democrats used racism to destroy the third party. Populists called for an alliance between poor blacks and whites. Their platforms denounced lynching and convict leasing and asked for guarantees of black suffrage. White Democrats charged that the unholy alliance of blacks and whites would corrupt southern morality and return the hated Republican Party to power. Meanwhile, southern conservatives shamelessly bought and intimidated black voters and used the free machinery of the state to cheat or "count-out" from office many successful Populist candidates.

After the death of Leonidas Polk of North Carolina in June 1892, southern Populists lacked a popular presidential contender. James B. Weaver, the old Greenbacker from Iowa, won the nomination in 1892. Conservatives reclaimed much of what they had lost in 1890, and in no southern state did Weaver win 40 percent of the vote. The panic of 1893 refueled the Populist charge. Democrats defeated their greatest challenge in 1894 by seizing silver as an issue, exploiting racism, proposing moderate reform, and controlling party machinery. In 1896 silver forces controlled the Democratic convention and nominated William Jennings Bryan, who carried the South but not the nation, and Populists saw their victories of 1892 and 1894 melt away as white, upland farmers returned to the Democratic Party.

The Democrats and their opponents, however, needed to chain the unleashed racism. Conservatives and liberals alike argued that politics could not be purified until blacks were disfranchised. Consequently, southern politicians began with poll taxes and continued through Jim Crow laws, carving out a separate and unequal society. The poll-tax legislation that disfranchised blacks did the same to most poor whites. Conservatives thus used the specter of Reconstruction to restrict the Left in the South. They convinced small farmers to reject third parties and their own economic welfare by threatening "Negro domination," and they convinced the same group to disfranchise part of their own numbers and to remain in support of conservative politics to keep the black in a subordinate position. The Left never overcame the myth of Negro domination.

Consequently, the two great events of 19th-century southern history, the Civil War and the agrarian revolts, left the Democratic Party in control; political wars pitted one faction of that party against another. Occasionally the Left would secede briefly and challenge the Democrats. Socialism claimed voting strength ranging from 20 percent of the electorate in Oklahoma to 32 percent in South Carolina in 1912. The xenophobia produced by World War I, however, ended the socialist crusade in the South as elsewhere. Likewise, negrophobia, in particular the outcry in the region against Booker T. Washington's friendship with Teddy Roosevelt, eliminated any appeal that the National Progressive Party might have had in the South. The first three decades or so of the 20th century thus saw the Left organize the Farmers' Union, voluntary acreage associations, and economic cooperatives and support such moderate reformers as Hoke Smith of Georgia and Braxton B. Comer of Alabama.

Conservatives retained control of the South until the New Deal. Franklin Roosevelt's policies galvanized southern politics because the region was so poor. Conservative Democrats came quickly to fear that the New Deal threatened their control of the southern economy with legislation like the Tennessee Valley Authority and the activities of the Department of Agriculture. They identified the Congress of Industrial Organizations, the Southern Tenant Farmers' Union, and the Farm Security Administration as political threats. Conservatives believed rightly that these federal and radical organizations sprang from the New Deal reform impulse.

Once more, conservatives turned to race to protect their economic interests. Many southern whites resented the New Deal's drive to win over urban voters and its consequent appeal to northern blacks. Although certainly not color-blind, the New Deal offered economic and social programs that included endorsement of a Fair Employment Practices Commission, antilynching legislation, and repeal of the poll tax; later came Harry Truman's Fair Deal, integration of the armed services, and civil rights legislation. The conservative wing of the Democratic Party struck back. In 1944 corporation lawyers, well-to-do businessmen, representatives of industry, and Black Belt conservatives organized the Jeffersonian Democrats in Texas, Mississippi, and South Carolina. In 1948 others in the Deep South joined this group and ran South Carolina governor Strom Thurmond for president on a Dixiecrat ticket. Dixiecrats carried only South Carolina, Alabama, Mississippi, and Louisiana, but battle lines were once more drawn, and race was once more the central issue of southern politics.

As southern conservatives cooperated with the Republican Party in the national Congress, supported Dwight D. Eisenhower in 1952 and 1956, and criticized the northern Democrats as being anti-South, the southern Left endorsed and fought for the national Democratic Party. Liberal southerners created such organizations as the Democrats of Texas and endorsed such politicians as Senator Ralph Yarborough (Tex.) or William Fulbright (Ark.)—all activities designed to commit southern Democrats to the national party's goals. A major goal after 1954 was, increasingly, an integrated society, and the cause of the southern Left became first and foremost integration. Conservatives' goals were to prevent it. Racism was used, as against Populism, as a barrier to any economic or social reform.

In the 1960 presidential race, Richard Nixon formulated the "southern strategy," implying there would be federal foot-dragging on integration in exchange for a conservative, Republican South. It was not successful in 1960, but in 1972 Nixon succeeded and the Solid South in some places is now more solidly Republican than Democratic.

The Republican Party in the South is composed largely of whites. Partly this is in reaction to the civil rights movement of the 1960s, a crusade endorsed by the southern Left. As the Student Nonviolent Coordinating Committee, the Congress of Racial Equality, and the Southern Christian Leadership Conference fought for equality, and Dr. Martin Luther King Jr., Stokely Carmichael, and James Farmer advocated civil rights, their cause dominated all other liberal concerns. The national Democratic Party endorsed these goals, and it won the support of southern blacks and other minorities. The 1960s witnessed triumphs for equality: the Civil Rights Act of 1964, the Voting Rights Act of 1965, the end of the poll tax, and an increase in black and brown voters. The Left predicted that a political coalition of blacks, browns, feminists, poor whites, liberals, and progressives would seize the South and bring about a myriad of reforms. Then, in the late 1960s, the antiwar movement swept the country and hopes of a broad coalition collapsed, as southern whites rebelled against black power, the student movement, feminism, and reform.

George Wallace led a major southern protest movement in the late 1960s and early 1970s, drawing supporters from a white backlash against the black freedom movement and liberal reform activities in general. Wallace was the charismatic governor of Alabama who first came into office in 1962 vowing "segregation forever." Using populist rhetoric and appealing to rural and working-class voters, Wallace mounted a major third-party effort in 1968, carrying Alabama, Arkansas, Georgia, Louisiana, and Mississippi in the presidential campaign. After an assassin's bullet crippled Wallace in 1972, his influence on national politics waned, but he remained a force in Deep South politics until the late 1970s.

By 1984 the Left in the South, as well as in the nation, was in disarray. "De jure" segregation, but not "de facto," ceased to exist. Civil rights no longer was the bellwether of reform. The Left concentrated simply on defeating maneuvers of Republicans to roll back the New Deal, Fair Deal, Great Society, and Supreme Court mandates for civil rights. Most southern blacks were Democrats, and most southern whites were Republicans. Consequently, party battles, in the South as in the nation, revolved around a liberal Democratic versus a conservative Republican Party rather than third parties or a Solid South.

The 1990s witnessed the rise of a cultural populism, rooted in the Wallace movement and its white constituency frustrated by social changes in the South. The Populist movement of the late 19th century saw economic activities as closely related to the maintenance of traditional values. Populists were profoundly skeptical of "progress," as defined by the forces of economic development, which they feared would threaten democratic control of government and an egalitarian society.

The late 20th-century Republican Party in the South appealed to white rural voters on social issues. The party's upper-income and suburban constituencies favored ties to, and support of, big business, but rural working-class whites responded to the party's labeling of the Democratic Party as a collection of elites, far removed from their social concerns. Such voters opposed abortion, gun control, gay rights, affirmative action, and welfare. While supporting school prayer, the Religious Right made evangelical Protestant churches a driving force in organizing these voters, who had a significant impact in electing and reelecting George W. Bush and in supporting countless congressional and state legislative candidates.

ROBERT A. CALVERT
Texas A&M University

Numan Bartley, *The Rise of Massive Resistance: Race and Politics in the South during the 1950s* (1960); Dan Carter, *From George Wallace to Newt Gingrich: Race in the Conservative Counterrevolution, 1963–1994* (1996); Joseph Crespino, *In Search of Another Country: Mississippi and the Conservative Counterrevolution* (2007); Carl N. Degler, *The Other South: Southern Dissenters in the Nineteenth Century* (1982); Lawrence Goodwyn, *Democratic Promise: The Populist Moment in America* (1976); Dewey Grantham, *Southern Progressivism: The Reconciliation of Progress and Tradition* (1983); James R. Green, *Grass-Roots Socialism: Radical Movements in the Southwest, 1895–1943* (1978); John B. Kirby, *Black Americans in the Roosevelt Era: Liberalism and Race* (1980); Alexander P. Lamis, ed., *Southern Politics in the 1990s* (1998); Christopher Lasch, *The True and Only Heaven: Progress and Its Critics* (1991); Robert C. McMath, *The Populist Vanguard: A History of the Southern Farmers' Alliance* (1975); Wayne Parent and Peter Petrakis, in *The Rural South since World War II*, ed. Douglas Hurt (1998); Theodore Saloutos, *Farmer Movements in the South, 1865–1933* (1960); Harvard Sitkoff, *The Struggle for Black Equality, 1954–1980* (1981); Samuel L. Webb, *Two-Party Politics in the One-Party South: Alabama's Hill Country, 1874–1920* (1997).

Race and Southern Politics

Race in the American South is the single biggest divisor in politics, education, and culture. Today the South is still home to the nation's largest African American population. According to the 2000 U.S. Census, roughly 54 percent of all American blacks live in the South, about 15.8 million of the 30 million in total. Political schisms based on race are not a new phenomenon for the South. Largely because of slavery and race, southern political history includes war, Reconstruction, and a long era of second-class citizenship.

Black southern political history fits into six distinct epochs: slavery, the Civil War, Reconstruction, the post-Reconstruction Jim Crow era, the civil rights movement, and the post–civil rights era. Slavery was the most apolitical time for southern blacks, as bondage prevented them from even the most rudimentary political participation. While by and large blacks were not actually political participants, their presence was the great political issue. The slavery question framed the concepts of states' rights and federalism as well as debates about admission of states into the Union.

The Civil War was fought largely over slavery, and race was also central to Reconstruction, which lasted from 1865 to 1877. Because of Abraham Lincoln's Emancipation Proclamation and the Radical Republican–led ratification in the U.S. Congress of the Thirteenth, Fourteenth, and Fifteenth Amendments, blacks mostly voted Republican. The Thirteenth Amendment declared an end to slavery throughout the United States. The Fourteenth provided for equal protection and due process and clarified citizenship, overturning the notorious *Dred Scott v. Sandford* (1857) decision, which said the framers of the Constitution did not intend for blacks to be citizens. The Fifteenth declared the right to vote would not be abridged on account of race.

Reconstruction witnessed unprecedented black political growth in the South. Largely because of armed Union troops protecting voters and candidates from violence and intimidation, African Americans voted in large numbers and fielded candidates for all levels of political office. At this time, blacks, being in the majority in Mississippi and South Carolina, were able to use this numerical advantage to elect their own to the U.S. Congress, including Senator Hiram Revels of Mississippi in 1870.

Yet, this political surge ended almost as quickly as it began. Following the Compromise of 1877, white southern elites, known as "Bourbon" Democrats, used the conclusion of Reconstruction to their advantage. These plantation elites instituted a series of laws and regulations that served the purpose of removing blacks from political power and planting a whole host of day-to-day humiliations on the black population. The Supreme Court's decision in *Plessy v. Ferguson* (1896) provided national sanction to the doctrine of separate-but-equal in public transportation.

Jim Crow quickly retarded the political progress made by blacks during Reconstruction. There were several Jim Crow political restrictions, and most harmful and pernicious were those that limited the vote. American states generally could impose restrictions on the vote because judicial interpretation of the U.S. Constitution at this time regarded voting as a "reserved" power belonging to the states, not a fundamental right belonging to all American citizens.

Many states instituted literacy tests, which the Supreme Court found legal in *Williams v. Mississippi* (1898). Written in a race-neutral manner, but mostly applied to blacks and very poor whites, these tests required voters to interpret a legal statute or clause of the state constitution. Whites were often exempted from the rigors of these tests through an "understanding clause," which gave the voting registrar wide discretion to deem who was fit to vote on an individual basis. Particularly good at nullifying the right to vote was the poll tax. This tax

"TIME WORKS WONDERS."

IAGO.(JEFF DAVIS.) "FOR THAT I DO SUSPECT THE LUSTY MOOR
HATH LEAP'D INTO MY SEAT: THE THOUGHT WHEREOF
DOTH LIKE A POISONOUS MINERAL GNAW MY INWARDS." — OTHELLO.

Cartoon published in Harper's Weekly, 9 April 1870, showing Jefferson Davis looking over
his shoulder at Hiram Revels seated in the U.S. Senate. (Thomas Nast, Library of Congress
[LC-USZ62-108004], Washington, D.C.)

was a fee to vote, and since most blacks during the Jim Crow era were in the economic underclass, it served the purpose of discouraging many from voting. The grandfather clause dictated that unless a person's grandfather was eligible to vote then that person was not eligible to vote, although *Guinn v. United States* (1915) declared this particular practice unconstitutional. State legislators often wrote these laws in a race-neutral manner, but rarely were they applied as such.

An additional form of voting discrimination was the white primary. The period 1876–1944 saw one-party voting in which the Democratic Party dominated in local, state, and national elections. As a result of the ineffectiveness of the Republican Party in the era, general elections were largely irrelevant because the Democratic primary was the real election. To exclude black voters, the Democratic Party declared itself a private organization that could limit participation in its internal affairs, resulting in the white primary. This lasted until *Smith v. Allwright* (1944), when the Supreme Court declared that the Democratic Party was not actually private.

Nonetheless, Jim Crow persisted throughout the first half of the 20th century. Characteristic of the legal struggle for equality during this time was the failure of the Dyer antilynching bill, which died in the U.S. Senate in 1918. Southern senators were able to kill legislation making lynching, a form of mob punishment, a federal crime. Southern congressmen were generally successful at keeping the federal government out of civil rights and out of the South until the civil rights movement prompted federal intervention.

Eradication of Jim Crow segregation and political restrictions was the larger goal of black protest. To that end, the civil rights movement, a large-scale effort led by southern blacks emphasizing nonviolent resistance, affected all Americans. Among the many southern blacks who played a particular role were Ralph Abernathy, Medgar Evers, James Farmer, Rev. Martin Luther King Jr., John R. Lewis, James Meredith, and Rosa Parks. The NAACP, the Congress for Racial Equality (CORE), the Student Nonviolent Coordinating Committee (SNCC), the Little Rock Nine, the Greensboro Four, and countless other individuals and groups combined to end Jim Crow in the South.

The first successful moments of the civil rights movement came from the Legal Defense Fund of the NAACP. Based in New York City and led by Charles Hamilton Houston and later Thurgood Marshall, these legal eagles sued to end Jim Crow racial discrimination in public accommodations, public transportation, and voting. Arguably, the most important case was *Brown v. Board of Education* (1954), which declared separate-but-equal in public education unconstitutional.

Of the many notable events of the civil rights movement, five are particularly significant, along with the numerous individuals who sacrificed time, energy, money, and, in some instances, their lives. On 1 December 1955 in Montgomery, Ala., police arrested Rosa Parks for refusing to give up her seat on a bus to a white man and violating the city's law requiring segregation on its buses. Cast into a role of national prominence, Rev. Martin Luther King Jr. helped lead a 381-day boycott of the Montgomery bus system. Eventually, the courts held segregation on intrastate public transportation unconstitutional and ended the boycott.

In 1957 the Little Rock, Ark., school board voted to integrate their school system, but segregationist governor Orval Faubus thwarted the plan. The integration plan was relatively benign, as the school board permitted just nine students to integrate Little Rock's Central High School. This form of token integration was common in the South following the Supreme Court's 1955 order to desegregate with "all deliberate speed." Governor Faubus's actions, including withdrawing protection for the nine students, prompted a constitutional crisis, and President Dwight Eisenhower sent troops from the 101st Airborne Division to protect the students from mob violence.

Countless incidents similar to Little Rock played out throughout the South in the ensuing years as blacks tried to integrate local schools. Many whites took a laissez-faire approach, yet many more, perhaps emboldened by the Strom Thurmond–penned "Southern Manifesto," fiercely resisted. The White Citizens' Councils best epitomize this massive resistance. First formed in Indianola, Miss., in 1954, members resisted efforts to integrate public life in the South.

Nonetheless, blacks and white liberals persistently attacked southern Jim Crow. The Freedom Riders in 1961, an integrated collection of northern college students, attempted to ride public buses from Washington, D.C., to New Orleans. Beaten, bloodied, and arrested in Alabama and Mississippi, the riders did not reach Louisiana. In 1963, during Freedom Summer, northerners attempted to register black Mississippians to vote. The murder of three of these civil rights workers cast a pall over the effort. However, these events stigmatized the South while also encouraging moderate whites in Congress eventually to take decisive action.

Prompted in part by Sheriff Eugene "Bull" Connor's 1963 unleashing of police dogs on civil rights demonstrators in Birmingham, Ala., the 1964 Civil Rights Act was intended to protect individuals against arbitrary discrimination. Passage of this legislation was not easy. Enacted after the longest filibuster (83 days) in Senate history, the act outlawed discrimination in hotels, motels, restaurants, theaters, and all other public accommodations engaged in interstate commerce; guaranteed equal protection for blacks in federally funded programs by prohibiting discrimination on the basis of race; banned discrimination in employment in any business on the basis of race; and established the Equal Employment Opportunity Commission.

Following passage of the 1964 Civil Rights Act, advocates still sought legislation protecting the franchise for blacks. Despite the Fifteenth Amendment's outlawing the abridgement of voting rights based on race, southern states in particular used numerous tactics to discourage blacks from voting, including literacy tests, poll taxes, and intimidation. The weakness of the Civil Rights Act of 1957 was evident by the paucity of black voters in the South. The 1965 Voting Rights Act became the single most important piece of legislation for increasing political participation of southern blacks. Between March 1965 and November 1988, the black-white gap in registration narrowed almost completely.

As written, the Voting Rights Act allowed federal registrars to enroll voters in areas where less than 50 percent of eligible voters were actually registered. These so-called covered jurisdictions were required to obtain preclearance from the Justice Department before they changed, or implemented any changes in, their voting practices to prevent any return to past discriminatory practices, or "retrogression."

The increase in black voter registration and office holding during the 1960 election altered the South's political scene. In 1960, 1,414,052, or 28 percent, of eligible black adults voted. By the end of the decade, 64.3 percent participated in the electoral process. Tennessee (92.1 percent), Arkansas (77.9 percent), and Texas (73.1 percent) were the southern states with the highest numbers of registered black voters.

In 1975 the number of black elected public officials in the South stood at 1,600. Within five years the number had jumped to nearly 2,500, and by January 1985 there were 3,233 black elected officials in the South. By 1993 there were 4,924 African Americans holding office in the South, representing 60 percent of the black officials in the nation. In 2001 there were 6,179 black elected officials in the South, representing 68 percent of the nation's total.

In the post–civil rights era, southern black partisanship has been reliably Democratic. Since President Lyndon B. Johnson signed the 1964 Civil Rights Act into law, southern blacks have voted overwhelmingly Democratic, with 1964 serving as a realigning election. Republican nominee Barry Goldwater, famous for his opposition of the 1964 Civil Rights Act, won only five states, his home state of Arizona and the four Deep South states of Louisiana, Mississippi, Alabama, and South Carolina.

Even so, for most white southerners the move from Democratic to Republican partisanship was gradual. An important distinction is the ideological difference between southern and national Democrats. Until the 1994 congressional elections, southern Democrats were considerably more conservative than their national counterparts in Washington, D.C., and enabled white southerners to vote in a bipartisan manner, yet consistently vote for the conservative candidate. Not until the 1980 election of Ronald Reagan did Republicans attract conservative southern candidates at the state and local level. Nonetheless, while the GOP is the dominant party in the South today, Republican hegemony in the South is not nearly as ubiquitous as Democratic hegemony was during the Solid South era. For instance, Democrats still control the Mississippi House, although it remains a reliably conservative legislative body.

In the post–civil rights era, two issues are particularly relevant to southern black politics: affirmative action in education, and criminal justice. Affirmative action policies are designed to correct past practices of discrimination against racial minorities. Two Supreme Court cases provide guidelines on affirmative action as it relates to higher education. First, in UC Regents v. Bakke (1978), the Supreme Court declared a special admissions program for minorities unconstitutional and specified that quotas violate the equal protection clause of the Fourteenth Amendment. In order to justify affirmative action as a remedy, a plaintiff had to show that a particular institution engaged in past discrimination. However, universities were allowed to use race as a "plus factor" along with numerous other factors. More recently, in Gratz v. Bollinger (2003) the Supreme Court affirmed a university's right to use race as a plus factor in admissions to obtain a "critical mass" of minority students, because diversity in higher education could be a compelling governmental interest as long as the program was "narrowly tailored" to achieve that end. In a companion case, Grutter v. Bollinger (2003), the Supreme Court stated the Constitution "does not prohibit the law school's narrowly tailored use of race in admissions decisions to further a compelling interest in obtaining the educational benefits that flow from a diverse student body." Justice Sandra Day O'Connor wrote, however, that universities should not allow affirmative action a permanent status but work instead to implement a "color-blind" policy.

The penal system, the death penalty in particular, has hit African American males particularly hard. Roughly 10.4 percent of all black males between the ages of 25 and 29 are either incarcerated, paroled, or on probation. Out of the 1,066 executions in America between 1976 and 2007, 363, or 34.1 percent, were black defendants; blacks now comprise 41.8 percent of death-row inmates. The death penalty is most prevalent in the South. Of the 1,066 executions, 749, or 70.3 percent, took place in the South, and out of the 363 black executions, 275, or 75.8 percent, took place in the South. This is particularly significant given the large number of exonerations, although southern states have been slow to embrace the death-penalty moratorium movement currently sweeping the nation.

Today the issue of race and politics in the South is more than just black and white. The region is a dynamic and changing environment, as exemplified by the sizable number of recent immigrants from Mexico and beyond. This influx has emerged as the next great challenge to the South.

MARVIN P. KING JR.
University of Mississippi

Numan V. Bartley, *The Rise of Massive Resistance: Race and Politics in the South during the 1950s* (1969); Earl Black and Merle Black, *The Rise of Southern Republicans* (2002); David A. Bositis, *Black Elected Officials: A Statistical Survey* (2001); Dan T. Carter, *From George Wallace to Newt Gingrich: Race in the Conservative Counterrevolution, 1963–1994* (1996); Joseph Crespino, *In Search of Another Country: Mississippi and the Conservative Counterrevolution* (2007); Robert A. Goldwin, *A Nation of States: Essays on the American Federal System* (1961); Ira Katznelson, *When Affirmative Action Was White: An Untold History of Racial Inequality in Twentieth-Century America* (2005); V. O. Key, *Southern Politics in State and Nation* (1949).

Reconstruction

Reconstruction was the period from 1865 to 1877 when national efforts were concentrated on incorporating the South back into the Union after the Civil War. The period involved important constitutional and political issues, but from the viewpoint of cultural history Reconstruction's underlying significance was its effort to remake southern culture. Neither before nor since have Americans had the opportunity to refashion a particular region within the nation. Some northerners approached this in a spirit of vengeance, seeking to punish southerners for the war; others had political motives for wanting to reduce southern influence and ensure Republican Party dominance and patronage for themselves; others were adventurers out to earn their fortune; still others were idealistic reformers hoping to aid freedmen adjust to their new status. Organizations such as the Freedmen's Bureau, the American Missionary Association, the northern Protestant denominations, the Republican Party, and the Union League represented the forces of the North. The image of the Yankee schoolmarm in the South was a prime example of this effort at cultural transformation. The Union soldier was another symbol of the effort: under the Reconstruction Act of 1867 the South was divided into five military districts and troops enforced government decisions. The cast of characters also included rapacious carpetbaggers, traitorous native scalawags, and ignorant freedmen.

This at least was the mythic view of Reconstruction. According to the myth, for a decade after 1867, carpetbaggers, scalawags, and freedmen ran the governments of the southern states, looting their financial resources, passing high taxes, denying whites a role in government, and spreading terror throughout the region. Only with the withdrawal of federal troops in 1877 did the terror end. Historian William Dunning and his students produced numerous state studies of Reconstruction that codified this interpretation in the early 20th century. Claude Bowers spoke for a generation of historians when he called Reconstruction "the tragic era."

Beginning in the 1950s modern historians such as Kenneth Stampp, C. Vann Woodward, and others challenged and revised this mythic view. They built on W. E. B. Du Bois's earlier work, *Black Reconstruction* (1935). Reconstruction, for example, did not last as long in most states as the myth suggests. Southern conservative, white-dominated governments took power in Virginia and North Carolina in 1870, in Georgia in 1871, in Arkansas, Texas, and Alabama in 1874, and in Mississippi in 1876. Federal troops were not withdrawn from South Carolina, Louisiana, and Florida until 1877. Moreover, actual military rule ended in 1868 in all the states except Virginia, Mississippi, and Texas, where in each case it ended in either 1869 or 1870. Civil state governments were in charge after that, except for brief periods of reliance on the militia or federal troops. No more than 20,000 federal troops were involved in the process.

Fraud surely occurred in elections, but the same was true of elections elsewhere in that period and under the conservative regimes that followed the Reconstruction governments. Only 150,000 whites were disfranchised under the initial military phase of Reconstruction, out of an 1868 white registration of approximately 630,000. Few whites voted and many blacks did, and more than disfranchisement, this explains the character of the participants in the governments. Blacks held offices during Reconstruction, mostly at the local level, but only in South Carolina was there a black on the Supreme Court and only the South Carolina and Louisiana legislatures had a majority of blacks. And no black served as a southern governor.

"The tragedy of Reconstruction is that it failed," wrote Carl N. Degler in *Out of Our Past: Forces That Made Modern America* (1970). Degler points out that modern historical scholarship rejects the idea of Reconstruction as a unique period of bad government and oppression, but one should remember that generations of southerners believed the myth, which nurtured in them the belief in regional differences and a consciousness of past abuse at the hands of northerners and their own former slaves. At the end of the war, southern whites were forced to accept the end of slavery, but Reconstruction showed their real commitment to a racial color line. This, not slavery, was a life-and-death matter. The thought of black social and political equality was unacceptable to most whites. Southern whites united in the 1870s in resisting northern-imposed radical change designed to end white supremacy. After the war, in fact, the defense of white supremacy became more clearly a southern position than before. In the proslavery argument, the defense of white supremacy had been couched in the broader defense of slavery, but race itself became the key issue in the post-bellum era.

Reconstruction was a struggle fought on many fronts. The same conflicts and issues seen in political life were also present in other areas of the culture. The Protestant denominations, for example, experienced trouble between blacks and whites, northerners and southerners. The spirit of Christian brotherhood did temper religious disputes more often than political conflicts. The northern missionary was an important symbol of Reconstruction. Missionaries came south to convert the freedmen and succeeded in convincing blacks to join several northern-based, predominantly black denominations. The missionaries also expected that southern whites would reunite with the northern churches, but southern whites exercised their spiritual self-determination during Reconstruction by preserving their regionally organized churches—the Southern Baptist Convention; the Protestant Methodist Episcopal Church, South; and the Presbyterian Church in the United States of America.

Education also reflected issues of Reconstruction. Northern teachers believed education would end the ignorance and brutality that abolitionists said existed in the South. Schools would promote democracy and class equality in good American, idealistic fashion. Blacks responded enthusiastically to the opportunities but faced the opposition of southern whites, who ostracized the northern teachers. Sometimes blacks also faced condescension of northern teachers who had their own racist preconceptions about southern blacks. Ultimately, though, the Radical Reconstruction program for public education was accepted. The southern white-controlled governments that came after Reconstruction did not reject black education, although they insisted on racially segregated systems of instruction.

In the development of southern black culture, the Reconstruction period should not be seen as a failure. Much progress occurred in the development of vital institutions: in education and landowning, in particular, and in community development. New leadership was tested for the future. Scholars have shown that the family survived slavery and in Reconstruction became a typi-

Members of the White League and Ku Klux Klan shake hands over a shield labeled "Worse than Slavery" depicting an African American couple with their dead baby and a man hanging from a tree. Published in 1874. (Thomas Nast, Library of Congress [LC-USZ62-128619], Washington, D.C.)

cally southern focus for individual endeavors. There was, to be sure, a debate on approaches toward the future. Was the best strategy racial self-help or interracial cooperation? Some black leaders worked for civil and political rights, while others—and probably the majority of the freedmen themselves—favored land and education.

Efforts by southern whites to end Reconstruction began almost as soon as the Radical Republican state governments took power. Not until northern weariness with enforcing Reconstruction took hold could much be done. Virginia was the first state "redeemed," a term southern whites used. Redemption was the process of replacing the Radical governments with conservative southern white governments. It was a well-organized political effort that also involved economic intimidation, community ostracism, political fraud, and violence. The Ku Klux Klan was the group most commonly involved in the violence. The Klan was a terrorist group that used violence against blacks and white Republicans in the name of preserving the morality and virtue of white civilization. Conservative whites eventually favored disbanding the Klan, which Nathan Bedford Forrest, its grand wizard, did in 1869, charging that outlaws had diverted it from its once high mission. Groups such as the Knights of the White Camellia and the White Brotherhood carried on the Klan's tradition, and Congress passed three Enforcement Acts in 1870–71 to deal with their violence. Nonetheless, the use of violence and other tactics led to the election of white southern conservatives, who maintained power thereafter, ending the threat to white supremacy. These methods of regaining power were called the "Mississippi plan," because they were perfected in that state in 1875–76. The Compromise of 1877, an informal, extralegal arrangement between southern Democrats and northern Republicans, brought the removal of federal troops from the South and the official end of Reconstruction.

Reconstruction had a positive legacy for the South. New state constitutions were written, many of which are still in effect as the basic documents of the states. It brought reforms in judicial systems, in codes of government procedure, in operation of county governments, in procedures for taxation, and in methods of electing government officials. Education was advanced, laying the basis for free public education. And constitutional amendments passed in that era supported the 20th-century civil rights movement's use of federal force to change the South's system of legal segregation.

Recent work on Reconstruction builds on the postsecessionist historians of the 1980s, who focused on shortcomings of Reconstruction state governments, including corruption, disastrous tax policies, and black disunity. They also criticized the limitations of northern reform efforts, seeing the supposed "radicalism" of the federal government as essentially conservative, with the U.S. Army and the Freedmen's Bureau working too closely with southern whites to push needed reforms.

Ongoing Reconstruction scholarship, which traditionally focused on political issues, has incorporated more social and cultural perspectives, broadening the understanding of the political. Eric Foner argues that class conflicts were as important as racial conflicts in interpreting Reconstruction. The upcountry white yeomen, a key constituency in postwar Reconstruction politics, were undergoing an economic transformation that coincided with the Reconstruction period, leaving them without their former independence rooted in their local, subsistence economies. Class and economic concerns weakened the yeomanry's long-term commitment to biracial politics. Foner points out that for a moment in time, "despite racism, a significant number of southern whites were willing to link their political futures on those of blacks."

Gender has also become a central concern in Reconstruction historiography, with women newly acknowledged as actors in the Reconstruction drama. The postwar redefinition of the household shaped Reconstruction politics, with such matters as legal marriage and control over women's labor and that of one's children becoming political issues.

CHARLES REAGAN WILSON
University of Mississippi

Dan T. Carter, *When the War Was Over: The Failure of Self-Reconstruction in the South, 1865–67* (1984); LaWanda Cox and J. H. Cox, *Reconstruction, the Negro, and the New South* (1973); Robert Cruden, *The Negro in Reconstruction* (1969); Laura F. Edwards, *Gendered Strife and Confusion: The Political Culture of Reconstruction* (1997); Eric Foner, *Reconstruction: America's Unfinished Revolution, 1863–1877* (2001), *A Short History of Reconstruction* (1990); John Hope Franklin, *Reconstruction: After the Civil War* (1961); Thomas Holt, *Black over White: Negro Political Leadership in South Carolina during Reconstruction* (1977); James M. McPherson, *Ordeal by Fire: The Civil War and Reconstruction* (1991); Michael Perman, *The Road to Redemption: Southern Politics, 1869–1879* (1984); Howard N. Rabinowitz, ed., *Southern Black Leaders of the Reconstruction Era* (1982); George C. Rable, *The Role of Violence in the Politics of Reconstruction* (1984); James G. Randall and David Donald, *The Civil War and Reconstruction* (1961); Heather Cox Richardson, *The Death of Reconstruction: Race, Labor, and Politics in the Post–Civil War North, 1865–1901* (2001); Kenneth M. Stampp, *Era of Reconstruction, 1865–1877* (1965); Daniel Stowell, *Rebuilding Zion: The Religious Reconstruction of the South, 1863–1877* (1998); Mark W. Summers, *Railroads, Reconstruction, and the Gospel of Prosperity: Aid under the Radical Republicans, 1865–1877* (1984); C. Vann Woodward, *Reunion and Reaction: The Compromise of 1877 and the End of Reconstruction* (1951).

Redemption

Over the past half century, the term "Redemption" has gained currency among historians of the South. When a historical term appears frequently in the literature, it usually means that it is becoming accepted as the most accurate or appropriate way of describing a particular historical period, episode, event, development, or trend. In this way, terms like "the Progressive Era," "the Civil War," "the Early Republic" become orthodox terminology for the thing they refer to. In the case of Redemption, however, the term is now employed generally, but the episode it categorizes is not agreed upon. Redemption can allude to two different things. It can either refer to the overthrow of Reconstruction between 1870 and 1876, or to the era after Reconstruction ended, from 1877 to the turn of the century. Thus, Redemption may be either a brief episode in the 1870s or a period, an era, of much longer duration.

The publication in 1951 of C. Vann Woodward's *Origins of the New South, 1877–1913* marked the beginning of historians' encounter with the notion of Redemption, because Woodward alluded to the men who came to power after the end of Reconstruction as "the Redeemers." By this, he meant to imply that these were new men, not the same elite that had formed the Confederacy and dominated it during the war. Historians before Woodward had designated these leaders "Bourbons," suggesting that, like the French royal family of that same name who returned to the throne after Napoleon, they had "learned nothing and forgotten nothing." They were therefore conservatives, even traditionalists, though they were not, of course, men with a particular taste for Kentucky whiskey! By introducing the new term "Redeemers," Woodward was arguing that this leadership cadre looked to the future and intended to redirect the southern economy toward manufacturing and railroads and to usher in an urban, industrial society, in effect, moving it toward a "New South." The end of Reconstruction marked, therefore, something of a break with the past, a discontinuity in the course of southern history.

Since the Redeemers were in power in the decades after Reconstruction, many historians began to refer to this era as "Redemption," sometimes as "the Redeemed South." All the same, the idea of these years as "the era of Redemption" or "the Redemption period" has never really been suggested in so many words. And indeed, Woodward himself never proposed it. After all, his book was entitled *Origins of the New South*, not "The Redemption" or "The Redeemer Era," so he never went so far as to coin a new phrase to apply to the period covered by his book. Thus, the term "Redemption" has been used to describe this period, but it has not really become accepted as, or attained the status of, a historical period.

More frequently, the word has alluded to the overthrow of Reconstruction in the 1870s. A collection of essays covering each Reconstructed southern state was edited by Otto H. Olsen in 1980 and called *Reconstruction and Redemption in the South*, while Michael Perman's *The Road to Redemption: Southern Politics, 1869–1879* (1984) employed the term both in the book title and in the title of its part 2. The problem with the terms "Redemption" and "Redeemers" is that they were first coined by the opponents of Reconstruction and applied to themselves. In fact, the phrase "the road to redemption" was introduced as early as 1870 by John Forsyth, editor of the *Mobile Register*, who was a virulent opponent of Reconstruction. These former Confederates conceived their task to be the redemption of the white South from "Radical rule," that is, to save the South, or perhaps reclaim it, from the evils of Republican government. By calling it Redemption, they were sanitizing and justifying their overthrow, often by violent means, of duly elected governments.

On the other hand, Redemption does provide a name for the active and organized campaign undertaken by Reconstruction's opponents that lasted a number of years, ultimately toppling every one of the Republican-controlled governments and thereby ending Reconstruction. Historians have often attributed the failure of Reconstruction to shortcomings among the southern Republicans themselves, such as internal rivalries, public corruption, poor political judgment, racial discrimination, and the like. Too often underemphasized, however, has been the ruthlessness and tenacity of Reconstruction's Democratic opponents and the massive onslaught they mounted against the Republican governments they considered illegitimate and alien.

Although it might not be the most appropriate expression, Redemption therefore refers to this campaign by the Democrats, the party of the South's economic and social elite, to eliminate the Reconstruction government, state by state. The process took place in three stages. The first occurred between 1868 and 1870. As the new governments created by Congress's Reconstruction Act of 1867 were being formed in the defeated South and a new electorate of black voters was being created, the opposition's strategy was noncooperation and abstention. They refused to cooperate with the federal authorities and they tried to defeat the new constitutions by abstaining from voting on them, thereby preventing the new governments from forming (a majority of the eligible voters had been required to participate under the terms of the Reconstruction Act of 1867, but Congress then changed the requirement). Once the governments were able to take office, the Democrats intimidated the newly enfranchised voters through violence carried out by the Ku Klux Klan, and they also acquiesced in the assassination of many of the leaders of the new Republican Party.

The second phase, from 1870 to 1873, involved public acceptance by the Democrats of the new Reconstruction governments and engagement in normal electoral competition with the Republicans who controlled them. At the same time, this overt accommodation to the reality of the new party and its new voters was accompanied by a less benign tactic. The Democrats began to subvert the Republican Party by encouraging dissension within its ranks by various means, both fair and foul. Then, whenever a division occurred and a bolt ensued, they threw their support to the bolting independents at election time, a tactic that was called "fusion." By 1873 this two-pronged strategy of apparent acceptance, but actual destabilization, of the Republican Party had resulted in the defeat of the Republicans in Georgia, North Carolina, Virginia, Arkansas, and Texas.

In the final phase, from 1874 to 1877, Reconstruction's opponents abandoned their tacit collaboration and campaigned instead as out-and-out Democrats determined to destroy the remaining Reconstruction governments, which were located in those states with large proportions of African American voters—Alabama, Mississippi, South Carolina, Louisiana, and also Florida. They played the race card vigorously so as to force whites to identify with and vote for the party of white supremacy, while they also unleashed violence and intimidation against the Republicans' black voters. Riots were instigated against blacks just before the elections in villages like Clinton, Miss., in 1875 and Hamburg, S.C., in 1876. Meanwhile, armed Confederate veterans on horseback, such as Wade Hampton's Red Shirts in South Carolina, paraded through black neighborhoods threatening likely Republican voters and sowing fear. As a result, the remaining Reconstruction governments fell to the Democrats.

This was how the South was "redeemed from Negro rule," as the instigators of these tactics described their movement. While it is useful to have a term to describe this aggressive and successful campaign by the Democrats to overthrow Reconstruction, "Redemption" is nonetheless an unfortunate epithet. Even though a historically authentic word, it is essentially a euphemism coined by its perpetrators to justify and sugarcoat their subversive and illegal actions. And therefore it is a problematic and pejorative term, rather like "carpetbagger" and "scalawag," which were coined by their detractors, the very same Democrats who overthrew Reconstruction and called it Redemption.

MICHAEL PERMAN
University of Illinois at Chicago

Edward Ayers, *The Promise of the New South* (1992); Eric Foner, *Reconstruction: America's Unfinished Revolution, 1863–1877* (1988); Glenda Elizabeth Gilmore, ed., *Who Were the Progressives?* (2002), *Gender and Jim Crow: Women and the Politics of White Supremacy in North Carolina, 1896–1920* (1996); J. Morgan Kousser, *The Shaping of Southern Politics: Suffrage Restriction and the Establishment of the One-Party South, 1880–1910* (1974); James Tice Moore, *Journal of Southern History* (August 1978); Otto H. Olsen, ed., *Reconstruction to Redemption in the South* (1980); Michael Perman, *The Road to Redemption: Southern Politics, 1869–1879* (1984), *The Struggle for Mastery: Disfranchisement in the South, 1888–1908* (2001); W. Scott Poole, *Never Surrender: Confederate Memory and Conservatism in the South Carolina Upcountry*

(2004); George C. Rable, *But There Was No Peace: The Role of Violence in the Politics of Reconstruction* (1984); C. Vann Woodward, *Origins of the New South, 1877–1913* (1951); Richard Zuczek, *State of Rebellion: Reconstruction in South Carolina* (1996).

Religion and Southern Politics

To the extent that there has ever been any truth to the term "Solid South," it has come from the distinctive relationship between religion and politics that has been a defining feature of the region. Pervasively Protestant, dominated from early times by evangelical groups, southern religion has tended strongly toward tradition and orthodoxy, being more biblical in belief, more emotional in practice, and more moralistic in its attitudes about the world than religion in other parts of the country. Over the last century, this conservative religion has contributed to the conservative politics of the region, as an alliance between evangelical and mainline white Protestants has provided a strong core of support for conservative political parties beginning with the southern Democrats of the early 20th century and continuing with the Republicans of our own time. Even so, the relationship between religion and politics in the South has been far from monolithic, as demonstrated especially by the divergent religious and political views of black and white Protestants. Moreover, with recent inmigration, southern religion has become less overwhelmingly Protestant, and this growing religious diversity has been reflected in the increasing political influence of Catholics in particular but also those of other faiths, as well as the secular unchurched.

From the time of earliest European settlement, Protestantism has exercised dominant political power in the South. Although Roman Catholics arrived first, establishing a foothold in Spanish Florida from the early 16th century, English-speaking settlers brought the Church of England with them, and it gained state support in every southern colony, beginning with Virginia in 1624. Although institutionally weak in many areas, especially along the southern frontier, the Anglican Church was strong enough in the most populated places to effectively assert its authority to collect parish taxes and compel attendance at some services, sparking determined protests from religious dissenters led by Baptists and Methodists. Following the American Revolution, these separatist sects flourished, encouraged by sympathetic political leaders such as James Madison, who led the campaign to disestablish Anglicanism (now the Protestant Episcopal Church) in Virginia and who penned the provision in the Bill of Rights preventing the establishment of a state church in the new nation. While some evangelicals continued to engage in political protest, including resistance to slavery, many more accommodated to mainstream norms, and by the early 19th century most had adopted attitudes that sanctioned and even sanctified the patriarchal, slave-owning family. In the antebellum period, evangelicals became still more supportive of the existing social order, as Baptists, Methodists, and Presbyterians articulated a biblical defense of slavery and broke from their national church organizations to form distinctly southern denominations. By 1861 any separation between church and state had all but disappeared, as southern clergymen in large numbers supported the Confederacy, describing the impending war as a crusade for righteousness and a "baptism in blood."

After the Civil War, Protestant political hegemony continued but came to be manifested in a variety of ways, with differences dependent on race and, to some extent, class and gender. Among white Protestants, church leaders contributed to the creation of a southern civil religion, the "religion of the Lost Cause," which combined Christian and Confederate imagery to reiterate the righteousness of the war and provide spiritual support for the racial segregation of the postwar period. Mixing moralism with a sense of white superiority, middle-class church members participated in prohibition and Sunday-closing campaigns while also advocating the creation of Jim Crow laws. In some churches, particularly those in the poorest parts of the rural South, Populists applied religious rhetoric in attempts to achieve economic reform. By the 1920s, however, with fundamentalism becoming a force in the South, increasingly conservative churchgoers directed their energies to outlawing the teaching of evolution in the public schools and defeating Al Smith, a Catholic, in the presidential election of 1928. Black Protestants, by contrast, responded to their loss of political power in the post-Reconstruction period by relying on newly created African American church denominations to act as agencies of social change: teaching literacy, providing social services, and creating a black leadership class, including many women, to exercise influence within the increasingly segregated black community. Some southern church women, black and white alike, brought about political reform through their participation in the antilynching crusade and the suffrage movement. Finally, a few Protestants—sometimes combining with Catholics and Jews—created interdenominational and interracial organizations, such as the Southern Christian Tenant Farmer's Union and the Fellowship of Southern Churchmen, to work for economic reform and racial progress.

In the mid-20th century, the South emerged from regional seclusion to play a more prominent role on the national stage, in large part because of its ability to combine religion and politics in new ways. From the time of the Montgomery bus boycott, the black church was inextricably tied to the civil rights movement, providing not only its biblically based philosophy of nonviolent protest but also an extensive infrastructure of buildings, community support, and politically skilled preachers led by Rev. Martin Luther King Jr. With few exceptions, white church leaders provided little support for the movement, and local pastors like Rev. Jerry Falwell insisted that the church separate itself from politics and concentrate instead on the winning of souls. By 1980, however, with the growth of evangelical and fundamentalist church membership, and with increasing concern among religious conservatives about social issues such as abortion, homosexuality, and changing roles for women, Falwell was exhorting his followers to become active in politics by participating in the movement of preachers and politicians that would come to be called "the New Christian Right." Led by televangelists Falwell and Marion "Pat" Robertson, institutionalized in national organizations such as the Moral Majority and Christian Coalition, and making use of local churches to distribute election guides and mobilize conservative voters, this religious-political movement rapidly became a force in national and regional politics, providing strong support for Ronald Reagan in the 1980 and 1984 elections while mustering millions of votes for conservative candidates in elections at the state and local level. With Pat Robertson's failure in the 1988 Republican presidential primaries, the movement lost strength, falling victim to tensions between Falwell's fundamentalists and Robertson's Pentecostals and to the endemic tendency of evangelicals to avoid politics altogether. Yet in spite of divisions and defections, the New Christian Right continued to exercise political power, primarily within the Republican Party, so that studies from the 1990s showed that activists associated with the movement controlled or held substantial influence in nine southern state party organizations and that voters sympathetic to it comprised up to 35 percent of the Republican electorate in some southern states.

In the South today, religion and politics continue to combine in distinctive but constantly changing ways. Maintaining the strong support of evangelicals and fundamentalists while also reaching out to mainline Protestants as well as to growing numbers of southern Catholics and Jews, the Republican Party has sought to solidify its control over the politics of the region. Simultaneously, black churches have continued to carry on the legacy of the civil rights movement, acting as part of a coalition of minorities—including Hispanic Catholics, Jews, and seculars—that provides the core constituency of the Democratic Party in the South. The result has been religious and racial polarization, as seen in the presidential election of 2000, when Republican George W. Bush won the support of 84 percent of observant white evangelicals in the South while Democrat Albert Gore received the vote of 96 percent of southern black Protestants.

Beyond electoral politics, however, patterns are more complex and diverse. On some social issues, white and black evangelicals hold similar views and at the state and local level have made alliances in campaigns against casino and race track gambling, the sale of liquor by the drink, and state-sponsored lotteries. Catholics have contributed to the complexity as well, combining with conservative evangelical Protestants to protest abortion while also acting in liberal interfaith alliances to oppose the death penalty. Other religious groups, even those small in size, have exercised disproportionate political power in other ways, as when Santerians in Florida won a precedent-setting case in the U.S. Supreme Court allowing them to engage in animal sacrifice as part of their religious practice. The growing presence of religious groups new to the region, including large numbers of Latino Catholics and small but steadily increasing numbers of Buddhists, Hindus, and Muslims, portends even less predictable political ramifications. For the foreseeable future, with the continued growth of evangelical and fundamentalist churches, and with the rapid in-migration of new faiths, the South promises to become both more distinctive and more diverse in its religious politics, and alliances of believers can be expected to play a defining part in southern politics in the 21st century.

MICHAEL LIENESCH
University of North Carolina at Chapel Hill

Kenneth K. Bailey, *Southern White Protestantism in the Twentieth Century* (1964); Glenn Feldman, ed., *Politics and Religion in the White South* (2005); John C. Green, in *The 2000 Presidential Election in the South*, ed. Robert P. Steed and Laurence W. Moreland (2002); John C. Green, Lyman A. Kellstedt, Corwin E. Smidt, and James L. Guth, in *The New Politics of the Old South*, ed. Charles S. Bullock III and Mark J. Rozell (1998); Christine Heyrman, *Southern Cross: The Beginnings of the Bible Belt* (1996); Evelyn Brooks Higginbotham, *Righteous Discontent: The Women's Movement in the Black Baptist Church, 1880–1920* (1993); Samuel S. Hill, *Southern Churches in Crisis* (1966), ed., *Religion and the Solid South* (1972); C. Eric Lincoln and Lawrence H. Mamiya, *The Black Church in the African-American Experience* (1990); John Shelton Reed, *The Enduring South* (1972); Charles Reagan Wilson, *Baptized in Blood: The Religion of the Lost Cause, 1865–1920* (1980); Charles Reagan Wilson and Mark Silk, eds., *Religion and Public Life: In the Evangelical Mode* (2005).

Republican Party

The Republican Party in the American South, now dominant in most national elections in the region, took a long, hard road to achieve this position. For nearly 100 years following the Civil War, the Republican Party was unwelcome in the South, but a party realignment in the middle portion of the 20th century reversed the party's fortunes. It is now stronger and deeper than its Democratic Party rival is, but it is not dominant in the same manner the Democratic Party once was during the days of the Solid South.

Following the Civil War, the Republican Party had little support among native white southerners. The common perception was that the Republican Party, through President Abraham Lincoln, had brought ruin and destruction upon the South in the war. First, Lincoln's election prompted South Carolina and then the other Confederate states to secede in response to the perceived threat of an imposing federal government. Then Lincoln's 1863 Emancipation Proclamation freed slaves in areas rebelling against the Union. For these reasons alone, white southerners generally felt nothing but hostility for Republicans. Reconstruction made matters worse.

Reconstruction, lasting from 1865 to 1877, was a period of massive social and political upheaval for the South. Elected with a veto-proof, two-thirds majority in both houses of Congress, Radical Republicans chafed against Reconstruction plans of President Andrew Johnson of Tennessee. The Radical Republicans split the South, excepting Tennessee, into five military districts, and Union troops occupied much of the region for the next decade. The Republicans in Congress also required the former Confederate states to ratify the Fourteenth Amendment as a condition for readmittance into the Union. This amendment contains several important clauses: guarantees of American citizenship, requirements that states provide equal protection and due process to their citizens, as well as certain political prohibitions on former Confederate officers. Despite ratification, for years many southerners argued that the Fourteenth Amendment had no "moral legitimacy" in the South because a "rump" Congress imposed it.

The backbone of Republicans during Reconstruction was a motley assortment of scalawags, carpetbaggers, and blacks. "Scalawag" was a pejorative term for a southern white who joined the Republican Party during Reconstruction. "Carpetbagger" was a derisive term for an opportunistic northern white who went to the South following the war. Blacks saw the Republican Party as the party of freedom and opportunity. The Fourteenth Amendment forbade many white southern males from seeking office after the war, and with a Union troop presence protecting black voters and candidates from intimidation, southern Republicans achieved electoral success.

Predictably, with the large majority of white southern natives finding circumstances intolerable, Republican hegemony quickly ended following Reconstruction. Violence and intimidation, aimed at blacks and white sympathizers, quickly transformed the Republican Party into a shell of its former self, and it remained weak until the mid-20th century. Bourbon Democrats sought to return the South to its antebellum roots and, through Jim Crow and the doctrine of white supremacy, largely succeeded. In this atmosphere the Republican Party languished for generations. It did have a few strongholds, however, and retained popularity in the hills and mountains of eastern Tennessee and western North Carolina. Primarily, though, the GOP, through its association with Lincoln and the Civil War, was a political nonfactor.

GOP weakness remained in effect through the Great Depression and Franklin Roosevelt's long presidency. However, during the 1930s and 1940s fissures started developing among southern Democrats that would sow the seeds for the later fracturing of the Democratic Party. The South was arguably the hardest hit region during the Depression, but finding acceptable means for recovery did not come easy. New Deal Democrats supported FDR's expansion of the federal government during this period, while conservative southern Democrats worried that intrusive federal measures would weaken the social, paternalistic, political, and economic order of the South. Most important were concerns of how federal largesse might upset the Jim Crow regime of the South. Thus, a long-lasting coalition developed between Jim Crow–supporting southern Democrats and economic laissez-faire Republicans. While not ready to change partisanship, Republicans and southern Democrats shared a distrust of an onerous federal state that led to an alliance between them.

Civil rights proved divisive for Democrats in 1948. Anger over inclusion of a pro–civil rights plank on the Democratic platform led to a walkout of the entire Mississippi and half of the Alabama delegation at the Democratic National Convention. South Carolina's Strom Thurmond led the revolt with an insurgent presidential campaign against President Harry Truman. While Thurmond's candidacy failed, it clearly set in motion the process whereby southern Democrats would abandon the Democratic Party over the civil rights issue. Although Thurmond returned to the Democratic Party, he became a Republican in 1964, and many more southerners would follow his lead. Modern Republican success at the subpresidential level can trace back to the 1960 election of Texan John Tower to the U.S. Senate. His election heralded a limited but auspicious rebirth of the GOP in the South. Tower won by portraying the national Democratic Party as being too liberal and out of touch with mainstream Texans.

The 1964 presidential campaign pitted incumbent Democrat Lyndon B. Johnson of Texas against Senator Barry M. Goldwater, Republican of Arizona. Despite his southern roots, Johnson generally sided with the underclass, and it showed in his domestic policy efforts. LBJ's forceful support for the Civil Rights Act of 1964, which greatly expanded the federal government's role in protecting civil rights for all Americans, especially for minorities, drew the enmity of many southern whites. Senator Goldwater strongly opposed this legislation, arguing against it, he claimed, not for reasons of racism, but as an issue best left to the states. This appeal to federalism and states' rights had strong attraction to Deep South whites. Nonetheless, President Johnson won reelection handily, with Goldwater winning only his home state of Arizona and four Deep South states, Louisiana, Mississippi, Alabama, and South Carolina. Though Goldwater lost in an Electoral College rout, the election served as a harbinger of things to come.

The 1964 election foreshadowed the slow but steady growth of the GOP in the South. The party was first successful in presidential elections and over time experienced electoral victories at the state and local levels. Several reasons explain the slow transition from Democratic identification to Republican identification in the South.

First, many scholars assert that partisanship is a psychological attachment. Once a partisan bond is established and transmitted from one generation to the next, it does not fade easily. Thus, native white southerners, who always considered themselves and their kind as Democrats, could not readily forgo that identification. Second, even though native white southerners may have felt abandoned by the Democratic Party, they made an important distinction between the national Democratic Party and the state and local Democratic Party. While the national party supported expansive civil rights for minorities, southern congressional representatives bitterly resisted federal efforts to expand civil and voting rights; highlighting their resistance was an 83-day filibuster in the Senate. Most important, southerners supported conservatives, and at the state and local level Democrats remained conservative.

Yet change slowly took place. First in states of the Rim South and then in the Deep South, voters elected a handful of Republicans to Congress in the 1960s and 1970s. By 1980 the perception of Republicans had changed, thanks to Californian Ronald Reagan. Understanding white southerners' attraction to Reagan significantly helps in explaining the political change that occurred in the South. Reagan's immense popularity in the region made it more palatable to claim Republican identification. This mental hurdle was an especially high barrier in many places where native southern, conservative whites were beginning to vote Republican but were reluctant to identify publicly as Republicans.

Originally an FDR Democrat, Reagan switched to the GOP in the 1950s because he believed it was the more anticommunist of the two parties. In 1964 Reagan proved he was a bona fide conservative with an extraordinary taped endorsement of Goldwater at the Republican National Convention. In 1980

Reagan won the presidency by campaigning as an optimistic conservative who favored tax cuts, a smaller federal government, and credible appeals to the nascent Christian Right movement, which had strong roots in the South. All these appeals, as well as his strong anticommunism, played well among white native southerners. At a campaign appearance at Mississippi's Neshoba County Fair, Reagan gave a speech that harkened back to Goldwater and made an unmistakable appeal to native southerners: "I believe in states' rights. I believe we have distorted the balance of our government today by giving powers that were never intended to be given in the Constitution to that federal establishment." Later in the speech, Reagan intoned that he would "restore to states and local governments the power that properly belongs to them."

Once the South turned the mental corner on electing Republicans, southern Republicans quickly transformed the national political scene. The watershed election occurred in 1994. Following 40 years of Democratic control of the U.S. House, Republicans took control of it primarily on the strength of their victories in the South. Of the 125 southern members of Congress in the 103rd Congress, 77 were Democrats and 38 were Republicans. Following the 1994 midterm elections, 64 Republicans and 61 Democrats comprised the southern delegation. After five Democrats switched their party affiliation, it was a 69 to 56 Republican advantage. The total Republican advantage in the U.S. House was 26 seats, with fully half of that advantage coming from the 11 southern states.

The most visible leader of the 1994 Republican takeover was Newt Gingrich. First elected from Georgia in 1978, Gingrich steadily worked his way up the Republican hierarchy. His vision of Republican prominence in the South and in the nation, coupled with the "Contract with America," catapulted him in 1994 to Speaker of the House. Gingrich best exemplified the southern preeminence within the GOP. In the House, Richard "Dick" Armey (Texas) was majority leader and Tom DeLay (Texas) was majority whip and later majority leader. The Senate, led by Trent Lott (Mississippi) and later by Bill Frist (Tennessee), a typically more restrained and august body, nonetheless moved in a rightward direction.

The impact of southerners on the Republican Party was unambiguous. The GOP placed more emphasis on curbing perceived liberal excesses, such as reforming welfare and pursuing deregulation in several industries. Additionally, there was much more emphasis on many divisive cultural issues (e.g., gay marriage, abortion, and euthanasia).

Perhaps the most memorable early moment of Republican control of Congress occurred, however, in late 1995 and early 1996, when Congress repeatedly challenged President Bill Clinton, himself a southerner from Arkansas, on the

TABLE 3. *Republican Strength in the South, 1951–1994 (Percentages)*

Year	Presidential Election	Senate	Governor	House	State Senate	State House
1956	52	0	0	7	3	4
1958		0	0	7	2	2
1960	26	5	0	7	3	4
1962		5	0	10	3	5
1964	37	9	0	15	5	7
1966		14	18	22	11	12
1968	45	18	18	25	13	13
1970		23	18	25	12	13
1972	100	32	36	31	14	17
1974		27	36	24	10	12
1976	9	23	18	25	9	12
1978		27	27	29	11	14
1980	91	45	45	36	14	18
1982		50	18	29	13	18
1984	100	45	18	37	16	22
1986		27	45	34	18	24
1988	100	32	45	34	23	27
1990		32	36	34	26	28
1992	71	45	27	38	31	31
1994		59	55	51	37	37

Sources: Charles S. Bullock III, in *The South's New Politics: Realignment and Dealignment*, ed. R. H. Swansbrough and D. M. Brodsky (1989); U.S. Bureau of the Census, *Statistical Abstract of the United States: 1994* (1994); Kae Warnock, press release for the *National Conference of State Legislatures*, Denver, Colo., 30 November 1994; *Washington Post*, 10 November 1994.

federal budget. While most Americans normally pay little attention to the day-to-day partisan wranglings on Capitol Hill, this time was different because the budgetary disputes led to the temporary closure of several federal agencies. This brought the dispute home to many Americans, and the net result was Clinton's winning the public relations battle as he successfully portrayed the Republican Congress as mean-spirited with its budget and insensitive to the needs of many Americans. Ideological consistency lost in a battle against pragmatic governing.

Despite that setback, Republicans kept a safe but small control of Congress for the next decade. Not until the 2006 congressional elections did the GOP relinquish control of Congress. This control never reached the largest margins that the Democratic Party mustered in its dominant heyday because the Republican Party was never as popular outside the South as it was inside. In other words, success at the congressional level never matched the party's success at the presidential level. During the 109th Congress (2005–7), when Republicans still retained control of the U.S. House, they enjoyed a 30-seat margin; however, in the South alone the margin was 27 (79–52) seats. Outside of the South the two parties were thus nearly even; it was solely on the basis of its southern dominance that Republicans controlled Congress. Following the 2006 elections, Democrats had a 33-seat advantage, but Republicans still had a 23-seat advantage in the South (76–53). Outside the South, Republicans were at a 56-seat disadvantage. In 2006 the northern deficit grew too much for the South to make up.

Today, the Republican Party in the South relies on a coalition of rural, pro-gun, social-conservative, and religion-friendly voters, along with members of the business community. Baptist religiosity of the South no doubt benefits the GOP. These so-called values voters identify with the GOP because it is willing to include socially conservative issues on the party's platform. Racially, the party is primarily white. Limited support comes from Asian Americans and Latinos, and the GOP continues to struggle to get the black vote.

The future of the Republican Party in the South is bright. National prospects are solid but circumspect, yet in the South, the GOP has a large, natural constituency that is socially conservative and still wary of a large, interventionist federal government. For those reasons, the GOP will remain competitive to dominant in the South for the foreseeable future.

MARVIN P. KING JR.
University of Mississippi

Earl Black and Merle Black, *The Rise of Southern Republicans* (2002); Joseph Crespino, *In Search of Another Country: Mississippi and the Conservative Counterrevolution* (2007); John Ehrman, *The Eighties: America in the Age of Reagan* (2005); V. O. Key Jr., *Southern Politics in State and Nation* (1949).

Segregation, Defense of

The 17 May 1954 Supreme Court decision in *Brown v. Board of Education* is frequently perceived as the start of both the Second Reconstruction and the white South's struggle to maintain the racial status quo. To be sure, the *Brown* decision had the type of crystallizing impact in the South that the Court's ruling a century earlier in *Dred Scott v. Sandford* had had in the North. Both decisions were followed by regional efforts to thwart the law of the land. Still, the perception that the Supreme Court in 1954 inaugurated a new era of federal involvement on behalf of the nation's black citizens is false. Moreover, southern resistance to federal attacks on segregation was ongoing.

During the decade prior to the *Brown* decision, for example, the Supreme Court had invalidated the white primary, ordered blacks admitted to all-white graduate and law schools, struck at racial segregation on interstate carriers, and barred states from enacting legislation designed to enforce racially restrictive property covenants. The President's Committee on Civil Rights was created by President Truman in 1946. Truman also ordered the desegregation of the armed forces.

Although all the aforementioned actions had not occurred prior to the 1948 National Democratic Convention, southern politicians clearly knew by that date the way the wind was blowing. Of special concern to white southerners was the report of the President's Committee on Civil Rights. *To Secure These Rights* (1947) contained 35 recommendations that touched upon virtually every facet of racial discrimination, including education, the armed forces, employment, and voting rights. When a majority of the delegates to the party's 1948 national convention adopted a strong civil rights platform, the entire Mississippi delegation and much of the Alabama delegation bolted the convention. A few days later segregationists from the South held a convention in Birmingham, where they created the States' Rights Democratic Party (Dixiecrats) and nominated Governor J. Strom Thurmond of South Carolina as their presidential candidate. The hope of the Dixiecrats was to secure enough electoral votes to prevent victory by either the Republicans or Democrats; the election would then be decided in the House of Representatives. In the House, according to the plan, the South would be able to negotiate a regional compromise that would protect the southern pattern of race relations. Although the States' Rights Democrats failed, they did focus attention on the "threat from Washington."

In many ways the Supreme Court decisions of the 1940s, the adoption of a civil rights platform by the Democrats in 1948, and the actions of President Truman were a prelude to the events that would follow the *Brown* decision. Indeed, the cumulative effect of the actions of all three branches of the national government was to abolish legal racial discrimination. Such a drastic change over a short time was, of course, resisted by many white southerners. The southern effort to resist change was based on an outdated philosophy and involved legal tactics, economic pressure, and violence.

Southern ideology had at its core the interrelated ideas of racial superiority and the natural order of things. According to the natural order argument, everything in nature had its proper place. In the words of a Florida jurist, "fish in the sea segregate in schools of their kind." The judge, as noted by Numan Bartley in *The Rise of Massive Resistance* (1969), used the example in an opinion that justified segregation. White southerners generally believed that the natural place for blacks was below that of whites. Quite simply, whites believed that blacks were inherently inferior.

The primary disseminators of literature that focused on the alleged inferiority of blacks were the Citizens' Councils of America (CCA) and the various state Citizens' Councils. These organizations had their beginning in Mississippi as part of the reaction to the *Brown* ruling. At first the Citizens' Councils concentrated on the school issue, but as the civil rights protest expanded, council members fought to maintain all forms of segregation. Unlike the Ku Klux Klan, the Citizens' Councils rejected the use of violence.

Convinced that the average white northerner held essentially the same racial beliefs as white southerners, the CCA embarked upon a propaganda campaign designed to demonstrate black inferiority. One tract cited in Neil R. McMillen's *Citizens' Council* (1971) lists the "eleven most essential differences between the two races." As was the case with racist literature of an earlier era, the CCA handbook contended that there were differences between the eyes, ears, hair, lips, noses, cheek bones, jaws, skulls, and voices of whites and blacks. Of special significance was an alleged difference in brain weight. *Racial Facts*, a publication of the Mississippi Council, asserted that the IQ of blacks was between 15 and 20 points below the average for whites.

Segregationists were especially prone to utilize the writings of Carleton Putnam and Carleton Coon. Putnam, a native of the North and a retired airline executive, was the author of *Race and Reason: A Yankee View* (1961). He first came to the attention of segregationists in 1958 through an open letter to President Eisenhower in which he defended segregation. In *Race and Reason* Putnam asserted that blacks were intellectually inferior and that the American public had been misled by a "pseudo-scientific hoax" put forth by anthropologists who were advocates of "racial equipotentiality."

Coon, a former president of the American Association of Physical Anthropologists, was the author of *The Origin of Races* (1962). In this study Coon concluded that over 500,000 years ago one species of man, *Homo erectus*, existed. According to Coon, *Homo erectus* evolved into *Homo sapiens* at different times and in different geographic locations. Five such evolutionary processes occurred. His research also led Coon to conclude that Caucasoids were about 500,000 years ahead of Negroids in terms of evolutionary development.

Segregationists, both those belonging to Citizens' Councils and those holding political office, frequently cited the writings of Coon and Putnam. Southerners were interested in the two men because of the belief that such individuals gave credibility to the segregationists' perspective. Credibility was essential to any campaign designed to convince northerners that the South should be allowed to continue its way of life.

From a political perspective, southerners resorted to the compact theory of government in their effort to overturn the *Brown* decision and to protect regional values. Drawing upon the writings of Jefferson and Calhoun, southern theorists concluded that the *Brown* ruling was unconstitutional. According to this rationale, public education was constitutionally a function of the states and not the federal government. Therefore, the Supreme Court had exceeded its authority by amending the Constitution, rather than merely interpreting it. In the effort to nullify the Court's action, southern politicians proposed to utilize the tools of massive resistance and interposition.

Interposition, a doctrine adopted by eight southern states in 1956 and 1957, was designed to defeat court-ordered desegregation. Under the plan, the sovereignty of the state would be interposed between the federal courts and local school officials. Advocates of the doctrine were convinced that federal judges would not issue contempt of court citations and jail governors and other elected state officials who refused to obey desegregation orders. Critical to the success of the plan was regionwide noncompliance. Total or near-total opposition to desegregation would persuade northerners to abandon efforts to force the South to give up its way of life.

The campaign for massive resistance was encouraged by southerners serving in Congress. In 1956 all but 27 of the southerners in Congress signed a "Southern Manifesto" in which they urged the states to resist integration. Likewise, pressure was brought to bear upon newspaper editors to ensure that they not encourage compliance with the law. And in Orangeburg, S.C., economic pressure was applied to those black parents who had petitioned to have their children attend desegregated schools; the schools in Orangeburg remained segregated. Meanwhile, schools in portions of some states (Prince Edward County, Va., for example) were closed to prevent integration. Several states favored the idea of closing the public schools and providing tuition grants to students who would attend private segregated schools. Finally, in four states (Alabama, Mississippi, Florida, and Georgia) the doctrine of nullification was implemented as legal action was taken to declare the *Brown* decision to be null and void. In these four states, as well as others in the old Confederacy, over 450 new segregation measures were passed. The new laws protected segregation and made desegregation illegal.

With the coming of the sit-in movement and the freedom rides of the 1960s, violence began to characterize part of the resistance to change. In *SNCC: The New Abolitionists* (1964), Howard Zinn describes the violence that confronted civil rights workers. Among the more prominent acts of violence perpetrated upon civil rights workers were the firebombing of a bus carrying freedom riders at Anniston, Ala. (1961), the murders in Mississippi of Medgar Evers (1963) and of three civil rights field-workers—Andrew Goodman, James Chaney, and Michael Schwerner (1964)—and the violence of law enforcement officials in Birmingham, Ala. (1963). In Birmingham, police used fire hoses and police dogs against demonstrators, many of whom were children. The use of force against civil rights activists was counterproductive. Each night citizens throughout the land who watched the evening news on television witnessed acts of violence being perpetrated upon fellow Americans. Northerners, as well as many white southerners, were shocked by the tactics of Birmingham officials. Equally disturbing to Americans was the bombing of Birmingham's Sixteenth Street Baptist Church, an incident that killed four black children who were attending Sunday school. Without a doubt, the acts of violence destroyed any sympathy that southern propagandists had created in the North and stimulated the passage of the Civil Rights Act of 1964.

By the mid-1960s the civil rights movement had moved beyond the limits of the South and into the North's ghettos. Here the frustrations associated with joblessness, poverty, and hopelessness led to the long, hot summers of rioting, burning, and looting. As the nation's great cities burned, a white backlash against blacks became apparent. Governor George Wallace of Alabama exploited this backlash, as well as a growing working-class anger with student demonstrators, antiwar activists, and the nation's welfare system. Using a "law and order" argument that had strong racial overtones, Wallace emerged as a national political force. As the candidate of the American Independent Party in 1968, he won 46 electoral votes and 13.5 percent of the popular vote.

Recent scholarship presents a nuanced picture of southern white responses to the threat of desegregation. Most white southerners did not identify with violent resisters to the civil rights movement, but their fearful silence allowed a militant defense of segregation to proceed. Moderates were unable to respond to the pace of social change, except with inaction.

In the final analysis, southern attempts to maintain legal segregation failed.

Indeed, not one of the tactics employed brought eventual success. Americans rejected the outdated belief that blacks are inherently inferior. Interposition ultimately forced whites to decide that desegregated schools were far preferable to no schools. Violence was counterproductive. And even a majority of the South's voters rejected the third party candidacies of Thurmond in 1948 and Wallace in 1968.

Just as there was no clearly defined beginning to the South's resistance to change, there is no clearly defined end. As legal segregation was abolished, patterns of de facto segregation emerged. Whites fled to the suburbs, argued in favor of neighborhood schools, and opposed court-ordered busing of students to achieve racially balanced schools. In the final analysis, the types of race-related problems that now exist in the South are essentially the same as those that exist elsewhere in the nation.

WILLIAM J. BROPHY
Stephen F. Austin State University

Pete Daniel, *Lost Revolutions: The South in the 1950s* (2000); George Lewis, *Massive Resistance: The White Response to the Civil Rights Movement* (2006); Jason Sokol, *There Goes My Everything: White Southerners in the Age of Civil Rights, 1945–1975* (2006).

Social Class and Southern Politics

Class patterns imported from England took root in the South back in the colonial era. The earliest settlers included few members of the British aristocracy or large-landed proprietor class; the organizers of these expeditions were for the most part adventurous, ambitious, talented people from the middle ranks of British society who sought opportunities not open to them at home in 17th-century Britain. A combination of circumstances made large-scale agriculture—or the plantation economy—not only possible but highly desirable. The planter "aristocrat" (later designated "cavalier") became the southern upper class and was the natural source of political leadership. A pattern of rural-based, planter-dominated politics was established and then extended as the South expanded into the areas south and west of the Chesapeake Bay area. This pattern was not completely broken (despite all the vicissitudes of the region's history) until the 20th century.

At the opposite end of the social scale, of course, was the black slave. Introduced into Virginia by a Dutch trader in 1619 as long-term indentured servants, blacks provided a permanent source of agricultural labor that served the expanding plantation cash-crop system. The enslavement of blacks soon followed, and by the middle of the 17th century the practice was made legal in Virginia. From there slavery moved to other areas, seemed in decline during the relative stagnation of the Tidewater plantations from soil depletion in the late 18th century, and developed and expanded again after 1795 with the invention of the cotton gin and the growth of the Deep South states. Slavery thus provided the plantation system a labor supply that was locked into a permanent state of economic and social immobility, rendered totally dependent, and excluded from the possibility of citizenship and participation in politics. It was ironic that upper-class slave owners like Thomas Jefferson would, in the 18th century, revolt (in the name of individual freedom and a new order of republican government) against the feudal remnants of inherited privilege. A further irony was the democratization of that republican form of government in the following century, as the South was beginning its self-conscious defense of slavery.

One other social class more or less formally identified as such well before the American Revolutionary era and continuously recognized as part of the social structure ever since was the southern "poor white." In 1728 William Byrd II headed a commission to establish the boundary between North Carolina and Virginia. Among other extensive descriptions of places and events in his *History of the Dividing Line* (not published until 1841, but circulated soon after it was produced) Byrd included a graphic account of a singularly unprepossessing group of people in the border backwoods who were referred to as "lubbers." Undernourished and unhealthy, indolent and dirt poor, ignorant and unskilled to the point of surviving only through low native cunning, the "lubber" became the prototype for what, under various derogatory ascriptions, was in effect a declassed, poverty-stricken, rural southern white. Though not clearly fixed by sociological definition, and relatively small in number even when extended to include economically marginal hill farmers, "poor whites" became such a literary convention that many people outside the South (and some inside it) think stereotypically that the South is composed of only three social classes—the planter aristocrat, the poor white, and the black.

In point of fact, through much of southern history the middle class was numerically dominant, because it included the yeoman farmer as well as the small-town merchant and professional person. The planter became both an idealized type and a real wielder of economic, social, and political power, and the economic importance and potential in democratic politics of the middle class was not effectively recognized until the 20th century.

Throughout the colonial period the planter aristocratic tradition continued to hold sway in politics (most notably in Virginia and South Carolina), and public service was considered a part of the continuing obligation of that class. In the more prominent families, males prepared for this role by joining a classical education to the study of law. The tradition produced a remarkable collection of early political leaders whose contributions to the American Revolution, the framing and adoption of the Constitution, and the early experience in making the Republic work are incalculable. Out of this class Virginia alone furnished the draftsman of the Declaration of Independence (Jefferson), the chief military commander of the Revolution who was later the presiding officer of the Constitutional Convention (Washington), that convention's most effective recorder and interpreter (Madison), four of the first five presidents of the United States (Washington, Jefferson, Madison, and Monroe), and the chief justice of the U.S. Supreme Court (Marshall) who did more than anyone to shape that branch of the national government into the powerful instrument it became. Prominent figures from the South were leaders in developing the Federalist Party, and Jefferson and Madison were the founders of the opposition Republican Party, which later became the Democratic Party. Jefferson's ideas had as much influence on the transition of the American Republic into a constitutional democracy as those of any other single person.

But if it was aristocrats such as Jefferson who provided much of the impetus for American democracy, it was left for the descendants of the "plain folk" settlers of the first American frontier (what are now the states of the Upper South) to make the practical transition in the form of Jacksonian democracy. From roughly the time of Jackson's election to the presidency in 1828 until the breakup of the party system in 1860, the South was part of national two-party politics in which the competition between the Democrats and Whigs was close, and the division in party adherence tended to be along social class lines that are still familiar. The Jacksonian Democrats found support in an expanding electorate moving toward universal white manhood suffrage, and the bulk of its supporters were farmers and laborers. The traditions of Jeffersonian agrarianism and decentralization of political power by way of geographically based pluralism also kept many planters in the Democratic fold. The Whigs, who displaced the moribund Federalists, tended to reflect the growth of the business and professional middle classes that were part of the incipient industrial development. Early in this period the New England reform movement, of which antislavery was simply one part, combined with the rapidly growing commercial and manufacturing interests in the Northeast to produce increasing sectional tensions that often turned on the way the North-South political and economic balance was to be maintained in the face of the slave-state versus free-state issue.

On the eve of the Civil War, an Alabama lawyer-planter and sometime Chicago businessman, Daniel R. Hundley, published a book entitled *Social Relations in Our Southern States* (1860). The study may well be the first attempt at a systematic analysis of the structure of social classes in the South. Hundley goes beyond the use of basic demographic characteristics in developing his taxonomy, identifying traits of character that affect political behavior and the social types he perceived. Although the southern gentleman is his ideal type, being a planter at a certain economic level is not enough to place one in this category. Two other types may be economically successful, yet never attain the nobility of character, the appropriate sense of honor, and the other virtues that would qualify them as gentlemen. These "cotton snobs" and "southern Yankees" in their respective ways were interested more in getting and spending wealth than in the conduct of individual and social life, according to the higher standards of the gentleman. Similarly, Hundley analyzes the middle classes, the primary categories being those in the towns (merchants and so on) and the yeoman farmers, with considerable range in each category in terms of social and economic functions as well as moral considerations. Two other categories that rank low on Hundley's scale of character traits are the "southern bully" (who may range widely in economic status) and "poor white trash"—the extended lubber image. Hundley also includes the "Negro slaves" in his discussion, but mainly for purposes of comparing the social condition of the slaves in the South favorably with the exploited "free" laborers elsewhere.

Hundley's book provided a solid sense of the complexity of the social structure of the pre–Civil War South and revealed the extent to which the South remained traditionally status-based in its social hierarchy rather than moving toward a social structure comparable to that in the northeastern states. The South held to the plantation-agrarian ideal as opposed to contractual foundations of social, economic, and political relations. *Social Relations in Our Southern States* anticipated the restoration in the post-Reconstruction South of something as close to the social structure of the antebellum South as the emerging ruling elite of planters, lawyers, doctors, merchants, and bankers could manage.

The South's "politics as usual" after Reconstruction was a one-party politics in which blacks were, by the end of the 19th century, removed from direct participation. Blacks were used as a symbolic threat to keep white voters in line when economic or other issues that generated divisions along class lines produced electoral challenges to the dominant structures of political power. Voter participation in elections at all levels declined as large numbers of poor whites (as well as virtually all blacks) were disqualified, and a large portion of those who were qualified did not bother to turn out for elections. Intraparty competition was carried on through various types of factional alignments, with the primary elections for nomination of candidates the point at which the real competition (if any) took place.

From time to time various political movements threatened to break the long-standing pattern of control by the Bourbon-planter class. In the 1890s the "farmer's revolt" made some headway in the South (as it did in the Midwest) when the Populist Party challenged the Bourbon-planter hegemony. Although Populism's main sources of support were the small farmers and laboring classes, it was never able to generate a voter coalition strong enough to sustain the few successes it had at the polls, partly at least because the possibility of uniting blacks and whites in the common effort was diverted by appeals to white racial unity within the Democratic Party. Vestiges of Populism appeared in factional form from time to time after 1900, most notably in the case of the Long faction in Louisiana, where economic issues overrode racial ones for a considerable period of time. Southern Progressivism, more of an urban middle-class phenomenon, also constituted reformist challenges to the dominant forces on occasion, but the voter divisions here tended to be less identifiable along class lines than in the case of Populism.

In the 20th century the South began to concentrate more on its economic development, which was interrupted by the Depression but stimulated by the New Deal reforms and by World War II. A new generation of southern political leaders emerged after the war, and the national Democratic Party began to take some initiative in advancing both party and national governmental programs against racial segregation.

The actions along these lines in the 1948 Democratic convention led to a walkout on the part of some of the southern states that was the beginning of the breakup of the "old" southern one-party politics and of the social practices that had such an important role in its long perpetuation. The subsequent civil rights movement, the rapid urban-industrial growth in the South, the centralization of governmental power, and all of the related changes have gradually produced political alignments among voters in the South that are more congruent with "normal" American tendencies to vote along economic and social class-interest lines than was the case during the era of the solid Democratic South. The nearest thing to a complete political mobilization of a socially identifiable group is the steady support of 90 percent and upwards of the black vote for Democratic candidates in straight contests between regular party candidates. A steady growth has occurred in middle-class, urban-suburban southern Republicanism. The "cultural wars" of the 1990s brought ideological divisions that sometimes blurred social class lines. It remains to be seen whether the "new" politics will mean continuing movement toward convergence in the social class patterns of support for parties, factions, individual candidates, and issues in the southern and nonsouthern states or whether new, but still distinctive, ones will emerge.

WILLIAM C. HAVARD
Vanderbilt University

Jane Dailey, Glenda Elizabeth Gilmore, and Bryant Simon, *Jumpin' Jim Crow: Southern Politics from Civil War to Civil Rights* (2000); Daniel R. Hundley, *Social Relations in Our Southern States* (1860); Jacqueline Jones, *The Dispossessed: America's Underclass from the Civil War to the Present* (1992); V. O. Key Jr., *Southern Politics in State and Nation* (1949); J. Morgan Kousser, *The Shaping of Southern Politics: Suffrage Restriction and the Establishment of the Old-Party South, 1880–1920* (1974); Richard Nisbet and Dov Cohen, *Culture of Honor: The Psychology of Violence in the South* (1996).

Taxing and Spending

Southern state governments were long distinguished by their relatively low levels of government spending and taxation and by the often regressive nature of their tax systems. Southern states spent, for example, an average of $1,657 per pupil for education in 1977–78, while the national average was $2,002. The average southern state spent 0.11 percent of its total expenditures on land and water quality control during the same year while the national average was 0.31 percent. In another example, the average southern state's Aid to Families with Dependent Children grant received an "adequacy score" of 8.09 percent in 1977 while the national average was 13.58 percent.

Southern states generally still obtain a greater share of their operating revenue from sales taxes than other states do, and their income-tax structures are often less progressive. In fact, one of the few southern governmental innovations was the sales tax itself, pioneered by Mississippi in 1934, and Alabama today has the most regressive tax structure of any state. These tax patterns have long helped to account for the widely held perception than the southern states are not normally as active, vigorous, or "forward-thinking" as the rest of the country.

Perhaps because governments are often evaluated on the basis of their taxing and spending policies, much research has been devoted to a systematic analysis of the causes and effects of the distinctive southern patterns of taxing and spending. An appreciation of the issues addressed in these studies is necessary to understand the extent to which southern cultural traditions and circumstances are related to the fiscal policies so readily observed.

The most frequently cited explanation for southern taxing and spending patterns is the traditional absence of effective party competition. V. O. Key Jr. suggested that one-party states spend less on social programs than states with a competitive structure simply because a single dominant party does not have to advocate and implement responsive policies in order to win elections. This notion appeared to have considerable validity when it was advanced in the 1940s, because it was consistent with impressionistic and anecdotal accounts of one-party politics and because it was derived from a straightforward theory of parties and government. The degree of party competition and the level of government spending for various social programs were statistically associated when all states were compared, and this provided additional support for Key's argument.

Key's theory became widely accepted and provided a solid foundation for linking basic southern political characteristics to public policy choices. Certainly, the tradition of Democratic Party dominance is a fundamental part of the southern political heritage, and it was not surprising that government expenditures reflected its influence. However, by the 1960s a different view was presented by other scholars, particularly Thomas R. Dye. Low government spending and regressive taxation could be explained by economic variables. According to Dye, "when the effects of economic development are controlled . . . almost all of the association between party competition and policy disappears."

This finding, and the voluminous research that it spawned, was unsettling to many students of politics because it suggested that basic political factors, such as party competition, were not important in terms of public policy. It also directly challenged the notion that the special character of southern politics and culture was fundamentally important in explaining why southern governments behaved differently; Dye's research indicated that any poor, rural state would adopt the taxing and spending patterns associated with the South.

The most compelling responses to Dye's line of reasoning emphasized political culture. Daniel Elazar suggested that three political subcultures can be identified among the American states—moralistic, individualistic, and traditionalistic. The southern states generally are dominated by traditionalistic subcultures, according to Elazar, which means that their governments should be expected to "maintain traditional patterns" and to be generally conservative in public policy. Conversely, moralistic states, such as Minnesota, Oregon, and Wisconsin, use government to further a representative conception of the good of the "commonwealth." Individualistic states have both moralistic and traditionalistic traits.

In 1969 Ira Sharkansky performed a systematic comparison of the states Elazar identified as moralistic, traditionalistic, and individualistic to determine whether they actually were different in the ways Elazar predicted and, more important, to determine whether the differences were simply a result of differences in economic and industrial development. Sharkansky found that the cultural differences were still important after the effects of the economic variables were taken into account. Southern states, with traditionalistic cultures, spent less on certain social programs and had fewer public employees per capita than other states, even those with similar economic circumstances.

The regional norms thus identified were persistent. Sharkansky reports that "during 1952–1974, per capita personal income in the old Confederacy went from 68 percent of the national average to 83 percent of the national average. Meanwhile, state expenditures per capita moved only slightly, from 87 percent to 88 percent of the national average." Although the economy in the southern states during the 1990s was more prosperous than ever before, the dominance of conservatives, both Democrat and Republican, resulted in state expenditures remaining behind those in other parts of the United States. The 1990s saw the growing popularity of a new revenue source in the South—gambling tax revenues, from lotteries and casinos. While controversial in the Bible Belt, these activities have taken root in Georgia, Louisiana, Mississippi, and other southern states, with revenues dedicated either fully or in part to funding public education. Other states outside the regions have also embraced gambling as a revenue source, so little regional distinctiveness appears.

States across the nation have had to increase expenditures since the 1980s in two particular areas—environmental management and health care. The rise of a "New Federalism" in the last few decades has meant federal programs that often mandate increased state spending.

The distinctive southern character identified by novelists, essayists, and journalists apparently has a real effect on the most tangible and concrete aspects of government—taxing and spending. Southerners remain less likely than their northern compatriots to turn to government for various social purposes or to redistribute income, even when their states become economically developed. Analysis of the more simplistic versions of V. O. Key Jr.'s ideas indicates, however, that the effect of southern culture on government policy is complicated and that economic factors are critical in explaining much regional variety.

MARCUS ETHRIDGE
University of Wisconsin at Milwaukee

Council of State Governments, *The Book of the States* (2004); Thomas R. Dye, *Politics, Economics, and the Public: Policy Outcome in the American States* (1966); Daniel Elazar, *American Federalism: A View from the States*, 2nd ed. (1972); Virginia Gray, Herbert Jacob, and Kenneth Vines, eds., *Politics in the American States: A Comparative Analysis* (1983); V. O. Key Jr., *Southern Politics in State and Nation* (1949); Ira Sharkansky, *The Maligned States: Policy Accomplishments, Problems, and Opportunities*, 2nd ed. (1978); Kevin B. Smith, ed., *State and Local Government, 2007* (2007).

Violence, Political

No other major section of the country can match the South's record of violence, political and otherwise. Southern political violence, like organized violence nationally, has featured repression by social and political elites of those who threatened (or were perceived to threaten) their control. The rare colonial insurrections—Bacon's Rebellion in Virginia (1675–76) and Culpepper's Rebellion in North Carolina (1677–78)—were in the main middle-class or upper-class revolts against ruling factions in their respective colonies and involved very little bloodshed. The Regulator movements of North and South Carolina in the 1760s and 1770s arose out of frontier conditions in the backcountry. The North Carolina movement sought to force the colonial authorities in the East to provide more responsible government in the West. The rebels were defeated on the battlefield of Alamance in 1771, after which six of their leaders were hanged. The South Carolina Regulators were vigilantes, organized to suppress anarchy and to force the colonial authorities in Charleston to bring government to the frontier. Neither movement aimed seriously to modify the structure of colonial government, much less to overthrow it.

In fact, many backcountry settlers felt a greater kinship with England after 1775 than with the eastern planters who led the movement for independence. Organized North Carolina Loyalists were decisively defeated at the battle of Moore's Creek Bridge in 1776, but partisan warfare raged between Whigs and Tories for several years in some interior districts of the Carolinas and Georgia.

Antebellum vigilantism, aimed at actual or suspected slave insurrections and their white instigators, was not political, strictly speaking. But the goal of keeping the slaves in subjection, by force if necessary, and the day-to-day requirements of slave discipline conditioned southerners to the use of force as a regular instrument of policy. Even greater discord followed in the wake of southern secession in 1861. Unionist sentiment existed in varying measure throughout the South, reflected in active or passive opposition to the Confederacy. It was strongest in the border states and in the mountain areas of Virginia, North Carolina, Tennessee, Georgia, Alabama, and Arkansas. Opinion was not uniform in these regions, however, and warfare of family against family, even brother against brother, was not unknown. Such hostilities engendered bitterness that lasted for many years, sometimes in the form of blood feuds.

These wartime differences were translated after the war into political party divisions: former Unionists became Republicans, and ex-Confederates affiliated with the Conservative or Democratic Party. Federal Reconstruction policy introduced the Republican Party to the South in 1867 as the champion of Unionism, black freedom, and civil rights. Regional opposition to these goals drew heavily on prewar precedents.

It was but a short step from the militia musters and the slave patrols of the 1850s to the Ku Klux Klan and the so-called home guards, white leagues, and red-shirt clubs of the Reconstruction era. All were designed to enforce white supremacy. For more than a decade after 1865, therefore, white southerners of a certain age and disposition felt it their duty and privilege to continue the twin struggles against Unionism and for white supremacy, now joined as a crusade against the "Black Republican" party. The crusade took several forms. All were more or less inspired, organized, and led by the middle and upper classes, appearances sometimes to the contrary notwithstanding.

The most spectacular form of resistance, but the least effective in the long run, was the midnight raiding of the Ku Klux Klan and its kindred organizations. Formed in Tennessee in 1866, the Klan spread throughout the South in the spring of 1868 as congressional Reconstruction policies went into effect. It killed, flogged, and intimidated hosts of black and white Republicans in the areas where it flourished, but by 1872 it was put down by a combination of state and federal judicial and military action. The Klan helped to impeach and remove Governor William W. Holden of North Carolina, but it failed to end Reconstruction in any state.

Probably the most successful form of political violence was the urban riot. Seventy-eight have been counted for the years 1865 through 1876 in cities like Memphis and New Orleans and villages like Camilla, Ga., and Clinton, Miss. Generally planned in advance, they often resulted in the death or banishment of Republican leaders of both races and the demoralization of their followers. Such riots occurred throughout the Reconstruction period and sporadically afterward, the last of them in Wilmington, N.C., in 1898 and Atlanta in 1906.

Closely related to the urban riots were the activities of the white league, red-shirt club, and other paramilitary groups that dispensed with the bizarre disguises of the Ku Klux Klan and operated in broad daylight. They rode about before elections, breaking up Republican meetings and intimidating Republican candidates and voters. Georgians pioneered this tactic in 1870, and it was

Ku Klux Klan members supporting Barry Goldwater's campaign for the 1964 Republican
Party presidential nomination (Warren K. Leffler, photographer, Library of Congress,
[LC-U9-12250M-13A], Washington, D.C.)

repeated with increasing sophistication throughout the Deep South from 1874
to 1876. With the urban riots, it was largely responsible for bringing southern
Reconstruction to a close by 1877.

From the 1870s to the 1890s southern Democrats controlled their respective
states by means of honest electoral victories (where possible) and partial disfranchisement, fraud, and violence (where necessary). Republicans were permitted to vote and to elect candidates in the mountains and the Black Belts,
but only as long as they did not threaten statewide Democratic control. In the
1890s, after a variety of agrarian insurgent movements, sometimes featuring
coalitions with Republicans, Democrats began more systematically to disfranchise their opponents through constitutional or legislative action. Henceforth,
the law would accomplish peacefully what riots and red-shirt campaigns had
done through threats and violence. The generation after 1890 saw the climax
not only of black disfranchisement but of lynching and enforced racial segregation as well.

The violence of the second Ku Klux Klan in the 1920s was not primarily
political, and except for such isolated events as the assassinations of Governor
William Goebel of Kentucky in 1900 and Senator Huey P. Long of Louisiana in
1935, substantial political violence did not return until the advent of the civil
rights movement, or Second Reconstruction, of the 1950s and 1960s. The civil

rights laws of 1957–64, and especially the Voting Rights Act of 1965, helped return millions of black voters to the polls after the lapse of three generations.

The civil rights movement used nonviolent protest as a means of winning public opinion throughout the country to peaceful change. Most of the violence that came was directed by whites against the desegregation of schools, businesses, and public facilities rather than the voting booth. It was not, therefore, specifically political until Martin Luther King Jr. and his colleagues shifted their emphasis in 1964 to black voter registration. The killing of Michael Schwerner, Andrew Goodman, and James Chaney in the registration drive in Mississippi and other acts of violence in 1964 hastened congressional passage of the Voting Rights Act the following year.

In 1979 members of the Ku Klux Klan and the American Nazi Party shot and killed five Communist Workers Party demonstrators at Greensboro, N.C. Unlike most of the political violence since the Civil War, this event had little or no direct racial bearing; the perpetrators and the victims were all white. The incident dramatized the enmity that developed after World War II between political fringe groups of the far left and far right. The enmity was most volatile in the South, where violence-prone Klansmen and Nazis were most in evidence.

The reasons for the South's affinity for violence are not easy to pinpoint with assurance, but surely racial dissension has played a central role. So too, perhaps, has the region's rural, scattered population, which traditionally encouraged hunting, self-protection, private settlement of grievances, and attendant carrying of weapons. Politically, the South has experienced more bitter conflict, arising from deep racial and class divisions, than any other section of the country. Even when these conditions change and internal differences abate, old cultural patterns retain a life of their own.

ALLEN W. TRELEASE
University of North Carolina at Greensboro

Richard Maxwell Brown, *Strain of Violence: Historical Studies of American Violence and Vigilantism* (1975); Jane Dailey, Glenda Elizabeth Gilmore, and Bryant Simon, *Jumpin' Jim Crow: Southern Politics from Civil War to Civil Rights* (2000); Hugh Davis Graham and Ted Robert Gurr, eds., *Violence in America: Historical and Comparative Perspectives* (1969); Michael K. Honey, *Southern Labor and Black Civil Rights: Organizing Memphis Workers* (1993); Steven F. Lawson, *Black Ballots: Voting Rights in the South, 1944–1969* (1976); George C. Rable, *But There Was No Peace: The Role of Violence in the Politics of Reconstruction* (1984); Bryant Simon, *A Fabric of Defeat: The Politics of South Carolina Millhands, 1910–1948* (1998); Allen W. Trelease, *White Terror: The Ku Klux Klan Conspiracy and Southern Reconstruction* (1971); Christopher

Waldrep, *Roots of Disorder: Race and Criminal Justice in the American South, 1817–1880* (1998); Wilcomb E. Washburn, *The Governor and the Rebel: A History of Bacon's Rebellion in Virginia* (1957).

Voting

"Among the great democracies of the world," V. O. Key Jr. noted in 1949, "the Southern states remain the chief considerable area in which an extremely small proportion of citizens vote." Yet the South has not always been the most backward, least democratic region in the Western world. Although other countries have, gradually or in sudden spurts, expanded the proportion of their citizens who enjoy and exercise the right to vote, the United States has followed a zigzag, not a linear, path. Born comparatively free, America contracted as well as expanded its suffrage thereafter. In its patterns of voting participation, as in other facets of society, the South exaggerated national trends.

Suffrage theory of the colonial South, like that of the colonial North, mimicked Britain's. "The laws of England," the Virginia legislature declared in 1655, "grant a voice in such election only to such as by their estates real or personal have interest enough to tie them to the endeavor of the public good." Accordingly, during most of the colonial period, only property holders could vote. Because of the much greater availability of land in the New World, however, freehold suffrage in practice enfranchised a much higher proportion of the free adult males in America than in the mother country. Substantial majorities, in Virginia as well as in Massachusetts, could and did vote. Property restrictions for office holding, some class deference, and the common interest of large and small planters, in addition to the wider reputations and greater availability of time and money enjoyed by the economic elite, guaranteed men of standing a disproportionate share of the political posts. Yet their tenure existed only at the sufferance of their neighbors (social inferiors, but often political near equals), and they failed to pay at least rhetorical tribute to white male equality at their peril.

Two factors—legal restrictions on suffrage and the degree of party competition—have chiefly determined voter turnout levels in the South, and, of these, the former has been much more important. The pattern of voter participation in the 11 ex-Confederate states was quite similar to that in the other states of the Union from 1840 through the 1880s. The massive divergence that Key noted opened up only after 1892, as southern states passed laws and standardized administrative practices that disfranchised large proportions of blacks and poorer whites. Designed to have a disproportionately adverse impact on the Repub-

THE FIRST VOTE.—Drawn by A. R. Waud.—[See next Page.]

"The First Vote," a wood engraving published on the title page of Harper's Weekly, *16 November 1867 (A. R. Waud, Library of Congress [LC-USZ62-19234], Washington, D.C.)*

lican and Populist Parties, the restrictive laws virtually ended party competition in most of the South, thereby further discouraging people from voting. Even though literacy tests and other restraints on suffrage were employed in the North as well as the South, the qualifications were not applied as severely above the Mason-Dixon line. Since 1940, as blacks gradually regained the vote and as Republicans contested more and more elections in the South, participation rates in the two sections have converged. By 1980 the difference in turnout was only 8 percent.

Although the sectional gulf between the years 1890 and 1965 is most striking, other facets of the pattern also deserve attention. In this as in many cases, the choice of the denominator presents a moral problem. Few free black males and no male slaves or women of any status were allowed to vote before 1860. Had black males, slave and emancipated, instead of only adult white males, been included in the antebellum denominators, southern turnout would have been only about two-thirds as high as northern in the antebellum period. Had women been counted, both lines would have shifted downward.

Following convention by calculating turnout on the basis of all males, regardless of race, in the denominator from 1860 to 1908, adding females in a few nonsouthern states in 1912 and 1916 and in all states thereafter, also hides two shifts that did not take place in the South. There were no overall voting declines as a result of the addition of freedmen and women to the voting polls. In 1860, 67 percent of the southern adult white males voted. In 1868, in the seven southern states that held elections, 70 percent of southern adult males, black as well as white, turned out. When compared to the political behavior of the early or mid-19th-century British or the late 20th-century American voter of lower social status, it seems amazing that such a large portion of the poverty-stricken, largely illiterate, recently enslaved population should have voted. Just as impressive, they overwhelmingly opposed the wishes of their former owners and then-current landlords. And whereas northern turnout dropped by more than 10 percent with the expansion of woman suffrage, southern women appear to have bounded off their pedestals to participate in politics in approximately the same—very low—proportion as the men.

Figure 2 lays to rest two other hoary notions. First, the left section of the graph shows that the high level of antebellum southern turnout was not merely a product of contests for the presidency or of Jacksonian democracy. Southern governors' races attracted large majorities of the adult white males long before battles for the White House did and continued to attract somewhat higher proportions of voters than presidential elections after the Old Hero retired. Second, although the Democratic primaries constituted the real elections in the first half of the century, the right portion of Figure 2 shows that turnout in those races barely exceeded that in southern presidential contests: only about one out of three southern white adults generally managed to cast ballots. Competition unstructured by parties did not foster participation; blacks were not the only ones deterred by the post-Populist southern political system.

In 1938 Ralph Bunche estimated that but 4 percent of southern blacks could vote. Legal attacks on the white primary, the poll tax, and other restrictive devices, culminating in the passage of the 1965 national Voting Rights Act, in

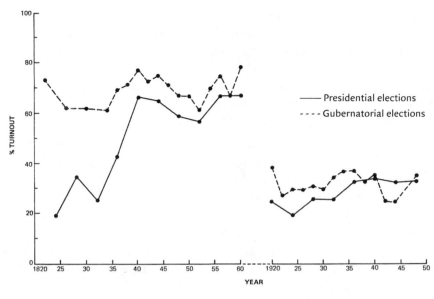

FIGURE 2. *Voting Turnout, Whites Only, in the Eleven Ex-Confederate States.*
Source: *U.S. Commission on Civil Rights, Political Participation (1968).*

addition to the return to the South of a Republican Party that was almost the negative image of its Reconstruction-era predecessor, vastly increased political activity among all groups, whites as well as blacks and Latinos. The vote brought change, real and symbolic. Public services expanded and were more freely available to all. Black and Spanish-surnamed southern mayors and congressmen became almost common. Former race-baiters kissed black babies and black homecoming queens. Yet in many rural areas and small cities, harsh discrimination persisted; and electoral structures, such as at-large provisions, which had the intent and effect of diminishing minority political power, discouraged blacks and Latinos from voting and diluted the impact of their franchises when they did turn out.

The Voting Rights Act was strengthened in 1982, and southern legislatures drew black majority districts. The Supreme Court cases *Shaw v. Reno* (1993) and *Miller v. Johnson* (1995) showed a conservative Court ruling that any redistricting could not have a predominantly racial intent. The number of minority candidates elected has not significantly declined since these court decisions. African American turnout in elections today is about 10 percent lower than white turnout. Well-organized voter registration drives continue to increase the number of African American and registered voters, but southern white voter registration has also increased in the last two decades.

J. MORGAN KOUSSER
California Institute of Technology

Robert E. Brown and B. Katherine Brown, *Virginia, 1705–1786: Democracy or Aristocracy?* (1964); Ralph J. Bunche, *The Political Status of the Negro in the Age of FDR* (1973); Robert M. Goddman, ed., *Reconstruction and Black Suffrage: Losing the Vote in Reese and Cruikshank* (2001); V. O. Key Jr., *Southern Politics in State and Nation* (1949); Alexander Keyssar, *Southern Exposure* (Winter 2002–2003); J. Morgan Kousser, *The Shaping of Southern Politics: Suffrage Restriction and the Establishment of the One-Party South, 1880–1910* (1974); Steven F. Lawson, *Black Ballots: Voting Rights in the South, 1944–1969* (1976); U.S. Commission on Civil Rights, *Political Participation* (1968), *The Voting Rights Act: Ten Years After* (1975), *The Voting Rights Act: Unfulfilled Goals* (1981); Chilton Williamson, *American Suffrage from Property to Democracy, 1760–1860* (1960).

Women in Southern Politics

The South has added distinctive connotations to the definition of women's "proper sphere" in the United States. An examination of southern politics confirms that, even though constrained by powerful cultural, legal, social, economic, and psychological forces, women have steadily moved from a predominantly private family role into public political activities. Historians have recently expanded the understanding of "political" beyond electoral activities, suggesting organized women's groups have had political significance.

The culture of the Old South, although never monolithic, generally restricted women to a narrow orbit circumscribed by the ascendant symbol of "the lady." Inspired by a variety of literary and historical sources, as well as by practical considerations, the complex image of "the lady" magnified the prevalent 19th-century national "cult of true womanhood," which prescribed piety, purity, submissiveness, and domesticity as preeminent female virtues and consigned women to the special province of the home. Southern shibboleths about women created an elaborate rationale dedicated to the defense of the peculiar institution of slavery and infatuated with the medieval code of chivalry. Submissiveness translated into inferiority, polemics superseded reason, myth obscured reality, and idealization became repression.

Disfranchised and denied orthodox political influence, women developed unconventional methods to challenge the male-dominated system. In time southern women proved particularly ingenious in their devices, but few opportunities existed in the society before 1860. In South Carolina, the Grimké sisters represented the dilemma of antebellum dissenters, who frequently took the path of imposed or self-imposed exile.

After 1865 southerners were compelled by education, industrialization, and urbanization to reconsider women's proper place. Voluntary associations, often affiliated with the authoritative institution of the church, enabled southern women to gain confidence as administrators and public speakers. From the 1870s they participated openly if not powerfully in state political organizations.

Female leaders of both races in the late 19th century organized into women's clubs and other groups that worked to combat disease, inadequate public schools, and civic disorder. With black men disfranchised and excluded from formal political life after the 1890s, middle-class black women played a new role, as ambassadors to the white community. Working with white women, especially in the Woman's Christian Temperance Union, black women promoted racial uplift and interracial cooperation, pursuing political objectives outside electoral institutions.

Ideologically quite different from these reformers, other southern women in the late 19th century also broadened the understanding of political activity through work to preserve traditional southern culture. Formed in 1894, the United Daughters of the Confederacy had 20,000 members by the early 20th century and used its attachment to the South's Lost Cause to pressure textbook committees to adopt books with pro-Confederate interpretations and to lobby state legislatures for support of Confederate veterans homes. And they persuaded school boards to honor the Lost Cause—demonstrating how they used social position and leadership skills to shape the region's public culture.

The campaign for woman suffrage and the crusade against lynching epitomized the strengths and weaknesses of the political efforts of southern women. To avoid the abusive epithet "short-haired women," they painstakingly displayed ladylike demeanor and selectively deferred to tradition in their appearance and action. Racism, states' rights, and pragmatic elitism compromised both the Southern States Woman Suffrage Conference, created in 1913 by Kate Gordon of New Orleans, and the Association of Southern Women for the Prevention of Lynching, launched in 1930 under the leadership of Jessie Daniel Ames of Texas. Torn between the desire for change and the perceived need for social control, southern reformers acquiesced to the dogma of white supremacy. The failure, except for ephemeral and fragile coalitions, to transcend the race question prevented the achievement of gender solidarity. Although

Arkansas, Tennessee, and Texas among the former Confederate states secured partial woman suffrage through legislative enactment and also ratified the Nineteenth Amendment, only the dreaded federal intervention brought full citizenship in 1920. Many veterans of the suffrage wars competed successfully for state political positions, but inexperience and prolonged socialization impeded the acquisition of real power. Toleration, not equality, most accurately described the condition of southern women.

The political culture after 1920 accentuated three southern phenomena: women as appointed male successors, women as male proxies, and women as mirrors of male political authority. Occasionally a successor established her own political identity, but most women appointed to office exerted marginal influence. Appointed U.S. senators, Rebecca Felton of Georgia, Hattie Caraway of Arkansas, Rose Long of Louisiana, and Dixie Graves of Alabama upheld the accepted image of southern women. Caraway won two complete terms in the elections of 1932 and 1938, but the precedents she set in the Senate had limited significance. The classification of "gracious southern lady" survived in the career of Representative Corinne "Lindy" Boggs of Louisiana, who initially triumphed in 1973 in a special election for her missing husband's congressional seat.

Two dramatic examples typify the southern woman as male proxy. Elected governor in Texas in 1924 and 1932 as a substitute for her disqualified husband, Miriam "Ma" Ferguson unabashedly offered voters two Fergusons for the price of one. Lurleen Wallace's brief administration as nominal governor of Alabama caricatured women in politics. Exploited by her ineligible husband, Governor George C. Wallace, who emerged victorious in her name in 1966, she stoically endured subordination until her death in 1968.

An exceptional model of women who are mirrors of male political authority, Rosalynn Carter attracted unusually intense scrutiny during her husband's presidency. All presidents' wives derive prestige from their relationships, but Carter's southern background marked her as "the iron magnolia," a superficial but telling delineation that popularly symbolized the contradictory impact of southern culture on women in politics.

In the era of the Second Reconstruction after World War II, organized attacks on race and sex discrimination reappeared. Awareness of racism stimulated consciousness of sexism, and again the South figured prominently in the battle. Women activists in student and civil rights groups publicized the common injustices, but the struggles allied women temporarily rather than permanently, and expectations of fairness and equality remained unmet.

Southern women have played a part in their own victimization by their equivocal attitudes. Both enthralled by and at odds with the stereotypical claims of their peculiar morality and virtue, they tailored their arguments to gain maximum advantage. Conflicting demands for liberation and the preservation of special protection negated each other.

The South played a major role in the defeat of the equal rights amendment, with women mobilizing after 1972 to pressure southern legislatures to defeat the amendment. Conservative women from the region became leaders in such groups as the Eagle Forum and the Republican Party, helping to elect conservative candidates such as Sue Myrick of Charlotte, N.C., to the U.S. House of Representatives. North Carolina's Elizabeth Dole served as a cabinet member to conservative presidents Ronald Reagan (as secretary of transportation) and George H. W. Bush (as secretary of labor), became the first viable woman candidate for the presidency in 1999, and was elected senator from North Carolina in 2004.

With the enfranchisement of African American voters in the 1960s, the South witnessed the election of growing numbers of black elected officials, including women. By 1993 there were 48 black women serving in the legislatures of 11 southern states. There were nine black women serving in Congress in 1993, including four from the South. By 2000, black women represented 35 percent of black elected officials. The number of women serving in 11 southern state legislatures went from 39 in the mid-1970s to 92 in 2004. In 2006 there were eight women serving as governors in the United States, but only one, Louisiana's Kathleen Blanco, was from the South. Four women served in 2007 as U.S. senators from the South.

Alteration, not transformation, has distinguished the political status of southern women. Evolutionary and revolutionary, conservative and radical, conformist and iconoclastic, pragmatic and idealistic, racist and egalitarian, their causes have embodied many of the paradoxes of the regional heritage that have influenced contemporary cultural patterns. Ambivalent about women's roles, the South sanctions sexual politics and the illusion of change, while the southern cultural tradition continues to inhibit genuine participation by women in its politics.

BETTY BRANDON
University of South Alabama

Julia Kirk Blackwater, in *The American South in the Twentieth Century*, ed. Craig S. Pascoe, Karen Trahan Leathem, and Andy Ambrose (2005); Sara Evans, *Personal Politics: The Roots of Women's Liberation in the Civil Rights Movement and the New Left* (1979); Glinda E. Gilmore, *Gender and Jim Crow: Women and the Politics of*

White Supremacy in North Carolina, 1896–1920 (1996); Jacquelyn Dowd Hall, *Revolt against Chivalry: Jessie Daniel Ames and the Women's Campaign against Lynching* (1979); Sharon Harley and Rosalyn Terborg-Penn, eds., *The Afro-American Woman: Struggles and Images* (1978); Julie Roy Jeffrey, *Feminist Studies* (Fall 1975); Gerda Lerner, *The Majority Finds Its Past: Placing Women in History* (1979); Donald G. Mathews and Jane Sherron De Hart, *Sex, Gender, and the Politics of the ERA: A State and the Nation* (1990); Lynne Olson, *Freedom's Daughters: The Unsung Heroines of the Civil Rights Movement from 1830 to 1970* (2001); Anne Firor Scott, *The Southern Lady: From Pedestal to Politics, 1830–1930* (1970); A. Elizabeth Taylor, *The Woman Suffrage Movement in Tennessee* (1957); Marjorie Spruill Wheeler, *New Women of the New South: The Leaders of the Woman Suffrage Movement in the Southern States* (1993).

All the King's Men

The 1946 novel *All the King's Men*, by Robert Penn Warren, is one of the most significant creative expressions about politics in the American South. The story of the rise of Willie Stark from a small-town idealistic do-good reformer to a demagogic governor parallels the fortunes of Louisiana governor Huey P. Long, but Warren also highlights another character, Jack Burden, the descendant of old Delta money who becomes Stark's aide and is caught up in the complex moral and political issues that Warren explores.

Warren began teaching at Louisiana State University in 1933 and observed close at hand Long's political career. The story of the Longlike figure Willie Stark began as a Warren verse play called *Proud Flesh*, with a politician named Willie Talos. The novel, which won the Pulitzer Prize in 1947, shows Stark as a local reformer trying to pass a school bond, but he is transformed after he discovers the state political machine had manipulated him into running for governor in order to drain off votes from another candidate. He comes to see himself as a savior for the "hicks," those working-class people that are his people. Jack Burden, who grew up the privileged son of money and opportunity, nonetheless had repeatedly sought to escape this world of privilege, ending up as a skeptical newspaper reporter who covers Long's rise and later becomes his aide. As Daniel Singal has noted, Burden is an existential character whose attempts to gain meaning in life lead him "toward the sordid and brutal world of politics." Burden discovered in that world, according to Singal, "the capricious character of the universe and man's essential helplessness within it."

Stark, who is frequently referred to as "the Boss," assumes that moral standards remain in perpetual flux, depending on historical circumstances. Southern religiosity, in the form of a Calvinist-inspired dim view of human nature, is part of Stark's moral vision. "Man is conceived in sin and born in corruption," he says, "and he passeth from the stink of the didie to the stench of the shroud." Facing a state power structure that has held back progress for his people, Stark finds easy justification for using any method to achieve his noble ends. He sometimes acts outside the law, using graft and blackmail to persuade opponents to support his plans. His bodyguard, Sugar Boy, is a brutal embodiment of physical force, and Stark keeps his greedy political cronies around to use when needed. Stark believes in the essential goodness of his reform efforts, and his own idealism shows in his unwillingness to cut corners in the building of the hospital that he sees offering true hope for poor people. In the end, a childhood friend of Burden's, Adam Stanton, who has been disillusioned by Stark's affair with his sister and Stark's questionable methods, assassinates him, again paralleling the violent end that faced Huey P. Long.

This story was the basis for two motion pictures. Robert Rossen directed the 1949 version of *All the King's Men*, which won three Academy Awards that year: Best Picture, Best Actor (Broderick Crawford), and Best Supporting Actress (Mercedes McCambridge).

Broderick Crawford as Willie Stark (far right) at a campaign rally, in a scene from All the King's Men (1949) (Film Stills Archives, Museum of Modern Art, New York, New York)

The film played down the specifically southern connections to the story, with no southern accents to be found and the demagogic story nationalized into one that could have been in almost any part of the nation. Still, for viewers who had read the novel and knew of the Long connections, the film dramatized a compelling saga of southern politics. Steven Zaillian was writer and director of a 2006 film version of *All the King's Men*, which starred Sean Penn as Stark and Jude Law as Burden. The novel had been set in the Depression, which was important background to the ability of an insurgent politician to achieve success, but this later film version moved the setting from the Depression to the 1950s. Penn attempted a drawl, but most critics saw it as unsuccessful. The cam-

era did dwell on the southern setting to the story, with evocative images of swamps, back roads, the Louisiana state capitol, and the French Quarter.

Composer Carlisle Floyd adapted the novel as a grand opera called *Willie Stark*, which premiered at the Houston Grand Opera in 1981. The 1996 novel *Primary Colors: A Novel of Politics* by "Anonymous," who turned out to be the journalist Joe Klein, was influenced by Warren's novel. Inspired by Bill Clinton's first presidential campaign in 1992, the novel echoes characters' names from the earlier novel, with a southern governor named Jack Stanton and an aide named Henry Burton. Burton faces similar complex issues of idealism and realism that Jack Burden wrestled with in Warren's novel, suggesting its continuing relevance in understanding philosophical matters related to politics in the South.

CHARLES REAGAN WILSON
University of Mississippi

Jack Temple Kirby, *Media-Made Dixie: The South in the American Imagination* (1978); Daniel Joseph Singal, *The War Within: From Victorian to Modernist Thought in the South, 1919–1945* (1982).

Ames, Jessie Daniel

(1883–1972) SOCIAL REFORMER.
Jessie Daniel Ames, born 2 November 1883, had moved three times in Texas by the time she was a teenager. Her father, a stern Victorian eccentric, migrated from Indiana to Palestine, Tex., where he worked as railroad stationmaster, and in 1893 the Daniels moved to Georgetown, Tex., the site of Southwestern University, from which Ames later graduated.

The brutal Indian Wars and vigilantism of the period created a violent atmosphere, which strongly affected the sensitive young Jessie. A strong-willed child, she had resisted the perfect table manners expected of her and often was sent to the kitchen. In the Daniels' kitchen, young Jessie heard about a lynching nearby in Tyler, an event she remembered for years and that influenced her lifelong efforts to abolish the practice.

In June 1905 Jessie Daniel married a handsome army surgeon, Roger Post Ames, who later died in Guatemala. In 1914 she rose to prominence in Texas as an advocate of southern Progressivism and woman suffrage. Unlike most suffragists in the early 1920s, she understood the grave injustice against blacks in this country. She served as a vital link between feminism and the 20th-century struggle for black civil rights.

In 1924 she became field secretary of Will Alexander's Atlanta-based Commission on Interracial Cooperation. She immediately began organizing against lynching in Texas, Arkansas, and Oklahoma. Alexander brought her to Atlanta in 1929 as director of women's work for the Commission, and in 1930 she founded Southern Women for the Prevention of Lynching, which in nine years had 40,000 members. Alerted by friendly law officers and her contacts in the press when a lynching threatened, Ames contacted women in that county who had pledged to work against violence. Her work was not always appreciated. Opposition came from women as well as men. The Women's National Association for the Preservation of the White Race claimed that Ames's women "were defending criminal Negro men at the expense of innocent white girls."

Ames did not support the federal antilynching bill in 1940 as being practical. She said it would pass the House, and southern senators would then defeat it. She was soon at odds with her boss, Dr. Alexander, as well as her old allies in the NAACP.

From May 1939 to May 1940 in the South, for the first time since records had been kept, not a single lynching occurred. World War II, however, dealt a death blow to Southern Women for the Prevention of Lynching, just as it did to the attempt to abolish the hated poll tax in the South. The alliance between women and victimized blacks, which Ames hoped for, was postponed.

In 1943 Southern Women for the Prevention of Lynching was absorbed by the newly formed Southern Regional Council, as was the Interracial Commission. Ames wanted to work for the new agency but found her services were not needed.

In the foothills of the Blue Ridge Mountains, Ames set about to rebuild her life. Elected superintendent of Christian Social Relations for the Western North Carolina Conference of the Methodist Church, she welcomed the opportunity "to get back into public life and be remembered." She later returned to Texas and was honored in the 1970s as a pioneer who combined feminism with civil rights activism. Jessie Daniel Ames died on 21 February 1972 at the age of 88.

MARIE S. JEMISON
Birmingham, Alabama

Jessie Daniel Ames Papers, Texas Historical Society, Dallas, Texas State Library, Austin, and Southern Historical Collection, University of North Carolina, Chapel Hill; Papers of the Association of Southern Women for the Prevention of Lynching and the Commission on Interracial Cooperation, Trevor Arnett Library, Atlanta University; Jacquelyn Dowd Hall, *Revolt against Chivalry: Jessie Daniel Ames and the Women's Campaign against Lynching* (1979).

Baker, Ella Jo

(1903–1986) CIVIL RIGHTS ACTIVIST. Ella Jo Baker, the daughter of Georgianna and Blake Baker, was born in 1903 in Norfolk, Va. When she was seven, Baker's family moved to Little-

ton, N.C., to live with her maternal grandparents, who owned a plantation where they had previously worked as slaves. The absence of adequate public schools for blacks in rural North Carolina and her mother's concern that she be properly educated resulted in Baker's attending Shaw University in Raleigh. There, she received both her high school and college education. Following her graduation in 1927, she moved to New York City to live with a cousin, where she worked as a waitress and, later, in a factory.

The product of a southern environment in which caring and sharing were facts of life and of a family in which her grandfather regularly mortgaged his property in order to help neighbors, Baker soon became involved in various community groups. In 1932 she became the national director of the Young Negroes Cooperative League and the office manager of the *Negro National News*. Six years later, she began her active career with the National Association for the Advancement of Colored People (NAACP), working initially as a field secretary in the South. In 1943 she was appointed national director of the branches for the NAACP. In both capacities Baker spent long periods in southern black communities, where her southern roots served her well. Her success in recruiting southern blacks to join what was considered a radical organization in the 1930s and 1940s may be attributed, in part, to her being a native of the region and, therefore, best able to approach southern people. Baker, who neither married nor had children of her own, left active service in the NAACP in

1946 in order to raise a niece. A short while later she reactivated her involvement with the organization, becoming president of the New York City chapter in 1954.

In 1957 Baker went south again, this time to work with the Southern Christian Leadership Conference (SCLC), a newly formed civil rights organization. The student sit-in movement of the 1960s protested the refusal of public restaurants in the South to serve blacks and resulted in Baker's involvement in still another civil rights group. As the coordinator of the 1960 Nonviolent Resistance to Segregation Leadership Conference, which brought together more than 300 student sit-in leaders and resulted in the formation of the Student Nonviolent Coordinating Committee (SNCC), Baker is credited with playing a major role in SNCC's founding. Severing a formal relationship with SCLC, she worked with the Southern Conference Educational Fund. In recognition of her contribution to improving the quality of life of southern blacks and to the founding of the Mississippi Freedom Democratic Party, Ella Baker was asked to deliver the keynote address at its 1964 convention in Jackson, Miss.

Ella Baker spent the remainder of her life in New York City, where she served as an adviser to a number of community groups. Prior to the release of Joanne Grant's film *Fundi: The Story of Ella Baker*, few people outside of the civil rights movement in the South knew about Baker's long career as a civil rights activist, but since then a number of leadership programs and grassroots organizations, such as the Children's

Defense Fund's Ella Baker Child Policy Training Institute and the Bay Area's Ella Baker Center for Human Rights, have been named in her honor. Nevertheless, she is probably less well known than many other civil rights workers, because she was a woman surrounded by southern men, primarily ministers, who generally perceived women as supporters rather than as leaders in the movement, and because of her own firm belief in group-centered rather than individual-centered leadership.

SHARON HARLEY
University of Maryland

Ellen Cantarow and Susan Gushee O'Malley, *Moving the Mountain: Women Working for Social Change* (1980); Clayborne Carson, *In Struggle: SNCC and the Black Awakening of the 1960s* (1981); Joanne Grant, *Ella Baker: Freedom Bound* (1999); Barbara Ransby, *Ella Baker and the Black Freedom Movement: A Radical Democratic Vision* (2003).

Baker, Howard, Jr.

(b. 1925) POLITICIAN.

Howard Baker Jr. is the heir to a rich tradition of Republican politics. His family has lived in mountainous east Tennessee since the 1700s, and Baker still makes his home in the small town of Huntsville. Both his father and his stepmother served in the House of Representatives, and Baker's father-in-law, Republican Everett Dirksen of Illinois, was Senate minority leader in the 1950s and 1960s. Republicans have won every congressional election since 1858 in Baker's native second district. A World War II veteran, he returned from the war to earn a law degree at the University of Tennessee and began a lucrative practice with the law firm his grandfather had established in 1885. Banking, coal, and real estate investments made him a wealthy man.

Baker entered elective politics in 1964 as a candidate for the U.S. Senate. Defeated after a strong campaign, he ran again two years later and became the state's first popularly elected Republican senator. Baker's success heralded a Republican surge in Tennessee that enabled the party to capture the state's other Senate seat and the governor's mansion in 1970. Baker is a bridge between two important sources of Republican strength in the South. Through his family he is linked to the mountain Republicanism that has flourished in Tennessee since the Civil War, but he is also popular with educated, affluent, white business and professional people across the state who have built the southern Republican Party into a significant force.

Baker first attracted national attention with his skillful performance as the ranking Republican on the Senate Watergate Committee in 1973. Three years later he won the post of minority leader and became majority leader when the Republicans took over the Senate after the 1980 elections. Ambitious for national office, Baker was frequently considered for a vice presidential nomination, but his bid for the White House in 1980 fizzled early in the campaign. The hallmark of Baker's Senate career was an emphasis on leadership through consensus. A centrist by instinct, his temperate rhetoric and charming manner made him highly effective in

the clubby atmosphere of the Senate, although some conservative members of his own party were skeptical of his ideological leanings. He retired from the Senate in 1985 but returned to the national scene in 1987 as President Reagan's chief of staff. Proud to be called a professional politician, Baker typified the moderate stance long characteristic of Tennessee politics.

DAVID D. LEE
Western Kentucky University

James Annis, *Howard Baker: Conciliator in an Age of Crisis* (1994); Jack Bass and Walter DeVries, *The Transformation of Southern Politics: Social Change and Political Consequence since 1945* (1976).

Barnett, Ross

(1898–1987) POLITICIAN.
Ross Robert Barnett became a symbol of resistance to integration as governor of Mississippi (1960–64) because he precipitated a riot on the campus of the University of Mississippi against federal marshals attempting to register the first black in a "white" Mississippi educational institution. Born the last of a Civil War veteran's 10 children in the Standing Pine community of Leake County, Barnett struggled against poverty to educate himself. While a student of the county agricultural high school, he worked as a janitor and a barber. He continued those occupations and sold aluminum cookware in the summer during his years at Mississippi College. After graduation he taught school and coached in Pontotoc before attending law school at Vanderbilt and the University of Mississippi. Moving to Jackson in 1926, he opened an independent prac-

tice. In 1943 he was elected president of the state bar association and by 1951 was secure enough to attempt to fulfill his boyhood dream of becoming governor. Without political experience and never having held a public post, he launched his first campaign for the state's highest office. He lost badly in the primaries of 1951 and 1955. But in 1959 the Citizens' Council wanted an ardent segregationist as its candidate, and Barnett was a complete racist.

While other candidates temporized by calling blacks "niggras," Barnett openly said "nigger" and told audiences, "The Negro is different because God made him different to punish him." Aside from his racism, Barnett was known for his folksy humor, but not all of it was intentional. He once told the Beth-Israel Temple in Jackson that "there is nothing finer than a group of people meeting in true Christian fellowship." Asked what could be done about (the disputed Chinese islands of) Quemoy and Matsu, Barnett responded, "Well, I expect we could find a place for them in the Fish and Game Commission."

The first year of his administration was less than successful. His was good-old-boy-style government, and he fought with the legislature for control of state agencies in order to provide the jobs needed to reward supporters. His primary contribution as governor was to promote industrial development through effective, prompt government service to industry, using his sales skills over promotional breakfasts with businessmen at the mansion.

When the federal courts ordered the University of Mississippi to admit James Meredith, a black man, Barnett defied the courts and was found in contempt. He answered Washington's demands with public assertions of state sovereignty while he secretly dealt with President John Kennedy and Attorney General Robert Kennedy. But the secret deal failed because Barnett could not resist playing to the public at an Ole Miss football game just prior to Meredith's enrollment. With over 40,000 people waving Confederate flags and singing "Go, Mississippi" to the tune of his campaign song, Barnett said, "I love Mississippi. I love our people. I love our customs." His campaign publicist has written of the moment, "As he stood there, smiling, acknowledging the cheers of the multitude, he was more than just a governor of Mississippi. He was a symbol of the South, with the red blood of his Confederate soldier father running through his veins. He represented the traditions that emerged after Reconstruction, a way of life that white southerners had vowed to continue." After some of the cheering crowd returned to Oxford to riot against federal authority, Barnett surrendered to overwhelming military force.

Despite his surrender, Barnett was enormously popular at the end of his term, a symbol of defeated but unbowed resistance to integration. Political observers predicted that he would dominate state politics for years, but he chose not to run for the U.S. Senate immediately, and as the story of his secret dealings with the Kennedys leaked out, his popularity waned. Another segregationist defeated him in the next gubernatorial primary, and Barnett was reduced quickly to a dated relic of a discredited philosophy. He appeared regularly at the Neshoba County Fair to entertain with stories and songs but had no more role in politics.

DENNIS J. MITCHELL
Mississippi State University at Meridian

Erle Johnston, *I Rolled with Ross: A Political Portrait* (1980); Robert Sherrill, *Gothic Politics in the Deep South* (1968).

Bilbo, Theodore

(1877–1947) POLITICIAN.
Theodore Gilmore Bilbo was born at Juniper Grove in Pearl River County, Miss., on 13 October 1877. He attended public school in Pearl River County and took courses but never earned a degree at Peabody College, Vanderbilt University, and the University of Michigan. He first entered politics in 1903 but was defeated for county clerk by a one-armed Confederate veteran. Displaying a sense of humor that would be a part of his political style, Bilbo confided to friends that he "started to vote for him myself."

Bilbo's 40-year political career was punctuated by victories and defeats. He served as state senator from 1908 to 1912. He became famous statewide for his involvement in "the Secret Causes" of 1910, during which he accepted a bribe in order to gain evidence that James K. Vardaman's opponents were bribing legislators. A vote to expel him from the state senate fell one vote short of the two-thirds necessary. In 1911 he was elected lieutenant governor and thereby became the presiding officer of the senate. Although implicated in a conflict-of-interest scandal while lieutenant governor, Bilbo was elected governor in 1915. His first administration was tainted by charges of sexual improprieties, and he lost a bid for U.S. Congress in 1918. In 1922 he postponed a bid for a U.S. Senate seat because he was jailed by a federal judge for refusing to honor a summons to testify in the seduction and breach of promise suit filed against Governor Lee Russell by a former secretary. Instead, Bilbo announced his candidacy for governor in 1923 but was defeated. In 1927 he ran again and won.

During his second administration, 1928–32, Bilbo became deeply involved in the governance of higher education. After the legislature refused to restructure the governing boards and relocate the University of Mississippi from Oxford to Jackson, Governor Bilbo, as chairman of the three existing governing boards, ordered extensive personnel changes at most of the state's colleges, but especially at the state university, the agricultural college, and the women's college. Bilbo's intrusion into personnel matters was neither new nor unusual. The state's institutions of higher learning had long been subject to the fury of factional politics. It was the epic sweep of his purge and his disdain for the Southern Association of Colleges and its accrediting standards that prompted several accrediting agencies to censure or withdraw their accreditation from the Mississippi institutions of higher learning.

After Governor Bilbo's second term expired, he organized a campaign for the U.S. Senate. In 1934 he was elected and then reelected in 1940 and 1946. Early in his senatorial career he was an ardent New Dealer, but as relief and recovery gradually gave way to reform, his ardor waned. He did, however, strongly endorse President Franklin D. Roosevelt's war policies.

In 1946 Senator Bilbo was confronted by two very serious challenges to his seat. First, a Senate investigating committee had prepared conflict of interest charges against him and planned to challenge his right to be sworn in for his third term. Second, a group of black Mississippians had filed suit seeking to overturn his reelection in 1946 on the grounds that large numbers of blacks had been systematically denied the right to vote in the Democratic primary.

However, before either of those two challenges could be resolved, Senator Bilbo, whose health had been declining rapidly during the previous several months, was admitted to Ochsner's Clinic in New Orleans. He died on 21 August 1947.

DAVID SANSING
University of Mississippi

Theodore Bilbo, Manuscripts, University of Southern Mississippi; A. W. Green, *The Man Bilbo* (1963); Chester M. Morgan, *Redneck Liberal: Theodore G. Bilbo and the New Deal* (1985).

Boggs, Lindy

(b. 1916) POLITICIAN.

Marie Corinne Morrison Claiborne was born 13 March 1916 at Brunswick Plantation, near New Roads, in Pointe Coupee Parish, La. She graduated from St. Joseph's Academy at New Roads in 1931 and earned her B.A. from Sophie Newcomb College of Tulane University in 1935, after which she became a teacher. She married Thomas Hale Boggs Sr. and, after his presumed death in an airplane that disappeared, she was selected in a special election in 1973 to succeed him as Democratic U.S. Representative from the Second District in New Orleans. Boggs was elected, with 82 percent of the vote, to a full term in 1974 and was reelected, serving nine terms. Boggs had 30 years of behind-the-scenes political activism before her election, working with her husband to raise money, run campaigns, and manage his Washington office.

While in Congress, Boggs served on the House Appropriations Committee and the Select Committee on Children, Youth, and Families, and she chaired the Joint Committee on Bicentennial Arrangements and the Commission on the Bicentenary of the U.S. House of Representatives. Boggs promoted legislation on civil rights, children and families, and equal pay for women. She was one of the founders of the Women's Congressional Caucus and was the first woman to chair the Democratic National Convention. President Bill Clinton appointed her the U.S. ambassador to the Vatican, where she served from 1997 to 2001. In 2006 Boggs received the Congressional Distinguished Service Award. Her political and family life is documented in *Lindy Boggs: Steel and Velvet*, a 2007 film by Louisiana Public Broadcasting and Blackberry Films.

CHARLES REAGAN WILSON
University of Mississippi

Lindy Boggs, with Katherine Hatch, *Washington through a Purple Veil: Memoirs of a Southern Woman* (1994); Thomas H. Ferrell and Judith Haydel, *Louisiana History* (Fall 1994).

Bush, George W.

(b. 1948) U.S. PRESIDENT.
Texas governor and 43rd president of the United States, George Walker Bush was born in New Haven, Conn., on 6 July 1946. Two years later Bush moved with his family to Texas where he grew to maturity in the conservative, oil-producing town of Midland. The grandson of a U.S. senator and son of the 41st president, Bush graduated from Phillips Academy in Andover, Mass., Yale University, and Harvard Business School. He served in the Texas National Guard during the Vietnam War, then opened an oil company, and later was the managing partner of the Texas Rangers Major League baseball team.

Despite coming from a wealthy family and attending elite private schools, Bush strongly identified with the working-class culture of Texas and the American South. He embraced staunchly conservative values and evangelical Christianity, both of which strongly influenced the direction of his life. Even while managing his business interests, Bush was intensely interested in politics. In 1994 he challenged Democratic incumbent Ann Richards for the Texas governorship and, to the surprise of many who dismissed him as inconsequential, won the election with 53 percent of the vote. Working with the Democratically controlled Texas legislature, Governor Bush successfully passed

a series of conservative reforms, including welfare law amendments, educational improvements, and stringent law enforcement (131 Texas men and women were legally executed during his tenure, earning Texas the reputation as "the nation's busiest executioner").

On the basis of his successful governorship, Bush won the Republican presidential nomination in 2000 and went on to defeat Democrat Al Gore in one of the most contentious national elections in American history. Bush's "compassionate conservatism" and expressions of deep religious faith struck a chord with white southerners who were dismayed by the excesses of the Clinton presidency. As a result, they comprised 40 percent of Bush's total vote for president. Although white southerners supported the newly elected president, many others did not. A pall of illegitimacy settled over the White House until the terrorist attacks on New York and Washington, D.C., on 11 September 2001. Bush's vigorous response to the terrorist attacks, especially the invasion of Afghanistan and the toppling of the Taliban regime, endeared him to many Americans who believed he was an effective war leader.

Expanding the global war on terror to include Saddam Hussein's Iraq, Bush launched a preemptive invasion of that nation in March 2003. Largely because of his image as a strong commander-in-chief, Bush received widespread support for the Iraqi invasion and won reelection in 2004. However, as the violence in Iraq intensified and American casualties mounted, it became increasingly difficult for Bush to maintain popular enthusiasm for the war, and his administration's failed response to the Hurricane Katrina devastation led to critical questioning of its competency for handling crises. By the end of 2006, disenchantment with the president's policies allowed Democrats to gain control of the House of Representatives and the Senate in midterm elections. Despite the rise of antiwar sentiment, Bush refused to significantly alter his strategy for prosecuting the war. In this way he exemplified the southern penchant for stubbornly clinging to a cause widely perceived to be lost.

G. WAYNE DOWDY
Benjamin L. Hooks Central Library
Memphis, Tennessee

Paul Burka, *Texas Monthly* (June 1995); Colin Campbell and Bert A. Rockman, eds., *The George W. Bush Presidency: Appraisals and Prospects* (2004); James C. Cobb, *Away Down South: A History of Southern Identity* (2005); Fred I. Greenstein, *The George W. Bush Presidency: An Early Assessment* (2003); Kevin P. Phillips, *The American Prospect* (February 2004).

Byrd Machine

The Byrd machine of Virginia (1922–65) was an expression of the unique cultural and political heritage of the Old Dominion, which cherished elitist and traditional values. Created by Harry Flood Byrd Sr. and other members of the state Democratic Party during the 1920s, the machine took advantage of restrictive electoral regulations that made it possible for a small percentage of conservative rural and small-town white voters to control elective offices. Byrd served successively as state party chairman,

governor, and U.S. senator (1933–65). At his retirement in 1965, Byrd arranged to have his Senate seat passed to his son, Harry Flood Byrd Jr.

During the 1930s, Byrd joined other southern Democratic and Republican conservatives to oppose the more liberal politics of the New Deal administration of Franklin D. Roosevelt. However, as urban areas in northern and southeastern Virginia developed after World War II, the control of the machine was gradually eroded. The machine's last stand was to organize a "massive resistance" campaign to oppose court-ordered integration of public schools after 1954. By the time Byrd retired from the Senate in 1965, the machine was ill-defined and many of its former loyalists had defected to the growing ranks of the southern Republican Party.

RAYMOND H. PULLEY
Appalachian State University

Harry Flood Byrd Sr. Papers, University of Virginia; Ronald L. Heinemann, *Harry Byrd of Virginia* (1996); Raymond H. Pulley, *Old Virginia Restored: An Interpretation of the Progressive Impulse, 1870–1930* (1968); Francis M. Wilhoit, *The Politics of Massive Resistance* (1973); J. Harvey Wilkinson III, *Harry Byrd and the Changing Face of Virginia Politics, 1945–1966* (1968).

Calhoun, John C.

(1782–1850) POLITICIAN AND
POLITICAL PHILOSOPHER.
Born of Scots-Irish ancestry in the South Carolina upcountry in the wake of the American Revolution, John Caldwell Calhoun traveled north for his education. He graduated from Yale and read law with Federalist judge Tapping

Reeve in Litchfield, Conn. Calhoun returned home, practiced law, won a seat in the state legislature, and then was elected to represent South Carolina in the U.S. Congress from 1811 to 1817. A devout nationalist during this phase of his career, Calhoun was a war hawk and an avid supporter of the War of 1812. He voted for a protective tariff in 1816 and introduced the bill chartering the Second Bank of the United States in 1817. He served as secretary of war in James Monroe's cabinet and in 1824 won election as vice president of the United States.

Calhoun was reelected vice president in 1828 and entered the administration of Andrew Jackson as heir apparent to the presidency. Within four years, however, Calhoun and Jackson were bitter enemies; Calhoun resigned his office and became an ardent sectionalist. Calhoun's *South Carolina Exposition and Protest* was the philosophical underpinning of the nullification movement in South Carolina. During the nullification crisis and after, Calhoun devoted his energies and considerable talents to the minority interests of the South. During a brief term as John Tyler's secretary of state (1844–45) and as a South Carolina senator (1845–50), Calhoun was the South's political champion and spokesman.

In a sense, Calhoun's career in public life embodied the course of southern political behavior. A nationalist during the Virginia dynasty, he became a sectionalist when he came to believe that nationalism conflicted with southern interests. To his death in 1850 Calhoun fought the South's political battles with considerable skill. His greatest sig-

nificance, however, lay in his capacity for political thought and analysis. His prime concern was for minority interests in American democracy. He believed the Union to be a compact; southern states had entered the compact when they ratified the Constitution, and they were free to dissolve the compact and leave the Union if they so chose. However, Calhoun revered the Union and attempted to discover some moderate constitutional course that would preserve both southern interests and the Union, one that would offer the minority South some alternatives to submission and secession. He never resolved the dilemma, but in the process of defining and articulating the southern political stance, Calhoun became a constructive critic of American democracy and, in the judgment of some historians, the foremost American political thinker of the 19th century.

EMORY THOMAS
University of Georgia

Gerald M. Capers, *John C. Calhoun, Opportunist: A Reappraisal* (1960); Margaret L. Coit, *John C. Calhoun: American Portrait* (1950); Richard N. Current, *John C. Calhoun* (1963); Ross M. Lence, ed., *Union and Liberty: The Political Philosophy of John C. Calhoun* (1992); John Niven, *John C. Calhoun and the Price of Union: A Biography* (1988); Clyde N. Wilson, ed., *The Papers of John C. Calhoun*, 28 vols. (1959–2003); Charles M. Wiltse, *John C. Calhoun, Nullifier, 1829–1839* (1949).

Carter, Jimmy

(b. 1924) U.S. PRESIDENT.
"I am a Southerner and an American," Jimmy Carter wrote in his campaign

autobiography, *Why Not the Best?* It would be difficult to quarrel with either assertion. Born and reared in the heart of the southwest Georgia Black Belt, James Earl ("Jimmy") Carter Jr. could trace both his American and southern ancestry back to the early 17th century when the first Carters arrived in Virginia. By the decade of the 1780s, ancestors of the future president had made their way to Georgia, eventually settling in Sumter County, where Jimmy Carter was born and raised.

The son of a moderately wealthy landowner and businessman, Carter, like many of the other progeny of upper-middle-class southerners, aspired to a military career. After completing his elementary and secondary education in Plains and matriculating for a year at Georgia Southwestern College in nearby Americus, he enrolled in the naval ROTC program at the Georgia Institute of Technology prior to securing an appointment to the U.S. Naval Academy in Annapolis. There the young cadet did well, finishing in the upper 10 percent of his 1946 graduating class. Thereafter, he entered the submarine service after completing his required two years of surface duty.

The young naval officer's promising military career ended in 1953, however, when he returned to Plains to manage the family's business affairs after the death of his father. Within a few years of his return, he was deeply involved in a variety of community affairs and soon was campaigning for the state senate seat once held by his father. After two terms in the Georgia General Assembly, Carter ran unsuccessfully for the Democratic gubernatorial nomination in 1966 before succeeding in the same quest four years later.

On the first day of his governorship, Carter attracted national attention by dramatically proclaiming that the time for racial discrimination in Georgia had ended. During the next four years Carter promoted a moderately liberal, progressive reform program, which included state government reorganization, judicial reform, consumer protection, welfare reform, tax reform, and environmental concerns. Following through on earlier commitments, he also appointed numerous black Georgians and women to important positions in state government. Unable to succeed himself in the governorship, Carter in 1974 began laying the groundwork for a successful run for the presidency of the United States. His 1976 campaign focused national attention on changes in the South in the previous decade. Carter played a crucial role within the South in strengthening, at least temporarily, a black-white coalition in the Democratic Party. He won black support and also appealed to the white rural South. For the first time since 1964, Democratic politicians across the South enthusiastically supported their party's presidential nominee.

Once installed in the presidential office, Carter, with less success, sought to push the same type of reforms that he had sponsored during his governorship. Domestic economic programs and international crises contributed to Carter's presidential woes, however, and in 1980 he was repudiated by the same voters, many of them southerners, who had supported him four years earlier. Several weeks later he was back in Plains, from which he had launched his meteoric rise to national prominence a few years earlier.

An unorthodox politician in many ways, Carter nevertheless was clearly a product of the southern culture into which he was born and in which he was raised. An inherited sense of noblesse oblige, which he shared with numerous others in the southern elite, combined in Carter with religious convictions (he was a "born again" Baptist) and a sense of history to produce a code of social ethics that permitted him to transcend the race issue that had been the burden of so many other white southerners. In so doing, symbolically at least, Carter's rise to the presidency represented the ultimate reunification of the South with the rest of the nation.

Since leaving the presidency, Carter has been a freelance ambassador on international missions, monitoring contested elections, negotiating peace agreements, and initiating relief efforts. He founded the Carter Center in Atlanta in 1982 to address issues of democracy and human rights. He received the Nobel Peace Prize in 2002. He has also been a grassroots participant in Habitat for Humanity's house-building programs and has authored 14 books, including works on faith, the outdoor life, and a series of memoirs.

GARY M. FINK
Georgia State University

Peter G. Bourne, *Jimmy Carter: A Comprehensive Biography from Plains to Post-Presidency* (1997); Douglas G. Brinkley, *The Unfinished Presidency: Jimmy Carter's Quest for Global Peace* (1998); Jimmy Carter, *An Hour before Daylight: Memoirs of a Rural Boyhood* (2001), *The Personal Beliefs of Jimmy Carter: Winner of the 2002 Nobel Peace Prize* (2002), *Sources of Strength: Meditations on Scripture for a Living Faith* (1998); Gary M. Fink, *Prelude to the Presidency: The Political Character and Legislative Leadership Style of Governor Jimmy Carter* (1980); David Kucharsky, *The Man from Plains: The Mind and Spirit of Jimmy Carter* (1975); William L. Miller, *Yankee from Georgia: The Emergence of Jimmy Carter* (1978); Kenneth E. Morris, *Jimmy Carter: American Moralist* (1996).

Carter, Lillian

(1898–1983) PUBLIC FIGURE.
Born in Richland, Ga., on 15 August 1898, Lillian Jackson Carter was the daughter of James Jackson, a Richland postmaster from whom she inherited an active interest in social justice and liberal politics. She remembers, for example, her father bringing meals from the local hotel, which served whites only, to blacks who waited at the post office.

In 1923 she married James Earl Carter. The Carters had four children: James Earl Jr., Gloria, Ruth, and William Alton. A trained nurse, Lillian Carter worked in a Plains, Ga., hospital during the 1920s and 1930s, helped with the Carter family business, served as house-mother to an Auburn University fraternity during the 1950s, later managed a nursing home, and served in the Peace Corps in India from 1966 to 1968. In 1978 she and Gloria Carter Spann published *Away from Home: Letters to My Family*.

Devotion to family characterized

Lillian Carter. She never disguised her ambitions for her son Jimmy Carter nor her pride in his accomplishments. She campaigned for his elections, from the Georgia legislature to the presidency. She had earlier helped in her husband's race for the state legislature. When James Earl Carter Sr. died in 1953, she was offered his legislative seat but declined. She later claimed that she might have accepted had she not been so grief stricken.

A staunch supporter of civil rights, Lillian Carter stood firmly with the national Democratic Party throughout the 1960s. In 1964 she served as cochair of President Lyndon Johnson's Americus, Ga., campaign office and suffered harassment for her leadership. In explaining her actions, Lillian stated, "I just couldn't stand to see a Negro mistreated." In 1977 the Synagogue Council of America awarded her its Covenant of Peace award, and in 1980 she was named honorary chair of the Peace Corps National Advisory Council. Religious but not puritanical, Lillian Carter preferred small-town life, hated to dress up, liked bourbon, and admitted that the only luxury she wanted was "a good-looking car." She died of cancer in Americus–Sumter County Hospital at the age of 85.

JULIA KIRK BLACKWELDER
University of North Carolina at Charlotte

Good Housekeeping (April 1977); *Ms.* (October 1976); *Newsweek* (4 and 26 July 1976); *Redbook* (October 1976), *Time* (3 January, 28 February 1976); *Who's Who of American Women*, 12th ed. (1981–82).

Clinton, Bill

(b. 1946) U.S. PRESIDENT.
William Jefferson "Bill" Clinton was born on 19 August 1946 in "a place called Hope," a small town in southwestern Arkansas. His father, William Jefferson Blythe III, died in a car accident just three months before his birth. While his mother, Virginia Cassidy Blythe, studied nursing in Louisiana to help provide for her son, his grandparents, who ran a country store in Hope, cared for him. When Billy, as he was called, was in early grade school, his mother returned, and they moved to Hot Springs, where Virginia married Roger Clinton. Because of Roger's gambling and alcohol addiction, Billy and his younger half brother, Roger Jr., depended even more on the strength and sacrifice of their mother.

Despite his tumultuous childhood, Clinton excelled in leadership roles and academics, and in high school he attended Boys Nation and met President Kennedy at the White House. He left Arkansas to attend Georgetown University, earning a bachelor's degree in international affairs. He was awarded the Rhodes Scholarship, which took him abroad to study in Oxford at a time when many of his classmates were being drafted to serve in Vietnam. Upon his return, he attended Yale Law School, where he met Hillary Rodham.

After law school, he came back home to Arkansas and began a life of public service. While teaching law at the University of Arkansas, Clinton wed Hillary Rodham in 1975, and their daughter, Chelsea, was born in 1980. Clinton won his first office, attorney general of Arkansas, in 1976. Two years later, at the age of 32, Clinton was elected governor, becoming the youngest governor in the nation at that time. During his tenure, Clinton positioned himself as a moderate Democrat, insisting on balanced budgets while trying to improve key services, such as public education.

Clinton entered the 1992 presidential race with the same centrist blueprint that guided his six terms as governor. Calling his approach "New Democrat," he aimed to slash the deficit, put 100,000 more police officers on the streets, create millions of new jobs, and reform the welfare and health care systems. While Clinton's message resonated with party loyalists, Democrats were equally interested in selecting a candidate whose appeal could reach conservative white southerners. After emerging victorious in the primaries, Clinton selected Senator Al Gore of Tennessee as his running mate. The addition of Gore, a fellow Southern Baptist, made it the first time in more than a century that a major party chose two southerners as nominees. Although they overwhelmed President George H. W. Bush in the electoral count, Clinton and Gore won only a third of the South's electoral votes.

During his first two years in office, Clinton succeeded in getting much of his agenda through the Democratic-controlled Congress, including his Family and Medical Leave Act, anti-crime bill, and deficit reduction package. By the midterm elections of 1994, however, backlash against his universal health coverage program and tax increases gave Republicans control of both houses of Congress for the first time since the Eisenhower administration. Moreover, Republicans now held a majority of the South's congressional seats, a feat not seen since Reconstruction. Yet Clinton rebounded as the public perception of his handling of the budget battles with the Republican-controlled Congress, which caused two government shutdowns in 1995, steered in his favor. Bolstered by an improved national economy, Clinton won another electoral landslide in his 1996 reelection campaign against Senator Bob Dole. During his second term, Clinton worked vigorously to broker and sustain peace agreements in the Balkans, Northern Ireland, and the Middle East.

Accusations of personal indiscretions dogged Clinton throughout his presidency, but none cost him politically or legally until he gave testimony in Paula Jones's sexual harassment suit against him in 1997. Testifying before a grand jury, Clinton lied about his sexual relationship with a White House intern, Monica Lewinsky. The House impeached Clinton on charges of perjury and obstruction of justice, making him the second president, and the first elected president (Andrew Johnson ascended to the presidency following Abraham Lincoln's assassination), to be impeached. Although the Senate failed to convict Clinton, allowing him to serve out his remaining term, the scandal crippled the president's political agenda and did not end his legal troubles. After Clinton settled with Jones, paying her $850,000, a federal judge found him in contempt of court for lying in a deposition. Rather than face disbarment hearings, Clinton surrendered his law license for five years.

After leaving the White House, the Clintons continued their roles as public servants. New Yorkers elected Hillary Clinton to the Senate in 2000 while the former president, through the Clinton Foundation, has worked to promote multilateral solutions to the world's problems, particularly fighting poverty and AIDS in Africa. The Clinton Presidential Library, which houses a museum and archive, opened in Little Rock in November 2004.

C. DALTON LYON
University of Mississippi

E. H. Crump, mayor of Memphis, Tenn., c. 1940 (Tennessee State Library and Archives, Nashville)

Bill Clinton, *My Life* (2004); John F. Harris, *The Survivor: Bill Clinton in the White House* (2005); Joe Klein, *The Natural: The Misunderstood Presidency of Bill Clinton* (2002); David Maraniss, *First in His Class: A Biography of Bill Clinton* (1996); Dewayne Wickham, *Bill Clinton and Black America* (2002).

Crump, E. H.

(1874–1954) POLITICIAN.
Born and raised in Holly Springs, Miss., Edward Hull Crump moved to Memphis as a young man. His business efforts prospered, especially his insurance firm, and Crump eventually built a sizable personal fortune. Politically active almost from his arrival in Memphis, Crump was elected mayor in 1909, 1911, and 1915, but his refusal to enforce Tennessee's Prohibition law prompted the state to initiate legal proceedings, which resulted in his resignation in 1916. Despite the setback, Crump continued to build a political machine that, by the mid-1920s, utterly dominated the large Shelby County vote. In 1932 the Crump-backed candidate for governor won election, and for the next 16 years the Memphis boss and his organization influenced the outcome of most major statewide races. Finally, in 1948, insurgents led by Estes Kefauver and Gordon Browning defeated the Crump choices for senator and governor in the Democratic primary. His power across Tennessee substantially weakened, Crump still controlled Memphis politics until his death in 1954.

A self-described progressive, Crump stressed efficient government and improved public services, policies that generally kept him in good stead with respectable Memphis business leaders, as did his bitter opposition to unions.

At the same time, however, the Crump machine was closely linked to the Bluff City's seamy vice trade, a prime source of money and votes for organization candidates. The Crump machine also included the local black community, tied to the boss by his special blend of patronage and coercion. Consequently, Memphis was one of the few places in the South that tolerated black voting during the segregation era. W. C. Handy celebrated Crump in his "Memphis Blues" (1912), a catchy tune that the mayor then used to gain black and white votes. "Mister Crump don't 'low no easy riders here," it said. Crump delighted in conducting well-publicized charity drives to benefit various causes, but he dealt harshly with potential opponents. City bureaucrats and policemen harassed his critics, while curious reporters and persistent labor organizers occasionally encountered strong-arm tactics. Although many Crump policies and practices were generally typical of machine politics in other parts of the country, Crump himself struck the pose of the paternalistic southern gentleman. Dapper and flamboyant, he was an unusually visible political boss who often castigated his enemies in splashy newspaper advertisements. A uniquely skillful politician, Crump wielded more power outside his own city than any other urban boss in the South.

DAVID D. LEE

Western Kentucky University

William Miller, *Memphis during the Progressive Era, 1900–1917* (1957), *Mr. Crump of Memphis* (1964); David Tucker, *Memphis since Crump: Bossism, Blacks, and Civic Reformers, 1948–1968* (1980).

Davis, Jefferson

(1808–1889) CONFEDERATE STATES OF AMERICA PRESIDENT.

"The man and the hour have met," a distinguished secessionist proclaimed when Jefferson Davis became president of the Confederate States of America. In most ways Davis seemed ideally suited to directing the South's struggle for independence. Born in Fairview, Ky., in 1808, Davis moved with his family to Wilkinson County, Miss., when he was still a boy. Experienced in warfare and politics, he had attended the U.S. Military Academy (graduating in 1828), participated in the Black Hawk War, commanded a regiment of Mississippi volunteers and been wounded in the Mexican War, served as President Franklin Pierce's secretary of war, and headed the U.S. Senate's Military Affairs Committee. A brave, bold, erudite agrarian who believed in slavery and the right of secession, Davis worked tirelessly for the Confederacy. Against the localism of certain governors and congressmen, he advocated measures for the Confederacy such as a military draft, conscription of blacks into the army, impressment of private property, government management of railroads and blockade-runners, and an income tax.

But his inability to maintain the support of the Confederate Congress and his unwillingness to delegate authority except in certain areas created problems; so did his direction of military strategy and tactics. Ironically, it may have been in military affairs, where so much was expected of him, that Davis failed. He picked only one outstanding army commander, Robert E. Lee; other commanders proved to be unsuccessful, distrusted by Davis, or both. Squabbles among generals and over military politics hampered the Confederate war effort, and as Union armies advanced, Confederate morale deteriorated. Davis hoped that his defensive-offensive strategy would save the South, yet in practice it became little more than a series of courageous but costly attacks on enemy forces until dwindling manpower forced the Confederates to go on the defensive after 1863.

Davis may have been "perverse and obstinate" and "an indifferent judge of men," as his critics claimed, but he maintained during the last months of the war an unfailing will to win and even tried to continue the war as the Confederacy collapsed. Captured in May 1865 and imprisoned for two years without a trial, he became in the North the symbol of the South's treasonable sins. In the *Rise and Fall of the Confederate Government*, which he wrote after release from prison, Davis shared much of the blame for Confederate defeat with others. Throughout the remainder of his life, he neither repented nor asked forgiveness for himself or for the cause he led.

GRADY MCWHINEY
Texas Christian University

Donald E. Collins, *The Death and Resurrection of Jefferson Davis* (2005); William J. Cooper, *Jefferson Davis, American* (2000); William C. Davis, *Jefferson Davis: The Man and His Hour* (1991); James T. McIntosh, ed., *The Papers of Jefferson Davis* (1971–); Dunbar Rowland, ed., *Jefferson Davis* (10 vols., 1923); Robert Penn Warren, *Jefferson Davis Gets His Citizenship Back* (1980).

Durr, Virginia

(1903–1999) SOCIAL REFORMER.
Born on 6 August 1903, Virginia Foster Durr spent childhood summers on her grandmother's plantation in Union Springs, Ala., where antebellum customs were preserved virtually intact. Her father had been destined to inherit the mantle of the slave-owning aristocracy; instead he was reduced to genteel poverty, first as a Presbyterian minister and then as an insurance salesman in Birmingham. Although an inheritance from her grandmother eventually allowed the family to pursue a fashionable social life in Birmingham, they were never altogether secure. "You see," she recalls, "we lived in this half way stage between being benevolent despots . . . and trying to make a living . . . and the poorer we got, the more snobbish we became." By the time she reached adolescence, Virginia Foster had absorbed the lessons of ladyhood: the sexual inhibitions, aristocratic pretensions, and racial taboos that went along with good manners and noblesse oblige.

The events of the 1920s and 1930s, however, exposed what Durr calls "the contradictions, the total contradictions" in her parents' world and set her on a profoundly different path. In 1920 she went north for two years of college at Wellesley where, for the first time, she met black students as equals. In 1926 she married a young lawyer named Clifford Judkins Durr; a year later their first daughter was born. Working for the Red Cross and the Junior League during the Depression, Virginia saw Birmingham's unemployed iron ore and steel workers "literally starving to death" because the city fathers refused to provide adequate relief.

Meanwhile, Virginia Durr's sister Josephine had married Hugo Black, who was elected to the U.S. Senate in 1920 and appointed to the Supreme Court in 1936. Black's recommendation helped Clifford Durr secure a job in Washington, where he became assistant general counsel of the Reconstruction Finance Corporation and then a member of the Federal Communications Commission (FCC). In Washington, the Durrs joined a lively circle of like-minded young southerners. She had four more children during these years and reveled in the excitement of the early New Deal. While she attended the La Follette Committee hearings on antilabor violence in Birmingham, her compassion for the poor turned to outrage at the Tennessee Coal and Iron Company, the United States Steel subsidiary that dominated her hometown. After the death of her only son, she became increasingly involved in politics in her own right, first in the Woman's National Democratic Committee and then in the Southern Conference for Human Welfare (SCHW).

Virginia Durr was a founding member of the SCHW and director of its Washington Committee, the most vital of its local organizations. The committee raised funds, united the capital's southern contingent for action on issues affecting the South, and conducted a vigorous congressional lobbying campaign. As executive vice president of the National Committee to Abolish the Poll Tax, she helped lay the groundwork for eliminating a major device by which blacks and poor whites were barred from the polls.

The postwar years brought a swing to the right and the beginning of the Cold War. In the 1948 presidential campaign, Virginia Durr left the Democratic Party to serve on Henry Wallace's platform committee and to run for governor of Virginia on the Progressive Party ticket. Clifford refused reappointment to the FCC because of his objections to President Harry Truman's loyalty program. Smeared as a "Communist sympathizer," he soon gave up his effort to practice law in the capital and moved to Denver to take a job with the Farmers' Union. When Virginia Durr signed a petition critical of the Korean War, Clifford was forced to leave that job, too. Reluctantly, the Durrs moved back to Alabama, where Clifford established a law practice in Montgomery and Virginia worked as his secretary.

Living with Clifford's parents in Montgomery and then moving to their own home in Wetumpka, the Durrs struggled to overcome their isolation and integrate themselves into the community they had left two decades before. In 1954, however, Virginia was pulled back into the political limelight when she was subpoenaed to appear at Senate Internal Security Commission hearings, presided over by Mississippi's James Eastland, on Communist influence in the Southern Conference Education Fund (an offshoot of the SCHW). A year later the civil rights movement began in earnest when Rosa Parks, a friend of the Durrs and a longtime stalwart of the NAACP, set the Montgomery bus boycott in motion. "It was a terrifically thrilling period," Virginia Durr recalls. "I wouldn't have missed it for anything." Clifford took civil rights cases. Virginia joined Dorothy Tilley's "Fellowship of the Concerned" and published articles on the movement. The Durr home became a mecca for lawyers, journalists, and civil rights workers. In the late 1960s Virginia brought her political experience to bear once more in the Alabama National Democratic Party, founded in opposition to the George Wallace–controlled regular Democrats.

Rosa Parks, Virginia Durr once observed, is "a remarkable woman . . . really what you would call the perfect Southern lady." And so, to be sure, was Virginia Foster Durr. Peeling away ladyhood's repressive conventions, she kept its informing spirit: gracious, generous, and attuned to the nuance of individual lives even as she pursued justice and gloried in the rough and tumble of a political fight. In that sense, she was part of a little-known tradition—the southern lady as radical, embodying the past while fighting for a different future. Fittingly, a statement issued by President and Mrs. Clinton following Virginia Durr's death in 1999 said, "A white woman born to privilege in the Deep South, Mrs. Durr refused to turn a blind eye to racism and intolerance in our society. Her courage and steely conviction in the earliest days of the civil rights movement helped change this nation forever."

JACQUELYN DOWD HALL
University of North Carolina at Chapel Hill

Hollinger F. Barnard, ed., *Outside the Magic Circle: The Autobiography of Virginia Foster Durr* (1985); Virginia Durr Papers, Schlesinger Library, Radcliffe College; Tom Gardner, *Southern Exposure* (Spring 1981); Patricia Sullivan, *Days of Hope: Race and Democracy in the New Deal Era* (1996); Sue Thrasher and Jacquelyn Dowd Hall, Southern Oral History Program, University of North Carolina, Chapel Hill, 1975.

Edelman, Marian Wright

(b. 1939) CIVIL RIGHTS LAWYER. Marian Wright Edelman is founder and president of the Children's Defense Fund, based in Washington, D.C. Born 6 June 1939 to a Bennettsville, S.C., Baptist minister and his wife (who also raised her four brothers, her sister, and 14 foster children), Edelman in 1983 was named by *Ladies' Home Journal* one of the "100 most influential women in America." In 1985 she received a MacArthur Foundation award of $228,000, which she promptly devoted to her Children's Defense Fund to make the needs of children—especially poor children—a top priority on America's agenda. She is a voice for children who cannot vote, lobby, or speak out for themselves. Edelman is concerned with every aspect of childhood health and education, infant mortality, teenage pregnancy, and child abuse. Her work graphically details the effects of poverty on the minds and future of America's children.

Awards and accolades for Marian Wright Edelman have cascaded in a steady stream since her undergraduate days at Spelman College in Atlanta, where a Merrill Scholarship afforded her a year's study at the Universities of Paris and Geneva. She now serves as chair of Spelman's Board of Trustees.

In the intervening years, she has fulfilled her early promise as one of *Mademoiselle* magazine's "four most exciting young women in America" (1965) and as *Vogue*'s "Outstanding Young Woman of America (1965–66)." During those years, many pieces of civil rights legislation were forged under the force of her determination and penchant for detail. Her brilliant congressional testimony, her lobbying for and drafting of legislation, and her highly focused intellect and energy led former vice president Walter Mondale to call Marian Wright Edelman "the smartest woman I have ever met."

Marian Wright grew up in a close-knit southern family for whom civil rights represented an American ideal. Her father's final days in 1954 were spent with a radio at his side, listening to news of the school desegregation case (*Brown v. Board of Education*) being argued before the Supreme Court. His last words to Marian, a week before the decision came down, were, "Don't let anything get between you and your education."

Edelman graduated from Spelman as valedictorian in 1960, won a John Hay Whitney Fellowship to Yale University Law School, received her LL.B. in 1963, and joined the NAACP Legal and Education Defense Fund as staff attorney in New York. From 1964 to 1968 she served as director of the fund's Jackson, Miss., office, where in 1965 she became the first black woman admitted to the Mississippi bar.

In Mississippi during the thick of the civil rights movement, she organized Head Start programs throughout the state for the Child Development Group of Mississippi (CDGM) and developed a keen awareness of the effects of poverty and hunger on the lives of young children. Her advocacy drew national attention to children suffering from hunger and malnutrition in America. As a Field Foundation Fellow and partner in the Washington research project of the Southern Center for Public Policy, she became a principal architect of and successful lobbyist for the Food Stamp Act of 1970. That year she became an honorary fellow at the University of Pennsylvania Law School and won the Louise Waterman Wise Award, and in 1971 *Time* magazine named her one of 200 outstanding young American leaders. From 1971 to May 1973 she served as director of the Center for Law and Education at Harvard University—a position she left to form the Children's Defense Fund.

Edelman's research on the plight of children in America is quoted in the major media, cited by congressional committees, and used in state and federal programming. She is the author of three books, *Children out of School in America* (1974), *School Suspensions: Are They Helping Children?* (1975), and *Portrait of Inequality: Black and White Children in America* (1980), all published by the Children's Defense Fund, as well as numerous articles and scholarly papers.

MARY LYNN KOTZ
Washington, D.C.

Governor Faubus addresses protesters at Arkansas state capitol in Little Rock, 1959, two years after the initial integration of Central High School. (John T. Bledsoe, photographer, Library of Congress [LC-U9-2919-25], Washington, D.C.)

Harry A. Ploski and James Williams, eds., *The Negro Almanac* (1983); *Psychology Today* (June 1975); *Who's Who in America*, 43rd ed. (1984–85); *Who's Who in Black America*, 4th ed. (1985).

Faubus, Orval

(1910–1994) POLITICIAN.
Six-term governor of Arkansas (1955–67), Orval Eugene Faubus gained notoriety around the world in 1957 for his defiance of the federal government in preventing the integration of Little Rock Central High School. Faubus quickly became one of the powerful symbols of southern resistance to desegregation, embodying in his person—and especially in his rhetoric—much that was of value to the South. Of humble origins, Faubus communicated effectively his distaste for the city and for the "Cadillac brigade" that wielded power there. He was a strong individualist who spoke the language of the states' rights advocates and the opponents of big government. Faubus earned the admiration of many southerners (and others) for standing up to the powerful forces that

threatened the traditional values of his region. An ambivalent leader who vacillated in his own mind between liberalism and conservatism, Faubus reflected the southern tension between the forces of continuity and change. His folksy manner, his defiant tone, his regard for the common folk, and his orientation toward the past all exemplified a southern cultural style, and all contributed to making Orval Faubus a kind of hillbilly hero.

Born in 1910 in the tiny Ozark Mountain community of Combs, Ark., Orval Eugene Faubus was reared in an environment of poverty and political radicalism (his father was a follower of the socialist Eugene V. Debs). After three years of military service, the young schoolteacher and newspaperman came to the attention of another GI reformer, the liberal governor Sid McMath, and landed a job on the Arkansas Highway Commission. In 1954 Faubus ran against an incumbent governor and won in one of the most scurrilous elections in Arkansas history. His opponent labeled him a communist because of his early association with the Commonwealth College. Faubus's first term was uneventful, and he ran successfully for a second term against an archsegregationist, whom he characterized as a "purveyor of hate." Hardly a model of political conservatism, Orval Faubus approached 1957 with a solid reputation as a moderate.

As Orval Faubus would say years later, 1957 overshadowed everything. His defiant stand against the forces of change and racial injustice earned him momentary fame, six terms as governor,

and tremendous power in his own state, but eventually it left him a captive of his image as a racist and an opportunist.

ELIZABETH JACOWAY
University of Arkansas at Little Rock

Orval Eugene Faubus, *Down from the Hills* (1980); Willard B. Gatewood Jr. and Timothy Donovan, eds., *The Governors of Arkansas: Essays in Political Biography* (1981); Roy Reed, *Arkansas Historical Quarterly* (Spring 1996).

Felton, Rebecca

(1835–1930) POLITICIAN AND WRITER.

Rebecca Ann Latimer Felton was a strong-willed, outspoken individual who defied the tradition that women should not become involved in politics. She played an active role in the career of her husband, Dr. William H. Felton, an early leader of Georgia's Independent Democrat Party. She managed his campaigns, helped draft bills, advised him on legislative strategy, and responded to his critics with innumerable letters to newspapers. She was perfectly capable of vehemently attacking male opponents, but when they responded she condemned them for criticizing a woman. The extent of her role in her husband's career is illustrated by the comment of one of Dr. Felton's opponents that he had been defeated "by the political she of Georgia" and by a newspaper headline that read "Mrs. Felton and Husband Returned."

Felton supported the temperance movement, worked to abolish the convict lease system, and defended state-supported schools against attacks by denominational colleges. She cam-

Rebecca Latimer Felton, Georgia politician and writer, c. 1920s (Photographer unknown, Library of Congress, [LC-USZ-62-20175], Washington, D.C.)

paigned for vocational training for poor white girls and agitated for admission of women to state universities. She wrote three books and was a columnist for the rural editions of the *Atlanta Journal*. In her columns she defended working conditions in southern cotton mills and criticized child labor laws, Jews, Catholics, and the theory of evolution. Early in the 1900s she became active in the woman suffrage movement, arguing that giving women the vote was necessary to keep power out of the hands of aliens and blacks. Her attacks on blacks were especially virulent. When the Wilmington, N.C., race riot broke out after she had defended lynching, she responded to criticism of her views by advocating that 1,000 blacks be lynched every week if necessary to prevent rapes. When Georgia's U.S. senator died in office, Felton was appointed to com-plete his term. She served for one day before resigning in favor of the senator-elect.

Rebecca Latimer Felton defies any simple categorization. Although she shared the conservative economic views and intense racial prejudice of many of her southern contemporaries, her feminism set her apart. Unlike many southern women who were involved in the temperance and suffrage move-ments, she did not move on to work for improved race relations. A rural woman, she enjoyed her role as one of the two lady managers from Georgia at the World's Columbian Exposition in Chicago. Her dogged determination, energy, and outspoken nature resulted in an unusually active public life and made her a force to be reckoned with in her native state.

JANE WALKER
Dekalb Community College

Rebecca Felton, *Country Life in Georgia in the Days of My Youth* (1919), *My Memoirs of Georgia Politics* (1911); John E. Talmadge, *Rebecca Latimer Felton: Nine Stormy De-cades* (1960); LeeAnn Whites, *Georgia Historical Quarterly* (Summer 1992).

Folsom, James

(1908–1987) POLITICIAN.
James Elisha "Big Jim" Folsom won the Alabama governorship in 1946 and 1954. He introduced classic southern Populist campaign techniques to the state, using country music, powerful symbols, and humorous parables to appeal directly to the voters. Folsom used campaigns as a platform from which to educate the electorate about the need to fight for their rights against the "Big Mules,"

Postcard of Alabama governor "Big Jim" Folsom and his family (Charles Reagan Wilson Collection, Center for the Study of Southern Culture, University of Mississippi)

meaning the elite. He spoke of the evils of racial discrimination, the need for reapportionment on a one-person, one-vote basis, women's rights, improved education, and better roads.

His forthright and principled campaign speeches were followed by vigorous but mainly unsuccessful attempts as governor to transform rhetoric into reality. His opponents were entrenched in a gerrymandered legislature controlled by Black Belt and Jefferson County (Birmingham) politicians. His efforts were also inhibited by the image, and often the reality, of corruption that surrounded his administrations and by a drinking problem that sapped his strength and ruined his judgment.

Folsom was born in 1908 in Coffee County, Ala., in the southeastern corner of the state known as the "Wiregrass." The Wiregrass had a small-farm economic base, low concentrations of

blacks, and a strong Populist political tradition. Folsom's many Populist-oriented challenges to the state's political elite and his racial moderation had clear origins in his Coffee County upbringing.

His political beliefs were strongly influenced by three people. His father, Joshua Folsom, held many county elective offices and introduced him to courthouse politics. Folsom's uncle, John Dunnavant, a Populist Party activist, was a brilliant storyteller who spoke glowingly of Grandfather Dunnavant's freeing of his slaves and of his opposition to the Civil War. Folsom's first father-in-law, probate judge J. A. Carnley, was another active and articulate Populist advocate, but one who stayed within the Democratic Party.

Folsom was not a pure Populist. His political views were also influenced by the Great Depression. He received an especially clear perspective on the suffering of that period in his position as Civil Works Administration director in north Alabama's Marshall County. From then on, he favored large-scale government assistance programs. Moving to north Alabama in the late 1930s, Folsom went to a region of the state with a political culture similar to that of the Wiregrass. His election victories united these two very similar regions against the state's Black Belt.

In 1962 Folsom was defeated in a reelection bid by George Wallace, who used race-baiting rhetoric to win.

CARL GRAFTON

ANNE PERMALOFF

Auburn University at Montgomery

Carl Grafton and Anne Permaloff, *Big Mules and Branchheads: James E. Folsom and Political Power in Alabama* (1985).

Fulbright, J. William

(1905–1995) POLITICIAN.
James William Fulbright moved to Fayetteville, Ark., from Summer, Mo., in 1906, a year after his birth on 9 April 1905. He spent his childhood in the University of Arkansas town, eventually attending college there and graduating with a B.A. in political science in 1925. His father, a highly successful businessman, owned the local newspaper, as well as a bank, a lumberyard, and a bottling company. His mother, a journalist and businesswoman, worked as editor of the family paper.

The fall after his graduation from Arkansas, Fulbright enrolled at Oxford University in England on a Rhodes scholarship and received his M.A. in 1931. He went on to earn a law degree in 1934 from George Washington University in Washington, D.C., passing the bar exam the same year. After serving as an attorney for the Department of Justice Anti-Trust Division from 1934 to 1935 and then briefly as a professor at George Washington, Fulbright returned to Fayetteville in 1936 to teach at the University of Arkansas Law School. He became president of the university in 1939, at the youthful age of 34.

Fulbright entered politics in 1942 when he was elected to the U.S. House of Representatives. He became a member of the Foreign Affairs Committee in January of 1943, and that September the House adopted the Fulbright Resolution, an international peace-keeping mechanism that became the United Nations Organization in 1945. He won a bid for Senate in 1944 and in 1946 introduced legislation that established the Fulbright Exchange Program, a student/teacher/scholar-exchange program sponsored by the Bureau of Educational and Cultural Affairs of the U.S. Department of State with the purpose of "contributing to mutual understanding between the United States and countries around the world." By 2007 approximately 105,400 individuals from the United States and 174,100 from other countries had participated in the program. "If large numbers of people can learn to know and understand people from nations other than their own," Fulbright said, "they might develop a capacity for empathy, a distaste for killing other men, and an inclination for peace."

In 1949 Fulbright became a member of the Senate Foreign Relations Committee, of which he was chair from 1959 to 1974, the longest serving chair of that committee in history. While Fulbright was an extremely popular senator, his congressional career was marked by opposition to the U.S. government's foreign and domestic policies. In 1954 he cast the sole dissenting vote against an appropriation for the Permanent Subcommittee on Investigations, chaired by Senator Joseph R. McCarthy, and he was outspoken in his objection to President Kennedy's invasion of the Bay of Pigs in 1961. While he signed the Southern Manifesto, which opposed racial integration in the South, Fulbright opposed the prejudiced policies of southern radical-Right leaders such as Strom Thurmond.

Fulbright may perhaps be best remembered, though, for his frank questioning of U.S. policy toward Southeast Asia during the Vietnam War. In 1966 he led the Senate Foreign Relations Committee in unprecedented televised hearings on the war, which began a nationwide debate on its merits. In 1967 he published *Arrogance of Power*, a book in which he condemns what he considered delusional and imperialistic justifications for the war in Vietnam and Congress's failure to set limits on that conflict. The book sold 400,000 copies.

In 1974, after 30 years of service in the Senate, Fulbright lost his seat to Arkansas governor Dale Bumpers. For the next 20 years he worked as counsel to the Washington, D.C., law firm of Hogan and Hartson and remained active in supporting the Fulbright Program. He received numerous awards from governments, universities, and educational organizations around the world for his work in promoting understanding between cultures and countries. In 1993 President Bill Clinton awarded him the Presidential Medal of Freedom.

William Fulbright died on 9 February 1995 in Washington, D.C., and is buried in Evergreen Cemetery in Fayetteville, Ark.

JAMES G. THOMAS JR.
University of Mississippi

William C. Berman, *William Fulbright and the Vietnam War: The Dissent of a Political Realist* (1988); J. William Fulbright, *Advice and Dissent* (1985), *The Arrogance of Power* (1966); Haynes Johnson and Bernard Gwertzmann, *Fulbright: The Dissenter* (1968); Randall Bennett Woods, *Fulbright: A Biography* (1995).

Gingrich, Newt

(b. 1943) POLITICIAN.
Born in Harrisburg, Pa., on 17 June 1943, Newton Leroy Gingrich moved to Georgia in 1960 with his family. As the civil rights movement swept across Georgia and the South, Gingrich became a Republican Party activist while a student at Emory University in Atlanta. Gingrich earned a doctorate in European history from Tulane University and returned to Georgia to teach at West Georgia College in Carrollton.

The social revolutions of the 1960s had a profound effect upon Gingrich, like many white southerners. Embracing conservative values, Gingrich deplored federal welfare programs and excessive government regulation. As a staunch Republican, he longed to "break the Democratic machine" in the nation's capital. In 1978 he was elected to the House of Representatives from Georgia's sixth congressional district. Gingrich wasted little time in attacking congressional Democrats. "The Democratic Party is now controlled by a coalition of liberal activists, corrupt big city machines, labor union bosses, and House incumbents who use gerrymandering, rigged election rules, and a million dollars from taxpayers per election cycle to buy invulnerability." Along similar lines, Gingrich distributed to Republican activists a list of words to use in describing Democrats. The list included such terms as "bizarre," "sick," and "traitors."

From Gingrich's point of view, the most outrageous example of Democratic Party corruption was the activities of Speaker of the House Jim Wright. In 1987 Gingrich charged that the Texas Democrat was guilty of financial improprieties related to campaign contributions. Largely due to Gingrich's efforts, Wright resigned from Congress in 1989. In the wake of his victory, Gingrich was widely perceived to be one of the most powerful Republicans in Washington. This image was enhanced when House Republicans elected Gingrich minority whip shortly before Wright's resignation. As his status within political circles grew, Gingrich worked aggressively to secure a Republican majority in the House.

During the congressional elections of 1994 Gingrich announced the Republican Party's "Contract with America"— an ambitious plan to cut taxes, eliminate government regulations, enact welfare reform, adopt a balanced budget amendment, and establish term limits

for members of Congress. Gingrich's "Contract" sparked the imagination of voters dissatisfied with progress made by President Bill Clinton and the Democratic-controlled House and was a major factor in the Republicans' winning majorities in both the House and Senate. As a result of the Republicans' stunning victory, Gingrich was elected Speaker of the House, serving from 1995 to 1999, and under his leadership much of his agenda was quickly adopted. However, with the exception of eliminating the Aid to Families with Dependent Children welfare program, the "Contract with America" stalled in the Senate and never became law.

Gingrich's position was further weakened when President Clinton won reelection in November 1996, and in January 1997 a congressional committee concluded that the Speaker had violated ethics rules, and he was ordered to pay a substantial fine. Gingrich was reelected Speaker shortly thereafter but was never able to again command the influence he had before 1996. Although reelected to the House in 1998, Gingrich stunned political observers when he announced, shortly after the election, his resignation from Congress.

Except for modifying the federal welfare program, Gingrich's congressional career did not result in the passage of major pieces of legislation. Nevertheless, he did have a profound effect on the American political landscape. The demonizing of Democrats by Gingrich and his conservative followers contributed greatly to the coarsening of American political discourse and further eroded the people's confidence in government. In this way, Newt Gingrich was not all that different from other southern firebrand politicians who attacked their adversaries without mercy, only to wreak havoc on the political process.

G. WAYNE DOWDY
Benjamin L. Hooks Central Library
Memphis, Tennessee

Dan T. Carter, *From George Wallace to Newt Gingrich: Race in the Conservative Counter-revolution, 1963–1994* (1996); Lewis J. Gould, *Grand Old Party: A History of the Republicans* (2003); Mel Steely, *The Gentleman from Georgia: The Biography of Newt Gingrich* (2000).

Gore, Al, Jr.

(b. 1948) U.S. VICE PRESIDENT AND ENVIRONMENTAL ACTIVIST.
Albert A. "Al" Gore Jr. was born in Washington, D.C., on 31 March 1948 to a politically prominent family. Gore's father was a Democrat who served the State of Tennessee as a member of the U.S. House of Representatives and then of the U.S. Senate. The senior Gore served in Washington for over 30 years, and the young Al Jr. spent most of his early years living there with his parents.

In 1969 Gore received a B.A. degree in government from Harvard University. During the Vietnam War he was an army reporter stationed in Vietnam. After serving in the military, Gore attended Vanderbilt University, where he studied religion. He then worked as a reporter for the *Nashville Tennessean*. In 1976 a seat in the U.S. House became open, and Gore sought and won the seat as a Democrat. He served in the House for four terms and was then elected to

the Senate in 1984. As a senator, Gore focused primarily on two issues: national security and the environment.

In 1988 Gore made a bid for the Democratic nomination for president. He ran as a "New Democrat" and attempted to appeal to moderates in the party. Although he won several primaries and caucuses, he was unable to expand his appeal outside the South, and he eventually withdrew from the race. In 1990 he was reelected to the Senate seat from Tennessee and began considering another run for the 1992 Democratic nomination for the presidency. But at that time, incumbent president George H. W. Bush was high in the polls and appeared unbeatable, so Gore decided to forgo a run for the office.

In 1992 the Democratic Party nominee for president, William Jefferson Clinton, chose Gore as his vice presidential running mate. This surprised many observers, because Clinton and Gore were both from the South and were ideologically compatible, whereas, ordinarily, the vice presidential selection reflects a balancing of the ideology or regional base of the party. The Clinton-Gore ticket won the election, and Gore went on to become one of the nation's most influential vice presidents. President Clinton relied heavily on Gore, who took the lead in environmental policy, government reorganization (the "reinventing government" movement), and, at times, U.S.-Russian relations.

In 2000 Gore won the Democratic Party nomination for president, and during the campaign he tried to distance himself from the popular but much criticized Bill Clinton. Despite peace and prosperity, Gore lost the 2000 election to George W. Bush. The election outcome was not decided until over a month after the election, as disputed returns in the state of Florida caused confusion and much legal wrangling. Eventually, in *Bush v. Gore*, the Supreme Court settled the dispute in Bush's favor, and Vice President Gore accepted the Court's decision with grace.

Gore remained active in politics through the environmental movement and was featured in the documentary *An Inconvenient Truth* (2006), a film (directed by Davis Guggenheim) that received a great deal of attention for its alarming and graphically stunning portrayal of the dire consequences of global warming. Gore published a book version of the film in 2006, a follow-up of his best-selling *Earth in the Balance* (1992), and the film went on to win an Academy Award for Best Documentary Feature.

In October 2007, Gore was awarded the Nobel Peace Prize for his effort "to build up and disseminate greater knowledge about man-made climate change." He shared the prize with the Intergovernmental Panel on Climate Change, and despite cries for him to run for U.S. president, Gore maintained that he could best serve the country and the planet as a private citizen.

MICHAEL A. GENOVESE
Loyola Marymount University

James W. Caesar and Andrew E. Bush, *The Perfect Tie: The True Story of the 2000 Presidential Election* (2001); David Maraniss and Ellen Nakashima, *The Prince of Tennessee: The Rise of Al Gore* (2000).

Hamer, Fannie Lou

(1917–1977) CIVIL RIGHTS ACTIVIST. Fannie Lou Townsend Hamer was the last of 20 children born to Jim and Ella Townsend, sharecroppers in Montgomery County, Miss. The family moved two years after her birth to Sunflower County, where she worked in the cotton fields from the age of six and attended public school through junior high. In 1945 she married Perry Hamer, a tractor driver on the W. D. Marlon plantation located four miles east of Ruleville. She labored as a field hand on the Marlon plantation until it was discovered that she could read and write. Then she was promoted to timekeeper. She was fired in 1962 because she had attempted to register to vote. Forced to leave the plantation, she received shelter in the home of William Tucker in Ruleville but had to flee from there after the house was attacked and riddled with bullets.

In 1963 she passed the Mississippi literacy test and became a registered voter. She then became a field secretary for the Student Nonviolent Coordinating Committee, organizing voter registration campaigns and working to obtain welfare and other benefits for underprivileged black families. She also worked with the National Council of Churches in creating Delta Ministry, an extensive community development program in Mississippi. While returning by bus from one voter registration workshop, she was arrested and severely beaten for attempting to use the restroom in a bus station in Winona.

Because the regular Democratic Party of Mississippi refused to accept black members, Hamer joined with black and white protesters in 1964 to form the Mississippi Freedom Democratic Party (MFDP). She was a member that year of the MFDP delegation that challenged the seating of the regular Mississippi delegation to the Democratic National Convention, and in her testimony before the credentials committee she vividly described the brutal reprisals she and other blacks had suffered in Mississippi because of their efforts to register people to vote and to exercise other civil rights. Her testimony was dramatically presented to the nation by television. Thereafter, she was in great demand, both as a speaker and as a performer of civil rights songs and spirituals.

The MFDP was unsuccessful in replacing the regular Democratic delegation in 1964, but that convention pledged that no delegation that barred blacks would be seated in future conventions. Hamer became a member of the delegation of the Mississippi Loyalist Democratic Party (the successor of MFDP), which unseated Mississippi's regular delegation at the Democratic National Convention in 1968. Back in 1964 she had attempted to run as the MFDP candidate for the U.S. House from Mississippi's Second Congressional District, but her name was not allowed on the ballot. Consequently, she, along with Victoria Gray and Annie Devine, on 4 January 1965, challenged the entire Mississippi delegation in the House of Representatives as unrepresentative of the people of the state. Their challenge failed.

In 1965 Hamer was the plaintiff in a suit that resulted in the U.S. Fifth Circuit of Appeals setting aside the local elections in Sunflower and Moorhead Counties because blacks had not been allowed to vote. She served on the Democratic National Committee from 1968 to 1971. In 1969 she founded and became vice president of Freedom Farms Corporation, a nonprofit venture designed to provide social services, to help needy black and white families produce food, to promote minority business opportunities, and to provide scholarships. She became chair of the board of directors of Fannie Lou Hamer Day Care Center, founded in Ruleville by the National Council of Negro Women in 1970. She also served as a director of the Sunflower County Day Care and Family Services and the Garment Manufacturing Plant, chair of the Sunflower County Voter's League, a member of the policy council of the National Women's Political Caucus, a trustee of the Martin Luther King Center for Social Change, and a member of the state executive committee of the United Democratic Party of Mississippi.

Fannie Lou Hamer received honorary degrees from Tougaloo College, Shaw University, Morehouse College, Columbia College, and Howard University. She also received the Mary Church Terrell Award from Delta Sigma Theta Sorority and the Paul Robeson Award from Alpha Phi Alpha Fraternity. In 1976 the mayor of Ruleville declared a Fannie Lou Hamer Day. She died of cancer in Mound Bayou Hospital on 14 March 1977.

CLIFTON H. JOHNSON
Amistad Research Center
New Orleans, Louisiana

Black Enterprise (May 1977); John Egerton, *Progressive* (May 1977); Fannie Lou Hamer Papers, Amistad Research Center, New Orleans, La.; Susan Johnson, *Black Law Journal* (Summer 1972); June Jordan, *Fannie Lou Hamer* (1972); Chana Kai Lee, *For Freedom's Sake: The Life of Fannie Lou Hamer* (1999); Kay Mills, *This Little Light of Mine: The Life of Fannie Lou Hamer* (1993); J. Todd Moye, *Let the People Decide: Black Freedom and White Resistance Movements in Sunflower County, Mississippi, 1945–1986* (2004); *Never Turn Back: The Life of Fannie Lou Hamer* (Rediscovery Productions film, 1983); *Sojourners* (December 1982); C. J. Wilson, *New South* (Spring 1973).

Hampton, Wade, III

(1818–1902) PLANTER, CONFEDERATE GENERAL, AND POLITICIAN.

Born in Charleston, S.C., Wade Hampton III grew up as a member of one of the wealthiest families in the South and went on to become a Confederate military commander and the epitome of the late 19th-century Lost Cause politician.

Hampton may have been the wealthiest planter in the antebellum South, with large holdings in South Carolina and Mississippi. He served in the South Carolina legislature from 1852 until 1861, advocating economic development and supporting railroads and manufacturing. He thought secession unnecessary for the protection of southern rights, but when South Carolina left the Union he raised his own regiment, the Hampton Legion, and fought from the battle of Manassas to Sherman's March. In August 1864 Hampton became commander of the cavalry of the Army of Northern Virginia, playing a key role in the defense of Richmond.

Postwar found Hampton's fortunes in decline, and he declared bankruptcy in 1868. As a heroic embodiment of the Confederacy, he found a new career in politics. He emerged in the early 1870s as a leader of the Bourbons, the traditional white leadership group of his state. He entered a political world in considerable turmoil, with white Democrats and mostly black Republicans in a bitter struggle for political control. Democratic rifle clubs, known as the Red Shirts, had initiated much violence leading up to the 1876 gubernatorial campaign, which featured Hampton as the Democratic nominee. He was a moderate and led a march across the state, eschewing violence and drawing on the rituals and symbols of the Lost Cause and southern tradition but also appealing for black votes. The disputed election results left Hampton and his Republican opponent Daniel Chamberlain both claiming victory. The national Compromise of 1877 brought Hampton and the Democratic Party to power in South Carolina and helped end Reconstruction.

Hampton's administration was fiscally conservative but alienated many ordinary people by ignoring the worsening situation of rural people. Hampton was reelected in 1878 and then served in the U.S. Senate from 1879 to 1891. The rise of Ben Tillman and his rural, anti-black, Carolina upcountry insurgency toppled Hampton and other Bourbon politicians in the early 1890s. Hampton ended life financially destitute and died in Columbia, S.C., 11 April 1902.

CHARLES REAGAN WILSON
University of Mississippi

William Brian Cisco, *Wade Hampton: Confederate Warrior, Conservative Statesman* (2004); W. Scott Poole, *Never Surrender: Confederate Memory and Conservatism in the South Carolina Upcountry* (2004).

Hays, Brooks

(1898–1981) POLITICIAN AND RELIGIOUS LEADER.

Brooks Hays personified, during his more than 50 years in public service, the Christian layman in politics. Born 9 August 1898 near Russellville, Ark., to Sallie Butler and Steele Hays, he graduated from the University of Arkansas (B.A., 1919) and George Washington University (LL.D., 1922). After serving in World War I, he married in 1922, the year he was admitted to the bar.

Hays was an assistant attorney general of Arkansas, twice an unsuccessful reform candidate for governor of that state and once for Congress, before he went to Washington as an attorney for the U.S. Department of Agriculture in 1935. A prominent member of the Southern Baptist Convention, he became an influential religious leader during his years as a member of Congress from Arkansas (1943–59). Washington, D.C., ministers chose him as their "Layman of the Year" in 1951, and he was later named "Churchman of the Year" by the Religious Heritage Foundation. He served on the Southern Baptist Christian Life Commission for 15 years and was its chair in 1957 and 1958. He was president of the Southern Baptist Convention from 1957 through 1959.

His long-standing and widely publicized support of civil rights for southern blacks involved him in his congressional district's 1957 controversy over the integration of Little Rock Central High School. Attempting to moderate the passions on all sides, he was the victim of what was most likely an illegal write-in vote that stripped him of his seat in Congress at the height of the passionate battle in 1958.

The following year, as his prestige grew through what was considered a "political martyrdom," Hays became a director of the Tennessee Valley Authority. With the return of Democrats to the White House in 1961, he became special assistant to President Kennedy and then to President Johnson for "congressional relations, international relations, federal-state relations, and church-state relations." In this capacity he carried his appeal for Christian brotherhood throughout the nation and around the world from 1961 to 1964.

Between 1964 and 1974, Hays taught government at Rutgers and the University of Massachusetts, ran unsuccessfully for governor of Arkansas, directed the first Baptist Ecumenical Institute at North Carolina's Wake Forest University, and ran unsuccessfully for Congress from North Carolina. He died at his home in Chevy Chase, Md., 12 October 1981.

JAMES T. BAKER
Western Kentucky University

James Baker, *Brooks Hays* (1989); Brooks Hays, *A Hotbed of Tranquility* (1968), *Politics Is My Parish* (1981), *A Southern Moderate Speaks* (1959), *This World: A Christian's Workshop* (1958); C. Fred Williams, *Baptist History and Heritage* (Fall 2006).

Helms, Jesse

(b. 1921) POLITICIAN.

Jesse Alexander Helms Jr. was born 18 October 1921 in the Piedmont North Carolina community of Monroe, the son of the town's police and fire chief. Following a Tom Sawyer childhood, a summer at a tiny Baptist college, and a year at Wake Forest, Helms dropped out of college to become a sports reporter with the *Raleigh News and Observer*. During World War II he served with the naval reserve. After the war he was briefly city editor with the *Raleigh Times* and then worked as a reporter with a Roanoke Rapids radio station before returning to Raleigh as news director at WRAL radio station.

While with WRAL, Helms became involved in the successful 1950 Democratic senatorial runoff primary campaign of Raleigh lawyer Willis Smith against Frank Porter Graham, the respected former president of the University of North Carolina, who had been appointed to the Senate in 1949. The Smith-Graham campaign was one of the dirtiest in North Carolina history. Smith literature depicted Graham as a communist sympathizer and integrationist, exhorting, "White People, Wake Up!" and warning of "Negroes working beside you, your wife and daughter, in your mills and factories," should Graham be elected. In later years, critics claimed that Helms had played a significant role in the Smith campaign—a charge Helms has consistently denied.

Whatever his role in the campaign, Helms became Smith's administrative assistant and served until the senator's death in 1953. Following a brief stint as aide to Smith's successor, Helms returned again to Raleigh and became executive director of the North Carolina Bankers Association and editor of its conservative monthly bulletin. From 1957 to 1961 he also served on the Raleigh city council.

In 1960 Helms became an executive, editorialist, and minor stockholder with WRAL radio and television stations. Over a 12-year period, he delivered some 2,700 five-minute commentaries over WRAL and the Tobacco Radio Network, a hookup of some 70 rural stations, railing against growing federal power, school desegregation, welfare fraud and waste, and racial "agitators." His *Viewpoint* editorials made Helms a familiar and popular figure in thousands of North Carolina homes. In 1970 he changed his party registration to Republican and in 1972 became the first Republican elected to the Senate from North Carolina since 1894. With the slogan "Elect Jesse Helms—He's One of Us," he won 54 percent of the vote against moderate Durham congressman Nick Galifianakis, the son of Greek immigrant parents.

During his first term, Helms was little more than a Senate curiosity, opposing abortions and sex education and defending school prayer, curbs on the federal courts, capital punishment, defense spending, and United States support for the white minority government of South Africa, but rarely exerting meaningful influence. At the same time, however, his outspoken sympathy for "pro-family" and other religio-political causes of the radical right began to attract a national following. Moreover, his Congressional Club, organized initially to retire a 1972 campaign debt, became an extremely successful political action committee, providing funds and technical assistance for a variety of conservative causes and candidates. The club spent over $7 million on Helms's 1978 reelection, outspending his opponent 30 to 1, and over $4 million on Ronald Reagan's 1980 presidential campaign.

The election of President Reagan and a Republican Senate majority in 1980, combined with the conservative national mood the 1980 election results seemed to reflect, gave Helms's movement respectability and the senator considerable national influence. By 1983, however, his position had seriously eroded. Relations with the Reagan administration—its policies and personalities entirely too moderate for Helms's tastes—had become strained at best. In the Senate, colleagues unsympathetic to his intransigence on "pro-family" issues and opposition to food stamps had countered with attacks on tobacco and other price-support programs important to North Carolina's agricultural economy. At home, every 1982 congressional candidate sponsored by the Congressional Club lost, with that organization's exorbitant spending and negative campaign strategy perhaps the major election issue.

In 1984, however, Helms won reelection over Governor James B. Hunt in the most expensive congressional campaign yet waged. Helms's campaign strategy was reminiscent of that employed so successfully against Frank Graham a quarter-century earlier. Hunt was condemned for supporting a national holiday honoring Martin Luther King Jr. and depicted as a tax-happy racial and political liberal, the candidate of "the bloc vote," "gays, porno kings, union bosses, and crooks." Campaign leaflets featured photographs of Hunt with Jesse Jackson and Helms with President Reagan, noting the "stark contrast." The ploy worked. Aided by Reagan's lengthy North Carolina coattails, a $15 million campaign chest, and Hunt's liberal image, the senator won 52 percent of the total vote, 63 percent of whites, but less than one percent of the black electorate.

With the Republican capture of the Senate in the 1994 elections, Helms became more powerful, serving as chair of the Agriculture Committee and then the Foreign Relations Committee. He became a leading political force in the Christian Right. Helms served longer than any U.S. senator in North Carolina history, deciding not to seek reelection in 2002. Wingate University is the repository of his official papers, and Liberty University opened the Helms School of Government in 2005.

TINSLEY E. YARBROUGH
East Carolina University

Ernest B. Ferguson, *Hard Right: The Rise of Jesse Helms* (1986); Wayne Greenhaw, *Elephants in the Cottonfields: Ronald Reagan and the New Republican South* (1982); Ferrel Guillory, *Southern Cultures* (Spring 1998); Jesse Helms, *Here's Where I Stand: A Memoir* (2005); Bill Peterson, *Washington Post* (national weekly edition, 3 December 1984); Peter Ross Range, *New York Times Magazine* (8 February 1981).

Col. Oveta Culp Hobby (right), first director of the Women's Army Corps, talks with Auxiliary Margaret Peterson and Capt. Elizabeth Gilbert at Mitchel Field on Long Island, New York (Al Aumuller, photographer, Library of Congress [LC-USZ62-118263], Washington, D.C.)

Hobby, Oveta Culp

(1905–1995) GOVERNMENT ADMINISTRATOR.

Born 19 January 1905, in Kileen, Tex., Oveta Culp Hobby achieved renown as the first commander of the Women's Army Corps (WAC), the first secretary of the Department of Health, Education, and Welfare, and the publisher of the *Houston Post*. Hobby's father was a lawyer and Texas state legislator who educated her in his interests. He was elected to the legislature in 1919, and the 14-year-old Oveta accompanied him to Austin and frequently observed the legislative activities. She read widely in

history and the law at an early age, and the Speaker of the Texas House of Representatives appointed her legislative parliamentarian when she was 20. She studied at Mary Hardin Baylor College in Belton, Tex., and earned a law degree in 1925 from the University of Texas at Austin. She worked in various political campaigns and ran unsuccessfully for the Texas legislature at age 25. The next year she married former Texas governor William Pettus Hobby.

Oveta Culp Hobby became active in civic affairs in Houston and worked with her husband on the newspaper they bought, the *Houston Post*. Hobby headed the Women's Interest Section of the War Department's Bureau of Public Relations from 1941 to 1942, and General George Marshall then asked her to head the Women's Army Corps. She organized and supervised this agency that commanded more than 150,000 volunteer women serving in Africa, Europe, Asia, and at other places around the world. She became the first woman to achieve the rank of colonel in the American military and resigned at war's end to return to Houston, working as director of KPRC radio and television in Houston and becoming vice president of the *Post*.

When Dwight Eisenhower ran for president in 1952, Oveta Culp Hobby and her husband became active in the national Democrats for Eisenhower movement. After Eisenhower's election, he appointed her chair of the Federal Security Agency and then, in 1953, named her the first secretary of the new cabinet department of Health, Education, and Welfare. She organized the new agency, overseeing the retirement funds of millions of Americans, outlining a building program for schools to accommodate the postwar baby boom generation, and supervising the distribution of the Salk polio vaccine.

In 1955 Hobby left government to return to Houston and work with the newspaper, continuing to be involved in civic affairs. She died on 16 August 1995.

CHARLES REAGAN WILSON
University of Mississippi

James Barron, *New York Times* (17 August 1995); Ann Fears Crawford and Crystal Sasse Ragsdale, *Women in Texas* (1982); Marguerite Johnston, *Houston: The Unknown City, 1836–1946* (1991).

Hull, Cordell

(1871–1955) DIPLOMAT.

It is a long way from the Tennessee mountains to the State Department corridors, and there was little in Cordell Hull's Overton County roots that prepared him to be the leading diplomat in Franklin Roosevelt's foreign-policy entourage. In fact, in his memoirs Hull mentioned two experiences that prepared him for world affairs; both were outside Tennessee. One was a year and a half of college in Ohio, where he was able to meet people with different habits and ideas; the other was his Spanish-American War service in Cuba, where he became aware of the wider world in which the United States would have to exist.

Hull had broad-ranging experience at the state, national, and international levels. A graduate of the law program at Cumberland University, he practiced law briefly before serving two terms in the state legislature. After serving in the Spanish-American War, Hull was a circuit court judge for four years and then was elected to the U.S. House of Representatives, serving from 1907 to 1930 (except for 1921–23). Among his many legislative accomplishments was the proposal of a graduated income tax measure in 1913. In 1930 Hull was elected to the U.S. Senate and served until his appointment as secretary of state.

During his 11 years as secretary of state (1933–44), Hull showed his Tennessee roots. Contemporaries dwelled upon such superficial points as his penchant for telling stories about his days in Tennessee, the colorful profanity that dotted his private conversations when he was angered, and his quiet, almost taciturn demeanor. Like other staunch southern Democrats of his day, Hull worked diligently for a program to lower tariffs. But Secretary of State Hull's views on trade were not those of the local politician who had to protect his constituents. He took a loftier view that a free-trading world would progress while an autarchic world order where nations conquered and hoarded markets and resources would lead to economic stagnation. As secretary of state, Hull engineered the Reciprocal Trade Agreements Act, worked especially to improve Latin American relations, helped shape the Good Neighbor policy, supported strengthening of America's military preparedness, and proposed an international diplomatic organization. Called by President Truman the "Father of the United Nations," Hull received the Nobel Peace Prize in 1945.

If Hull's worldview went beyond the parochial views of most of his fellow Tennesseans, he brought to the Department of State a faith in absoluteness drawn from his early years in the Cumberland Mountains, where certainty mattered above all. To the men of his region during the Civil War, Hull recalled, it made little difference whether you fought in the Confederate or Union armies as long as you fought. His father personified the certainty of right and wrong when he tracked down and publicly killed a man who had informed on him during the war, an act for which his father was neither prosecuted nor chastised.

Even as a law-and-order judge riding circuit in Tennessee, Hull showed he had absorbed this black-white view of life. There were good people and bad people, and it was as simple as that. Similarly, during World War II Secretary Hull saw Nazi Germany and Imperial Japan in this black-white view.

JONATHAN G. UTLEY
University of Tennessee

Harold B. Hinton, *Cordell Hull: A Biography* (1942); Cordell Hull, *The Memoirs of Cordell Hull*, 2 vols. (1948); J. W. Pratt, *American Secretaries of State*, vols. 12, 13 (1964).

Jackson, Andrew

(1767–1845) U.S. PRESIDENT, FRONTIERSMAN, PLANTER.
Born near the border of North and South Carolina—the exact spot is in dispute—Andrew Jackson moved to frontier Tennessee in 1788 at the age of 19, an early pioneer in a significant migration pattern that eventually redrew the boundaries of "the South." Tennessee at the time, and throughout Jackson's life, was more western than southern. Although he developed substantial landholdings near Nashville, held slaves, and lived the life of a gentleman planter at "The Hermitage," Jackson as late as the 1840s considered himself a westerner and a nationalist, never a southerner, and he was so perceived by his contemporaries.

Nonetheless Jackson's career was rife with consequences for the South. His defeat of the British at New Orleans and of the Seminoles in Florida nailed down southern borders once and for all. He

Andrew Jackson, frontier hero and U.S. president, date unknown (Tennessee State Library and Archives, Nashville)

cratic impulse whose egalitarian values and reform tendencies were ultimately subversive of the southern slavery system.

Although Jackson's Scotch-Irish parents had only recently emigrated at the time of his birth, his formative years in the Carolina upcountry doubtless contributed to his fierce combativeness, his attraction to the law and the militia, his love of horses and horse racing, and his patrician style. It was as frontier lawyer and politician, militia leader and military hero, that he rose to fame, an ardent Unionist and an instinctive democrat.

RICHARD H. BROWN
Newberry Library
Chicago, Illinois

H. W. Brands, *Andrew Jackson: His Life and Times* (2005); James Curtis, *Andrew Jackson and the Search for Vindication* (1976); Burke Davis, *Old Hickory: A Life of Andrew Jackson* (1977); Robert V. Remini, *The Revolutionary Age of Andrew Jackson* (1976).

moved carefully on the issue of expansion into Texas while in office, but his passionate interest in the area eventually resulted in extension of the southern frontier westward.

The Democratic Party that he led to the presidency and institutionalized around issues important to him represented an alliance of "Southern Planters and Plain Republicans of the North," as Martin Van Buren put it; it was rooted in the "Old Republican" ideology of Thomas Jefferson and coupled with a strong overlay of western pragmatism. Committed to the Union and to strict construction of the Constitution, the party served for decades as a shield for southern slave owners against the rising antislavery clamor. Paradoxically, it also embodied and promoted the demo-

Jackson, Jesse

(b. 1941) CIVIL RIGHTS ACTIVIST, MINISTER, POLITICIAN.
Called "the most famous Black man in America today" by one admiring biographer, a position confirmed by the more scientific conclusions of major national polls, Jesse Louis Jackson was born 8 October 1941 in Greenville, S.C. His mother was Helen Burns, and his father was Noah Louis Robinson, to whom his mother was never married. Charles Henry Jackson became the husband of Jesse's mother, and young Jackson's stepfather provided him with a comfortable home and stable family life.

Jesse Jackson surrounded by marchers carrying signs advocating support for the Hawkins-Humphrey
Bill for full employment, 1975 (Thomas J. O'Halloran, photographer, Library of Congress
[LC-U9-30656B-10], Washington, D.C.)

Jackson grew up in Greenville, where he was sensitive to the racism and segregation of the times and exhibited an inquisitive mind, street savvy, athletic ability, and discipline. He left the University of Illinois after one year when he was told by coaches that a black man could not play quarterback, and he turned down a professional baseball contract when he was offered less than a white counterpart. He became active in the sit-in demonstrations organized by the Congress of Racial Equality (CORE) in Greensboro, N.C., where he had come to enter all-black North Carolina A&T University on a football scholarship. At A&T, he was a star quarterback, honor student, student body president, and fraternity leader. He was elected president of the North Carolina Inter-Collegiate Council on Human Rights,

and by his senior year assumed broader responsibilities as the southeastern field director of CORE. Jackson accepted a Rockefeller scholarship to the Chicago Theological Seminary, having decided that the pulpit was a better platform than the courtroom to realize his developing ambitions and commitments.

Jackson's prominence in the civil rights movement is tied to his apprenticeship under Martin Luther King Jr. Jackson met King while in college, but he did not join the staff of the Southern Christian Leadership Conference (SCLC) until 1965, helping to organize the Selma marches and demonstrations just prior to King's Chicago campaign. King later appointed Jackson as director of SCLC's Operation Breadbasket, an economic development coalition of ministers and business people using such direct action tactics as boycotts and mass demonstrations.

The assassination of King on 4 April 1968 led Jackson to assume national leadership, an opportunity he seized with vigor. Jackson emerged as the aggressive spokesperson of a movement in disarray. Operation Breadbasket moved away from its parent organization, SCLC, and proclaimed itself the leading civil rights organization in the nation. After a flurry of boycotts in which "covenants"—agreements to provide jobs, develop businesses, place deposits in black banks, and advertise in the black media—were signed, Operation Breadbasket was renamed Operation PUSH in December 1971. Jackson's tactics were reminiscent of the "Buy Black Campaign" and the "Don't Buy Where You Can't Work" protests of the 1930s in Chicago and other cities.

Jesse Jackson's greatest achievement was his 1984 presidential campaign. Jackson had run for mayor of Chicago in 1971 and had been active in such national political forums as the National Black Political Assembly in 1972 and 1973. He showed himself to be knowledgeable on a wide range of issues, articulate in televised debates, and adept in seizing media attention with such feats as his extrication of a black navy pilot from Syria. Jackson galvanized black community sentiment, and the results were quite unexpected. With a very small campaign war chest, Jackson gathered almost 20 percent of the vote (3.5 million) in the Democratic primaries and won 465.5 convention votes. More important, his campaign spurred voter registration, stirred local debate

and activity, and challenged Democratic Party rules that seemed unfair. His achievement led to an invitation to deliver a keynote to the Democratic National Convention in San Francisco.

Looking toward the 1988 campaign, Jackson sought to fashion his "rainbow coalition" into a more viable organization, which he did, attracting 6.9 million votes and winning five southern states on Super Tuesday, 8 March 1988, yet ultimately losing the Democratic Party nomination to Michael Dukakis. Following the 1988 election Jackson moved from Chicago to Washington, D.C., where he ran for "statehood senator," which he won, choosing to serve only one term in that position (1991–96).

In 2000 Jackson wrote and published, with his son Congressman Jesse Jackson Jr., *It's About the Money!: How You Can Get Out of Debt, Build Wealth, and Achieve Your Financial Dreams!*, a how-to guide for achieving a more secure financial future. Jesse Jackson was awarded the Presidential Medal of Freedom the same year.

RONALD BAILEY
University of Mississippi

Lucius J. Barker, *Our Time Has Come: A Delegate's Diary of Jesse Jackson's 1984 Presidential Campaign* (1988); Roger Bruns, *Jesse Jackson: A Biography* (2005); Rod Bush, ed., *The New Black Vote: Politics and Power in Four American Cities* (1984); Marshall Frady, *Jesse: The Life and Pilgrimage of Jesse Jackson* (2006); Adolph Reed Jr., *The Jesse Jackson Phenomenon: The Crisis of Purpose in Afro-American Politics* (1986); Barbara A. Reynolds, *Jesse Jackson: America's David* (1985); Hanes Walton, *Invisible Politics: Black Political Behavior* (1986).

Jefferson, Thomas

(1743–1826) U.S. PRESIDENT,
WRITER, PLANTER, SCIENTIST,
ARCHITECT.

Thomas Jefferson was born on the edge of the frontier in colonial Virginia. He went on to acquire as fine an education as America offered, graduating from the College of William and Mary in 1726. He studied law under George Wythe and practiced at the bar until the Revolution. He was elected to the Virginia House of Burgesses in 1769. Already the inheritor of large landholdings, he increased his property greatly through the dowry of his wife, Martha Wayles Skelton, whom he married in 1772. They had two daughters who survived to maturity.

In 1774 Jefferson drew political attention with his pamphlet *A Summary View of the Rights of British America*, the best remonstrance against the king and defense of colonial rights that had yet been seen. He carefully controlled his writing style so that any literate reader might follow his argument. Then, in 1776, Jefferson—now a member of the Continental Congress—was chosen to write the Declaration of Independence. It is his masterpiece and America's fundamental political document. In succeeding years he was elected governor of the state of Virginia and member of Congress and was appointed minister to France. From 1790 to 1793 he served under Washington as the first secretary of state.

Jefferson's only book, *Notes on the State of Virginia*, was published in 1785. In it he recorded the milieu of early America. Jefferson was an advocate of the scientific method, and his book included efforts to classify botanical, geological, and paleontological specimens. He showed the confident Enlightenment belief that science could promote progress. His collection and classification of items reflected the practical need of a farmer to know the environment, as well as simply the desire to satisfy his curiosity. He agonized over the question of slavery (he held many slaves), echoing most of the persistent stereotyping of blacks so noticeably American. Controversies over Jefferson's relationship with his slave Sally Hemings have reverberated from his time to the contemporary era. Yet he was a true Enlightenment man, also voicing—as in the Declaration—the finest of ideals concerning justice, religious freedom, and equality.

He was paternalistic, not only at home but in his attitudes toward Indians, blacks, women, and commoners. Thus, his long political service was noblesse oblige. He was elected third president of the United States in 1801 (a second term followed). While president he arranged the Louisiana Purchase (1803), doubling the size of the nation.

Always busy, he designed his mansion, Monticello, the Virginia capitol at Richmond, and, late in life, the University of Virginia. He designed an Episcopal chapel in Charlottesville, dozens of Virginia country homes, simple and functional courthouses, and even jails in Cumberland and Nelson counties. He accumulated an architectural library of 50 titles in French, Italian, German, and English. His architectural achievement was to adapt classical forms to Virginian and southern needs.

Jefferson personified character, vision, grace, scholarship, and leadership—the qualities of the early southern gentleman that are part of his legacy. Students of southern culture look to him as the exemplar of major themes, ideals, and achievements of the region as well as the nation.

WILLIAM K. BOTTORFF
University of Toledo

R. B. Bernstein, *Thomas Jefferson* (2003); Julian P. Boyd et al., eds., *The Papers of Thomas Jefferson* (1950–); Fiske Kimball, ed., *Thomas Jefferson, Architect: Original Designs in the Coolidge Collection of the Massachusetts Historical Society, with an Essay and Notes* (1968); Dumas Malone, *Jefferson and His Time*, 6 vols. (1948–81).

Johnson, Andrew

(1808–1875) U.S. PRESIDENT.
Andrew Johnson was born on 29 December 1808 in Raleigh, N.C. Raised in poverty and informally educated while working as a tailor's apprentice, Johnson left home at a young age, eventually settling in Greeneville, Tenn., and opening his own tailor shop. He married Eliza McCardle on 17 May 1827 and began participating in debates at the local academy. As his business improved, Johnson's tailor shop became a local meeting place for lively discussions on politics. Encouraged by his wife and his debating success, Johnson entered politics.

Within two years Johnson became mayor of Greeneville, and by 1835 he was elected to the Tennessee House of Representatives. He lost his seat in 1837 but was reelected in 1839. Following his second term, Johnson won a seat in the Tennessee Senate. A supporter of free laborers' rights, champion of the common man, and an opponent of a law that allowed increased representation to slaves, Johnson also supported a bill that provided farms to the poor. While serving as senator, Johnson motioned to create a new state, to be named Frankland, out of the adjoining Appalachian lands of North Carolina, Virginia, Georgia, and Tennessee. The motion, of course, failed. He went on to win the governorship of Tennessee in 1853 and 1855, and in that position provided his state with a public school system and public libraries.

In 1857 Johnson was elected to the U.S. Senate. He was a steadfast supporter of the Constitution over states' rights. During the crisis over secession, Johnson remained loyal to the Union, and when Tennessee seceded he remained in the Senate (the only southerner to do so), being labeled a traitor by many southerners. Nonetheless, he had supported Stephen Douglas for president in 1860, championed the Fugitive Slave Law, and defended slavery. Uniquely open to both sides' point of view, Johnson warned against secession and abolition, believing that both were threats to the Constitution and the Union.

In 1862 President Lincoln appointed Johnson military governor of Tennessee, and after large parts of the state fell to Union forces Johnson worked to effectively silence anti-Union sentiments. In 1864, sensing an impending end to the Civil War, the Republicans nominated

Johnson for vice president in place of Lincoln's first-term vice president, the passionate abolitionist Hannibal Hamlin, even though Johnson was an old-fashioned southern Jacksonian Democrat.

After Lincoln's assassination, Vice President Johnson became the 17th U.S. president and was assigned the unenviable tasks of reconciling the North and South and reconstructing a region that remained hostile to the U.S. government. While the Senate was out of session he reconstructed the Confederate States and pardoned all who would take an oath of allegiance, although he required government officials and men of wealth to take a special presidential pardon.

Despite these oaths of allegiance and the abolition of slavery (established by the Thirteenth Amendment), prewar southern leaders initiated "black codes" to restrict freedmen's rights, which Johnson supported, and Radical Republicans in Congress restructured Johnson's program by refusing to seat any prewar representative or senator in Congress. As well, Congress passed the Civil Rights Act of 1866, which forbade discrimination against the newly freed blacks and made them full citizens of the United States. The Fourteenth Amendment was passed soon after. It allowed that no state could "deprive any person of life, liberty, or property, without due process of law," and no ex-Confederate state but Tennessee initially consented to its ratification.

The congressional elections of 1866 resulted in an overwhelming victory by the Radical Republicans. The following March, a Radical Republican Congress placed the South under military rule and passed the Tenure of Office Act, which forbade the president to remove civil officers without senatorial consent. The act was an effective attempt to wrest control of Reconstruction from the hands of the president and place it squarely in the control of the largely Republican Senate. When Johnson dismissed the Lincoln-appointed secretary of war, Edwin M. Stanton, Congress voted to impeach him. He was acquitted by one vote.

Johnson completed Lincoln's term but did not receive his party's nomination in 1869. He went home to Greeneville, Tenn., and in 1875 returned to the U.S. Senate. He suffered a stroke later that year, and on 31 July 1875 Andrew Johnson died. As well as the passing of the Thirteenth and Fourteenth Amendments, Johnson's presidential legacy includes the addition of Nebraska as a state and the purchase of the Alaska territory. His childhood home still remains in Raleigh at the Mordecai Historic Park.

JAMES G. THOMAS JR.
University of Mississippi

Howard Beale, *The Critical Year: A Study of Andrew Johnson and Reconstruction* (1958); Albert Castel, *The Presidency of Andrew Johnson* (1979); Noel Gerson, *The Trial of Andrew Johnson* (1977); Chester G. Hearn, *The Impeachment of Andrew Johnson* (2000); Andrew Johnson, *The Papers of Andrew Johnson* (1979); Eric McKitrick, *Andrew Johnson and Reconstruction* (1967); Glenna Schroeder-Lein, *Andrew Johnson: A Biographical Companion* (2001); James Selton, *Andrew Johnson and the Uses of*

Constitutional Power (1980); Brooks Simpson, *The Reconstruction Presidents* (1998); Hans Trefousse, *Andrew Johnson: A Biography* (1989).

Johnson, Lady Bird

(1912–2007) FIRST LADY OF THE UNITED STATES AND CONSERVATION ADVOCATE.

Claudia Alta Taylor Johnson was born on 22 December 1912 near Karnack, a small east Texas town. Her parents were Thomas Jefferson Taylor, a landowner and country storekeeper, and Minnie Lee Pattillo, both Alabama natives. Lady Bird, so named by a nursemaid, was the youngest of three children and the only daughter. When she was five, her mother died and her Aunt Effie Pattillo, a genteel Alabamian, moved to "the Brick House," the family home in Karnack, to care for her. Lady Bird Taylor was educated in local public schools, graduating from Marshall High School in 1928. She attended St. Mary's Episcopal School for Girls in Dallas and then received two bachelor degrees (liberal arts and journalism) from the University of Texas at Austin. In 1934 she married Lyndon Baines Johnson, the secretary of a Texas congressman, after a two-month courtship. Washington, D.C., was home for the Johnsons almost continuously from 1934 until 1969. They had two daughters, Lynda Bird, born on 19 March 1944, and Luci Baines, born on 2 July 1947.

Lady Bird Johnson emerged as a public figure when her husband became vice president in 1961. As the nation's "second lady" she earned a reputation as a gracious hostess who skillfully combined superb good taste with down-home southern hospitality. Her role as national hostess and decorator was enlarged when she became first lady in November 1963. As a political helpmate, she made a special appeal to the Deep South, which she traversed in a whistle-stop tour during her husband's campaign in 1964. Aware of the importance of her position, she began to record on tape aspects of her personal and public life; one-seventh of the resulting transcript has been published in the 800-page *A White House Diary* (1970). The journal is a testament to Lady Bird Johnson's keen sense of family, devotion to the principles espoused by her husband, and commitment to her own special concerns—national beautification, conservation, education, and children.

Lady Bird Johnson attributed her love of land, nature, and nation to her early years of growing up in the east Texas piney woods and Alabama cotton lands and to her later life in the Texas hill country, where the ancestral Johnson family home is located. For her First Lady's Committee for a More Beautiful Capital she tapped prominent architects, conservationists, and philanthropists who landscaped Washington with seasonal plantings and groves, refurbished memorials, and improved parks and school yards in the inner city. The Highway Beautification Act of 1965 translated into public policy her programs for control of billboards, the screening of junkyards, and the planting of flowers along highways. Following the retirement of President Johnson in 1969 and his death in 1973, Lady Bird Johnson devoted her time to her daughters and seven grandchildren and to her extensive holdings in Texas television and other media, begun in the 1940s with the purchase of station KTBC in Austin. She continued to focus her public work on roadside beautification, conservation, and the arts.

In 1982 more than 100 historians who rated first ladies on the basis of their leadership, intelligence, value to country, and independence ranked Lady Bird Johnson third, following Eleanor Roosevelt and Abigail Adams. Lady Bird Johnson died on 11 July 2007.

MARTHA H. SWAIN
Texas Women's University

Elizabeth Carpenter, *Ruffles and Flourishes: The Warm and Tender Story of a Simple Girl Who Found Adventure in the White House* (1970); Lewis L. Gould, *Lady Bird Johnson: Our Environmental First Lady* (1999); Lady Bird Johnson Papers, Lyndon Baines Johnson Library, Austin, Tex.; Lady Bird Johnson, *Texas: A Roadside View* (1980), *A White House Diary* (1970); Ruth Montgomery, *Mrs. LBJ* (1965); Jan Jarboe Russell, *Lady Bird: A Biography of Mrs. Johnson* (1999); Marie Smith, *The President's Lady: An Intimate Biography of Mrs. Lyndon B. Johnson* (1964).

Johnson, Lyndon B.

(1908–1973) U.S. PRESIDENT.
Convinced that a southerner could not be elected to the presidency in his lifetime, Lyndon Baines Johnson sought to minimize his southern credentials. Describing himself as an American, a westerner, a Texan, and, only lastly, a southerner, he attempted to divorce himself from the region and its conservative racial and social image. As a southerner, a congressional leader with a mixed civil rights record, and the successor to a slain president whose reform image loomed larger in death than in life, Lyndon B. Johnson sensed a special need to convince the nation that he too was dedicated to the cause of equality and a decent standard of living for all Americans. Pursuing this goal during the five years of his presidency (1963–69), he pushed through the Congress the most significant civil rights legislation since Reconstruction—the legislation outlawing discrimination in education, public accommodations, voting, employment, and housing. Armed with authority to cut off federal funds to segregated public schools, his administration integrated the schools at a pace that repeated court decisions had largely failed to effect. And his 1965 voting rights legislation produced a 50 percent increase in southern black voter registration by 1966—an increase that facilitated the election of black officeholders (387 in Mississippi alone by mid-1980) and ultimately moderated the region's racial politics.

The administration's War on Poverty attempted to cope, moreover, with the plight of the poor in the South and the rest of the nation. For children, Johnson created the federal school breakfast, Head Start, day care, and foster grandparent programs; for the elderly, Medicare and special housing; for the unemployed, the Job Corps; for the myriad problems confronting the poor, Volunteers in Service to America (VISTA) and the Community Action Program. Nor were such programs intended only for economic relief. They also provided a political base for minorities, especially in the South. Many VISTA volunteers, for example, became heavily involved in southern politics; and the Community Action Program through which federal poverty funds were channeled to largely private, minority-related agencies was designed in part to bypass the traditional federal, state, and local power structures.

While president, Lyndon Johnson was never able to convince most civil rights leaders and social activists of his commitment to reform. For them, as for his critics on the right, he was simply a calculating politician posturing for liberal and minority votes. More critically, urban riots, rising inflation, the growing national preoccupation with Vietnam, the merging of the civil rights movement with the antiwar effort, and the increasingly radical character of the two movements largely derailed Johnson's social programs and dampened public enthusiasm for further civil rights reform. Ironically, too, though he was a creature of the Solid Democratic South, his administration probably did more to drive white southerners into the ranks of the GOP than all the efforts of Republican presidents and presidential aspirants. Whatever its direction, however, his impact on southern politics was to be truly profound. In later years, moreover, liberals would develop a more sympathetic image of his presidency and its role in social reform. That image moved former SNCC leader and caustic Johnson critic Julian Bond to describe the former president in 1972 as "an activist, human-hearted man [who]

had his hands on the levers of power and a vision beyond the next election. He was there when we and the Nation needed him, and, oh my God, do I wish he was there now."

TINSLEY E. YARBROUGH
East Carolina University

Robert Dallek, *Flawed Giant: Lyndon B. Johnson, 1960–1973* (1998), *Lone Star Rising: Lyndon Johnson and His Times, 1908–1960* (1991), *Lyndon B. Johnson: Portrait of a President* (2003); Robert A. Divine, ed., *Exploring the Johnson Years* (1981); Ronnie Dugger, *The Politician: The Life and Times of Lyndon Johnson* (1984); Eric Goldman, *The Tragedy of Lyndon Johnson* (1968); Doris Kearns, *Lyndon Johnson and the American Dream* (1976); Nick Kotz, *Judgment Days: Lyndon Baines Johnson, Martin Luther King Jr., and the Laws That Changed America* (2005).

Jordan, Barbara

(1936–1996) LAWYER AND POLITICIAN.

Barbara Charline Jordan first came to national prominence in November 1972 when she was elected to the U.S. House of Representatives from the 18th Congressional District in Houston, Tex. She and Andrew Young, who was elected that same year from Atlanta, Ga., were the first two blacks from the Deep South to win national office since the turn of the century.

Born 21 February 1936, the youngest of three daughters, to the Ben Jordans in Houston, Barbara Jordan grew up in a devoutly religious environment. Her parents and grandparents were lifelong members of the Good Hope Baptist

Church in Houston's predominantly black Fifth Ward. As a child, she was a bright student with a natural flair for speaking. Her high school teachers encouraged her to develop her talent by participating in various oratorical contests. Although the Houston school system was segregated, the precocious youngster took many honors in citywide matches. She graduated magna cum laude from Texas Southern University and earned her law degree at Boston University in 1959.

Returning to Houston, the fledgling barrister worked three years before being able to open her law office, but the lure of politics was already beckoning her. She became active in the local Democratic Party. In 1966, following redistricting, Barbara Jordan was elected to the Texas Senate, the first woman to win a seat in the upper chamber of that legislature. During her six years in the senate, she earned the admiration of her white male colleagues for her ability to get along well with others and to influence the passage of such legislation as the Texas Fair Employment Practices Commission, improvement of the Workmen's Compensation Act, and the state's first minimum wage law. In 1972 Barbara Jordan made history when the senate unanimously elected her president pro tempore. On 10 June 1972, in the traditional "Governor for a Day" ceremonies, she became the first black woman governor in U.S. history.

In 1971 her supporters in the state senate carved out a new congressional district to include a majority mixture of blacks and Hispanics. In November 1972 that electorate gave her a sweeping victory as their representative to Congress from the 18th District. She was assigned to the important House Judiciary Committee. In the wake of the scandals growing out of the Watergate break-in on 17 June 1972, the Senate Select Committee on Presidential Campaigning, under the chairmanship of Sam Ervin of North Carolina, began holding hearings in May of 1973. One year later, on 9 May 1974, the House Judiciary Committee under Peter Rodino opened impeachment hearings against President Richard Nixon.

During the House hearings, Barbara Jordan became a household name throughout America. As *Time* magazine said, "She voiced one of the most cogent and impassioned defenses of the Constitutional principles that emerged from the Nixon impeachment hearings." Opinion polls soon listed her as among the 10 most influential members of Congress, and Democratic Party leaders chose her, along with Senator John Glenn, to give a keynote address to its 1976 national convention.

Always realistic, Barbara Jordan firmly resisted all efforts to draft her as a candidate for the vice presidential nomination that year. She believed the country was not ready for such a development, although it was slowly inching toward the goal of equality in race relations. For personal reasons, Jordan retired from politics in 1978, accepting a position as the Lyndon B. Johnson Centennial Chair in National Policy at the LBJ School of Public Affairs at the University of Texas at Austin. Barbara

Jordan has left a legacy of great accomplishments in public service, both legislatively and personally. President Bill Clinton awarded her the Presidential Medal of Freedom in 1994. She died in 1996. *Texas Monthly* magazine in 1999 named her the Role Model of the Century for the state she served.

ETHEL L. PAYNE
Washington, D.C.

Ira B. Bryant, *Barbara Charline Jordan: From the Ghetto to the Capitol* (1977); *Ebony* (February 1975); *Houston Post* (21 July 1976); Sandra Parker, ed., *Barbara C. Jordan: Selected Speeches* (1999); Mary Beth Rogers, *Barbara Jordan: American Hero* (1998).

Kefauver, Estes

(1903–1963) POLITICIAN.

Carey Estes Kefauver, U.S. senator from Tennessee for 14 years and Democratic vice presidential nominee in 1956, is credited with having influenced incorporation of more direct popular appeal in presidential campaign methods, as contrasted with traditional reliance on local political organizations. Less tangible but probably more important was his possible influence on elimination of the customary stance and image of the southern senator.

Before Kefauver's consistently controversial career in the U.S. Senate, the image of the verbose gentleman with flowing hair and tie—like his first Tennessee senate colleague, K. D. McKellar—was not universally applicable to southern politicians, but it was associated with a solid bloc of Dixie legislators whose votes on certain issues, especially civil rights legislation, were predictable. Kefauver's refusal to conform to that image never lessened his popularity, and his stances probably undermined the assumption that southern senators and congressmen are distinct from—and often opposed to—the mainstream.

Kefauver's almost unheard-of challenge to an incumbent administration of his own party in plunging into the 1952 presidential race against the will of then-president Harry Truman also marked the beginning of the end of the once traditional axiom that "no southerner can ever become president." He did not make it that far himself, but four southerners, Lyndon B. Johnson, Jimmy Carter, Bill Clinton, and George W. Bush, attained the office after his death. An unacceptable liberal to southern colleagues, yet not liberal enough for northern Democratic leaders, Kefauver won successes both in the Senate and on the campaign trail almost exclusively through his ability to appeal directly to the voters, not only in his own state but nationwide.

A Yale graduate who left a successful Chattanooga law practice for a decade in the House of Representatives, Kefauver reached the U.S. Senate in 1948 through a successful challenge to the statewide political hegemony of Memphis's E. H. Crump. He was boosted into the 1952 presidential picture by his televised investigation of organized crime, and his soft voice and unavoidable handshake gave him name recognition second only to that of Dwight D. Eisenhower, according to a Gallup poll. After his second failure, in 1956, to win the

Democratic presidential nomination, Kefauver spent the rest of his career leading a series of Senate investigations, the most notable into antitrust violations and prescription drugs.

CHARLES L. FONTENAY
Nashville, Tennessee

Charles L. Fontenay, *Estes Kefauver: A Biography* (1980); Richard Harris, *The Real Voice* (1964); William Howard Moore, *The Kefauver Committee and the Politics of Crime, 1950–1952* (1974).

Key, V. O., Jr.

(1908–1963) POLITICAL SCIENTIST. V. O. (Valdimer Orlando) Key Jr. was born on 11 March 1908 in Austin, Tex. Key was known as one of the early pioneers in the behavioral movement in American political science for his studies of the American electorate, public opinion, and voting behavior.

Key received his undergraduate education at McMurray College and then at the University of Texas at Austin, where he received his B.A. in government with high honors in 1929 and his M.A. in government in 1930. He spent the next four years studying in the political science department at the University of Chicago, where he received his doctorate in 1934 and wrote his dissertation, "The Techniques of Political Graft in the United States." In 1934 Key married another political scientist, Luella Gettys, in Chicago.

Key took his first teaching position in the fall of 1936 at UCLA. While teaching in Los Angeles, Key started a research study with fellow UCLA professor Winston W. Crouch that was published

in 1939 as *The Initiative and the Referendum in California.*

Key left his teaching position at UCLA in 1936 when he was invited to join the staff of the Social Science Research Council in Chicago, for whom he produced a report entitled *The Administration of Grants to States* at the behest of the Social Security Administration. In 1937 Key went to work for the National Resources Planning Board in the U.S. Department of the Interior.

In 1938 Key was hired as an assistant professor of political science at Johns Hopkins University. He continued to publish many important articles in academic journals. In 1942 he published his first textbook, *Politics, Parties, and Pressure Groups*, which examined the relationship between political parties and interest groups. During World War II he was employed by the Bureau of the Budget of the Committee on Records of War Administration under the direction of Pendleton Herring. The committee's work was published as the *United States at War* in 1946.

In 1946 Roscoe Martin persuaded Key to undertake a study of the electoral process in the southern United States at the University of Alabama, which was financed by a $40,000 grant from the Rockefeller Foundation. Key oversaw the study while two young scholars, Alexander Heard and Donald Strong, traveled around the various southern states doing the initial research for it. In 1949 all of this research culminated in the writing of Key's seminal book, *Southern Politics in State and Nation.* The work was a systematic study, state by state, of the southern electoral process. Key used many interviews with prominent southerners and also statistically analyzed southern electoral results.

In 1949 Key accepted the Alfred Cowles Chair of American Government at Yale University and became the chair of the department of political science there. His tenure at Yale between 1949 and 1951 was tumultuous and resulted in his accepting a long-standing offer to become a faculty member in the department of government at Harvard University in 1951.

While teaching at Harvard in 1954, Key published a how-to textbook on research techniques entitled *A Primer of Statistics for Political Scientists*. In 1956 he followed up his *Southern Politics in State and Nation* with a study of all of the states north of the Mason-Dixon Line entitled *American State Politics: An Introduction*. Key also acted as the political science editor for the Alfred A. Knopf publishing house and continued to publish many important articles in major academic journals throughout his years at Harvard. He also served as the president of the American Political Science Association in 1958 and 1959.

Hoping to advance his statistical and survey skills, Key spent the 1959–60 academic year at the Survey Research Center at the University of Michigan, and his studies there resulted in another influential work, *Public Opinion and American Democracy*. In April of 1963 Key became seriously ill and was hospitalized. He died on 4 October 1963 at Beth Israel Hospital in Brookline, Mass. Prior to his death, Key's research focused on how voters rationally choose which candidates to vote for in elections, and the work was posthumously published in 1966 as *The Responsible Electorate*.

ANDREW M. LUCKER
Case Western Reserve University

Andrew M. Lucker, *V. O. Key Jr.: The Quintessential Political Scientist* (2001).

Lewis, John R.

(b. 1940) CIVIL RIGHTS ACTIVIST AND POLITICIAN.

Born in rural Pike County, Ala., John R. Lewis rose from his sharecropper origins to become one of the most effective voices for nonviolent social change in the United States during the 1960s and beyond. He attended college at the American Baptist Theological Seminary and at Fisk University in Nashville, Tenn., where he joined hundreds of other college students in the local sit-in movement. Lewis first received widespread national attention in 1961 when, as one of the Nashville students who had traveled to Alabama to revive the integrated Freedom Rides, television and newspaper cameras captured his vicious beating outside of a Montgomery bus terminal at the hands of white segregationists.

Lewis became chairman of the Student Nonviolent Coordinating Committee (SNCC) in 1963 and held the post until 1966, when he was voted out of office amidst members' calls for whites to leave SNCC and organize in the white community. Lewis wanted the organization to remain interracial and committed to nonviolent direct action and community organizing programs.

Left to right: Bayard Rustin, Andrew Young, Rep. William Fitts Ryan, James Farmer, and John Lewis, 1965 (Stanley Wolfson, photographer, Library of Congress [LC-USZ62-121285], Washington, D.C.)

He represented SNCC at the 1963 March on Washington for Jobs and Freedom and penned a speech that demanded, "Which side is the federal government on? The revolution is at hand, and we must free ourselves of the chains of political and economic slavery. . . . We cannot be patient, we do not want to be free gradually. We want our freedom, and we want it *now*." If senior organizers of the march had not censored Lewis and forced him to deliver a toned-down version of the speech in front of the Lincoln Memorial, it might have initiated a dramatic shift in the movement. Instead, Lewis's words have been forgotten in favor of Martin Luther King Jr.'s "I have a dream" speech.

Lewis remained committed to the cause of raising a "nonviolent army" to attack Jim Crow. When SNCC and the Southern Christian Leadership Conference highlighted the denial of voting rights to Alabama blacks in 1965, Lewis led 600 protesters across the Edmund Pettus Bridge in Selma toward the state capitol in Montgomery. On "Bloody Sunday," as news cameras again clicked and whirred away, state troopers attacked Lewis and the marchers with billy clubs and tear gas. The melee sparked national anger that helped cement popular support for what would become the Voting Rights Act of 1965, arguably the crowning achievement of the national civil rights movement.

Lewis took his commitment to equal civil rights for all Americans and desire to create "the beloved community" to elected office in 1981, when he was elected to the Atlanta city council. He has represented Georgia's Fifth District (metropolitan Atlanta) in the U.S. House of Representatives since 1987, having won 10 reelection bids at this writing. Lewis's commanding moral conscience established him as a power player in the national Democratic Party. The House Democratic caucus has elected Lewis to several leadership positions, including his current post of senior chief deputy whip. Lewis's annual reenactment of the march across the Pettus Bridge had become such an important rite of passage for aspiring political candidates that Lewis played kingmaker in March 2007, juggling requests from the Hillary Clinton and Barack Obama presidential campaigns for prominent spots among the marchers.

Lewis's approach to politics at the dawn of the 21st century has owed much to his experience as a young organizer. He has continued to work to build coalitions among people of color, the poor and working-class, and white liberals and to empower people to solve their own problems. He has neither apologized for nor wavered from his lifelong commitment to racial justice and integration. "I took a position then, and I take it today: that the idea of integration, of the beloved community, is an idea that we must struggle to make real," he told a 1999 audience. "If I'm the last person in America believing in integration, then I will be that person."

J. TODD MOYE
University of North Texas

Raymond Arsenault, *Freedom Riders: 1961 and the Struggle for Racial Justice* (2006); David Halberstam, *The Children* (1999); John Lewis with Michael D'Orso, *Walking with the Wind: A Memoir of the Movement* (1998).

Long, Huey P.

(1893–1935) POLITICIAN.
Governor of Louisiana, U.S. senator, and popular leader during the Great Depression, Huey Pierce Long emerged from the relatively poor hill country of northern Louisiana to transform forever the politics of his state. After eight years as a member of the Public Service Commission, he was elected governor in 1928 as the champion of the common people against the Old Guard, the oil interests, and the planter elite. Although his opponents often decried his radicalism, Long was in many respects a rather conventional progressive reformer. He oversaw a massive public works program, an improvement of state educational and health facilities, and a modest reform of the tax codes. But if Long was relatively moderate in his legislative aims, he was decidedly immoderate in the means he adopted to attain them. In his eight years as leader of Louisiana—four as governor and four as U.S. senator, from which position he continued to control the state through carefully chosen surrogates—he created a political machine without precedent in American history. By skillful use of both his wide popularity and his official powers, he won total mastery of the state legislature; from there, he proceeded to transform state government—through a series of constitutional amendments and other devices—to concentrate virtually all power in his own hands.

After entering the Senate in 1932, Long quickly rose to national prominence as well—first as a supporter and then as a foe of Franklin Roosevelt, but always as an advocate of redistribution of wealth. As leader of his own national political organization—the Share Our Wealth Society—he mobilized a following that alarmed even the president himself. At the peak of his power, positioning himself for a national campaign in 1936, Long was assassinated in September 1935 by a Baton Rouge physician, whose motives remain unknown.

Long was both a classic example of and a radical departure from the southern demagogue. Like others, he rose to power on the basis of explicit, if crudely expressed, class grievances. Like others, he drew from the traditions of Populism, defending the sanctity of local communities against the encroachments of powerful interests. But unlike most southern demagogues, Long translated his popular appeal into lasting and far-reaching political power; he compiled a record of substantive accomplishment; and he achieved and maintained authority without exploiting the issue of race. No southern politician of his era, moreover, could match Long's popular appeal outside the region. Long's career exposed in the starkest possible form both the dangers and the opportunities of effective Populist appeals to the discontented and dispossessed. He used his popularity to accumulate great and menacing power, but at the same time he turned the gaze of troubled Louisianans (and many others as well) away from the cultural, religious, and racial issues that had dampened economic progress and social reform in the past, and elevated to prominence basic questions of power and wealth. After Huey Long, Louisiana's conservative oligarchy would never rest entirely comfortably again.

ALAN BRINKLEY
Harvard University

Garry Boulard, *Huey Long Invades New Orleans: The Siege of a City, 1934–36* (1998); Alan Brinkley, *Voices of Protest: Huey Long, Father Coughlin, and the Great Depression* (1982); William Ivy Hair, *The Kingfish and His Realm: The Life and Times of Huey P. Long* (1991); Huey P. Long, *Every Man a King* (1933), *My First Days in the White House* (1935); Keith Ronald Perry, *The Kingfish in Fiction: Huey P. Long and the Modern American Novel* (2004); Allan P. Sindler, *Huey Long's Louisiana* (1956); Richard D. White Jr., *Kingfish: The Reign of Huey P. Long* (2006); T. Harry Williams, *Huey Long* (1969).

Lott, Trent

(b. 1941) POLITICIAN.
Born 9 October 1941 in Grenada, Miss., Chester Trent Lott is the only child of Chester Paul and Iona Watson Lott. Lott's father was a laborer and farmer and later a worker at Ingalls Shipbuilding in Pascagoula, while his mother taught elementary school. Lott was educated in the public schools of Pascagoula and at the University of Mississippi, where he earned an undergraduate degree in public administration (1963) and a law degree (1967). At Ole Miss he was a member and president of the Sigma Nu social fraternity and a varsity cheerleader. Lott's Ole Miss friends have remained trusted associates throughout his years in politics. After receiving his law degree, Lott returned to Pascagoula to practice law.

Lott entered politics as the Republican Party rose to power in the South. As many white Mississippi voters grew disenchanted with the Democratic Party's perceived sympathies to the civil rights movement and liberal social policies, they began voting for Republican presidential candidates, then congressional candidates, and finally state and local candidates. Lott and other southern Republicans in the 1970s and 1980s entered the scene as overt appeals to race were no longer part of the southern political landscape. Instead, the Republican Party claimed to better represent the conservative positions that the majority of the state's voters favored. Before seeking office himself, Lott served for four years as administrative assistant to a striking example of the old breed of Mississippi politician: Democratic representative William Colmer, a 40-year veteran of the House, the powerful chair of the Rules Committee, and a segregationist who had supported the Dixiecrat ticket in 1948. In 1972, when Colmer retired, Lott decided to run for his seat. Local Republicans courted Lott, who announced that he would run as a Republican, claiming to find his new party a much more ideologically congenial home. Colmer crossed party lines to offer Lott his endorsement. The 1972 elections provided a preview of the Republican future of Mississippi politics: Richard Nixon received 78 percent of the state's votes; both Lott and Thad Cochran, now the senior senator from Mississippi, were elected to U.S. House seats.

Lott served in the House from 1973 until 1989 and developed a strong interest in tax and budget matters. He served from 1975 to 1989 on the Rules Committee and from 1981 to 1989 as House minority whip, where he gained a reputation as an effective and well-

organized tactician and as a coalition-building deal-maker. In 1988, upon the retirement of long-serving Democratic senator John C. Stennis, Lott ran for the seat. In a hard-fought campaign, Lott defeated Representative Wayne Dowdy, a Democrat and former mayor of Mc-Comb, winning 54 percent of the vote. Lott did not face a serious challenge in his reelection bids in 1994, 2000, and 2006. When Lott took his seat, Mississippi was represented in the Senate by two Republicans for the first time since Reconstruction.

Throughout his years in the House and Senate, Lott maintained a consistently conservative voting record. In 1994 he became Senate majority whip and in 1996 was elected majority leader, a position that he held with one brief interruption until 2002. Lott was criticized by some Republicans for his lack of partisanship, especially in his handling of the impeachment trial of Bill Clinton, a difficult task, given the impossibility of finding two-thirds of the Senate to vote for conviction.

In December of 2002 Lott gained national notoriety for his apparently well-intentioned but ill-chosen remarks at the 100th birthday party of Senator Strom Thurmond of South Carolina. Lott noted that the state of Mississippi had supported Thurmond's 1948 Dixiecrat presidential campaign and speculated that the nation would be better off had other states followed Mississippi's example. Critics immediately called the remarks racially insensitive or worse. Lott offered several apologies for his comments, but beset by critics in the media and from both parties, he resigned the majority leadership. The White House conspicuously failed to come to Lott's assistance. The controversy did little to damage Lott's popularity in Mississippi; he was overwhelmingly reelected in 2006. His national political fortunes revived when in 2006 he was elected by one vote over Lamar Alexander of Tennessee as Republican minority whip.

Like other southern conservative politicians, Lott worked assiduously to bring federal spending to his state. His old 5th Congressional District on the Gulf Coast received generous amounts of defense spending. He argued with Republican presidents to protect highway construction and military bases in Mississippi. Lott also worked to recruit aerospace industries and other employers to the state. Citing a desire to "do something else," Lott unexpectedly resigned his Senate seat in December 2007, five years before his term was set to expire.

TRENT WATTS
University of Missouri at Rolla

Trent Lott, *Herding Cats: A Life in Politics* (2005); Jere Nash and Andy Taggart, *Mississippi Politics: The Struggle for Power, 1976–2006* (2006).

Lynch, John Roy

(1847–1939) POLITICIAN AND LAWYER.

Lynch was born on 10 September 1847 in Concordia Parish, La., the son of an Irishman, Patrick Lynch, and a slave, Catherine White. His father bought and intended to set free his whole family, but death and the treachery of a friend intervened, so that Lynch was not freed until 1863 by the Union army in Natchez. Lynch was self-educated, except for four months of formal schooling in 1866. He early became active as a Republican, and in 1869 Governor Adelbert Ames appointed him a justice of the peace. That same year Lynch was elected to the Mississippi House of Representatives. Reelected in 1871, he was chosen as Speaker of the House, which he ruled, according to a unanimously passed resolution, "with becoming dignity, with uniform courtesy and impartiality, and with marked ability." The occasion of the resolution was Lynch's departure from the Mississippi House for the U.S. House of Representatives, where he took his seat in December 1873, after handily defeating the Democratic candidate. In all, he served three terms, though his third term was cut short by the necessity of having to contest the election of his Democratic opponent; Lynch was finally declared the winner.

Following defeat for reelection in 1882, Lynch went home to Adams County to run his plantation. Still active as a Republican, he was a delegate to the Republican National Conventions of 1884, 1888, 1892, and 1900; even earlier, while still a member of the Mississippi House, he had been a delegate to the 1872 Republican National Convention. Democrat Grover Cleveland offered Lynch a minor appointive office, which he turned down; but in 1889 he accepted from Republican president Benjamin Harrison the position of fourth auditor of the treasury and served until the return of Democrats to national power in 1893.

About this time, Lynch began the study of law, and in 1896 he was admitted to the Mississippi bar. From 1893 till 1896, though, Lynch largely busied himself with his Adams County plantation and with real estate speculation in Natchez. From 1896 to 1898 he practiced law in Mississippi and in Washington, D.C., with the firm of Robert H. Terrell. With the outbreak of the Spanish-American War in 1898, Republican president William McKinley appointed Lynch as a paymaster of volunteer forces, with the rank of major; in 1901 he was appointed to the same position and rank in the regular army, in which he served till 1911, when he retired.

Lynch then settled in Chicago, where he practiced law and traded in real estate. In 1913 he published his *Facts of Reconstruction*, which is commonly regarded as the best account of Reconstruction by a black participant. His last years were spent writing *Reminiscences of an Active Life*, which was not published till 1970, under the editorship of John Hope Franklin. Lynch was married twice. His 1884 marriage to Ella Somerville, by whom he had one daughter, ended in divorce, and in 1911 he married Cora Williams, who survived him.

CHARLES E. WYNES
University of Georgia

John Hope Franklin, ed., *Reminiscences of an Active Life: The Autobiography of John Roy Lynch* (1970).

Maddox, Lester

(1915–2003) POLITICIAN.
In January 1967, with the South in the midst of dramatic change initiated by the civil rights movement, Lester Garfield Maddox was elected governor of Georgia. For a decade prior to his election, he had made himself a symbol of white resistance to integration. Each Saturday in the Atlanta newspapers he advertised his fried chicken restaurant, the Pickrick, and purchased space for a political column that attacked liberals as enemies of America, God, individual freedom, and states' rights. His particular brand of right-wing thinking combined religious fundamentalism with racism and classical laissez-faire doctrines. The combination proved to be appealing to many Georgians who shared aspects of his background.

Maddox was born in Atlanta in 1915, one of seven children of parents who had left rural Georgia to seek better employment opportunities in Atlanta. His father worked in a small steel factory and found it difficult to support his family during the Depression. Lester dropped out of high school, married at an early age, and worked at a variety of jobs before starting a small restaurant that he and his wife turned into a highly successful enterprise. Active in the Baptist Church and several fraternal orders, Maddox began in the 1950s to challenge the racial moderation that characterized Atlanta's political leadership. In 1964 he attracted national attention when he refused to obey the recently passed Civil Rights Act by denying service to blacks at his restaurant. Brandishing a pistol and distributing ax handles to his supporters, he forcibly turned away blacks from his door. When the federal courts ordered him to end discrimination, he sold the restaurant to friends rather than operate it on an integrated basis.

Maddox's highly visible defiance of federal authority served as a springboard for his pursuit of the governorship in 1966. With little financial support and no assistance from established political leaders, he launched his campaign in rural areas of central and southern Georgia. On fence posts and pine trees he nailed signs announcing, "This Is Maddox Country," and on election day his claims were supported. In the Democratic primary he toppled a former governor, Ellis Arnall, whose moderate stance on racial issues and long-standing opposition to the Talmadge forces in Georgia politics proved to be handicaps. In the general election Maddox was opposed by Republican Howard "Bo" Callaway, a millionaire segregationist who had recently left the Democratic Party. Neither man received a majority in the election because 7 percent of the electorate, blacks and white liberals, wrote in the name of Ellis Arnall. The Georgia legislature convened in January to decide between the two leading candidates; the outcome was not in question as rural Democrats who dominated the proceedings cast their votes for the intrepid Atlanta gadfly, Lester G. Maddox.

As governor, Maddox did not effect any significant changes in the state's institutions. He did not close the public schools nor use the powers of his office to challenge federal authority. White Georgians continued the slow process of adjusting to the end of segregation while their governor delivered regular verbal assaults on those who had brought about the change. In 1968 Maddox made an abortive two-week campaign for the presidential nomination of the Democratic Party; afterwards he supported the independent candidacy of George Wallace. When he completed his term as governor and could not succeed himself, he handily won election as lieutenant governor. But in 1974 the voters rejected his bid for the governor's office in favor of a moderate, George Busbee. The majority no longer wanted the state to be led by an extremist defender of the old order of segregation.

JAMES C. LANIER
Rhodes College

Numan Bartley, *From Thurmond to Wallace: Political Tendencies in Georgia, 1948–1968* (1970); Marshall Frady, *Southerners: A Journalist's Odyssey* (1980); Lester Maddox, *Speaking Out: The Autobiography of Lester Garfield Maddox* (1975).

Madison, James

(1751–1836) U.S. PRESIDENT AND POLITICAL PHILOSOPHER.
James Madison defended the interests of Virginia and the South within the framework of the federal government that he helped create. Educated by private tutors at plantation schools in Orange County, Va., and at the College of New Jersey (now Princeton University), he became an effective spokesman for his state and region. In the Continental Congress, 1780–83 and 1787–88, he worked to ensure Virginia's cession of western lands to the Confederation government on conditions favorable

to his state. He urged that the United States secure navigation rights to the Mississippi River—then controlled by Spain—which he recognized as crucial for the South's economic development.

At the 1787 Constitutional Convention Madison urged that the federal government be strengthened with delegated powers while the states retained reserved powers. As a congressman he worked to establish the new government while opposing efforts by the Federalist administration for further consolidation of national powers. His 1798 Virginia Resolutions defended civil liberties and asserted the right of states to interpose their authority to declare unconstitutional the Federalist-sponsored Alien and Sedition Acts. Those resolutions became the foundation of states' rights doctrine for early 19th-century Republicans.

Sectional divisions and his own Republican scruples over legislative supremacy impeded Madison as fourth president of the United States, 1809 to 1817. Long-standing disputes with Great Britain finally erupted in the War of 1812, which was supported in the South but unpopular in the North. In retirement, Madison was embarrassed when—during the 1828–33 South Carolina nullification controversy—states' righters invoked his Virginia Resolutions. He objected that his proposals for interposition meant only cooperation among the states to repeal federal laws or amend the Constitution. He advised President Andrew Jackson and cabinet officers on responding to the nullifiers.

Madison deplored slavery but remained economically dependent on the slave labor of his plantation. He was a founder and president of the American Colonization Society, which worked to return free blacks to Africa. His interests ranged beyond political theory and practice to architecture, the visual arts, and education. Madison supervised additions to Montpelier, his Orange County house, which he filled with his collection of books and paintings. He worked with his lifelong friend and political confidant, Thomas Jefferson, to establish the University of Virginia, which he served as visitor and second rector. Throughout an extraordinarily long career, Madison advanced the political and cultural life of his state, region, and nation.

THOMAS A. MASON
Indiana Historical Society

Irving Brant, *James Madison*, 6 vols. (1941–61); William T. Hutchinson et al., eds., *The Papers of James Madison*, 26 vols. (1962–); Ralph Ketcham, *James Madison: A Biography* (1971); Drew R. McCoy, *The Last of the Fathers: James Madison and the Republican Legacy* (1991); Robert A. Rutland, *James Madison: The Founding Father* (1987).

Monroe, James

(1758–1831) U.S. PRESIDENT.
James Monroe was born in Westmoreland County, Va., in 1758. In 1774 he entered the College of William and Mary. When the American Revolution erupted, the young Monroe enlisted in the Third Virginia Infantry in 1776 and soon found himself participating in the fighting in New York, New Jersey, and Pennsylvania. Monroe served with General George Washington and the Continental Army until 1778, rising to

the rank of major. Following his tour of duty, Monroe returned to Virginia, where he became the military commander for Virginia.

Monroe then left military life and entered politics, first as a state assemblyman in 1782 and then as a congressman from Virginia in the Confederation Congress, where he served from 1783 to 1786. As a member of Congress, Monroe helped to defeat the Jay-Gardoqui Treaty that would have closed the Mississippi River to American commerce. Monroe left Congress to resume his studies and became a successful lawyer in Virginia. He was elected to the House of Delegates in 1787, and he served in the Virginia ratifying convention, which ratified the Constitution in 1788. In 1790 Monroe was elected to the U.S. Senate, where he served until 1794. Monroe worked closely with James Madison and Thomas Jefferson, becoming an important leader and spokesman in the Senate for the developing Republican Party.

Monroe's life and career changed course yet again, when President Washington offered him the position of minister to France in 1794. Monroe arrived in France in July 1794, after the overthrow of Robespierre by the Thermidorean reaction and served until 30 December 1796. He returned to Virginia and resumed his life as a small planter and lawyer. Monroe wrote *A View of the Conduct of the Executive in the Foreign Affairs of the United State Connected with the Mission to the French Republic during the Years 1794, 5 & 6*, which appeared in 1798.

Monroe returned to elective politics in 1799, when he was elected governor of Virginia. He remained governor until 1802, when he decided to return to his legal career. Monroe had little time to resume his career because President Jefferson nominated him to be an envoy extraordinary to France to assist in the negotiations for the Louisiana Purchase. Jefferson then appointed him minister to Great Britain, where he served from 1803 to 1807. Monroe made an abortive run for the presidency in 1808, but the Republican caucus in Virginia preferred Madison. Monroe's candidacy caused a split in Republican ranks that took several years to heal. He served in the Virginia Assembly from 1810 to 1811, and he was again elected governor in 1811.

His tenure as governor was brief. Madison nominated him as secretary of state in 1811, to replace Samuel Smith. Monroe served in that office until 1817, when he became the fifth president. Monroe had the distinction of serving as secretary of state and acting secretary of war during Madison's second term as president, a period that coincided with the War of 1812.

Monroe's presidency from 1817 to 1825 has been characterized as the "Era of Good Feelings." The Republican Party stood alone, the Federalist Party having disintegrated after the War of 1812. This era witnessed a burst of American nationalism as the nation moved westward. Several new states joined the Union, including Mississippi (1817), Illinois (1818), Alabama (1819), Maine (1820), and Missouri (1821). The United States also acquired Florida from Spain in the Transcontinental Treaty. There was nationalism in

Supreme Court decisions, such as *Mc-Culloch v. Maryland* (1819), *Cohens v. Virginia* (1821), and *Gibbons v. Ogden* (1824), as the Supreme Court stressed the supremacy of federal law over state law. The Monroe Doctrine of December 1823, though written by Secretary of State John Quincy Adams, warned European powers not to attempt to recolonize the South American republics that had recently gained their independence from Spain. There were problems, though, in these years. The Panic of 1819 plunged many Americans into unemployment or bankruptcy and left a lingering antibank sentiment in the South and West. Slavery became a major issue when Missouri petitioned for statehood in 1818, and the Missouri Crisis of 1819–21 threatened to rend the Union along a North-South line. When Monroe left office in March 1825, he was the last of the "Virginia Dynasty," which had included Washington, Jefferson, and Madison. After his presidency, Monroe returned to private life. He did serve Virginia in one final capacity, as president of the state constitutional convention in 1829. Monroe moved to New York City to live with his daughter and died there on 4 July 1831.

JAMES C. FOLEY

St. Andrew's Episcopal School
Ridgeland, Mississippi

Harry Ammon, *James Monroe: The Quest for National Identity* (1971); *Biographical Directory of the American Congress, 1774–1971* (1971); Noble E. Cunningham Jr., *The Presidency of James Monroe* (1996).

Moral Majority

The Moral Majority was an educational, lobbying, and fund-raising organization dedicated to conservative Christian causes. Founded in 1979 with the assistance of "New Right" leaders, the Moral Majority was led by Jerry Falwell, pastor of the 18,000-member Thomas Road Baptist Church in Lynchburg, Va.

Nationally, Moral Majority maintained a legislative office near the capitol in Washington, D.C., monitored legislation, issued regular appeals to its members for political action through letter writing, lobbied Congress on behalf of specific legislation, and published the *Moral Majority Report*, a small monthly newspaper. Legally, Moral Majority was comprised of three separate organizations: Moral Majority, a lobby; the Moral Majority Foundation, an educational foundation; and the Moral Majority Legal Defense Foundation, an organization that offered legal assistance and funds to various conservative religious groups, such as Christian schools that regularly did battle with secular authorities.

Moral Majority operated a political action committee during the 1980 national campaign but abandoned it after spending only $20,000. The national organization was loosely replicated at state and local levels by Moral Majority chapters variously centered in election districts, counties, or major population centers. Lobbying, publication of voting records and newsletters, and organized action were also undertaken at the local level. The national Moral Majority was active in establishing local chapters and in training their leaders, often by sponsoring regional training programs in conjunction with the Committee for the Survival of a Free Congress. Voter registration, involving participation of local churches, was also a major concern at all levels.

Although the basic source of support for Moral Majority was from independent fundamentalist churches, often Baptist, the organization saw its agenda as moral, not religious. It welcomed and cooperated with all who shared its views regardless of their religious orientation. Moral Majority sought to "return the nation to moral sanity," to revitalize those values "which made America great." It opposed abortion, homosexuality, pornography, the exclusive teaching of evolution, feminism, the welfare state, and secularism in general. Issues supported included prayer in public schools, state support for private (particularly religious) education, recognition of parents' and churches' rights to educate children without outside interference, a strong national defense coupled with an aggressively anticommunist foreign policy, and a laissez-faire capitalism at home that subordinated itself to the national interest abroad.

Geographically, Moral Majority drew its major support from the South and Midwest and its most effective leadership from the South. It represented a "going public" and an attainment of national influence on the part of southern religion. Moral Majority's political activism constituted a significant revision of the traditionally separatist and nonworldly tendencies of its supporting churches, but not necessarily a reversal or a sharp break. Moral Majority perpetuated a southern Protestant tradition of selective social activism on a narrow range of issues centered upon personal morality. In so doing, it reflected fundamentalism's holiness roots and the conviction that social well-being is born of individual purity. The call for national repentance as a cure for impending disaster (God's rejection of America) coupled with its Manichaean sense of rigid good and evil in all matters, religious, social, or political, reflected a tradition of revivalism that moved its converts from total depravity to thorough regeneration.

Moral Majority consisted of a wedding of fundamentalist religion with a "chosen people" style of civil religion, which represented a major tie between religion and mythology in the region. It was convinced that America's success as a nation depended upon its people, rendering obedience to God's law as understood in a fundamentalist reading of the Bible. Moral Majority supporters regarded themselves as a saving remnant, calling the nation back to faithfulness, to its covenant with the biblical God who, although once so near to rightfully forsaking America, awaited a sign of repentance that would again allow him to bless that bastion of true religion and return it to its rightful, dominant place in world affairs. Jerry Falwell's two books, *How You Can Help Clean Up America* (1978) and *Listen, America!* (1980), give a summary of the Moral Majority's aims and its "action programs for decency" in the nation.

Moral Majority had failed by the late 1980s to gain key legislation to support its agenda, and Falwell dissolved the organization in 1989. After that, Pat Robertson supplemented Falwell as leader of the Christian Right, and the Christian Coalition emerged in the 1990s to advance many of the moral and family values that Moral Majority had championed.

DENNIS E. OWEN
University of Florida

Gabriel Fackre, *The Religious Right and the Christian Faith* (1982); Samuel S. Hill and Dennis E. Owen, *The New Religious Political Right in America* (1982); William Martin, *With God on Our Side: The Rise of Religious Right in America* (1996); Peggy Shriver, *The Bible Vote: Religion and the New Right* (1981).

New South Governors

In southern politics, 1970 marked a watershed. That year saw the election of moderate governors across the South who changed the way the nation looked at the region and at southern state chief executives. Southern politicians of a new style were elected governor: from the ranks of Democrats came a "no-liquor-no-tobacco Panhandle Presbyterian elder" named Reubin Askew in Florida; John C. West, a racial moderate who rose through the ranks of the South Carolina Democratic Party; a self-styled "country lawyer" in Arkansas's Dale Bumpers; peanut farmer Jimmy Carter of Georgia; and Terry Sanford and James Hunt of North Carolina. Republicans A. Linwood Holton in Virginia and Tennessee's Winfield Dunn also represented this new style of

governor. And so did Democrat Albert Brewer, who inherited Alabama's governorship in 1968 but was not reelected in 1970. Just as the post–World War II economic boom transformed the southern economy, the combination of the civil rights movement, the Voting Rights Act of 1965, the subsequent political party realignment, and the rise of moderate southern governors changed the South's political landscape in 1970.

These governors benefited from paramount changes in southern politics. When he wrote *Southern Politics in State and Nation* in 1949, V. O. Key Jr. asserted that for the South to experience a political revival it had to gain its freedom from four major institutions that had constricted the region's political development for decades: disfranchisement, the one-party system, malapportionment of state legislatures, and Jim Crow segregation. Three decades later, *Brown v. Board of Education* (1954), the civil rights movement, and the subsequent legislation expanding voting and civil rights had sounded the death knell for the traditional, one-party, segregated South.

Perhaps the event most important to the rise of "New South" governors was the 1965 Voting Rights Act. African American votes were crucial in these governors' defeats of segregationist opponents. Before the 1965 legislation, African American voters were virtually nonexistent in the region. By 1967 the number of African American voters in the South skyrocketed. As a whole, the region's black voter registration grew by more than 70 percent. The result of such massive increases in black voters was the creation of new majority coalitions in state legislatures and new faces in state government, especially the governor's office. The change was so dramatic that by 1972 every southern state except Alabama had elected moderate governors who avoided racial rhetoric and advocated progressive policies. But the progressivism of the 1970s class of new southern governors was limited largely to their views on race and reform of state governmental structures. On economic issues they could be quite conservative, reflecting the antitax mood of their day. These governors were often less progressive than the Populist, segregationist governors of the earlier 20th century. Although contemporary journalists may have labeled these state chief executives as "populists" or "progressives," such titles are misleading. The 1970s class of governors' reforms more closely resembled governors who reflected "business progressivism" of the 1920s, which emphasized highway improvement, educational expansion, health reform, and general expansion of public services. But even this comparison is tenuous. The progressivism of the post–civil rights era New South governors rarely extended beyond racial moderation, reform of state governmental structures, prison reform, mental health programs, and education reform.

The 1970 class of governors was succeeded in later years by a second group of New South governors that included South Carolina's Richard Riley, Florida's Robert Graham, Georgia's George Busbee, Louisiana's David Treen, Mississippi's William Winter, Tennessee's Lamar Alexander, Virginia's Charles Robb, Arkansas's David Pryor and Bill Clinton, and the North Carolina triumvirate of James Holshouser, Jim Hunt, and Jim Martin.

GORDON E. HARVEY
University of Louisiana at Monroe

Gordon E. Harvey, *A Question of Justice: New South Governors and Education, 1968–1976* (2002); Alexander Lamis, *The Two-Party South* (1990); Larry Sabato, in *Contemporary Southern Politics*, ed. James F. Lea (1988); Randy Sanders, *Mighty Peculiar Elections: The New South Gubernatorial Campaigns of 1970 and the Changing Politics of Race* (2002).

Pepper, Claude

(1900–1989) POLITICIAN.
The oldest of four children, Claude Denson Pepper was born on the family farm near Dudleyville, Ala. "Full grown" before he had ever traveled on a paved road, when he accompanied his debate team to Chapel Hill, N.C., as a college freshman, it was the farthest north he had ever been. A southerner, a Baptist, and a lifelong unwavering Democrat, a New Deal liberal who in a 1950 smear campaign was branded a "leader of radicals" and "advocate of treason," Pepper was nevertheless hailed as a representative American, "the nearest thing this country has to a national congressman."

Pepper's wide ambition and indomitability surfaced early. A schoolteacher for a time in Dothan, Ala., then a steel-mill worker, he continued to hold down a part-time job while attending the University of Alabama. He graduated Phi Beta Kappa in 1921 and, after receiving a law degree from Harvard in 1924, taught for a year at the University of Arkansas before setting up practice in Perry, Fla. In 1929 he was elected to the Florida House of Representatives but was defeated two years later and resumed his law practice, this time in Tallahassee.

After an unsuccessful bid for the U.S. Senate in 1934 (lost by only 4,000 votes), Pepper filed for a vacancy two years later and was nominated by his party, unopposed. Committed to Roosevelt's economic programs for the good of the South and the nation, Pepper gained the president's support for election to his first six-year term in 1938. He consistently risked antagonizing both big business and social conservative interests in Florida by opposing racism and by favoring minimum wage laws, national health insurance, old age pensions, and federal aid to education.

Pepper was reelected in 1944, but his postwar record that included such things as encouraging rapprochement with the Soviet Union, early backing of Dwight Eisenhower against Truman, opposition to union-regulating Taft-Hartley legislation, and support for anti–poll tax laws led his enemies to close ranks in 1950. Florida boss Edward W. Ball, assisted with funds gleaned nationally, groomed Representative George A. Smathers to run against Pepper in what has been called "the most elaborate crusade for political annihilation ever conducted in Southern politics." Coupled with slanderous slogans and speeches, a pamphlet, "The Red Record of Senator Claude Pepper," circulated throughout Florida. On election night, when Pepper had lost by 67,000 votes, people passing his house shouted obscenities and applauded his defeat.

With law offices in Tallahassee, Washington, and Miami, Pepper again returned to a successful private practice but was discontented being out of office. In 1962 he ran for and won a House seat newly created for the Miami congressional district. He was consistently reelected after that.

As congressman, Pepper remained responsive to a diverse constituency that included Haitian refugees, blacks, Hispanics, and many white retirees. He introduced legislation to support housing projects and cancer research, crime prevention programs, and economic aid to South Americans. Undaunted by Reagan administration pressure to cut social programs, Pepper continued to pursue his maverick policy in an era of conservatism. As chair of the House Select Committee on Aging, he became a particularly staunch defender of government responsibility for the elderly: "I refuse to believe that a country as rich and powerful as ours can't afford to guarantee the basic comfort and security of its older citizens. I know we can do it," he added, characteristically, "and I intend to be long and loud about it."

ELIZABETH M. MAKOWSKI
University of Mississippi

Tracy E. Danese, *Claude Pepper and Ed Ball: Politics, Purpose, and Power* (2000); John Egerton, *New York Times Magazine* (29 November 1981); Claude Denson Pepper, with Hay Gorey, *Pepper: Eyewitness to a Century* (1987).

Polk, James Knox

(1795–1849) U.S. PRESIDENT.
For most Americans, James Knox Polk, the 11th president of the United States, is an obscure historical personality whose administration is remembered because he waged an unpopular war with Mexico—but did little else.

That is unfair to him. He did a great deal more. Surely he is the nation's most unappreciated president. In a single term in office he engineered the annexation of Texas, bluffed the British out of the Oregon Territory, waged that unpopular war with Mexico to win California and New Mexico, and, with all of that, enlarged the nation's landmass by a full third. It was, finally, James Knox Polk who made the United States a continental nation, "from sea to shining sea."

Polk, at a critical moment, also reformed the nation's monetary system. As he came into office, the country's economic policy was in transitional shambles, and he knew it. As a member of Congress and as Speaker of the House, Polk had helped President Andrew Jackson, his political guru, win the so-called war against the Second Bank of the United States. Old Hickory had stripped from the "Monster" bank all federal deposits on which the institution had paid no interest and with which it had corruptly influenced politics. Jackson's administration distributed those government funds among what soon became known as "pet banks." Many of them turned out to be as mismanaged and as corrupt as the "Monster." Polk ended all of these prob-

lems. As president, he pushed through Congress a measure creating an independent treasury that placed all federal funds in government vaults where they were kept safe and administered only to pay bills and meet payrolls.

Martin Van Buren had first pushed the idea after he succeeded Old Hickory—but he could not sustain it. Polk did. The Independent Treasury remained in place for more than six decades until it ultimately was replaced in 1913 by the present Federal Reserve System.

These were great achievements. But was Polk a great president? "Presidential greatness" is a term of elastic and elusive definition. Some may be surprised to learn that American historians, in polls conducted every decade since the 1940s, have consistently ranked Polk somewhere between seventh and twelfth among great and near-great presidents. Harry Truman, the only White House occupant to evaluate his predecessors, listed Polk among his "eight best" chief magistrates. "He was a great president!" said Truman.

Polk's presidency was one thing. His personality was something else again. To read his presidential diary, which he kept with remarkable fidelity over three years, is to confront a brooding and humorless politician. He wrote his diary with effortless clarity and opinionated candor that reveals the shadowed side of a conflicted personality. He seems demanding to the point of unreasonableness, determined to the point of stubbornness, and at times self-righteous to the point of paranoia.

His intense partisanship emerges in the diary. So does his ego. Any member of the Whig opposition party was suspect, reactionary, wedded to money, probably corrupt, and an enemy. Democrats who flirted with Whigs also were castigated in his diary. He branded a Presbyterian minister who had criticized him as "a knave without vital religion or a fanatic without reason."

Secretary of State James Buchanan is repeatedly held up to ridicule by Polk's acidic pen. He also wrote scorching criticisms of his two leading Mexican War generals, Zachary Taylor and Winfield Scott. Outnumbered by Mexican troops, they won battle after battle—but Polk branded them selfish, misguided Whig soldiers ambitious to use their military success politically. He was right about that, of course. During the 1844 campaign, he had pledged that he would not seek reelection—and he kept his word. It pained him deeply when General Taylor was elected to succeed him as president.

Whatever his flaws of personality (and they are obvious to those who read the diary) there is much to admire in the career of James K. Polk. He loved his country and served it well. Only Jefferson, Jackson, and Lincoln among the 19th-century presidents exercised the power of the executive as effectively.

It hardly seems fair that Polk, who left the White House at age 53, ill and worn from overwork, went home to Nashville and died from cholera three months later.

JOHN SEIGENTHALER
The First Amendment Center
Vanderbilt University

Wayne Cutler, ed., *James K. Polk Correspondence*, vol. 7, January–August 1844 (1989); J. George Harris, *Polk Campaign Biography* (1990); Allan Nevins, ed., *Polk: The Diary of a President, 1845–1849, Covering the Mexican War, the Acquisition of Oregon, and the Conquest of California and the Southwest* (1929); Robert V. Remini, *Andrew Jackson and the Course of American Empire*, vol. 1, 1767–1821 (1977); Arthur M. Schlesinger, *The Age of Jackson* (1945); John Seigenthaler, *James K. Polk, 1845–1849* (2003).

Prohibition

Although closely identified with the southern ethos in the 20th century, the movement to limit the sale and use of alcoholic beverages has never been an exclusively southern endeavor. The first areas touched by this effort were in the East and Midwest in the antebellum period. Prohibition, as an ideal, originated in the voluntarism of the early temperance movement. After the Civil War more advocates adopted the policy of abstinence, or "teetotalism," and followed the legislative example of the state of Maine. Such groups as the Woman's Christian Temperance Union and the Anti-Saloon League of America organized for the fight.

In the first decade of the 20th century, dry sentiment gained momentum in the South as Georgia enacted statewide prohibition. By 1910 over two-thirds of southern counties were dry. Nationally, the economic exigencies of World War I combined with the denouement of Progressivism to bring about passage of the Eighteenth Amendment and the start of the Prohibition period (1920–33), during which the manufacture and sale of alcoholic beverages were forbidden.

Various interpretations have been offered for this monumental struggle against liquor. Until the early 1970s liberal historiography scorned prohibitionists in general, and the southern variety in particular, as misguided provincials who eschewed genuine reform, advocating prohibition instead as a panacea for their fears about a changing America.

Recent scholarship has been more sympathetic to the prohibitionist cause, finding a greater degree of diversity among its adherents. For example, not all members of the liturgical churches opposed prohibition. Patrick Henry Callahan, a leading southern Catholic layman, actively supported prohibition. Moreover, studies of individual psychological crises of the late 19th and early 20th centuries indicate that alcohol abuse did, indeed, cause severe economic and social distress. Alcoholism particularly attacked the prevalent middle-class ideal of family autonomy. In effect, the methods now used to study the drug subculture are being applied to alcoholism, past and present.

The presidential election of 1928 solidified the southern consensus favoring prohibition. Many southerners voted against Al Smith because of his lack of support for prohibition, though their votes were read as anti-Catholic. After the repeal of national prohibition in 1933, the South became the bastion of dry support in the nation. While Mississippi opted for statewide prohibition, other southern states adopted some form of local option and allowed municipalities and counties, even pre-

cincts, to decide the issue. Will Rogers once commented that "southerners will vote dry as long as they can stagger to the polls." More southerners still live in areas of strict alcohol control than any other region of the United States.

Consequently, the bootlegger and moonshiner have continued to ply their trades, often with the full cooperation of local authorities. Most southern communities have legends about the classic confrontations between moonshiner and revenue agent.

With the development of tourism and urbanization, legalization of liquor without restriction has become more common. However, conservative and fundamentalist Christian groups oppose such change in southern mores and often still muster enough votes to win local wet-dry elections.

WILLIAM E. ELLIS
Eastern Kentucky University

Edward Behr, *Prohibition: Thirteen Years That Changed America* (1996); Jack S. Blocker Jr., *American Temperance Movements: Cycles of Reform* (1989); Paul A. Carter, *Another Part of the Twenties* (1977); Norman H. Clark, *Deliver Us from Evil: An Interpretation of American Prohibition* (1976); James H. Timberlake, *Prohibition and the Progressive Movement, 1900–1920* (1963).

Radical Republicans

"Radical Republicans" was a frequently used, but often imprecisely defined, term applying to one faction of the Republican Party in the South after the Civil War. In 1867, at the outset of the congressional program of Reconstruction, the nature of southern Radicalism was reasonably clear: Radicals favored guaranteed equal rights for the freedmen, the establishment of public schools, and fairly sweeping disfranchisement of former Confederates. In some states the Radicals insisted that schools be nonsegregated and that public accommodations be open to both races. The Radicals' opponents, the moderate Republicans, would extend political and civil equality, but nothing more, to the freedmen and hoped to attract part of the native white electorate with a program of economic development. Political alignments and party factionalism make generalization somewhat difficult, but on the whole northern-born white people who came to the South after 1861 (referred to by southerners as "carpetbaggers"), along with the freedmen, were most likely to belong to the Radical faction. However, the majority of the native white Republicans (referred to as "scalawags"), many with Whig loyalties from the antebellum years, were moderates. Also, as a general rule, the larger the black voting majority in a given district, the greater was the likelihood that Radical candidates—either carpetbaggers or blacks—would be elected.

Southern Radicalism owed much to northern influence, through the power of the carpetbaggers in the party hierarchy and in its commitment both to racial justice and, on occasion, to the social equality of the races. In the 1870s, after some Republican governments had fallen to the Conservatives (or Democrats) and those remaining were under assault, southern Radicals looked to their northern counterparts to inter-

vene once more in southern affairs and salvage their political power, if not the broader goals of Reconstruction. Further intervention, however, was an impossibility after 1872. Finally, the fluidity of political alignments and the serious divisions between moderate and Radical Republicans that weakened the federal government's commitment to Reconstruction also plagued and weakened the southern parties. Radical Republicanism was an artificial development in the South, introduced by outsiders, and, despite its name, it proved to be less than truly radical in its dedication to the freedmen.

Radical strength varied in the southern states, but it was best embodied in the administrations of Adelbert Ames in Mississippi (1874–76), William P. Kellogg in Louisiana (1873–77), and Edmund J. Davis in Texas (1870–74). On the other hand, Radicalism was fairly weak in Florida, North Carolina, and Georgia, where nearly all prominent Republicans were scalawags, and was almost nonexistent in Virginia. In most states, however, Republican parties were divided and greatly weakened by factional and ideological struggles and found it difficult to combat the increasingly strong challenges from Conservatives. White southerners came to equate Radicalism with Republicanism, thereby rejecting the party of the freedmen, drawing a clear color line in politics, driving most whites into the Democratic Party, and helping to create a solidly Democratic South, which lasted until the 20th century.

JOHN M. MATTHEWS
Georgia State University

Warren A. Ellem, *Journal of Southern History* (May 1972); Eric Foner, *Reconstruction: America's Unfinished Revolution, 1863–1877* (2002); Richard L. Hume, *Journal of American History* (September 1977).

Randolph, John

(1773–1833) POLITICIAN.

John Randolph of Roanoke represented the interests of traditional slaveholding Virginians in Congress and expressed the aristocratic style of the Virginia past in American public life from the early Republic through the Jacksonian period. Randolph entered public life as part of the Jeffersonian opposition to the Adams administration and was a prominent member of the congressional leadership in Jefferson's first administration. He broke with Jefferson and, along with purist republicans, formed an extreme group called the "tertium quids" within the party.

Beginning with an uncompromising assertion of states' rights, in time they became suspicious of democracy as well as American nationalism, detecting in the growth of the federal government an ultimate threat to slavery and the plantation way of life. Randolph's career was largely one of opposition, although he sometimes found allies on particular issues. He was probably the first important American statesman to stake out the positions that came to characterize the secessionist southern view of the Union. Although he dismissed Calhoun's metaphysics, he influenced the South Carolinian's development as a sectional leader.

Randolph's notorious, exciting, and eccentric public persona, his witticisms and verbal challenges, and his stinging contempt for the barbarities of American democratic public life contributed to the mythology of southern blue bloods and hotbloods. Randolph seized the American imagination, North and South, in a pattern that would come to characterize the southern hold on the American imagination.

In his antidemocratic and anticommercial conservatism, his states' rights consistency and republican purity, and his prophetic sense of where southern slaveholding interests must lie, Randolph earned his place in the pantheon of southern activists. In his extravagant and dramatic eccentricity, his keen eye for the appetites of the democratic electorate, and his attempt to embody the Virginia heritage, Randolph earned a lasting place as a mythic southerner.

ROBERT DAWIDOFF
Cornell University

Henry Adams and Robert McColley, *John Randolph* (1882, 1995); William Cabell Bruce, *Randolph of Roanoke: A Biography Based Largely on New Material*, 2 vols. (1922); Robert Dawidoff, *The Education of John Randolph* (1979); Adam L. Tate, *Virginia Magazine of History and Biography*, no. 3 (2003); William R. Taylor, *Cavalier and Yankee: The Old South and American National Character* (1961).

Rayburn, Sam

(1882–1961) POLITICIAN.

Sam Taliaferro Rayburn, congressman from a rural northeast Texas district from 1913 until his death in 1961, was one of the most powerful congressmen in the 20th century. Born in Roane County, Tenn., on 6 January 1882, the son of a Confederate soldier, he moved to Fannin County, Tex., at the age of five. He was educated in country schools and attended Mayo College in Commerce, Tex. After a brief stint as a schoolteacher, Rayburn was elected to the Texas House of Representatives in 1906. In 1911 he was elected Speaker of the Texas House, and during reapportionment in that year he carved a congressional district that was to elect and reelect him for 25 terms.

In his early years Rayburn was a follower of the charismatic Texas senator Joseph Weldon Bailey. With Bailey's fall from power, Rayburn's ambitions for higher statewide office were thwarted. He became a lieutenant of the influential Texas congressman John Nance Garner and in 1932 directed Garner's campaign for the presidency. Rayburn was heavily involved in the negotiations that led to the Roosevelt-Garner ticket.

After Roosevelt's election Rayburn became a workhorse of the New Deal through his role as chairman of the Interstate and Foreign Commerce Committee. His southern populist leanings led him to support most of Roosevelt's economic policies, and his committee handled such legislation as the Truth-in-Securities Act (1933), the Securities Exchange Act (1934), the Federal Communications Act (1934), the Public Utility Holding Company Act (1935), and the Rural Electrification Act (1936).

In 1937 he was elected majority leader of the House of Representatives, and in 1940, upon the death of William Bankhead of Alabama, he was elected Speaker. With the exception of the four years that the Republicans controlled

the House, Rayburn was Speaker from 1940 to 1961. During those years his primary goal was to serve as a bridge in the House between the southern and northern wings of the Democratic Party.

He worked closely with southern committee chairmen, presidents, and his protégé in the Senate, Lyndon B. Johnson, to build the coalitions necessary for national policy-making. Rayburn was a strong supporter of defense preparedness, prolabor legislation, public power, and farm programs. Although a segregationist, he supported the 1957 Civil Rights Act and counseled moderation in the reaction to *Brown v. Board of Education.*

Though a national leader, he maintained a strong tie to his district and to the rural South. He died of cancer of the pancreas on 16 November 1961, in Bonham, Tex.

ANTHONY CHAMPAGNE
University of Texas at Dallas

Anthony Champagne, *Congressman Sam Rayburn* (1984); C. Dwight Dorough, *Mr. Sam* (1962); H. G. Dulaney, Edward Hake Phillips, and MacPhelan Reese, eds., *Speak, Mr. Speaker* (1978); Alfred Steinberg, *Sam Rayburn: A Biography* (1975).

Richards, Ann

(1933–2006) POLITICIAN.
Ann Richards, the energetic and quick-witted feminist Texas Democrat, first burst onto the national political stage when she delivered the keynote address during the 1988 Democratic National Convention in Atlanta. Speaking of the wealthy incumbent U.S. vice president George H. W. Bush, who also called Texas his home, Richards quipped,

Ann Richards, the boisterous Texas governor, obtained a license to ride a motorcycle at the age of 60 (Courtesy Texas State Library & Archives Commission)

"Poor George. He can't help it. He was born with a silver foot in his mouth." The line would prove to become one of her most memorable, and the popularity she gained from it perhaps helped propel her to the highest office in the state of Texas.

Born Dorothy Ann Willis in Lakeview, Tex., to a father who, Richards always claimed, came from Bugtussle and a mother who, as she also claimed, came from Hogjaw, Richards moved with her family to Waco so she could attend Waco High School. While at Waco

High, Richards attended Girls State, a summer citizenship and leadership conference in Austin. She also attended Girls Nation in Washington, D.C., where she toured the White House and met President Harry Truman.

After high school Richards dropped the name Dorothy and married her high school sweetheart, Dave Richards. The couple enrolled at Baylor University in Waco the following fall. Richards earned her B.A. in 1954. The couple moved to Austin following graduation, and Richards taught government at a junior high school while her husband attended law school at the University of Texas. Her husband earned his law degree, and the couple moved again to Washington, where he worked for the U.S. Civil Rights Commission, and then to Dallas, where she settled in as a homemaker and became politically active as a campaigner for gubernatorial candidates Henry B. Gonzalez and Ralph Yarborough.

In the early 1970s Richards went on to do campaign work for Texas candidates, including Sarah Weddington, a lawyer running for a seat in the Texas House who had successfully argued *Roe v. Wade* before the U.S. Supreme Court. In 1976 Richards decided to stage her own campaign for public office and ran for Travis County commissioner, and she won. She was reelected to the position in 1980, won an election for state treasurer in 1982, and was reelected in 1986. Yet, during this period of political ascension, Richards's personal life was plummeting into ruin. Her marriage had ended in divorce, and her drinking grew out of control. She entered and completed rehabilitation, and in 1990 Richards succeeded in becoming the second-ever woman governor of Texas (the first being Miriam "Ma" Ferguson in the 1920s and 1930s). During the first few years of her governorship "a New Texas," Richards claimed, had been born.

A slew of achievements ornamented Richards's term as an effective, progressive, and culturally liberal Texas governor, including increasing the number of women and minorities appointed to state government posts, revitaliz-

ing the Texas economy, instituting the state lottery, introducing insurance and environmental reform, establishing a substance-abuse program for inmates, and lowering the number of violent inmates released.

In what was widely considered an uninspired reelection campaign, Richards lost the governorship to the son of the vice president whom she had jokingly put down in 1988, George W. Bush. Although Bush was inexperienced as a politician, despite his paternal background, he ran a cunning and successful campaign that pitted a number of Richards's liberal, yet then-popular, achievements against her. Republicans who had crossed the party line to elect her governor returned to their GOP roots, citing fiscal irresponsibility and a lax attitude toward criminal punishment among their reasons for abandoning her.

After leaving office, Ann Richards worked as a public speaker and as a lobbyist for a high-profile Washington law firm. In 2006 she died of esophageal cancer and was laid to rest in the Texas State Cemetery in Austin.

JAMES G. THOMAS JR.
University of Mississippi

Ann Richards and Peter Knobler, *Straight from the Heart: My Life in Politics and Other Places* (1989); Mike Shropshire and Frank Schaeffer, *The Thorny Rose of Texas: An Intimate Portrait of Governor Ann Richards* (1994); Sue Tolleson-Rinehart and Jeanie R. Stanley, *Claytie and the Lady: Ann Richards, Gender, and Politics in Texas* (1994).

Russell, Richard B.

(1897–1971) POLITICIAN.
Richard Brevard Russell, a dominant
force in the U.S. Senate for almost four
decades, was born in Winder, Ga., on
2 November 1897. After earning a law
degree at the University of Georgia in
1918, he began practicing law in his
hometown.

The son of a state legislator who
became the chief justice of the Georgia
Supreme Court, Russell began his public career in 1921 when he won election
to the Georgia House of Representatives. By the time he was 30 he was the
Speaker of that assembly, and in 1931
he became Georgia's youngest chief
executive. His two years as governor are
remembered for the reorganization that
reduced the number of agencies and
departments.

When the incumbent U.S. senator
died in 1932, Russell won the special
election to replace him. From 1933 until
his death on 21 January 1971, he served
on the Appropriations Committee,
rising through the seniority system to
become its chair during his last two
years. Of perhaps greater note was his
service on the Naval Affairs Committee
and, after the 1947 Legislative Reorganization Act, on the Armed Services
Committee, which he chaired for 16
years prior to 1969. From this base
Russell developed his reputation as a
leading Senate expert on national defense. Although an advocate of a strong
military, he opposed the commitment
of American troops to Southeast Asia.
Nonetheless, once his advice was rejected, he staunchly supported the military action.

The other major feature of Russell's
career—the second longest in Senate history—was his leadership of the
southern wing of the Democratic Party.
He was a master of the chamber's rules,
which he used to thwart liberal policy
initiatives. He was the chief strategist
in southern efforts to defeat, or at least
weaken, civil rights bills. Although
Russell became a leader of the bipartisan Conservative Coalition, he began
his career as a New Deal Democrat.
Once the economic crisis receded,
Russell, like many southern members of
Congress, backed away from additional
welfare proposals and government
regulations.

In 1948 and 1952 Russell's name was
placed in nomination for the presidency
at the Democratic National Convention.
Considered a gifted political leader,
Russell was ambitious for the presidency and frustrated at never gaining
it. He and many political commentators
blamed this failure on his being southern; his opposition to civil rights legislation did, in fact, effectively limit his
national appeal. Russell was instrumental in promoting the career of Lyndon
Johnson, much of whose presidency
Russell came to oppose.

CHARLES S. BULLOCK III
University of Georgia

Harry Conn, *New Republic* (12 May 1952);
Gilbert Courtland Fite, *Richard B. Russell Jr.,
Senator from Georgia* (1991); John A. Gold-
smith, *Colleagues: Richard B. Russell and
His Apprentice Lyndon B. Johnson* (1998);
Harold H. Martin, *Saturday Evening Post*
(2 June 1951); *New Republic* (6 February
1971); Richard B. Russell, Calvin M. Logue,
and Dwight L. Freshley, *Voice of Georgia:*

Speeches of Richard B. Russell, 1928–1969 (1997); *Time* (1 February 1971); Jeff Woods, *Richard B. Russell: Southern Nationalism and American Foreign Policy* (2006).

Secession

The politics of secession consisted of the separate actions of individual southern states in late 1860 and early 1861 and did not represent a unified South acting as a concerted whole. Secession was triggered in November 1860 by the election of Lincoln to the presidency, at the head of a sectionalized Republican Party that was publicly committed to prohibiting the expansion of slavery into the federal territories and pledged—though recognizing slavery in the states where it already existed—to the ultimate extinction of slavery. Secession itself occurred in two distinct waves; in each it generally received its strongest support from those areas with the heaviest concentrations of slaves.

After a series of hastily called, highly localized, and often closely contested elections, delegates chosen on a county-wide basis attended state conventions convened to decide the question of secession. Seven states had left the Union by 1 February 1861. This first wave—South Carolina, Mississippi, Florida, Alabama, Georgia, Louisiana, and Texas—comprised the original Confederate States of America, the provisional constitution for which was adopted in Montgomery, Ala., on 7 February 1861.

In the meantime Unionist sentiment remained dominant in the states of the Upper South. Here the proportion of slaves to the total population was but half that of the Lower South (25 as op-posed to 50 percent), fears of slave uprisings were less intense, economic and cultural ties with the free states were deeper, and the prosecessionist wing of the Democratic Party did not control local politics. Secession was temporarily halted. Nonetheless, virtually all political factions in the Upper South conceded the legal right of secession and agreed that any effort to coerce a seceded state back into the Union should be resisted.

Lincoln was inaugurated in early March, and any lingering opportunity for reunion floundered over the issue of the expansion of slavery. The second wave of secession was unleashed when Fort Sumter fell to the Confederacy in April and Lincoln called for state militia to put down what the North believed was a rebellion. Four additional slave states from the Upper South—Arkansas, North Carolina, Virginia, and Tennessee—joined the Confederacy rather than bear arms against fellow southern whites.

The secessionists had appealed successfully to values of individual autonomy, freedom from arbitrary power, and political self-determination. Embedded within America's 19th-century political culture and most often applied to whites only, these values could be used either for or against the Union and either to attack or defend slavery. The politics of secession ensured that this debate would be settled only by a civil war.

WILLIAM L. BARNEY
University of North Carolina at Chapel Hill

Christopher J. Olsen, *Political Culture and Secession in Mississippi: Masculinity, Honor, and the Antiparty Tradition, 1830–1860* (2002); David M. Potter, in *The Impending Crisis, 1848–1861*, ed. Don E. Fehrenbacher (1976); Ralph A. Wooster, *The Secession Conventions of the South* (1962); Bertram Wyatt-Brown, in *Religion and the American Civil War*, ed. Randall M. Miller, Harry S. Stout, and Charles Reagan Wilson (1998).

Smith, Frank

(1918–1997) POLITICIAN.

Frank Smith represented white southerners who rejected segregation during the 1950s and 1960s. Despite being born and reared in the Mississippi Delta, where segregation of the races was the unquestioned social system, Smith developed "liberal" social and political attitudes. Educated at Sunflower Junior College and the University of Mississippi, Smith went to war in 1942 as a private and returned a captain, a veteran of General Patton's Third Army. He came back to the Delta, to Greenwood, to help establish the liberal *Morning Star* and entered the state senate in 1947. Leaving the newspaper, he worked in John Stennis's Senate campaign and went to Washington as Stennis's assistant.

In 1950 Smith ran for the Delta's congressional seat and defeated a states' rights candidate. Smith established himself through constituent service and good congressional relationships as a strong representative. Keeping his belief in racial integration secret, he worked to mitigate the effects of segregation. In Congress, he also worked for free-trade and consumer-protection laws, such as the act requiring content labeling on clothing. Although he obscured his liberalism as much as possible from Delta voters, voting analysis exposed his record, and following the *Brown* decision in 1954 his "moderation" became more evident as Mississippi withdrew from national politics. Smith's adherence to the national Democratic Party's platforms and his backing of John F. Kennedy alienated many supporters. In 1962 the segregationists redistricted Smith into a race that he would not win.

Smith's defeat coincided with the integration crisis at the University of Mississippi. Because Smith publicly condemned the state's segregationist government, he was effectively exiled from the state by a power structure that saw him as a traitor. Kennedy appointed Smith to the Tennessee Valley Authority (TVA) board of directors; from that office Smith wrote an autobiography to explain his development into a liberal and advocated integration and voting rights for blacks. During Smith's years at TVA (1962–72) he wrote increasingly about environmental issues. Through his books and his position he worked for intelligent management of natural resources, doing battle with both industry and preservationists.

He continued to work toward leading Mississippi and the South into the American mainstream socially and politically. During his exile from Mississippi, Smith discreetly encouraged a moderate group within the Mississippi Democratic Party and worked for cooperation with newly enfranchised black voters. Leaving TVA, Smith ran for Congress in a new district of central Mississippi. Defeated and denied appointive positions in Mississippi, he turned to academic posts in Illinois and Virginia. In the first, he dealt with a plan for environmental education, and in the second, he examined southern politics.

Although Smith published a book of essays outlining his philosophy entitled *Look Away from Dixie*, he did not look away. Instead, he ended his years of public service as special assistant to Governor William Winter of Mississippi (1980–84). In a sense his life's work was realized, because metaphorically Mississippi had rejoined the Union.

Smith's personal correspondence is filled with letters from Mississippians praising his defiance of the segregationist power structure and lamenting their forced silence. Smith clearly was a spokesman for southern white integrationists and moderates offended by the excesses of the segregationists. He was important as a symbol for whites because he was undeniably a Mississippian. Other integrationists were dismissed as outsiders who did not understand, but Frank Smith was one of their own and an integrationist. After retiring from politics, Smith ran a bookstore in Jackson.

DENNIS J. MITCHELL
Mississippi State University at Meridian

Dennis J. Mitchell, *Mississippi Liberal: A Biography of Frank E. Smith* (2001); Frank Smith, *Congressman from Mississippi* (1964), *Look Away from Dixie* (1965), *The Politics of Conservation* (1966), *The Yazoo River* (1954).

Southern Governors' Association

The Southern Governors' Association was born at the urging of President Franklin D. Roosevelt for an organization that would foster cooperation among southern states in a unified effort to address the economic conditions of the South, judged in the 1930s to be the nation's top problem. The association was created after five southern governors met with Roosevelt to discuss the inequitable railroad rate-differential system. Within a few weeks following the 1934 meeting, the association started up with five charter members. By 2006 membership included Alabama, Mississippi, Louisiana, Texas, Georgia, Arkansas, Missouri, North Carolina, South Carolina, Tennessee, Virginia, West Virginia, Kentucky, Maryland, Oklahoma, Puerto Rico, and the U.S. Virgin Islands.

The first issue tackled by the association, the crippling railroad rate-differential system, was reflective of the region's colonial status in the national economy. Northern owners of southern capital restricted the southern economy to producing raw materials for northern manufacturing. And southerners chafed that the region with almost a third of the nation's population was contributing less than 15 percent to the national economy, which resulted in poverty, low wages, poor working conditions, and desperation among the region's leaders for improvement. In effect, railroad shipping rates were low when the South shipped raw materials to the North but high for finished goods. And it was less expensive for northern firms to ship finished goods to the South.

The first resolution emanating from the Southern Governors' Association called for Congress and the president to end such discriminatory rate policies.

Although it took much longer than expected, the association succeeded in ending the rate-differentials years later. Since then, the association has focused on other complex issues facing the region and its residents. By 1982, the association realized it could better represent the regional interests if it relocated its headquarters from Atlanta, Ga., to Washington, D.C.

The Southern Governors' Association served to unify southern state chief executives behind a common purpose—the economic and social uplift of the region. And from the rate-differential issue that first brought them together to dealing with the aftereffects of Hurricane Katrina in 2005 and 2006, the association has addressed the region's biggest challenges in its existence: from infant mortality to education reform, atomic power to economic development. Offshoots of the association, which focus exclusively on several such issues, include the Southern Growth Policies Board, the Southern Regional Educational Board, the Southern Regional Project on Infant Mortality, and the Southern States Energy Board.

GORDON E. HARVEY
University of Louisiana at Monroe

James C. Cobb, *The Selling of the South: The Southern Crusade for Industrial Development, 1936–1990*, 2nd ed. (1993); Carole E. Scott, *Essays in Economic and Business History*, vol. 9 (1991); Gavin Wright, *Old South, New South: Revolutions in the Southern Economy since the Civil War* (1986).

Southern Strategy

Southern politics underwent a watershed in the 1960s with the congruence of several factors. The landmark legislation of the civil rights movement, specifically the Civil Rights Act of 1964 and the Voting Rights Act of 1965, and the thousands of African Americans who registered with and voted for the Democratic Party, transformed the southern political landscape. White southern conservatives reached the conclusion that "their" party was changing, and they sought other outlets for their political support.

In 1950 not a single Republican could be found among the region's U.S. Senate delegation. In 1964 Barry Goldwater's defeat of Lyndon Johnson in the South using a racially charged presidential campaign broke the power of the Democratic Party over the region and began the switch from solidly Democratic to solidly Republican in presidential voting by 1980. Richard Nixon's "southern strategy" serves as an important stage in the growth of the Republican South.

Into this late-1960s political flux marched George Wallace. In 1968 Wallace's American Independent Party campaign shocked political observers with his criticism of "pointy headed intellectuals" and his attacks on Washington "bureaucrats" from both parties. He appealed to a white, working-class electorate that felt overburdened with taxes, ignored by their elected representatives, and discriminated against in favor of African American voters. He garnered almost 13 percent of the vote and 46 electoral votes in the general election—mostly from "Deep South" states. Wallace won 40 percent of the southern white vote to Nixon's 45 percent. In the South, Wallace's support came from those white conservatives who were in an apolitical limbo of sorts, not comfortable in the "new" Democratic Party, but not yet trusting enough in the Republican Party to dive fully in.

Nixon's early use of the southern strategy came in the 1968 election and was perfected in the years leading up to his 1972 reelection campaign. Advised by South Carolinian Harry S. Dent, Nixon began to appeal to southern conservatives with coded language and with hollow commitments to racial progress. At once, Nixon issued vague endorsements for racial equality while resisting the implementation of policies designed to meet that goal. Nixon also criticized "forced" busing to achieve school integration and insisted the Justice Department pursue integration at a slower pace than before. He spoke of the need for more "law and order" and increased prosecution for drug use. More telling was the Dent/Nixon strategy of desegregating the South, but seeing to it that federal judges and Democrats were blamed for it. Thanks to Dent's suggestion, the Nixon administration shifted desegregation cases to the courts and then blamed "activist judges" for the decisions.

When Abe Fortas resigned from the U.S. Supreme Court in 1969, Nixon furthered his appeals to southern conservative sentiments by his nomination of South Carolina's Clement Haynsworth to the Court. Haynsworth had little chance of confirmation since his racial views were controversial and well known. Nixon then nominated Florida's

G. Harrold Carswell, whose nomination was doomed by a similar racist paper trail. After blaming Democrats for the failed nominations, Nixon then nominated Minnesota's Harry Blackmun, who received unanimous confirmation to the Court.

Nixon's landslide reelection in 1972 saw the South vote solidly Republican for the first time. The southern strategy had succeeded marvelously, and white conservatives had found their presidential home, while the Republican Party had found the foundation to its presidential and later congressional electoral success in later decades.

GORDON E. HARVEY
University of Louisiana at Monroe

Joseph A. Aistrup, *The Southern Strategy Revisited: Republican Top-Down Advancement in the South* (1996); Earl Black and Merle Black, *The Rise of Southern Republicans* (2003); Dan Carter, *The Politics of Rage: George Wallace, the Origins of the New Conservatism, and the Transformation of American Politics* (1995); Michael Schaller and George Rising, *The Republican Ascendancy: American Politics, 1968–2001* (2002).

Talmadge, Eugene

(1884–1946) POLITICIAN.
Born in Forsyth, Monroe County, Ga., the son of Thomas and Carrie Talmadge and father of U.S. Senator Herman Talmadge, Eugene Talmadge served several terms as governor of Georgia during the period of ferment in which he dominated Georgia politics (1926–46). He was known for his fiery political style that evoked fanatical loyalty from thousands of agrarian supporters who

Eugene Talmadge on the Georgia campaign trail, 1936 (Georgia Department of Archives and History, Atlanta)

responded to his appeals in celebration and defense of rural Georgia's embattled culture and lifestyle.

As his political style evolved from populistic agrarianism to virulent racism, Talmadge gained notoriety as the stereotype of a southern demagogue, a "Cracker buffoon," a "redneck racist." At the peak of his popularity, Talmadge drew crowds of 20,000 to 30,000 for campaign rallies in small towns throughout Georgia. Country folk from everywhere in the state came to stand in the hot Georgia sun and eat barbecue, sneak a swig or two of corn liquor, listen to "Fiddlin' John" Carson's country music, and take in "Farmer Gene's" political road show. With the appropriate southern drawl and proper quotations from the Scriptures, Talmadge conjured up vivid images of a blessed but embattled rural lifestyle, condemned the farmers' enemies as if he were a country preacher railing against Satan, and promised "he-man" action in the farmers' interests against the minions of such alien forces as "mastadon trusts" and Wall Street.

Talmadge's rural political style represented in many ways a significant agrarian response to the vast changes associated with the emergence of modern America. In a process begun in the late 19th century, the older America of autonomous rural communities was breaking down before the new centralized bureaucratic order, which served "the regulative hierarchical needs of urban-industrial life." "Farmer Gene's" response was similar to the earlier efforts of the Southern Farmers' Alliance and the Populist Party led in Georgia by Thomas Watson.

Both Talmadge and Watson made cultural appeals to Georgia farmers at times when their rural lifestyle seemed seriously threatened by circumstances largely beyond their control. In many ways Talmadge's style reflected his support of southern agrarian culture. This can be said about his appeals to his fellow Georgians' fundamentalist religious beliefs, to their habits of "macho" individualism and personal violence, and to their localistic lifestyle centering on long-term attachments to specific places and specific people. Moreover, many of his actions seemed to be designed to preserve Georgia's rural culture in the face of powerful assaults from the outside world, including his attacks on the New Deal federal government. Talmadge always based his defense of rural Georgia on traditional Democratic Party principles: the "classical" economic doctrines of Adam Smith and the political doctrines of Thomas Jefferson and the Jacksonian Democrats. When "Farmer Gene" burst upon the Georgia political scene, the Bourbon Democratic establishment supported the New

South creed, which celebrated the union in the South of the American pastoral and industrial images described by Leo Marx in *The Machine in the Garden*. Talmadge's political style rejected the Bourbons' ideological synthesis and constructed a sacred mysticism out of the elements of southern rural culture. Earlier, "Farmer Gene's" Populist precursors had called for variation in the traditional principles of the Democratic Party when they proposed legislation and other actions requiring significant government power to bring the party's outlook into line with changing realities. Once this effort failed, however, their defense of the rural lifestyle and of the traditional Democratic principles turned into something akin to an irrational emotional response to attacks on a sacred mysticism.

At the zenith of his career, Talmadge was bold enough to muster his agrarian forces against President Franklin D. Roosevelt, but something went awry and "Farmer Gene's" rural political style failed to hold enough supporters firmly to his banner to carry him through the fight. Under normal circumstances his style offered great promise of success. It focused on the cultural issues (tied to rural Georgians' "personally structured value systems"), which, along with purely local concerns, usually dominated American politics before the New Deal. After such a serious crisis as the Great Depression allowed economic issues to capture the voters' attention, however, Talmadge's rural and political style declined in effectiveness from its peak of the mid-1930s. In his later campaigns, "Farmer Gene" focused on the race issue as he tried to find another cultural issue that could earn him votes in rural Georgia.

KARL RODABAUGH
East Carolina University

William Anderson, *The Wild Man from Sugar Creek: The Political Career of Eugene Talmadge* (1975); Sarah Lemmon, "The Public Career of Eugene Talmadge, 1926–1936" (Ph.D. dissertation, University of North Carolina, Chapel Hill, 1952); Calvin McLeod Logue, *Eugene Talmadge: Rhetoric and Response* (1989); Karl Rodabaugh, *Southern Studies* (Spring 1982).

Taylor, John

(1753–1824) POLITICAL PHILOSOPHER, WRITER, AND PLANTER.

John Taylor, born in December 1753 in Caroline County, Va., is referred to as "John Taylor of Caroline"; he was one of the fathers of southern politics. He was more famous in his own time than later; his prestige was such that he was several times elected U.S. senator from what was then the most powerful state in the Union without campaigning and against his wishes. He was a soldier in the American Revolution who died regretting that the Revolution had ended in the construction of a federal government more dangerous to the colonies than that of Great Britain. He retired from a lucrative law practice to become not only a highly successful planter and agricultural reformer but the foremost political defender and philosopher that American agriculture ever had. He was an eloquent advocate of economic, political, and religious freedom for the citizen and an unbending defender of slavery.

Taylor may even be said to have been a pioneer figure in southern literature. His books and pamphlets are not only full of keen political and economic analysis but are written in a colloquial style—full of satire, hyperbole, and front-porch digressions—highly suggestive of the oral tradition evident in later southern writers.

Taylor embodied many persistent and recurrent tendencies and themes of southern politics. He represented both a conservative allegiance to local community and inherited ways and a radical-populist suspicion of capitalism, "progress," government, and routine logrolling politics. He was at the same time more radical and more conservative than his friend, admirer, and fellow Virginia planter Thomas Jefferson. Taylor was Jefferson's down-home side—exactly what Jefferson would have been like had he been less cosmopolitan and less of a practical politician. In many respects Taylor was a more authentic voice of Jeffersonianism than was Jefferson himself. Taylor's Old Republican defense of states' rights, strict construction, and intelligent farming and his opposition to federal power, judicial oligarchy, paper money, stock jobbing, taxation, and expenditure were reflexive, reluctant defenses of native soil and were based upon the unyielding conviction that an unoppressed and predominantly agricultural population was the only possible basis for free government.

At the core of Taylor's thinking was a

belief that the world is divided between producers and parasites. The producers are decent folk who labor in the earth for their daily bread and produce everything of real economic and moral value in society. They are subject to endless depredations from those that Taylor referred to as "aristocrats." By aristocrats he meant not people of good birth but people, mostly northerners, whose main business was manipulating the government for artificial advantages for themselves. This view of the world, as much a folk attitude as a philosophical position, is a recurrent theme in much of southern culture and behavior.

Taylor's more important works are *Definition of Parties; or, the Political Effects of the Paper System* (1794), *An Enquiry into the Principles and Tendency of Certain Public Measures* (1794), *A Defense of the Measures of the Administration of Thomas Jefferson* (1804), *Arator, Being a Series of Agricultural Essays, Practical and Political: In Sixty-Four Numbers* (1814), *An Inquiry into the Principles and Policy of the Government of the United States* (1814), *Construction Construed, and Constitutions Vindicated* (1820), *Tyranny Unmasked* (1822), and *New Views of the Constitution of the United States* (1823).

CLYDE N. WILSON
University of South Carolina

M. E. Bradford, introduction to *John Taylor, Arator* (1977 reprint); Charles William Hill, *The Political Theory of John Taylor of Caroline* (1997); Eugene T. Mudge, *The Social Philosophy of John Taylor of Caroline* (1939); Robert E. Shalhope, *John Taylor of Caroline: Pastoral Republican* (1980).

Taylor, Zachary

(1784–1850) GENERAL AND U.S. PRESIDENT.

Although Zachary Taylor was a landed southerner and slaveholder, he was a fervent nationalist, and during his brief yet tumultuous tenure as U.S. president preceding the Civil War he was prepared to hold the Union together at any cost.

Taylor grew up on a plantation in the frontier settlement of Louisville, Ky., after his family relocated there from Virginia when he was still an infant. During his early childhood, his family home was a modest cabin in the woods, but as his father grew more prosperous he accumulated a substantial amount of land and slaves, eventually building his family a larger brick home, which young Zachary shared with his seven siblings. Even during his early years Taylor aspired to military life, and he eventually enlisted. In 1808 he earned his first commission as an officer. His assignment was commander of the garrison at Fort Pickering, located where the city of Memphis is today.

In 1810 Taylor married Margaret Mackall Smith, and for the next 30 years she and their children followed him from military post to military post, finally settling in Baton Rouge, La., in 1840, where he served as fort commander. Military life provided Taylor with only the scantest financial stability, yet he shrewdly turned the 300 acres given him by his father into sizable landholdings in Mississippi, Louisiana, and Kentucky.

In 1845, when Texas achieved statehood, Mexico challenged the United

States' annexation of the territory, and President James Polk sent General Taylor into Mexico where he won great victories at Monterrey (September 1846) and Buena Vista (February 1847) in what had become the Mexican-American War. On the field of battle Taylor earned the designation of "Old Rough and Ready" because of his willingness to endure the same physical conditions that his troops did, and he soon became celebrated as a national hero.

With the 1848 presidential election looming and the issue of slavery's spread into new territories weighing heavily upon the nation's conscience, Taylor, a wealthy slave owner now, seemed an obvious choice as a southern candidate. At the same time, Taylor appealed to northerners because of his dedicated service to the Union during the war. While Taylor supported slavery, he prevaricated on its spread into the new western territories, but he also opposed secession as a solution to America's slavery problem. In the end Taylor accepted the Whig Party's nomination, with the New Yorker Millard Fillmore as his vice presidential running mate. That November Taylor won the presidency, beating the Democratic Party's candidate, Lewis Cass, and the Free Soil Party's candidate, the former president Martin Van Buren, whose party opposed any extension of slavery into new states and territories.

During his presidency the issue of slavery's western expansion became increasingly heated. Taylor grew to oppose the expansion, in part because of the Whig Party's solid opposition to it. His solution to the problem was to let the new territories apply for statehood and thus allow each state to vote on whether to allow slavery. California had applied for statehood as a free state, and it was expected that New Mexico would follow suit. As Taylor's loyalty to the opposition of western slavery grew unyielding, southern senators began to call for secession. Taylor, ever the nationalist, made it clear that he would not hesitate to use the U.S. military to suppress any form of rebellion.

Taylor's ultimate solution became known as the Compromise of 1850. Much to the displeasure of southern states, who had counted on the equal balance between the number of free and slave states, Congress admitted California as a free state, but as a concession to the South the territories of Utah, New Mexico, Nevada, and Arizona were to be organized without any federal restriction on slavery, thus leaving the door open to that possibility once they did apply for statehood. Also, a second Fugitive Slave Law mandated that all states participate in the return of any escaped slaves to their rightful owners. Before 1850 that responsibility rested solely with the federal government, and the new law made recovery of fugitive slaves considerably easier. This relaxation of the first Fugitive Slave Law (1793) infuriated northern abolitionists, further fanning the flames of the slavery controversy.

Later that year, before Taylor could fully comprehend the effects of his compromise, he fell ill at a Fourth of July celebration in Washington, D.C., and five days later he died. He is buried in Louisville, Ky., in the Zachary Taylor National Cemetery. His only son went on to fight as a general for the Confederacy in the Civil War between the free North and slave South that Taylor had tried so desperately to prevent.

JAMES G. THOMAS JR.
University of Mississippi

K. Jack Bauer, *Zachary Taylor: Soldier, Planter, Statesman of the Old Southwest* (1993); Michael F. Holt, *The Rise and Fall of the American Whig Party: Jacksonian Politics and the Onset of the Civil War* (1999); Silas Bent McKinley, *Old Rough and Ready: The Life and Times of Zachary Taylor* (1946).

Thurmond, Strom

(1902–2003) POLITICIAN.
Born in Edgefield, S.C., on 5 December 1902 of a prominent political family, Strom Thurmond was active in politics for more than half a century. Personifying the conservative nature of the region, Thurmond was an ageless institution reminiscent of W. J. Cash's metaphorical South, "a tree with many age rings . . . bent and twisted by all the winds of the years, but with roots in the Old South."

The formative influences on Thurmond began with his father and were enhanced by the deep political and historical forces of his native Edgefield. William Watts Ball, editor of the *Charleston News and Courier*, once observed that Edgefield "had more dashing, brilliant, romantic figures, statesmen, orators, soldiers, adventurers, and daredevils than any county of South Carolina." This rural county has produced 10 governors, half as many lieutenant governors, and a number of

Strom Thurmond, Dixiecrat candidate for the presidency and longtime Republican U.S. senator. Photo taken in the 1980s. (Senate Office, Strom Thurmond, Washington, D.C.)

U.S. senators. Additionally, Edgefield harbors a deep strain of violence, which originated in the 18th century and has been rather proudly maintained into the 21st. There is also in the area a core of evangelical fundamentalism, which emerged in Thurmond's personality and value system.

The blood feuds of the 19th century and the code duello that characterized much of the South have approached a cultural norm in South Carolina. In 1856 Congressman Preston Brooks of Edgefield caned Senator Charles Sumner of Massachusetts into insensibility because of a Sumner speech that Brooks regarded as slanderous. Strom's father "had to kill a man" as a result of a political feud. Senator Benjamin Ryan Tillman, also from Edgefield, and a close personal friend of Thurmond's father, initiated a fist fight on the Senate floor with a colleague. A less spectacular example of the Edgefield tradition occurred when Strom Thurmond twice pinned Senator Ralph Yarborough outside a committee room in order to prevent a quorum.

Thurmond made his national reputation as a presidential candidate in 1948, leading a dissident band of segregationists in their defection from the national Democratic Party. Thurmond and his Dixiecrats were manifestations of the stress inherent in the New Deal coalition bequeathed to Harry Truman. Thurmond's secession in 1948 was reminiscent of pre–Civil War tensions when regional candidates bolted the democracy to close ranks behind defenders of southern values and their peculiar institution. Not since the days of John C. Calhoun had the South seen such a popular symbolic leader as Thurmond. Indeed, Thurmond as a neo-Calhounite added a fascinating historical dimension as the South faced its "Second Reconstruction."

By a kind of historic osmosis Thurmond absorbed the ethos of familial and regional values. The development of his personal value system mirrored his social environment. Thurmond's conceptual interaction with the world around him was essentially fundamentalist. As a literalist he saw things in absolute terms. A Manichaean by nature, Thurmond had a vision of events dominated, as Robert Sherrill put it, by "metaphysical absolutes" where there is "one Eden, one Hell, one Heaven, one Right, one Wrong, and one Strom." The most revealing source of Thurmond's political fundamentalism,

vision of history, and analysis of contemporary political events is his book, *The Faith We Have Not Kept*, published in 1966.

To some, Strom Thurmond was nothing more than a segregationist with a penchant for young women. However, deeper analysis shows Thurmond to possess a prismlike quality through which national issues are refracted, making him a symbolic figure of a South in transition. After the Voting Rights Act of 1965 and the increase of black voters in South Carolina, Thurmond ended his overtly segregationist rhetoric and began seeking black votes. The South of 1948 is light-years from the South of today, and the evolution of Thurmond and the South have stood as twin testaments to a man and a region that achieved some accommodation with their history.

The appeal of Strom Thurmond was best captured by the reply of a millworker, when asked why he was voting for Thurmond: "Strom stands up for what he believes in, even when he's wrong." In sum, Thurmond was the quintessential southern politician: enduring yet resilient, simple but canny, militaristic yet biblical, and always the candidate.

Thurman died on 26 June 2003. Shortly afterward, his illegitimate daughter, Essie Mae Washington-Williams, came forward, revealing her father's secret support for her over the years and revealing a new aspect of the complicated life of a major southern political leader.

JAMES G. BANKS
Cuyahoga Community College

James G. Banks, "Strom Thurmond and the Revolt against Modernity" (Ph.D. dissertation, Kent State University, 1970); Jack Bass and Walter DeVries, *The Transformation of Southern Politics: Social Change and Political Consequence since 1945* (1976); Jack Bass and Marilyn W. Thompson, *Ol' Strom: An Unauthorized Biography of Strom Thurmond* (1998).

Tillman, Benjamin Ryan

(1847–1918) POLITICIAN.
Born in the Edgefield district of upcountry South Carolina, Ben Tillman grew up in a well-off farm family and went on to become the prototype of the southern rural demagogue. As a youth, he lived through the turmoil of the Civil War but first made his political mark during Reconstruction. He was a member of a rifle club movement, later known as the Red Shirts, which worked to restore white rule. Tillman took part in the Hamburg Massacre in July of 1876, during which whites murdered black militia members. It fractured peace between Democrats and Republicans and contributed to the electoral crisis of 1876–77, which eventually brought an end to Reconstruction. The white leaders who came to power, led by Wade Hampton III, were a coalition of planters, merchants, railroad developers, and others who became a new ruling class called the Bourbons, or Redeemers.

Tillman became a leader of a Farmers' Alliance in the mid-1880s, portraying himself as the advocate for common farm folk against the powers that be. He was a rabble-rouser, denouncing his state's political leadership as backward-looking aristocrats who were out of touch with ordinary people. He urged changes in taxation and legislative apportionment and became popular as the promoter of a "farmer's college." He claimed the mantle as spokesman for the upcountry against the lowcountry.

South Carolina voters elected Tillman governor in 1890 and reelected him in 1892. He achieved modest reforms in railroad-rate regulation and restrictions on child labor. He imposed state control of liquor sales and created a whites-only Democratic Party primary. He identified himself with the Farmers' Alliance but distanced himself from the Populist Party, which he saw as radical in its call for a greater government role in the economy and in its promotion of black voting rights. Tillman's racist outlook brought him his greatest notice. He was a leader of disfranchisement of African American voters at the 1895 South Carolina Constitutional Convention. He became a U.S. senator that same year, and his racist rhetoric made him infamous in other parts of the nation. He delivered a speech countless times in which he discussed southern race relations and admitted he would gladly take part in a lynch mob against any black man accused of rape. Tillman also spoke out against corporations and trusts, opposing the "money power" that he believed worked against agrarian interests. He opposed American territorial expansion as benefiting only corporations.

Tillman was a colorful and flamboyant politician. He had gained the nickname "Pitchfork Ben" as a result of threatening to stick a pitchfork in

Grover Cleveland when the two disagreed. His extreme rhetoric, blatant racism, and justification of violence stirred mass emotions among his struggling white farm constituents. He was significant as a leading southern insurgent who threatened the existing state and local power structure that often ignored the plight of the plain folk in the closing decades of the 19th century.

CHARLES REAGAN WILSON
University of Mississippi

Stephen Kantrowitz, *Ben Tillman and the Reconstruction of White Supremacy* (2000); Francis Butler Simkins, *Pitchfork Ben Tillman: South Carolinian* (1944).

Voting Rights Act (1965)

Two things have changed the modern South: Air-conditioning and the Voting Rights Act. Unfortunately, Americans have a better understanding of how air-conditioning functions than they do the Voting Rights Act.

Because discriminatory administration of state laws and constitutional amendments undermined federal protection of the rights of minority voters, Congress passed the Voting Rights Act in 1965. The act changed the landscape of electoral politics in America, overthrowing three generations of disfranchisement. After the Civil War and Emancipation, Reconstruction brought to formerly enslaved African Americans freedom, citizenship, and the right to vote under the Thirteenth, Fourteenth, and Fifteenth Amendments. Yet, when Reconstruction ended, these constitutional amendments did not ensure a fair and equal vote. Recalcitrant whites, including organizations such as the Ku

Klux Klan, used terrorist and fraudulent antisuffrage activities to deny African Americans the right to vote. A series of court cases systematically dismantled the civil and voting rights legislation of the first Reconstruction. Legal methods of disfranchising African Americans included gerrymandering, at-large elections, registration and secret ballot laws, the poll tax, literacy tests, and the white primary. By the early 20th century, these methods had effectively disfranchised millions of African Americans. In 1958 the Civil Rights Commission reported that there were 44 counties in the Deep South where there was not a single black voter registered. Many of these counties had large African American populations; some had black American majorities.

The 1965 Voting Rights Act banned literacy tests, facilitated lawsuits to prohibit discriminatory laws or practices, and sent federal voting registrars into intractable areas. In addition, section 5 of the Voting Rights Act required "covered jurisdictions," all initially in the South, to obtain "preclearance" from the U.S. Department of Justice for any change in their electoral procedures. An immediate effect of more minority voters was the replacement of blatant bigotry in electioneering with more subtle racial appeals. A longer-term effect has been the election of minority citizens to almost every level of government.

South Carolina, joined by other southern states, challenged the Voting Rights Act in 1966 in *South Carolina v. Katzenbach*, claiming that the act violated its right to control and implement elections. After the Supreme Court rejected this challenge, Mississippi and Virginia filed *Allen v. Board of Elections* (1969), contending, again unsuccessfully, that the act protected only the right to cast a ballot, not the right to have nondiscriminatory election structures, such as district elections. Congress renewed all the provisions of the Voting Rights Act in 1970 and 1975, amending it in 1975 to include, in section 203, provisions to protect language minorities, such as Asian, Hispanic, and Native American voters.

After its initial victories in court, the Voting Rights Act began to suffer defeats. In *Beer v. U.S.* (1976), the Supreme Court ruled that section 5 of the act did not prevent discriminatory election laws generally, but only those that resulted in a "retrogression" of minority influence. For instance, after African Americans were enfranchised by the act, a local jurisdiction could shift district lines in order to ensure a continuation of all-white government, and the Department of Justice had to allow the change to go into effect. Even more significant, a four-person plurality of the U.S. Supreme Court ruled in *Mobile v. Bolden* (1980) that no election law violated section 2 of the act or the Fifteenth Amendment to the Constitution unless it could be shown that the law had been adopted with a racially discriminatory intent. During the First Reconstruction, in 1874, Mobile, Ala., had instituted at-large elections; after the passage of the act in 1965, many other southern localities switched from district to at-large elections. In such elections because whites who outnumber minorities

generally vote for whites (i.e., racial bloc vote), minorities had a much more difficult time getting elected, and under *Bolden*, minority plaintiffs had a much more difficult time winning lawsuits.

In 1982 Congress not only renewed the preclearance provision of section 5 for 25 years, it also effectively overturned *Bolden* by making clear that a proof of intent was unnecessary to win a section 2 case. Moreover, it weakened *Beer* by instructing the Justice Department not to preclear state or local laws that were discriminatory in either intent or effect. Ironically, in view of the heated two-year struggle in Congress, this strongest version of the act passed by much more overwhelming congressional majorities than ever before. Even more surprising, within two days of the signing of the renewed act, the Supreme Court in *Rogers v. Lodge* announced an effect standard for the act that was nearly identical to that just passed by Congress and that implicitly repudiated the *Bolden* decision of 1980.

Along with the one-person, one-vote ruling of the Supreme Court in *Reynolds v. Sims* (1964), the Voting Rights Act has added another dimension to the politics of redistricting following each decadal census. Once a secretive, unchallengeable practice, redistricting is now played out in courtrooms, as well as back rooms, often ending up before the Supreme Court. The most startling Court decision was *Shaw v. Reno* (1993). Disfranchisement had prevented African Americans from electing a single member of Congress from North Carolina from 1898 to 1965; after 1965 the state's leaders had repeatedly rearranged district boundaries to keep the 11-member delegation all white in a 23 percent black state. But after the 1982 amendments strengthened the Voting Rights Act, a newer generation of North Carolina leaders, under pressure from the U.S. Department of Justice, drew two districts in which 54 percent of the voters were African American. In order to preserve the seats of white Democratic incumbents, North Carolina legislators drew new black-majority districts in even stranger shapes than the districts they replaced. Ignoring previous pro-white racial gerrymandering in the state, five members of the Supreme Court denounced the most integrated congressional districts in North Carolina's history as "segregated" and declared them unconstitutional. White-majority districts could take any shape, the same five justices wrote in a later case from Texas (*Bush v. Vera*, 1996), but black-majority districts could not look "bizarre" to judges. And in a Georgia case, *Miller v. Johnson* (1995), the Supreme Court by the same 5–4 vote announced that black-majority districts could not be drawn with a predominantly racial intent and that white-majority districts could not be challenged under this standard. Finally, in two cases from Bossier Parish, La., the five-person Supreme Court majority ruled that the Justice Department under section 5 of the act had to preclear any election law change, unless it made minorities worse off than before the change. Bossier's school board could thus remain all white.

The Voting Rights Act rid the country of the most outrageous forms of voter disfranchisement. Equal voting rights has meant representation for a large minority of citizens and has brought a tremendous increase in minority elected officials, particularly Native Americans in the West, Hispanics in California and Texas, and literally the election of thousands of African American officeholders across the old Confederacy. The Voting Rights Act is a success story. Designed to increase minority voter registration, it has done so. It has also reduced election-related violence, increased responsiveness and the provision of services to minorities, made the political resources of the minority community, especially African Americans in the South, more available to society as a whole, made it possible for southern solons to support civil rights, made racial politics unfashionable, and opened opportunities for minorities to pursue careers in politics. Despite its significant weakening by a 5–4 majority of the U.S. Supreme Court in the 1990s, the Voting Rights Act continues to have a tremendous influence on American, and especially southern, political life.

ORVILLE VERNON BURTON
University of Illinois at Urbana-Champaign

Chandler Davidson and Bernard Grofman, eds., *Quiet Revolution in the South: The Impact of the Voting Rights Act, 1965–1990* (1994); David Garrow, *Protest at Selma: Martin Luther King Jr. and the Voting Rights Act of 1965* (1978); Nick Kotz, *Judgment Days: Lyndon Baines Johnson, Martin Luther King Jr., and the Laws That Changed America* (2005); J. Morgan Kousser, *Color-blind Injustice: Minority Voting Rights and*

the *Undoing of the Second Reconstruction*
(1999); Steven F. Lawson, *Black Ballots: Voting Rights in the South, 1944–1969* (1976).

Wallace, George

(1919–1998) POLITICIAN.

No other person had as much impact
on Alabama politics in the 20th century
as George Wallace. Born the son of a
farmer on 25 August 1919 in Clio, Ala.,
Wallace attended Barbour County High
School, where he developed his skill at
boxing. He later won the state bantam
weight Golden Gloves championship,
a feat that provided him fodder for his
political rhetoric years later—often
referring to himself as the "fighting little
judge."

In 1937, at the age of 18, Wallace enrolled in the University of Alabama Law
School and supported himself by waiting tables, driving a taxicab, and boxing
professionally, especially after his father
died of Brill's disease shortly after his
arrival at Tuscaloosa. In 1942 Wallace
graduated from law school and enrolled
in the U.S. Army Air Corps. The next
year he married his sweetheart, Lurleen
Burns. While in the service, Wallace
made the first of many calculated political moves, forgoing an opportunity to attend officer training school,
reasoning that his war record would
appear stronger to Alabama voters if
he remained an enlisted man. In 1945
Wallace was medically discharged
from the army suffering from "severe
anxiety."

In 1946 Wallace won his first campaign and represented Barbour County
in the Alabama House of Representatives, where he pursued a liberal agenda

of industrial development, education
reform, and racial moderation. From
1953 until he ran for governor in 1958,
Wallace served as the Third Circuit
Court judge. In 1958 he ran for governor against John Patterson, following a
moderately liberal platform—along the
style of Governor James E. "Big Jim"
Folsom—even refusing the support of
the Klan. Although he ran a tireless
campaign, Wallace lost resoundingly to
Patterson, who appealed to racism and
openly embraced the KKK. Stung by this
defeat, Wallace promised that "no other
son-of-a-bitch will ever out-nigger me
again."

In 1962, after running the most
openly segregationist campaign in state
history, political chameleon Wallace
won a landslide election for governor,
defeating Jim Folsom and a young politician named Ryan deGraffenreid. In his
inaugural address, he delivered a speech
for which he would be forever known,
promising "segregation now, segregation tomorrow, segregation forever."
Less than six months after his 1963 inaugural address, Wallace made another
stand for segregation—this time in the
schoolhouse door of the University of
Alabama. A year later, Wallace made
his first foray into presidential politics,
showing well in the Wisconsin, Maryland, and Indiana Democratic presidential primaries, capturing a third of the
vote in the Wisconsin primary.

Constitutionally forbidden to succeed himself, and desperately needing
a platform from which to launch his
national political aspirations, Wallace
convinced wife Lurleen to run for governor. She won a landslide victory and

Governor George Wallace attempting to block integration at the University of Alabama, 1963 (Warren K. Leffler, photographer, Library of Congress [LC-U9-9930-20], Washington, D.C.)

George became her adviser, even staffing his own office.

In May of 1968 Lurleen Wallace died of cancer, leaving Lt. Governor Albert Brewer in charge. Lurleen's death devastated Wallace while motivating him to pursue the presidency. In 1968 Wallace's American Independent Party campaign shocked political observers with his criticism of "pointy headed intellectuals" and his attacks on Washington "bureaucrats" from both parties. He appealed to a white, working-class electorate that felt overburdened with taxes, ignored by their elected representatives, and discriminated against in favor of African American voters. He garnered almost 13 percent of the popular vote and 46 electoral votes in the general election and set the foundation for Richard Nixon and the Republican "southern strategy" of later years.

Although Wallace had promised Albert Brewer that he would not challenge him for governor in 1970, he nonetheless decided to run. The 1970 Alabama Democratic gubernatorial campaign is considered the nastiest in state history, as Wallace played on racial fears and stereotypes to defeat the moderate Brewer and win the governor's chair for the second time. This time he could succeed himself, thanks to a 1968 constitutional amendment allowing consecutive terms.

Wallace made two other forays into presidential politics, in 1972 and 1976. Although the nation began to moderate racially, Wallace's former statements about race and segregation haunted him as he defended himself by claiming he had always been a moderate. He changed his message to appeal to economic dissatisfaction and parental concern about busing to integrate schools, while also calling for the enforcement of "law and order." Wallace's campaign was cut short when Arthur Bremer shot him at a 1972 Maryland political rally. Paralyzed from the waist down and in constant pain, Wallace still won primaries in Maryland, Michigan, Tennessee, and North Carolina, though he lacked enough support for the nomination, and settled for another term as Alabama governor.

Wallace "retired from the governorship" in 1979, following his third term, but returned for one last campaign in 1982, which marked a remarkable conversion of sorts. He spoke more about God and his relationship with his Savior, sought forgiveness from civil rights leader John Lewis, and made calculated appearances before African American groups, offering a standard apology for his past actions. And they forgave him by giving him their votes for a fourth term as Alabama governor in 1982. Wallace had paid scant attention to his state after 1970 while running for president, but his health forced him to do even less after 1982 as he remained bedridden and suffering from failing health. After his last term ended in 1987, he retired, constantly suffering from the effects of the Bremer shooting. He died on 13 September 1998.

GORDON E. HARVEY
University of Louisiana at Monroe

Dan Carter, *The Politics of Rage: George Wallace, the Origins of the New Conservatism, and the Transformation of American Politics* (1995); Marshall Frady, *Wallace: The Classic Portrait of Alabama Governor George Wallace* (1996); Jeffrey Frederick,

"Command and Control: George Wallace, Governor of Alabama, 1963–1972" (Ph.D. dissertation, Auburn University, 2003); Stephan Lesher, *George Wallace: American Populist* (1995).

Washington, George

(1732–1799) U.S. PRESIDENT.
George Washington was born into a well-established and prosperous Virginia family in 1732. By his own efforts and by his marriage to Martha Dandridge Custis he entered the ranks of the First Families of Virginia. In his youth his loyalties were to Virginia and the British Empire. He became a surveyor as a young man and at 19 became a commander of one of the military districts in Virginia, later playing a prominent military role in the French and Indian Wars. Convinced that it was wrong for one people to have power to tax and to dominate another, he came to the forefront of the Virginia patriots.

Washington served in the Virginia House of Burgesses from 1759 to 1774 and was elected as a delegate to the First Continental Congress. As commander in chief of the Continental Army, he was one of the first to indicate that he desired independence from Britain. He built a sizable army from often raw frontier colonists, maintained the army's discipline and morale under trying circumstances, and kept it in the field until the surrender of Lord Cornwallis's force at the Battle of Yorktown in 1781 ended the war.

In the fall of 1775 he referred to America as "my country" and "my bleeding country." He gave utter allegiance thereafter to the American Republic. In the 1780s Washington referred to Virginia as a "middle" state rather than a southern one. He condemned the Articles of Confederation because they gave the central government insufficient power, and he was the most influential champion of the Constitution. As president he steadily and effectively toiled to assure the safety and growth of the nation, creating, without precedent, executive departments and a sense of national identity. He denounced sectionalism of every sort, in particular condemning all efforts to set the emerging sections, North and South, against each other. It is fair to say that he was an ardent Federalist in his last years.

Washington was a land speculator and a farmer rather than a planter, for he turned away well before 1775 from emphasis upon tobacco growing to general husbandry. He was an agrarian reformer who promoted early efforts at crop rotation, invented a special plow to combat soil erosion, and experimented with fertilizers. He marketed wheat and fish in the West Indies. With the years, he became increasingly hostile to black slavery. He declared that it ought gradually to be abolished, said that he would vote for emancipation, and arranged in his will to free his slaves and those of his wife.

JOHN R. ALDEN
Duke University

John R. Alden, *George Washington: A Biography* (1984); Joseph J. Ellis, *His Excellency: George Washington* (2004); James T. Flexner, *George Washington*, 4 vols. (1965–72); Douglas Southall Freeman, John A. Carroll, and Mary W. Ashworth, *George Washington: A Biography*, 7 vols. (1948–57); Paul Johnson, *George Washington: The Founding Father* (2005).

Watson, Tom

(1856–1922) POLITICIAN.
Thomas Edward Watson spent most of his life in the village of Thomson, Ga. As a young man he taught in country schools, later becoming a highly successful lawyer who practiced in small towns. He succeeded in part because he knew country people well and spoke in a colorful, rural idiom. For Watson the ideal society embraced the life he had known as a young boy, when his grandfather had owned a valuable plantation. After the Civil War his family lost that estate and sank into poverty. Although Watson became a wealthy lawyer, he knew that many southern farmers—plagued by falling cotton prices and increasing tenancy—faced hard times. He did not believe that the New South creed, with its call for industrialization and urbanization, would help them. Instead, Watson championed the ideal of a South that consisted largely of prosperous farmers.

With the rise of the Farmers' Alliance in the 1880s, Watson hoped that its programs could help country people. In 1890 he won a seat in Congress as an Alliance candidate, and during his one term he introduced a resolution that eventually resulted in free delivery of rural mail. In 1891 Watson joined the People's Party and became a leading spokesman for southern Populism, a movement of landowning farmers and tenants who wanted to improve rural life by making reforms in the prevailing economic system. To achieve his goals, Watson called on blacks and whites to join forces in working for economic reforms. He did not advocate social equality between the races, but his attempt to win black votes caused white Democrats to denounce him and his fellow Populists as threats to white supremacy. During the congressional elections of 1892 and 1894, the Democrats resorted to massive fraud to ensure Watson's defeat. In the face of that harsh treatment, Watson remained loyal to the People's Party; in 1896 he served as its vice presidential candidate.

Following his defeat in that election, Watson retired to private life, where he devoted himself to practicing law, writing history, and editing several magazines. Between 1900 and 1920 he continued to use his influence with former Populists to determine the outcome of Georgia elections, and near the end of his life he served for two years in the U.S. Senate. After 1900 he no longer demonstrated the idealism that he had displayed as a Populist leader in the 1890s. Instead of encouraging blacks and whites to work together for common political objectives, he advocated the disfranchisement of blacks. He also became a leading proponent of anti-Catholicism and anti-Semitism. When he died in 1922, the newly revived Ku Klux Klan held him in high esteem.

WILLIAM F. HOLMES
University of Georgia

Walter J. Brown, *J. J. Brown and Thomas E. Watson: Georgia Politics, 1912–1928* (1988); Ferald J. Bryan, *Henry Grady or Tom Watson?: The Rhetorical Struggle for the New South, 1880–1890* (1994); Charles Crowe, *Journal of Negro History* (April 1970); William F. Holmes, in *A History of Georgia*, ed. Kenneth Coleman (1991); Robert Saunders, *Georgia Historical Quarterly* (Fall 1970); Thomas E. Watson Papers, Southern Historical Collection, University of North Carolina, Chapel Hill; C. Vann Woodward, *Tom Watson: Agrarian Rebel* (1938).

Wilson, Woodrow

(1856–1924) U.S. PRESIDENT.

Born in Virginia and raised in Georgia, South Carolina, and North Carolina, Woodrow Wilson was one of the South's most influential leaders in American history. His first memories, he once said, were of the news of Lincoln's election and the outbreak of the Civil War. The most important influence on his early life was his father, Joseph R. Wilson, a prominent Presbyterian minister who helped form the Presbyterian Church in the United States and ardently defended slavery. Woodrow Wilson later declared that "the only place in the country, the only place in the world, where nothing has to be explained to me is the South."

Wilson began his education at Davidson College in North Carolina, completed his undergraduate work at Princeton, and pursued his legal training at the University of Virginia under John B. Minor. For a brief time in Atlanta he practiced law, which he found at odds with his primary interests—history and literature. During this period he met his first wife, Ellen Axson Wilson, herself the daughter of a distinguished family of southern Presbyterian ministers. He left Atlanta to do doctoral work at the Johns Hopkins University, where he received a Ph.D. for his work *Congressional Government*.

Southern observers watched with pride as Wilson steadily achieved fame and influence as an educator, historian, man of letters, and political commentator, and his successful campaign for the White House in 1912 was due in great measure to his ability to portray himself paradoxically as both a southerner and a national figure.

In fact, he was both. He retained southern attitudes toward women throughout his life but insisted on a college education for his own daughters. He shared the racist values of American society of his day and as president (1913–21) presided over the segregation of federal agencies, yet never trafficked in blatant racism. In his historical writing he lauded the South for its adherence to principle in fighting the Civil War but described both the institution of slavery and the South's understanding of the Constitution as doomed by the progressive forces of history. He disciplined himself and his wife to drop their southern accents, although his southern political alliances brought him to national power.

Wilson's political achievements include breaking the Republican hold on the White House in the post–Civil War period and bringing the South into national politics. But perhaps the greatest irony is that this son of a region known for its parochialism should have laid the foundations for America's self-understanding in world affairs. Ellen Axson Wilson praised him for being "an infinitely better, more helpful son to her [the South] than any of those who cling so desperately to the past and the old prejudices." "I believe," she said, "you are her greatest son in this generation and also the one who will have the greatest claim on her gratitude."

JOHN M. MULDER
Louisville Presbyterian Theological Seminary

Thomas J. Knock, *To End All Wars: Woodrow Wilson and the Quest for a New World Order* (1992); Arthur S. Link, *Journal of Southern History* (February 1970), *Wilson: The Road to the White House* (1947); John M. Mulder, *Woodrow Wilson: The Years of Preparation* (1978); J. A. Thompson, *Woodrow Wilson: Profiles in Power* (2002).

Young, Andrew

(b. 1932) MINISTER, CIVIL RIGHTS ACTIVIST, POLITICIAN, AND DIPLOMAT.

Andrew Jackson Young Jr. was born 12 March 1932 in New Orleans to the middle-class household of Andrew Jackson Young Sr., a dentist, and Daisy Fuller Young. He attended Dillard University (1947–48) and Howard University, where he received his B.S. in biology (1951). After leaving Howard, Young attended Hartford Theological Seminary, where he received a degree in divinity (1955). He was ordained by the Congregational Church before returning south to pastor churches in Georgia (Beachton and Thomasville) until 1957. That year, unfulfilled with his small-town ministry, he became executive director of the National Council of Churches' New York–based Department of Youth Programs. In that capacity he hosted the nationally televised, youth-oriented series *Look Up and Live*.

Then, captivated by the burgeoning southern civil rights movement, Young returned south again as head of the United Church of Christ's (UCC) voter registration program headquartered in Alabama. While working with the UCC, Young joined the staff of the Southern Christian Leadership Conference (SCLC) in 1961 at the request of its president, Martin Luther King Jr. Young acquired the reputation of being a moderating force within King's spirited inner circle. While other King lieutenants played firebrand roles during the initial stages of campaigns in such cities as Birmingham and Selma, Young came in later as SCLC's negotiator in meetings with segregationists. Young served as SCLC's executive director and its executive vice president, and he drafted versions of the 1964 and 1965 Civil Rights Acts. He left SCLC in 1970 to make the transition from protest politics to electoral politics.

Young's initial campaign for Georgia's Fifth Congressional District seat was unsuccessful, but he won in 1972. He and Barbara Jordan, who was elected to the House of Representatives from Texas in the same year, thus became the first southern blacks since 1898 to win congressional elections. Young was reelected in 1974 and 1976. During his tenure as congressman, Young opposed the Holt Amendment, which sought to prohibit federal withholding as a means to compel school desegregation. He actively supported the extension of the Voting Rights Act of 1965, citing the

Andrew Young, civil rights activist, Georgia congressman, UN ambassador, and mayor of Atlanta. Photo taken in the 1980s. (Mayor's Office, Atlanta, Georgia)

increase in black registration (from 29 percent in 1964 to 56 percent in 1972) in states affected by this law. He also favored the subsequent broadening of the act to include language minorities, and he served on the House Banking and Currency Committee and Rules Committee.

Young was one of the first nationally known black leaders to support Jimmy Carter's 1976 bid to become the first modern president from the Deep South. Young, as Carter's major adviser, allayed the suspicions of many black leaders and voters about Carter and his southern background. Young came to Carter's defense, nullifying criticism of the former Georgia governor, when he made a campaign blunder by stating his support for the "ethnic purity" of white neighborhoods. When some 90 percent of the more than 6 million black voters cast their ballots for Carter, providing him with his slim margin of victory over Gerald Ford, Young's active support was seen as pivotal by many. In fact, Carter stated that Young was the only person to whom he owed a political debt.

Carter appointed Young U.S. ambassador to the United Nations. In this position, Young was able to create a viable dialogue between the U.S. government and the Third World after a period of intense alienation during the Nixon-Ford years. In particular, relations between Africa and the United States bettered as a result of Young's efforts to do away with apartheid. His negotiations contributed to the coming of majority rule to Zimbabwe in 1980. Young's time in the United Nations was marked by a bluntness unusual to diplomacy. His statements that Britain had institutionalized racism and that Cuban troops were a stabilizing force in Angola, among others, created much controversy. Young resigned his post in 1979 when an uproar occurred after he met with a Palestine Liberation Organization representative, counter to official U.S. government policy. He came back to Atlanta and was elected its mayor in 1981 and reelected in 1985.

Expressing the conviction that for-eign and domestic policies of the Reagan administration were "clear failures," Young's mayoral career was characterized by continued support for Atlanta's affirmative action programs ("good business" as well as the law) and attempts to link the gateway city economically with the "new frontier" markets of Latin America, Africa, and the Middle East.

Young ran unsuccessfully for governor of Georgia in 1990 and later became co-chair of the Centennial Atlantic Games Committee, which brought the summer Olympics to Atlanta in 1996. Today he is co-chair of Goodworks International, a consulting firm that works with corporations and businesses in Africa and the Caribbean.

VINCENT D. FORT
Morehouse College

Robert H. Brisbane, *Black Activism* (1974); Andrew DeRoche, *Andrew Young: Civil Rights Ambassador* (2003); James Gaskins, *Andrew Young: Man with a Mission* (1979); *New York Times* (3 January 1982); Howell Raines, *My Soul Is Rested: Movement Days in the Deep South Remembered* (1977); Eddie Stone, *Andrew Young: Biography of a Realist* (1980); Andrew Young, *An Easy Burden: The Civil Rights Movement and the Transformation of America* (1996).

Page numbers in boldface refer to articles.

Criminal justice, 12, 16, 19, **30–33**
Criminal law, 12, **33–36**
Crouch, Winston, W., 361
Crump, E. H., **327–28**, 360
Cuba, 196
Culpepper's Rebellion, 297
Culture wars, **177–81**, 293
Cumberland University, 348

Dabney, Robert L., 220
Dalton, Ga., 208
Danforth, John C., 132
Daniel, Peter V., **87–88**
Danville, Va., 180
Darrow, Clarence, 123, 125
Davis, Benjamin J., Jr., 99
Davis, "Cyclone," 220
Davis, Edmund J., 380
Davis, Jeff, 170, 182, 184, 244
Davis, Jefferson, 72, 85, 107, 134, 220, 243, **328–29**
Dawson, R. H., 28
Dayton, Tenn., 123, 125, 126
Death penalty. *See* Capital punishment
Declaration of Constitutional Principles, 57, 171
Declaration of Independence, 132, 140, 204, 218, 291, 353
Deep Dark River (Rylee), 53
Degler, Carl N., 267
deGraffenried, Ryan, 402
DeLay, Tom, 229, 246, 282
Delta Ministry, 341
Demagogues, 151, **182–85**, 244–45, 365, 398
Democracy in America (Tocqueville), 225
Democratic National Committee, 189, 342
Democratic National Convention, 55, 153, 186, 188, 190, 280, 285, 319, 342, 352, 382, 385
Democratic Leadership Council, 229
Democratic Party, 73, 108, 138, 144, 153, 160, 162, **185–89**, 216, 219, 221, 223–24, 225, 229, 235, 236–40, 254, 273, 274, 291, 299, 350; conservatives in, 145, 147, 236, 257; Bourbons in, 146, 226, 243; promi-

nence of, 148, 152, 168, 170, 171, 205, 224, 226–27, 232, 234, 253, 262, 284, 295, 380; liberalism of, at national level, 159, 206, 258, 339; abandonment of, 161; and issues of race and civil rights, 163, 172, 179, 188, 206, 245, 277, 280, 281, 293, 323, 389; and Southern Alliance, 248, 255; and Populists, 255–56, 293; and New Deal, 280. *See also* States' Rights Democratic Party
Democratic-Republican Party, 236
Dent, Harry S., 187, 390
Derbigny, Pierre, 113
Desaussure, Henry, 119
Detroit, Mich., 59, 115, 209
Devine, Annie, 342
Digest of Civil Laws Now in Force in the Territory of Orleans, 113
Dinnerstein, Leonard, 95
Disfranchisement, 15, 147–48, 150, 151, 256, 267, 299, 301, 399, 400
Divorce, 10, 38–40
Dixiecrats, 55, 67, 143, 153, 187, **189–90**, 257, 285, 397
Dixon, Frank, 190
Dixon, Thomas, 52, 53
Dodd, William E., 217, 220
Dole, Bob, 326
Dole, Elizabeth, 308
Dorsey, Hugh, 97
Douglas, Stephen A., 219, 354
Dowdy, Wayne, 163, 366
Dred: A Tale of the Great Dismal Swamp (Stowe), 51
Du Bois, W. E. B., 19, 193, 267
Dukakis, Michael, 352
Dukes of Hazzard, The, 60
Dunn, Winfield, 374
Dunnavant, John, 336
Dunning, William, 267
Durham, N.C., 98
Durr, Clifford Judkins, 329, 330, 331
Durr, Virginia, **329–31**
Duval County, Fla., 60
Dye, Thomas R., 295

Catholics, 275; and Santerians, 278; and secession, 386

Floyd, Carlisle, 312

Flush Times of Alabama and Mississippi, The (Baldwin), 52

Flynt, J. Wayne, 147

Folsom, James, **335–37**, 402

Folsom, Joshua, 336

Foner, Eric, 270

Food Stamp Act of 1970, 332

Fool's Errand, A (Tourgee), 116

Ford, Jesse Hill, 53

Foreign policy, **195–201**

Foreman, Percy, **94–95**

Forrest, Nathan Bedford, 270

Forsyth, John, 273

Fortas, Abe, 390

Fourteenth Amendment, 13, 14, 19, 72, 75, 82, 83, 85, 92, 110, 134, 139–40, 145, 227, 260, 265, 279, 355, 399

Fourth Amendment, 118

France, 110, 353, 371

Frank, Andre Gunder, 151

Frank, Leo, case, **95–97**

Frankfort, Ky., 26

Frankfurter, Felix, 118

Franklin, John Hope, 368

Franklin College, 84

Freedman's Bureau, 8, 266, 270

Freedom Farms Corporation, 342

Freedom Rides, 20, 99, 263, 362

Freedom Summer, 263

Frémont, John C., 192

Frist, Bill, 282

Fugitive Slave Act of 1793, 87

Fugitive Slave Act of 1850, 72, 85, 87, 354, 395

Fulbright, J. William, 170, 257, **337–38**

Fulbright Exchange Program, 337

Fulton County, Ga., 60

Futurama, 54

Gaines Leathers v. Blackwell Durham Tobacco Co., 46

Galifianakis, Nick, 345

Galveston, Tex., 46

Garner, John Nance, 170, 382

Geer, John, 99

Genovese, Eugene D., 145, 205

George, James Z., 255

Georgetown University, 325

George Washington University, 102, 337, 344

Georgia: and criminal code, 12, 34; voting districts in, 15; and convict lease system, 26–27, 28; and criminal justice, 32; and family law, 37, 39; and slavery, 43, 44, 129; and massive resistance, 57, 156; county politics in, 175; and Latinos, 207, 208, 211; black electorate of, 228; and Reconstruction, 267; taxing, 296; and Unionism, 297; prominent figures of, 323–25, 334, 338–40, 368–69, 390–93, 405–6, 407–9; prohibition, 378; and secession, 386

Georgia, University of, 48, 49, 156, 385

Georgia Commission on Education, 68

Georgia General Assembly, 181

Georgia Institute of Technology, 323

Georgia Supreme Court, 44, 89

Gerrymandering, racial, 16, 22–23, 163, 401

Gingrich, Newt, 162, 180, 206, 229, 239, 246, 282, **338–40**

Glaise, Joyce, 180

Glenn, John, 359

Globalization, 211, 212

Glover, Nat, 60

Goebel, William, 299

Goldwater, Barry M., 161, 187, 227, 237, 264, 280–81, 389

Gonzales, Henry B., 384

Goodman, Andrew, 288, 300

Gordon, John B., 255

Gordon, Kate, 306

Gore, Albert, Jr., 65, 66, 170, 189, 229, 239, 277, 320, 326, **340–41**

Government administration, **201–3**

Grady, Henry W., 150

Graham, Frank Porter, 345

Graham, Robert, 375

Grant, Joanne, 315
Graves, Dixie, 307
Gray, Victoria, 342
Great Britain, 371
Great Depression, 152, 156, 209, 221, 293, 336, 364, 392
Greenbackers, 254
Greenberg, Kenneth, 242
Greeneville, Tenn., 354, 355
Greensboro, N.C., 262, 300, 351; sit-ins, **98–99**
Greenville, Miss., 66
Greenville, S.C., 83, 351
Gressette, L. Marion, 68
Grier, Robert, 86
Griffith, Andy, 54
Griffith, D. W., 52
Grimké sisters, 306
Grisham, John, 54

Habitat for Humanity, 324
Hahn, Steven, 191
Hamburg, S.C., 274, 398
Hamer, Fannie Lou, **341–42**
Hamilton, Alexander, 110, 218, 236
Hamlin, Hannibal, 355
Hampton, Wade, 274, **343**, 398
Hampton Roads, Va., 85
Handy, W. C., 328
Harlan, John Marshall, 116, 118
Harrington, William, 54
Harris, Joe Frank, 97
Harrison, Benjamin, 367
Harvard University, 49, 90, 134, 136, 320, 332, 340, 362, 375
Hawaii, 196
Hawkins, 53
Haynes, Richard "Racehorse," 95
Haynsworth, Clement, 118, 390
Hays, Arthur Garfield, 123
Hays, Brooks, **344**
Head Start, 332, 357
Health, Education, and Welfare, Department of, 82, 347, 348
Heard, Alexander, 361

Heflin, Thomas, 170, 182
Helms, Jesse, 65, 228, **345–46**
Hemings, Sally, 221, 353
Henry, Patrick, 52, 71, 119, 242
Herndon, Angelo, case, **99–100**
Herrenvolk democracy, 144–45, 205
Herring, Pendleton, 361
Highway Beautification Act, 356
Hill, Anita, 132
Hill, Lister, 170
Hispanics, 207–11
History of the Dividing Line (Byrd), 290
Hobby, Oveta Culp, **347–48**
Hobby, William Pettus, 347
Hodges, Luther, 157
Hofstadter, Richard, 183, 226
Hogg, James S., 248, 255
Hoke v. Henderson, 122
Holden, William W., 298
Hollings, Ernest S., 245
Holmes, Oliver Wendell, 62, 84, 138
Holshouser, James, 375
Holton, A. Linwood, 374
Homestead laws, 6–7, 38
Hopwood v. Texas, 92
Houston, Charles Hamilton, 26
Houston, Tex., 32, 54, 95, 102, 358–59
Houston County, Tex., 247
Houston Post, 347, 348
Howard University, 121, 407
How You Can Help Clean Up America (Falwell), 373
Huebner, Timothy, 120
Hull, Cordell, **348–49**
Humphrey, Hubert, 186, 187
Hundley, Daniel R., 292
Hunt, James B., Jr., 245, 346, 374, 375
Hunter, James Davison, 177
Huntsville, Ala., 213, 315
Hurricane Katrina, 321, 389
Hussein, Saddam, 320
Hutchison, William R., 179

Ideology, political, **204–6**
Illinois, 126

Missouri Territory, 39
Mobile, Ala., 84, 85, 400
Mobile Register, 273
Mondale, Walter, 332
Monroe, James, 196, 291, 322, **370–72**
Monroe Doctrine, 196, 372
Montesquieu, 34
Montgomery, Ala., 20, 103, 114, 263, 330, 362, 386
Montgomery Improvement Association, 115
Moorhead County, Miss., 342
Moral Majority, 161, 177, 180, 228, 277, **372–74**
Moral Majority Report, 372
Moreau-Lislet, Louis, 113
Morgan, Charles, Jr., **112**
Morgan, Edmund S., 144
Morgan, John Tyler, 197, 199
Morgan, J. P., 197
Morganton, S.C., 90
Morial, Ernest, 228
Morning Star, 387
Mossler, Candy, 95
Multnomah County, Ore., 59
Murray, Pauli, 193
Myrdal, Gunnar, 145
Myrick, Sue, 308

Napoleonic Code, **112–14**
Nashville, Tenn., 86, 87, 208, 349, 362
Nashville Agrarians, 218, 221
Nashville Tennessean, 340
Natchez, Miss., 368
National Association for the Advancement of Colored People (NAACP), 14, 19, 53, 66, 69, 82, 83, 108, 114, 121, 132, 181, 262, 313, 314, 330, 332
National Black Political Assembly, 352
National Committee to Abolish the Poll Tax, 330
National Council of Churches, 341
National Council of Negro Women, 342
National Economist, 247
Nationalism, 161, 371

National Labor Relations Act, 10, 231
National politics, **225–30**
National Prison Association, 27
National Urban League, 19
National Women's Political Caucus, 342
Negro National News, 314
Neshoba County, Miss., 57
New Deal, 9, 19, 46, 152–53, 154, 161, 221, **230–31**, 247, 256–57, 280, 293, 321, 382, 392, 397
New Federalism, 296
New Mexico, 377, 395
New Orleans, La., 36, 54, 83, 85, 138, 139–40, 298, 319, 349
New South governors, **374–75**
New York, 32, 64, 207
New York City, 95, 100, 200, 262, 314, 315, 320
New York Times, 66
Nicholls, Francis, 138
Nineteenth Amendment, 251, 307
Nixon, E. D., 114
Nixon, Richard M., 90, 102, 112, 116–18, 161, 168, 180, 187, 227, 257, 359, 366, 389–90, 403
Nixon v. Sirica, 121
Nobel Peace Prize, 324, 341, 349
Nonviolent Resistance to Segregation Leadership Conference, 315
Norfolk, Va., 83
North American Free Trade Agreement (NAFTA), 211, 212
North Carolina: and homestead laws, 7, 38; voting districts in, 15, 400–401; and convict labor, 28; and criminal justice, 31; and family law, 38, 39, 40; and child labor, 45–46; and school prayer, 67; prominent figures of, 90, 100–101, 122–23, 345–46; and slave patrols, 129; county politics in, 175; and Latinos, 207, 208, 209, 211; and Populists, 249; and Reconstruction, 267; Regulators, 297; and Unionism, 297; and secession, 386
North Carolina A&T University, 351
North Carolina Central, 50

Prince Edward County, Va., 287
Princeton University, 105, 406
Principles of Pleading (Tucker), 134
Progressivism, 45, 205, 244, **250–52**, 293, 313
Prohibition, 11, 35, 251, **378–79**
Protestant Methodist Episcopal Church, South, 268
Protestants, 11, 15, 179, 228, 247, 251, 258, 268, 275–76, 373
Protest movements, **253–59**
Provincials, The (Evans), 63
Pryor, David, 375
Public Opinion and American Democracy (Key), 362
Public Utility Holding Company Act, 382
Public Works Administration, 231
Pudd'nhead Wilson (Twain), 51
Puerto Rico, 197
Pulitzer Prize, 94, 311
Putnam, Carleton, 286

Race, and southern politics, **259–66**
Race and Reason (Putnam), 286
Racial Facts, 286
Racism, 13, 30, 52, 73, 83, 127, 144, 257, 317. *See also* Segregation; Violence
Radical Republicans, 145, 175, 269, 355, **379–80**
Rainach, Willie M., 68
Raleigh, N.C., 345
Raleigh-Durham, N.C., 208
Raleigh News and Observer, 345
Raleigh Times, 345
Randolph, Edmund, 87
Randolph, John, 169, **381**
Raulston, John T., 123, 125
Ray, James Earl, 95
Rayburn, Sam, 170, 245, **381–82**
Reagan, Ronald, 22, 76, 132, 161, 168, 180, 188, 200, 206, 228, 239, 246, 265, 277, 281–82, 308, 316, 346
Reciprocal Trade Agreements Act, 349
Reconstruction, 6, 13, 81, 146, 150, 153, 175, 205, 216, 236, 243, 253, 260, **266–71**, 273–74, 279, 298, 355, 380
Reconstruction Act of 1867, 266, 273
Reconstruction and Redemption of the South (Olsen), 272
Redeemers. *See* Bourbon Democrats
Redemption, 269, **271–74**
Red Rock (Page), 52
Red Shirts, 274, 343, 398
Reeve, Tapping, 322
Rehnquist, William, 76, 118
Religion, 11, 63–67, 76; and southern politics, **275–78**. *See also* Protestants; School prayer
Religious Right, 177, 179, 180, 181, 206, 228, 258, 277
Reminiscences of an Active Life (Lynch), 368
Report on Economic Conditions of the South, 152
Republican National Convention, 135, 177, 281, 367
Republican Party, 108, 139, 153, 216, 223, 224, 236–40, 258, 273, 274, **278–84**, 291, 298, 299, 380; and peonage, 29; prominence of, 159, 162, 172, 235, 265, 326; conservatives in, 161, 189; race in, 163, 236, 245; and culture wars, 180; unpopularity of, 186, 226, 232, 244, 253, 266; and "southern strategy," 187–88, 206; and Jeffersonian tradition, 219; and Populists, 249; women in, 308
Research Triangle (North Carolina), 160
Resettlement Administration, 230
Responsible Electorate, The (Key), 362
Revels, Hiram, 243, 260
Rhett, Robert Barnwell, 170, 243
Richards, Ann, 320, **382–84**
Richmond, Va., 72, 83, 87, 88, 110, 117, 121, 343, 353
Richmond Times Dispatch, 241
Right-to-work laws, 47
Riley, Bob, 212
Riley, Richard, 375